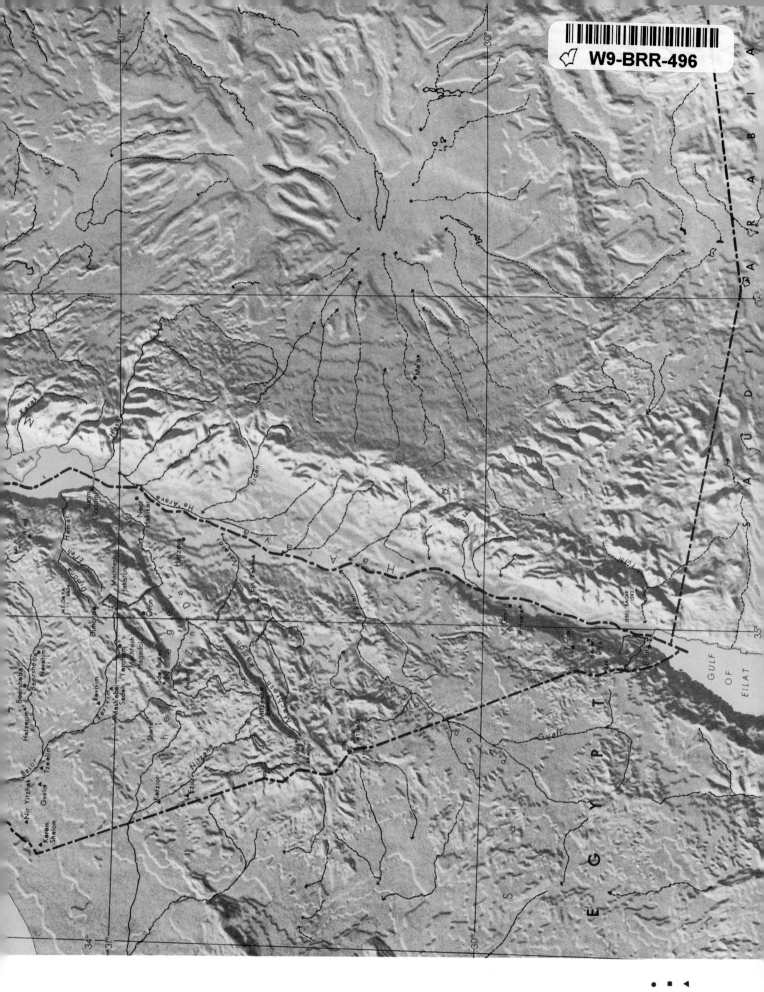

Town ●

Moshav ■

Kibbutz ▲

SAUDI ARABIA

EGYPT

GULF OF EILAT

The Negev Desert

Beersheba

Dimona

Beersheba

Eilat

JEBEL BAQR
1592

Sinai

Ma'an

Karak

THE JEWS IN THEIR LAND

The Jews in their Land

conceived and edited by

David Ben-Gurion

Translated from the Hebrew by Mordechai Nurock, Misha Louvish

A Windfall Book
Doubleday & Company, Inc.
Garden City, New York

Editor: David Ben-Gurion

Text Editor: Jeremy Robson   Art Editor: Felix Gluck

ISBN: 0-385-06152-8

Library of Congress Catalog Card Number: 73-10589
First published in 1966 by Aldus Books Limited
Aldus House, Conway Street, Fitzroy Square, London W.1.
First published in the United States of America in 1966 by
Doubleday & Company Inc., Garden City, New York
Library of Congress Catalog Card Number: 66-11274
New revised edition 1974
© 1966, 1974 Aldus Books Limited, London
Printed and bound in Yugoslavia by Mladinska Knjiga,
Ljubljana.

Contents

Note: The term B.C.E. used throughout the text denotes "Before the Christian Era"; the term C.E. denotes "Christian Era".

Foreword

The historiography of the Jewish people is as old as the cultural history of the people itself. Biblical historiography accompanied the nation from its very beginnings and immortalized its spiritual and political development up to and during the Babylonian Exile, the days of the Return to the Land, and the consequent renewal of autonomy. Since religious creativeness was the supreme expression of the Jewish genius during the period of the nation's independence, some scholars have held that the Roman destruction of that independence and the emergence of Christianity from Judaism marked the end of Jewish history: they ignored the fact that even after independence had been crushed, and the bulk of the nation had been scattered over the globe, the unity and uniqueness of Israel survived and its people continued to hope for the renewal of independence in the Land.

In recording the life of this nation, therefore, modern historians have sought to cover also the long period during which the stage of Jewish activity was the entire world: for geographic dispersion did not destroy the spirit that kept the nation virtually intact as a single historical entity. This volume is significant in that it presents the continuous story of the Jewish people *within* the borders of its homeland. It covers both the periods of its independence—when it created the original culture that was to give it its permanent place in the annals of mankind—and the periods when strangers ruled the Land and the Jewish population consisted only of the remnants and the beginnings of the incessant waves of those returning from the Dispersion.

The changes seen by this tiny land were many. After the Romans came Persians, Muslims, Christians, Mamelukes, and Turks. And then came the League of Nations' Mandate, designed to establish the Jewish National Home.

Throughout all these changes the enduring link between people and homeland never weakened. There was hardly a crisis or decisive point in the history of the nation that did not augment Jewish return from the Diaspora. And every such wave of return was inspired by renewed

Messianic hopes. This process was crowned in the last quarter of the 19th century with heightened immigration and the beginnings of agricultural settlement, strengthened by the growth of the world movement of "Lovers of Zion" and the emergence of political Zionism. Then came the 20th century. In Europe, the nation suffered destruction more terrible than anything it had experienced in its long history of tragedy—the slaughter of 6,000,000 and the destruction of its vital cultural centers. In Palestine, the failing Mandatory regime was compelled to leave; Jewish sovereignty was regained, and there began a mass Return to Zion on a scale unmatched in any period of the past. And although the bulk of Jewry is still scattered over the globe, the State of Israel unites all Jews with the ties of the spirit.

The inspiration of reborn Israel is that same ancient heritage that inspired Jewish spiritual life throughout the ages, and the great Jewish contribution to humanity—the Scriptures, and the vision of Israel's Prophets proclaiming the oneness of God and the equality of human beings created, all, in his image. In these books of the Bible are formulated the moral principles that have become the ideals of civilized man. Out of this Judaism, Christianity was born and Islam grew. In all churches, men pray with the words of the Psalmist. The call of the Hebrew Prophets for social justice and peace among nations has become, today, the aspiration of all humanity. The Messianic idea, crowning glory of biblical prophecy, envisaging the return of Israel to its Land and the redemption of mankind from oppression and war, is the challenging goal of this generation and of generations to come. It is the fervent belief of those who are reviving the Jewish homeland in our day, and renewing the sovereignty of Israel, that the vision of the Prophets of old will be the guiding star lighting Israel's future and the future of mankind.

Zalman Shazar,

former President of Israel.

But the Lord was wroth with me for your sakes, and would not hear me: and the Lord said unto me, Let it suffice thee; speak no more unto me of this matter. Get thee up into the top of Pisgah, and lift up thine eyes westward, and northward, and southward, and eastward, and behold it with thine eyes: for thou shalt not go over this Jordan. But charge Joshua, and encourage him, and strengthen him: for he shall go over before this people, and he shall cause them to inherit the land which thou shalt see.

Part One

Professor Yohanan Aharoni

Entry to Exile

1200 B.C.E. -587 B.C.E.

Compared with the large Middle Eastern lands, such as Egypt and Mesopotamia, that played so vital a part in the early development of human civilization, Palestine was, in biblical times, small in size and poor in natural resources. The ancient Land formed a narrow strip stretching along the Levant: in the east it was bordered by the western fringe of the great Syrian-Arabian desert; in the south the wilderness of Sinai separated it from Egypt; in the north the country's extreme was marked by the city of Dan, near the main source of the river Jordan at the foot of Mount Hermon. The total distance from the northernmost point of Dan to Beersheba in the south (where sedentary habitation generally ended) is approximately 140 miles, and nowhere—from sea to steppe—was the country more than 80 miles wide, making a total area of about 11,340 square miles. (Modern Israel has an area of 7992 square miles.)

The long and stormy chapters of Palestine's history contrast sharply with its size. Time and again this minute country has figured prominently in the world's history. And what has given it this special role is its geographical position at the crossroads of the Middle East.

In global terms, the Land is situated in the heart of the continental bridge from Asia to Africa. At the same time, its coastline faces westward to Europe. In the south (through the Gulf of Eilat) it is linked to the Red Sea and the Indian Ocean, where navigation lanes lead to the Far East and East Africa. (Though geographical horizons may have been narrower in the past, the route through Palestine was nevertheless of major importance, connecting, as it did, the great ancient civilizations of Egypt, Assyria, and Babylon, which remained unrivaled until the rise of Greece and Rome.) To the east of Palestine lies Mesopotamia, land of the Euphrates and the Tigris; to the south, Egypt, land of the Nile; to the north, the highlands of Hittite Anatolia; to the west, Cyprus and the Aegean Isles.

It is easy, then, to appreciate the emphasis on communication in Palestine's history, and the country's prominence as an international highway. One main axis of traffic was from north to south, a junction with Mesopotamia and Anatolia on the one hand, and Egypt on the other. This was the Romans' *Via maris*, the vital route rising from Egypt along the entire length of the Mediterranean coast and forking (through the Valley of Jezreel) into branches that ran northward through the Valley of the Lebanon toward Damascus and toward Tadmor (Palmyra).

Alongside the major Middle Eastern trade routes stood three of Palestine's most powerful cities: Gaza, Megiddo, Hazor. Control of the routes was the constant dream of ambitious rulers, and countless military campaigns were waged over them—by the pharaohs, by the kings of Assyria, Babylon, and Persia, by Alexander the Great, the emperors of Byzantium, the Arabs, the Crusaders, the Mamelukes, the Turks, and so on—through to Britain's Field Marshal Allenby in World War I. So this small country became a corridor and battleground for the mighty powers that surrounded it, which is why its spells of independence and tranquillity were almost always brief. In the era of Rome and Byzantium, for example, Palestine was on the fringe of the western world, subject to unceasing pressures from Mesopotamia and Arabia; in the Hellenistic era, it was a constant bone of contention between Ptolemid Egypt and Seleucid Syria. Whenever Assyria, Babylonia, or Persia was dominant, Egypt was invariably scheming to undermine their rule in Palestine and to invade the country. And Egyptian domination of Palestine in the second millennium Before the Christian Era (B.C.E.) constantly led to wars with the Hurrites of Mitanni and with the Hittite kingdom.

These interminable combats naturally caused widespread destruction, and the ensuing rule of imperial Rome exhausted Palestine's resources further. Nevertheless, because of its geographical position, the country continued to contribute generously to the civilization of the ancient East.

For millennia conquerors following the *Via maris* have left monuments at Nahr el Kelb, near Byblos, Syria. Above, the reliefs of Rameses II of Egypt, from the 13th century B.C.E. (right), and of Shalmaneser III of Assyria, from the ninth century B.C.E. Below, a map showing the *Via maris* and Palestine's position in the Middle East.

—————— Main Highways
- - - - - - Other Routes

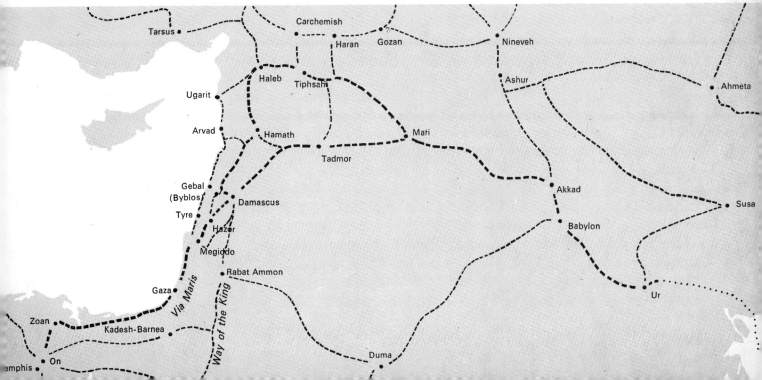

WEDGED as it is between sea and desert, Palestine is influenced by two contending forces, and its terrain and climate have inevitably taken on their characteristics. In winter strong westerly winds bring rain from the sea, while in summer scorching dust clouds blow in from the east. Whereas in Phoenicia (the Lebanon) the marine impact has been strongest (there are numerous small bays that form natural harbors for boats, as well as mountains that keep the desert in check), in Palestine the desert climate has most influence. A long, almost unindented coast-line and shifting dunes make it difficult for boats to land; and east of the Jordan—and in the Negev—the desert merges indistinguishably with the cultivated areas.

Palestine is within the subtropical zone. It has a rainy season in winter and a dry season in summer, but the rainfall varies considerably from region to region. Only in a narrow strip of land along the Mediterranean is the rainfall appreciable, but even here the transition to arid steppe in the south is abrupt. The higher ground in the north gets the most rain, for the lower the terrain (and the more southerly or distant from the sea) the swifter the falling-off in precipitation. Rainfall varies greatly from year to year. Furthermore an appreciable percentage of the total rainfall can fall in just a few days, and droughts are frequent over a substantial part of the country. On rainy days the creeks tend to fill rapidly, and water pouring down from the hills soon chokes the gullies. Thereafter a succession of hot days may quickly dry up the soil.

Most of Palestine's rivers are seasonal, and carry water only for a few days during rainy weather. But the Yarmuk and the Jabbok (in the east), and the Harod (in the west), flow perennially into the Jordan, and the Arnon and the Zered into the Dead Sea. At one time the Yarkon, flowing from a rich source at the foot of the ancient fortress of Antipatris, reached the Mediterranean, but most of its waters have now been piped down to the Negev desert. Elsewhere, smaller rivers (including the Kishon) are unreliable.

Generally speaking, the country is mountainous. Most of its rock formations are limestones of relatively late geological creation, though more ancient crystalline rocks can be found near the Gulf of Eilat in the south. The north east (particularly Bashan and the eastern part of Lower Galilee) contains areas covered by volcanic rocks, the product of volcanic eruptions.

In parts the mountains rise to over 3000 feet—from 3962 feet (the highest peak in Galilee) to 5641 feet in the Highlands of Edom. Between them, geological faultings have produced deep valleys. The largest and deepest of these is the Jordan Valley, part of a long rift stretching from Northern Syria to East Africa. The Jordan Valley drops from 656 feet below sea-level at Lake Kinneret (the Sea of Galilee) to 1312 feet below sea-level at the Dead Sea, the lowest point on the earth's surface. Lesser rift valleys abound, especially in the north. The most remarkable of these is the Valley of Jezreel, which divides Galilee from the Hills of Ephraim and provides the only easy passage inland from the coast to the Lebanon Valley and Damascus. North of it, the mountains of Galilee and Lebanon make transit difficult. (In fact the only other eastward route of any importance is about 156 miles further north, in the Valley of the Eleutheros—now Nahr el Kabir—situated north of the Lebanon mountains.)

Because of the highly pervious nature of the limestone that forms the greater part of Palestine's surface, water is absorbed swiftly and deeply into the ground until it is trapped in impermeable rock layers and forced to flow along them. Only a little water, therefore, breaks through to the surface again in springs. Most of the few springs that do exist are associated with geological faults. (Not until recently has it become possible to reach and exploit the deep-lying underground water by pumping from wells.)

THE NATURAL VEGETATION OF ISRAEL

MEDITERRANEAN

SEA

LEBANON

SYRIA

Sour
(Tyre)

Kiryat Shmona

Safad

Jordan

SEA OF
GALILEE

Acre

Haifa • Kiryat Yam

Tiberias

Yarmuk

Mt. CARMEL

Valley of Jezreel

Nazareth

Afula

Hadera
Hadera

Jenīn

Bet
She'an

Netanya

Herzliya

Nābius
(Shechem)

Zarqā

Tel Aviv-Jaffa
Bat Yam
Holon

Yarkon

Petah
Tikva

JORDAN

Rishon Le Zion •

Lydda

Ramleh

Amman

Rehovot

Jericho

Jordan

Soreq

Jerusalem

Ashkelon

Bethlehem

Gaza

Hebron

DEAD SEA

Mujib

Besor

Rafah

Beersheba

Beersheba

Zin

Hasā

The Negev

Zin Desert

Ha 'Arava

Machtesh Ramon

Ha 'Arava

Paran

Ma'an

EGYPT

Paran Desert

Sinai

Girafi

Eilat

GULF
OF
EILAT

▨	Desert
▨	Semi-desert
▨	Savannah
▨	Mediterranean
▨	Prairie
▨	Deciduous
▨	Coniferous
▨	Mountain

The mountain ranges and the deep Jordan rift divide the country into four distinct geographical regions: the coastal plain, the central highlands, the Jordan depression, and the highlands of Transjordan. The coastal plain is widest in the south, narrowest in the north. Thus an intermediate zone of low hills—the Shefela (debased or lowly zone)—appears in the south between the complex of mountains and the coastal plain. Near the coast the Via maris is forced to swing east to avoid a belt of shifting sand-dunes, several miles wide. As a result, most of the big coastal towns were built slightly east of the seashore. By and large the coastal and other plains of the Land are covered by deep and fertile alluvial soil, swept down from the highlands.

North of the river Yarkon, in the same coastal region, lies the Sharon plain. Red sandy soil covers its western parts, and dense forests grew there until quite a late period. Mount Carmel, sloping down to the sea, screens the Sharon from the Valley of Acre (which adjoins the Valley of Jezreel). The Acre Valley also stretches north-ward along the coast and ends in the ridge of Rosh Hanikra (Ras en-Nakura), which reaches the coast and forms precipitous cliffs—these cliffs are known as the Ladder of Tyre, since it is necessary to ascend this ridge to reach Tyre from the south. (A modern railway tunnel running beneath it was blocked when Israel's War of Independence began in 1948.)

The central highlands rise rapidly above the coast and the Shefela; their much-dissected table-lands tend to be narrow in the south and wider and more accessible in the north. Considerable areas of this mountainous region were originally forested, but when settlement started most of the thickets were uprooted and replaced by terraces for fruit trees. Then, when the country was devastated and its habitation declined, the terraces collapsed for lack of care and a great deal of the fertile soil was swept away, leaving the hills barren. Today the eroded slopes are suitable only for afforestation—and so the cyclic process of soil-formation recommences.

The highlands are divided into Galilee, Ephraim (Samaria), and Judaea. Upper Galilee is a mountain complex with its highest parts in the south east; its most fertile and convenient sectors extend northward, reaching as far as the deep canyon of the river Qasimiye (Litani) that separates Upper Galilee from the mountains of the Lebanon. A narrow and deep valley divides Upper Galilee from Lower Galilee; the flattest areas of the regions are the broad valleys that cut from east to west and form intermontane basins.

The hills of Ephraim and Judaea are also much-dissected plateaus with a great many ridges and small valleys. Their main watershed (which sends water eastward to the Jordan Valley and westward to the Mediterranean) is in the eastern part of the range. Near the watershed, and almost parallel to it, runs the main route crossing the hills from south to north, and on it are situated the main towns of the region: Hebron, Bethlehem, Jerusalem, Beth-el, and Shechem. Other, less important routes are found on a series of plateaus in the hills of Ephraim; around Jerusalem these plateaus are narrow, and deep ravines, plunging east and west, hindered the making of an alternative route. Thus Jerusalem, throughout its history, held a unique position, dominating the north-south and east-west mountain routes, and severing Ephraim from Judaea.

The Jordan rift is closed in on both sides by precipitous mountain sides, heavily dissected by deep gorges. In the center of the valley the Jordan has carved a deep, winding bed for itself in the thick and soft calcareous sediments that cover the valley; but the river is not navigable (and in earlier times, when methods of irrigation were primitive, its waters could not be used for cultivation). The river is bordered on both sides by a narrow strip of dense and tangled vegetation that forms a rich nature reserve where, in biblical times, lions roamed (JEREMIAH XLIX: 19). The climate is hot and the rainfall slight, but there are a number of perennial springs and brooks—in the Beisan Valley, for example—that flow to the Jordan. Tropical agriculture flourishes here, in Jericho, and along the Jordan's eastern bank.

The Desert Areas

The river Jordan runs into the Dead Sea (in Hebrew, Yam Hamelah—the Sea of Salt). The high percentage of salts produced by massive evaporation makes it impossible for any creature to live in these waters—hence their name. To the west and east great rock walls, furrowed by ravines, predominate and (except for a lush patch at Ein-Gedi and one or two smaller oases) the Dead Sea is surrounded by desert, scorching hot for most of the year. The wilderness of Judaea (west of the Dead Sea) with its canyons and virtually inaccessible caves and rock-dwellings, often served as a place of refuge for rebels and outlaws, and in recent years many ancient scrolls and documents have been discovered in its dry caverns.

The Arava, a southern extension of the Jordan rift from the Dead Sea to the Gulf of Eilat, is also largely desert: particularly important are the mines of copper ore in some of the gorges on both sides of the valley, and the north-south highway.

More than any other zone, the Transjordan highland has retained the look of a level plateau. It consists mainly of layers of Senonian and Cenomanian limestone and chalk beds. In the west it falls in much-dissected precipitous slopes toward the valley; to the east, it slopes gradually and merges into the Syrian-Arabian desert. (Bashan, with its volcanic soil, is especially fertile.) The Gilead was once thickly wooded, especially north of the river Jabbok. East of the Dead Sea (as far as the river Arnon in the south) the plateau takes the form of a fertile tableland; at one time it was a bone of contention between Israel and Moab. Edom is characterized by mountains, and most of its rock formations are hard—limestone, Nubian sandstone, and (in the south) granite.

As can be seen, the country's geological and topographical diversity make it distinctive. Within short distances of one another are regions that differ widely—wet and hilly Galilee, the tropics of the Jordan Valley, the fertile Transjordan highland, the arid Negev, and so on. Mountain gradients are harsh, and make natural partitions between the different zones.

Natural resources have always been scarce. What chemical wealth there was (such as the minerals of the Dead Sea and the phosphates of the Negev) could not be exploited in biblical times, and only the copper mines in the Arava were important. Naturally, the intercontinental highways were important economically, but they also brought their own troubles; the constant battles fought over them impoverished the country time and time again and eventually destroyed the great fortified towns that lined the Via maris.

Agriculture was the unrivaled spearhead of the economy: grain-growing in the valleys, fruit trees on the hills, grazing in the marginal areas, and tropical crops in the Jordan Valley (especially rare herbs and spices). As described in the Bible, this was ‹ A land of wheat, and barley, and vines, and fig trees, and pomegranates; a land of oil olive, and honey › (DEUTERONOMY VIII: 8), a description that exactly portrays the agrarian diversity of the land. Except in the comparatively small area where irrigation was possible (for example, in the Jordan Valley), everything depended on the winter rainfall—which meant that drought and famine were frequent.

The deep bond that existed between the farmer, the soil, and his God is expressed in these words: ‹ For the land, whither thou goest in to possess it, is not as the land of Egypt, from whence ye came out, where thou sowedst thy seed, and wateredst it with thy foot, as a garden of herbs: But the land, whither ye go to possess it, is a land of hills and valleys, and drinketh water of the rain of heaven: A land which the Lord thy God careth for: the eyes of the Lord thy God are always upon it, from the beginning of the year even unto the end of the year › (DEUTERONOMY XI: 10-12).

The face of the Land: above, the fertile Jezreel Valley—the citrus fruit (above right) grown here and in the Sharon Valley constitutes a major part of Israel's economy.

Below, the barren Judaean desert (where David hid from Saul) and its drop to the Dead Sea—where there is now a thriving *kibbutz*. Below right, the parched soil of the Negev gullies.

Above, the hills of Judaea, with the outskirts of Jerusalem in the distance. Centuries of neglect and soil erosion have left these once fertile hills barren, and suitable only for afforestation.

Below, the Arava, the rift valley stretching for 106 miles from the Dead Sea to the Gulf of Eilat: many of the Arava's gorges are rich in copper ore.

Excavations at Jericho reveal massive fortifications built in the Neolithic period—some 6000 years before the Israelites entered Canaan.

THE LAND to which the Children of Israel came (which was then called Canaan) was an ancient one, and the price they had to pay for settlement was more or less continual warfare and suffering. According to the Bible, the first town to fall to the Israelites was Jericho, seven miles north of the Dead Sea—the oldest town of all. Recent discoveries confirm that even in the Neolithic Age (8000-5000 B.C.E.) Jericho was greatly advanced in art, architecture, and administration. Most of the other Canaanite towns were built toward the end of the fourth millennium B.C.E.—that is, 2000 years or so before the Israelite conquest—and by the third millennium they were both prosperous and strong.

At that time the dominant centers of civilization were to the north and south, in Mesopotamia and Egypt, and Canaan provided the vital corridor between them. These neighboring countries, with their plethora of rivers and fertile plains, were extremely prosperous, and their inhabitants were highly civilized—for the art of writing (Babylon's cuneiform characters and the Egyptian hieroglyphics designed for writing on papyrus) had been developed even before the rise of the first kingdoms of Sumeria and Egypt. The history of these dynasties has, therefore, been accurately preserved in numerous documents; many of these have since been unearthed in palaces, temples, and tombs.

About the turn of the second millennium a great wave of people (the Amorites of the Bible) speaking a west-Semitic dialect had invaded the Middle East: they were

The Land of Canaan

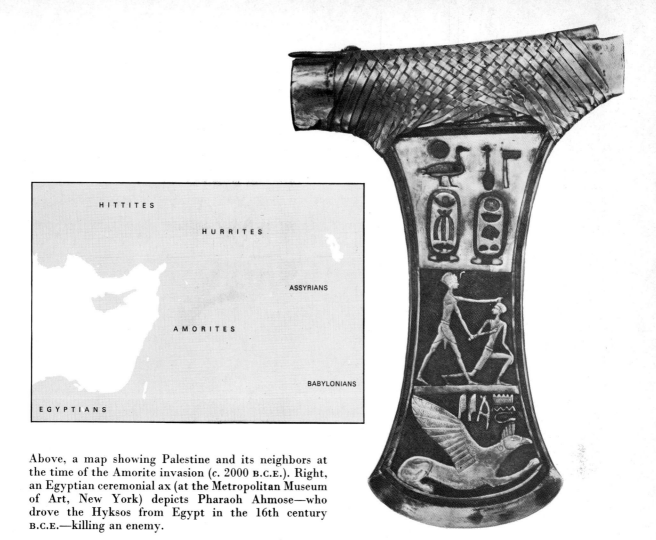

Above, a map showing Palestine and its neighbors at the time of the Amorite invasion (*c.* 2000 B.C.E.). Right, an Egyptian ceremonial ax (at the Metropolitan Museum of Art, New York) depicts Pharaoh Ahmose—who drove the Hyksos from Egypt in the 16th century B.C.E.—killing an enemy.

called the *Amurru* by the Akkadian inhabitants of Mesopotamia, a word that means « the people of the west. » The Amorites overran every kingdom and city they attacked, and eventually built new towns on the mounds of the destroyed kingdoms. These Amorite towns were progenitors of the Canaanite towns of the Bible. The oldest inscriptions concerning Canaan belong to the period of the Egyptian Middle Kingdom (that is, the 20th century B.C.E.), when the pharaohs sought to control Canaan. A delightful description of Canaan appears in the *Story of Sinuhe*, the autobiography of an Egyptian who fled to Canaan in the middle of that century and found asylum there with one of the ‹ governors of the foreign lands. › Later, Sinuhe himself became governor of one of Canaan's provinces. He describes it thus: ‹ He [the protecting governor] let me choose for myself of his country, of the choicest of that which was with him on his frontier with another country. It was a good land, named Yaa. Figs were in it, and grapes. It had more wine than water, plentiful was its honey, abundant were its olives. Every kind of fruit was on its trees. Barley was there, and emmer. There was no limit to any [kind of] cattle . . . . › Clearly, this was the beginning of a remarkably fertile era in Canaan, and the Egyptian stranger seems to have accurately listed its main products—fruits, grain, and cattle. The biblical description of the Promised Land is almost identical.

The decline of the Middle Kingdom during the 18th century B.C.E. and the conquest of Egypt by the Hyksos, did not affect Canaan greatly; on the contrary, a number

Recent excavations in northern Israel reveal the ancient city of Hazor. The most powerful northern Canaanite city during the period of the Israelites' settlement in Canaan. Hazor faced the mountains of the Golan (east of Galilee) and commanded the main northeastern approaches to the Land.

of large, fortified Canaanite towns flourished in this period. These centers, surrounded as they were by enormous slopes of beaten earth, were apparently modeled on the giant Hyksos strongholds that are known to have existed at Qatna (in Syria), at Hazor (in Israel), at Tel-el-Yahudiyeh (in Egypt), and at Carchemish on the Euphrates (in northern Syria). The area of these Canaanite towns was 10 times that of most in the ancient world. (Megiddo, for example, an important town, occupied about 15 acres, while the area of Hazor was 200 acres.) Apparently the fortified enclosures around the towns were used for stabling war horses and for storing the war chariots that had become all-important in battle.

The town of Hazor is the only one mentioned in the archives of the Amorite kingdom of Mari, on the Euphrates, powerful in the 18th century B.C.E. when the Babylonian king Hammurabi reigned. The mention—in connection with commercial transactions and royal envoys—occurs in the very same line as allusions to such important royal centers as (among others) Carchemish, Yamhad (Aleppo), and Qatna. The Bible (JOSHUA XI: 10) stresses that at one time Hazor was ‹ the head of all those kingdoms, › which is accurate, since it was then unrivaled by any city in Canaan. In the armies of the kings of Canaan, which the Tribes of Israel were to encounter during the conquest, the principal weapon was the chariot, and its use involved the training of special charioteers. These charioteers (the *maryanu*, in Indo-European) were, in fact, the mainstay of the Canaanite monarchy; they were given large estates and eventually became a nobility. This led to the emergence of a kind of feudal system, with a supreme monarch backed by vassal « kings » who depended, in their turn, on the charioteer-aristocracy and landowners. And bound to the landowners' estates was a population of farmers *(hofshi)*, the « freemen » of Akkadian documents. The language spoken in Canaan was a western Semitic dialect, extremely close to biblical Hebrew. But (as inscriptions show) many Canaanite kings bore Hurrite and Indo-European names. Egyptian inscriptions refer to the country itself as the Land of Hurru—that is, of the Hurrites, whom they considered the ruling class.

Egyptian Rule

When the 18th dynasty was established in Egypt in the middle of the 16th century B.C.E. by Ahmose (Aahmes), Egypt's New Kingdom took over control of Canaan. Its rule was to last for nearly 400 years. At this point the term « Land of Canaan » first appears in historical sources. The term originated somewhere on the Phoenician coast, and inscriptions from the 15th century B.C.E. use it to refer to a class of wealthy merchants—possibly dealers in the rare blue and purple dyes that were extracted from sea-snails. This narrow connotation is preserved in certain passages of the Bible, to signify either merchants and notables (ISAIAH XXIII: 8; HOSEA XII: 7-8; ZEPHANIAH I: 11), coastal dwellers generally, or the inhabitants of the northern part of the Jordan Valley (NUMBERS XIII: 29; JOSHUA V: 1, and XI: 3; JUDGES XVIII: 7, 28; and ISAIAH XXIII: 11). However, the term was eventually used to designate the entire Egyptian province of Canaan. Thus the king of Babylon could write to pharaoh: ‹ Canaan is thy land and its kings are thy servants › *(el-Amarna* 8, 25): and the king of Alashia (Cyprus) could refer to ‹ the governorate of Canaan › *(el-Amarna* 36, 15). The four centuries of Egyptian domination in Canaan were by no means smooth ones, and the vicissitudes left their mark on the country's history. The peak of Egyptian power was reached under Thutmose III, who defeated an alliance of the

Below left, a Syrian captive—a carving (*c.* 1350 B.C.E.) from the head of a ceremonial walking stick found in the tomb of Pharaoh Tutankhamen. Below, a reconstruction—at the Haifa Museum of Ancient Art—of a Canaanite burial cave uncovered during excavations near Haifa: the cave dates back to the Late Bronze Age (14th-13th centuries B.C.E.).

The Egyptian conquest of Canaan was completed in the 15th century B.C.E. by Thutmose III. In a relief from the temple of Amon at Karnak (above) Thutmose is shown slaying captives. In the excerpt below—from a commemorative stela found at Jebel Barkal, in Egypt—he recalls the tribute received from his vanquished enemies at Megiddo. Right, another Karnak relief lists towns taken by the later Pharaoh Sheshonk (945-924 B.C.E.)—among them is a place named "Abram's Field."

Then that enemy and the princes who were with him sent out to my majesty, with all their children carrying abundant tribute: gold and silver, all their horses which were with them, their great chariots of gold and silver, as well as those which were painted, all their coats of mail, their bows, their arrows, and all their weapons of warfare. It was these with which they had come from afar to fight against my majesty, and now they were bringing them as tribute to my majesty . . . giving praise to my majesty, seeking that the breath of life might be given to them—Thutmose III, from the Barkal Stela.

kings of Canaan decisively at Megiddo in 1468 B.C.E. At the head of the alliance were the kings of Kadesh (on the Orontes) and Megiddo, and it was supported by the kingdom of Hurrite Mitanni—Egypt's rival for rule in Syria during the 16th and 15th centuries B.C.E. But the situation deteriorated during the reign of Thutmose's son Amenhotep II, who was compelled to crush a rebellion in central Canaan in which the kingdom of Mitanni was again involved.

The Hittites

At the beginning of the 14th century B.C.E. a new enemy challenged Egypt in the north—the Hittites, centered in Anatolia. In the *el-Amarna Letters* (the Egyptian archives from the capital city of the Pharaoh Ikhnaton, who ruled in the first half of the 14th century) there is frequent mention of Hittite uprisings in both Syria and the Valley of the Lebanon. This unrest led to an inevitable decline in Egyptian power abroad, since the Egyptians were far too preoccupied with their own internal troubles to concentrate on events in Canaan.

With the establishment of the 19th dynasty (at the beginning of the 13th century B.C.E.) the Egyptians renewed their efforts to dominate Canaan and Parts of Syria (ancient Syria). To that end, they transferred their capital to Zoan, the old Hyksos headquarters in the northern Delta, and renamed the town Pi-Rameses (after Rameses II). This is Raamses, the town the Israelites helped to build (EXODUS 1 : 11). The struggle with the Hittites for command of Canaan reached its climax in the reign of Rameses II. The crucial battle, fought at Kadesh (about 1286 B.C.E.), ended in defeat for the Egyptians. But the long-drawn-out warfare had exhausted both powers, and in the 21st year of Rameses' reign (about 1270) they signed a peace treaty accepting the *status quo* in Parts of Syria and Canaan.

The treaty (both the Egyptian and Hittite versions are extant) lacks any description of the boundaries agreed upon by the signatories. But other contemporary sources show that they were south of Kadesh and north of Damascus. This description tallies with the delineation of the borders of the Land of Canaan given in the Bible (NUMBERS XXXIV: 1-12). The terms of the treaty were observed until the beginning of the 12th century, when the Hittite kingdom was shattered by an invasion of « people of the sea, » among them the Philistines, who even reached the borders of Egypt itself. As Egyptian authority waned in the middle of the 12th century, two contenders for control of Canaan were left: the Philistines and the Israelites.

Canaanite Culture   The Egyptians had never regarded their rule over Canaan as anything more than the imperial management of an inferior race. They hardly ever meddled in its domestic concerns or attempted to impose their customs or forms of worship. Indeed, they were interested only in the larger towns and those valleys that contained strategic highways. As a result their administration was never imposed evenly, and the Israelites were able to penetrate the more barren hinterland and the sparse mountain areas. In the *el-Amarna* period two powerful rivals, Shechem and Jerusalem, already controlled the central mountain range. In the north we hear of Hazor overrunning Upper Galilee, and of Ashtarot (the capital of Bashan), two central towns also mentioned in accounts of the Israelite conquest. These royal cities ruled many smaller towns and wide areas of land with varied and sparse populations—conditions that greatly assisted the Israelites in their search for land.

Nevertheless, the culture of Canaan was surprisingly uniform, highly developed, and cosmopolitan, with Egyptian and Mesopotamian influences (and even Mitanni, Hittite, Cypriot, and Aegean influences) evident. Recent discoveries confirm this cosmopolitanism: a fragment of the Babylonian *Epic of Gilgamesh*, for example, was

An ivory carving (dated to 1350-1150 B.C.E.) found at Megiddo, in the Jezreel Valley—it is thought to depict the triumphal celebration of a king's victory.

Left, a Canaanite maiden and, above, the dwarf Bes—in Egyptian lore the protective genie of pregnant women, children at play, and people asleep: two ivory carvings found at Megiddo (from the 14th-12th centuries B.C.E.).

discovered at Megiddo in Northern Israel; and slabs of basalt and orthostats revealing Hurrite and Hittite presence were found at Beit She'an in north-east Israel, and even further north at Hazor. Indeed, Egyptian scarab seals and typical Mycenaean imported wares have been unearthed in all the Canaanite settlements of that period.

The beautifully constructed Canaanite cities were surrounded by massive walls with magnificent double or triple towered gates at the main entrances. The king's palace stood at the highest point (a fortress within a fortress) and around the palace were scattered the luxurious mansions of his courtiers. In the opulent interiors thin layers of ivory covered the furniture, and utensils were made of gold, silver, lapis lazuli, or alabaster. The store house of gems and vessels of the *el-Amarna* period, and the wealth of ivories from the 13th and 12th centuries B.C.E. found in the cellars of the palace at Megiddo represent the most splendid craftsmanship of the time.

One part of every city was set aside for a temple or temples, each dedicated to a different divinity, and remained sacrosanct for generations. (A splendid example is given by the Square of Holiness at Megiddo, a complete row of Canaanite temples dating from the beginning of the third millennium to the close of the 12th century B.C.E.) The forms of Canaanite worship and the mythological rites linked with it

24

This is the message of Baal Puissant,
the word of Him who is Puissant among Warriors:

Now do thou banish warfare from the earth,
and love do thou emplant within the land!
Now do thou weave no longer on the earth
tissues of lies, but rather threads of peace;
I bid thee, twine no longer in the land
a mesh of guile, but rather skeins of love!

Now haste, now hurry, now bestir thyself,
and let thy feet come speeding unto me,
yea, let thy steps now haste to where I am.
For there's a rede that I would rede to thee,
a word that I would fain relate to thee;

That word it is which wind-swept trees repeat,
which pebbles in the whispering brooks receive,
which, like the murmur of a threnody,
heaven repeats to earth, and deeps to stars.

Yea, I, installed as godhead of the North,
will fashion now upon that hill of mine,
a lightning such as heaven doth not know,
a voice the like of which men do not know,
greater than all mankind yet understand.

Come thou, and I, even I, will light a flame
upon that holy place which evermore
shall be the hill of mine inheritance,
upon that lovely place which evermore
shall be the mount where my puissance rests!

—Baal, god of rainfall and fertility, calls to
the goddess Anat (from a 14th-century B.C.E.
Canaanite epic poem found at Ugarit in Syria).

Right, a basalt pillar from a 14th- to 13th-
century B.C.E. Canaanite sanctuary at Hazor
—the carving of hands raised toward a crescent suggests worship of the moon.

are revealed in a library found in the 14th century B.C.E. temple of Ugarit, a coastal
town in the north (Syria). The Temple was discovered in 1928.

The Canaanite Religion All the Canaanite religions had « El » as their chief deity—a vague, distant presence,
who played little part in worship. The most revered of the gods was Baal, master
of the forces of nature, who inhabited a lofty mountain in the far north (though
he was continually identified with local phenomena). The goddesses Astarte (in
Hebrew, Ashtoreth), Asherah, and Anat symbolized the cult of fertility, and were
worshiped with sensual practices. At the heart of Canaanite mythology lay the
legends of the victory of Mot (god of Hell) over Baal, of Baal's salvation and
resurrection as a result of the warrior-goddess Anat's help, and of their marriage—all
this representing Nature's yearly cycle of death and rebirth. To the Tribes of Israel,
the sensual fertility ritual and the temple prostitution that went with it proclaimed
the moral degeneracy of Canaanite rites. Nevertheless, trees representing the goddess
Asherah and figurines of the goddess Ashtoreth appeared in Israelite homes.
As we saw earlier, the western-Semitic dialect spoken throughout Canaan was
similar to biblical Hebrew; but the language used in diplomatic circles was Akkadian,

25

Above, a sandstone sphinx (15th century B.C.E.) from the temple of Serabit el Khadem in Sinai. The inscription (in Proto-Sinaitic, perhaps the earliest alphabetic script) contains the dedicatory phrase *Ib'll*—"for Baalit." The chart (below) traces the development of the alphabet.

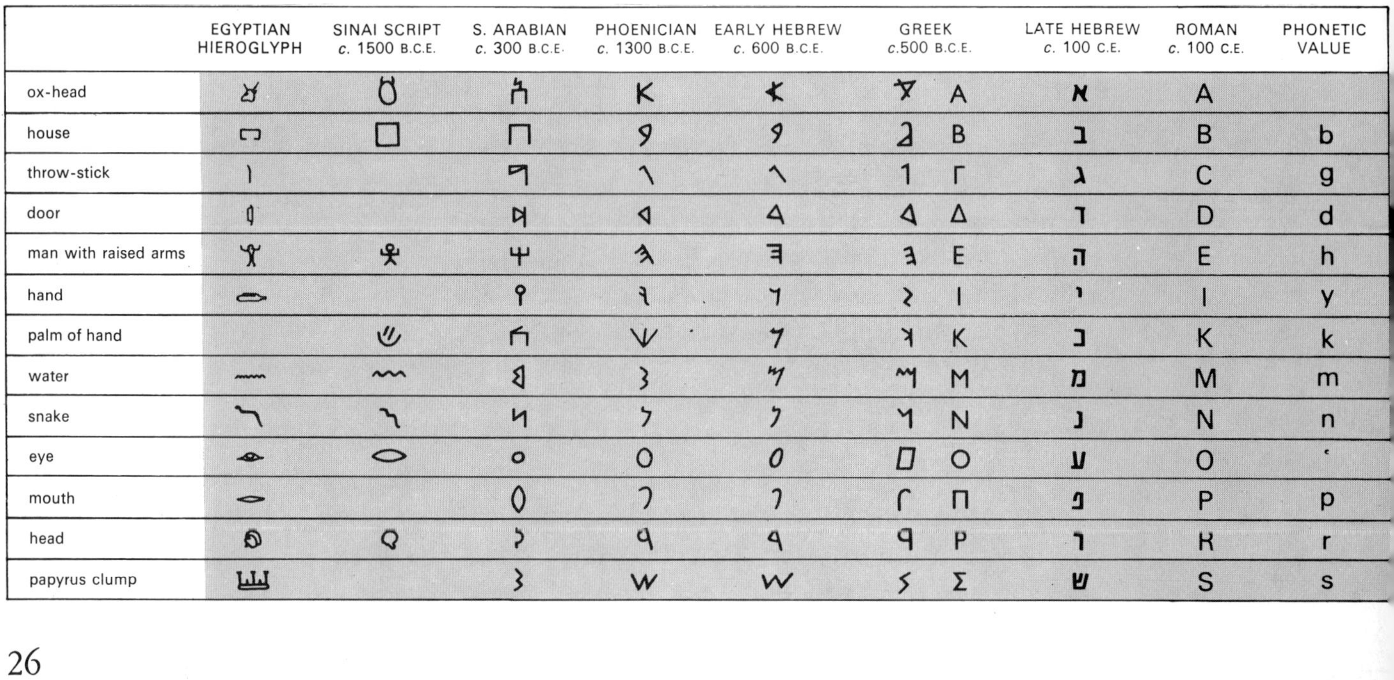

	EGYPTIAN HIEROGLYPH	SINAI SCRIPT c. 1500 B.C.E.	S. ARABIAN c. 300 B.C.E.	PHOENICIAN c. 1300 B.C.E.	EARLY HEBREW c. 600 B.C.E.	GREEK c.500 B.C.E.		LATE HEBREW c. 100 C.E.	ROMAN c. 100 C.E.	PHONETIC VALUE
ox-head	ᛃ	ठ	ḥ	K	ⱊ	ⱅ	A	א	A	
house	⌐	□	Π	9	9	⅃	B	⅃	B	b
throw-stick	∖		⅂	∖	∧	⌐	Γ	⅄	C	g
door	◁		◁⟍	◁	△	◁	△	⅂	D	d
man with raised arms	Ψ	ⱷ	Ψ	ⱬ	⪉	⪉	E	π	E	h
hand	⌾		ⴹ	ⴹ	⅂	⤳	I	י	I	y
palm of hand		ⱳ	⌐	Ⅴ	⅂	ⴽ	K	כ	K	k
water	⌁	⩜	ⴼ	⟩	ⱳ	⩜	M	מ	M	m
snake	⌐	⟍	ⴷ	⅂	⅂	ⴹ	N	נ	N	n
eye	⌾	◯	○	O	0	☐	O	ⴹ	O	'
mouth	⌐		0	⅂	⅂	Γ	Π	⅂	P	p
head	⌾	Q	⅂	�	�	⅂	P	⅂	Ʀ	r
papyrus clump	ⴤ		⅂	W	W	ⵑ	Σ	ש	S	s

and the Canaanite kings all had scribes who knew its cuneiform alphabet. The Canaanites were also familiar with Egyptian hieroglyphics (to judge from Egyptian inscriptions discovered in Syria and Palestine) and at Byblos in Syria attempts were made to develop a syllabic script, perhaps based on the Egyptian hieroglyphic script.

The Early Alphabet

Before the middle of the second millennium a distinct form of alphabetic writing had been created in Canaan—one that could contain and transcribe the national dialect. The first evidence of the existence of this script came from inscriptions of the 15th century B.C.E. found at Sinai, and further evidence (from the 17th to the 13th century B.C.E.) came to light later in Canaan, at Lachish, Gezer, Beth-Shemesh and other sites. It seems that under the influence of the new script a second alphabetic form of writing (based on the cuneiform style) evolved in the north of Syria. Inscriptions in that form have been found in Ugarit and elsewhere.

The Canaanite script was the first truly alphabetic script. Its invention made it possible to transcribe the language in from 22 to 32 letters, as opposed to the Egyptian and Mesopotamian methods that involved hundreds of signs. Later it was borrowed by the Greeks, and eventually transformed the art of writing into something that could be practiced by everyone.

When the Israelites entered Canaan, then, they were confronted by royal cities of great age, and by a progressive and advanced society. Canaan was not only a desired objective; it was also Israel's great teacher, and brought with it a rich and massive legacy—one that Israel found difficult to absorb and adjust to its own unique spirit.

The Patriarchs

Biblical historiography preserves the tradition that the Tribes were familiar with Canaan long before the conquest—that they were, in fact, returning to the land where their ancestors had once dwelt, in order to fulfill an ancient purpose and promise. This view is substantiated by archaeological evidence. The names of the Patriarchs and also their ways and customs clearly belong to the second millennium B.C.E.

The dealings of the patriarch Abraham with Eliezer and Hagar become clear in the light of a Hurrite ordinance of the 15th century B.C.E., discovered at Nuzi in northern Mesopotamia; the ordinance prescribes the rights of slaves and adopted servant-maids as possible heirs. And other second millennium customs throw light on Jacob's arguments with Laban, and on Rachel's theft of her father's idols.

There is a good deal of evidence to show that the Patriarchs originated in Mesopotamia. According to tradition, Abraham was born in the Chaldean town of Ur, an important center in southern Mesopotamia. (The name « Chaldees » is, in fact, an anachronism; the Chaldees did not enter that area until the 11th century B.C.E.) Abraham's father, Terah (the son of Nahor and grandson of Serug), went to live in Haran, and it was from there that Abraham departed for the Promised Land (GENESIS XII: 1-4). Isaac's wife Rebecca came from the town of Nahor (GENESIS XXIV) and Jacob's father-in-law, Laban the Aramite, came from Haran—all places in northern Mesopotamia, near the river Balih. Haran and Nahor are mentioned repeatedly in Mari inscriptions of the 18th century B.C.E., and two other towns, Tel Turihi (Tel Terah) and Serugi (Serug), are known from later Assyrian sources. The Patriarchs were tribal chieftains wandering with their flocks and chattels from Mesopotamia to Egypt along the margins of the fertile crescent. Their beast of burden was the donkey, and their source of livelihood was sheep and also, perhaps, trade (GENESIS XXXIV: 10). They were unaware of frontiers, and their domain was the whole tract of settlement stretching between Mesopotamia and Egypt, ‹ from the river of Egypt unto the great river, the river Euphrates › (GENESIS XV: 18). This picture is typical of the Amorite nomads who, in the first centuries of the second millennium B.C.E., infiltrated into all the settled areas that lay between Babylon and Egypt—some settling on the land, others continuing to live as nomads.

A caravan of Amorite nomads—details from a wall-painting (c. 1890 B.C.E.) from the tomb of Pharaoh Khnum-hotep III at Beni Hasan in Lower Egypt. The complete painting incorporates the inscription 'the arriving, bringing eye-paint, which 37 Asiatics brought to him.' The bellows carried by the two donkeys may indicate that some of the nomads represented here are metalworkers.

The parts of Canaan most frequently referred to in the stories of the Patriarchs are in the central mountain range, in the Negev, and in Transjordan: Shechem, Beth-el, and Dothan in the Hills of Ephraim; Hebron (Mamre) and Jerusalem (Salem) in the Hills of Judaea; Mahanaim, Penuel, and Succoth to the east of the Jordan; and, most important, Beersheba and Gerar (its neighbor) in the Negev, the towns from which the Patriarchs drifted southward to the wells and oases in the desert. Some of these sparsely populated parts of Canaan, such as Gilead and the Negev, were famous for their grazing land.

For the most part the Patriarchs were on friendly terms with the local inhabitants, and from time to time they lived within town borders and received certain forms of patronage: Abraham purchased a burial-place for himself near Hebron (GENESIS XXIII), Isaac dug wells near Gerar and practiced seasonal farming successfully (GENESIS XXVI). But they had a sizable military force behind them and Abraham could, when pressed, recruit 318 warriors called *hanichim* (GENESIS XIV : 14). (The Hebrew word *hanichim*, meaning trained servants or professional soldiers, occurs in a 15th century B.C.E. letter from Taanach, in which an Egyptian envoy complains that his garrison has received no « hanukku. »)

The story of Jacob's homecoming to Canaan is revealing. The Bible states that he moved at a leisurely pace through Transjordan with his family and his great herds, and that when he approached the Canaanite town of Shechem he pitched his tent just outside its limits while his sons spread out in the fields with the livestock. Then he bought a plot of land where he could build an altar to the God of Israel (GENESIS XXXIII)—it is interesting to note that the Patriarchs bought land only for worship and burial. But when the family honor was slighted, Jacob's sons did not hesitate to attack Shechem, killing all the male inhabitants of the town; then, to escape Canaanite vengeance, they resumed their migration (GENESIS XXXIV).

It is difficult to find an example among other nations of the preservation of historical traditions from so ancient a period, and one that preceded the settlement and organization of the nation in its own land. This historical consciousness, characteristic of the Jews from their beginning, sprang from a certain spiritual philosophy. It is no coincidence that the first people to believe in a single God was also the first to develop an historical literature and to preserve historical traditions from the time of its inception.

EGYPTIAN EMPIRE 1450 B.C.E.

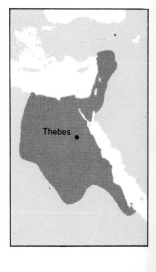

Thebes

The belief that a personal covenant existed between the tribal leader and the special divinity who guided his steps seems to have been widespread among nomadic societies. Take, for example, the abundance of Amorite names in which a word meaning either « father, » « brother, » or « people » replaces the word « god »—words like *Avi-ezer* and *Ahi-ezer*, meaning « my father is my help » and « my brother is my help. » It is as though a pact had been made between the leader and the divinity that turns the tribe into the god's family; the god takes the tribe under his aegis, and in return the tribe pledges itself to worship only that god. In this light the exceptional phenomenon of « the god of Abraham, Isaac, and Jacob, » which belonged to the phase of ancient nomadism, can be understood. God's recurrent promise to the Patriarchs—on the one hand to defend the tribe and multiply its descendants, and on the other to settle it in an inhabited land—express the primordial longings of roving tribesmen.

The Hebrews

The Patriarchs are styled « Hebrews, » a name that can presumably be identified with that of a group (variously called « Apiru, » « Hapiru, » « Habiru, » or « Khapiru ») that became known for the first time from the *el-Amarna Letters*—though opinions as to the connection, if any, between the two diverge widely. But it is clear that the Khapiru were not a homogeneous ethnic group. They appear in different sources throughout the second millennium B.C.E., from places as divergent as Ur in South Mesopotamia, Mari, Nuzi, Anatolia, Syria, Canaan, and Egypt. Yet the allusion is always to aliens without rights to land or property. Occasionally they form part of the town population, but more often they are semi-nomads dwelling on the fringes of towns. Time and again they figure as mercenaries or merchants; or even, on occasions, as serfs.

The status of the Patriarchs in the Bible narrative is very similar. In Hittite contracts we find the phrase « God of the Khapiru, » which is very like « the God of the Hebrews » in the Bible, a title only used when Moses appealed to pharaoh (EXODUS III: 18ff). This is not a paradox; although the Khapiru did not constitute a nation but a social class emerging at different times and in different places, it is possible to treat the references to them in Canaan, on the eve of the period of the Israelite invasion, as information bearing directly upon the Tribes of Israel. For it is as Khapiru, or Hebrews, that they made their entry.

A number of Khapiru were already in Canaan before the 13th century B.C.E. The first definite mention of them occurs in the reign of Amenhotep II (about 1430 B.C.E.) in a list of captives compiled after two of the pharaoh's campaigns, thus: 127 governors, 179 brothers of governors, 555 sons and daughters of governors, 550 maryanu and 240 of their wives, 640 Canaanites (all these belonging to the ruling classes); 3600 Apiru, 15,200 Shasu (Bedouin) and 36,300 Hurrites. Apart from the ordinary inhabitants of Canaan (the Hurrites) two new elements become evident: Shasu and Apiru. The proportion (taken from the list of captives, not the overall population) is 66 per cent Hurrites, 27.5 per cent Shasu and 6.5 per cent Apiru. By the 15th century B.C.E., the Bedouin and the Hebrews already represented a third of the total, and the proportion undoubtedly rose in the next two centuries.

The *el-Amarna Letters* frequently mention the Khapiru as sworn foes of Egyptian administration; the neighboring kings accused one another of allying with them, of furnishing them with arms and provisions, and of aiding them to subjugate parts of the country, particularly the hill-country. The king of Hazor joined with the Khapiru to over-run regions in Upper Galilee; Labaya, king of Shechem, was charged with helping the Khapiru, and admitted as much in writing (*el-Amarna* 254). Shuwardata, king of Gath, is accused, together with the king of Gezer of leading the Khapiru in battle (*el-Amarna* 290); Abdi-Khaipa, king of Jerusalem, claimed that the kings of Gezer, Ashkelon, and Lachish aided them with supplies;

Syrian prisoners and their Egyptian guard—from a Memphis relief (14th century B.C.E.), which depicts Syrian captives being led before the pharaoh.

and the queen of Zaphon, in the central Jordan Valley, reported that the Khapiru had encroached on Ajalon and Zorah and threatened her realm. (These were areas where the Patriarchs ranged, and the first centers of Israelite settlement.)

The tribe of Asher in the north is mentioned in Egyptian sources from the early 13th century B.C.E., and a stela of the reign of Seti I (about 1300 B.C.E.), discovered in Beisan, talks of the suppression of Apiru disturbances ‹ on the mount of Yarumtu. › (This is the Jarmuth, belonging to the tribe of Issachar, north of the Valley of Jezreel—JOSHUA XXI: 29.) The town of Shunem (at the foot of the Hill of Moreh) was destroyed in the *el-Amarna* period by King Labaya of Shechem, and in one missive the king of Megiddo announces that he is plowing the lands of Shunem, under Egyptian orders, with the help of « tribute men » (indentured labor) brought from Yapu (Japhia) near Nazareth, on the boundary between Issachar and Zebulun (JOSHUA XIX: 12). Shunem is a town of Issachar (JOSHUA XIX: 18), founded exactly as Jacob's blessing testifies: ‹ Issachar is a strong ass couching down between two burdens: And he saw that rest was good, and the land that it was pleasant; and bowed his shoulder to bear, and became a servant unto tribute › (GENESIS XLIX: 14-15).

Thus the traditions of the Patriarchs reflect the movements of the Hebrews in the Land hundreds of years before the Israelite conquest. Among these Hebrews (or Khapiru) were the clans from which the Tribes of Israel sprang. The Hebrews had infiltrated in various ways according to circumstances of time and topography, either militantly or as serfs in Canaanite service. The feelings of an Egyptian envoy at the moment of crossing the mountain passes between Megiddo and the Sharon are preserved in a manuscript from the 13th century B.C.E. *(Papyrus Anastasi I)*, ‹ The defile is dangerous, full of Shasu hidden among the thorns; their height is four or five cubits from heel to head, their faces are thunderous, their hearts hard. › Here, perhaps, is an echo of Israelite occupation of the hills.

The Israelites

The Israelites first emerge as a people in the middle of the 13th century B.C.E. During their servitude in Egypt they built Pithom and Raamses (EXODUS I: 11) which, as we have seen, became the capital of the 19th Egyptian dynasty. Across the Jordan they found the organized kingdoms of Edom, Moab, and Ammon: archaeological discoveries show quite definitely that these areas were not settled before the 13th century B.C.E., and the Bible confirms that all the events occurred in the reign of the first king of Moab (NUMBERS XXI : 26).

In towns mentioned in the accounts of the conquest, excavation reveals signs of devastation from the end of the later Canaanite period (that is, the 13th or, at the very latest, the early 12th century B.C.E.): they are Beth-el, Lachish, Debir, Eglon, and Hazor. In the layer that marks the overthrow of Lachish, an inscription came to light from the fourth year of an unnamed pharaoh's reign. The inscription cannot be from an earlier reign than that of Mernephtah, son of Rameses II, which means that Lachish was not reduced before 1220 B.C.E. Excavation also points to the founding of a great many settlements in the hill-country of Canaan during the 13th century B.C.E.—for example in Transjordan, in Galilee, and in the southern range of Ephraim—and these are undoubtedly connected with the Israelite settlement. There is further confirmation in a stela (from the fifth year of his reign) in which Mernephtah declares that he has triumphed over the people of Israel in Canaan, sure proof of Israelite presence there about 1220 B.C.E.

It is remarkable that the Israelite tradition should fail to mention any encounter with the Egyptians in Canaan, or to provide any hint that Egypt was the supreme ruler of the area at that stage. This omission may well be because the Tribes initially encroached upon the mountainous and inland regions that were distant from Egyptian headquarters. But the nature of contemporary sources is also to blame, for, rather than a continual historical record, they present a sequence of traditions dealing with a variety of clans, places, and periods, compiled after a long interval of time. It is natural that such subjective accounts should concern only certain towns and fail to provide a broad background of Canaan and its surroundings.

The Bible demonstrates clearly the way in which events that belong, in essence, to one or other of the Tribes become attributed first to the whole nation, and then to Joshua as he assumed the position of leader. Thus the seizures of Hebron by Caleb and of Debir by Othniel (JOSHUA XV: 13-19) are also ascribed to Judah (JUDGES I: 10-11), and eventually to Joshua and all Israel (JOSHUA X: 36-39).

The first chapter of the Book of Judges contains a great deal of fragmentary information about the Tribes' movements. The tribe of Judah goes up to Bezek (Khirbet Ibzik in the Hills of Ephraim) and then on southward through Jerusalem to the Judaean Hills. The tribe of Dan journeyed from the south across the Hills of Ephraim to Laish (Dan) in the north, plundering and robbing as it went, despite the fact that the area was already settled by various Israelite tribes (JUDGES XVIII). The Book of Judges also records the capture of Beth-el by the house of Joseph, of Hormah by the tribe of Simeon, of Arad by the Kenites—all cities catalogued in the list of « kings of the Land » conquered by Joshua and the Children of Israel (JOSHUA XII). The inference is that we can generally take as authentic those traditions that have come down to us—authentic, that is, as episodes (not always recounted in strict chronological order) concerning individual tribes rather than the people as a whole.

The same problems are presented by the traditional story of the going-down to Egypt, the enslavement there, and the miraculous Exodus. No Egyptian documents

THE PHARAOHS (1991–525 B.C.E.)	
Dynasties XII-XIII	*1991–1720*
Hyksos Rule	*1720–1570*
Dynasty XVIII	*1570–1303*
Ahmose	1570–1545
Amenhotep I	1545–1525
Thutmose I	1525–1508
Thutmose II	1508–1486
Hatshepsut	1486–1468
Thutmose III	1468–1436
Amenhotep II	1436–1410
Thutmose IV	1410–1402
Amenhotep III	1402–1364
Amenhotep IV (Ikhnaton)	1364–1346
Tutankhamen	1346–1333
Haremhab	1333–1303
Dynasty XIX	*1303–1213*
Seti I	1303–1290
Rameses II	1290–1223
Mernephtah	1223–1213
Dynasty XX	*1200–1065*
Rameses III	1175–1144
Rameses IV-IX	1144–1090
Dynasty XXI	*1065–935*
Siamon	964–947
Dynasty XXII	*935–725*
Shishak (Sheshonk) I	
	935–914
Dynasties XXIII–XXIV	
	725–751
Dynasty XXV	*751–656*
Shabaka	710–696
Taharka	685–663
Assyrian Rule	*671–663*
Dynasty XXVI	*663–525*
Necho II	609–593
Psamtik II	593–588
Psamtik III	526–525
Persian Conquest	*525*

naming the Children of Israel or any of the Tribes as such exist, though contemporary inscriptions frequently refer to the passage of nomads along frontier fortresses (Shur of Egypt) to the Delta area; and Rameses II refers to the fact that Apiru were working on the construction of the new capital. It is clear that the « Egyptian chapter » only concerned a relatively small group of people, probably the house of Joseph, which held an important position in Egypt. And it would also seem that the sojourn in Egypt was brief, since, except for a few Egyptian names in Moses' family, absolutely no signs of Egyptian influence can be traced, either in biblical accounts or in excavations of ancient Israelite settlements.

The Exodus

THE EXODUS seems to have taken place during the reign of Rameses II, probably following his unsuccessful campaign against Kadesh (about 1286 B.C.E.). The first staging posts mentioned in the Book of Exodus, Migdol and Baal-Zephon, are to the north of the Delta, and the « Sea of Reeds » (Red Sea) appears to have been one of the lagoons in that vicinity, perhaps the Serbonian Lake. The Hebrews were warned not to pass through ‹ the way of the land of the Philistines, although that was near; for God said, Lest peradventure the people repent when they see war, and they return to Egypt › (EXODUS XIII: 17). But this is an anachronistic reference to the southern branch of the Via maris (stretching from Egypt to the southern coast of Canaan) where the Philistines settled afterward. The stretch was full of Egyptian camps and fortresses, and no band of refugee Khapiru could possibly have escaped that way.

Tradition links the Exodus with the revelation on Mount Sinai. In their speech to pharaoh, Moses and Aaron state that they wish to go into the wilderness and hold a feast to the Lord (EXODUS V: 1-4): ‹ The God of the Hebrews hath met with us: let us go, we pray thee, three days' journey into the desert, and sacrifice unto the Lord our God. › The Tribes gather in a holy place of assembly below Mount Sinai, and there Moses brings them the Lord's revelation.

The beginning of Israel's history is dominated by the colossal figure of Moses. Though we know little of his origins and early life, his personality is clearly defined

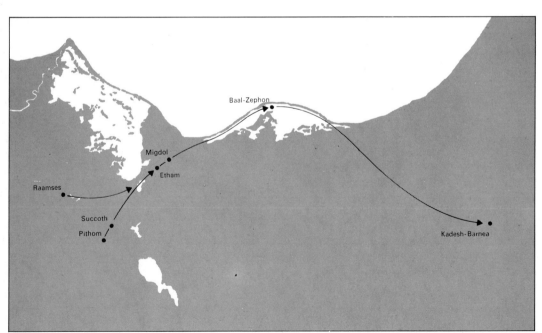

Above, a map tracing the Israelite Exodus from Egypt. Above right, Moses leads the Children of Israel across the Red Sea—from a Jewish prayer book (Hamburg, 1427 C.E.). Right, the Bardawil Lake in northeast Egypt. Some scholars hold that the Israelites' Red Sea crossing was made here, and that the tribes actually crossed the marshes between the lake and the Mediterranean.

by his deeds. He formed the confederacy of the Twelve Tribes of Israel at Sinai, and made an eternal covenant between them and the One Invisible God, Yahweh—a name that signifies « creator » or « maker of being. » Yahweh is identified with the divinity of the Patriarchs, and the new covenant was very like those made by the Patriarchs. But at Sinai a new religion was born; belief in a single, formless, universal God, a God of righteousness who guided the course of peoples—the pure monotheistic faith bequeathed by Israel to the world.

The view that the law proclaimed in the Ten Commandments was essentially the work of Moses himself is generally accepted nowadays. Many of the Bible's ordinances are also ancient, and the « Book of the Covenant » (EXODUS XXI-XXIII) in its form recalls the law codices of Sumeria, Babylon, Assyria, as well as those of the Hittites of the third and second millennia B.C.E. But it differs considerably in substance, representing an essentially classless patriarchal society.

At Sinai, the Israelites became a nation, and the tribal confederacy that was to occupy Canaan was born. The tradition of this covenant could not have taken shape under the schismatic conditions that existed within the Land itself. After Sinai the Tribes were united in a common idea, and the promise of settlement in their own Land was an inherent part of it. Although they generally acted independently, the memory of a mutual and holy Covenant was always behind them. Thus their different and disconnected victories tend to sound like the work of a collective, single-minded army of conquest.

The first center of the Covenant may well have been at Kadesh-Barnea (DEUTERONOMY I: 46), the great oasis on the southern borders of Canaan, and accepted burial ground of the family of Moses (NUMBERS XX: 1). From there spies were sent into the Land, and from there too (according to tradition) began the advance on Canaan.

The first attempt to move directly into Canaan was thwarted by King Arad's vigorous resistance (NUMBERS XIV: 40-45; XXI: 1; XXXIII: 40; and DEUTERONOMY I: 41-44). After that the Tribes swung eastward into Transjordan, an under-populated region outside the confines of the Egyptian province, providing excellent pasturing land. The Israelites were not the first people to settle there. The Ammonites, Moabites, and Edomites had already moved into the south of Transjordan and the desert margin. It appears that they had taken and re-populated mainly vacant areas containing only scattered and broken towns like Rabbah (captured by the Ammonites and made into their capital, Rabbath-Ammon). These events confirm that the Israelite conquest was not a random and arbitrary occurrence, but part of a great wave of « colonization » that swept the territories of the Fertile Crescent at the turn of the 13th century B.C.E., similar to the massive Amorite invasion of a previous age.

This was the Aramaeo-Hebrew « shock of conquest » that was felt throughout Canaan and Syria (and as far as Mesopotamia), and gave rise to assertions of affinity with the Aramaeans and such Hebraic elements as the inhabitants of Transjordan. The causes or circumstances that created these migratory convulsions are not known, but the Tribes' switch from their old Bedouin ways to a sedentary life can only be understood in terms of this general movement of peoples.

In other parts of Transjordan, the Tribes of Israel also found kindred Hebrews who had entered in an earlier period and who now joined them. It seems that the tribe of Gad belongs to these earlier settlers (classed in clan genealogy as sons of handmaids or concubines, i.e. the sons of Zilpah, who was Jacob's concubine and the handmaid of his wife Leah), who occupied so much land that the terms « Gilead » and « Gad » became almost synonymous. Northern Gilead and the boundaries of Bashan were overrun by tribal raiders at different times—by the clan of Jair, for instance, which gave its name to settlements called « farmsteads of Jair, » and apparently was an offshoot of a powerful confederacy of tribes that

**Fighting
for
the
Land**

34

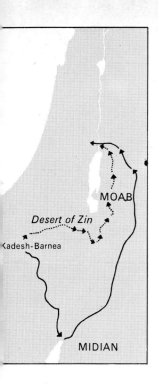

Left, a map showing the movement of the Tribes into Canaan. Above, the wilderness of Zin crossed by the Israelites during their wanderings.

(according to Assyrian inscriptions) also invaded the country around the Euphrates. (The traditions of the wars against the giant King Og of Bashan certainly belong to that former phase, for they are shared by the Ammonites.)

Conquest of Gilead

Edom, Moab, and Ammon quickly established monarchical forms of government, and provided a formidable barrier to Israelite progress. Sihon, king of Heshbon (one of the few royal cities in southern Gilead) extended his realm at Moab's expense, robbing the first king of Moab of all the plainland as far as the river Arnon (NUMBERS XXI: 26ff.). The Tribes, who surrounded the kingdoms of Edom and Moab in the south-east, attacked from the desert and took Heshbon.

The tribe of Reuben seems to have played a central part in the assault; it was the oldest of the Tribes of Israel, by tribal lineage, and now established itself in and around Heshbon (NUMBERS XXXII: 37). This victory also gave the Tribes the plains around Heshbon, and from then on the river Arnon became the recognized boundary between Moab and Israel, though the Moabites never resigned themselves to the situation, and constantly strove to regain the lost area. The whole of Gilead was now wide open to the Israelite settlers. It is interesting to note that (according to tradition) it was in Gilead, between Mahanaim and Penuel on the river Jabbok, that Jacob was given the name Israel (GENESIS XXXII: 28).

Most of the Tribes soon moved west of the Jordan, though historical information here is fragmentary. The stories of the overthrow of Jericho and Ai echo popular folklore, but many archaeologists doubt whether such tales contain the least grain of historical fact. In the 13th century B.C.E., Jericho was at best a weak unfortified settlement, and Ai had been destroyed in the earlier Canaanite period, more than a thousand years before the coming of the Tribes. (Incidentally Ai means « the ruin »; it is therefore possible that the legends were connected with some particularly large mounds of debris evident in the area.)

But possibly there is something in the theory that the Israelite confederacy was centered near Jericho in the ancient sanctuary of Gilgal, on the banks of the Jordan.

זה שער העיר ויולד עד האמצע

An imaginary plan of Jericho, made by the Spanish scribe Elisha Ben Avraham Crescas (in the 14th century c.e.) for his illuminated bible—the famous "Farhi Bible."

Many years later the first of Israel's kings was crowned at Gilgal (I SAMUEL XI: 14). Nor was it by chance that the Israelites later turned back to Gilgal, the first focus of the Covenant in Canaan, for it recalled a tribal unity that had broken down during the period of the Judges. Accordingly, the history of the conquest preserves mainly those stories connected with Gilgal. There is even an intriguing hint of the transfer from Gilgal: ‹And an angel of the Lord came up from Gilgal to Bochim . . . › (JUDGES II: 1). After this the divergent Tribes established different centers, and traditionalists who believe in a general Israelite alliance must link Saul's reign with the Gilgal period, erasing or blurring the intervening period.

The Second Stage

The other campaigns described in the Book of Joshua—the wars against the Gibeonites, the seizure of the cities of the Shefela, the war in Galilee—were not part of the first invasion of Canaan, but a second stage of conflict with surviving Canaanite strongholds. (The Tribes already occupied their respective estates.) Only extremely sketchy descriptions of the Tribes' penetration into the Land are contained

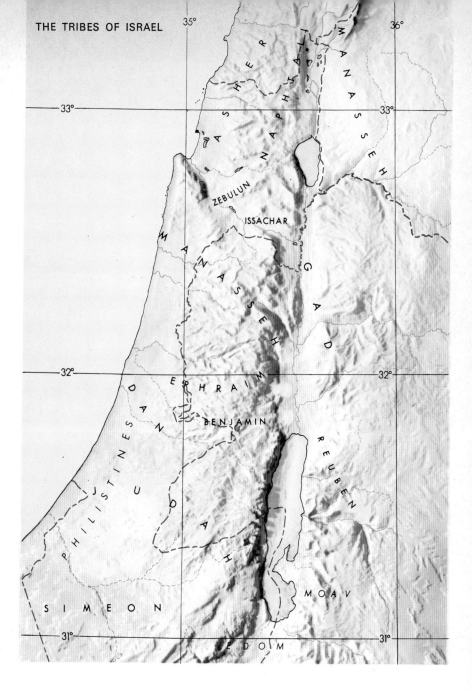

And Joshua gathered all the tribes of Israel to Shechem, and called for the elders of Israel, and for their heads, and for their judges, and for their officers; and they presented themselves before God. And Joshua said unto all the people, Thus saith the Lord God of Israel, Your fathers dwelt on the other side of the flood in old time, even Terah, the father of Abraham, and the father of Nachor: and they served other gods. And I took your father Abraham from the other side of the flood, and led him throughout all the land of Canaan, and multiplied his seed, and gave him Isaac. And I gave unto Isaac Jacob and Esau: and I gave unto Esau mount Seir, to possess it; but Jacob and his children went down into Egypt. I sent Moses also and Aaron, and I plagued Egypt, according to that which I did among them: and afterward I brought you out. And I brought your fathers out of Egypt: and ye came unto the sea; and the Egyptians pursued after your fathers with chariots and horsemen unto the Red sea. And when they cried unto the Lord, he put darkness between you and the Egyptians, and brought the sea upon them, and covered them; and your eyes have seen what I have done in Egypt: and ye dwelt in the wilderness a long season. And I brought you into the land of the Amorites, which dwelt on the other side Jordan; and they fought with you: and I gave them into your hand, that ye might possess their land; and I destroyed them from before you. . . . And ye went over Jordan, and came unto Jericho: and the men of Jericho fought against you, the Amorites, and the Perizzites, and the Canaanites, and the Hittites, and the Girgashites, the Hivites, and the Jebusites; and I delivered them into your hand—JOSHUA XXIV: 1-11.

in the first chapter of the Book of Judges. The one item concerning the clan of Joseph is the capture of Beth-el (confirmed by recent excavation and the unearthing of a Canaanite town, destroyed in the 13th century B.C.E. and covered by a layer characteristic of early Israelite settlement). Beth-el was in the southern part of Ephraim's estate, near the boundary with Benjamin.

There is no evidence of invading warfare elsewhere in the Hills of Ephraim. But it is evident that Israelite tribes had settled there, and it is there that the tribal center in the period of the Judges was situated—first, it seems, in the neighborhood of Shechem ‹ under an oak, that was by the sanctuary of the Lord › (JOSHUA XXIV: 26), where the Tribes were already congregated (so tradition says) in Joshua's time. Later the center was at Shiloh, between Shechem and Beth-el. Here, no doubt, were forerunners of the Hebrews who had come to the region in the *el-Amarna* days and who were now prepared to ally themselves with them.

Apparently fighting also went on elsewhere, as the list of conquered Canaanite towns given in JOSHUA (XII: 7ff.) indicates. Alongside Beth-el in the Hills of Ephraim are mentioned Tappuah and Tirzah, which indicates that the compiler had heard accounts of battles at these towns not recorded in the Bible. Take the reference to Tappuah in one passage: ‹ Now Manasseh had the land of Tappuah: but Tappuah on the border of Manasseh belonged to the children of Ephraim › (JOSHUA XVII: 8).

37

This implies an interesting linkage of events in the neighborhood of Tappuah, and slightly shifts the veil that covers the complexities of conquest and settlement: Manasseh settled within the territory of the Canaanite town (mainly to the north of it); but the town itself fell into the hands of Ephraim.

It is doubtful whether there was ever any widespread fighting in the Hills of Ephraim, presumably because the scattered nature of the Canaanite towns, and Israelite infiltration into the areas between, made it difficult for the towns to organize a collective « front. » The towns of Shechem, Tirzah, and Canaanite Hepher in the Sharon are cited as belonging to Manasseh (JOSHUA XVII: 2-3), and the implication is that they were eventually absorbed into the Israelite tribal organization. The story of Abimelech who turned against his people to become king, assisted by the ‹ men of Shechem › (JUDGES IX), suggests that at this time Shechem was still mainly a Canaanite city, and the ‹ men of Shechem › were apparently the Canaanite lords of the town. Thus it would seem that these towns accepted Israelite dominion.

The first great Canaanite alliance came into being farther south under the leadership of the king of Jerusalem, who succeeded in uniting under a single command his neighbor Hebron and three more distant cities, Jarmuth, Lachish, and Eglon (JOSHUA X: 1-15). It is reasonable to suppose that Joshua was connected with this episode. As victor in the first large-scale campaign against a Canaanite alliance, he came in the course of time to be considered the central figure in the traditions of the conquest. The fact that he was buried in Timnath Serah (Heres) in the Hills of Ephraim confirms that the campaign was fought by the clan of Joseph.

In his attempt to form a united Canaanite alliance the king of Jerusalem met with the refusal of the Gibeonites, who surrendered to the Tribes; and when he attempted to subdue them, Joshua attacked, cut his line of retreat to Jerusalem, and pursued the fleeing Canaanite troops down the famous declivity of Beth-Horon as far as the Valley of Ajalon. (The episode has been immortalized in an ancient song.) The Canaanite reverse in Gibeon opened the way for the Tribes in the south, who were then able to approach the Hills of Judaea directly from the Negev and the Arava. Hebron and its neighboring towns fell to the sons of Caleb (according to tradition, as reward for Caleb's resoluteness in the mission of the spies—NUMBERS XIII); and the area of Debir in the south-eastern Shefela fell to the kindred clans of Kenaz. Caleb and his family also established themselves in the southern parts of the Hills of Judaea and in the Negev. During David's reign there are references to sectors of the Negev belonging to Caleb, Jerachmeel, the Kenites, and others. The fact that these tribal families shared many names with the Hurrite families of Edom points to common origins. Of the Kenites it is said that they came to the neighborhood of Arad from ‹ the city of palm trees › (JUDGES I: 16): the reference is not to Jericho, but to Tamar (or Zoar) south of the Dead Sea.

Judah came from the north, as related briefly in JUDGES (I: 4ff.), by way of Bezek (cf. Saul's journey from Bezek to Jabesh-Gilead—I SAMUEL XI), and destroyed Jerusalem. The Tribes were often able to capture and raze Canaanite towns in this way, but they rarely had the strength or the technical skill to occupy them at once and to erect the necessary buildings and encircling walls. Thus Jerusalem seems to have fallen again a little later to the Jebusites, by all indications people of Hittite or Hurrite descent, who formed a powerful alien enclave in this period (cf. JUDGES XIX: 10-12), splitting the Tribes of the south from the Hills of Ephraim. The tribe of Judah settled south of Jerusalem, and Bethlehem, mentioned in the *el-Amarna Letters* as being within the region of Jerusalem, became its center.

Simeon seems to have followed a similar route from the north (JUDGES I: 3). At any rate, his place in the traditional tribal covenant shows that, like Judah, he was associated with the Tribes of Israel before the settlement (see GENESIS XXXIV: 25).

Simeon settled in the neighborhood of Beersheba (already the center of Hebrew activity in the Patriarchs' era) and from there expanded eastward, capturing Canaanite Hormah (JUDGES I: 17).

Settlement of the Shefela

From the narrow confines between Jebus and the territory of Caleb, the families of Judah expanded westward toward the Shefela. In the north of the Shefela they penetrated mainly as settlers, and assimilated the Canaanite elements of the area; in the southern plain, a number of towns were conquered, among them Lachish and its neighbors Makkedah, Libnah, and Eglon (JOSHUA X, and XV: 39-42). And it is no doubt true that Horam, king of Gezer, tried to aid Lachish (JOSHUA X: 33), for even in the *el-Amarna* period these were the largest towns in the area.

Excavation of sites in the Shefela shows that the Tribes did not rebuild ruins immediately after conquest; a period of time had to elapse before habitation was renewed, and then it was renewed only by degrees. There is no question but that Israelite settlement started with the downfall of the towns (perhaps even earlier in parts), but the Tribes were not capable of reestablishing the complex structure and organization of urban life immediately.

Lachish, as we saw, was conquered some time after 1220 B.C.E., a dating that fits the general political context—for during the period of decline that followed the collapse of the 19th Egyptian Dynasty (about 1210-1175 B.C.E.) the country plunged into domestic disorder and, despite the attempts of Rameses III to sustain it, the great empire finally disintegrated. Canaan was left to its own devices, and in the zones where Israelite penetration and Canaanite capitals clashed, conditions were explosive. It is to this period that we can assign the capitulation of the southern towns of the Shefela and the fiercest of the Galilee battles.

A letter from the prince of Jerusalem to the Egyptian pharaoh (probably Amenhotep III), *c.* 14th century B.C.E.—it was found at Tell-el-Amarna in 1887.

To the king, my lord, say: Thus Abdu-Heba, thy servant. At the feet of my lord seven times and seven times I fall. Let my king know this matter! Milkilu and Tagu have caused their troops to enter the town of Rubutu. . . . Let my king know that all the lands are at peace but that there is war against me. So let my king take care of his land! Behold the land of Gezer, the land of Ashkelon, and Lachish, they have given them grain, oil, and all their requirements; and let the king thus take care of his archers! Let him send archers against the men who transgress against the king, my lord. If there are archers here in this year, then the lands and the governors will still belong to the king, my lord; but if there are no archers, the lands and the governors will no longer belong to the king! Behold this land of Jerusalem: it was not my father and not my mother who gave it to me, but the arm of the mighty king which gave it to me. Behold, this deed is the deed of Milkilu and the deed of the sons of Lab'ayu who have given the land of the king to the Apiru. Behold, O king, my lord, I am right! . . . Addaya has left, together with the garrison and the Egyptian officer which my king had given me. Let the king know! . . . So send me a garrison this year, and send me a commissioner likewise, O my king—the prince of Jerusalem.

The Bible refers to two northern wars, the Battle of the Waters of Merom (JOSHUA XI) and the Battle of Deborah (JUDGES IV-V); in both, Jabin, king of Hazor, led the Canaanite alliances. Hazor was already the capital of Canaan in Hyksos days, and up to the 13th century B.C.E. its name appears in most important Egyptian sources. Archaeological finds show conclusively that until then it was the greatest of the northern Canaanite cities, but that it declined swiftly at the close of the century and was wiped out soon afterward. Primitive Israelite settlements were started among the ruins, but did not endure (which was the usual order of things), and Hazor remained derelict until the reign of Solomon. Archaeological excavation confirms that Hazor was destroyed either at the end of the 13th or at the turn of the 12th century B.C.E.

Both the northern wars were probably waged after the collapse of the 19th Egyptian dynasty, against royal alliances of a similar make-up. Apart from Hazor, accounts of the battles at the Waters of Merom name only three cities: Shimron in the northern Valley of Jezreel, Achshaph in the Valley of Acre, and Merom in Upper Galilee. There follows a reference to ‹ the kings that were on the north of the mountains, and of the plains south of Chinneroth, and in the valley, and in the borders of Dor on the west › (JOSHUA XI: 2).

This might imply that the accounts specify only the principal cities, and that there was still a general alliance of cities from the northern valleys and Galilee. The Song of Deborah (JUDGES V) speaks of a pact only between the kings of Canaan under Sisera, the commander of Hazor's army. But since the fighting took place between Taanach, Megiddo, and Mount Tabor (JUDGES IV: 6 and 14; V: 19), the same or nearly the same league of the northern kings must be intended, possibly an even larger one. The list of « the kings of Canaan » given in the Book of Joshua preserves a fuller catalog of the parties participating in the pact, namely (according to the Septuagint): Hazor, Shimron, Merom, Achshaph, Kadesh, Taanach, Megiddo, Jokneam, Dor, and « Galilee of the Gentiles, » a collective name for the whole territory ruled by Sisera (JOSHUA XII: 19-23).

Analysis of the nature of the wars, of their geographical progress, and of their outcome, reinforces the view that the war waged by the prophetess Deborah preceded that of the Waters of Merom, for hers was the first victory of the Israelites over a large concentration of Canaanite chariots, an adversary that the Tribes usually feared and disliked facing. (For this reason, and also because the Canaanites had managed to dominate the Galilean tribes for some time, her victory left a deep impression and was immortalized in the Song of Deborah.)

Deborah, and Barak son of Avinoam, marshaled the tribal forces at Mount Tabor, a holy and well-protected place (DEUTERONOMY XXXIII: 19) bordering on the estates of Naphtali, Issachar, and Zebulun. Sisera mobilized his chariots and advanced. Doubtless he thought that the sight of his chariots would scatter the Tribes; perhaps this maneuver had been successful on previous occasions. But his open emergence on to the plain beneath the mountain robbed the chariots of their principal power, the element of surprise. Barak chose exactly the right moment to attack, forced Sisera's troops to withdraw, and drove them into the floodwaters of the river Kishon. No important Canaanite town appears to have fallen as a result of this victory, but the balance of strength in the north was radically altered in Israel's favor from this point on.

The battle of the Waters of Merom was fought in Upper Galilee, scarcely nine miles from Hazor. It appears that Canaanite forces had been rushed there in an attempt to save Hazor and Upper Galilee. But the Canaanites were defeated, and Hazor soon capitulated to the encircling Tribes. The biblical version, associating the extinction of Hazor with the war at the Waters (JOSHUA XI: 10-15), is an accurate record of the events.

An aerial view of Mount Tabor, where Deborah and Barak defeated the armies of the Canaanite kingdom of Hazor.

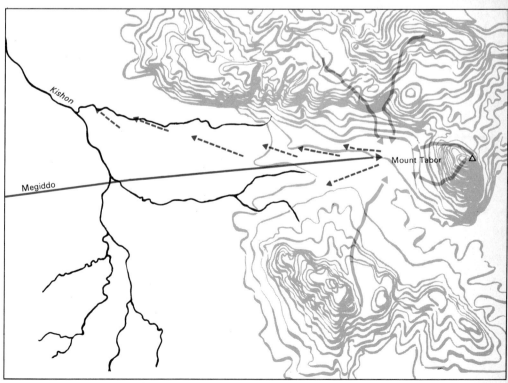

And Sisera gathered together all his chariots, even nine hundred chariots of iron, and all the people that were with him, from Harosheth of the Gentiles unto the river of Kishon. And Deborah said unto Barak, Up; for this is the day in which the Lord hath delivered Sisera into thine hand: is not the Lord gone out before thee? So Barak went down from mount Tabor, and ten thousand men after him. And the Lord discomfited Sisera, and all his chariots, and all his host, with the edge of the sword before Barak; so that Sisera lighted down off his chariot, and fled away on his feet. But Barak pursued after the chariots, and after the host, unto Harosheth of the Gentiles: and all the host of Sisera fell upon the edge of the sword; and there was not a man left—JUDGES IV: 13-16.

JUST as it would be wrong to regard this long chapter of warfare as a single and combined operation of conquest, so it is wrong to regard the settlement of the Tribes as a single, simple course of events. Presumably, the transition to agriculture and permanent dwellings began with the first entry of the Tribes into their respective territories. But it was a slow process, since the Tribes simply did not possess the resources to occupy the urban territories they conquered: ‹ And the Lord thy God will put out those nations before thee by little and little: thou mayest not consume them at once, lest the beasts of the field increase upon thee › (DEUTERONOMY VII: 22). The Tribes first sought to occupy the hill region where the Canaanite settlements were sparse and their war chariots ineffective. (The Bible constantly emphasizes the fact that this or that tribe could not occupy a valley because of the Canaanite ‹ chariots of iron ›; see JOSHUA XVII: 12-18; JUDGES I: 19.) In the books of Joshua and Judges, names of cities the Tribes could not take are given; among them are Jerusalem, Gezer, and the towns of the northern Shefela within the ‹ territory of Dan ›; and in the north, the chain of strongholds in the valleys of Acre and Jezreel. When the Israelites did enter the valleys, they were generally forced to pay tribute to the Canaanite towns or to become their serfs, like Issachar and Asher in Western Galilee, who dwelt ‹ among the Canaanites › (JUDGES I: 32).

But some Canaanites still remained in the hill country between the Israelite settlements, and not only in the cities of the Gibeonites that had come to terms with the Israelites. We saw earlier, particularly from the genealogical list of the tribe of Manasseh, how Canaanite towns were annexed to the Tribes; Zaphon, too, in the Jordan Valley (NUMBERS XXVI: 15) appears to have joined the Tribes, and there must have been many other similar cases. The conquest of the remaining cities did not take place at once, as is made clear by the inter-tribal frontiers, which are generally defined by the names of important Canaanite towns: Jerusalem and Kirjath-Jearim between Judah and Benjamin; Beth-el and Gezer between Benjamin and Ephraim; Tappuah between Ephraim and Manasseh; Jabneel and Adama on the southern border of Naphtali; and Hannathon and Jokneam between Zebulun and Asher. If these had been taken before settlement began, they would have become tribal centers and not boundary-marks.

The question of land was an urgent one for the Tribes. The solution was expressed by Joshua in answer to the complaints of the children of Joseph: ‹ If thou be a great people, then get thee up to the wood country, and cut down for thyself there in the land of the Perizzites and of the giants, if Mount Ephraim be too narrow for thee . . . But the mountain shall be thine; for it is a wood, and thou shalt cut it down: and the outgoings of it shall be thine . . . . › (JOSHUA XVII: 15-18). These phrases express a revolutionary concept in the settlement of Canaan. The Land had been continually invaded throughout its long history; but each new invader had only brought a fresh ethnic element to merge with the existing ones, and the pattern of settlement never altered materially. The Israelites were the first people to be dissatisfied with city conquest alone, which, in any case, they only partly achieved. They proceeded to lay their hands on great tracts of forest and virgin soil in the wooded regions; and these acquisitions re-cast the map of settlement and literally transformed the Land of Canaan into the Land of Israel, thus crystallizing the distinctiveness of the Jews in their Land.

The country was now spotted with settlements, particularly in the mountainous areas that, until then, had been forested. Exploration has revealed that these settlements existed throughout Galilee, in the Hills of Ephraim, in Judaea, and in Transjordan. Usually they were small, unfortified, or weakly fenced; but invariably they were situated close to arable land. The tools used by the Israelites were a crude copy of Canaanite tools, and the Israelites learned the arts of building and pottery from their neighbors in Canaan. Characteristic forms (differing from north to south) were quickly developed, which make it easy to identify early Israelite settlement. The establishment of dense and continuous Israelite zones near Canaanite habitations helped to safeguard a national identity and its development, both spiritually and materially, while allowing for assimilation of Canaanite culture and techniques. The filling of the gaps between settlements also tended to modify the local geo-political situation. Apart from the increase in the economic potential as a result of the expansion of cultivated areas, and the doubling and even tripling of the population, the gaps between the regions (which had been a serious obstacle to internal political unity) were bridged. As a result, the economic and political value of east Transjordan and the mountain areas rose markedly, and they became a vital hinterland in times of emergency. The fact that the Israelites were eventually able to weld the greater part of the Land into a single kingdom for the first time in its history was an outcome of their full settlement of the interior.

The peopling of the hills and the clearing of forests were made much easier by the invention of impermeable cisterns (which ended the need to depend on nearby springs) and durable iron tools; neither of these inventions can be credited to the Tribes. Impermeable cisterns existed at the end of the Canaanite period; and iron, first used by the Hittites, appears to have been brought to Canaan by the Philistines. The cisterns were an essential feature of close hill-settlement, for they enabled rain and flood water to be stored. Iron, on the other hand, made the felling of trees and the preparation and plowing of fields a good deal easier. The Philistines, of course, tried to retain a monopoly of the manufacture of iron implements, but the Bible shows that iron tools and weapons soon formed an integral part of the Israelite economy, and that the Israelites were prepared to buy them whatever the price (I SAMUEL XIII: 19-21).

This network of small settlements was suited to the patriarchal form of administration, and helped to prolong its existence. The system was based on the patriarchal households and family units that made up each tribe; blood relationship was the all-important consideration, territorial allegiance was secondary. Family elders and tribal chiefs were the judges when disputes arose between households and families, and were commanders in time of war. Each tribesman was considered a guardian of his fellow's safety: to wound the individual was to wound his tribe, and revenge could be swift and furious. Though the transition to fixed settlement necessarily weakened tribal unity, the small settlements could not yet afford to abandon the collective protection on which their safety depended. On the other hand, the tribes had to adapt themselves to their new existence. Changes began to develop in their composition, and new alliances were formed between neighbors.

Dividing the Land

Throughout the period of the judges there was constant change in the tribal names, composition, and places of settlements. Some of the names of the new tribes indicate that they were formed as the result of some geographical or special circumstance. For instance Benjamin (which means « son of the south ») was the southernmost of the tribes settled in the Hills of Ephraim, and Issachar (meaning « the man of payment ») was the name given to a tribe that paid tribute to Canaanite overlords. It would seem that Ephraim existed as a geographical name before the arrival of the tribe of Ephraim (originally part of the house of Joseph). Even during Deborah's campaign, the tribe of Machir was mentioned alongside Ephraim (JUDGES V: 14), and only at a later stage, when many families from Machir wandered to the north of Gilead, did the tribe become divided.

Manasseh was the name given to the western tribe, and the rest of the tribe became either Ben Manasseh (meaning « the son of Manasseh ») or Avi Gilead (literally « the father of Gilead, » though « inhabitant of Gilead » is implied). The names of the remaining sons of Manasseh (Abiezer, Helek, Shechem, Shemida, and so on)

43

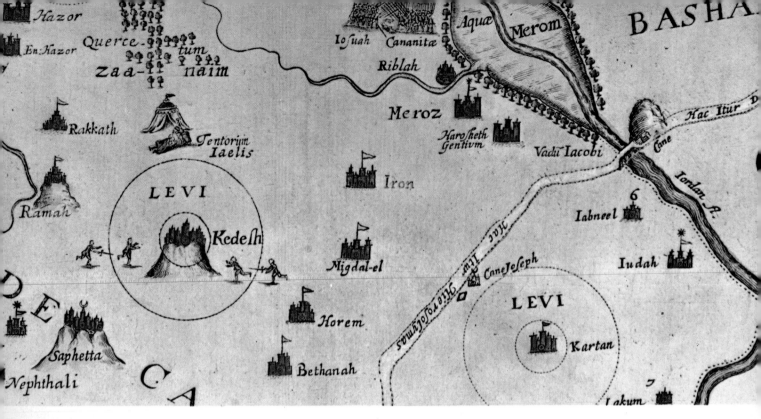

Part of a map of Palestine in biblical times (drawn by the 17th-century English engraver, Thomas Fuller) showing the Levite sanctuary towns.

And among the cities which ye shall give unto the Levites there shall be six cities for refuge, which ye shall appoint for the manslayer, that he may flee thither : and to them ye shall add forty and two cities—NUMBERS XXXV: 6.

are still known as geographical administrative units in Samarian shards from the time of Jehu (842-814 B.C.E.). This is the origin of the genealogical list given in the Book of Joshua (XVII: 1-3) for the daughters of Zelophehad (the son of Hepher, the son of Gilead, the son of Machir, the son of Manasseh), reflecting lengthy and intricate vicissitudes of settlement.

The only extant account of tribal wandering concerns the tribe of Dan. The tribe was prevented from gaining a foothold in the northern Shefela by the Amorite cities, and moved on through the Hills of Ephraim to the northern end of the Jordan Valley, where it captured the Canaanite town of Laish. The tribe renamed the town Dan, and made it the center of its new territory (JUDGES XVII-XVIII). This, too, is an account not of the migration of an entire tribe, but of the movements of one part of the family of the Danites —JUDGES XVIII: 11. (Samson came from the tribe of Dan, though the legends that surround his name must belong to the later period when the Tribes were in conflict with the Philistines in that area.)

The existence of identical family names in different tribes and the distinct geographical links with distant places show that the wanderings of families and households from area to area were a common occurrence, for the migrants naturally retained their family names. For example, Asher's territory was in Western Galilee, but its family names were connected with places in the southern region of the Hills of Ephraim, and one of its principal families, the Beriah, was counted among the families of Ephraim and Benjamin.

The biblical accounts of the Tribes' activities convey something of their dynamism; but the descriptions of their territories belong to a later stage. From these it is possible to reconstruct a picture of the tribal alliances as they were formed during the period of settlement. Most important is the description of the tribal boundaries

Tribal Boundaries

in the Book of Joshua (xv-xix). The compiler used several sources, but what concern us particularly are the passages that describe the boundaries and indicate adjacent geographical points. Even though the town lists may be drawn from different periods, the precise fixing of inter-tribal boundaries must have been done by the Tribes at the time of settlement to avoid conflict and rivalry. Some scholars believe that this boundary list could not have been compiled until the time of King David (who made Jerusalem an important city), since the descriptions of the boundaries around Jerusalem are detailed, while those of the boundaries elsewhere in Palestine are much briefer. But it would seem that the original list was edited and abridged in David's reign, and that the list in the Book of Joshua is the later.

The original account probably gave exact particulars of the springs, hills, groves, and so on that bounded the tribes in each area, but the abridged (and later) version retained only the names of towns near frontiers, often without specifying on which side of the frontier they were situated. In the case of the northern tribes in particular, there is often no more than a reference to the frontier of the adjacent tribe—in this way: ‹ reacheth to Zebulun on the south side, and reacheth to Asher on the west side › (JOSHUA XIX: 34).

The boundaries of some other tribes are described vaguely, if at all. Simeon, for instance, was simply recorded as being ‹ within the inheritance of the Children of Judah › (JOSHUA XIX: 1); Dan is said to have traveled northward and settled near Naphtali (JOSHUA XIX: 47); and the boundaries of Issachar and of the tribes in Transjordan are not described at all.

The Northern Tribes

The tribes of the Hills of Ephraim and Galilee were formed into a tribal alliance; and a further alliance, made on the ‹ altar over against the land of Canaan, in the borders of Jordan, › linked them with the tribes of Transjordan (JOSHUA XXII). The whole body of the southern tribes—« Judah »—probably included many elements that were outside the early confederacy. The link between the southern and northern tribes was made tenuous by the hostile enclave that stretched from Jebusite Jerusalem through the Gibeonite cities to Gezer.

The northern alliance, which had its headquarters at Shiloh, mid-way between Beth-el and Shechem (JUDGES XXI: 19), adopted the name of « Israel. » It possessed both the original Ark of the Covenant and the ‹ tabernacle of the tent of the congregation › from the days of the desert wandering. By the time the monarchy was established, Israel and Judah had become completely autonomous powers, governed by permanent institutions of elders; and they supplied separate contingents in time of war. After this the term « Israel » becomes ambiguous: it either refers to the whole people or (more accurately) to the northern alliance only.

Little is known about the administration of the tribal alliances, but the stable condition of the Tribes at the time of the monarchy's creation suggests that their authority was substantial. The northern alliance was centered around the sanctuary of Shiloh, where a priestly house, claiming descent from Moses' brother Aaron, officiated. The alliance was presided over by the priests and presidents of the Tribes, who seem to have been elected by an assembly of elders. In times of emergency, the community would come under the control of the military leaders, « the men of Israel, » and a supreme military command would be established.

The judges occupied a special place within the framework. The great judges were inspiring, almost prophetic spiritual leaders who in times of crisis would assume control of the people as God's representatives. Later they became the leaders of the tribal alliances. In addition there were a number of « minor judges » who were not concerned with war (JUDGES X: 1-5; XII: 8-15). Thus it may well be that a permanent judicial appointment, held by the chieftains of the Tribes in turn, existed within the organizational framework, and that this post assumed greater authority in time of war. The discussions that took place between Jephthah and the elders of Gilead show that this is likely: Jephthah stipulated that he would return and lead the people against Ammon only if they would let him continue, after victory, as the chief of the elders of Gilead (JUDGES XI: 5-11).

If the appointment of a great judge, elected by the will of God, did not lead to the immediate establishment of a monarchy, it was because the patriarchal system was so deeply rooted. For this reason, Gideon's son, Abimelech, failed in his attempt to become king. His power was bolstered by a company of ‹ vain and light persons › (JUDGES IX: 4), that is to say, by a troop of mercenaries with no position in Israelite society. Furthermore, he was supported by the Canaanites of Shechem, who hoped that he would help them to regain their supremacy in the Hills of Ephraim. (In fact, they were the first to rebel when Abimelech refused to obey their instructions; as a result he destroyed their ancient city—JUDGES IX: 23-45.) Thus Abimelech failed to establish a lasting authority within the Israelite settlement, and it is almost certain that his leadership would have been short-lived even if he had not been killed in Thebez when a ‹ certain woman cast a piece of a millstone › upon his head.

The tribal alliance, by its very nature, was weak: it possessed neither administration nor a standing army, and the judges could only marshal a large force at moments of extreme peril. Even then the clans often sent small contingents. At the end of the fighting (as the biblical historian records) ‹ the children of Israel departed ... every man to his tribe and to his family .... In those days there was no king in Israel: every man did that which was right in his own eyes › (JUDGES XXI: 24-25). But Israel had no really large enemy at the time, and the alliance was adequate for the defense of the new settlements that were springing up. No power had yet replaced the waning Egypt. The Land of Israel, Syria, and the countries of the Euphrates were seething with Hebraic and Aramaean tribes struggling to gain entry into the settled areas. Nowhere was there any strong resistance. As we saw, most of the Canaanite towns were weakened after a number of fierce and decisive battles at the end of the 13th century B.C.E., and though a few still retained their independence and former boundaries, they no longer constituted a threat to the Tribes. The « peoples of the sea, » and in particular the Philistines, who began to arrive about 1170 B.C.E. were themselves in a phase of settlement and consolidation, and it was years before they became a first-class military power.

The wars described in the Book of Judges were against neighboring Hebraic monarchies or invading nomads who exploited every opportunity to trespass and enlarge their domains. But none of these could stand up to the Tribes. The wars of Ehud against Moab, of Gideon against the Midianites, and of Jephthah against Ammon are typical examples. Whether or not the events were recorded in correct chronological order is arguable, but they clearly occurred during the 12th century B.C.E. or, at the very latest, at the beginning of the 11th.

For the most part this was a peaceful period of settlement and stabilization in which hundreds of Israelite villages sprang up. The Israelite farmer was primarily interested in his soil, and would relinquish his plow to answer the Judge's call to arms only when he had no choice. So long as no grave danger threatened, he was satisfied with the existing tribal organization and unwilling to exchange it for another that might constrict his personal liberty.

The risk of being assimilated into Canaan and of being swallowed by its culture (as had happened to so many others of its conquerors) was a grave one. Indeed, Israel borrowed all its material culture from the Canaanites, and the sophisticated and cosmopolitan Canaanite cities inevitably had an effect. But the gravest threat was to the Israelite religion.

Consolidation

The Influence of Baal

46

The God of Israel and of the Patriarchs had helped the Chosen People to conquer Canaan. Now many of the early places where Baal had been worshiped were converted into « high places » for the worship of Yahweh. The fertility cult of Ashtoreth offered one temptation, though a minor one, since as we saw the simple tribesmen were shocked by the sexuality associated with the cult: nevertheless, they were quick to admit figurines of the goddesses Asherah and Ashtoreth into their homes. Much more dangerous was the worship of many *Baalim*, local variants of the one Baal who dwelt in the far north, and who might have become identified with, or even have replaced, Yahweh. Names containing the word « Baal » became common in Israel; for example, Jerubbaal (another name for Gideon) and Ishbaal the son of Saul, who was also called Ishui or Ish-yo (I SAMUEL XIV: 49). That is to say, the radical « Baal » was often substituted for the radical « Yo » or « Yah. »

Biblical historiography regards all setbacks that occurred during the period of the Judges as punishment for the worship of Baal. And not without cause. Mobilization of the Tribes for a national war necessarily involved a renewed address to the national divinity who fought Israel's battles. This religio-national awakening is movingly expressed in the Song of Deborah with its reference to the great and invisible God, who had accompanied his people ever since the time of the Patriarchs. It was to this God that the Tribes turned in times of trouble.

Despite all temptations the Tribes were surprisingly successful in preserving their internal forms of administration, traditions, and creed—a success largely due to the exceptional circumstances of Israelite settlement. Israel did not conquer Canaan in one sweep, and many of its new settlements were founded on largely virgin soil in independent geographic clusters near Canaanite settlements. These were ideal conditions in which the Israelites could borrow ideas from their neighbors, and adapt what they had learned to their own spirit. Thus when the time came to overrun the remaining cities and to unite the country into a single, national territory, the Tribes were no longer primitive nomads attacking from the desert. In this sense the period of the Judges was an era of growth, refinement, and stabilization that gave birth to the new and special characteristics of Israel.

Conflict with the Philistines

MID-WAY through the 11th century B.C.E., a formidable rival to supreme power in Canaan emerged to face the Israelites—the Philistines. And the grim and fateful conflict that ensued eventually gave rise to monarchical rule in Israel.

The Philistines first came to Canaan in about 1170 B.C.E., a few generations after the Tribes. Their migration is described in the records of Rameses III, who tells of his fierce war with the « peoples of the sea » during the eighth year of his reign. Evidently the Philistines moved eastward from the islands of Greece and Asia Minor before the force of the Doric invasion. (The Dorians, one of the main branches of the ancient Greek peoples, came to the Peloponnese from north-west Greece in the 11th century, conquering the remnants of the Mycenaean Empire.) The Philistines swept aside all obstacles, including the Hittite kingdom and a number of Syrian cities, and even threatened Egypt itself. After a tremendous struggle, Rameses III was finally able to beat them back to the southern coast of Palestine, where they settled. They rapidly became the undisputed masters of this rich region; and Gaza, the Egyptian provincial capital, was soon one of their principal cities. Findings of Philistine pottery (a late type of Mycenaean ceramic influenced by Egyptian and local forms) indicate that there was widespread settlement in the southern coastal valleys, stretching as far north as the river Yarkon.

Except for scanty references in the Bible, little is known about the Philistines' settlement in Palestine, or of their history. The Philistine conquerors quickly adopted the Canaanite way of life, accepting the speech, customs, culture, and religion.

47

A 12th-century B.C.E. relief from Medinet Habu in Egypt depicts a naval battle between the forces of Rameses III and the Philistines (distinguishable by their more ornate helmets).

Philistine ceramics begin to disappear in the middle of the 11th century B.C.E., and even the Philistine gods (as we know them from the Bible), Dagon and Baalzebul—or Baalzebub—were in fact ancient Canaanite gods.

But the Philistines retained a military supremacy that was based on rigid organization and superior weapons. The Bible speaks of the existence of a federation of five cities: Gaza, Ashkelon, Ashdod, Gath, and Ekron. At the head of each of these cities stood a single autocratic leader or *seren* (a word close in origin to the Greek word *tyrannos*). The warriors fought with heavy iron weapons, and wore armor that made their champions—like the giant Goliath—resemble the Trojan heroes of the *Iliad*. (As noted earlier, the Philistines were probably responsible for bringing the art of iron-working to Palestine; they quickly gained a monopoly of iron weapons and took great care to prevent the Israelites and Canaanites from producing their own.)

Philistine Expansion

During their first century in Canaan the Philistines were satisfied with the territory they owned. They began to expand toward the boundaries of Israelite settlement only in the middle of the 11th century B.C.E., and the subsequent fighting in the eastern Shefela (the ancient inheritance of Dan) provides the historical background to the legend of Samson. The bravery of the lone Israelite champion and his tragic fall do not change the basic picture of the Philistine military superiority, which was only too real, and their strangulation of the cities of Judah (JUDGES XV: 9ff.). Eventually the northern tribes, too, were involved in a crucial battle with the Philistines at a point between Aphek (at the source of the Yarkon, on the Philistine boundary) and Israelite Eben-Ezer (I SAMUEL IV). The Israelites were routed, the Ark of the Covenant was captured, and the Philistines enjoyed the full fruits of victory: Shiloh (as excavation and later hints show) was destroyed.

The Philistine victory completely shattered the alliance of the northern tribes. It is true that the Israelites later regained the Ark of the Covenant and returned it to Beth-Shemesh in Judah; but since there was no tribal center there, it was kept at Baalah (Kirjath-Jearim) on the southern frontier of the confederation (JOSHUA xv: 9; xviii: 14). The prophet Samuel, Israel's leader, strove to continue the tradition of Israelite unity, concentrating his attention on Beth-el, Gilgal, Mizpeh, and even his own city, Ramah, on the border of Benjamin (I SAMUEL vii: 16-17). But despite the great victory attributed to Samuel (I SAMUEL vii: 7ff.), his rule was basically a spiritual one, and even in the later years of his leadership there was still a Philistine garrison at Geba, near Gibeah, the main town of Benjamin (I SAMUEL xiii: 3). The presence of an enemy garrison in a central position on the southern boundary of the Hills of Ephraim could only mean that the Philistines controlled even the areas of Israelite settlement in the hill country: the complete conquest of Canaan by the Philistines seemed imminent.

*When the Philistines took the ark of God, they brought it into the house of Dagon, and set it by Dagon. . . . And when they arose early on the morrow morning, behold, Dagon was fallen upon his face to the ground before the ark of the Lord; and the head of Dagon and both the palms of his hands were cut off upon the threshold—*I SAMUEL v: 2-4.

A wall-painting from the third-century c.e. synagogue at Dura Europos, in Mesopotamia, represents the triumph of Judaism over paganism: it was inspired by the biblical story of the Philistine idol toppling before the captured Israelite Ark of the Covenant (quoted above).

This was the Tribes' blackest moment. Their alliances had been torn to shreds, and suddenly they found themselves dominated by an alien power. The result was the birth of a monarchical regime that once again tilted the scales in Israel's favor. The Philistines, in reality, were only a small minority in spite of their efficient, well-equipped army. Once the tenacious Israelite farmers had been shaped by a strong leader into a compact striking force, the Philistines could not match them.

That leader was Saul, the last of the judges and first of the kings. His first campaign was not against the Philistines, but against the Ammonites who were threatening Jabesh-Gilead. (It is not known whether the Philistines knew of this campaign or whether they merely looked upon Saul as a faithful vassal and, as such, did not object to this expedition east of the Jordan.) But far from disbanding his troops after the battle, Saul raised the standard of Israel against the Philistines, and Samuel anointed him king in Gilgal before the Lord (I SAMUEL XI, 14-15).

The place of anointment was significant. Gilgal, a sanctuary close to the boundary between Judah and the northern tribes, was associated with the oldest traditions of the alliance of the Tribes from the time of the conquest of Canaan. Thus, by associating itself with them, the monarchy strove to reunite Judah and Israel.

Saul proceeded to destroy the Philistine garrison at Gibeah of Benjamin, which then became his capital, Gibeah of Saul—*Givat-Shaul* (I SAMUEL XIII). The Philistines advanced immediately and camped at Michmash. From there they dispatched three columns of soldiers, to the north, to the west, and to the east, planning to make the Tribes panic. Saul's son Jonathan crossed the deep dividing ravine in a daring assault and surprised the enemy; the Philistines were beaten back and fled through Beth-Horon to their bases. The fighting in the Shefela continued throughout Saul's lifetime (I SAMUEL XIV : 52), but by the time of his death the Philistines had been completely driven from the hill country.

Saul's reign is not well documented. The stories recounted in the Bible (mostly of quarrelsome encounters with David) present a one-sided and tendentious portrait. He was a strong and able commander; not only did he free Israel and drive the Philistines from the Israelite zone of settlement, but he also put an end to the raids of hostile tribes from Transjordan, and of the nomadic Amalekites in the south (I SAMUEL XIV: 47-48). There is no doubt that Saul was extremely popular, and the tales of his conflicts with David show how powerful his authority was, even in Judah. (In Saul's time there was no direct mention of the separate existence of Israel and Judah.) So long as Saul lived, David was unable to win the sympathy of even his own tribe. He had to flee to the wilderness, and was eventually forced to seek asylum with the hated Philistines.

Saul's great ambition was to unite and liberate the entire Israelite population of the Land. He was not at all interested in ruling the foreign settlements that existed within Israelite areas, and even Jebusite Jerusalem, so near to his capital, caused him little concern. The only foreign people he attacked were the Gibeonites, for he considered their presence in the territory of Benjamin a danger, since their cities divided Judah and the northern tribes, and were close to Jerusalem.

The image of Saul that emerges from the biblical descriptions reveals a brave and noble man, ‹ higher than any of the people from his shoulders and upward › (I SAMUEL X: 23), uncompromising but not arrogant. Samuel, spokesman of the priests and the tribal alliance, urged that Saul should be crowned because it was clear that the alliance was not strong enough to revitalize itself and throw off the Philistines. Nevertheless Samuel was faithful to the tribal spirit. He shared the general feeling that the monarchy might harm the freedom of the family and the individual, and even the absolute authority of the God of Israel; but he was prepared to accept it as the lesser of two evils, a dichotomy that explains the eventual split between Samuel and Saul.

Saul responded to the call of the Lord, but from then on he was not prepared to make any concessions to the tribal alliance or to the laws of the priesthood that were bound up with it. Because he knew that the priests had not completely relinquished their rights, he suspected their intentions, and he massacred the priests of the house of Eli for helping David. He left the Ark of the Covenant in Kirjath-Jearim so that the priesthood would not be strengthened, and so that there would be no encouragement to return to the early organization of the northern tribes. The mistrust that Saul felt for the priests was extended to David. At first he tried to befriend David as a means of stabilizing and broadening his own power in Judah; but he suffered from what he considered to be David's betrayal, which he took to be rebellion by the house of Judah.

Eventually this first and noble king of Israel was destroyed by the torments of his own heart. He came to regard the smallest criticism of his actions, or of the monarchy, as open treason. And if Saul's image is lit with a tragic light, it is precisely because of the strange contrast between these inner torments and the admiration and loyalty shown him by the Israelites—feelings that are expressed so movingly in David's dirge (II SAMUEL 1: 17-27).

David and Saul

DAVID was graced with qualities Saul never possessed; consequently his achievements were even more brilliant. His early youth was spent at Saul's court where he was ‹ cunning in playing, and a mighty valiant man, and a man of war, and prudent in matters, and a comely person › (I SAMUEL XVI: 18). After his victory over Goliath he quickly won royal favor, and became Saul's son-in-law and a regimental commander. When he fell from favor and had to flee to escape Saul's jealousy, he gathered together a band of oppressed, hunted, and embittered men. For a while he succeeded in ruling part of the desolate wilderness of Judaea, which by its very nature provided ideal protection for outlaws.

But even there David felt unsafe from Saul's avenging arm, and he took refuge with Achish, the king of Philistine Gath. This step gravely compromised his future; but the fact that he could return later, his fame and favor undiminished, shows how flexible and *politique* he could be—a far cry from Saul's naivety and obstinacy.

When David was with the Philistines, Achish gave him Ziklag, an outlying town on the border of the Negev desert: David made it a tiny satellite kingdom within the Philistine protectorate. David determined to gain the affection of the southern tribes by attacking the Negev Bedouin and by gifts; and though the Bible does not say so directly, it may be inferred that Achish was quite content with this situation, for David was a valuable thorn in Saul's side. David's policy was a risky one, for on the face of things it aggravated schismatic trends in the new monarchy. But David possessed more than courage, cunning, and intelligence; luck, too, was on his side. Sixteen months after his arrival in Ziklag, Saul and three of his sons were killed in battle by the Philistines at Mount Gilboa. (At the last moment David was spared the necessity of taking part in the battle as a vassal in the service of the Philistines—I SAMUEL XXIX: 3-4). The balance of power was temporarily upset, and it looked as though the Philistines would dominate the country again. The Israelites lost the Hills of Ephraim, and the survivors of Saul's house tried to maintain their rule from Mahanaim in Transjordan.

Distraught, the southern tribes appealed to David, and he was anointed king of Judah in Hebron (c. 1006 B.C.E.). The Philistines did not react immediately, which

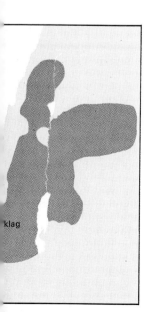

klag

A map showing Saul's kingdom and the position of Ziklag, given to David by the Philistine king.

51

suggests that they still considered David to be their ward, and were glad of this deepening of the rift between Judah and Israel.

The quarrel between David's opponents—Ishbaal (Ishboshet), Saul's son, and Abner, the commander of the host—and their eventual death, helped David greatly. Once they were dead, David had no serious rival, and the elders of Israel went to Hebron and anointed him king over Israel as well.

One of his first acts was to capture Jebusite Jerusalem and make it the capital of his kingdom. This wise and far-sighted action alone would have assured David's immortality. Apart from being an ancient royal city in the center of the Land, Jerusalem was a neutral zone on the boundary between the northern and the southern tribes. Thus it made the ideal capital for a monarchy that set itself above inter-tribal feuding. From this point on, the Jebusite citadel of Zion was the City of David by right of conquest; the house of David and its capital Jerusalem became synonymous terms, symbols of the unified kingdom.

David hoped to make up for his earlier divisive behavior by this act, and he began a new policy of annexing the remaining alien regions within Israel. By the time the Philistines realized what had happened, it was too late for them to act effectively. David defeated them in two successive battles in the Valley of Rephaim near Jerusalem, and drove them from the hill country. After these reverses, the Philistines were reduced to a minor power and were no longer a danger to Israel.

Expanding the Kingdom

In the years that followed, David overcame all his surrounding enemies one by one, and gradually expanded his kingdom; he captured the Canaanite cities in the valleys, overcame the Amalekites and the Bedouin, and annexed the principalities of Transjordan, Moab, Edom, and Ammon. His only serious rivals in Syria and Palestine were the Aramaeans and the Phoenicians. (At that time Aram-Zobah in the Valley of the Lebanon was the chief Aramaean power.) David won several victories over the Aramaeans, and annexed their territory to his kingdom. He was on peaceful terms with Phoenician Tyre, though he restricted the city's activities. From this point Tyre's interests swung westward, and it became the most important maritime power in the Middle East.

Before very long, David's kingdom had become all-powerful: its boundaries stretched from Levo-Hamath in the Valley of the Lebanon to the river of Egypt, and David's control of trade routes in the north stretched as far as Tadmor and Tiphsah (on the Euphrates).

The material and spiritual revolution that unfolded in Israel during the reigns of David and of Solomon, his successor, was remarkable; no praise could be too great. A nation of peasants that had lived until then in comparatively isolated and depressed regions became, almost overnight, lords of an empire that commanded the most valuable commercial communications in the Middle East. The king's merchants sold and transported chariots, war horses, weapons, and luxury goods to Egypt, Syria, and Mesopotamia. Command of the Gulf of Elath (Aqaba) on the Red Sea led to trade in precious spices with southern Arabia; and from there—with the help of Phoenician ships and sailors—the Israelite merchants could reach the harbors of Africa and India. As more and more money poured into the royal treasury, the Israelites' standard of living began to rise dramatically. Edom, Moab, Ammon, and the countries of Aram-Damascus and Aram-Zobah were vassal states, and as such were forced to pay heavy annual tributes, while other neighboring kingdoms, such as the neo-Hittite Hamath and the Philistines, had to buy their independence. David and Solomon's great objective was to impose permanent organizational forms on this complex kingdom, and the forms had to be created virtually from scratch. Naturally they could learn from their neighbors—from Egypt in particular, and from the old Canaanite cities. It is hardly coincidental that many of Israel's dignitaries had foreign names, for David was quick to employ the Canaanite notables of the various cities, and to draw on their experience. The army, too, was reformed: in addition to the tribal contingents that were only called upon in times of emergency, a regular army of « champions » and mercenaries was formed, entirely under the king's command. A second and radical innovation was the use of war chariots, an expensive addition that necessitated the construction of special chariot towns and stables, and the training of special charioteers. These professional soldiers soon surpassed the tribal contingents as a fighting force, and eventually supplanted them. In David's time, Joab was still general of the Israelite host, and Benaiah commanded the mercenaries (II SAMUEL XX: 23); but by Solomon's reign, Benaiah had become sole commander (I KINGS IV: 4).

An equally revolutionary innovation was the *corvée*, entitling the king to call up anyone to work on state projects for a certain length of time, an ancient practice in Canaan and Egypt. Naturally the burden fell mainly on the non-Israelite population of Palestine, but as the rate of construction rose in Solomon's reign, the corvée inevitably came to embrace the Israelites too.

David was the great conqueror, Solomon the great builder. The buildings he constructed in Jerusalem and elsewhere were in part splendid and luxurious edifices, as was fitting for so outstanding a monarchy, and in part functional buildings intended to fortify the frontiers and the central cities. Solomon was advised by Phoenician architects from Tyre, and advanced Phoenician architecture soon became common throughout the country. After the 10th century B.C.E., we find dressed stone, Phoenician-Israelite column-capitals (known as Proto-Aeolic), burnished pottery, and so on.

And when the queen of Sheba heard of the fame of Solomon . . . she came to prove him with hard questions. And she came to Jerusalem with a very great train, with camels that bare spices, and very much gold, and precious stones—I KINGS X: 1-2.

A 19th-century Abyssinian portrayal of the tradition of the Queen of Sheba: the last two lines depict the queen's visit to King Solomon.

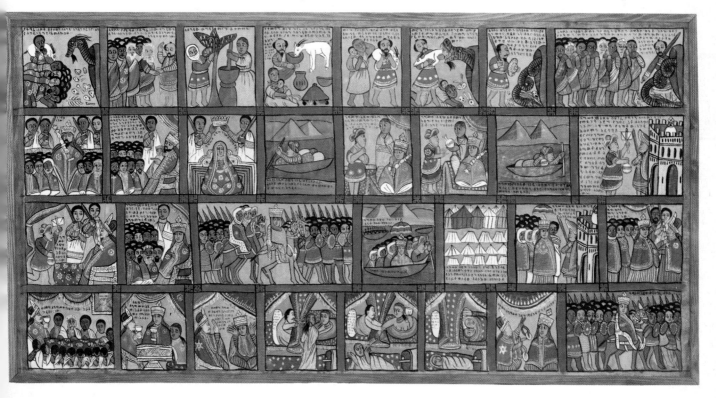

By far the most enduring of all David and Solomon's works was the Temple of Jerusalem. The removal of the Ark of the Covenant to Jerusalem symbolized the city's new status as the holy center of the tribal Covenant, the heir of both Shiloh and Hebron. The Temple was only one of the splendid royal buildings built by Solomon in Jerusalem, and by no means the largest, but it enshrined the new national spirit and became identified with the existence of the people in its Land.

Though the Temple was built to the familiar Canaanite-Phoenician pattern and its liturgical forms were greatly influenced by Canaanite patterns of worship, it remained wholly Israelite in its spiritual essence. It represented and revived the ancient tradition of the Twelve Tribes of Israel and their wandering in the wilderness; and the God of Israel who came to dwell in the holy of holies (the Temple in Jerusalem) was the same supreme imperceptible Being who had guided them in the wilderness. The house of David and the kingdom of Israel forged a permanent bond with the worship of Yahweh in a sanctified Jerusalem, and from then on the people thronged to worship there on festival days. The Temple's sway was extended by the settlement of Levite families (loyal to the house of David and familiar with the rituals of religious observance) in key points throughout the Land. The Levites served ‹ in all the business of the Lord, and in the service of the king › (I CHRONICLES XXVI: 30).

Under the monarchical regime, the Temple became the center of the new national unity and spirit, and of the tradition of Israel in Canaan. Creativity flourished around the Temple; new heights were reached in religious and national poetry, and in historical literature that sought to reveal the mysterious motivations of God. The monarchy was seen as representing the fulfillment of the Lord's promises and of his omnipotence. The king was seen as God's servant, chosen by him, and subservient, like every man, to his commandments. (There are few historical parallels to the extraordinary stand taken by the prophet Nathan against the all-powerful David, and to his devastating words: ‹ Thou art the man ›—II SAMUEL XII.)

Foundations were laid during this period for the Bible that was to become the unique

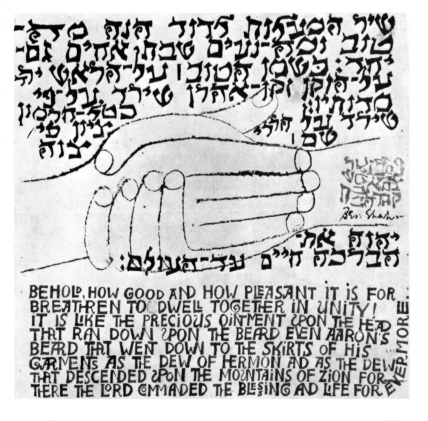

Left, an illustration of Psalm 133, a Song of David, by Ben Shahn.

Right, the temple and palaces of David and Solomon—based on a modern reconstruction (from both biblical tradition and recent archaeological findings) by Julius Jotham Rothschild. A key is given below.

A : The Temple and the Temple area
(II CHRONICLES III : 1)
B : The Royal Palace and Harem (I KINGS VII : 1-8)
C : Palace of the Daughter of Pharaoh
(I KINGS VII : 8)
D : The House of the Forest of Lebanon
(I KINGS VII : 2)
E : The Porch of the Pillars (I KINGS VII : 6)
F : Royal Horse Stables (I KINGS IX : 19)
G : Arsenal and Army Stores (I KINGS IX : 22)

and eternal creation of the Children of Israel. To David's reign belong the most sublime and sensitive chapters of the Bible. The religious poetry of the Bible (the Psalms) attributed by tradition to David, and the works of wisdom ascribed to Solomon (Proverbs and Ecclesiastes) each present a philosophy reflecting the character of the two great kings. Though the unified kingdom lasted for only two generations, its tremendous intellectual achievements have survived to this day.

Waning Power

By the time Solomon came to the throne (968 B.C.E.) the great kingdom of Israel had already begun to contract. Egypt was stirring again, and it appears that the Pharaoh Siamon marched from the Nile and took Gezer, the key city of the northern Shefela (I KINGS IX: 16). Solomon managed to regain the city by signing a treaty with the Egyptians, and he cemented the treaty with a political marriage. But the scriptures are vague here, and hide more than they reveal.

From this point on, Gezer became a boundary, and supreme control of the land of the Philistines (the south-west) passed once again into Egyptian hands. The adverse balance of trade with Tyre damaged Solomon more and more, and to pay his debt to its king he was forced to concede ‹ twenty cities in the land of Galilee › (I KINGS IX: 10-13). East of the Jordan he was harassed by a number of risings, and Hadad raised a revolt in Edom, with Egyptian help. In Damascus too, Rezon, son of Eliadah rebelled and established the nucleus of a kingdom that was soon to present a formidable challenge to Israel.

Solomon could see no alternative to strengthening the border fortresses and key cities. But the work involved exhausted his treasury and compelled him to press an ever-increasing number of his people into corvée. As a result, domestic tensions grew fiercer, and a number of insurgents from the Tribes turned to Egypt for help and asylum (I KINGS XI: 40). But the revolutionary spirit that now infected the kingdom was not new. It sprang from a deep-rooted tension between a centralized monarchy and the traditional tribal ways, and was evident throughout David's reign. This tension had, in fact, led to Absalom's revolt against David.

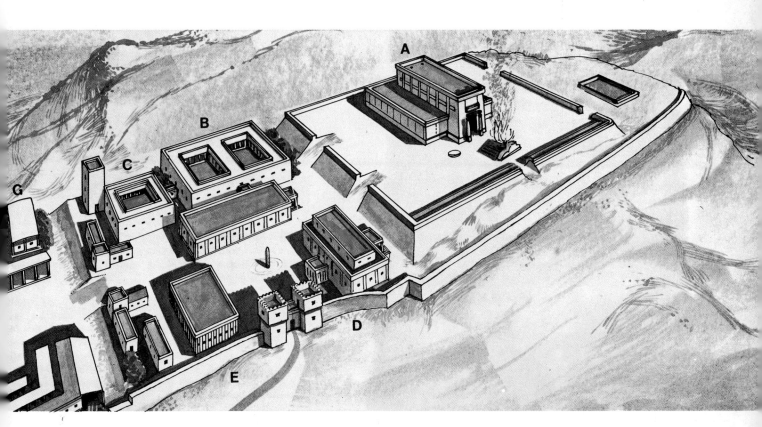

WHEN Solomon died (about 928 B.C.E.), the country was divided once again—more than 300 years after the conquest. The new kingdom of Judah was to survive another 300 years, the kingdom of Israel only 200. The days of relative peace, when no great powers struggled for control of Syria and the Land of Israel, were past. Egypt was now watching events in the Land closely, and tried to intervene at every opportunity. A new rival arose to challenge Israel in the north, Aram-Damascus, though the threat was overshadowed by Assyria's growing power.

But it would be wrong to see this period as one of continuous conflict and decline. Both kingdoms had a good deal of material and intellectual prosperity before them. Outwardly, there was not a great deal of change, for, as will be seen later, the true spirit of Israel was personified by the prophets, who generally defied the kings and rebelled against all stereotyped forms of government.

The two halves into which the kingdom now split had always really existed, despite the apparent unification. What now happened was that Benjamin joined Judah, probably because that tribe was so close to Jerusalem, which was left the capital of the southern kingdom. The Transjordan tribes joined the northern kingdom, for both geographical and historical reasons. The rest of Solomon's empire crumbled away. Aram-Damascus (which had won its freedom during his reign) dominated the Valley of the Lebanon and the north of Transjordan. For a while Ammon and Moab accepted Israel's rule, but the monument of Mesha, king of Moab, records that Moab soon broke away. (Moab was only recaptured in the days of Omri.)

The Kingdoms of Israel and Judah

KINGDOM OF ISRAEL	
Jeroboam I	928
Nadab	907
Baasha	906
Elah	883
Zimri	882
Omri	882
Ahab	871
Ahaziah	851
Joram	850
Jehu	842
Jehoahaz	814
Joash	800
Jeroboam II	785
Zechariah	749
Shallum	748
Menahem	748
Pekahiah	737
Pekah	735
Hoshea	731
Fall of Samaria	722

The Moabite Stone: this stela—found in southern Transjordan in 1868—was erected by King Mesha of Moab, to commemorate his successful rebellion in 849 B.C.E. against the rule of Israel. Part of it is translated below.

> . . . As for Omri, king of Israel, he humbled Moab many years, for Chemosh was angry at his land. And his son followed him and he also said, 'I will humble Moab.' In my time he spoke thus, but I have triumphed over him and over his house, while Israel hath perished for ever! . . . Now the men of God had always dwelt in the land of Ataroth, and the king of Israel had built Ataroth for them; but I fought against the town and took it and slew all the people of the town—from the Moabite Stone (or Mesha stela).

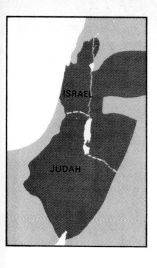

The kings of Judah attempted to rule Edom and as far as Elath, but Edom managed to free itself and was not reconquered until the reign of Asa or Jehoshaphat. In practice, two small domains were left, and the boundary between them ran south of Beth-el (about 10 miles north of Jerusalem).

Judah remained faithful to the house of David, and as a result its government was generally stable. In the last years of Israel's existence, four dynasties ruled in rapid succession, and kings replaced one another almost overnight, hastening the kingdom's break-up. Israel was the larger and stronger of the two kingdoms, and at times the kings of Israel could look on the kings of Judah as their vassals; but they had no ambitions to overrun Judah. When Joash conquered Jerusalem (in the days of Amaziah), for example, he only destroyed part of the walls, and he never attempted to annex the city or kingdom to his own. Israel's own sanctuaries in Beth-el and Dan replaced the central Temple in Jerusalem.

There is no doubt that Israel's two sanctuaries were associated with the ancient traditions of the Covenant of Shiloh, and they must not be thought of as idolatrous; the gold calves set up there by Jeroboam were not meant to represent the Invisible God. In all probability they were no more than a pedestal over which the deity was imagined as standing invisibly, just as he was imagined as sitting over the cherubim of Jerusalem. (In the same way, Hadad, or Baal, the god of the wind, was portrayed as standing on a calf or a bullock.) But obviously the similarity of the symbols encouraged syncretism. Indeed, even Jerusalem was not free from similar phenomena, or from the practice of alien forms of worship, a consequence of the political marriages of various kings.

But the influence of the Temple and of the ancient rites always remained supreme in Judah: it was there that the tradition of the unity of the Twelve Tribes was nurtured and the spirit of ancient Israel was perpetuated and became for ever linked with Jerusalem and the house of David.

The kings of Judah seized every chance to extend their power over the whole of the Land, especially after the downfall of the kingdom of Israel. For half a century the two kingdoms competed and quarreled, enfeebling themselves and opening the way to external domination. Five years after Rehoboam succeeded Solomon as king (928 B.C.E.), Shishak (Sheshonk) king of Egypt invaded the Land. The results of his campaign can be learned from the list of captured towns inscribed upon the walls of the temple of Amon at Karnak. As the Bible story relates (I KINGS XIV: 25-28; II CHRONICLES XII: 1-12), Shishak did not conquer Jerusalem, and was content with a heavy tribute. After approaching Jerusalem, he turned north to the Hills of Ephraim, to the valleys of Succoth and Jezreel, and to the Sharon. The second part of the list concerns the Negev. The Egyptians turned southward, apparently to Ezion Geber on the Gulf of Elath. Though Jeroboam had been crowned king of Israel with Egyptian help, Shishak attacked both kingdoms with equal force. It is obvious that his intention was to gain control over the important commercial routes—the Via maris in the north and the highways of the Negev. A fragment of a monument erected by Shishak, found in Megiddo, shows that the Egyptians maintained control of these areas for some time.

Throughout the reigns of Rehoboam and Jeroboam, the wars between Israel and Judah were continuous. Abijah son of Rehoboam succeeded during his short reign in capturing Beth-el and the neighboring towns for Judah (II CHRONICLES XIII: 19). But when Baasha (of the tribe of Issachar) overthrew Jeroboam's sons in Israel, the balance of power shifted. In about 885 B.C.E., Baasha recaptured the lost towns and penetrated into Judah, capturing the northern fortress of Ramah (six miles from Jerusalem) and strengthening its walls. Asa, the king of Judah, was forced to turn to Ben-Hadad I, king of Aram-Damascus, for help. Aram seized this chance to invade Israel, captured many cities in Galilee (I KINGS XV: 18-20), and destroyed

57

Solomon's fortifications at Hazor. As a result of the fighting, a new boundary dividing the weakened kingdoms was established between Mizpeh and Beth-el.

The third Israel dynasty was founded by Omri in about 882 B.C.E. Under him, the kingdom prospered considerably. Omri's first act was to establish a new capital in Samaria, some eight miles north-west of Shechem (previously the capital had been variously at Shechem, Penuel, and Tirzah). In this way he ended the jealousy between different centers, an action similar to David's occupation of Jerusalem.

Omri appears to have created the revolutionary policy that was pursued so successfully by his son Ahab. He united the forces of his kingdom against the main enemy, Aram-Damascus, and strengthened his ties with Judah and Tyre, bolstered by dynastic intermarriages. The fact that Jehoshaphat, king of Judah, fought under the leadership of the kings of Israel in their recurring wars proves that Judah accepted its severance from Israel, and recognized Israel's political and military superiority.

Omri succeeded in retaking Moab, and his son Ahab won a series of battles against Ben-Hadad, regaining the towns of the north for Israel. In 853 B.C.E., Ahab joined forces with his enemy Ben-Hadad to fight against Assyria at Karkar on the Orontes, as recorded in an inscription of Shalmaneser III. Ahab brought 2000 chariots to the battle, more than half the chariot-strength of the allies. From this can be gauged Israel's great strength in this period, and also Ahab's political intelligence in recognizing Assyria as the chief danger.

Excavation in Samaria, Megiddo, and Hazor confirms that this was a period of prosperity in Israel, a prosperity that was reflected in palatial buildings. But the inevitable consequences were social unrest and a strengthening in the autocratic nature of the monarchy. According to Israelite law, the king had no right to dispossess a farmer of his vineyard, even if it were next to his own palace.' But when Naboth the Jezreelite refused to sell his vineyard to Ahab, the king's wife Jezebel (daughter of the king of Tyre) brought false charges against Naboth and he was stoned to death. The cry of the prophet Elijah, ‹ Hast thou killed, and also taken possession? › echoed Nathan's words to David—‹ Thou art the man! › In addition to this growing autocracy, the pure Israelite religion was being contaminated by its contact with other religions, especially as the prestige of Baal, God of Jezebel's Tyre, grew. Consequently the prophets, in their dedication to the God of Israel and to social justice, became fierce opponents of the monarchy.

These conflicts were less pronounced in Judah. The reigns of Asa (908-867) and of Jehoshaphat (867-851) especially, were characterized by fortification and internal organization, and the division of the kingdom (apparently for the first time) into 12 regions, as listed in the Book of Joshua (xv: 21-62 and xviii: 25-28). Judah was now at peace with Israel, and was able to channel its energy into the south. Once again we hear of Jehoshaphat ruling the Arava and Edom, and trying to renew the sea-trade from the Gulf of Elath (I KINGS XXII: 48-49). Strongholds from this period have been uncovered in Arad and in Ezion-Geber.

The second half of the ninth century B.C.E. was a period of decline for both kingdoms. Aram-Damascus reached the peak of its power, combining all the territories of its satellite states in Inner Syria into one kingdom (I KINGS XX). In 853 B.C.E. (as we saw) Ben-Hadad succeeded in uniting most of the kings of the region, including Ahab, king of Israel, and the alliance defeated Shalmaneser near Karkar. But Ahab and Ben-Hadad were soon at war again over the territory of Ramoth-Gilead. (It was in this battle that Ahab, disguised as an ordinary soldier, was killed.) But even before this fatal battle, Mesha, king of Moab, had rebelled against Ahab; and the combined armies of Joram, son of Ahab, and of Jehoshaphat, king of Judah, could not crush him (II KINGS III). Eventually, in the days of Jehoram (851-843), son of Jehoshaphat, Edom also broke free from Judah (II KINGS VIII: 20-22).

58

The House of Jehu

In about 842 B.C.E., after much bitter fighting, the house of Jehu took over the throne of Israel. Jehu, helped by the widespread opposition to the house of Ahab and the support of the prophets, cruelly stamped out all forms of Baal worship. Following the murders of Jezebel and Ahaziah, relations between Tyre and Judah deteriorated. In Judah, Athaliah, daughter of King Ahab, reigned briefly. But even though the house of David was restored after her reign, relations with Israel never returned to their former happy state.

Throughout this period the Assyrians harassed Damascus continuously, and in 841 B.C.E. Shalmaneser succeeded in breaking through to the boundaries of Damascus and northern Transjordan. Among the names of those forced to pay tribute to Assyria appears that of ‹ Jehu, son of Omri, king of Israel. › (The Assyrians first came into actual contact with Israel in the days of the house of Omri, and for them this remained the name of the kingdom until its destruction.) The presence of the Assyrian giant in Syria and Palestine was now only too real, and overshadowed the territorial conflicts of the local kings.

On this occasion King Hazael (who came to power at the same time as Jehu) managed to stand his ground against Shalmaneser's advance, and Damascus was spared. During the next 40 years Assyrian pressures were checked, and the Aramaeans gained the upper hand in the conflict between Aram and Israel. In the last years of Jehu's reign, and during the reign of his son Jehoahaz, Israel declined rapidly. The Aramaeans controlled the whole of Transjordan and the north, and the kingdom of Israel was virtually locked in the narrow confines of the Hills of Ephraim (II KINGS X: 32-33; AMOS I: 3). In one sally (about 815 B.C.E.) Hazael advanced as far as Gath in the Shefela, and King Jehoash had to pay a large tribute to halt the invasion of Judah (II KINGS XII: 18).

Below, Shalmaneser III of Assyria (858-824 B.C.E.) receives tribute from the king of Israel—from a monument at Nimrod, his capital. Below left, king Hazael of Aram-Damascus, who checked the Assyrian invasion of his kingdom (a ninth-century B.C.E. ivory, found at Arslan Tash in Turkey).

By contrast with Aram-Damascus, Israel and Judah were now minor protectorates: Israel's chariot strength had been reduced to 50 horses and 10 chariots (II KINGS XIII: 7). But, ironically, Israel and Judah were saved at this point by the Assyrians, who renewed attacks on Aram-Damascus in 802: ‹And the Lord gave Israel a saviour, so that they went out from under the hand of the Syrians: and the children of Israel dwelt in their tents, as beforetime › (II KINGS XIII: 5). The « saviour » was Adadnirari III, king of Assyria; but the salvation was to be only temporary. Though the yoke of Damascus had been thrown off and Israel and Judah could breathe freely again, the last buffer between them and the Assyrian Empire had gone; their turn was next. For the moment, however, Assyria concentrated on its internal affairs, and until Tiglath-Pileser III succeeded to the Assyrian throne in 745 B.C.E., the kingdoms of the Land and of Syria enjoyed a final spell of peace and prosperity. Under Jehoash, son of Jehoahaz, and his son Jeroboam II, Israel not only broke away from Damascus, but eventually came to rule its territory. Jeroboam ‹ restored the coast of Israel from the entering of Hamath unto the sea of the plain › (II KINGS XIV: 25); that is, from Levo (Labweh) in the Valley of the Lebanon, on the border of the kingdom of Hamath (the boundary even in the days of the Land of Canaan) down to the region of the Dead Sea in the south.

Judah, too, seized the chance to extend its frontier to the south and west. Previously King Amaziah (799-786) had managed to regain control of part of Edom with the king of Israel's help, but the expedition ended in a split, and Israel eventually gained control of the « king's way » in Transjordan (II KINGS XIV: 1-14). This was not a serious setback for Judah, and under Amaziah's son Azariah (Uzziah), its boundaries were expanded on an unprecedented scale. Azariah conquered more Philistine territory, routed the Arabians and Maonites in the south, and completed the conquest of Edom, including Elath (II CHRONICLES XXVI: 6-10). In the expanse of the Negev and the wilderness of Judaea, he established a network of strong fortresses that dominated the boundaries and roads, and settlements sprang up around them.

For Judah, this was an era of economic progress, military strength, and political tranquillity furthered by Azariah's far-sighted domestic schemes: ‹ Also he built towers in the desert, and digged many wells: for he had much cattle, both in the low country, and in the plains: husbandmen also, and vine dressers in the mountains, and in Carmel: for he loved husbandry › (II CHRONICLES XXVI: 10). Judah and Israel now occupied together approximately as much territory as David had ruled over.

Assyrian charioteers, one of a series of bronze friezes depicting Shalmaneser III's victories over the neighboring kingdoms (from the gates of the temple of Imgur-Bel, at Bulawat, Iraq—ninth century B.C.E.).

Relations between the two kingdoms were good, and both had intelligent and capable monarchs. Even though Azariah fell ill with leprosy half-way through his reign, and affairs of state were entrusted to his son Jotham, it seems that he remained firmly in control for the duration of his long reign.

The story of Solomon and Ahab repeated itself. Once more economic well-being widened social differences and—especially in the northern kingdom—estranged the people from the traditions of the ancient Israelites, and from the worship of Yahweh. In Samaria, Megiddo, and Hazor archaeologists have uncovered splendid and luxurious buildings. Amos speaks of ‹ the winter house › and of ‹ the summer house › and of ‹ the houses of ivory › (III: 15) meaning, presumably, the palaces of Jezreel and Samaria. Remnants of the ivory inlay from these palaces were found in Samaria, engraved in the finest Phoenician manner, and similar articles have been found in the homes of the wealthy—some of them doubtless imports from Phoenicia. When an area of merchants' dwellings was dug up in Hazor, for example, beautifully engraved bone and ivory objects were discovered. To this period, too, we assign the appearance of the first « prophets of writing, » whose warnings must have seemed anachronistic and uncalled-for in such prosperous times.

The Assyrian Threat

Jeroboam II died about 749 B.C.E., and the murder of his son Zechariah ended the rule of the house of Jehu, which had given Israel its kings for almost a century. After this, rulers came and went in swift succession, and the ensuing instability hastened the kingdom's end. In 745, Tiglath-Pileser III assumed power in Assyria. He heralded a great era of expansion, and a new policy that involved the placing of conquered territories under the rule of governors, and large-scale transplantation of populations. A strong alliance of the kings of Syria and of the Land, under the leadership of Azariah, king of Judah, held him off, which indicates that Judah assumed control of the region as Israel grew weaker. Azariah died in 742, and his grandson Ahaz became king of Judah.

In the same year, Pekahiah, son of Menahem, was killed by Pekah, son of Remaliah, who then tried to organize a new anti-Assyrian alliance together with Rezin, king of Aram-Damascus. When Ahaz, the king of Judah, declined to join the alliance, the two entered Jerusalem and attempted to put their puppet on the throne. Judah's neighbors seized their chance: Edom broke free, Elath was lost, and the Philistines extended their boundaries in the Shefela to the foothills (II KINGS XVI: 6; II CHRONICLES XXVIII: 17-18). Political change in the Land was startlingly rapid: only

THE ASSYRIAN EMPIRE 650 B.C.E. THE BABYLONIAN EMPIRE 550 B.C.E.

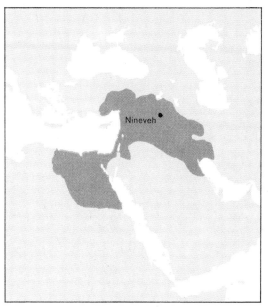

ISAIAS·E Z E
IPHETA·CHIAS
REX

The prophet Isaiah and King Hezekiah—from the Imperial crown (*c.* 962 C.E.) of the Holy Roman Empire. Isaiah holds a scroll containing his words to the king: 'I will add unto thy days fifteen years.'

three or four years after Azariah had emerged as champion of the kingdoms of Syria and of the Land, the territory of Judah had become smaller than ever.

In his despair Ahaz turned to Assyria for help, though the prophet Isaiah, who realized how serious the Assyrian hazard was, had advised him not to. Tiglath-Pileser moved swiftly. In his first invasion of the Land in 734 he advanced south along the coast to Philistia; in his two subsequent expeditions (733-732) he took Damascus and the northern portions of Israel, turning them into Assyrian provinces, and exiling many of their inhabitants.

Here were the beginnings of the Assyrian provinces (in the Land and in Syria) that remained virtually unaltered under the Assyrian rule and were eventually inherited by the emperors of Babylonia and Persia. During the reign of Tiglath-Pileser, three provinces were created in Israel: Dor in the Sharon, Megiddo in the Valley of Jezreel, and Gilead in central Transjordan.

Only the assassination of King Pekah of Israel in 731, and the subsequent surrender of his successor Hoshea, saved the Hills of Ephraim. But the surrender was only temporary; and after Tiglath-Pileser's death, Hoshea rebelled. Then his dreams of freedom were shattered by the Assyrians: Shalmaneser V marched on Samaria in 724, and Hoshea was forced to capitulate. But his surrender came too late. In 722 Samaria was conquered after a siege that lasted three years, and Sargon (now king of Assyria) turned the remainder of the kingdom of Israel into an Assyrian province, banishing many Samarian notables to northern Mesopotamia and Media, and replacing them with exiles from Babylon and Syrian Hamath.

The newcomers quickly adopted the local ways, dialects, and beliefs. But they also brought their own cults and customs, which naturally became intermingled with existing practices. From this time, the people of the Hills of Ephraim were known as Samaritans. They inherited the ancient enmity to Judah, but moved far away from the original spirit of Israel. (This explains why the Israelite population in the areas that had become Assyrian provinces in the days of Tiglath-Pileser—Galilee and Gilead, for example—was less contaminated, and now looked toward Judah.)

Invasion of Judah

Although Judah became an Assyrian satellite in every respect, it escaped Israel's fate. That Sargon's military adventures passed by Judah was largely due to Isaiah's moderating influence. But when Sargon died in 705, the Assyrian Empire was shaken to its foundations. Revolts erupted everywhere, and Hezekiah, king of Judah, encouraged by Egypt and by the envoys of King Merodach Baladan of Babylonia, revolted as well. Most of his help came from Philistine Ashkelon; but he was also joined by Ekron, which deposed its king, Padi, handing him over in chains (as we learn from the inscriptions of Sennacherib).

It was four years before King Sennacherib of Assyria could organize a punitive expedition to the Land; and Hezekiah had not been idle in the interval. The fortifications of Jerusalem were strengthened, and the famous tunnel of Siloam was pierced to ensure a supply of water during siege. The boundaries of Judah were enlarged, the army was reinforced, chariots and store-cities were built.

The national revival was also bound up with religious reforms and the purification of the religious service, which had been tainted by foreign rites and customs. A sanctuary built within the royal Judaean citadel of Arad, on the southern border of the kingdom, was partially destroyed during Hezekiah's reign (cf. II KINGS XVIII : 4). Hezekiah also tried to extend his influence in the north and carry out reforms in the Assyrian provinces around Israel (II CHRONICLES XXX : 1-12).

Sennacherib entered Judah in 701 B.C.E.. He swept aside the Egyptian army that had come to aid insurgents in the coastal plain near Eltekeh, forced Ashkelon to submit, occupied Ekron, and then turned toward Jerusalem. In his state records, he speaks of capturing 46 towns of Judah, and some are catalogued in the prophecies of MICAH (I: 10-16) and ISAIAH (X: 28-32). The conquest of Lachish is detailed in relics from the ancient city of Nineveh, Assyria. Hezekiah hurriedly dispatched an enormous tribute, but it had no effect: Sennacherib besieged Jerusalem and demanded its unconditional surrender.

Hezekiah rejected the ultimatum, and the prophet Isaiah (who had always opposed any rising against Assyria) now supported him wholeheartedly. Isaiah knew that the capture of Jerusalem would mean the extinction of the kingdom of Judah. Exactly how the campaign ended is not certain, but we know Jerusalem was not taken, and Judah escaped once more, a miracle that gave new and infinite vigor to faith in the one, omnipotent God in whose hands even Assyria was but clay.

The Assyrian siege of the Judaean city of Lachish (*c.* 701 B.C.E.)—part of a relief from the palace of Sennacherib at Nineveh (Kuyunjik) in Mesopotamia: Lachish was one of 46 towns taken by the Assyrian king in his punitive expedition against the rebellious King Hezekiah of Judah.

Hezekiah died shortly after this fighting, and his son Manasseh (who reigned from 697 to 642) submitted completely to a now all-powerful Assyria. Thus Esarhaddon was able to overrun Egypt as well in 671. Sennacherib's invasion had left deep scars, especially in the Shefela, but the boundaries of Judah were largely unchanged and slowly life returned to normal.

After the death of Ashur-Banipal the Assyrian Empire began to crumble. Judah could now enjoy its last years of prosperity under Josiah, an intelligent and daring ruler of exceptional ability whose aim was to restore the kingdom of the house of David over the whole of the Land.

The expansion of Judah, connected as it was with the collapse of Assyrian power, was accompanied by an intensification of religious feeling. When Ashur-Banipal died, Josiah took the first step toward political freedom and the ending of foreign forms of worship. Four years later, in the 12th year of his reign, he carried out a wholesale purge, not only in Judah and Jerusalem but also ‹ in the cities of Manasseh, and Ephraim, and Simeon, even unto Naphtali . . . throughout all the land of Israel › (II CHRONICLES XXXIV: 6-7). Assyria was now fully occupied with internal troubles, and in 626 Babylon also broke free. Josiah made the most of his opportunities and extended his rule over the entire Land. (A contemporary Hebrew letter, discovered in a citadel near the coast between Yavneh and Ashdod, shows that Josiah ruled even the northern part of Philistia.) Within the space of 20 years, most of the Land of Israel was again united under one powerful king.

Josiah's military and political accomplishments warrant comparison with those of David. But his greatest achievements were spiritual, and as in David's day they were associated with the sublime mission of Jerusalem. In the 18th year of his

THE ASSYRIAN EMPIRE

Ashurnasirpal II	883–859
Shalmaneser III	858–824
Shamshi-Adad V	824–811
Adadnirari III	811–783
Shalmaneser IV	783–773
Ashurdan III	773–755
Ashurnirari V	755–745
Tiglath-Pileser III	745–727
Shalmaneser V	727–722
Sargon II	722–705
Sennacherib	705–681
Esarhaddon	681–669
Ashur-Banipal	669–612
Fall of Nineveh	612

THE NEO-BABYLONIAN EMPIRE

Nabopalassar	625–605
Nebuchadnezzar	605–562
Nabonidus	555–539
Persian Conquest	539

64

reign (622) a scroll of the Law was found in the Temple while renovations were in progress. This book was to become the official law of Judah and the nucleus of the Book of Deuteronomy, the great work in which all the ancient historical sources were gathered into a single religio-national history, steeped in the spirit of the prophets. Essentially, the author advocated a return to the pure and simple monotheistic law, the worship of Yahweh alone, and unchallenged concentration of that worship in Jerusalem. Thirty-five years before the destruction of the First Temple, this purified creed was triumphant in Judah, and Jerusalem became the national and spiritual center of the People of Israel.

The Last Days of Judah

The last days of the kingdom of Judah are described with surprising clarity in contemporary inscriptions—surprising, that is, because the Land is generally poor in written records. Most monuments and inscriptions were destroyed in the numerous disasters, and the widely-used parchment and papyrus could not endure in ordinary conditions. The few extant inscriptions include the stela of Mesha, king of Moab, from the middle of the ninth century B.C.E., the Siloam inscription from the time of Hezekiah, the short epitaph on the tomb of a royal steward of Judah from the end of the eighth century B.C.E., and a fragment from Samaria containing the single word *asher* (« which »). Recently scrolls of parchment and papyrus have been discovered in the dry caves of the wilderness of Judah, but so far (except for a few disjointed words on a palimpsest) these have been from subsequent periods.

As knowledge of writing spread, people naturally began to make wider use of cheap sherds of clay for letters and accounts. The first to be unearthed were Samarian sherds from the Jehu dynasty in Israel, mainly receipts for wine and oil from the royal estates. Others were dug up in the strongholds of the kings of Ezion Geber and Arad—these were mainly documents and letters dating from the eighth and seventh centuries B.C.E.

A letter, apparently from the period of Josiah, and found in a fortress on the coast between Yavneh and Ashdod, throws some light on an administration that centered around the king's fortresses, garrisons, and generals. The letter was written to the local governor by a man at work on the harvest; he was complaining because his garment had been taken unjustly. It is doubtful whether the complaint ever reached the governor, for Egyptian columns destroyed the citadel at about this time and ended Judaean rule of the area.

By far the most important and dramatic documents to be discovered are the *Letters of Lachish*, found beneath a thick layer of ashes in a guard-room at the city gates. Apart from displaying a style similar to Jeremiah's and that of other compositions of the period, the contents of these letters throw revealing light on the last stage of Judah's long struggle for freedom. Some speak of a prophet who went down to Egypt, and of a general who pursued him (compare the story of Urijah in JEREMIAH XXVI: 20-23); others discuss the words of men who come to weaken the morale of the people.

It is particularly interesting to note that most personal names in the Letters end with the name of God *(Yahu)*—names such as Gemaryahu, Hatzilyahu, Yaazanyahu—and that none preserves the element *Baal*, though this was still commonplace in the sherds of Samaria. This important change was undoubtedly connected with the intense religious revival that occurred in Josiah's reign.

Judah's last days of greatness were brief. With Assyria's final downfall, Babylon and Egypt were left to vie for control of Syria and the Land. Judah was quickly obliterated in this battle of the giants. Josiah made a last effort to bar the passage of Pharaoh Necho II (who had moved northward to help the remnants of the Assyrian army), but he was killed at Megiddo in 609 B.C.E.

An ivory (found at Arslan Tash) shows a woman—possibly the goddess Astarte—framed in a window: it is thought to be part of the booty taken from Aram-Damascus by the Assyrians in the eighth century B.C.E.

Egyptian Domination

For the next four years the Land was under Egyptian domination, and Judah was forced back to its former boundaries. The Egyptians crowned Jehoiakim king of Judah, and he retained his throne even when his country fell to Babylon. But despite the warning of the prophets, and of Jeremiah in particular, the last kings of Judah would not resign themselves to servitude. The great fortress or palace built by Jehoiakim at Ramat Rahel (possibly the ancient Beth Hakerem), half-way between Jerusalem and Bethlehem, was certainly bound up with the revolt he was planning against Babylon (JEREMIAH XXII: 13-19). It was built in the best Phoenician-Israelite tradition, which shows how optimistic the ruling classes in Judah were, and how Phoenician architectural styles were preserved until the end of the kingdoms.

The palace is outstanding for its great smoothed and dressed stones and many Proto-Aeolic capitals, the first of their kind to be discovered in Judah, and also for the window balustrades that embellish the front of the building. These balustrades are made of pillars decorated with falling leaves, and the capitals are voluted exactly as in a familiar Phoenician ivory plaque of a woman in a window resting against a similar balustrade. Jeremiah's description was amazingly accurate: ‹ and cutteth him out windows; and it is cieled with cedar, and painted with vermilion › (XXII: 14). Above the capitals unearthed by archaeologists there had been a wooden beam, and red paint was still discernible on the white stone.

Hopes were many, but the consequences bitter. In 597 B.C.E. the Babylonian army stormed Jerusalem. Jehoiakim died, and his son Jehoiachin capitulated and was exiled to Babylon, together with many of the aristocracy and craftsmen of Jerusalem. His submission had saved Judah once again, and Nebuchadnezzar, king of Babylon, crowned Jehoiachin's uncle, Zedekiah, in his place—though Judah was now reduced to a fraction of its original size. But Babylon's continued cruel oppression soon led to further rebellion; again Egypt encouraged the Judaeans, and again Jeremiah protested in vain. In 589 B.C.E. Zedekiah, a weak king, was persuaded to rebel. That was the end. The Babylonians took and sacked the cities of Judah one after the other, and besieged Jerusalem.

In a Lachish Letter, Hoshaiah, commander of a fortress on the road to Jerusalem, wrote to his master Jaush, commander in Lachish: ‹ And let [my lord] know that we are watching for the signals of Lachish, according to all the indications which my Lord hath given, for we cannot see Azekah. › It would be impossible to find a closer parallel to the biblical account of the days of Jeremiah: ‹ When the king of Babylon's army fought against Jerusalem, and against all the cities of Judah that were left, against Lachish, and against Azekah: for these defenced cities remained of the cities of Judah › (JEREMIAH XXXIV: 7).

The Fall of Jerusalem

Jerusalem was captured in the summer of 587 B.C.E. A month afterward (according to tradition, on the ninth day of the Hebrew month of Av) the Babylonians destroyed and burned all its walls and buildings. The First Temple lay in ruins. The surviving citizens were exiled to Babylon, except for the poorest classes—the vine-growers, the vine-dressers, and the farmers—who stayed in the villages. Gedaliah, son of Ahikam (a Jerusalem notable), was left in charge by the Babylonians. But soon afterward Gedaliah was murdered, together with the Babylonian garrison of Mizpeh, and the remaining organized Jewish population fled to Egypt. Judah's independence had finally ended.

It is incredible that only 25 years elapsed between Josiah's death and the quenching of the last flicker of Judaeo-Israelite independence. The devastation was frightful. Every town since excavated in Judah can be seen to have been totally demolished in that period, and to have remained in ruins for years. The great mass of the people had been banished, the remainder dwelt ‹ in the wastes ... in the open field ... in the forts and in the caves › (EZEKIEL XXXIII: 27). But the Judah of Josiah and of Jeremiah had forged the tools that sustained the Jewish nation even after this holocaust—its faith constant, its eyes forever turned to the destroyed Jerusalem.

Assyrian soldiers lead the people of a defeated town into captivity (from a Nineveh relief, seventh century B.C.E.).

Behold, the days come, saith the Lord, that the plowman shall overtake the reaper, and the treader of grapes him that soweth seed; and the mountains shall drop sweet wine, and all the hills shall melt. And I will bring again the captivity of my people of Israel, and they shall build the waste cities, and inhabit them; and they shall plant vineyards, and drink the wine thereof; they shall also make gardens, and eat the fruit of them. And I will plant them upon their land, and they shall no more be pulled up out of their land which I have given them, saith the Lord thy God.

AMOS IX: 13-15

Part Two

Dr. Eliahu Auerbach

The Prophets

The classical heritage of the prophecy of Israel is of vital importance both in its own history and in the history of mankind. Apart from being essential to an understanding of the basic characteristics of the Jewish people, prophecy itself has had a vital influence on the historical development of the Jewish nation. The ideas of the prophets, springing from the most deeply rooted forces of the Judaic soul, gradually transformed Israel completely; because of these ideas the nation came to adopt a unique attitude to its own destiny—an attitude that played a decisive role in determining its fate.

The Hebrew word for prophet—*navi*—means literally a « speaker » or a « teller. » The biblical use of the word denotes a particular style of speech—words spoken in an ecstatic state of mind, the cry of men through whom God speaks. So the passive phrase « to be a navi » means « to be inspired or driven to prophesy » (as in AMOS III: 8, or JEREMIAH XI: 21 and XXIII: 25). The meaning is made even clearer in the reflexive form *hitnabeh*—« to make oneself out to be a prophet » or « to behave as a prophet »—a word that is synonymous in Hebrew with *hishtage'a*— « to go mad » or « to act as a madman » (as in JEREMIAH XXIX: 26—« every man that is mad, and maketh himself a prophet »). The prophet and the madman are set beside one another and on occasions the prophet is simply referred to as « the madman » (2 KINGS IX: 11).

Nevi'im appear in the most ancient historical and legendary tales of the Scriptures, living in groups, and moving around the country—playing their deafening music and dancing ecstatically (1 SAMUEL X: 5). The enthusiasm of the nevi'im was infectious, and often swayed people, as it did King Saul when he met them (1 SAMUEL X: 10). But in general they were regarded with mixed feelings of awe and slight contempt.

Such self-styled « prophesiers » (common figures in many primitive societies) may seem, in principle, to have little to do with such true prophets as Moses, Elijah, Amos, and Jeremiah. Yet their presence at the beginnings of the tradition exactly typifies the profound characteristics of the Jewish people. The phenomenon that arose in Israel was so radically transformed and deepened that nothing remained of the primitive element except the name. The same process occurred with the development of the great Judaic moral code, which—as the result of a continual struggle—was raised from the level of elemental tribal loyalty and blood-vendetta to the level of a supreme ethic.

Literary Prophecy

Prophecy as a historical phenomenon is limited by definite boundaries of time and place, and the significance of these limitations has not yet been fully recognized. Generally the limitation of time is understood to be something accidental or external. We are acquainted with the literary prophets only through their writing, and so regard the first to write down his prophecies—Amos (eighth century B.C.E.)—as the first of the prophets. The writing itself was an integral part of the original phenomenon known as « literary » or « classical » prophecy, and not just a question of transcribing the spoken words. Literary prophecy ended at the time of the Babylonian exile (toward the end of the sixth century B.C.E.) or just after, and the later prophetic books (such as the books of Daniel and Zechariah) already belong to the Apocalyptic literature.

The geographical limitations are just as important. The exponents of literary prophecy came from the southern tribes—that is to say, from Judah and its neighbors.

Right, the Prophet Isaiah, a relief (c.1140) from the church of Souillac, in southwest France. In Isaiah's writings, literary prophecy attained its finest expression.

Zechariah's vision of the four chariots, a drawing from the 10th-century Catalan Roda Bible.

*And I turned, and lifted up mine eyes, and looked, and, behold, there came four chariots out from between two mountains; and the mountains were mountains of brass. In the first chariot were red horses; and in the second chariot black horses; And in the third chariot white horses; and in the fourth chariot grisled and bay horses. Then I answered and said unto the angel that talked with me, What are these, my lord? And the angel answered and said unto me, These are the four spirits of the heavens, which go forth from standing before the Lord of all the earth—*ZECHARIAH VI: 1-5.

Amos addressed himself entirely to the kingdom of Israel, though he came from Tekoa, situated between Bethlehem and Hebron at the edge of the Judaean desert. Jeremiah came from Anathoth « in the land of Benjamin » but as a priest of the tribe of Levi he belonged to the southern tribes. And Hosea was his neighbor from the same mixed area, where there had been close contact between the northern and southern tribes since the time of Saul.

The fact that literary prophecy occurred only among the southern tribes, and was part of their distinctive spiritual qualities, is confirmed by the opposite fact that « ecstatic » prophesying occurred only in northern Israel, and was quite unknown in the south. The barrier of time and place between these two phenomena—prophesying and prophecy—are quite distinct. The roots of prophesying go back to the primitive Canaanite inhabitants of the Land. (Even non-biblical writings—such as the description of Ven-Amon's journey in the Golenisheff Papyrus from about 1100 B.C.E.—confirm that this was so.) Prophecy, on the other hand, is closely bound up with the philosophy and ideals of the nomadic desert peoples.

Transition and Evolution

The transition from the prophesier to the prophet may perhaps be seen in the mighty figure of Elijah, Amos's predecessor. Elijah still displayed the characteristic features of the prophesier—his group-living with « sons of the prophets, » his dress, his sudden appearances and disappearances, his restlessness, and his ecstatic trances and movements (1 KINGS XVIII: 42, 46). But at the same time the character of his work was truly prophetic. He fought for the Israelite God against the Canaanite gods of Queen Jezebel and her court, and he reproached King Ahab for killing Naboth the Jezreelite and taking his vineyard. Elijah's indignant cry ‹ Hast thou killed, and also taken possession? › remains a supreme expression of the prophetic conscience (1 KINGS XXI: 19).

Elijah's creed was contained in his phrase: ‹ The Lord, He is God! › He would not compromise in any way with Baal-worship, and despite persecution and danger he clung to the worship of God. Like all the true prophets he was compelled to proclaim God's word. And when he despaired and cried out in his suffering, the voice of God answered him with the command: ‹ Go, return on thy ways. › Elijah was a true prophet—though not a literary one. He was alone in his period and his environment, but this isolation distinguished him from the « prophesier » and brought him closer to the prophets, who were also always withdrawn and isolated. The men we term « prophets » were few and far between, and in the course of 200 years—from the time of Amos to the destruction of Jerusalem—we know of only six: Amos, Isaiah, Micah, Zephaniah, Nahum, and Jeremiah. And if their influence was nevertheless revolutionary and long-lasting, it was because the unity of purpose displayed by all the prophets deepened the impression made by each individually—and also because their prophecies were written down in such a memorable form. The influence of the prophetic books was even greater than that of the men themselves, doubling and redoubling their impact.

External Influences

Some scholars contend that the threat of an all-powerful Assyria and the imminence of disaster were responsible for the birth of prophecy. However, attractive as this theory may be, it attempts to suggest a rational explanation for prophecy which, by its very nature, was irrational. In actual fact, Amos appeared in the days of Jeroboam the Second (785-749 B.C.E.), when the kingdom of Israel was at the height of its prosperity and power. His prophecies never even mention Assyria, then far too preoccupied with its own internal problems to pay attention to the west. Nevertheless, Amos foretold Israel's decline.

Similarly, Jeremiah appeared at a time when Judah was flourishing—in the days of Josiah, the restorer of David's kingdom; and he prophesied disaster at the very time when the death of Ashur-Banipal, king of Assyria (626 B.C.E.), paved the way for Judah's political ascendancy. Nor is there any need to recall the happy political situation that existed in the days of Isaiah and Micah, who foretold the decline of Judah 180 years before it came. If these prophets foretold disaster, it was not because danger threatened but because they were inspired by profound spiritual sources unrelated to external events.

Another view prevalent among scholars is that the prophets were the product of social conditions. And it is obvious, from the way in which all the prophets, from Amos to Jeremiah, condemned the luxury of the wealthy and attacked the inhuman oppression of the weak, that they were acting as leaders and spokesmen of the oppressed classes, and that this social concern was the driving force behind their activities. Indeed, many believe that the prophets arose out of the social upheavals that shook the monarchy—a view that lacks historical substantiation.

The prophets' own testimonies on contemporary events must be treated cautiously, for theirs was not an objective assessment of the situation but a supremely idealistic, subjective, and exalted demand. In the light of their denunciations all the people appear as idolators, and it would seem that the worship of Baal was dominant. But historical sources affirm that Yahweh held undisputed sway over the Israelites, and that their forms of worship were only slightly tainted by Canaanite culture. So the prophetic indictments of the people's moral standards cannot be taken at their face value; if they could, we would have to regard the Israelites as a rabble of sinners for whom extinction was the only cure, though the very existence and activity of the prophets contradict this verdict. The trial of Jeremiah (in 608 B.C.E.) indicates that a high standard of justice and integrity existed, and it could have done so only among a people living on a high moral plane.

The kingdoms of Israel and Judah suffered no real social upheavals. If we examine the reasons for this remarkable phenomenon we find, first of all, that the democratic regime of the ancient nomadic tribes (based on the tribe and the family) survived for centuries and prevented sharp social clashes. There never were large estates in Israel and the fact that agriculture was the basis of the economy helped to avert internal conflict, as did the absence of large cities (even Samaria and Jerusalem, to judge from their fortifications, were comparatively small, with no more than 20-25,000 inhabitants), the consequent absence of a landless proletariat, and the comparatively minor importance of maritime trade at that time.

The prophets also helped to preserve social equilibrium, acting as safety valves for social tensions, and preventing dangerous explosions. The strength of their influence can be judged from the impression made on King Jehu (10 years after the event) by Elijah's condemnation of Ahab's dealings with the Jezreelite farmer Naboth (2 KINGS IX: 25-26). Further proof of this influence is the legal framework given to the demands of the eighth-century prophets by the Book of Deuteronomy. Thus the relationship between prophecy and social conditions helped to preserve Israel from greater social upheavals, and was far from passive. The roots of prophecy lay in the souls of the people whose sons the prophets were. Only in this context of growth from within can the development and influence of prophecy be understood.

THE MOVE from the desert to the Promised Land radically altered every aspect of Israelite life. During their first few hundred years in Canaan the Israelites mingled constantly with the existing Canaanite population and might easily have lost their identity, as other nomadic tribes had done, but for the fact that they had a history and a culture of their own: the testament of Moses. They were united by a religious idea, they preserved a patriarchal tradition that went back to Egypt and Kadesh, and they had their own writings. It was this distinctive and closely guarded heritage that enabled them to preserve their spiritual independence.

Judah remained closer to the desert than Israel. Because of the nature of their territory, the southern tribes were cattle breeders rather than farmers and led a semi-nomadic existence over a large, sparsely populated area. Since there were no large Canaanite habitations in the vicinity, their numbers were swelled mainly by tribes from the south: Calebites, Kenites, Rechabites, and Jerahmeelites.

But in Israel, too, there was a stirring of conservative forces that opposed the growing Canaanite influence and clung to the desert traditions. The nomadic tribal and family system remained for centuries the foundation of social life. The patriarchal legends, which were closely bound up with the south (through Abraham and Isaac) and Transjordan (through Jacob), helped to maintain a living bond with the desert, the Ark of the Covenant, and the Tent of Meeting; and the sanctuaries at Shiloh and Gilgal served as centers for the development of the Mosaic tradition. As a result, a tension was created between the present and the past, between life and tradition. The fate of these tensions—whether they would weaken or grow steadily stronger—depended on the « accident » of historical development.

In this context the establishment of the monarchy was decisive in determining the spiritual life and future of the people of Israel. Through the union of north and south—established in the days of King Saul, and developed further by David and Solomon—the south became the dominant element, and the southern tribes exercised most influence on Israel's cultural development. It was in this period that the great work of the Pentateuch (the Five Books of Moses) was created. This work assembled the Israelite national traditions according to the views of the southern tribes, and gave them a literary form. The Pentateuch, steeped as it was in the Mosaic desert tradition, deepened the existing gulf and conflict between the life of the present and the ideal of the past.

In Judah, too, the conflict deepened as a result of contact with the north. The more national consciousness was intensified, and the more the customs and cults of the northern population penetrated to the south, the more obvious it became that these powerful influences were alien to the revered heritage of the Patriarchs. It was natural that the first discharge of tension should occur in the south, in Elijah's courageous revolt.

Southern Dominance

A son of the desert, Elijah naturally championed the ideal of the desert tradition against the religious and social manifestations of a culture typified by Phoenician Baal-worship. Elijah's pilgrimage to the primeval source of his strength, to the Lord in the Sinai desert, was profoundly significant. Within a few years Israel was shaken by the rising of Jehu, in which this king-killer was joined by two religious groups: the disciples of Elijah and the sect of the sons of Rechab, both devoted to the ideals of the desert.

At this point the leadership of the spiritual movement that was to end in prophecy passed into the hands of the south. If any political development was connected with this change, it was not the approach of the Assyrian danger, but the southward advance of two successive kings of Judah—Amaziah (799-786 B.C.E.) and Azariah (or Uzziah—786-758 B.C.E.)—and the close ties existing between Judah and the friendly tribes of the Negev and the Sinai peninsula. The connection in time is also very clear. In about 790 B.C.E., Amaziah took Sela, in the territory of Edom; shortly after 770 Azariah reached the Red Sea. And in 763 the first of the great literary prophets appeared from the south: Amos of Tekoa.

What, then, was the desert ideal of the prophets and their predecessors? Was it no more than a reactionary devotion to the past, an adherence to an outdated way of life? In fact it was nothing of the kind. While it is true that the past was illuminated in the golden light of the ideal, the question we must ask is: what was this life described as « ideal »?

First of all it was the desert life of simplicity, sincerity, and rectitude, against which all the possessions of the settlers were seen as illusion and self-indulgence rather than as progress. The structures and code of behavior adopted by the sons of Rechab, which resembled those of the Nabateans and of the first Muslims in later generations, are particularly enlightening:

‹ Ye shall drink no wine . . . . Neither shall ye build house, nor sow seed, nor plant vineyard . . . but all your days ye shall dwell in tents › (JEREMIAH XXXV: 6-7). By contrast, Amos castigates the women of Samaria—those ‹ kine of Bashan . . . which say to their masters, Bring, and let us drink › (AMOS IV: 1)—for leading gluttonous, drunken, and idle lives, and then lashes out at their masters ‹ That lie upon beds of ivory, and stretch themselves upon their couches . . . That drink wine in bowls, and anoint themselves with the chief ointments › (AMOS VI: 4-6).

The importance of the desert tradition lay, essentially, in its presentation of Israel's earliest epoch, before the entry into Canaan, as a golden age of nearness to God. The forging of the Tribes into one nation, in the desert and through the covenant with Yahweh, was a fundamental religious experience, and one that left an indelible impression on the national memory. In the hearts of those who preserved this tradition, the desert period was remembered as one of pure and unquestionable devotion to the God of Israel. This concept was shared by all the prophets, and expressed repeatedly by each in turn (AMOS II: 10; MICAH VI: 4; JEREMIAH II: 2).

The lives of Israel's forefathers were also held as exemplary in all social and moral spheres. The simple and severe morality of the desert nomads, the responsibility of all for each, the equality of poverty—all these stand out resplendently against the confusion, vulgarity, and evil of more modern ways of life. However, the desert ideal did not crave a return to nomadism for its own sake, but the preservation of Israel's primeval life in the desert. The desert ideal was not a reactionary social ideal, but a historic and traditional one.

The principle of the desert ideal stimulated the development of prophecy and enabled the prophets to feel and present everything that was new and vigorous, everything that erupted from their innermost being, as something ancient. Through their bond with the desert ideal, the prophets came to regard themselves as disciples of Moses and continuers of his work. And this very real historic attachment was above all a dedication to the immortal and exclusive covenant existing between Israel and its God. It was only the desert ideal that made the Israelites regard all elements in Canaanite life as intrinsically alien.

Thus the desert ideal, for all its retrospection, became a guiding force in prophecy. It preserved everything that had been handed down and acted as a touchstone for the development and fusion of the past and the present. In the souls of the prophets these conflicting forces merged with a dynamic and tempestuous force that acted as a stimulus to progress.

*And Elijah the Tishbite, who was of the inhabitants of Gilead, said unto Ahab, As the Lord God of Israel liveth, before whom I stand, there shall not be dew nor rain these years, but according to my word. And the word of the Lord came unto him, saying, Get thee hence, and turn thee eastward, and hide thyself by the brook Cherith, that is before Jordan. And it shall be, that thou shalt drink of the brook; and I have commanded the ravens to feed thee there—*I KINGS XVII: 1-4.

Left, the ravens bring food to Elijah at the brook of Cherith—a 12th-century French miniature. *Bodleian Library, Oxford (MS. Bodley 270b, f.168).* Right, the traditional Elijah's Tree, in the Sinai desert, where the prophet rested during his flight from Queen Jezebel (I KINGS XIX: 4-6).

JUST AS human beings are endowed with different qualities and talents, so nations too display their own distinct qualities. And though national talents must be assessed cautiously, the nature of the talents, especially among the historic peoples, is usually quite particular. The distinctive feature of Israel, its history, and its specific spiritual emphasis, is rooted in the constant growth of the moral urgency. This urgency can be felt pulsating behind the covenant made by Moses between God and his people; it molded Israel's conception of the nature of the divine, a nature that, in Israel, has always been sought in the sphere of morals; it is echoed throughout the pages of the Bible; it was the supreme arbiter, and it confronted every king of Israel who became drunk with his own power.

The form in which the moral demand was expressed varied with the personality of each prophet, but with all of them it was the basic driving force. The morals imperative or urgency was characterized by its power: always it was intended to change the existing order, to reshape the Israelites' way of life. This was its overriding principle, and if the desert ideal was the vessel into which prophecy chose to pour its concepts, the moral imperative was the vessel's content—a content that gave direction and depth to the prophets' ideas.

Prophecy brought about a decisive change in the concept of the divine. It is true that even in the basic Mosaic laws that concept was concerned mainly with the moral aspect, and later the moral concern expanded and deepened. But with the appearance of the literary prophets the moral idea became the principal element of divine perception, and God the embodiment of the moral imperative.

This profoundly serious concept of the divine is characteristic of Israel. The lighthearted bantering tone in which Homer, for example, described the weaknesses of the Greek gods is entirely foreign to the spirit of Israel, as expressed in prophecy. Consequently, an unbreakable bond was forged between God and humanity. As a result of this elevation of human morality to the divine sphere, and the impregnation of the divine with the moral, the moral became the force that sustained man's life in the universe.

This moral ideal is expressed repeatedly throughout the prophets' writings:

‹ Take thou away from me the noise of thy songs; for I will not hear the melody of thy viols. But let judgment run down as waters, and righteousness as a mighty stream › (AMOS V: 23-4).

‹ He hath shewed thee, O man, what is good; and what doth the Lord require of thee, but to do justly, and to love mercy, and to walk humbly with thy God? › (MICAH VI: 8).

‹ He judged the cause of the poor and needy; then it was well with him: was not this to know me? saith the Lord › (JEREMIAH XXII: 16).

The moral concept was certainly not the discovery or exclusive possession of the prophets or of the Jewish people as a whole. It belongs to mankind. But what particularizes it is the elevation of morality to the level of the supreme and omnipotent power that upholds and directs human life on all levels—the status of the individual, the relationship between man and his neighbor, the behavior of society as a whole, the relationship between nation and nation, and, finally, the relationship between man and his God.

Prophecy stood for the ultimate understanding of morality as a primal human instinct, capable of molding society and laying the basis for a true culture and civilization, the moral being conceived as a necessity of life. The supreme expression of this idea is found in Deuteronomy: ‹ That which is altogether just shalt thou follow, that thou mayest live › (XVI: 20).

The impulse to proclaim moral ideas is the force that moves the prophet and determines his fate: it is elemental and inescapable—‹ The lion hath roared, who will not fear? the Lord God hath spoken, who can but prophesy? › (AMOS III: 8).

Prophecy's historical importance lies in the tremendous power with which this compulsion to proclaim the Lord's word surges forward, renewing itself at every step, heedless of the people's readiness or ability to absorb it. The compulsion is reinforced by the magnificent unity of form in which each prophet echoes and adheres to his predecessor's demands, in his own voice and tone, and from a different point of view—though the content is always the same. One hammer blow is not enough to shape the steel. Blow after blow, falling repeatedly and with equal intensity, will eventually bend it and give it a new form. Nevertheless, whatever authority the prophets had may well have derived from the fact that the Israelites were at one with them in spirit and could be molded by their drive.

The Poetic Vision

ALL THE PROPHETS' writings are poetic in tone and highly ornate, though their form is never merely decorative. There is always the fusion of form and substance that makes for poetry. And it is a strange but significant fact that all the prophets were poets, so much so that any prose passages that appear in the prophetic writings must always be suspected of being later additions. This is not to say that the prophets always spoke in verse; but they always arranged their words and the rhythm of their words with the utmost sensitivity and accuracy.

Form is essential to the nature of prophecy, and leads to an understanding of it. It proves beyond doubt that the literary prophets, unlike their predecessors, were not men swept away by ecstasy, battling in an eloquent and unconscious frenzy. It shows that the words of the prophets were not bound up with oratory, that they were not instantaneous outpourings designed to produce a direct, immediate effect, but that they were used to form chiseled, polished poems.

If this is true, what then is the prophet's inspiration, the ‹ hand of God › that descends and guides him? Here we find a key to the riddle of prophecy: it is the poetic form itself that is felt to be divine, and the poet's intoxication is ‹ the hand of God. › It is only when the images descend upon the prophet and crystallize within him in the form of connected speech that he declares: ‹ Saith the Lord. ›

But form and style are not the final test. Poets think in terms of images, see visions, perceive symbols and their connections where the ordinary man would see nothing. Naturally, the prophet or poet is not always in this heightened state. There are days when he sees objects in a humdrum way—until the world suddenly takes on a new appearance, is full of secrets, symbols, and visionary power, and his eyes penetrate to depths and distances where he sees objects not as they appear but according to their significance. He is carried by an unknown force, he rises to new heights, images and sounds merge; the vision becomes a song, the poem flows and he can say: ‹ The word of the Lord came to me. ›

A classic description of this heightening transformation is given in the following quotation from Jeremiah (XVIII: 3-6):

Then I went down to the potter's house, and, behold, he wrought a work on the wheels. And the vessel that he made of clay was marred in the hand of the potter: so he made it again another vessel, as seemed good to the potter to make it. Then the word of the Lord came to me, saying, O house of Israel, cannot I do with you as this potter? saith the Lord. Behold, as the clay is in the potter's hand, so are ye in mine hand, O house of Israel—
JEREMIAH XVIII: 3-6.

Two visions of Jeremiah: left, the prophet is touched by the hand of God; right, his visit to the potter's house—drawings from the Roda Bible.

Here we can clearly see the sudden transformation of an everyday experience into a symbolic vision, at that very moment when the prophet says: ‹ Then the word of the Lord came to me. › But the presentation of the sudden, pictorial vision as a source of divine inspiration is expressed even more clearly in another passage from Jeremiah. In the middle of political discussions with King Zedekiah, the vision takes possession of the prophet (XXXVIII: 21-2):

‹ But if thou refuse to go forth [to submit to the Chaldeans], this is the word that the Lord hath shewed me:

‹And, behold, all the women that are left in the king of Judah's house shall be brought forth to the king of Babylon's princes, and those women shall say, Thy friends have set thee on, and have prevailed against thee: thy feet are sunk in the mire, and they are turned away back. ›

The image rises suddenly to the prophet's eyes and compels him to move, while speaking, from prose into verse. And at that same moment he says: ‹ the Lord hath shewed me. › Thus we can perceive (to the extent that it is possible to perceive and grasp religious and poetic experiences with the intellect) that while the prophet's divine inspiration always appears in poetic form, the converse is also true: the appearance of the poetic inspiration is interpreted by the prophet as a sign of the nearness and influence of God.

The same can sometimes be said of the prophets' « secular » poems, which contain no prophetic element. A beautiful example is presented by the sublime poem of Isaiah ‹ against the king of Babylon › (XIV: 4-23), which is divine only because it has been written by a divinely gifted poet. The same is true of Jeremiah: his cry of despair rises from the very depths of a tormented soul (XX: 7-9, 14-18), and his words are among the most deeply religious ever to have been written.

EVERYTHING spoken or written by the prophets in this classical period was inspired by one subject and one aim: concern for the fate of the Children of Israel. This concern is apparent in all their images and visions; it places the pen in their hands. Amos provides a perfect example of this social concern when he declares:

‹ I was no prophet, neither was I a prophet's son; but I was an herdman, and a gatherer of sycomore fruit:

Concern for the People

The hand of the Lord was upon me, and carried me out in the spirit of the Lord, and set me down in the midst of the valley which was full of bones . . . . I prophesied as I was commanded: and as I prophesied, there was a noise, and behold a shaking, and the bones came together, bone to his bone. And when I beheld, lo, the sinews and the flesh came up upon them, and the skin covered them above: but there was no breath in them. Then said he unto me, Prophesy unto the wind, prophesy, son of man, and say to the wind, Thus saith the Lord God; Come from the four winds, O breath, and breathe upon these slain, that they may live. So I prophesied as he commanded me, and the breath came into them, and they lived—EZEKIEL XXXVII: 1-10.

A mural depicting Ezekiel's vision of the valley of dry bones—from the third-century synagogue at Dura Europos, Mesopotamia. The large figures represent Ezekiel at different stages of the vision.

80

‹ And the Lord took me as I followed the flock, and the Lord said unto me, Go, prophesy unto my people Israel › (VII: 14-15). Amos's concern here is not for his birthplace, in the narrow sense of the term, but for the whole northern kingdom; and it is this concern that spurs him to action. Jeremiah is even more specific. He says: ‹ my heart maketh a noise in me; I cannot hold my peace, because thou hast heard, O my soul, the sound of the trumpet, the alarm of war › (IV: 19).

Concern for the people's fate dominates the prophets so completely that every thought, image, and vision is colored by it. All the prophetic writings contain the recurring theme: attachment to the people and love of the fatherland. Amos sees grasshoppers, a plumb line, a basket of summer fruit—and each becomes a symbol of the national tragedy. Jeremiah sees ‹ a rod of an almond tree, › a ‹ seething pot,› some ‹ clay vessels, › and ‹ baskets of figs ›—and they all become symbols of the people. Hosea's marriage is an unhappy one, and this too becomes a symbol of the nation's plight. The prophet is always haunted by this anxiety for his people: ‹ If I go forth into the field, then behold the slain with the sword! and if I enter into the city, then behold them that are sick with famine! › (JEREMIAH XIV: 18).

The prophets' concern for the nation's fate forced them to become leaders; not in the realm of politics, though they often pronounced on affairs of state; not in social conflicts, though they denounced social evils; but leaders in the way of righteousness, in ‹ the way of the Lord. ›

Concern for the people's destiny was only another aspect of the prophets' moral impulse. For in so far as morality is concerned with this world, it has to be realized in man's relations with his neighbor. In this light one can understand the grief and pain of the prophet who is compelled to proclaim the moral law and yet sees his people being destroyed because they will not accept its dominion. For, above all, the prophets were concerned with the inner fate of the people, and they saw external fate only as its consequence. And so the prophets admonished, denounced, exhorted, entreated, and despaired—and yet, in their heart of hearts, they believed in the exalted world of peace and the nearness of God. But they also believed that this new world could not be reached unless the Lord's people survived. Israel had to survive.

It is this moral concern that transformed the poet into a prophet: he had to place his power of vision, his brilliant intellect, his imagination, and his glowing images at the service of this one goal. Every prophet was a poet, but not every poet could

be a prophet unless every ounce of his spiritual energy was channeled in the one direction, toward the prophetic goal. Consequently the prophetic phenomenon was rare, even in Israel. It sprang, as we have seen, from four spiritual sources: the ideal of the desert; the moral idea; the poetic vision; and concern for the people's fate. In the overall picture of classical Hebrew prophecy, the desert ideal is the frame, the moral idea the subject matter, the poetic vision the color and form, the concern for the people's fate the raging cry of the soul. Together they provided the sublime image of the spirit of man, mirroring God himself.

THE GREEK parallel to the Hebrew word navi, *prophetes*, contains the idea that the man given this title is capable of foreseeing and foretelling the future. The Babylonians, Assyrians, Egyptians, Greeks, and Romans all planned their major policies according to the dictates of the prophets. But the prophets of Israel did not foretell the future in this way. To understand this, we must turn to the writings of the prophets themselves (for most stories about the prophets cannot be substantiated). Clearly it is important to consider whether any of their forecasts did not come true, for if the prophets were really gifted with second sight, they would not have made mistakes. Close examination of the prophetic books, however, reveals the fact that all the prophets made numerous forecasts that were never realized. A few of the most obvious ones can serve as examples.

In 734-3 B.C.E., Isaiah said of a child (born, at the latest, in 732):
‹ For before the child shall have knowledge to cry, My father, and my mother, the riches of Damascus and the spoil of Samaria shall be taken away before the king of Assyria › (VIII: 4). The prophecy was fulfilled in regard to Damascus; but at the time of the conquest of Samaria (in the year 721) the child would have been 11 years old, and certainly able ‹ to cry, My father, and my mother. ›
Jeremiah, too, made many wrong forecasts. In 626 B.C.E., he declared that the destruction of his people was imminent (IV and IX), but they survived another 40 years. After the battle of Carchemish (in 605 B.C.E.) he again prophesied the end (XIII, XIV, XVI, XVII); but 20 years passed before the prophecy was fulfilled. Jeremiah foretold that Jehoiakim, king of Judah, would receive ‹ the burial of an ass, › but in fact the king ‹ slept with his fathers › (2 KINGS XXIV: 6). There is also a discrepancy between Jeremiah's prophecy concerning Zedekiah's death and the historical facts. True, he writes, ‹ And thou shalt not escape out of his hand [the hand of the king of Babylon] . . . and thou shalt go to Babylon › (XXXIV: 3). But he goes on to say: ‹ thou shalt die in peace: and with the burnings of thy fathers . . . so shall they burn odours for thee; and they will lament thee, saying, Ah lord! › But the king's sons were slain in front of him; then his eyes were put out, and he was taken to Babylon where he died (2 KINGS XXV: 7).
It is clear, then, that when the prophets foretold the future they did not mean ‹ It will be so › but rather ‹ it must be › or ‹ it ought to be so. › The event is dependent on a condition; and the prophet's emphasis is on the condition, not the event. The prophets were convinced that a certain kind of behavior would lead to a certain event, and that if the cause changed, the effect changed with it.
None of the prophets ever described an event as something absolute and inevitable, but as something that involved a choice. So most of the prophecies are qualified by certain reservations. The prophets were really saying: if ye hearken to the voice of the Lord, ye shall be saved; but if ye do not hearken, ye shall perish.
The prophet, therefore, never foretold events. Whenever he appears to be foretelling the future, his prophecy is always conditional. And this difference between prophet and fortune teller illuminates the most profound aspects of the prophets' attitude to the world, to destiny, to choice, and to necessity.

The Greek *moira* and the Roman *fatum* denote an inescapable fate: in his desire to escape its fury, man succeeds only in bringing it down remorselessly upon himself (as Oedipus did). Biblical prophecy, on the other hand, regards man as master of his fate, and yet as being finally responsible to God. The source of the impending event lies in the hand of man: the moral world controls the world of events. Blind fate never rules; it is man who is called upon to fashion the world. This is the moral of the universal order, and it contains the essence of the Jewish philosophy.

False Prophecy

Here lies the answer to a difficult question: how to differentiate between the true and the false prophet. It is certainly wrong to say that the true prophet, unlike the false one, foretold the future accurately. For, as we have seen, the true prophet could often be mistaken, while forecasts of false prophets were often realized (DEUTERONOMY XIII: 1-5). Nor can one say that the true prophets were guided by divine inspiration, while the false prophet lied—for the false prophets claimed to be speaking the Lord's word, as the clash between Jeremiah and Hananiah illustrates (JEREMIAH XXVIII).

The dividing line is very slender, the essential difference lying in the moral content of the prophetic message. Jeremiah laid down only one distinction: that the true prophet prophesies ‹ of war, and of evil, and of pestilence, › while the false prophet ‹ prophesieth of peace › (XXVIII: 8-9). Strange though these words seem, they reach the heart of the matter. The true prophet has only one criterion—the moral law. And when he is faithful to it he cannot help but condemn the people and foresee that they will suffer.

The true prophet can fulfill his mission faithfully only by swimming *against* the stream. The false prophet, on the other hand, is guided by a number of criteria: the people's mood, political aims, mob enthusiasm. The true prophet is isolated, and sometimes hated, because he speaks without fear or favor. The false prophet is surrounded by cheering crowds; he is flexible and allows himself to be swept along by the tide. When disaster comes, he drowns in despair with the rest of the people. But the true prophet holds his ground—firm, upright, a pillar of strength—and comforts his people (JEREMIAH XXXI; EZEKIEL XXXIII-XLVIII; ISAIAH XL-XLV).

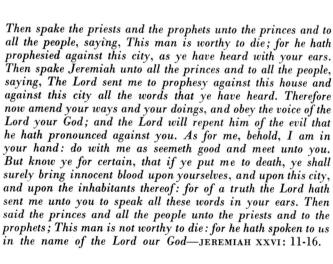

Then spake the priests and the prophets unto the princes and to all the people, saying, This man is worthy to die; for he hath prophesied against this city, as ye have heard with your ears. Then spake Jeremiah unto all the princes and to all the people, saying, The Lord sent me to prophesy against this house and against this city all the words that ye have heard. Therefore now amend your ways and your doings, and obey the voice of the Lord your God; and the Lord will repent him of the evil that he hath pronounced against you. As for me, behold, I am in your hand: do with me as seemeth good and meet unto you. But know ye for certain, that if ye put me to death, ye shall surely bring innocent blood upon yourselves, and upon this city, and upon the inhabitants thereof: for of a truth the Lord hath sent me unto you to speak all these words in your ears. Then said the princes and all the people unto the priests and to the prophets; This man is not worthy to die: for he hath spoken to us in the name of the Lord our God—JEREMIAH XXVI: 11-16.

Two illustrations from the Roda Bible. Left, Jeremiah on trial before the king. (Although the drawing shows him being stoned to death by the people, he was in fact acquitted, and died some years later in Egypt.) Right, the Prophet Jeremiah at the siege of Jerusalem—seated in the lower right-hand "corner" of the city.

FOR MOST ancient peoples, ritual was a direct manifestation of religion: in fact, the words « ritual » and « religion » were practically synonymous. To abolish ritual was to depose or destroy the deity. The Jewish people alone were prepared to regard ritual as a specific problem within the sphere of theology, and one that could be legitimately examined and criticized.

This astonishing intellectual advance was a direct result of biblical prophecy. Before its emergence no real criticism of ritual itself existed, even in Israel, and only very occasionally had the nation's spiritual leaders tried to purge the religion of its superstitious elements. The prophets' attitude to ritual, from Amos on, was more outspoken and rigid. Recognizing only one criterion, the moral law, the prophet regarded ritual as something immaterial and inessential compared to the all-essential moral imperative. And since the dominance of ritual and worship tended to divert the people's attention from the true way of the Lord, the prophets became expressly hostile to ritual. This hostility was voiced unwaveringly by all the prophets who lived before the Babylonian exile, starting with Amos:

‹ I hate, I despise your feast days, and I will not smell in your solemn assemblies.

‹ Though ye offer me burnt offerings and your meat offerings, I will not accept them: neither will I regard the peace offerings of your fat beasts.

‹ Take thou away from me the noise of thy songs; for I will not hear the melody of thy viols.

‹ But let judgment run down as waters, and righteousness as a mighty stream › (v: 21-24).

And Amos goes on to ask a vital question:

‹ Have ye offered unto me sacrifices and offerings in the wilderness forty years, O house of Israel? › (v: 25).

Here Amos, the defender of the desert ideal, assumes that everyone knows as a fact and accepts the tradition that sacrifices were unknown in the time of Moses. He was not the only prophet to make this assumption. Isaiah spoke similarly:

‹ To what purpose is the multitude of your sacrifices unto me? saith the Lord: I am full of the burnt offerings of rams, and the fat of fed beasts; and I delight not in the blood of bullocks, or of lambs, or of he goats › (I: 11).

‹ . . . cease to do evil; learn to do well; seek judgment, relieve the oppressed, judge the fatherless, plead for the widow › (I: 16-17).

Both these prophets are declaring the outward show and ritual of sacrifices and festivals to be worthless in themselves: they had to be backed by a moral outlook, termed ‹ judgment. › Micah's conception of the problem was more profound:

‹ Wherewith shall I come before the Lord, and bow myself before the high God? shall I come before him with burnt offerings, with calves of a year old?

‹ Will the Lord be pleased with thousands of rams, or with ten thousands of rivers of oil? shall I give my firstborn for my transgression, the fruit of my body for the sin of my soul?

‹ He hath showed thee, O man, what is good; and what doth the Lord require of thee, but to do justly, and to love mercy, and to walk humbly with thy God? › (VI: 6-8).

Here revulsion for the ritual of sacrifice is expressed completely. Ritual is said to be the way of the mistaken. God's will is different: he desires justice, mercy, and humility as a token of man's reverence for his maker. Micah was not saying that the ritual should be purified. He was questioning the value of ritual itself. (It should be remembered that his words were spoken in the days of King Hezekiah, who carried out far-reaching reforms in ritual.)

Hosea adopted the same categorical tone:

‹ For I desired mercy, and not sacrifice; and the knowledge of God more than burnt offerings › (VI: 6).

Elijah's offering is consumed by 'the fire of the Lord'—a fresco from the Dura Europos synagogue (third century c.e.). After this victory over the prophets of Baal, Elijah fled to Beersheba to escape Jezebel's vengeance.

So Ahab sent unto all the children of Israel, and gathered the prophets together unto mount Carmel. And Elijah came unto all the people, and said, How long halt ye between two opinions? if the Lord be God, follow him: but if Baal, then follow him. And the people answered him not a word. Then said Elijah unto the people, I, even I only, remain a prophet of the Lord; but Baal's prophets are four hundred and fifty men. Let them therefore give us two bullocks; and let them choose one bullock for themselves, and cut it in pieces, and lay it on wood, and put no fire under: and I will dress the other bullock, and lay it on wood, and put no fire under: And call ye on the name of your gods, and I will call on the name of the Lord: and the God that answereth by fire, let him be God. And all the people answered and said, It is well spoken—I KINGS XVIII: 20-24.

Jeremiah's Pronouncement

The prophets' attitude to ritual was most clearly expressed by Jeremiah. In his great oration in the Temple (in 609 B.C.E.), Jeremiah surveyed and appraised the reforms made by Josiah 13 years before. And, characteristically, his words indicated clearly that these major reforms had not swayed him an inch from the thinking and teaching of his predecessors.

Like Amos, Jeremiah denied that ritual was backed by the authority of Mosaic law:

‹ . . . Put your burnt offerings unto your sacrifices, and eat flesh.

‹ For I spake not unto your fathers . . . concerning burnt offerings or sacrifices.

‹ But this thing commanded I them, saying, Obey my voice, and I will be your God, and ye shall be my people . . .› (VII: 21-3).

Jeremiah scorned all worship, even the Temple itself, when the spirit was wrong:

‹ Trust ye not in lying words, saying, The temple of the Lord, The temple of the Lord, the temple of the Lord, are these.

‹ For if ye throughly amend your ways and your doings; if ye throughly execute judgment between a man and his neighbour;

‹ If ye oppress not the stranger, the fatherless, and the widow, and shed not innocent blood in this place, neither walk after other gods to your hurt:

‹ Then will I cause you to dwell in this place . . .› (VII: 4-7).

Jeremiah would not even accept the recently discovered Book of the Law as a reliable guide for Judah, and he expressly denied its authority:

‹ How do ye say, We are wise, and the law of the Lord is with us? Lo, certainly in vain made he it; the pen of the scribes is in vain.

‹ . . . lo, they have rejected the word of the Lord; and what wisdom is in them? › (VIII: 8-9).

The prophets' uniform attitude to ritual and their intellectual courage played a highly important part in shaping the historical development of the Jewish people. King Hezekiah and King Josiah could only bring about their reforms after many years of painful progress, whereas the prophets were centuries ahead of the people.

They did not reform ritual but hotly denied its value; they did not purify or purge it of evil elements, but stripped religious consciousness of all ritualistic elements. It is possible that the prophets—because of the extraordinary uniformity of their preaching over a period of 180 years—would ultimately have been able to enforce their ideas. As it was, the chain of biblical prophecy was broken with the destruction of the kingdom, and once this force was removed, the desire to refine and purify ritual prevailed. After Jeremiah, the people came under the spell of the priest Ezekiel, whose ritualistic ideas seem almost prehistoric beside those of the prophets. It was only because of the continued power of the prophets' writings that the prophetic outlook on ritual triumphed centuries later.

Those who regard the prophet as nothing more than the passive instrument of the divine message, with no will of his own, deny the human element of prophetic revelation. Fortunately history has recorded more than the passive aspects of the prophetic phenomenon: it demonstrates the considerable differences that existed between the characters of the prophets and the development of their prophecy, and also the close bond that existed between their historical influence, their personalities, and their modes of expression. Above all, the prophets (whom we will now consider individually) were living men of flesh and blood.

AT THE HEAD of Israel's history stands the colossal figure of Moses. His gaze is fixed on the future, his countenance illuminated by historical tradition, but the man himself is still wrapped in the cloak of legend. Here we must concern ourselves with a limited and cautious account of Moses' life and work, based only on reliable historical traditions.

Moses

To begin with, Moses was an actual historical personage, not a mythological creation. Though little is known of his childhood and early life (as with many great historical personages), it seems clear that he belonged to the tribe of Levi. Only this could explain the central position held by the Levites in Israel's ancient religious life. Moses was closely linked with Egypt. His name (which means « child » or « son ») is Egyptian, and is a component in the names of several pharaohs. In so far as a man's name indicates his cultural ties, Moses' name gives historical corroboration to the stories of his ties with the Egyptian royal house. And there is also historical evidence to show that he stayed in Midian.

Moses became leader of the Israelites on their departure from Egypt (in about 1260 b.c.e.). A good deal of reliable evidence substantiates the story of the crossing of the Red Sea—at its shallow northwestern arm—which was then directly connected with the Bitter Lakes: the waters were held back for a time by an east wind (EXODUS XIV: 21), and the pursuing Egyptians were surprised and drowned by the returning flood. There is a reference to this event in a short contemporary poem known as « the Song of Miriam » (EXODUS XV: 21).

In the Song of Deborah, written about 120 years after the Exodus, the number of men deemed fit for military service in the whole of Israel is given as 40,000. Calculating backward (and allowing for normal natural increase), we can reckon that some 3000 men of military age took part in the Exodus; this would put the total number of people who left Egypt at about 12-13,000. A company of that size could find room and sustenance in the oasis of Kadesh, which covered an area of 38 square miles and was watered by abundant springs. It was at Kadesh that the Twelve Tribes of Israel were consolidated into one people under Moses' firm leadership. And Kadesh became the cradle of Israel and its religion.

The Kadesh oasis, as its name implies (it derives from the Hebrew root meaning « holy »), had been a sacred place since ancient days, like Mecca in Arabia; and it

86

I am the Lord thy God. . . . Thou shalt have no other gods before me. Thou shalt not make unto thee any graven image, or any likeness of any thing that is in heaven above, or that is in the earth beneath, or that is in the water under the earth: Thou shalt not bow down thyself to them, nor serve them: for I the Lord thy God am a jealous God, visiting the iniquity of the fathers upon the children unto the third and fourth generation of them that hate me; And shewing mercy unto thousands of them that love me, and keep my commandments. Thou shalt not take the name of the Lord thy God in vain; for the Lord will not hold him guiltless that taketh his name in vain. Remember the sabbath day, to keep it holy. Six days shalt thou labour, and do all thy work: But the seventh day is the sabbath of the Lord thy God: in it thou shalt not do any work, thou, nor thy son, nor thy daughter, thy manservant, nor thy maidservant, nor thy cattle, nor thy stranger that is within thy gates: For in six days the Lord made heaven and earth, the sea, and all that in them is, and rested the seventh day: wherefore the Lord blessed the sabbath day, and hallowed it. Honour thy father and thy mother: that thy days may be long upon the land which the Lord thy God giveth thee. Thou shalt not kill. Thou shalt not commit adultery. Thou shalt not steal. Thou shalt not bear false witness against thy neighbour. Thou shalt not covet thy neighbour's house, thou shalt not covet thy neighbour's wife, nor his manservant, nor his maidservant, nor his ox, nor his ass, nor any thing that is thy neighbour's— EXODUS XX: 2-17.

Moses, by Michelangelo (1475–1564)—from the church of S. Pietro in Vincoli, Rome.

appears that the tribe of Levi had inhabited it in earlier days. That is why Levi was describ̧ed as ‹ a tribe of priests, › why Moses led the people to Kadesh, and why he reappointed the Levites as a tribe of priests (EXODUS XXXII: 26-9).

According to tradition, the Lord revealed himself to Moses at Kadesh. This was the site of the burning bush—in Hebrew, *sneh*. (It seems certain that the name for the Mount of the Revelation—Sinai, meaning thorn-shaped—came from the word sneh. The mountain's other name, Horeb—EXODUS III: 1—comes from the Hebrew *herev*, a sword, and means a sharp spike of rock.) Another, later tradition (DEUTERONOMY I: 2) places the Mount of the Revelation at 11 days' journey southeast of Kadesh, in the land of Midian, where active volcanoes existed in biblical times. (The description in EXODUS XIX could well be of a volcanic eruption.) In any case it was not situated in the arid wilderness of granite hills to the south of the Sinai peninsula, as many people now assume.

After 40 years, Kadesh became too small to contain the Israelites. Their numbers had doubled through natural increase and because other Israelite tribes had arrived from the desert. We hear of unrest among the people, of risings against the authority of Moses as leader and priest, of complaints about discrimination, and so on. It was at this point that the aged Moses conceived his daring plan to conquer Canaan, after he had heard from Transjordan that waves of Amorites had penetrated Canaan

Moses brings the two tablets of the Law to the Children of Israel—an illumination from the Sarajevo Haggada (executed in northern Spain in the 13th century C.E.).

*And Moses turned, and went down from the mount, and the two tables of the testimony were in his hand: the tables were written on both their sides; on the one side and on the other were they written. And the tables were the work of God, and the writing was the writing of God, graven upon the tables. And when Joshua heard the noise of the people as they shouted, he said unto Moses, There is a noise of war in the camp. And he said, It is not the voice of them that shout for mastery, neither is it the voice of them that cry for being overcome: but the noise of them that sing do I hear. And it came to pass, as soon as he came nigh unto the camp, that he saw the calf, and the dancing: and Moses' anger waxed hot, and he cast the tables out of his hands, and brake them beneath the mount—*EXODUS XXXII: 15-19.

from northern Syria and established two kingdoms, in northern Moab and in the Bashan. Moses perceived that the general chaos in Transjordan presented a unique opportunity. And he ordered the departure from Kadesh.

He planned to skirt the land of Edom, which had a well-organized army, to move north through Moab, and then to turn westward and break into Canaan. But a large section of the people (later known as « the tribes of the south ») separated from the main body on the eve of the departure from Kadesh, and moved directly northward. They occupied the south of Canaan, with the exception of Jerusalem; the sequence of events can be grasped from the account in Numbers (XXI: 1-3) and Judges (I: 16-36). Moses and the rest of his people passed through eastern Transjordan, overcame the Amorites, and turned westward toward Heshbon.

But Moses did not descend into the Valley of the Jordan. He died on the way, within sight of the Promised Land.

The Covenant	Moses' greatest political achievement was the establishment of the « Covenant of the Twelve Tribes of Israel » at Kadesh, the covenant that gave birth to the people of Israel. The number of tribes in the covenant is clearly laid down by tradition; but the list of tribes is not. In the south of the Holy Land lived tribes that were always regarded as Israelite (though they never belonged to the « sons of Jacob »): the Calebites, Kenites, Rechabites, and Jerahmeelites. On the other hand, it appears that the tribes of Asher, Reuben, and Gad were never in Egypt. (Historical sources indicate that they settled in Canaan earlier.)

The most authentic list of the participating tribes in the Covenant of Kadesh is given in Judges (I: 16-36). It names only 10 tribes—including Caleb and Kenaz (the Kenites)—but five of the «sons of Jacob» are missing. If we compare and fit together all the existing information, the list of tribes concerned in the Covenant of Kadesh appears as follows: Levi, Caleb, Kenaz, Rechab, Jerahmeel, Judah, Simeon, Zebulun, Dan, Naphtali, Ephraim, and Manasseh.

The tribal Covenant was conceived to end blood feuds and disputes between the tribes. It necessitated the institution of permanent laws and a judge with unquestioned authority. Moses understood and fulfilled both these requirements. We know of only two inter-tribal disputes during the next two centuries—in contrast to the perpetual strife and friction that was commonplace among nomadic tribes.

The fundamental law of the Covenant is undoubtedly contained in the Ten Commandments. But a general system of law and jurisdiction was needed as well, and the creation of this system was another of Moses' great achievements at Kadesh. Fragments of his « Book of the Covenant » giving details of his legislation have come down to us (EXODUS XXI-XXIII). Moses established a body of between 70 and 72 « elders, » about six from each tribe. Here, too, is an indication of how few the people were, for it would seem that each judge would hear the suit of no more than 50 families. Moses himself was the supreme judge (EXODUS XVIII: 26); but he was advised by his father-in-law, a wise Midianite priest (EXODUS XVIII: 24).

The Covenant was more than a pact between the tribes themselves, or between Moses and the tribes, and this is its unique feature. It was a pact between the people and their God. It was founded on the religious concept embodied in the name « Israel » (meaning « God fights »). God fights through the hosts of his people: the birth of the people and the birth of its faith were one.

The Ten Commandments	Moses stands out among the great figures of civilization because of the originality of his religious ideas. In an age when idols were manifold and gods were considered to be only slightly above the human level, he recognized that a true concept of the divine meant belief in a single divine entity. Moses did not bequeath specific philosophic definitions or religious principles; he gave only instructions—in the

form of the Ten Commandments—and these are the only source from which his religious ideas can be deduced.

The monotheism of Moses was pure and absolute. This is made clear in the first commandment, and even clearer in the second, which forbids any formal description of the deity. This prohibition is expressed with the utmost severity; Moses regarded any attempt to describe God as sacrilege. And in doing so he distinguished Israel from the world around and gave it a particular characteristic.

The third commandment is often misunderstood. The statement that the Lord's name must not be taken in vain means that it must not be used for magical ends in the practice of witchcraft, or to force the will of man on God. God's name may only be pronounced in prayer to him. The other commandments are concerned with human relationships. The injunction to rest from work on the seventh day is Israel's great gift to the world and a foundation of social development. The six commandments from the fifth to the tenth refer to the moral behavior of the individual and need no explanation; they are the basis of most civilized societies. A covenant is usually a two-sided agreement that binds both parties and can be dissolved by either of them. But in the Covenant of Kadesh the obligation falls only on the Children of Israel: it is through this Covenant that they became a nation. The moral commandments are the commandments of God. Man can only obey. And here, too, was a major human advance. Moses was the first man to comprehend the deity as a moral entity. The only definition of God was the moral one, and Moses would accept no other.

Moses' Achievement

Moses' monotheism triumphed once and for all over the era of magic and mythology. But in the sphere of ritual Moses belonged to his age. Adoration of God was expressed by animal sacrifice, and his decisions were obtained by questioning through the angels Urim and Thummim. (This left a great deal for the prophets to explain and interpret, for they based their activity on the ideas of Moses.) In the Ten Commandments, however, no rules of worship were set down, and even the injunction to observe the Sabbath was not ritualistic but socio-religious: it is a commandment to rest from work, to give the soul as well as the body respite.

Moses was alone in his greatness, an extraordinary phenomenon at odds with his age. His was an age and a world steeped in magic, superstition, and bloodcults, and these practices were linked with belief in various gods. Yet Moses could form the supreme concept of the one God, who could not be described and who demanded moral action. Moreover, he dared to accept the task of instilling this idea into the minds of nomads and serfs, and to set their imaginations aflame with it. He possessed

Behold, the days come, saith the Lord, that the plowman shall overtake the reaper, and the treader of grapes him that soweth seed; and the mountains shall drop sweet wine, and all the hills shall melt. And I will bring again the captivity of my people of Israel, and they shall build the waste cities, and inhabit them; and they shall plant vineyards, and drink the wine thereof . . . . And I will plant them upon their land, and they shall no more be pulled up out of their land which I have given them— AMOS IX: 13-15.

a great and colorful spectrum of talents that no one man, perhaps, has ever before or since possessed. He was a profound, original thinker, a statesman and commander capable of standing up to the gravest perils. He had an exceptional flair for wise judgment and rapid decision, the ability to give the correct order at the right time. When his work was imperiled (as in the episodes of the golden calf and Baal-Peor), Moses could be hard and even brutal; but nevertheless he bowed to the dictates of right and justice. Whenever he had to prevent his people from wandering off the chosen course, his anger could rise like a flame; yet at the same time he possessed unlimited patience, and forgave the frailties of the weak. For 40 years he was an untiring teacher and educator. And though he towered above the people, he was close to the most simple of his brethren, who would come to him with their griefs. He bore the burden of the whole nation.

Moses was not a visionary who cherished illusions about the future; he was a seer, who saw the future, like the prophets who became his heirs. It is hard to find anyone of equal stature, for he perfectly combined spiritual understanding and the ability to act and administer. He was the greatest of all the great prophets of Israel.

Amos

AMOS was a herdsman and a gatherer of sycamore fruit who came from Tekoa in Judah, situated between Bethlehem and Hebron at the edge of the Judaean desert— on the slopes of the Judaean hills that face the Dead Sea. He expressly denied affiliation with any bands of prophets who lived on alms, and was proud of his economic independence (VII: 14). Alone in the silence of the austere Judaean hills, he walked behind his flock, close always to the desert ways, his thoughts nourished constantly by the desert ideal of Israel's past.

But in no sense was he an uncultured semi-nomad. On the contrary, his vast knowledge casts a vivid light on the spiritual vitality of the shepherds and herdsmen that he typified. Amos was thoroughly familiar with the history and tradition of both his own and the neighboring peoples, with the various trends in the political life of his time, with the geography of Palestine and the encircling lands, with the stars in their courses, with religious customs.

It is strange that this peaceful man should abandon his tranquil life and leap into the whirlpool of prophecy. But his explanation was simple: ‹ And the Lord took me as I followed the flock, and the Lord said unto me, Go, prophesy unto my people Israel › (VII: 15). It was this command that stimulated him to preach his code of morality—and, remarkably, he turned to the northern kingdom. The disasters that overtook Amaziah, king of Judah, had brought the victorious northern kingdom

91

to Judah's notice: Amos could not fail to discern the extent to which the patriarchal morality had been abandoned there.

Amos was the prophet of wrath. He was impelled to proclaim God's anger and to announce that the day of judgment was imminent—and no more. His language is severe and trenchant; only here and there do we find a note of mercy or compassion (VII: 1-6). His outlook was as fierce and austere as the desert in which he was born. Amos was the first to formulate the idea of Israel as a chosen people, a choice that involved a mission, a burden, a responsibility: ‹ You only have I known of all the families of the earth; therefore I will punish you for all your iniquities › (III: 2).

For Amos, moral responsibility was a decree as inflexible as the laws of nature. No other prophet had so inflexible a view of the universal order of morality—a view that led him to see Israel as doomed: ‹ The virgin of Israel is fallen; she shall no more rise: she is forsaken upon her land; there is none to raise her up › (v: 2).

Amos adopted a universal attitude, looking beyond the immediate boundaries of his own people. According to him, the God of the universe did not need Israel to carry out his will. Before God all people were equal: ‹ Are ye not as children of the Ethiopians unto me, O children of Israel? saith the Lord. Have not I brought up Israel out of the land of Egypt? and the Philistines from Caphtor, and the Syrians from Kir? › (IX: 7).

Never again could « chosen » mean racial superiority—but rather a doubled and redoubled responsibility. And since (in Amos's critical eyes) Israel no longer met this demand, there could be no hope of salvation—though it pained Amos to admit so. Sacrifice and prayer could not save the people, only righteousness (v: 21-24).

Amos spoke in terse, biting words. He came when the spirit moved him, and when he was threatened by violence he returned to the tranquillity of his herds and his sycamore trees. This humble herdsman was a great poet; his language and imagery were overwhelmingly powerful. Unlike Elijah, Amos was not the zealous champion of Israel's one God—nor did he fight the foreign false gods: that battle had been won in a much earlier period. Amos sought only one thing—to see God's law reign among men, a law that demanded morality of the individual, social justice of the community: ‹ But let judgment run down as waters, and righteousness as a mighty stream. › (v: 24).

Hosea

HOSEA was slightly younger than Amos and came from an altogether different environment. He lived in a border area in the territory of Benjamin, close to Judah. But unlike Amos he was brought up in a progressive rural settlement, and was completely familiar with the literary culture of his day. He arrived at prophecy through his own personal misfortune—his marriage to an unfaithful woman, a marriage that he saw as symbolic of the relationship between Israel and its God.

Hosea was a man of intellect and reflection, unlike the strong-willed and deeply emotional Amos. His character was altogether milder. While they both prophesied the apparently inevitable destruction of Israel, Hosea was tortured and tormented by the prospect—as he was by the infidelity of his wife, whom he loved despite her betrayal. Consequently there is more pain and lamentation than anger in his words, and now and again a spark of hope leads him to believe that Israel might still be spared. He depicts God in his own image—as if God, too, punished Israel against his will, and in deep grief:

‹ How shall I give thee up, Ephraim? how shall I deliver thee, Israel? . . . mine heart is turned within me, my repentings are kindled together › (XI: 8).

A light shone from the depth of Hosea's suffering—the conviction (of paramount importance to the spiritual development of the Jewish people) that God loved Israel despite its sins, and that he could not bring himself to destroy it in his wrath.

92

He understood that God had loved his people from their earliest days, and those days became the golden age of Israel's past. Here is the desert ideal in all its purity: ‹ When Israel was a child, then I loved him, and called my son out of Egypt . . . . I taught Ephraim also to go, taking them by their arms . . . › (XI: 1-3).

Because of this affinity between God and his people, Hosea saw the people's conduct as a sin against God. This conception of Israel's history contains his most original idea, and it was to have a strong influence on future generations. Because Hosea often spoke about ritualistic matters, he has often been accused of being more primitive than Amos, who concerned himself only with the moral imperative. But in fact Hosea was the more modern. He realized, as Amos had not, that all the popular manifestations of the Israelite faith (including customs of worship) did not originate with the Israelites, but were a legacy from Canaan.

Hosea's attitude was creative in every sense of the word. It refused to allow the problem of Israel's original culture to be forgotten, and it motivated the reforms of subsequent periods. It led on the one hand to a progressively deeper conception of the spiritual foundations of religion, on the other to an increasingly rigorous rejection of Canaanite elements—as the reforms of Josiah, Ezekiel, and Ezra show. And Hosea displayed the same spiritual freedom in other spheres. He was not afraid to denounce the rebellion of Jehu (which had taken place a century earlier) as ‹ the blood of Jezreel › (I: 4), even though it had taken place with the prophet Elisha's blessing. Hosea considered that all blood was precious, even when shed—allegedly—for the greater glory of the Lord.

The same remarkable spiritual freedom is evident in Hosea's appraisal of the patriarchal chronicles, which by then had become legends that were believed in with implicit faith. Hosea considered that Jacob's example was a bad one:
‹ The Lord hath also a controversy with Judah, and will punish Jacob according to his ways; according to his doings will he recompense him.
‹ He took his brother by the heel in the womb, and by his strength he had power with God:
‹ Yea, he had power over the angel, and prevailed: he wept, and made supplication unto him: he found him in Beth-el, and there he spake with us . . . › (XII: 2-4).

Hosea was alone in his generation and, like all the prophets, far ahead of his time. He was shunned by his people and reviled for his attacks on religious customs. With profound grief he watched the kingdom of Israel disintegrating before his eyes. But his writings were saved and taken to Judah, where they had a profound effect. King Hezekiah's reforms were only the first attempt to realize Hosea's ideas.

Isaiah

ISAIAH's background was quite different from that of the simple herdsman Amos or of the refined, elegaic Hosea. Isaiah lived in Jerusalem, the capital, and apparently came from a distinguished family. He was well known to the two kings of his day—Ahaz and Hezekiah—and addressed them as equals. His language, always rich and carefully chosen, is that of an intellectual.

Isaiah's induction into prophecy occurred ‹ in the year that King Azariah died › which was a year of political unrest. Isaiah was young at the time, and the father of a small son. The prophet's induction and his description of it are characteristic: he was the first prophet to venture a description of God and his angels. But this incursion into the crude anthropomorphic territory of the popular imagination was conducted humbly, and raised the religious concept to a supreme, spiritual plane. There was such a cosmic sublimity in Isaiah's vision of God—‹ and His train filled the Temple ›—that the man, the prophet, felt himself to be small and unclean by comparison. But when the voice was heard calling ‹ Whom shall I send? › Isaiah answered with the assurance of a man who knows his strength: ‹ Here am I, send me! ›

Sennacherib's army fleeing from Jerusalem (a 16th-century Turkish miniature): Isaiah kneels on the right of the picture.

Therefore thus saith the Lord concerning the king of Assyria, He shall not come into this city, nor shoot an arrow there, nor come before it with shields, nor cast a bank against it. By the way that he came, by the same shall he return, and shall not come into this city, saith the Lord. For I will defend this city to save it for mine own sake, and for my servant David's sake. Then the angel of the Lord went forth, and smote in the camp of the Assyrians a hundred and fourscore and five thousand—ISAIAH XXXVII: 33-36.

Political Influence

In his first appearance before King Ahaz in 733 B.C.E. (VII), Isaiah already displayed the qualities that were to distinguish him during the 40 years of his ministry. He had great powers of perception and discernment—invaluable in that tortuous political world—that gave him great influence over his country's fate. Just as he had been quick to discern (in 733) that the threat of war with Ephraim and Aram was slight (VII), so he was right 20 years later when he condemned Hezekiah's leanings toward Babylon (XXXIX): he was right again in 711 when he dissuaded the king from plotting against Assyria (XX) and, above all, he was right in 701 when he detected Sennacherib's weakness, and saved Jerusalem (XXXVIII).

But apart from a powerful intellect, Isaiah possessed a decisive soul that looked toward the unseen and demanded implicit faith. These two qualities are revealed in his conversation with Ahaz: after delivering a prophetic analysis of the political situation, the prophet, suddenly sure that the Lord would not abandon his emissary, gave the hesitant king a sign: ‹ Ask thee a sign of the Lord thy God; ask it either in the depth, or in the height above › (VII: 11). For Isaiah, faith counted above everything: ‹ If ye will not believe, surely ye shall not be established › (VII: 9).

Isaiah considered faith to be the basis of religion, and held the truly prophetic belief that God purposefully directed the nations and their destinies. Hence he arrived at an all-embracing and universal monotheism. His God was truly ‹ the

94

God of heaven and earth, › and the nations were God's tools; even Assyria, mistress of the world, was only the rod of his wrath.

All Isaiah's words were imbued with this sublime conception of God, and as a result his whole personality became endowed with a special majestic grandeur. He walked among the affairs of everyday life with the fixed gaze of the visionary, in a fervent ecstasy that recalls the « prophesiers » of the past. (In contrast to Amos, Isaiah actually called himself a « prophet » and his wife a « prophetess. »)

The extreme nature of Isaiah's symbolic acts also recalls the « prophesiers.» For many months he walked the streets of Jerusalem ‹ naked and barefoot, › to make people aware of the fate that awaited anyone captured in battle. Like Hosea, he gave his sons names that vaguely indicated the future: one was called *Shear-jashub* (meaning « a remnant shall return»), and a second *Maher-shalal-hash-baz* (meaning « speedy the spoil, soon the booty »).

The "Messianic Days"	The conviction that historical events occurred according to a divine plan dominated Isaiah's mind whenever he described the future, and led him to conceive the idea of a perfect ending to the chronicles of mankind—the era that we call the « Messianic Days. » This idea, one of the most fruitful in the spiritual development of humanity, became the guiding and sustaining force of all social progress. It gave meaning to the life of society, which, in Israel, was dedicated for the first time to perfection rather than to power. That perfection was peace, the ending of all war the world over—an idea that became the eternal spiritual heritage of the Jewish people. Isaiah prophesied that even in nature there would be no more suppression of the weak by the strong:

‹ The wolf also shall dwell with the lamb, and the leopard shall lie down with the kid; and the calf and the young lion and the fatling together; and a little child shall lead them.

‹ And the cow and the bear shall feed; their young ones shall lie down together: and the lion shall eat straw like the ox.

‹ And the sucking child shall play on the hole of the asp, and the weaned child shall put his hand on the cockatrice' den › (xi: 6-8).

But even more sublime and moving is the vision of eternal peace for all mankind ‹ in the last days › when the vision becomes ripe for realization:

‹ And he shall judge among the nations, and shall rebuke many people: and they shall beat their swords into plowshares, and their spears into pruninghooks: nation shall not lift up sword against nation, neither shall they learn war any more › (ii: 4).

These tremendous words were spoken at a time when battles and bloodshed were rife, when Sargon the Assyrian literally flayed the king of Hamath, when Sennacherib impaled the members of the council of Ekron on stakes, and when the violent and aggressive policy of the Assyrian kings made brute force seem the only way to mold the course of history. Isaiah gave the people a great and onerous historic mission—to be both forerunner and fighter for the ideal of peace and righteousness: ‹ For out of Zion shall go forth the law, and the word of the Lord from Jerusalem. › But in Isaiah's eyes Israel was no longer worthy of this mission and would be destroyed (i and vi), with the exception of a small group of pure, deserving people— ‹ the remnant shall return › (x: 20-22). Thus the idea of the « choice » is made even more profound and spiritual since it was no longer a privilege granted by virtue of national origin, but a privilege granted only to those who had been purified through righteousness. Most important, this belief made Isaiah quite certain that Zion, the seat of the « remnant,» would not fall even to Sennacherib. (Later the concept degenerated into an almost superstitious belief in the invulnerability of the Temple and the Holy City, so that Micah was compelled to fight it, and Jeremiah to deny it altogether.)

Isaiah foresaw the era of mankind's happiness in the most concrete terms; and here he showed himself to be a man of his times, firmly rooted in the soil of reality. He visualized that the people of Israel, and consequently the entire world, would be governed by ‹ a rod out of the stem of Jesse › (XI: 1) whose image (as depicted by the prophet) has remained the image of the Messiah for the Jewish people.

It could well be that Isaiah's hopes were excited to the point of error, and that they caused him to receive with shouts of joy the birth of Hezekiah's son, which had been delayed for many years:

‹ For unto us a child is born, unto us a son is given: and the government shall be upon his shoulder › (IX: 6). Isaiah even saw in the infant ‹ the Prince of Peace. › No mistake could have been more tragic, for this son was Manasseh, the same Manasseh who set Judah back 100 years (from the spiritual point of view) and, according to legend, was responsible for the aged prophet's death.

Isaiah exercised a tremendous influence over his own period and over the thoughts of succeeding generations. He even intervened effectively in political affairs. In fact it is almost true to say that the axiom stating that *every* prophet is necessarily persecuted and reviled in his own day did not apply to him. The reason for this—apart from his aristocratic personality and his influence over the king—was the power of his prophetic message.

No other prophet had such a consummate command of language. Isaiah raised the artistic level of prophecy to its zenith, matching the rhythm of his words to their content with the skill of a virtuoso. The flow of his unforgettable images and similes was inexhaustible—and if (as can be assumed) Isaiah composed the great ballad against the king of Babylon (XIV: 4-23), then he stands among the truly great poets of the world. As so often happens, the glorious form of Isaiah's writing exalted the content, and ensured its permanence. For a century Isaiah's ideas reigned supreme in the world of the spirit. And then there arose a prophet of equal power.

Jeremiah

THE GREAT FIGURE of Jeremiah stands at the dividing point of two eras. His life, like those of so many other servants of humanity, was a hard one, though he was fortunate in one respect: he was able to entrust his work to the care of tradition and to make himself known to later generations through his faithful disciple Baruch the son of Neriah, who recorded details of his life. This record makes Jeremiah more substantial and real than any other man in Israel's ancient history.

Jeremiah came from a priestly family that lived in the village of Anathoth, north of Jerusalem. According to all the available evidence he was a descendant of Abiathar of the house of Eli—the high priest who was deposed by King Solomon and banished to Anathoth (1 KINGS II: 26). This would mean that he was directly descended from Moses and his family.

In the 13th year of Josiah's reign (in the spring of 626 B.C.E.), when Jeremiah was in his early twenties, he was visited by the spiritual experience that we call « dedication to prophecy. » In his earliest prophecies, Jeremiah already appears as a great poet—in the depth of his sensitivity, the power and the clarity of his expression, the vividness of his vision. His astonishing conception of the approaching disorder is one of the gems of literature:

‹ I beheld the earth, and, lo, it was without form, and void; and the heavens, and they had no light.

‹ I beheld the mountains, and, lo, they trembled, and all the hills moved lightly.

‹ I beheld, and, lo, there was no man, and all the birds of the heavens were fled.

‹ I beheld, and, lo, the fruitful place was a wilderness, and all the cities thereof were broken down . . .› (IV: 23-26).

He chants an elegy to himself, breathing new force into an ancient form:

‹ For death is come up into our windows, and is entered into our palaces, to cut off the children from without, and the young men from the streets.

‹ ... Even the carcases of men shall fall as dung upon the open field, and as the handful after the harvestman, and none shall gather them › (ix: 21-22). Here, for the first time, death is depicted as a reaper.

The originality of Jeremiah's images won them a place in the language of his own people, and in the languages of all civilized peoples—the greatest of poetic achievements. Their power and originality can be seen from these examples: ‹ O Lord ... that triest the reins and the heart › (xi: 20); ‹ What is the chaff to the wheat? › (xxiii: 28); ‹ as a bullock unaccustomed to the yoke › (xxxi: 18); ‹ Can the Ethiopian change his skin...? › (xiii: 23); ‹ as the stubble that passeth away by the wind of the wilderness › (xiii: 24); ‹ as the clay is in the potter's hand › (xviii: 6). And God is described as ‹ the fountain of living waters › (ii: 13).

Josiah's Reforms

The year 622 B.C.E., when Jeremiah came of age, marked a turning point in his life. In that year the scroll of Deuteronomy was discovered and as a result Josiah's great reforms were instituted. When Moses had reached maturity he had gone away into the desert for many years to be alone with himself, before bursting forth again like a scorching desert wind, full of the knowledge of God and an unquenchable creative ardor. Jeremiah, too, disappeared in just the same way, for 13 years.

Jeremiah certainly had every reason to be confused and shocked by the sudden reforms. Josiah had compelled the closure and destruction of every temple in the country, with the one exception of the Temple in Jerusalem. The ritual of the other temples was condemned as idolatry, and from then on Jeremiah, the man of Anathoth, the descendant of Abiathar and Moses, was—according to these laws—an idolater and a deposed priest.

Jeremiah was forced to consider how best to preserve his spiritual individuality. He had to meditate on the true bond between man and his maker, and to consider two problems: whether, indeed, God did dwell only on Mount Zion (where Jerusalem's Temple was situated) and whether the sacrifices of men like himself could be idolatrous while the sacrifices of others were not so—only because they were made on the ancient and holy rock.

So long as Josiah (whom he knew and respected as a diligent seeker after God) was alive, the prophet was silent. But when the king was killed (in 609 B.C.E.) and the spirit of his work collapsed with him, Jeremiah realized that this was not the road to inner sanctification and purification. And then, at the gate of the Temple, he delivered a powerful oration attacking all that was holy to his generation:

‹ Trust ye not in lying words, saying, The temple of the Lord, The temple of the Lord, The temple of the Lord, are these.

‹ For if ye throughly amend your ways and your doings; if ye throughly execute judgment between a man and his neighbour;

‹ If ye oppress not the stranger, the fatherless, and the widow, and shed not innocent blood in this place ... Then will I cause you to dwell in this place ... › (vii: 4-7). The people had begun to believe that under the shelter of purification ceremonies they could continue to sin with an easy conscience; the Temple had become a fetish, ‹ a den of robbers › (vii: 11); and ‹ Therefore will I do unto this house ... as I have done to Shiloh › (vii: 14).

Jeremiah was radically opposed to sacrifices, more so than any prophet before him. He denied that they had the sanction of Divine Law:

‹ For I spake not unto your fathers, nor commanded them in the day that I brought them out of the land of Egypt, concerning burnt offerings or sacrifices:

‹ But this thing commanded I them, saying, Obey my voice, and I will be your God, and ye shall be my people ... › (vii: 22-23).

97

The blind king Zedekiah of Judah is led into Babylonian captivity—a miniature from a 14th-century French bible. Zedekiah's desperate rebellion against Nebuchadnezzar led to the Babylonian invasion of Judah in 586 B.C.E. and the capture of Jerusalem. *Bodleian Library, Oxford* (MS. *Douce 211, f.213*).

And in the fourth month, in the ninth day of the month, the famine was sore in the city, so that there was no bread for the people of the land. Then the city was broken up, and all the men of war fled, and went forth out of the city by night by the way of the gate between the two walls, which was by the king's garden; (now the Chaldeans were by the city round about:) and they went by the way of the plain. But the army of the Chaldeans pursued after the king, and overtook Zedekiah in the plains of Jericho; and all his army was scattered from him. Then they took the king, and carried him up unto the king of Babylon to Riblah in the land of Hamath; where he gave judgment upon him. And the king of Babylon slew the sons of Zedekiah before his eyes: he slew also all the princes of Judah in Riblah. Then he put out the eyes of Zedekiah; and the king of Babylon bound him in chains, and carried him to Babylon, and put him in prison till the day of his death—JEREMIAH LII: 6-11.

Jeremiah's Vindication

Jeremiah met a great deal of opposition. Many people held that the scroll of the Law discovered in 622 B.C.E. required the offering up of sacrifices. Jeremiah replied: ‹ How do ye say, We are wise, and the law of the Lord is with us? Lo, certainly in vain [falsehood] made he it; the pen of the scribes is in vain › (VIII: 8).

The meaning of Jeremiah's words is quite clear. The prophet is proclaiming the discovered ‹ Book of the Law › (2 KINGS XXII: 8) to be the deceitful forgery of a scribe. As against the written word—the fruit of the «false» pen of the scribes—he sets, with all the sureness of the prophetic voice, the true ‹ word of the Lord. › (The Revised Standard Version of 1952 gives this more precise translation of the above sentence: ‹ But, behold, the false pen of the scribes has made it into a lie.›) Jeremiah's words are an example of spiritual freedom unequalled in those days. The fact that Jeremiah was not put to death by ‹ the priests and the prophets and all the people, › that he was given a fair trial before the council of the princes, and that their verdict was: ‹ This man is not worthy to die: for he hath spoken to us in the name of the Lord our God › (XXVI: 16)—all these facts show that respect for justice and the word of the Lord was still ingrained in the national conscience.

From this point on, Jeremiah was confronted by a dangerous enemy: the priesthood. He was forbidden to address the people within the bounds of the Temple, and this was virtually to stifle his spirit at times when his creative power was at its height, and he was under immense emotional tension. (It was during these few years— between 609 and 605 B.C.E.—that half of his poems were written.)

The obstacles encountered by Jeremiah at every step threw him into the depths of despair, but they could not break him. With a cry of victory his spiritual power burst upward from a sea of pain, and the world was given a sublime poem, a poem that records the struggle of man for his God, and with his God:

‹ O Lord, thou hast deceived me, and I was deceived: thou art stronger than I, and hast prevailed: I am in derision daily, every one mocketh me.

‹ For since I spake, I cried out, I cried violence and spoil; because the word of the Lord was made a reproach unto me, and a derision, daily.

‹ Then I said, I will not make mention of him, nor speak any more in his name. But his word was in mine heart as a burning fire shut up in my bones, and I was weary with forbearing, and I could not stay › (xx: 7-9).

The Fall of Judah

The critical battle at Carchemish was fought in 605 B.C.E. In that black hour, Jeremiah envisioned the clouds of the Babylonian tempest gathering and approaching with inexorable force: he believed that Judah's end had come. Within a few weeks, a flood of feverish poems burst from his pen: adjuring, warning, lamenting, denouncing:

‹ Say unto the king and to the queen, Humble yourselves, sit down: for your principalities shall come down, even the crown of your glory.

‹ The cities of the south shall be shut up, and none shall open them: Judah shall be carried away captive all of it, it shall be wholly carried away captive › (xiii: 18-19).

It was this certainty of imminent destruction that moved Jeremiah (in the autumn of 605 B.C.E.) to write down all his prophecies in a single scroll, with the aid of his disciple Baruch. True, the prophet was wrong—but the world should be grateful for the mistake that gave it this marvelous work. The scroll concludes with the majestic judgment:

‹ The sin of Judah is written with a pen of iron, and with the point of a diamond: it is graven upon the table of their heart, and upon the horns of your altars; . . . by the green trees upon the high hills.

‹ O my mountain in the field, I will give thy substance and all thy treasures to the spoil . . . .

‹ . . . and I will cause thee to serve thine enemies in the land which thou knowest not: for ye have kindled a fire in mine anger, which shall burn for ever › (xvii: 1-4). With all his fervor—especially after Zedekiah became king—Jeremiah implored his people to accept the yoke of Babylon willingly; for he saw in Babylon the only guarantee of his people's welfare—and he loved his people, despite his denunciations. He realized that only in an atmosphere of peace (and not in the turmoil of revolt and battle) could he hope to lead the Israelites in the way of God, and to deliver them from destruction. In his struggle, the prophet had to face opponents of increasing power. At first he overcame them. But in the end, disaster struck.

Jeremiah, then an old man of about 65, remained firm and upright, while the world collapsed around him. With supreme courage and determination he spoke what he believed to be true. He was threatened and bullied, but he would not recant.

When Jerusalem capitulated to the conqueror and despair reigned, Jeremiah alone would not submit. He felt pity and compassion for his people, convinced that the inhuman suffering that had been thrust upon them was enough to wipe out all guilt. He was the only person to see beyond the immediate situation, to foresee a happier future: the people of Moses and the prophets could not, must not, sink into oblivion. And as a concrete sign of his certainty of survival, Jeremiah bought from his uncle—shortly before the fall of Jerusalem—a field in Anathoth. And he carried out this strange transaction and all the necessary formalities before the gaze of mocking passersby, declaring: ‹ Houses and fields and vineyards shall be possessed again in this land › (xxxii: 6-15).

The lull that followed the tempestuous battle for Jerusalem encouraged Jeremiah to sing once again. And it was now that his genius rose to its last, perhaps its greatest, height, in songs of consolation and hope. Israel and Judah—brothers in destiny in the desert and the Promised Land, and now, too, in decline—were fused again in the prophet's eyes as he looked toward the future, foreseeing the resurgence of the entire people, of all Israel—Samaria and Zion together:

‹ Thou shalt yet plant vines upon the mountains of Samaria . . . .

‹ For there shall be a day, that the watchmen upon the mount Ephraim shall cry, Arise ye, and let us go up to Zion unto the Lord our God› (XXXI: 5-6).

The prophet moved to Ramah, and there the past and the future merged for him in a single ring of perfection. At Ramah, where Rahel died while bearing Benjamin, the prophet envisioned the mother of the nation bewailing the fate of Israel:

‹ A voice was heard in Ramah, lamentation, and bitter weeping; Rahel weeping for her children refused to be comforted . . . .

‹ Refrain thy voice from weeping, and thine eyes from tears: for thy work shall be rewarded, saith the Lord; and . . . thy children shall come again to their own border › (XXXI: 15-17).

But Jeremiah's last words—his prophecy of the new covenant—expressed his most profound ideas in the most simple of forms:

‹ Behold, the days come, saith the Lord, that I will make a new covenant with the house of Israel, and with the house of Judah:

‹ . . . I will put my law in their inward parts, and write it in their hearts; and will be their God, and they shall be my people › (XXXI: 31-33).

Instead of the law—the human heart; instead of the old covenant—the new. Jeremiah freed himself from the bonds of his age. Though he was steeped in his people and its fate, he was inspired by the essence of religion: devotion to God. He transcended all the concepts and manifestations of the priesthood, all forms of mediation between man and his God. In his eyes religion and morality were one (XXII: 16). But so were morality and happiness. He saw the sublime as something that resides in the heart of every man. These eternal ideas—grander than any government, kingdom, temple, or sacrifice—saved his people when all else had been destroyed.

Jeremiah died on foreign soil, and little is known about his end. But he lives to this day beside the sacred martyrs of humanity: a pure and ardent man; great, loyal, and merciful; a man of sorrows, a man accustomed to endure agony and grief.

SHORTLY before the Babylonian exile there arose the voice of a prophetic poet whom we call today « the Second Isaiah » (ISAIAH, chapters XL-LXVI). In his prophecies, the national pride of Israel reached its peak—and at the same time the prophetic vision came to encompass the entire human race. He wrote before the fall of Babylon (in 539 B.C.E.), but he envisaged the liberation of the exiles as an immediately impending event (XL: 1-11).

The Second Isaiah saw history as an orderly and preordained chain of events unfolding under divine leadership: whatever happened, happened according to the divine plan. Israel was the cornerstone in this plan. He saw sin in Israel; but this sin (and here he differed considerably from the dominant conception) had already been more than doubly expiated (XL: 2). The sin of the past did not depress him; the certainty of redemption elevated his spirit.

He regarded Cyrus the Persian not as one conqueror among others, but as a liberator. Even more remarkably, he saw him as an instrument in the hands of God (XLV: 1-4). The Lord, he said, calls Cyrus ‹ my shepherd › (XLIV: 28), and even gives him the ceremonious title of ‹ his anointed, › generally reserved for a descendant of the house of David (XLV: 1). So spoke the man who was full of burning pride for his people Israel—but a man whose feelings for universal peace were even greater than his national enthusiasm. The prophet did not see in Cyrus an idolatrous

The Second Isaiah

foreigner. Apparently he had come to the conclusion that Cyrus' Zoroastrian faith was close to the monotheism of Israel and its ethical doctrines. Still, he also recognized the duality on which that faith was based; and he clearly emphasized this profound difference when, in the same chapter in which he describes Cyrus as the Lord's anointed, he expressly rejects the Persian doctrine (XLV: 6-7):

‹ . . . there is none beside me. I am the Lord, and there is none else. I form the light, and create darkness: I make peace, and create evil: I the Lord do all these things.› This penetrating, new, untrammeled view of religion is at the same time a faithful continuation of the ideas of the great Isaiah. We can see why, when the books of the biblical canon were later assembled and determined, the songs of this anonymous prophet were thought fit to be called by the name of Isaiah the son of Amoz.

"The Servant of the Lord" Four songs are interpolated into the book of the Second Isaiah, which are like a foreign body in their environment, but have a close inner bond between them: they can be found in chapters XLII: 1-4; XLIX: 1-6; L: 4-9; and LII: 13 to LIII: 12. Usually they are called « The Songs of the Servant of the Lord. » The scholar Duehm was probably correct when he wrote (in 1875) that they should not be ascribed to the Second Isaiah, but should be regarded as the work of another poet, who bequeathed them to us as a highly important testimony to his age. Jewish tradition regards this « Servant of the Lord » as a symbol of the people of Israel; but in the light of the last song it might be assumed that here is the picture of a great personality.

Here is a new ideal of man, an ideal that could not have been conceived before the Babylonian exile: the man who suffers in silence, who walks humbly, but fearlessly holds his ground until righteousness conquers (XLII: 2-4). The power that fills him gives him a feeling of divine vocation and confidence in his final success (XLIX: 1-6) despite all obstacles, and even in moments of weakness. His suffering is great, he is almost overwhelmed by persecution, but he trusts in God (L: 5-9). In the fourth and longest of these songs (LII: 13 to LIII: 12), the speaker is no longer the Servant of the Lord himself, but the poet to whom the Servant is a religious manifestation. Here it becomes abundantly clear that the reference is not to the people of Israel symbolized in the person of the Servant of God, but to a specific living personality; for the God-fearing servant *dies* in his sufferings: ‹ And he made his grave with the wicked › (LIII: 9).

His disciple and herald wrestles with two difficult questions. First, how can God allow his servant to suffer for no crime? He replies that he has suffered and died not for his own sin but for ours: ‹ And the Lord hath laid on him the iniquity of us all. › Secondly, does the death of the righteous man mean that all is lost? Here, too, the reply (LIII: 10-12) is given in the form of a great idea, whose influence became apparent only at a later date: since God has accepted the sacrifice, his servant will be resurrected and will complete his work with victory. This consolatory idea was adopted by the Dead Sea sect and through it was passed on to Christianity.

Ezekiel OF ALL the prophets before the end of the Babylonian exile, Ezekiel was the only one who wrote prose. This was no accident; his way of thought was that of a scholar and a priest rather than of a poet or visual artist. On only two occasions did he succeed in creating a poetry rich in images: in his lament over Queen Hamutal (XIX) and in his tremendous vision of the dry bones (XXXVII).

While his predecessors drew their vision from the interpretation of everyday events, Ezekiel laid the foundations for a new form of religious literature: the Apocalypse. In later centuries this form grew considerably in importance through the writings of Zechariah, the Book of Daniel, and the Apocrypha. Ezekiel saw fantastic visions and described them in detail; he heard the voice of angels and reported their speeches at length. The description of the divine chariot alone fills a chapter of his book. Ritual, which the other prophets regarded as of secondary importance, had a great and primary significance for Ezekiel. In his great vision he saw the Temple, with all its details and dimensions, its staff and organization, its sacrifices (XL-XLVIII). The prophets before him always spoke to the people; but in the Babylonian exile man appears as an individual. Ezekiel's anxiety was for the soul of the individual, and he always insisted on a careful balance between guilt and punishment. He thus became one of the founders of « individual religion »: but his main demand (in contrast to that of the Servant of the Lord) is correct ritual and ritual purity. In one respect Ezekiel continued the tradition of Jeremiah: after the destruction of the kingdom he became a consoler of his people. He believed implicitly in the return to Zion and its revival (XXXIII-XLVIII), and he calls upon the people in exile to hold fast to this faith.

After the Second Isaiah and the Servant of God, the dominating spirit of prophecy dwindled and vanished. Though writings have come down to us of men known as « latter prophets »—such as Haggai, Zechariah, and Malachi—they never achieved the stature of the older, greater prophets.

The Last of the Prophets

Haggai, for example, had but one theme: to speed the construction of the Temple. To him delay was only a symptom of the abjectness of the repatriated Babylonian exiles. And salvation, he insisted, lay in the crowning of Zerubbabel of the house of David. But, by that emphasis, he may have been an unwitting factor in his favorite's subsequent downfall and disappearance.

Zechariah, another « apocalyptic, » also urged the building of the Temple and even prepared a coronet for Zerubbabel. (From his chapters VI, XII, and XIII there is no question that he had Zerubbabel in mind.) In the matter of worship, he was far more liberal than the priesthood of succeeding generations: for instance, he recommended that the days of mourning for the destruction of the Temple and of Jerusalem be replaced by festivals of rejoicing (VIII: 19).

At the end of the catalogue is Malachi, who saw in the neglect of Temple worship the root of all evil. At times his attack on this neglect could rise to grand and powerful prophetic utterance: ‹ Have we not all one father? hath not one God created us? why do we deal treacherously every man against his brother, by profaning the covenant of our fathers? › (II: 10).

Jonah

Though the brief Book of Jonah is usually admitted to the prophetical canon, it was not written by a prophet (although a prophet Jonah, son of Amittai, is mentioned—2 KINGS XIV: 25—in the reign of Jeroboam). The book is a legend of a prophet, full of morals; it parallels the folk tales of Elijah and Elisha, but is of considerably later composition. At the same time it conforms to the spirit of classical prophecy in its emphasis on the ‹ earth and the fulness thereto. ›

Only at the end does the real issue emerge: the relations between Israel and the surrounding peoples. Here the Book of Jonah reveals that characteristically prophetic tendency to swim against the stream, for its period was marked by Israel's unyielding aloofness from its surroundings. Even the remnants in northern Israel, the Samaritans, were left strictly alone.

The book re-emphasizes God's command to love and pity all men—even the dwellers in Nineveh, city of blood and wickedness. The « hero » of the tale is not a hero at all: he struggles to escape the burden that God assigns him, but in the end he learns his lesson. And the lesson contains one of the profoundest truths of Judaism: that the justice of God is not conditioned by a remorseless agency like the *moira* of Greece or the *fatum* of Rome. Man controls his own destiny: if he falls, by contrition and repentance he can rise again.

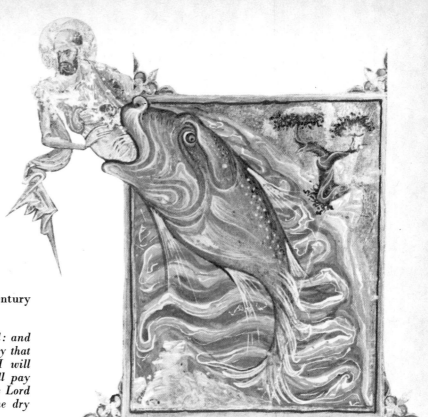

Jonah is 'vomited' onto dry land by the whale—a 13th-century Armenian miniature.

*When my soul fainted within me I remembered the Lord: and my prayer came in unto thee, into thine holy temple. They that observe lying vanities forsake their own mercy. But I will sacrifice unto thee with the voice of thanksgiving; I will pay that that I have vowed. Salvation is of the Lord. And the Lord spake unto the fish, and it vomited out Jonah upon the dry land—*JONAH II: 7-10.

The Prophetic Legacy

IN ANY SUMMARY of the fundamental ideas of prophecy and its effects upon civilization, its place in the religious development of the Jewish people must first be established. Moses, lawgiver and architect of the nation, ushered in a new epoch with his concept of the one God. From then on the idea of divinity gained a strength and power that it could never have where men worshiped a multitude of gods. Thus it is clear why this novel concept of the godhead must be indescribable, why every element of magic had to be expelled from it.

The Ten Commandments became a compelling and succinct code of conduct in human relationships. And classical prophecy in Israel injected the principles of faith into everyday life by presenting the moral imperative as the paramount requirement of God and as the measuring rod of all aspects of the nation's development. Only through ethical behavior may man walk « the way of God » and come into communion with him. Prophecy, the interpreter and instructor of this discipline, was the stimulus by which individuals came to love and fear their God, in the highest form of faith. The impact of prophecy can also be seen as a contribution to the evolution of Christianity and Islam. From his acquaintanceship with the Jews, Mohammed came to recognize the absolute uniqueness of God, and was always moved by the tales of the Patriarchs and by the teachings of the prophets on the moral imperative. But even more fundamental is prophecy's importance for Christianity. Largely through the personality of its founder, the Jew, Jesus of Nazareth, Christianity flows directly from Judaism. The New Testament quotes copiously from the words of the Prophets, both where Jesus himself is speaking and when the Apostles tell the story of his life and works. For Christians, the Books of the Prophets are Holy Writ.

But the prophets of Israel left an imprint upon civilization that extends far beyond the realm of religion. They were the first and greatest teachers of pure ethics, teachers who are still listened to by millions today. Their dreams of international peace have, in our own age, become an end toward which all humanity yearns and strives. For nearly 2000 years, their tireless appeal for social justice, for the protection of the weak, has been a mighty driving force in history, a powerful fulcrum of human progress. The words and concepts of the Prophets of Israel still retain the power to affect the minds and hearts of mankind.

Now in the first year of Cyrus king of Persia, that the word of the Lord by the mouth of Jeremiah might be fulfilled, the Lord stirred up the spirit of Cyrus king of Persia, that he made a proclamation throughout all his kingdom, and put it also in writing, saying, Thus saith Cyrus king of Persia, The Lord God of heaven hath given me all the kingdoms of the earth; and he hath charged me to build him an house at Jerusalem, which is in Judah. Who is there among you of all his people? his God be with him, and let him go up to Jerusalem, which is in Judah, and build the house of the Lord God of Israel, which is in Jerusalem.

Part Three

Professor Yehoshua Guttmann
and
Dr. Menahem Stern

From the Babylonian Exile
to the Bar Kochba Revolt
587 B.C.E. -135 C.E.

In the six centuries that passed between the destruction of the First Temple by the Babylonians and the destruction of Herod's Temple by the Romans, the fortunes of the Land of Israel were to rise and fall. The Land was to suffer in turn under Babylonian, Persian, Greek, Egyptian, Syrian, and Roman domination and its status was to vary from that of a downtrodden colony to that of a recognized kingdom. Great national heroes were to arise, many to die for the Land. Jerusalem was to become one of the most splendid cities of the east, only to be destroyed again. But through all these changes there ran one constant thread, a thread that was to be woven inextricably into Jewish history and Jewish life—the profound influence of religion and the *Torah*, the Mosaic law.

The conquest of Jerusalem in 587 B.C.E. and its consequences—the destruction
of the Temple, the exile to Babylon of thousands of the nation's leaders, and the exodus of multitudes to neighboring countries—brought great suffering to those who remained in the Land. The havoc and ruin that swept Palestine after Jerusalem's fall provide the main subject matter of the Book of Lamentations and many songs in Jeremiah, Psalms, and Ezekiel. But the songs also provide reliable evidence of the people's strength of spirit: in describing disaster and exile they express the deeply held conviction that the nation had suffered tragedy because of its religious and moral misdeeds, but that if it changed its ways and atoned, redemption—as depicted by the prophets of consolation—could still be attained.

Aftermath

Although a wealth of contemporary material reflects the mood of the people at this time of national disaster, we know very little from the writings of the time about the actual conditions of life of those who remained in Judah and Israel. But despite the scarcity of these records, there is sufficient evidence to establish that even in Judaea—and to some extent in Israel as a whole—spiritual and political life continued, often intensively.

After the destruction, two trends or moods became apparent in the life of Israel. One was the mood reflected in Lamentations and other elegiac writings of the time. The author of Lamentations was undoubtedly a resident of Jerusalem, an eye-witness of the national disaster. (One—and possibly two—of the chapters was written shortly after the destruction of the Temple, but other passages were composed much later: the last chapter was certainly written a number of years after the destruction.) The elegiac chapters of Lamentations describe the destruction of Jerusalem, and the sufferings and tribulations of its leaders, in the most concrete of terms. To emphasize the tragedy of their fall from the heights to the depths, the author dwells on their former glory and greatness—in complete contrast to the prophets of his generation, who rebuked the princes and nobles and held them responsible for the tragedy. Even after the immediate roar of the destruction had subsided, he continued to lament the ruination of the city and its Temple. Doubtless he found many listeners among Jerusalem's citizens, who also mourned the national disaster and called for prayer and repentance, cherishing hope of redemption.

The second trend, which found expression as early as the period of King Jehoiachin's exile (in 597 B.C.E.) and again after the destruction of the Temple, reflected a mood quite different from the nostalgia over the glory and splendor of the rich that we find in Lamentations. According to the prophet Ezekiel, the people of Jerusalem told the exiles who were expelled with Jehoiachin: ‹ Get you far from the Lord: unto us is this land given in possession. › After the destruction we find the same idea expressed again, in a different style: ‹ Abraham was one, and he inherited the Land: but we are many; the land is given us for inheritance. › From this it would appear that both in the days of Jehoiachin and in the period after the destruction, those who remained behind believed that since the exiles had been compelled to leave the Land, they had lost their right to it.

106

Ezekiel prophesying to the Elders of Israel in Babylon—from a 16th-century Turkish manuscript. Ezekiel was exiled to Babylon with many of the nation's leaders in 597 B.C.E.: in his early prophecies he castigated the people for their moral and religious laxity, but after the fall of Jerusalem he consoled the exiles and prophesied the return to Zion—describing in detail the rebuilt Temple and the redeemed nation (EZEKIEL XL–XLV).

The Exiles

Though scholars have tried to establish the actual number of Jews who went into exile, there is no satisfactory basis for their calculations. The list given at the end of the book of Jeremiah specifies that there were three Exiles: that of Jehoiachin in 597 B.C.E., involving 3023 exiles; that of Zedekiah in 587 B.C.E., involving 832; and a third and last in 582 B.C.E., involving 745—a total of 4600 exiles in all. But whether or not this list is reliable and whether it really includes all the exiles is impossible to say. Nor is there any definite information about the numbers of those who took part in the first return from Babylon in 537 B.C.E. The separate figures given in Ezra and Nehemiah total about 30,000, while the inclusive number given in both sources is 42,360—and the discrepancy is not explained.

Though it is difficult to make sense of these confused and often contradictory figures, it does seem that the great majority of the people remained in the Land: and that although the destruction of Jerusalem and many fortified cities in Judaea impoverished a number of areas and caused some internal movement of population, references to the transformation of the country into a desert are exaggerated.

107

Jerusalem, which suffered more than any other city at the time of the destruction, remained in the possession of its Jewish residents throughout; and there is no record of any attempt at penetration by foreigners. (The proclamation of Cyrus, king of Persia, who ordered the rebuilding of the Temple in 538 B.C.E., called on the exiles to ‹ go up to Jerusalem, which is in Judah; › and it appears that Jerusalem was an inhabited city when the first of the returning exiles reached it. In the south, too, it seems that the Edomites still ruled over several districts, and that the Jews continued to live there under them.)

The Babylonians generally displayed a close interest in the Land of Israel and its neighborhood, and a desire to retain command. Shortly after the conquest of Jerusalem, they began a siege of Tyre that lasted for some 13 years. During the same period, Nebuchadnezzar imposed his rule on Arad, Sidon, Gaza, and Ashdod. Babylonian documents of the period of Nabonidus (last king of the neo-Babylonian dynasty, 555-539 B.C.E.) refer to ‹ numerous armies in Gaza on the Border of Egypt › that the Babylonians maintained there. And so it may be assumed that Babylonian control over the Land and the neighboring countries led to the complete control of its Jewish community and the absolute acceptance of Babylonian rule. It was during the period of Babylonian rule that the division of the Jewish regions into districts occurred: these districts still existed a century later.

Little by little, contact was established between the *Yishuv* (the Jewish population of the Land) and the Jews of Babylon. News of the surrender of Jerusalem in the summer of 587 B.C.E., for example, was received by the Babylonian community from a refugee who was neither an exile nor one of the captives taken by the Babylonians (EZEKIEL XXXIII: 21). And even in the earlier stages of exile there were certainly many others who maintained contact between Babylonia and Palestine. We know from Babylonian sources that Jehoiachin retained the honorable title of king in exile, and that he and his family were maintained by the Babylonian authorities. After Nebuchadnezzar's death in 572 B.C.E., Jehoiachin's prestige rose still more. The new king of Babylon ‹ set his throne above the throne of the kings that were with him in Babylon . . . and he did eat bread continually before him all

In the seventh year [of Nebuchadnezzar] in the month of Kislev, the Babylonian king mustered his troops and, having marched to the land of Hatti, besieged the city of Judah. On the second day of the month Adar he captured the city and seized the king. He set up in it a king after his heart and having received its heavy tribute sent [them] off to Babylon—from the Babylonian Chronicle.

Part of the Babylonian Chronicle—a series of clay tablets containing the history of the Neo-Babylonian Empire. This tablet covers the years 605-594 B.C.E. and among other events describes the storming of Jerusalem in 597 B.C.E. In the excerpt above the deposed king is Jehoiachin, and the ruler chosen by Nebuchadnezzar is Zedekiah.

the days of his life › (2 KINGS xxv: 28-9). This improvement in Jehoiachin's position helped the Jewish community in Judaea considerably.

As more regular contact between Judaea and the exiles was established, relations between the poor who had stayed behind (and who cultivated the exiles' lands) and those who lived in Babylonia improved. The influence exercised by Jehoiachin and his associates at the Babylonian court on behalf of the community in Judaea also helped to weaken the antagonism toward the exiles that existed in Palestine after the destruction. The absence of any signs of dispute between those who eventually returned from exile and those who remained may be largely attributed to the gradual contacts made between the two communities during the Exile.

Religious Observance The destruction of the Temple caused many in Israel to turn from their religion and to reject the reforms of Josiah (see page 64). But the heathen rites of the « high places » never became popular again. Apparently there were no longer any priests to lead this type of worship, nor any following strong enough to reinstate it on a large scale. Instead of the former public worship, domestic rites began to spread among certain circles—worship of ‹ the queen of heaven › (JEREMIAH XLIV: 15-25), for instance, or the rites that Isaiah condemned. In some circles, however, Josiah's ordinances were studiously kept—or at any rate as far as was possible in the circumstances. There were memorial fasts and speeches to recall the day Jerusalem's walls were breached by the enemy, to mourn the Temple's destruction, and to mark the other tragedies that had befallen Israel. According to the Prophet Zechariah, these fasts, lamentations, and obsequies were observed for 70 years—until the Second Temple was completed in 515 B.C.E.—and always in the Temple area. Verses in Lamentations and Psalms, written in Judaea during the Exile, reflect the conflicting emotions of hope and despair that wracked the Yishuv at the time. They recall how, during the conquest of the Promised Land, the Children of Israel were succored by the strong right arm of the Lord, how the Lord made his light to shine upon his people. Yet they also contain a bitter protest to Heaven: ‹ Yea, for thy sake are we killed all the day long.... Awake, why sleepest thou, O Lord? › (PSALM 44: 22-3). Psalm 74 recalls the grandeur of God in creating the universe, and expresses the psalmist's faith that God will triumph over his adversaries, who are also Israel's. Elsewhere, however, a psalm exalting the Lord's glory and reiterating his pledge that the house of David shall be immortal is joined with the plaint: ‹ But thou hast cast off and abhorred, thou hast been wroth with thine anointed › (Psalm 89: 38). Belief in a glorious hereafter reaches its highest expression in Psalm 102, which again exalts the glory of the Creator: ‹ They [Heaven and Earth] shall perish, but thou shalt endure ... The children of thy servants shall continue, and their seed shall be established before thee › (26-28).

The power of the poetry written in Judaea at this time is most strikingly illustrated by the vision of Isaiah (XXI: 1-10). It was a vision that shook the prophet like the storms of the south (an allusion understandable only on the lips of a seer who himself dwelt in Judaea). By day and by night he gazes toward Babylon, until he finally receives news of its downfall and of the extinction of its idol host. In that collapse, he perceives the collapse of the kingdom of false gods the world over. Persia is beyond his vision. He sees Elam and Media as the destroyers of Babylon. His age precedes the rise of Cyrus, his place is Judaea and Judaea only.

Apart from their intrinsic value these various poetic works—dirges, prayers, and predictions, reflections on the people, on the Land and its God, on the world as it was known—must have forged a firm spiritual bond between Exile and Yishuv. Together with the prophecies of the prophets of consolation in exile they prepared the way for the return to Zion and the restoration of Jewish sovereignty over the Land in the days of the Second Temple.

As to the region from . . . as far as Ashur and Susa, Agade, Eshnunna, the towns Zamban, Me-Turnu, Der as well as the region of the Gutians, I returned to these sacred cities on the other side of the Tigris, the sanctuaries of which have been ruins for a long time, the images which used to live therein and established for them permanent sanctuaries. I also gathered all their former inhabitants and returned to them their habitations —from the Cylinder of Cyrus.

Right, the Cylinder of Cyrus, king of Persia (c. 536 B.C.E.): on it Cyrus refers to the capture of Babylon, and lists the measures he took to repair the wrongs done by its previous rulers. (Those described in the extract translated above included, presumably, the repatriation of the Judaean exiles and the restoration of the Temple in Jerusalem.)

Left, King Nebuchadnezzar of Babylon eating grass (from a 14th-century French bible). The book of Daniel relates how the king 'was driven from men, and did eat grass as oxen' as a punishment for his idolatry (IV: 33).

THE BELIEF that the power of Babylon would soon fade was widespread among both the Jews of the Land and those in exile. The pomp and ceremony, the annual New Year processions, the splendid temples of Babylon, all failed to impress the exiles. On the contrary, it was at this very time, within the sanctum of the Babylonian pantheon, that Israel's prophets uttered their most bitter condemnations of idolatry and of the idols of Babylon in particular, deriding and reviling both.

Babylon had trampled on all that was sacred to Israel: it had desecrated its Temple, slaughtered its priests and princes, judged its king. Nevertheless, the feeling spread that this would be the last of the realms of paganism, that this kingdom of idols with its lawless and vulgar regime that trusted only in force and tyranny would soon be destroyed—for it had profaned God's holy shrine, and mocked the creator of the world.

Both Isaiah and Jeremiah prophesied that Babylon would fall, and that its graven images would be cast down and destroyed. Isaiah foretold that Elam and Media would be the destroyers. Jeremiah named Ararat, Minni, and Ashchenaz, and peoples of the north. Jeremiah's prophetic verses—written before Isaiah XXI, in Judaea, during the period of the Exile—included radiant predictions of the return to Zion. But more than that, they contained a sweeping and confident prophecy of the disaster approaching Babylon.

It was in 550 B.C.E. that King Cyrus of Persia rebelled against his overlord, the king of Media, and seized control of the whole kingdom of the Medes. His sudden rise to power astonished his contemporaries, for as governor of an outlying province he was a comparatively insignificant vassal within a great empire. But in less than four years he had annexed Asia Minor, and it became clear that Babylon's days were numbered. The Greek historian Herodotus, writing at the end of the fifth century B.C.E., gives some impression of how this marvel of history struck the world. But earlier still, Aeschylus, in his tragedy *The Persians* (first performed in 472 B.C.E.), spoke of Cyrus as ‹ the mortal blessed by the gods: possessing might, he brought peace to all that were faithful to him, but the Lydians and the Phrygians he conquered and all Ionia he smote with his strength. ›

The Return

The Rise of Persia

And so it is not surprising that Isaiah, a contemporary prophet, should claim that Cyrus had been born ‹ For Jacob my servant's sake and Israel mine elect. › It was as though Cyrus had been anointed to fulfill ancient longings; as Isaiah saw it, the Almighty no longer felt the need to pour out his wrath on Israel. He would send no more Nebuchadnezzars (whom Jeremiah called the ‹ servant of the Lord ›) to wreak havoc in the Land because its inhabitants had gone astray and did not hearken to his word. Now the Lord had summoned a messenger, an envoy dedicated to a new task: the rebuilding of Jerusalem and its Temple. And every new development confirmed that this man, whom the Lord had raised up from the north, would appear ‹ from the rising of the sun › and call upon the name of the Lord.

Cyrus' Proclamation

Cyrus took Babylon in 539 B.C.E. In the summer of the following year he issued his proclamation on the rebuilding of the Temple: all Jews, whether in Exile or in the Land, felt that the heart-warming prophecies of Isaiah were at last to be fulfilled. Cyrus announced that the money needed for rebuilding the Temple would be drawn from the royal purse, and that all the vessels of gold and silver taken from the Temple by Nebuchadnezzar would be returned.

In that period it was customary to proclaim royal edicts through criers, and at the same time to record them in writing for the royal archives. Thus we have two versions of the proclamation—the oral and the written. It is certain that the oral proclamation was made in Hebrew, the language of the people addressed. (The text, as it is given in the book of Ezra, is evidently very close to the original, and must have been spoken to the exiles by a Jew in Persian service.) The documentary version was in Aramaic, the language normally used in Persian records.

The Persians were far from ready to govern a territory as vast as the one that now fell unexpectedly into their hands. Their language was not fully developed, and culturally they were generally less advanced than their western neighbors of Babylon, Syria, Palestine, and Asia Minor. The dualistic creed of Zoroastrianism had not yet become a state religion, nor did it possess qualities strong enough to pull the disparate regions of the empire together. Thus the Persian authorities tended to respect nations and civilizations more advanced than their own, and it was their

111

A relief (6th-5th century B.C.E.) from Persepolis in Persia depicts Ahura Mazda (later called Ormazd), god of Zoroastrianism, the religion of ancient Persia. Zoroastrianism taught that the world was torn between two deities: Ahura Mazda—the Wise Lord, creator of heaven and earth, light and life—who embodied the spirit of goodness, truth, and law; and Ahriman, the Evil Spirit, whose essence was falsehood and death.

policy to grant wide autonomy to the conquered. Moreover, the split between Nabonidus, who ruled Babylon jointly with Belshazzar (they were its last rulers) and the priests of Babylon—following Nabonidus' attempts to reform the religion and its ritual and to move idols from place to place—led the Persians to favor the restoration of transferred statuary to its original siting and to adapt their policy to the requirements of local worship. The proclamation of Cyrus reflected this attitude, and aimed to satisfy the petition presented by Jewish spokesmen. The first *aliya* (or return to the Land) appears to have taken place in 537 B.C.E. According to one source (EZRA I: 8), it was led by a prefect or prince appointed to govern Judaea on behalf of the Persian government: the prefect was Sheshbazzar (or Shenazar) son of Jehoiachin. Here, again, the Persians conformed to their general policy in naming a descendant of the house of David to administer the Land for them.

Sheshbazzar brought with him the Temple appurtenances that had been stored in Babylon for so long, as well as cedar wood for the new structure. In addition he recruited skilled carpenters and stonemasons from Sidon and Tyre. It appears that only the foundations of the Temple were completed by Sheshbazzar and that the remaining work was carried out by Zerubbabel, who succeeded him.
The work of construction soon began to attract the attention of the many alien tribes that had been transported to Palestine by the Assyrians after Samaria's downfall in 722 B.C.E. (see page 63). Zerubbabel and the « founding fathers » were unwilling to let them help in building the Temple—but not through any dogmatic objection to « self-proselytizing » strangers, for at that time Jews regarded converts with friendliness and approval. (Ezekiel, for example, had stated categorically when discussing the apportionment of estates: ‹ ye shall divide it by lot for an inheritance unto you: and to the strangers that sojourn among you, which shall beget children among you, and they shall be unto you as born in the country among the children of Israel; they shall have inheritance with you among the tribes of Israel. › And the Second Isaiah affirmed the same principle.) What Israel's leaders questioned were the ideals of those who now « volunteered » to build with the rest—and undoubtedly these were far removed from those that inspired the Jewish workers. To accept

Rebuilding the Temple

112

them as brothers in this vital cause might be to wreck the hopes placed on the collapse of Babylon and on the world to be born after the death of idolatry.

Work on the Temple was interrupted and hampered in every possible way. The carriers of vital materials were assaulted and robbed; there was endless conspiracy and lying against the Jews at the Persian Court. At the same time no dramatic improvements were evident in Judaea. Idols were still in evidence everywhere: idolatrous Babylon had merely been supplanted by a slightly less heathen Persia. The Jews themselves despaired of the undertaking, and work on the Temple stopped.

The Work Completed

It was only after protracted warfare had rocked Persia in 522-520 B.C.E., and Darius I had finally squashed the insurrection and restored order throughout the empire, that the Jews felt confident enough to renew their work. The prophets Haggai and Zechariah could not believe Judaea alone would be troubled now that peace had come to illuminate the whole world, could not believe that God would expend his anger on Judaea alone. Their trust and conviction were amplified by their belief that tempest and ensuing quiet were only an overture to mightier things than the kingdom of Persia had accomplished. As Haggai interpreted it: ‹ Yet once, it is a little while, and I will shake the heavens, and the earth, and the sea, and the dry land. . . . The glory of this latter house shall be greater than of the former . . . and in this place will I give peace, saith the Lord of hosts ›—HAGGAI II: 6-9.

Zerubbabel and Joshua, the high priest, were called upon to take courage and build the Lord's house, for the peace that Darius made was not true peace. True peace was the peace that only God would ‹ give in this place, › where there would be a house of greater glory than ever before in the past. And Zerubbabel would stand in its center: ‹ I will shake the heavens and the earth; And I will overthrow the throne of kingdoms, and I will destroy the strength of the kingdoms of the heathen . . . . In that day . . . will I take thee, O Zerubbabel , my servant, the son of Shealtiel . . . and will make thee as a signet: for I have chosen thee. . . . ›

The importance of the Temple in reshaping the nation's spiritual life and the immediate resolve to fulfill the prophetic visions of a glorious Israel explain why the prophet Zechariah came to consider the high priest as being second only to the « royal » leader, Zerubbabel: both would witness the disappearance of evil from the earth, and in their days ‹ many people and strong nations shall come to seek the Lord of hosts in Jerusalem. ›

The great leaders, together with the ordinary people, were stirred to action by the prophets, and by 515 B.C.E. the Temple had been rebuilt. As in Sheshbazzar's time, the people knew that next to the First Temple the new one was ‹ as nothing, › but still they hoped that finally ‹ The glory of this latter house shall be greater than of the former. ›

Life under the Persians

THE PEOPLE's hopes, bolstered as they were by the completion of the Temple, were soon to be shattered. With its walls destroyed, Jerusalem remained exposed to the attacks of nomadic tribes (« the sword of the wilderness ») that had so often plagued its citizens, even while Babylon ruled. Though the danger was perhaps not as great, it nevertheless remained. During the reconstruction of the Temple, the question of walling Jerusalem was considered; but nothing had been done. The antagonists of Israel's political and spiritual rebirth (‹ the adversaries of Judah and Benjamin, › as Ezra called them) were always active, and early in the reign of Xerxes (485-465 B.C.E.) they launched a bitter tirade—in the form of a defamatory letter—against the men of Judaea and Jerusalem. Under Artaxerxes I (465-424 B.C.E.), probably just before Ezra's return from Babylon, an attempt was made to build the wall, but a petition by the « adversaries » was granted by the Persians, and work halted.

The hopes that idolatry would end and that a new world would be created in the spirit of Judaism had not produced a new order of life: the old sinful ways were still followed to a disturbing degree. Jews in and beyond Judaea—particularly the exiles in Babylon—believed that only if a society based on the ideals of the Torah were established could the aspirations of the Temple's builders be realized. It was because he sensed the spiritual deterioration of the Yishuv that Ezra, a member of the priestly family of Zadok and a scribe in the Persian court, decided to bring a new party of settlers to the Land to establish the Mosaic law there. Just how concerned the Yishuv was may be inferred from the princely deputation that met Ezra on his arrival, begging him to end the abomination that the sons of Judaea were committing by taking alien women in wedlock. A yearning for a nobler way of life is perceptible in everything concerned with the « covenant of confession, » the agonizing reappraisal by which Judaea accepted a new discipline.

Official approval for the new reforms in Judaea and Jewish life could be obtained only by patient negotiation or pleading by the exiles at the Persian Court. Ezra, the priest and scribe, was chosen as spokesman: ‹ For Ezra had prepared his heart to seek the law of the Lord, and to do it, and to teach in Israel statutes and judgments. › Thanks to his great diplomacy, Ezra secured wide powers. His authorization from Artaxerxes I made him responsible for relations between Judaea and the imperial government as well as for relations between the Yishuv and Exile, and in particular he was given authority to untangle Judaea's domestic affairs. But Ezra's authority embraced the exiles, too, for the decree specified ‹ all the people that are beyond the river. › In the practical sense, relations between Judaea and the imperial government meant permits to transfer money and all manner of capital and chattels to Jerusalem for divine worship. We know that the government subsidized the Temple budget, and exempted its officiants from many local taxes. Ezra was empowered to ‹ set magistrates and judges › who knew and would apply the laws of Israel's God, the religious canons of Jewry. These magistrates were given wide powers and could punish by the seizure of property, fines, imprisonment, banishment, ostracism, or even death.

The outstanding question was that of intermarriage, and the application of the law to « strangers » who had intermarried with Jews. It is interesting to note that both Athens and Rome were equally concerned in this period with this aspect of the right of citizenship. In 451 B.C.E., Athens recognized the principle of limiting citizenship to children born of citizen parents, and Rome acted similarly.

In Israel the problem of assimilating or naturalizing strangers was complicated by the organization of the Yishuv on the basis of biblical law. Comparatively simple solutions such as the conferring of citizenship on persons entitled to judge or hold office—which had been commended by Aristotle in Greece—were inappropriate because of the far more stringent demands and qualifications needed in Judaea. The entire future of the reformed Yishuv was at stake, for it was obvious that if there were no limit to foreign contact and intermarriage, the whole future of a community struggling to conform rigidly to Bible teaching would be impaired.

Ezra was deeply disturbed by the conditions he found after his repatriation in 457 B.C.E.—particularly the extent of intermarriage. He knew in advance that he would have to instruct the people in the Torah and organize a biblical system of law and justice, but he had no particular knowledge of how the people lived. It is easy to understand his great shock, and his reaction. In frantic despair and flaring anger he rent his garments, plucked the hair from his head and beard, and sat all day, stunned and fasting: ‹ Then were assembled unto me every one that trembled at the words of the God of Israel. › The prayer that he recited in the courtyard

Ezra's Petition

Problems of Intermarriage

114

WALLS OF JERUSALEM

David and Solomon

Nehemiah

Suleiman

of the sanctuary, kneeling, his hands stretched to heaven, drew ‹ a very great congregation of men and women and children. › And then he said: ‹ Now therefore let us make a covenant with our God to put away all the wives, and such as are born of them, according to the counsel of my lord, and of those that tremble at the commandment of our God; and let it be done according to the law. ›

This drastic proposal was only partially carried out: Ezra himself did not draw on the full authority vested in him by Artaxerxes' decree, except to convoke all the citizens of Jerusalem (on the 20th of the Hebrew month of Kislev) for a three-day discussion. The gathering dispersed without effectual decisions, responsibility for action being handed over to the elders and judges of each town. Ultimately, 113 families undertook to obey the injunction to separate themselves from ‹ the [alien] people of the land. ›

How this was done, there is no means of knowing. But we do know that when Nehemiah became prefect of Judaea in 444 B.C.E., the problem still existed. The later « covenant of confession » says only that ‹ we would not give our daughters unto the people of the land, nor take their daughters for our sons. › Nothing is said of divorcing wives already wedded. Yet by the time power passed from Persia to Greece (in 332 B.C.E.) Judaea had developed a stable political and social organization, scrupulous in its conformity to the laws of the Torah. Somehow the question of intermarriage had been settled long before in the manner Ezra wished; the nation had accepted the settlement, and no external pressures had been required.

The New Wall

An important development was the construction of a new wall around Jerusalem—inspired and directed by Nehemiah: the wall made the city a political center once again. Nehemiah had been chamberlain at the court of Artaxerxes I, an important position usually given only to men of high aristocratic birth. But despite his office, he had remained dedicated to his own people and to the God of Israel.

115

The head of an inhabitant of Syria, possibly a Judaean—part of a fifth-century B.C.E. relief (from Persepolis) showing tribute bearers arriving before the Persian king.

PERSIAN KINGS

Cyrus	550-529 B.C.E.
Cambeses	529-522 B.C.E.
Smerdis (Gaumata)	
	522 B.C.E.
Darius I	522-485 B.C.E.
Xerxes I	485-465 B.C.E.
Artaxerxes	465-424 B.C.E.
Xerxes II	424-423 B.C.E.
Darius II Nothus	
	423-404 B.C.E.
Artaxerxes II	404-358 B.C.E.
Artaxerxes III Ochus	
	358-338 B.C.E.
Arses	338-336 B.C.E.
Darius III	336-330 B.C.E.

MACEDONIAN KINGS

Philip II	359-336 B.C.E.
Alexander	336-323 B.C.E.

Nehemiah felt that an unwalled Jerusalem was a slur on the nation, an ignominy that had to be removed without delay. Artaxerxes had recommended Nehemiah warmly to his governors in Palestine and his subsequent nomination as prefect of Judaea gave him the opportunity to carry out his plans. In the book of Nehemiah, the names of all those who obstructed Nehemiah are listed, but we can only speculate as to their motives. It appears, for instance, that Tobiah, whom Nehemiah calls ‹ the servant, the Ammonite, › was a descendant of one of the princely clans of Judah that fled from Jerusalem to Ammon at the time of the destruction with Ishmael, son of Nethaniah, and his followers. Presumably Tobiah held high office at the court in Ammon and founded the « Tobiad » family that is mentioned frequently in Jewish sources from the middle of the third century B.C.E. Tobiah's son Johanan, son-in-law of Meshullam the son of Berechiah, was listed as one of the builders of the wall— and this points to Tobiah's origin in Judaea and suggests that his family had never wholly given up its ancestral faith. But there is evidence to show that the family had pretensions to authority in Jerusalem and Judaea, that Tobiah's forefathers had been bested by the sons of Jehoiachin, and that Tobiah himself was rejected by those in power at the time—including Nehemiah himself.

The enmity of Sanballat, prefect of Samaria, is easier to understand: for him a revived Jerusalem would be a dangerous rival, particularly for domination of his own region. Geshem the Arabian presumably caused trouble because he had trade relationships with Tobiah and feared that a strong Judaea might damage them. Geshem (apparently a member of one of the tribes of Kedar) had been banished during the wars of Nebuchadnezzar and Nabonidus, and settled in the neighborhood of present-day Ismailia on the Suez Canal, where he traded on the spice highway from southern Arabia to the Hauran. It was presumably in this lucrative traffic that Geshem was associated with Tobiah and the Ammonites.

But no interference could frustrate Nehemiah's tremendous will and assertiveness, or the concerted determination of the people, who came forward from every corner of Judaea to raise the wall. Work went on from dawn to dusk. The Persian soldiers under Nehemiah's command not only protected the workers, but helped in the building themselves: in 52 days the wall was complete. Nehemiah was also instrumental in renewing the portals and precincts of the Temple. With a wall around Jerusalem and the Temple safe, the Yishuv could live at peace.

Caring for the Poor

Once the wall was finished, Nehemiah turned to the important task of rehabilitating the populace. Hordes of indigent farmers came to him with their complaints: the corn they had harvested barely sufficed to feed them and there was not enough for a new sowing; hunger had driven them to mortgage their fields, their vineyards, and their homes; worst of all, imperial taxation could no longer be met. In Jewish law it was not customary to enslave defaulting debtors—although impoverished individuals could sell themselves into slavery. But debts to the royal treasury always meant enslavement. Nehemiah was deeply disturbed by the thought that men might be forced to barter their freedom to pay their dues ‹ for the king's tribute. › His indictments of ‹ the nobles and the rulers ›—the landed and wealthy gentry—show that Jews, too, made money by trading in unhappy lives.

Hitherto it had been the accepted practice to ransom fellow Jews from Gentile custody with communal money, or with the help of private benefactors. Now (as Nehemiah passionately charged) there were men of Israel selling their brethren into bondage and saddling others with the task of liberating them. His talks with the rich resulted in the return of all mortgaged property to the debtors and the cancellation of all debts, in both cash and kind. And the creditors took an oath, saying: ‹ So God shake out every man from his house, and from his labour, that performeth not this promise, even thus be he shaken out, and emptied. › This, indeed, was a sign of unreserved willingness to accept the ordinances of the Torah.

The Great Assembly

The Bible indicates that the great concourse of the people—summoned by Ezra on the first day of the month of Tishri—took place very soon after the wall was finished. The purpose of the assembly was to recite the Torah in public, and the procedure followed is of very great interest. Ezra stood upon a high wooden dais, prototype of the synagogue *almemar* (dais) of later days. As the Scroll was unfolded, the people rose, and Ezra pronounced a blessing to God. The hands of all were uplifted and the whole congregation answered ‹ Amen, Amen, › and knelt. This ceremony of the glorification of the Torah became traditional, a form of divine worship that had nothing to do with sacrifices. It was purely a demonstration of respect for the law of God. The Greek author Hecataeus, a contemporary of Ptolemy I, was an eyewitness at the ceremony, and praised it as a symbol and model of a people's devotion and fidelity to the commands of their God.

On that inaugural day, the Reading of the Law lasted from sunrise to noon. It was an inspired and ecstatic occasion. The listeners wept, and Nehemiah, Ezra, and the Levites found it hard to comfort them and make them understand that this was a sacred day of rejoicing, not one of lamentation: ‹ for the joy of the Lord is your strength. › Slowly, under their persuasion, the tears changed to ‹ . . . great mirth, because they had understood the words that were declared unto them. › The following day, the leaders of the congregation assembled at Ezra's home ‹ even to understand the words of the law, › and to study and clarify the Torah.

On the 24th day of the month of Tishri a public meeting was called to acclaim the new covenant nationally. It was a day of fasting and mourning, of confession of the sins of the past and present generations. A quarter of the service was devoted to the Reading of the Law, and at one stage there was supplication by all ‹ with a loud voice unto the Lord their God. › The history of mankind since the Creation was surveyed, and in particular the history of Israel—from Abraham right up to the Persian conquest.

The covenant was primarily designed to ensure the proper observance of Temple worship, as can been seen from its concern that the rights of the officiants should not be curtailed in any way. But the opening clauses deal with other important issues such as the ban on marriage with aliens, the prohibition of buying or selling on the Sabbath, observation of the fallow year and, especially, abandonment in that year of ‹ the exaction of every debt. › The Torah is silent on the prohibition of buying and selling on the Sabbath, although the custom was very old (AMOS VIII: 5). We know that Ezekiel considered observance of the Sabbath to be among the most vital of the Torah's commandments. In a sermon to the elders of Babylon he declared: ‹ Moreover also I gave them my sabbaths, to be a sign between me and them, that they might know that I am the Lord that sanctify them. › And he went on to remind the people: ‹ And hallow my sabbaths; and they shall be a sign between me and you, that ye may know that I am the Lord your God. ›

For the Second Isaiah, also, Sabbath observance and loyalty to God's Covenant were equally vital. In his fierce condemnation of fasts that had no true moral content, he included only one of the commandments linking man with his maker—observance of the Sabbath day. Thus it would seem that after the destruction of the Temple (and the ensuing curtailment of ceremonial worship) the Sabbath took on special meaning. Recitals from the Torah and the accompanying ceremony may possibly have been a rule of the Sabbath in earlier times. But at any rate, by the beginning of the Hellenistic period (which followed Persian rule) the Sabbath had become sacrosanct again and its customs and strictures were strictly observed: no Jew would consider lifting a stone on the Sabbath, even to save his life.

The formal observation of the Sabbath had no basis in the written law; it came from the oral law that had evolved even before the covenant, and was expressed in it. Biblical interpretation and diligent study—to ‹ understand the words of the law ›—are the basis of other passages of the covenant. Succeeding *halachic* scholars were fully aware that many of the *halachot* (the legal parts of Jewish traditional literature) introduced by the authors of the covenant had no biblical sanction, and they sought to explain this fact in different ways. But the contemporary halachic scholars were certainly not concerned with literal interpretation of the Torah; they were concerned only with the ideals of Jewish prophecy and the principles and objectives set down in the Torah—and they settled the articles of the covenant accordingly. This can be seen from the phrasing of the oath they took: ‹ to walk in God's law, which was given by Moses the servant of God, and to observe and do all the commandments of the Lord our Lord, and his judgments and his statutes › (NEHEMIAH X: 29). The concluding verses of the same chapter deal with practical issues, but the essential concern is for God's Torah, in all its parts and precepts, as interpreted by the scholars.

The covenant of confession was sealed by a treaty that was signed by all the leaders of Judaea. From the politico-juridical aspect this was a contract binding all subjects owing allegiance to Judaea (and all the leaders of Judaea) to be loyal to the law of the state—the Mosaic law—and to perform all its commandments. Nehemiah names some 50 men of rank among the signatories, and follows his list with the phrase: ‹ And the rest of the people, the priests, the Levites, the porters, the singers, the Nethinims [Temple servitors], and all they that had separated themselves from the people of the lands unto the law of God. › From this it would seem that there were others in Judaea who had not so separated themselves, and who would

And the king said again unto Esther on the second day at the banquet of wine, What is thy petition, queen Esther? and it shall be granted thee: and what is thy request? and it shall be performed, even to the half of the kingdom. Then Esther the queen answered and said, If I have found favour in thy sight, O king, and if it please the king, let my life be given me at my petition, and my people at my request: For we are sold, I and my people, to be destroyed, to be slain, and to perish. But if we had been sold for bondmen and bondwomen, I had held my tongue, although the enemy could not countervail the king's damage. Then the king Ahasuerus answered and said unto Esther the queen, Who is he, and where is he, that durst presume in his heart to do so? And Esther said, The adversary and enemy is this wicked Haman. Then Haman was afraid before the king—ESTHER VII: 2-6.

A page from the 15th-century Italian "Rothschild" manuscript recording the tradition of the deliverance of Persian Jewry from the hands of Haman, chief adviser to King Ahasuerus (*c.* 480 B.C.E.). Haman ordered the death of all Jews in the empire, but the king's Jewish wife Esther and her kinsman Mordecai interceded—and Haman (and then his 10 sons) was hanged. The occasion is commemorated by the festival of Purim.

not sign. They certainly had no civil rights and must have been denied all opportunity of judicial office or public service: only those who followed God's law, as given by the hand of Moses, could enjoy either.

It is unlikely that each signatory was fully conversant with biblical canon, even though he swore to observe and keep it, but some among them must have understood ‹ the words of the law. › The Persian king, Artaxerxes, had urged Ezra to proclaim the laws of God to the untutored, but, as Ezra himself reported (VII: 25), he found knowledgeable men in the Land who could act as principals of the covenant, to teach halacha and expound its practice.

What little information we have concerning religious life in Judaea in the early Hellenistic period tends to confirm that generally (and not only with regard to the Sabbath) basic principles followed the lines of the written law, while the broad pattern of practice was derived from written exegesis and from the oral law. It is safe to assume that the group of men who drew up the covenant and presented it for endorsement and signature did not cease their labors on the 24th of Tishri. They undoubtedly continued their task of phrasing, exactly and in detail, the statutes incorporated in God's law; and it seems certain that from then on all such work required the approval of an authorized body.

An old tradition of the *Mishna* (the codification of the oral law—see page 179), asserts that the members of the Great Convocation formed the links in the chain of biblical tradition from the Prophets down to Antigonus of Socho (in the third century B.C.E.); this would appear to be historically correct. The injunctions concerning contributions, tithes, and first fruits demanded so much self-denial from the common people that they could hardly have been imposed without the assent of an authority empowered to legalize demands of that kind. Doubtless, congresses took place from time to time—in the manner of the first mass meeting—to draft halachot and publish them in a binding form; doubtless, all such enactments were obeyed without demur.

In the Persian period, Judaea was officially called by its Aramaic name of *Yahud*; in the Hebrew of the Bible it is *Yehuda*. (The Greek form « Ioudaia, » found in early Hellenistic literature, is taken from the Hebrew.) Seals unearthed in cities of Judaea confirm that the men appointed as prefects were Jews, and it is probable that some had a voice in translating biblical principles into « statutory » practice when the need arose; certainly they would have ratified any halachot, as Nehemiah did. Some of the prefects must have been biblical scholars: one—who lived, apparently, at the beginning of the Hellenistic period—has been identified as « Hezkiya » from a seal found in Beit-Tzur. He cannot be any other than Hezekiah, the « High Priest » Hecataeus spoke of as a great man esteemed by all his fellow Jews. (Hecataeus had witnessed the gatherings Hezekiah organized for Torah instruction.)

In Persian days, the bounds of Judaea were narrow: in the north it stretched just north of Beth-el; in the south it ended south of Beit-Tzur (near Hebron); in the east it reached the Jordan river; and in the west ran from Keilah northward to the west of Ono. But these bounds marked only the sovereign territory, populated by citizens obedient to the doctrines of the Torah: there was also close Jewish settlement in Transjordan. In southern Palestine there were a number of Jewish settlements— Beersheba, Kiryat-Arba, Gei-Hinom, and others. Nehemiah records that there was a Jewish settlement within the prefecture of Samaria; the book of Judith speaks of numerous Jewish settlements in the Valley of Jezreel.

What fragmentary information we have about the economy at this time indicates that most members of the Yishuv were farmers: the complaints made to Nehemiah of ill-treatment by nobles and princes were certainly the complaints of an agricultural people. But there were also jewelers and peddlers who made a good living, and who helped to build parts of Jerusalem's wall. Nehemiah mentions also perfumers and oven makers. Trade with Tyre was extensive, and as a result a number

The Judaeans

A Greco-Phoenician silver *drachma*, minted in Judaea in the fifth century B.C.E., shows a God seated on a winged chariot and holding a bird: it is one of the few extant examples of the coins minted by the Judaeans during the period of Persian rule.

of Tyrian merchants actually came to live in Jerusalem. (Nehemiah fought to ensure that the conduct of this trade did not desecrate the Sabbath in any way.) Israel as a whole, and Judaea within it, always exported oil and wines, and both these commodities must have played an important part in the trade with Tyre.

The spice-groves of Jericho also did a considerable trade; this, perhaps, is why the city was attacked when Artaxerxes III (358-338 B.C.E.) waged war on the towns of Syria and Israel, and why it was seized by the troops of Alexander at the beginning of his invasion of Syria in 332 B.C.E. Part of Jericho's harvest was consigned to Egypt where it was used, with pitch from the Dead Sea, in the process of embalming; the income from the pitch was high.

The Persians allowed Judaea the right of coinage—a further indication of its prosperity. Unfortunately only a handful of these coins exists today. The economy as a whole was still based mainly on a system of barter, but the fact that Judaea needed to mint its own currency suggests a reasonably developed economic system.

Nehemiah's Reforms

Nehemiah's reforms saved farmers the wretchedness of becoming hopelessly entangled in debt and distraint, or of being forced to mortgage their labor to wealthy masters. According to Hecataeus, restrictions on the sale of lands in Judaea remained in force for the next 130 years: the object was to prevent the formation of *latifundia*—great holdings in the hands of single owners—and we can envisage a husbandry of small-holders, each cultivating his own plot with his own resources. In accordance with the laws of the Bible (which were, in fact, national policy) there was no class distinction, no flavor of discrimination between citizens. But politico-juridical equality did not remove the division between rich and poor; the status of Temple attendants, for example, who were exempt from payment of imperial taxes, continued to grow. The state administration was by no means democratic. Central authority was exercised by the nobles and princes, and rural and municipal authority by representatives of the elders and clan heads. The prestige of the Temple gave the high priest a pivotal and directive place in the administration, whereas the office of *ethnarch* (president), held by a descendant of the house of David, gradually lost content and meaning. (Eventually its holder was excluded altogether from the conduct of affairs.)

The leaders of the state were assisted by Bible scholars whose chief concern, it seems, was to transcribe the Torah for general reading. Between them they were instrumental in developing Judaea's religious and social order; by the beginning of the Hellenistic period, this was safely established. The scribes and copyists also taught Bible law and expounded it in public. At first, these duties were concentrated in priestly hands. Little by little, however, laymen began to take over posts in what was quite a large establishment—but not until the Greeks occupied Palestine.

THE PERSIAN EMPIRE 500 B.C.E.

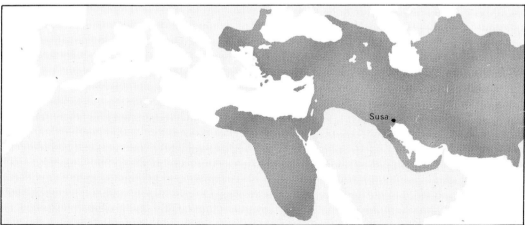

121

The Macedonian Conquest

IN 332 B.C.E. Alexander the Great marched into Palestine. His victory over the Persian armies completely changed the course of Israel's history. In many ways the period of Macedonian conquest reflected shifting balances of power after the Return to Zion. The foreign tribes that Assyria had planted in Palestine were grouped administratively around Samaria, the capital of the former kingdom of Israel, and its citadel, and had long since become known as Samaritans; but as yet they had shown no sign of developing into a homogeneous religious entity. (Both the sons of the prefect of Samaria at the end of the fifth century B.C.E., Daliya and Shlomiya, bore Hebrew names, testifying adherence to Judaism.) Some indication of the Samaritans' standing and influence is given by the appeal addressed to them by the Jews of the military colony in Egyptian Yeb (Elephantine) concerning renovation of a temple that the local priests had destroyed. (Yeb was a fortress town on the Egyptian-Ethiopian frontier, on the Nile opposite Aswan. Jews had lived there from 540 B.C.E., had their own Temple, and manned the garrison.)

Over the question of Jerusalem's supremacy as the national and religious center of Jewry, Judaea and Samaria were at odds. There is record of the Samaritan negotiations with Alexander during his siege of Tyre, which suggests that he found them a distinct sect with Shechem (called Neapolis under Macedonian rule—later Nablus) as their center. Nevertheless, the Samaritans followed the *Pentateuch* (the five books of Moses) meticulously, for they regarded it as the divine fount of life and prayer. Since the Bible does not specifically speak of Jerusalem as a religio-political capital, they felt free to choose Shechem and to reject Jerusalem. It is doubtful whether the Macedonians formally sanctioned the choice. But we can be certain (all sources are unanimous on this point) that the new lords of the Land gave Judaea and Jerusalem pride of place, and regarded Samaria only as a fort for a Macedonian garrison.

The Spread of Hellenism

With the Macedonian occupation, Israel was swept into the orbit of Hellenism, and came within range of the Greek writers and philosophers for the first time. References to Jews and Judaism by Greek writers at the beginning of the Hellenistic period were far from hostile. They describe the Jewish Torah as a philosophic conception of the world and its adherents as philosophers, and even compare the position of the Jews among the Syrians to that of the Brahmins among the Indians—an attitude quite different from the one generally adopted toward foreign nations

in Greek historical works. Hecataeus describes how Jews were ready to give their lives for the sanctity of their faith, how they would suffer every kind of torture and anguish, die the cruelest of deaths, rather than violate the Torah of their ancestors. Jewish history and philosophy were of particular interest to Demetrius of Phaleron, a distinguished pupil of Theophrastus (the successor of Aristotle in the peripatetic school of philosophy), who became famous in Athens as a legislator and statesman. Demetrius became so interested in the Bible that, when he was in political exile at the court of Ptolemy I, he initiated its translation into Greek.

If the attitude of Greek literature toward the Jews deteriorated later, it was because of conflicts that developed between the Jews and the hellenizing elements—in the Land and abroad.

AFTER Alexander's death in 323 B.C.E., a battle for power broke out between his two leading generals, Ptolemy and Seleucus, and Palestine became the center of a long and complicated series of battles. Ptolemy gained control of Egypt, while Seleucus won most of the lands that Alexander had conquered in Asia. Both the first Ptolemy and the first Seleucus claimed Palestine as part of their kingdom, but finally Palestine and part of Syria came under the dominion of the Egypt of Ptolemy, a dominion that lasted from 301 to 198 B.C.E. The only precise piece of historical information we have for this period—even though it was a vital one—apparently dates from the year 312 B.C.E. This information shows that meticulous observance of the Sabbath rest by the Jews of Jerusalem was responsible for their failure to resist Ptolemy I when he marched his troops into the city on the Sabbath day. Ptolemy occupied the city, dealt ruthlessly with its inhabitants, and carried many Jews off as captives to Egypt.

At that time Jerusalem had a very large population—far larger than it had in the time of Nehemiah. As the established spiritual rulers, the priests had acquired considerable status, and belonged to the moneyed class. Nor was priestly office confined to Temple worship or to the management of Temple affairs. The priests were the people's teachers; but they also monopolized the judiciary, since all questions of law and justice were settled according to biblical dictates. From the time of Ezra— who was both scribe and priest—the overwhelming majority of Bible scholars were to be found in the priestly caste.

The long period of Ptolemid hegemony in Palestine strengthened the nation in many ways. When the Ptolemies took over the Land they found there (or in the vicinity) political units that, to a greater or lesser degree, enjoyed some sort of internal autonomy. Across the Jordan, for example, were the « Tobiads » (members of the powerful Tobiah family that opposed the re-building of Jerusalem's Wall). Apart from being completely independent in their domestic affairs, the Tobiads had a private army of mixed nationalities at their command.

In their dealings with the king and his financial adviser, they assumed a virtually sovereign bearing. The general extent of autonomy in Israel is revealed in a contemporary document that records how a Jew—Yedoa—was able to defy the central authorities and win his suit.

About 30 « municipalities » possessed substantial rights of self-government, the majority of them along the coast, and many had long engaged in trade with Greece: among them were ancient cities like Acre, Ashkelon, and Gaza, where the upper classes had developed urban life on the Greek model. A few centers of settlement in the interior (such as Beit-She'an, Adoraim, and Marissa) were also autonomous, as well as some in Transjordan—Gadara, Gerasa, and Philadelphia, for example. Each autonomous unit contained the town itself and its suburbs or satellites, as well as villages and farmsteads within the urban confines; it was self-determining in local management and in the election of its leaders, and responsible to the central government only in fiscal matters.

No doubt the Ptolemies considered it wise to grant this generous measure of freedom to the vassal Land, and to the parts of Syria they ruled. Egyptian statesmen were aware that several of the commercial towns in both countries inclined to side with their rivals, the Seleucids, who controlled the trade routes to the east and parts of Asia Minor. There must have been a considerable body of opinion in Judaea favoring connections with the Seleucids—simply because Ptolemid domination jeopardized contact with the Jews in Mesopotamia, then a Seleucid satrapy. So it was a feature of Ptolemid policy to woo the friendship and loyalty of the subject peoples, and to gain dependable allies among them. In Egypt, the Ptolemies had taken over a homogeneous population, conditioned from time immemorial to government by central monarchy; in the Land and in Syria there were populations of great diversity, differing from each other in every possible way—in culture, in religion, in forms of government. Each place, every habitation, had its own idiosyncrasies, particularly with regard to economy and trade.

Spiritual Freedom

Judaea, which had a thriving community, closely-knit in faith and intellectual development, was looked up to by the Ptolemies, who went out of their way to enlist its favor to a much greater extent than they did the other self-governing "municipalities" and regions. The "Letter of Aristeas," written in Egypt by a Jew, describes meetings and discussions between Ptolemy II (285-246 B.C.E.) and the high priest of the day on relations between the Egyptian dynasty and Judaea, and on the translation of the Bible into Greek. Though the letter might be considered the artistic creation of a writer wishing to idealize Judaea and its regime, it is accurate enough in its general historical content and description. It tells how prisoners taken from Judaea to Egypt during the wars of the Diadochi (at the end of the fourth century B.C.E.) were released as a step toward improving relations between the two countries, and goes on to describe the many festive receptions given in the palace of Ptolemy for the high priest and his retinue of elders.

Judaea's spiritual sovereignty, then, was virtually complete, as was its political independence—at least with regard to its internal affairs. At the head of Judaea's administrative system stood the high priest, assisted by a council of elders, the *Gerusia*. Both jurisdiction and Bible instruction were prerogatives of the priesthood, although knowledge of the Bible was clearly widespread. Most contemporary writings and commentaries on the Torah concentrated on the sections dealing with man's behavior to his fellows, and touched only incidentally on those dealing with the relationship between man and his maker. This emphasis is apparent in the writings of the Jerusalem sage Ben-Sira, who wrote at the end of the Ptolemaic period (about 170 B.C.E.). The fact that he dwelt upon observance of Bible law and its commandments would seem to indicate that education toward such observance must have been a central concern of Judaean society. We may conclude that the Jewish « type » that had evolved during the Persian period took final form under the Ptolemies—that is, the Jew whose personality and characteristics were molded by a pre-ordained way of life and by submission to the Torah.

The most significant political event to occur in Judaea under the Ptolemies was the transfer of responsibility for tax collections to a member of the Tobiad family; the reasons for this move were both external and domestic. The high priest, Onias II,

Ptolemy II Philadelphus dictating the decree in which he liberated Jewish captives and announced his intention of authorizing a Greek translation of the Bible (the *Septuagint*) —from an 11th-century manuscript of the *Letter of Aristeas*.

King Ptolemaeus to Eleazar the high priest greeting and health. Forasmuch as there are many Jews settled in our realm who were forcibly removed from Jerusalem by the Persians at the time of their power, and others who entered Egypt as captives in the train of our father . . . we, then, have given liberty to more than a hundred thousand captives, paying their owners the proper market price, and making good any wrong which they may have suffered through the passions of the mob—part of a decree of Ptolemy II Philadelphus (285-246 B.C.E.), given in the Letter of Aristeas.

The tomb of a wealthy citizen of Beit She'an. In Hellenistic times, Beit She'an—situated at the juncture of the Jezreel and Jordan valleys—was the center of the Decapolis (the league of Ten Cities).

had refused to pay Ptolemy III (Euergetes—246-221 B.C.E.) the 20 talents of silver due annually on his own private property, thus endangering the safety of Judaea. According to the Jewish historian Josephus Flavius (first century C.E.) the Jews rightly resented the high priest's behavior. It seems that, although Onias refused to draw the money from his own coffers, he was quite prepared to pay it out of the public taxes. He remained unmoved by Ptolemy's threat to sequester lands and settle soldiers upon them—which might mean that Onias felt he could use the threat to coerce the people into accepting the extra liability. But it could well be that Onias intended only to rid himself of any personal responsibility for the payment of the royal taxes.

Ben-Sira tells us that at times the tension between the poor and the wealthy was alarming. He talks of a ‹ judge of oppression › dispensing judgment at will, and from this it would seem that the public was critical of a judiciary drawn from the priesthood, and even suspected it of corruption. We have seen that by the beginning of the Hellenistic era the priesthood was firmly entrenched, and that many of its members—especially those related to the high priest himself—had grown rich. So where a question of sharing the burden of taxation arose, the collectors and assessors would naturally fall suspect. Moreover, the concentration in priestly hands of all domestic control (in addition to the control of Temple affairs) eventually made the priesthood answerable for all the shortcomings in the administration that became manifest as time went on.

Judaea was rescued from its predicament by Joseph son of Tobiah, Onias' nephew. We saw earlier how intimately the Tobiads were involved in the economy and commerce of Transjordan and Egypt. Now Joseph was sent to Egypt, with Onias' consent, where he succeeded in settling all the outstanding issues. As a result, a

Tobiad Control

126

dichotomy was produced in Judaean administration. Jurisdiction and the Temple administration remained entirely in priestly hands, as did all forms of religious authority. But everything concerned with the king's taxes, all fiscal and financial discussions with Egypt, were now handled by Joseph and his kinsmen. Naturally their influence and prestige in Judaea rose considerably—and rose still more when the Tobiads were appointed to collect taxes in other parts of the Land. Their income became so great that they were able to adopt a more tolerant attitude to tax collection in Judaea itself. Moreover, they had to employ a large staff of officials to cope with their many and varied concerns, including their former interests in Transjordan, and this meant employing many Judaeans.

Josephus goes so far as to claim that Joseph changed the whole manner of Jewish life, erasing the poverty and degradation and creating a paradise in their place. The claim may be exaggerated, but it has some substance: many Jews became wealthy as partners or assistants in Tobiad affairs, and engaged profitably in the international trade that passed through Israel. In this period, too, intellectual levels rose considerably—and not only within the confined ranks of the priesthood; there were many scholars who devoted their entire lives to the study of the books of prophecy and wisdom (Proverbs, Ecclesiastes, and the Song of Solomon). Many scholars entered the service of princes and plutocrats where they made worldly use of their intellectual training and knowledge of the Torah to serve as scribes and aides, or traveled abroad.

A wall-painting of Solomon's Temple from the third-century c.e. synagogue at Dura Europos, in Mesopotamia: the Hellenistic style of the architecture would indicate that the artist was actually depicting a temple of his own period.

IN 200 B.C.E. the Land of Israel came under the domination of yet another foreign power. In that year the Seleucid ruler Antiochus III (223-187 B.C.E.) defeated the Ptolemaic armies near the headwaters of the Jordan (in Syria) and during the following two years made himself master of the entire Land of Israel. Once again the whole of Judaea, including Jerusalem, became a battlefield. The conflict in Judaea—where both the rival powers had partisan support—led to competing bids for allegiance by the two sides, and the possession of Jerusalem swung from one to the other. Within the family of Tobiah, there was an irreparable split. Earlier, when Judaea was still ruled from Egypt, Hyrcanus, Joseph's younger son, had won royal favor—against the family's wishes and in defiance of his father's explicit bidding—and was now left with a personal monopoly of his father's business interests within the Ptolemid empire. Naturally, the pro-Ptolemid elements rallied around him, but his brothers, supported by many Judaeans (under the leadership of the High Priest Simeon, son of Onias II), declared for the Seleucids and sided with them. Meanwhile there were signs of dissolution in Egypt, and the obvious weakness of Ptolemy IV's successor encouraged others to join the pro-Seleucid ranks; soon the Seleucid element formed a majority in Judaea.

The help given to Antiochus' forces by the Judaeans was considerable. They provided supplies for their soldiery and fodder for their combat-elephants; they drove the Egyptian garrison from its Jerusalem fortress, and greeted the triumphant Seleucid troops in Jerusalem with great enthusiasm. In recognition of this support, Antiochus authorized the repair of all war damage in the city, the distribution of funds to maintain Temple worship and to refurbish the sanctuary, the exemption of all citizens from taxation for three years, and the liberation of all Jewish captives. Antiochus made other concessions. The council of elders, the priests and scribes of the Temple, and the cantors were freed from both the poll tax and the salt tax. And, most important of all, the main clause of a royal charter approved Judaea's laws as the legal code of the Land: ‹ All the people shall determine their form of government in accordance with the laws of their forefathers. › Judaea, with its juridical and social system resting solidly upon the Torah, had received official endorsement of its regime from Persia in Ezra's days, and the Ptolemies had followed that policy scrupulously. Now, with the Seleucids in control of Judaea, its laws were reaffirmed for the third time.

The presence of a foreign garrison in Jerusalem during the fighting moved the Jews to ask Antiochus to issue an order affirming the sacredness of their shrines and holy belongings. The king did so, prescribing heavy penalties for any soldier who trespassed on the Temple enclosure or brought pollution into the city. His successor, Seleucus IV (187-175 B.C.E.), was equally careful to maintain good relations with Judaea: he issued further decrees, and although we have no details, it would appear that their overt intention was to curtail the rights of the ambitious Tobiads. Seleucus IV assigned the main role of government to a new Council of Elders, a body made up of clan heads, priests, and city elders; and the high priest was singled out for particular distinction and responsibility. Thus the privileges Onias II had once surrendered were restored again to the traditional leaders.

The change in policy evident under Antiochus Epiphanes (175-164 B.C.E.) was the outcome of a complex of internal events that were aggravated, in turn, by external involvements. The trouble was sparked off by an argument between the governor of the Temple and the high priest over the question of the former's authority in Jerusalem. But basically it was a question of funds in the Temple coffers. (On several occasions the Books of the Maccabees declare that these funds represented private deposits that the Temple management sometimes invested commercially.) The chief Seleucid minister was sent to Jerusalem to collect the funds and transfer them to the royal treasury: but, after investigating the matter, he sided with the

SELEUCID KINGS

Seleucus I	312-281 B.C.E.
Antiochus I	281-262 B.C.E.
Antiochus II	261-246 B.C.E.
Seleucus II	246-227 B.C.E.
Seleucus III	227-223 B.C.E.
Antiochus III	223-187 B.C.E.
Seleucus IV	187-175 B.C.E.
Antiochus IV	175-164 B.C.E.
Antiochus V	164-163 B.C.E.
Demetrius I	162-150 B.C.E.
Alexander Balas	
	150-145 B.C.E.
Demetrius II	145-140 B.C.E.
Antiochus VI	145-143 B.C.E.
Tryphon	143-138 B.C.E.
Antiochus VII	138-127 B.C.E.

Antiochus IV 175-164 B.C.E

high priest. The situation worsened, and Onias III decided to go to Antiochia himself, and to settle the issue once and for all; since he had already convinced the minister, he was sure that he would have little trouble in winning over the king. But at that moment the court was thrown into a turmoil by the death of Seleucus IV. He was succeeded by Antiochus Epiphanes.

In Jerusalem the opponents of Onias gained control of the Temple—apparently as a result of the change—and took the earliest opportunity to introduce radical administrative reforms that would enable them to carry out their plans, in the Temple, in Jerusalem, and throughout Judaea. Life in the capital was revolutionized completely, and alien manners, names, and forms of behavior were introduced. (For example, Joshua, the brother of Onias, and one of the leaders of the revolution, changed his name to Jason.)

The revolution was designed, principally, to make Jerusalem resemble a Greek city. The right of citizenship was restricted to a very few; only the children of the elect could be schooled in the new exclusive gymnasium and be coached there in athletics and wrestling. The gymnasium and its physical exercises were only an external manifestation of the central objective of this social revolution—the conversion of Jerusalem into a Greek city-state, where all power would be held by elite citizens. This meant placing authority exclusively in the hands of men attracted by the form of the Greek *polis*—especially in the towns of Israel that were large enough to rank as Greek city-states. The gymnasium was always the focus of such a town, and only around it could a city-state flourish.

For the revolutionaries, the new policy represented an escape from prison. Bible canon had cast a wall of quarantine around Judaea, had cut it off and isolated it from the world. The revolutionaries were sure that it would be easier, now, to form close ties with city-states far and near, if only Judaea organized its administration to correspond with theirs. But the innovation was too drastic for the Yishuv to accept: it knew that in neighboring city-states power was in the unyielding grasp of a minority of merchants and rich farmers. Such plutocracy was unthinkable in a Judaea indoctrinated by Nehemiah's economic reforms and an egalitarian Torah, a Judaea where every man was his fellow's equal under God, in civil and political rights, and where these principles had become the essence of Jewish life.

Ptolemy V   204-181 B.C.E.

THE SELEUCID EMPIRE 198 B.C.E.

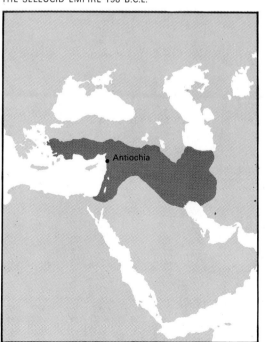

THE PTOLEMID EMPIRE 300 B.C.E.

The urge to expand the narrow boundaries of Judaea, established in Persian days, was actually stronger among those who held fast to the ordinances of the Torah than among the reformers. Though it may not, as yet, have taken tangible political shape, it nevertheless remained the healthy ambition of a flourishing faith: this desire was certainly not the monopoly of a few men accustomed to govern by virtue of material wealth, men whose wealth was dwindling, and who now sought to rehabilitate themselves at the expense of the common good. Vital to the whole philosophy of the Bible was the concept of the Land of Israel as holy soil, promised to Israel for an inheritance. It was the duty of those faithful to the Torah to cleanse the Land of ‹ the people of the lands . . . which have filled it from one end to another with their uncleanness › (EZRA IX: 11).

THE NEW masters of Jerusalem made no attempt to hamper Temple worship, which went on regularly. Even when Jerusalem's new city council sent a delegation to Tyre to attend a ceremony in honor of the town god Melkarth (Heracles)—as was the Greek custom among friendly cities—the envoys would not contribute toward the cost of the pagan festivities, but instead dedicated the gift of money they had brought to the needs of the Tyrian fleet.

At the outset, it seems that the inhabitants of Jerusalem were not wholly conscious of the municipal reforms; a small clique had always run the city, and transfer of authority from one clique to another was hardly noticed. At first the « city » system brought little change to the lives of those towns that adopted it. But it was different when Hellenism became stronger: new towns, identical in constitution to their Greek counterparts, were founded then—often upon ancient ruins—and the founders labored to give them a thoroughly Greek appearance.

The fact that the Jerusalem innovators had no genuine attachment to Hellenism in the modern sense of the word is obvious from all the historical sources of the period. In practice, there was no real conflict between Greek culture as such and devotion to the faith of Israel, and both cultures could exist together. Even the Tobiad faction, which had wrecked the traditional regime, was not aligned with Hellenism in spirit or thought. If Joseph, their leader, cultivated the customs of Hellenistic Egypt, it was out of a desire for its extravagances—and this may also be said of his sons and sympathizers, who were the architects and agents of the social revolution. They thirsted for the elegant and luxurious way of living that was then widespread in the Mediterranean lands.

The dispute that divided the ranks of the innovators for three years (from 174-171 B.C.E.) revealed the weakness of their hold on the popular imagination, and showed how desperately they needed to control public means—including the Temple funds. Socially isolated, they were pushed to wild extremes. When Menelaus, the brother of Simeon and governor of the Temple, was sent to Antiochia to discuss Judaea's affairs at court, he realized that Onias III—then a political exile in the sanctuary of Daphne, near the city—presented a grave threat to the new policy, and he contrived his assassination.

Shortly after, Joshua-Jason, the high priest, who had not yielded to the wishes of the out-and-out reformers, was superseded: Menelaus took his place as high priest. The citizens of Jerusalem discovered that on Menelaus' orders the men of the new regime were selling the gold vessels of the Temple. In the rioting that followed, Menelaus' brother, Lysimachus, was trampled to death by the mob. This was the beginning of fierce civil strife—still confined to Jerusalem, but already charged with the explosive ingredients that Seleucid interference in Judaea's affairs was about to ignite. And the blaze came soon enough when the Yishuv declared open war—not just on a faction of reformers, but on the whole of the Seleucid Empire.

THE HELLENISTIC PERIO

130

Below, the base of a second-century C.E. gold goblet, found in Rome: it is thought to depict some of the Jewish ritual objects taken from the Temple in Jerusalem. Left, a first-century C.E. relief from Ashkelon (in Israel) shows the Greco-Roman mother-goddess Isis with the god Horus, her son.

The conflagration was sparked off by Antiochus' visit to Jerusalem (in either 170 or 169 B.C.E.), after his campaign against Egypt: the minor insurrection in Jerusalem that ended in the death of Lysimachus was little more than a year old. The people had welcomed the king warmly—despite the fact that Menelaus had been exonerated from all responsibility for the outbreak and several representatives of the council of elders had been executed. But the real object of the king's visit soon became apparent: it was to despoil the Temple. No one could fail to see the difference between the dedication and loyalty of Onias III, who had prevented the Seleucid chief minister from tampering with the Temple funds, and Menelaus' mishandling of affairs. For a while, however, all was quiet on the surface. Joshua-Jason, who had been forced into flight when Menelaus usurped his place, was able to return with armed men and to recapture power. But in the public eye he was as responsible as anyone for all Judaea's present vexations—and citizen resistance, which now became apparent, was aimed at him as much as at Menelaus.

Growing Unrest
It is not easy to establish whether the disorders on Joshua-Jason's return preceded the looting of the Temple or followed it. But it is certain that matters came to a head when Antiochus decided to send his army into Jerusalem to keep order and to build a fortress there to assure Seleucid control of the region. In all probability, Menelaus, fearing for his own position, had urged the king to do this. But the main reason was the existing state of war between Antiochus and Egypt, and Antiochus' fears that Judaea would side with the Ptolemies: he could not fail to have noticed that Jewish sympathy for the Ptolemies was increasing daily.

According to the king's orders, local workmen were to be forced into building the fortress, but the commanding officer of the Mysian mercenaries, fearing disturbances, decided not to conscript residents in the usual way: at first, indeed, he kept the purpose of his coming a secret, and began the work suddenly, with pressed labor, on a Sabbath. He assumed that no Jew would interfere with the building on that day,

131

but he proved to be very wrong. By violating the holy rest of those Jews pressed into service, he provoked bloody riots in the streets of Jerusalem. From that point on, the authority of Joshua-Jason and Menelaus was upheld by the troops of Antiochus, and nobody who opposed it was safe; as might be expected, the insurgents went underground and began operations from their hiding-places.

The defenders of the Torah's sovereignty began to win widespread support and to gain strength rapidly: the Seleucids were quick to recognize that, if they wished to rid themselves of the causes of disorder and the opponents of royal decrees, they would have to declare war on the principal source of mischief—the religion of Israel. The text of Antiochus Epiphanes' proclamation can have differed very little, if at all, from the account given in the First Book of Maccabees (1: 41 *et seq.*). In general terms, the proclamation forbade any nation of the empire to set itself apart, and to disassociate itself from the other nations.

**Mounting
Opposition**

All the other nations within the Seleucid Empire—or indeed within the Ptolemid Empire—had retained their ancestral faith, but their gods were easily identified with the divinities of Greece. For them the proclamation was in line with an existing and accepted state of things, and they could acquiesce easily. It was, too, broadly in line with the desires of the Jason-Menelaus faction, which was anxious to draw nearer to Judaea's neighbors and to break down the « separatism » taught in the Bible. Antiochus must have issued precise instructions on the enforcement of the proclamation and on how to deal with recalcitrants.

It appears that the Seleucids were only vaguely aware of the make-up and numbers of the men of Judaea who were ready to die for the disciplines of the Torah: quite probably, Menelaus and his spokesmen persuaded the court that the critics of the alien city regime constituted only a sprinkling of bigots who could be dealt with easily. At any rate, the government went into operation with the forces it had in Jerusalem and in Judaea. From Jerusalem, where the fortress gave ample protection and provided a source of armament and ammunition, it was able to launch a series of victorious attacks against the Yishuv.

The Seleucid military measures led, finally, to sacrilege. On the 25th of the Hebrew month of Kislev, 167 B.C.E., an « abomination of desolation » was placed on the altar of the Temple: in the Lord's sanctuary, in Holy Jerusalem, the graven image of an earth-bound « god of the skies » (Zeus) was set up, and the heathens of the empire came to pay homage to it. The profanation took place when many of Jerusalem's Jewish inhabitants had already left the city. The « eternal lamp » of the Temple had not been extinguished: it was removed by force, and the pagan gods installed. This act was the prelude to fresh Seleucid oppressions, known collectively as the « Antiochean decrees. » The decrees forbade compliance with the laws of the Torah— including observance of the Sabbath, and circumcision—on pain of death. Jews everywhere were compelled to take part in idolatrous worship and to offer up sacrifices on altars erected for the purpose. Some submitted to the decrees; others fled to the desert. Many suffered martyrdom rather than violate the Torah's decrees.

THE UNDERGROUND groups formed a united front on the border between Judaea and Samaria under the leadership of Mattathias, a priest and member of the Hasmonean house from Modi'in. The first problem facing the rebel forces was whether or not they might sin against the Sabbath in self-defense. Strict observance of the Sabbath had brought many troubles. The soldiers of Antiochus were well aware that a pious Jew would give his life rather than desecrate the Sabbath, and time and again they chose that day for their attacks. Now, however, with the agreement of the « pietists » *(hassidim)*, dispensation was given to fight on the Sabbath—but

**The
Maccabean
Revolt**

When Judas heard of the king's coming, he . . . met the king, and pitched his camp in certain straits, at a place called Bethzachariah, at the distance of seventy furlongs from the enemy; but the king soon drew his forces from Bethsura, and brought them to those straits; and as soon as it was day, he put his men in battle array, and made his elephants follow one another through the narrow passes, because they could not be set sideways by one another. Now round about every elephant there were a thousand footmen and five hundred horsemen. The elephants also had high towers [upon their backs], and archers [in them]; and he also made the rest of his army to go up the mountains, and put his friends before the rest; and gave orders for the army to shout aloud, and so he attacked the enemy. He also exposed to sight their golden and brazen shields, so that a glorious splendour was sent from them; and when they shouted the mountains echoed again. When Judas saw this, he was not terrified, but received the enemy with great courage, and slew about six hundred of the first ranks. But when his brother Eleazar, whom they called Auran, saw the tallest of all the elephants armed with royal breastplates, and supposed that the king was upon him, he attacked him with great quickness and bravery. He also slew many of those that were about the elephant, and scattered the rest, and then went under the belly of the elephant, and smote him and slew him; so the elephant fell upon Eleazar, and by his weight crushed him to death— Josephus Flavius, Antiquities of the Jews.

A battle in the Maccabean War—a drawing from the 10th-century Roda Bible: in the left foreground is one of the combat elephants used by the Seleucid forces.

with a qualification: the Jewish fighters were only permitted to repel an assault, not to strip the dead or to seize booty. (In ancient usage, the term *hassid* denoted those Jews who were scrupulously attentive to the commandments of the Bible and who, by the way they conducted their own lives, demonstrated how the burden and sanctions of the Torah should be borne. Once the hassidim consented to the dispensation, it was accepted without question throughout Israel.)

Under Mattathias' leadership the ground was prepared for full-scale war. He did not engage the royal army in open battle, but concentrated on irregular guerrilla actions and on consolidating the rebel ranks. After his death the leadership passed to his son Judas, known as Maccabaeus, the greatest Jewish commander of the Second Temple period. When it became clear that the rebel intervention was endangering Seleucid rule in Judaea, the royal commanders stepped in to crush the incipient revolt. The first to clash with Judas was Appolonius, governor of Samaria: he was killed in battle and his forces were routed. A second attempt, on a larger scale, was made by Nicanor and Gorgias, who prepared to invade from the west. But this advance, too, was frustrated by Judas' military skill.

While most of the Seleucid troops remained encamped at Emmaus, a few picked legions, under the command of Gorgias, went up to the hills to track down the Jewish forces. Judas received detailed information from the surrounding villages of Gorgias' advance: the Seleucid general, however, had no means of knowing the rebels' position or movements. Judas chose to attack during the night-watch when—as he knew from his informants—Gorgias was away from the camp, hunting him with a large detachment of soldiers. The Jews charged, blowing rams' horns as the Bible advised in its « laws of war »: the leaderless garrison, shaken by the sudden alarm, may well have feared that the horns were summoning all the surrounding villagers to fall upon them.

Within a short while, the Jews had taken Emmaus and set the Seleucid camp on fire. When Gorgias and his detachment returned worn and weary from their fruitless search, they saw the flames rising from their camp and the Jewish forces drawn up for battle: they retreated in disorder, through hostile Jewish settlements, and only very few reached the coast. The spoils were vast, and Judas was able to organize a regular army, and to bring relief to the victims of the Antiochean decrees.

But Judas was still not powerful enough to withstand a full military expedition by the enemy: he had no cavalry, and he had no means of procuring combat-elephants. But as a spearhead, either within or on the frontiers, his men could be of tremendous value in defending Jewish minority groups in Gentile towns. He was able to extend the bounds of Judaea and annex to it areas of dense Jewish settlement in the south (including Hebron), and also areas of mixed population in the west. But it was the political consequences of his victories that mattered most. After the defeat of Gorgias, Antiochus' viceroy, Lysias, who had once governed all the western provinces of the empire while Antiochus was away fighting in the east, was sent to Judaea. Lysias tried to enter Judaea with a powerful army from the south, but he too was routed in battle, near Beit-Tzur. Lysias realized that the revolt could be suppressed only with great difficulty—especially as some of the Seleucid forces were engaged on the eastern front, under the command of Antiochus himself, and the empire was in bad financial straits. This fact (together with the threat of Roman intervention) induced the Seleucids to redress a policy that had brought them no benefit or political advantage: in the spring of 164 B.C.E., all previous dictates against Judaism were withdrawn, and all insurgents who returned to their normal occupations within a fortnight were granted a free pardon.

The Capture of Jerusalem

However, Judaea's representative in the negotiations had been Menelaus, and Judas Maccabaeus and his followers—distrusting the Seleucid promises—would not disarm. Instead, Judas marched on Jerusalem at the head of his forces, taking the city (but not the citadel) in 164 B.C.E. Three years after its pollution, Judas and his men were able to cleanse the Temple, and in memory of its re-dedication the festival of *Hanuka* was established for all generations. By this victory Judas became, in effect, the recognized head of Judaea. As such he conducted, with the support of his brothers, a series of operations against those foreign elements in the Land that endangered the peace of the Jewish population. He marched to Gilead at the head of a large force, struck at the enemies of the Jews in the area, and evacuated some of the Jewish inhabitants of Transjordan to Judaea. Meanwhile a second column under Simeon was operating in western Galilee, while other forces marched into Edom and toward the coastal strip.

A year later, after continuous fighting in the border regions, Judas decided that the time was ripe for an attack on the citadel itself in Jerusalem. This was blatant defiance of the central Seleucid government. On the face of it, Lysias had little

An 18th-century German *Hanuka* lamp, with oil burners: these are lit (one on the first night, one extra on each succeeding night) on the eight-day festival of Hanuka, held to commemorate the victory of Judas Maccabaeus and the subsequent rededication of the Temple—and also the miracle of the cruse of oil that was found and kept the Temple's Eternal Lamp alight for eight days.

choice but to deploy the whole military strength of the empire against Judas—and had he done so, he would have undoubtedly been victorious. But instead, displaying remarkable diplomatic skill, he restored to the Yishuv all the rights it had enjoyed under Antiochus III, thus reversing the Jason-Menelaus reforms. Menelaus was condemned as a traitor to the empire, and put to death. Judas was not touched, the fortress in Jerusalem remained, and Eliakim (Alcimus)—who was in Lysias' confidence—was made high priest. This settlement angered the Gentile townspeople of the coast, particularly the occupants of Acre.

Shortly after the change in Seleucid policy the empire was thrown into a ferment again. Both Lysias and the young Antiochus V were murdered, and Demetrius I succeeded to the Seleucid throne in 162 B.C.E. His policy was to support Alcimus (the Jewish high priest appointed by the Seleucids) in his struggle against Judas, but the brutality displayed by Alcimus and the Seleucid commanders re-united the majority of the people behind Judas. In 161 B.C.E., Judas won his last great victory against the Seleucid forces, whose commander, Nicanor, fell in battle on the 13th of the Hebrew month of Adar.

Judas, however, was not content with his military victory. He understood that Demetrius would not give up Judaea without a bitter struggle, and decided to ally himself with the all-powerful Roman Empire, Demetrius' enemy. The senate in Rome agreed to the alliance, which was officially concluded in 161 B.C.E. But it did not save the Jews from Demetrius' vengeance. In 160 B.C.E., a mighty Seleucid army invaded the country, and Judas Maccabaeus was killed in the ensuing battle. The loss of this great leader was a grievous blow to the nation. With the support of Alcimus, the high priest, the Seleucid conquerors surrounded the country with a ring of fortresses and began a campaign of oppression. But Judas' brothers Jonathan and Simeon, managed to unite the rebel forces and to establish a base in the Judaean Desert, which the imperial armies—despite several onslaughts—were unable to destroy. Jonathan transferred the field of action to Michmash, north of Jerusalem, and the Seleucid authorities, despairing now of victory, accepted that the only real power was in Hasmonean hands.

In the meantime, the unity of the Seleucid Empire was threatened by a pretender to the throne. Both the pretender (who was supported by Egypt and Rome) and the legitimate king, Demetrius, turned to Judaea for support. Jonathan bided his time, playing one off against the other, and using the lull to consolidate his position. In 152 B.C.E., on the Feast of Tabernacles, he appeared for the first time in the Temple as high priest, shortly after the Seleucids appointed him viceroy over a now wider Judaea. Jonathan's prestige increased rapidly. He very quickly made Hasmonean Judaea one of the most important military and political factors in southern Syria, using his great diplomatic skill to exploit the changing political circumstances. He not only consolidated his rule in Jerusalem and the former territory of Judaea, but expanded its boundaries. Jonathan's main achievement was probably the seizure of the Lydda area and two other districts in southern Samaria: he also took over the Ekron area. And when, in 143 B.C.E., Demetrius II was under threat from the citizens of Antioch and appealed to Jonathan for help, a Jewish force went north, gained control of Antioch, and rescued the king.

After Jonathan's death (he was treacherously murdered by a Syrian general), Simeon continued his brother's work. He took the citadels in Jerusalem, Beit-Tzur, and Gezer, expelled the foreigners from Jaffa and made it the main Jewish port. In 142 B.C.E. the independence of Judaea was recognized by Demetrius II. The climax came on the 18th of the Hebrew month of Elul, 140 B.C.E. On that day, before priests and people, leaders and elders, Simeon was proclaimed hereditary *nassi* (prince or president), high priest, and commander in chief, and was entrusted with all the concerns of the Temple and the Land. As commander in chief he was responsible for arms and fortifications. No meeting could be convened without his approval; all official documents had to bear his name; only he could appear in public robed in purple and wearing a bracelet of gold. So a new royal dynasty, the house of the Hasmoneans, was born. Once again the Yishuv could enjoy political independence. Simeon's appointment as nassi and high priest was for life—or until ‹ a prophet of truth should arise in Israel. › This exceptional proviso admitted an awareness that the full sovereignty enjoyed by Judaea fell short of perfection, and that the privileges vouchsafed to Simeon by the Great Convocation—especially in respect of his double title—were not to be thought of as equaling God's promise to David that his house should reign in perpetuity.

The Hasmonean State

JUST AS the formation of the Hasmonean state was conditioned by the political activities of the Seleucid kingdom, so its territorial expansion was influenced by the processes that were leading to Syria's disintegration. In most of its military clashes Judaea came face to face with the Seleucids' successors among the Hellenistic cities and with the various principalities that had seized control of the areas adjoining Judaea: it was only at the beginning of this period that the Seleucid kings appeared as Judaea's principal enemies. In general, the prolonged dynastic struggle completely undermined the foundations of the military and financial strength of the kingdom—or what remained of it—and left it impotent. One by one the great Greek cities broke away from the body of the kingdom. Tyre, Sidon, Byblos, Tripoli, Acre, Gaza, and Ashkelon all became autonomous, and by the end of the second century B.C.E. had severed all ties with the central government in Antiochia. For the most part they developed an urban life on the Greek model, but there were also some former Seleucid cities that fell under the rule of tyrants. This was the position in Dora and Strato's Tower, as well as in several important cities in Transjordan—in Philadelphia, for example.

Hasmonean Judaea was not the only state to take advantage of the disintegration of the Seleucid kingdom. There was a parallel advance in the status of the Nabatean kingdom, whose history bears directly on the development of Judaea. One of the Nabatean kings' main objectives was to control the roads that joined southern Arabia (through their capital, Petra) with Egypt and Gaza on the one hand, and with Damascus and the Phoenician cities on the other. At the time of the Maccabean revolt under Judas, the Nabateans allied themselves with the Jews against the common Seleucid enemy. However, in the heyday of the Hasmonean kingdom they were generally to be found among the Hasmoneans' principal opponents—mainly because both kingdoms were expanding in the same area.

Throughout the period, the Ptolemaic kingdom also remained a political factor affecting the development of the Land of Israel. It, too, suffered considerably from internal disputes, but unlike Syria, Egypt generally maintained its unity and its position as a power.

With the death of Antiochus Sidetes, the last great Seleucid king, in 127 B.C.E., the structure of the Seleucid kingdom collapsed completely. As a result, Johanan Hyrcanus (135-104 B.C.E.), the son and heir of Simeon, was able to begin his fight to restore Jewish rule throughout the Land. The wars of Johanan Hyrcanus were a continuation of the struggle begun by his predecessors. Like his father, he dreamed of repossessing the nation's « ancestral heritage »—that is, the entire Land of Israel. Johanan's military campaigns were conducted on three fronts—in the north, south, and east—and proved of major importance for the country's future. In the last 20 years of the second century B.C.E., he succeeded in annexing important areas

in the interior to the Judaean state. Of particular importance was his expansion to the south: the whole of Idumea (Edom) became a part of Judaea and its inhabitants were converted to Judaism. From then on, the Idumeans were an inseparable part of the Jewish nation, and their leading families occupied positions of authority in the Hasmonean state. Johanan also made conquests in Transjordan and advanced in the direction of Samaria, occupying the Samaritan center at Shechem and destroying their temple on Mount Gerizim.

In the last years of his life, Johanan renewed his campaigns and succeeded in conquering the important Hellenistic cities of Samaria and Scythopolis (Beit-She'an). Samaria was destroyed in about 107 B.C.E. and the road to Galilee was opened up to the Jewish armies. Johanan's son, Aristobulus I (104-103 B.C.E.)—one of the principal executors of his father's policy even in his lifetime—completed the occupation of Galilee and converted the Itureans to Judaism.

Left, the ancient Nabatean temple at Petra, in Transjordan: the rock-cut city of Petra was the Nabatean capital from the fourth century B.C.E.

Right, a bronze Nabatean oil-lamp, shaped like a man's head. found at Avdat—a Nabatean settlement in the Negev desert, where modern Israeli scientists have experimented with Nabatean farming systems and methods of irrigation.

The growth of the Jewish state was facilitated to some extent by the ties Johanan Hyrcanus succeeded in establishing with several of the great powers, especially the Roman republic and Ptolemaic Egypt, and with those claimants to the Seleucid throne who were allied to them. Johanan renewed the alliance that had been established with Rome by Judas Maccabaeus, and—thanks to the considerable influence of Egyptian Jewry at that period and its contacts with the royal court at Alexandria— was able to improve relationships with Ptolemaic Egypt. The alliance with Rome helped the Hasmonean rulers to develop further international ties, particularly with Pergamum in Asia Minor.

Alexander Jannaeus

The reign of Alexander Jannaeus (103-76 B.C.E.), the brother and heir of Aristobulus, was marked by the reunification of the country under Judaean rule. Under him, the Jewish kingdom of this Second Temple period grew as large as it was ever to be. After the conquest of Idumea, Samaria, and Galilee, came the conquest of the coastal region. In most of this area, the Jews did not have to face serious opposition. Only Acre in the north and Gaza in the south were capable of putting up any serious resistance, and a clash could be expected with the tyrannical rulers of Dora and Strato's Tower. These powers combined to block Jewish expansion—and they were supported by the Phoenician cities north of Acre and by Ptolemy Lathyrus, the ruler of Cyprus, who landed at the head of a large army. He succeeded in raising Alexander's siege of Acre, but failed in his plan to take Sepphoris.

Ptolemy then advanced through Galilee to Transjordan, where he defeated Alexander in battle; however, Alexander received military aid from Egypt and was able to halt the Cyprian's advance. Alexander was now free to deal with Ptolemy's former allies in Transjordan and on the coast, especially Gaza. He overran a number of cities in Transjordan—including Gadara, the most famous of the Hellenistic cities in the east of the Land—and then moved westward and down the coast. As was

139

expected, he met strong resistance only at Gaza: although the help promised to the people of Gaza by the king of the Nabateans never materialized, and internal disputes weakened the city's defense, it held out against Alexander's siege for an entire year. Gaza (which finally fell in about 96 B.C.E.) was Alexander's most difficult conquest. Once he had overcome it, he was able to continue his expansionist policy: a long line of Greek cities in Transjordan and in the Kinneret (Sea of Galilee) area fell to him. Among these were Philoteria, south of the Sea, the Golan, including the strong fortress of Gamala, and the city of Hippo (Susita). The extension of Judaean territory in the north-east and east was accompanied by expansion in the south and south-east. Alexander Jannaeus' last campaign was the siege of Regev, an important fortress in Transjordan that was taken a few days after his death in 76 B.C.E.

The important conquests made by Alexander toward the end of his reign were largely the result of the military superiority he managed to establish over the Nabateans. Only a few years before, the Nabateans had penetrated right into the interior of the country west of the Jordan and forced him onto the defensive. Now, at the end of his reign, Alexander succeeded in reversing the position and compelled the Nabateans to give up vital areas.

THE KINGDOM OF
ALEXANDER JANNAEUS

Queen Alexandra

Alexander was succeeded by his wife Alexandra (Shlom-Zion) who reigned from 76-67 B.C.E. Her foreign policy was mainly a continuation of her husband's, though the rate of conquest was slower. She maintained a large army and, in addition to recruiting a large number of mercenaries, doubled the Jewish armed forces. But despite the fighting force at her command, her most ambitious campaign, an attempt to take Damascus with a force under the command of her son Aristobulus, failed. Indeed, at one time during her reign the kingdom was in serious danger. This was when the king of Armenia invaded Syria with a powerful army and approached the borders of the Land. However, the danger passed when Roman legions invaded Armenia. From that point on, the Land of Israel, together with Syria, entered into the sphere of direct Roman expansion.

The Hasmonean conquests in effect halted the Greek domination of the Land and blocked the expansion of the Hellenistic cities and the mixed Semitic-Greek elements into the interior. Thanks to the success of the Hasmoneans' political policies, most of the country's Semitic inhabitants became part of the Jewish nation, and the islands of Jewish settlement scattered throughout the Land became part of the Jewish state. The name « Judaea » ceased to apply only to a limited area around Jerusalem; in this period it became the name of the entire Land of Israel. (It was still the official name of the country when Hadrian ruled in the second century C.E.). The new name reflected the ethnic changes and the relations of forces established during the period of the Hasmonean conquests. The territorial expansion had been gradual, until Johanan Hyrcanus and Alexander Jannaeus finally broke the back of the Hellenistic cities: through their victories, the Jews became a majority again in the Land; and they remained one even after the collapse of the Hasmonean state.

The Hasmonean conquests were accompanied by a migration of Jews from Judaea and the neighboring areas to the fertile lands of the Shefela (see page 14), to Galilee. and to Transjordan. The Shefela and the Sharon plain (see page 14) as far north as the Carmel range became areas of close Jewish settlement. With the expansion of the Jewish population throughout the country, local centers—such as Sepphoris in Galilee and the Jewish cities in Transjordan—also grew.

The constitutional development of Hasmonean Judaea was impelled by the people's decision of 142 B.C.E.—which recognized the status of the Hasmonean dynasty as the official leadership of the new Jewish state and made Simeon high priest, nassi, and military commander of Judaea. The Hasmonean dynasty held fast to the high priesthood. By doing so, it continued the tradition that had formed under

Persian rule, when the office became the most important in Judaea. The relinquishment of this office in favor of another would have greatly undermined the status of the Hasmoneans, for the nation was accustomed to regard the high priest as its principal leader: to the people, then, they remained high priests—though they assumed the title of ethnarch when dealing with neighboring powers. The radical change took place only in the days of Aristobulus I, who assumed the kingly crown to increase the prestige of the Hasmonean rulers.

The transformation of the Hasmonean state into a monarchy was accompanied by a gradual process by which the ruler's authority became greater than that of the institutions representing the nation. Even Jonathan and Simeon were given a more prominent place in official documents than the Gerusia (the council of elders). This enhancement of the ruler's status at the expense of the Gerusia produced a change in the composition and function of the latter: it was during the Hasmonean period that the Gerusia was given the new name of *Sanhedrin* (see page 148).

To defend the state and carry out their own political program, the Hasmoneans had to maintain an army that was strong enough to keep the neighboring forces at bay. For the most part the army was composed of Jews. (A Greek writer, Strabo, testifies to the high military potential of the Jewish population in the Yavneh—Jamnia—and Sharon areas.) We hear as well of the Hasmoneans maintaining legions of well-trained mercenaries. They also took great pains to fortify their towns. Indeed, the Hasmoneans were outstanding as builders of fortresses: Jerusalem, the capital, was known as an unusually strong city, and the Temple Mount within it was evidently a fortified area on its own.

Gradually, the Hasmonean royal court began to resemble, in manners, atmosphere, and external splendor, the courts of the other kings of the east. There were frequent struggles for the succession, and an atmosphere altogether different from the one of holiness and dedication to a cause that had been evident under Judas Maccabaeus and his brothers. At the same time a process of hellenization was evident: one obvious manifestation was the adoption by the rulers of Greek names in addition to their Hebrew ones. Their example was followed by most important officials in the political administration and in the army. But despite these considerable changes in the regime and its policies, the Hasmoneans could not submerge the fundamentally Jewish character of the kingdom—the product of a desperate religious war.

Agriculture and Trade

During the Hasmonean period, agriculture continued to be the basis of the Jewish economy, and the country's prosperity was generally dependent on the agricultural produce. A most important aspect of Hasmonean policy was the annexation of important agricultural areas in the Shefela, the Sharon, Samaria, and Transjordan. Apart from the ordinary farming, the groves of balsam trees in the Jericho and Ein Gedi areas provided the Hasmonean kings with a considerable income. Fishing also held an important place in the Jewish economy, and the city of Tarichea (west of the Sea of Galilee) was known for its preserved fish. The years of Alexandra's reign were generally outstanding for their agricultural yield and prosperity, though we also learn of periods of agricultural decline and drought and, naturally enough, of the damage done to the economy by the battles raging in the Land.

Side by side with agriculture and other associated occupations, handicrafts developed and trade prospered. Jerusalem itself was primarily a center of crafts, even before the Hasmonean revolt, and it continued to play an important part in international transit trade. The conquest of the coastal strip by the Hasmoneans increased the importance of Judaea's role in this traffic and led to the enrichment of those engaged in large-scale commerce through the country's ports. It is remarkable that, despite the political fragmentation and the prolonged wars, there was no interruption in the commercial prosperity of the area in which the Land of Israel was situated.

A model of a first-century B.C.E. Hasmonean warship (from the Haifa Maritime Museum): it is based on a contemporary wall painting discovered in a Jerusalem catacomb.

The Seleucid dynasty may have declined, but the successor states and cities developed a variegated economic life. And representatives of the coastal cities of Phoenicia and the Land were prominent in the commercial affairs of Delos and Athens.

The establishment of the Hasmonean state strengthened the status of the many Jewish communities of the *Diaspora*—those communities living in foreign lands, whose roots went back many generations. Hundreds of thousands of Jews continued to live in Mesopotamia and throughout the Mediterranean world. Natural increase, the absorption of converts, and the transfer of Jewish captives to foreign countries contributed to the growth of these Jewish communities, which achieved considerable political influence. Many of the powers that came into contact with Judaea had to remember that their own Jewish communities were loyal to Jewish national interests, that they believed in the unity of all Jews, and that they recognized the ruler of Judaea, who served as high priest in the Temple in Jerusalem, as leader of the entire Jewish nation.

Diaspora Jewry also assisted Judaea by providing financial support for the Temple: the half-shekel contribution, which Jews in various centers would collect and transfer to Jerusalem, became a regular source of income and support in Hasmonean times. The Temple and the supreme religious authority of Jerusalem provided a constant source of inspiration to the Jews abroad, and the great new festivals associated with the Hasmonean victories—such as Hanuka and Nicanor's Day— were also observed in the Diaspora.

At first, the Hasmoneans were swept forward on a wave of religious and national enthusiasm; but even then the seeds of future dissension were being sown. The extreme hellenizers, cut off from the body of the nation, lost ground, while the hassidim and their successors—who now stepped forward to oppose the dictates of the foreign empire—became powerful again. On the other hand, those members of the upper classes who had been only mildly Hellenistic, and who had stood loyally behind the Hasmonean House during the decisive struggle, also continued to be an important political factor: and their weight increased as the regime moved

The Pharisees and Sadducees

in the direction of monarchy. These latter two social groups found expression in the two sects that evolved and left their imprint on all the inner development of Judaea during the Second Temple period: the *Pharisees* and the *Sadducees*.

The Pharisees, continuing the tradition of the hassidim, represented broad popular circles and influenced the great majority of the people, who regarded them as their teachers and guides. Their leadership was in the hands of the great sages of the Torah. These sages endeavored to uphold the authority of the oral law side by side with the written law, and to popularize the Torah and establish its authority in all spheres of life: they combined faith in divine providence with a belief in the free will of man.

The Sadducees mainly represented the wealthier and more aristocratic circles in Jewish society, and their first leaders came from families that were close to the pre-Hasmonean high priesthood. The Sadducees opposed the upholding of the oral law as a source of legislation equal in authority to the written. Although the Sadducees were a minority group, they were an extremely powerful one as a result of their social standing and wealth.

Religious and social life during the Hasmonean period was highly diversified, and it would be a mistake to imagine that the Pharisees and Sadducees represented the only factors and factions in Jewish life at that time: there were a number of others. (The Essenes, for example, an ascetic sect, held a place of honor and influence in Jewish society, because of the strength of their organization, the sanctity of the members' lives, and their faith in their own prophetic power.) But the main struggle for the soul of the nation and the character of the state was conducted between the Pharisees and the Sadducees.

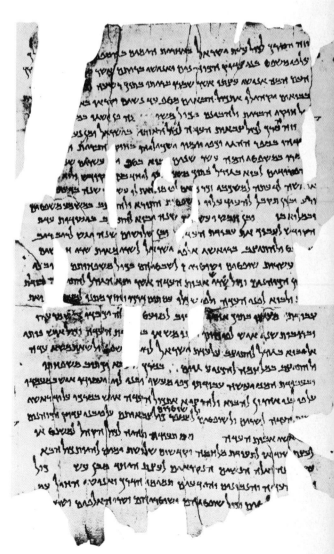

The Master shall teach the saints to live according to the Book of the Community Rule, that they may seek God with a whole heart and soul, and do what is good and right before Him as He commanded by the hand of Moses and all His servants the Prophets; that they may love all that He has chosen and hate all that He has rejected; that they may abstain from all evil and hold fast to all good; that they may practice truth, righteousness, and justice upon earth and no longer stubbornly follow a sinful heart and lustful eyes committing all manner of evil. He shall admit into the Covenant of Grace all those who have freely devoted themselves to the observance of God's precepts, that they may be joined to the counsel of God and may live perfectly before Him . . . and that they may love all the sons of light, each according to his lot in God's design, and hate all the sons of darkness, each according to his guilt in God's vengeance—from the Essene Community Rule.

The first page of the Essene *Community Rule*, found at Qumran, northwest of the Dead Sea (quoted above). The members of the Essene sect, founded in the second century B.C.E., considered contemporary Judaean society to be degenerate, and led an ascetic existence in the Judaean desert. They believed that by remaining pure and faithful to God's precepts they were preserving a nucleus of his elect for the Messianic Kingdom of God.

At first, the Hasmoneans were the natural leaders of those circles that were represented and influenced by the Pharisees, and until the time of Johanan Hyrcanus customs and laws were determined by Pharisaic rulings. The first clash between the Hasmonean rulers and the Pharisees came in Johanan's day: and the breach widened during the reigns of his sons until the Hasmonean dynasty eventually made peace with the Pharisees and, in Queen Alexandra's reign, raised them to power again. The causes of the split are easy to imagine: the secular atmosphere that began to dominate the royal court, the gradual hellenization of the kingdom, and various other features of Alexander Jannaeus' policy were far from compatible with the concept of holiness as developed by the Pharisees. Indeed, many of the Pharisees' followers were opposed to the transformation of Judaea into a monarchy—regarding a monarchical regime as irreconcilable with the traditional system of rule that recognized the high priests as the nation's leaders.

Despite all this, the Hasmonean dynasty retained a great deal of its prestige, and some Pharisaic leaders were prepared to compromise with it—on condition that some extreme features they objected to were removed. Their spokesman was Shim'on Ben Shetah, an illustrious sage and a man of action. It was he who, during the reign of Alexandra, brought about the restoration of Pharisaic domination and acceptance of the laws of the Pharisees as the laws of the state.

WHEN THE ROMANS appeared in Syria in 64 B.C.E. the political situation in the Land was already unsteady. Once Pompey, the Roman commander, decided to annex Syria, Roman intervention in Judaea became inevitable. The bitter struggle that broke out after the death of Alexandra between her two sons, Hyrcanus and Aristobulus, did no more than hasten this intervention and—to some extent—affect its character. Pompey decided in favor of Hyrcanus, whose supporters opened the gates of Jerusalem to the Romans; but he met determined resistance from Aristobulus' army on the Temple Mount. After a three months' siege, in which thousands of the defenders were killed, the Temple fortress was taken, and in 63 B.C.E. the whole of Judaea was absorbed into the political framework of the Roman Republic. Thus ended one of the most glorious periods in Israel's history. The Hasmonean State had maintained its independence for some 80 years, and in that time it had succeeded in consolidating the Land of Israel under Jewish rule.

Pompey's occupation of Jerusalem was followed by political changes that affected the whole country. Whereas Syria became a Roman province, Pompey allowed Judaea to remain autonomous: but he cut the country in size, confiscating most of Alexander Jannaeus' conquests and part of the areas occupied by Simeon and Johanan Hyrcanus.

The country was deprived of all its outlets to the sea, as well as part of Idumea and most of Samaria, and the government was entrusted to Hyrcanus II. The Romans planned to renew the influence of the Hellenistic elements and to weaken the Jewish community in that way. But their success was limited, and for a long time the Jews remained the largest and most powerful element in the Land.

Under Julius Caesar (who ruled Judaea from 45-44 B.C.E.) there was some improvement in relations between the Roman authorities and the Yishuv: Caesar was sympathetic to all Jews within the empire, and regarded them as allies. At the very beginning of his war with Pompey, Caesar planned to dispatch Roman forces to the Land under the command of Aristobulus. And after his victory (in 48 B.C.E.) Hyrcanus and his adviser, Antipater the Idumean, went over to Caesar's side, and gave him vital support when he was besieged in Alexandria by Ptolemy XII, King of Egypt. Once he had overcome Ptolemy's army, Caesar proceeded to set the affairs of Judaea in order. Hyrcanus was confirmed in office as high priest

Roman Rule

Augustus
Tiberius
Gaius
Claudius
Nero
Galba ⎫
Otho ⎬
Vitellius ⎭
Vespasian
Titus
Domitian
Nerva
Trajan
Hadrian
Antoninus Pius
Marcus Aurelius
Commodus
Pertinax ⎫
Didius Iulianus ⎬
Septimius Severus ⎭
Caracalla
Macrinus
Elagabalus
Alexander Severus
Maximinus
The two Gordiani ⎫
Pupienus and Balbinus ⎬
Gordian III ⎭
Philip
Decius
Gallus
Aemilianus
Valerian ⎫
Gallienus ⎬
Claudius
Quintillus ⎫
Aurelian ⎬
Tacitus
Probus
Carus
Carinus and Numerian
Diocletian (Maximian associated with him, 286)
Constantius and Galerius

144

and ethnarch, and the claims of Antigonus, son of Aristobulus, were rejected. The walls of Jerusalem, which had been destroyed by Pompey, were rebuilt, and the port of Jaffa was restored to Judaea.

The assassination of Caesar in 44 B.C.E. dragged Judaea into a war that engulfed the whole Mediterranean world: in particular, the Parthian invasion of Syria during 40 B.C.E. brought chaos to the Land. Antigonus the Hasmonean, who had been rejected by Caesar, seized the opportunity to ally himself with Rome's enemies and reclaim the throne of his fathers. The great majority of the Jewish nation supported Antigonus, who became king of Judaea, thus reviving the Hasmonean monarchy. As a counter-measure, the Roman generals Mark Antony and Octavian proclaimed Herod, the son of Antipater, as king. And once the Romans had routed the Parthians and were in a position to release large forces for operations against Judaea, Antigonus was doomed. In 37 B.C.E. Jerusalem fell to the legions after a five-month siege, and Antigonus, the last of the Hasmonean kings, was executed.

The kingdom of Herod that followed (37-4 B.C.E.) was bound up with Roman policy in the east. Its character and boundaries were fixed by the rulers of Rome to suit their own interests. In the same way, the Romans supported Herod because they considered him to be a man who could preserve order. The relationship established between Herod and Rome followed the pattern that was customary between the empire and its various vassal kingdoms. Herod was treated as an ally—although, in fact, his hands were tied in every matter of political importance. This was glaringly obvious in the sphere of foreign policy, which Rome controlled completely.

THE ROMAN EMPIRE 150 C.E.

27 B.C.E.–14 C.E.
14 C.E.–37 C.E.
37 C.E.–41 C.E.
41 C.E.–54 C.E.
54 C.E.–68 C.E.

68 C.E.–69 C.E.

69 C.E.–79 C.E.
79 C.E.–81 C.E.
81 C.E.–96 C.E.
96 C.E.–98 C.E.
98 C.E.–117 C.E.
17 C.E.–138 C.E.
38 C.E.–161 C.E.
61 C.E.–180 C.E.
80 C.E.–193 C.E.

93 C.E.–211 C.E.

11 C.E.–217 C.E.
17 C.E.–218 C.E.
18 C.E.–222 C.E.
22 C.E.–235 C.E.
35 C.E.–238 C.E.

38 C.E.–244 C.E.

44 C.E.–249 C.E.
49 C.E.–251 C.E.
51 C.E.–253 C.E.
53 C.E.–260 C.E.

60 C.E.–268 C.E.

68 C.E.–270 C.E.

70 C.E.–275 C.E.

75 C.E.–276 C.E.
76 C.E.–282 C.E.
82 C.E.–283 C.E.
83 C.E.–284 C.E.

84 C.E.–305 C.E.
305 C.E.

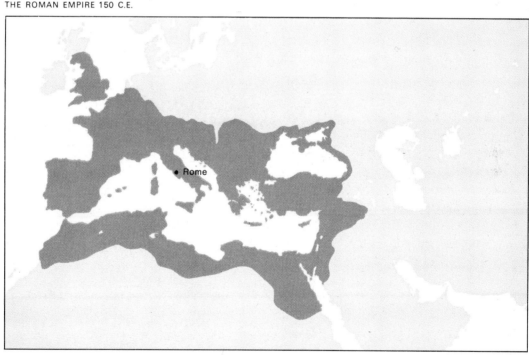

Roman soldiers lead captives before their emperor—from a first-century B.C.E. Roman sarcophagus.

145

During the rule of Augustus (27 B.C.E.-14 C.E.) Herod's kingdom covered almost the entire Land of Israel (with the exception of the Ashkelon enclave and the coastal strip north of the Carmel). It was extended in the year 23 B.C.E., when Augustus handed him Trachonitis, Bashan, and Hauran. Herod had absolute authority over his subjects. And despite Rome's fears that this authoritarianism might provoke the Jews into revolt, Herod generally succeeded in keeping the peace throughout his territory: popular resentment was never voluble enough to burst into open rebellion. A combination of iron rule and carefully timed concession, and the encouragement of those elements dependent on him for position and economic status enabled Herod to keep his throne until his death.

The security force at Herod's disposal consisted partly of foreign mercenaries, partly of soldiers from the large Greek cities founded in his day—especially Sebaste and Caesarea. In this way the importance of the foreign population of the Land was boosted at the expense of the Yishuv. The external splendor of Herod's reign was typified by his court, which resembled the courts of the Hellenistic kings of the east in every aspect. Many of Herod's principal officers were of Greek origin: in fact his private secretary was Nicolaus of Damascus, the great poet and historian (and a friend of Augustus) whose 144-volume universal history was written at Herod's suggestion. Herod's fame and international status attracted visitors from various parts of the Greek world to his court, and from time to time they played important roles in the internal relations of the royal house.

More than any Jewish ruler in the period of the Second Temple, Herod was concerned with building new cities and erecting splendid edifices: among his greatest achievements in this sphere was the establishment of new cities on the ancient sites of Strato's Tower (which became Caesarea) and Samaria (which became Sebaste). At Caesarea he built the country's largest port, which soon came to play a central part in its economic life. Sebaste was used as a place to settle soldiers after they had

Herod's Kingdom

Left, the remains of the deep-sea harbor at Caesarea. The harbor was constructed by Herod in 22-10 B.C.E., and later rebuilt by the Crusaders in the 13th century (with the original pillars cut by Herod's stonemasons). Above, a coin struck during the reign of Herod's son Archelaus (6 B.C.E.-4 C.E.): it shows the original harbor. Right, the Roman aqueduct at Caesarea, another example of the city's former splendor.

completed their service, though Herod persuaded many people from the surrounding areas to reinforce its population: both were organized on the accepted pattern of Hellenistic cities. Herod also built Herodion, south-east of Jerusalem, and added to the magnificence of Massada. Jerusalem itself was transformed into one of the most splendid capitals of the east. Herod rebuilt the Temple (which became known as Herod's Temple), erected a royal palace, built a theatre, an amphitheatre, and great towers in the Upper City.

From the beginning, Herod ruled against the will of the great majority of the Jews, and although he took steps to win the support of the people—helping Jews in the Diaspora, erecting a splendid Temple, lowering taxes from time to time—he never succeeded in overcoming the fundamental opposition to his regime. The foreign atmosphere that prevailed at Herod's court exemplified the great distance existing between king and people, and the establishment of new Hellenistic towns as fortresses for defense against the Jews emphasized the damage his policies had done. Herod's complete submission to the ideology of the Roman Empire, including the worship of Caesar and the building of temples in his honor (outside the centers of Jewish population), widened the gap. When he died there was a general feeling of relief, and revolts against his heirs broke out throughout the Land. The rebellion was quickly suppressed by the Roman army. Archelaus, Herod's son, was confirmed as ethnarch of Judaea, Idumea, and Samaria, while another son, Herod Antipas, was made ruler of Galilee and Jewish Transjordan.

Roman Administration Archelaus' rule, which lasted for 10 years, was characterized by a severity that eventually led to his removal from office by Augustus and his exile to Gaul. Augustus then decided to turn the territories ruled over by Archelaus into a Roman province, under a member of the Roman Equestrian order who commanded a detachment of the auxiliary forces. (In Judaea, these forces consisted mainly of inhabitants

of the foreign cities.) This ruler, who in the course of time became known as the « procurator, » was responsible for security, the administration of justice, and the orderly collection of taxes. His permanent seat was at Caesarea. The procurator did not have Roman legions to support him and whenever trouble threatened he was dependent on the assistance of the governor of Syria, who had a strong force of legions. As a result, Syrian intervention in the affairs of Judaea was frequent.

Roman rule left the local Jewish institutions with a considerable measure of autonomy, and used them to preserve order in the Land and to help in the collection of taxes. The most important of these institutions was the high court (or Sanhedrin) in Jerusalem, the supreme Jewish judicial and religious authority. In assessing the Sanhedrin's powers, it is necessary to distinguish between the attitude of the Jews—who regarded it as the principal ruling body in the nation—and its actual status at the end of the Second Temple period, when the Roman rulers limited its authority. Naturally, the Roman authorities would have found it almost impossible to sift the mass of litigation that required judicial decision, and they therefore left this to the local Jewish institutions. As a result, the administration of the towns and villages and the supervision of religion and worship remained in the hands of the Jews themselves. In capital crimes, the powers of the Jewish courts were undoubtedly abolished by the Romans—except, apparently, in cases directly concerned with the desecration of the sanctity of the Temple: in these matters, the Sanhedrin could pass the death sentence, though the representative of the Roman administration maintained some power of supervision. These powers varied according to the dictates and discretion of the procurator: Pontius Pilate, for example, exercised these powers to the full. But during periods of Roman leniency, the Jews were given free rein to try capital crimes connected with the Temple rites, and their powers were often extended to deal with religious offenses connected only indirectly with Temple worship.

The Sanhedrin consisted of 70 judges, including priests and *Levites* (descendants of the holy tribe of Levi). The senior priestly circles constituted a well-defined group, but the scribes—who really represented the Pharisee sages and who formed a separate group—were also prominent, and they became more and more so as their views gained popular support. Not all the Sanhedrin's members came from Jerusalem; some belonged to the provincial cities of Judaea, and we also hear of « elders » who came to the capital from their cities in Transjordan. Whenever the high priest was present at a sitting of the Sanhedrin, he acted as president. But the Pharisee group developed its own leadership, headed by the great personalities of the house of Hillel—Rabban Gamliel the Elder, and his son Rabban Shim'on. At no time in the Second Temple period could Jerusalem really be regarded as a Hellenistic city. Gymnasia and other cultural institutions on the Greek model did not exist, although the city's constitution provided for popular assemblies, at fixed times and places. On the other hand, the capital did adopt part of the urban terminology that was widespread in the Hellenistic-Roman kingdoms of the east. Thus, the Sanhedrin began to be referred to as the *boule* and its members as *bouleutae*, and some new institutions similar to these of the Greek cities in the Roman Empire were introduced. We also find, as in other cities of the Roman Empire, the *dekaprotoi*, the « ten first ones, » a committee of prominent citizens who were particularly associated with financial administration.

Tiberias, by contrast, was built and organized from the beginning on the pattern of the Greek city, despite its Jewish majority. It had a boule and a popular assembly, though the latter sometimes met in the synagogue. The executive authority was headed by an *archon* and economic life was controlled by the *agoranomos*. The city also had a large stadium.

THE HERODIANS

Herod the Great 37-4 B.C.E.

Herod Philip 4 B.C.E.-34 C.E.
Herod Antipas
            4 B.C.E.-39 C.E.

Herod Archelaus
            4 B.C.E.-6 C.E.

Herod Agrippa I 37-44 C.E.
Herod Agrippa II 50-93 C.E.

THE KINGDOM OF HEROD

148

A 19th-century lithograph showing the caves of the *Sanhedrin* in Jerusalem (first-second century C.E.)—the traditional burial place of the Sanhedrin's members.

In their efforts to find suitable ways of maintaining order in Judaea, the Roman authorities took considerable pains at first to consider the religious feelings of the Jewish population—by prohibiting, for example, the introduction of statues and pictures into Jerusalem. But the two sides often failed to arrive at an understanding, and the gap between the emotional attitudes of the Romans and the Jews intensified the hostility of the Jewish population to Roman rule. The period of the first Roman governors in Judaea passed reasonably quietly; but under Pontius Pilate (procurator from 26 to 36 C.E.) a series of clashes occurred between the Roman authorities and the Yishuv. The most serious flared up when a Roman unit tried to introduce banners bearing a portrait of the emperor into Jerusalem. The attempt aroused the entire nation, and Pilate gave way.

Desecration of the Temple

The first really grave break between the Yishuv and the Roman Empire came under the Emperor Gaius Caligula (37-41 C.E.). Knowing that the emperor was a fanatic who believed himself to be a god and who accepted the worship of Caesar as his due, the foreign minority at Yavneh (Jamnia) set up an altar to Caesar. The Jews of the city, who would not tolerate idolatry on the soil of Judaea, smashed the altar. The emperor retaliated by ordering, among other things, the erection of an enormous golden image in the Jerusalem Temple itself. When news of the edict spread, it aroused fury throughout the Yishuv: open revolt seemed imminent. An appeal to Caesar by Agrippa I, grandson of Herod, led to the withdrawal of the most extreme clauses in the edict, but it was only the assassination of the emperor in the year 41 C.E. that prevented the outbreak of a Jewish-Roman war. Even after Caligula's death, the memory of these events and the fear of their repetition cast a cloud over all relations between the Yishuv and Rome.

Even during Caligula's rule, Agrippa I was already the outstanding Jewish political personality in the Roman Empire. He had been educated in Rome, where he was able to mix in the upper circles of Roman society, and on Caligula's accession he was granted the tetrarchy of north-east Palestine and given the title of king. Agrippa I had more influence in Rome than any Jew before him—and he was also the only prominent Herodian monarch to place the interests of the Jewish people before his own. Throughout the seven years of his rule (37-44 C.E.) he acted in close cooperation with the great majority of the Jews and their recognized leaders.

After Caligula's assassination, Claudius, Agrippa's close friend, succeeded to the imperial throne: Agrippa was made king of the entire Land of Israel. Gradually, he began to consolidate his position in the east and (unlike the other Herodian kings, who remained loyal instruments of Roman rule) worked to create a Jewish army and to improve the Yishuv's means of defense. Agrippa's friendship with the emperor and with many prominent figures in Roman society encouraged the Yishuv to believe that his activities would not be interfered with. But when he tried to strengthen the fortifications of Jerusalem, the governor in Syria intervened and prevented the completion of the work.

Agrippa had worked tirelessly to strengthen and revitalize the Yishuv, and many regarded him as the heir of the Hasmoneans rather than the grandson of Herod. But after his death in 44 C.E., Judaea became a Roman province again, with all that this status involved. Twenty-two years were to pass between Agrippa's death and the Great Revolt, and they were marked by a gradual worsening of relations between the Roman procurators and the Jewish nation. Roman oppression grew ever more severe, clashes ever more frequent. Under Florus, the last procurator (64-66 C.E.), the situation became impossible. Roman rule in Judaea was bankrupt; the official Jewish institutions, despite their autonomy, lost all prestige and influence. Anarchy developed, both in Jerusalem and in the countryside.

An outstanding feature of these intervening years was the growing influence exercised by the extremist fighters for freedom over the lives of the Jews. (Though the fighters are sometimes referred to as « zealots, » at one stage the term referred only to an extreme wing.) The religious outlook of these rebel groups was based on Pharisee doctrines, but in some ways was more extreme. For instance, the rebels elevated political freedom to the plane of a religious principle—regarding submission to imperial rule as a grave *religious* transgression. In this, they differed also from the Hasmonean rebels who rose up against Antiochus, two centuries earlier. In the earlier period the Jews had rebelled only when there was no alternative, when the very survival of Jewry was in danger. For the extremists, however, freedom became the ideal—freedom irrespective of existing circumstances. Just as there could be no compromise with idolatry, so there could now be no concessions over submission to the emperor: the Kingdom of God had to be won by deliberate action, and the Almighty would help those who did his will. Inevitably, this outlook led to the continual advocacy of rebellion.

At the same time the older, more sober groups that were prominent in Hasmonean days continued to maintain their considerable influence over the Jews. The total number of Pharisees at the end of the Second Temple period is not known, but over 60,000 of them refused to take the oath of allegiance to the emperor and the king in the days of Herod—and their numbers were obviously far greater. Generally, the Pharisees were led by the distinguished sages of the day, such as Rabban Gamliel the Elder, Rabban Shim'on (his son), and Rabban Yohanan Ben Zakkai. But the very fact that the Pharisees had become the major force in the Land caused dissension in their own ranks: while they were united over the major principles of religion, they were divided over the major political issues. And it was from the ranks of the Pharisees that the leaders of the freedom movement emerged: together, Judah of Galilee and Zadok the Pharisee became prominent instigators of irreconcilable opposition to Rome.

The most powerful wing of the Pharisees was dominated by Rabbi Hillel, who had come from Mesopotamia and been active in the Land since the days of Herod. Hillel was the greatest sage of his generation. He was president of the Sanhedrin and founder of the school that was to have the greatest influence on the nation's life. His pronouncements in social, economic, and juridical spheres were recognized by the large majority of the general community as binding. Rabbi Hillel's great rival was Shammai, whose school seems to have been associated with the extreme zealots. (After Hillel's death, his grandson, Rabban Gamliel the Elder, succeeded him as president of the Sanhedrin in Jerusalem. He was responsible for pronouncements on various subjects, such as divorce and the determination of the leap year, and was acknowledged as a supreme authority on Jewish law. He had many disciples, some of whom played important roles in the Great Revolt. Rabban Gamliel's most distinguished associate was Rabban Yohanan Ben Zakkai.)

Rabban Gamliel, the son of Rabbi Yehuda Hanassi, said: 'It is good to follow a workaday occupation as well as to study the Torah, for between the two one forgets to sin. . . . Beware of the [Roman] authorities, for they make no advances to a man except for their own purposes. They seem friendly when it is to their advantage, but desert a man in trouble'—from the Mishna.

Rabban Gamliel the Elder with three of his disciples—an illumination from the 13th-century Sarajevo *Haggada*: Rabban Gamliel was president of the Jerusalem *Sanhedrin* in the first century C.E., and a leader of the Pharisee faction.

The Sadducees were led by the aristocratic families, such as the houses of Hanan and Baithos, that produced most of the high priests of the period. And they were joined by many of the upper classes outside the priesthood. The Essenes, whose origins also went back to the Hasmonean period, continued to exist—and sometimes to play a part in Jewish affairs. Philo, the Alexandrian philosopher, and Josephus tell us that members of the Essene sect were to be found in various towns and villages throughout Judaea. And the Roman scholar Pliny recorded that there was an Essene settlement to the west of the Dead Sea. Evidently they had no private property; some lived by tilling the soil, breeding sheep, or keeping bees; others preferred handicrafts. Whatever their occupation, the Essenes entrusted their wages to an elected treasurer, who purchased all their necessities. They abhorred trade of all kinds and the manufacture of weapons, and were against slavery. Very few of them married—and then only to perpetuate mankind.

Jewish Settlement

By the end of the Second Temple period, the Jews formed a majority in the Land, though we have no definite figures. Most lived in Judaea, Galilee, and Transjordan, but there was a considerable number in the Hellenistic cities on the coast—cities like Ashkelon, Caesarea, and Acre. Idumea was completely Jewish, and the Jews predominated in north-west Samaria. The only area without a Jewish population loyal to the Temple in Jerusalem was the interior of Samaria, around Shechem, where the Samaritans, distinct in their religion and origin, continued to form a wedge between the Jews of the north and south. Though the majority of Jews lived in the villages, a number of the urban centers—Jerusalem, Jericho, Sepphoris, and Tiberias, for example—were entirely or largely Jewish.

Because of Jerusalem's status, Judaea remained the most important Jewish area. Jerusalem's Temple made the city the hub of the entire Jewish people, and one of

151

the most famous cities of the civilized world. The second largest Jewish center was Galilee, which at the end of the Second Temple period was a highly prosperous area with many villages and towns. Galilee played a vital part in Jewish life, and was the source of some of the most significant religious and political movements. From Galilee (where Christianity was born) came some of the most extreme fighters for freedom. Among its chief cities were Sepphoris and Tiberias.

The Temple continued to be the religious and social center of the nation, and many thousands of Jews—men, women, and children—would crowd the Temple Mount at festival times. Thanks to the income from the Diaspora's half-shekel contribution, the Temple treasury had large funds at its disposal: these were often used to help meet the city's local needs (and they often aroused the avarice of the Roman procurators). The administration of the Temple's financial and other affairs was well organized by the high priest and his senior colleagues, assisted by officials. (The most important was referred to in the Greek writings as the *strategos*.)

THE OUTSTANDING characteristic of the Yishuv during this period was its fidelity to the Jewish faith, and in particular to the concept of monotheism as it had crystallized in previous generations. Monotheism was accepted absolutely, and there was no repetition of the earlier attempts by extreme Hellenists to adopt the religious faiths of others. Though individuals among the upper classes in the Diaspora might have abandoned the religion of their fathers, and though some religious syncretism was evident outside the Land, the Jews in Palestine remained unflinchingly faithful to Judaism. While it is true that beliefs, opinions, customs, and forms of organization in the Jewish world continued to be affected by foreign influences, these operated below the surface; there was no longer any deliberate pandering to foreign ideas: the influences operated in both directions. Nor was there any idolatry.

The Jewish monotheism of the Second Temple period was marked by a strong tendency toward abstraction. But while certain circles came to accept a more and more abstract concept of the Deity, the belief in angels—or in other mediators between God and the human world—also spread. At the same time the contrast between the ideal of justice and the actual world situation contributed to the emergence of quasi-dualistic ideas of a clash between the kingdom of God and the kingdom of Satan. But neither the emphasis on the activities of angels nor the importance given to this type of dualism affected the fundamental monotheistic belief.

The rule of the Torah was a particularly noticeable feature of Jewish religious development. It encompassed all spheres of human activity, becoming the basis of Jewish life everywhere: the bond that held the various parts of the nation together. All the Jewish literature of the period contains repeated praise of the Torah as the foundation of the world, and the people themselves were prepared, literally, to give up their lives rather than transgress its commandments. From the days of Antiochus Epiphanes, this devotion and readiness for martyrdom became an outstanding characteristic of Judaism, and an historical factor of the first importance, for it largely determined the Roman authorities' attitude to the Jews.

The Torah was the possession of the entire community. Study of its precepts began at an early age. (Josephus laid great stress on the Jewish practice of teaching children to read Hebrew at an early age, so that they could study the nation's history. He claimed that as a result, knowledge of the Torah was so deeply rooted in the nation that if anyone asked a Jew about the laws he would find it easier to reply than to give his own name.) The responsibility for education lay primarily with the parents, but in the later part of the period steps were taken to teach the children publicly. There is a well-known tradition that Shim'on Ben Shetah established

Religion and Literature

152

The remains of the second- to third-century synagogue at Capernaum (Kfar Nahum) on the northern shore of the Sea of Galilee: Jewish settlement probably continued here until the sixth century. Franciscan monks acquired the site in 1894, built a monastery, and partially restored the synagogue.

schools, and we are told that Yehoshua Ben Gamla, the high priest, appointed teachers in every town to instruct children between the ages of six and seven. The extensive world of the *halacha* began to develop at this time, and to dominate the development of Jewish faith and society. The halacha (the oral law) evolved on the one hand from custom rooted in tradition, and on the other from a system of logical principles and judicial procedures derived from interpretation of the written law (the Torah).

Of all the institutions created by the Jews during the Second Temple period, it was the synagogue that had the greatest influence on the development of their culture: gradually it became the center of Jewish religious and public life. At the end of the period there were synagogues at Tiberias and Kfar Nahum (Capernaum):

153

and in Jerusalem there were special synagogues for Jews from the Hellenistic Diaspora. The synagogue provided a unique setting for the worship of God—a worship freed from the bonds of elaborate and expensive ritual.

The development of religion and political affairs at this time was closely bound up with the Messianic concept. Eschatological and Messianic hopes had long formed an integral part of the Jewish philosophy, taking various forms in various periods. A characteristic feature of Jewish eschatology was the linking of national with universalist aspirations: not only Israel would be purified on the last day of judgment, not the enemies of Israel alone would meet with retribution on that day—the fate of all nations and all men would be decided. It was believed, also, that there would be dramatic changes in the physical universe, that a new and splendid world would replace the old. These universalist tendencies were accompanied by the development of individualism. The vision of the future satisfied both the yearning for national redemption and the longings of the individual—as expressed by widespread belief in the resurrection of the dead.

Christianity, like the other contemporary Messianic movements, was born of a belief that the world's end was approaching. But while the other movements faded away after the death or failure of their leaders, Christianity gathered strength after the crucifixion of its founder by Pontius Pilate. The death and teachings of Jesus, and the memory of his personality, continued to inspire his disciples, who were joined by many adherents—including Jews from the Hellenistic Diaspora living in Jerusalem.

HEBREW continued to be a living language in Jerusalem and apparently in other parts of Judaea as well. It seems that the establishment of the Hasmonean state led to a more widespread use of Hebrew. The Hebrew spoken was the new, Mishnaic Hebrew (that is, the Hebrew of the *Mishna*: see page 179), a popular, growing language, influenced by everyday life—not merely a continuation and imitation of the classical, biblical language. Aramaic, too, was used widely in daily life, and constituted the main medium of speech for the masses in the Jewish areas outside Jerusalem and Judaea. The upper classes and the Jews who lived in the Hellenistic towns also learned Greek.

Hebrew remained the main literary tongue of the Jews in Palestine: the great bulk of their literature was written in Hebrew, and only a minor part in Aramaic. As a rule Jews wrote Greek only when living abroad (as in the case of Josephus). The literature itself was extremely varied, and included history, fiction, poetry, apocalyptic works, and *midrashim* (commentaries and homilies on the scriptures). Some of the historians followed the biblical style, others abandoned traditional ways and adopted the current Greek methods of description and interpretation. The First Book of Maccabees provides an excellent example of the traditional approach. It was written in Hebrew (though it is extant in Greek translation only) during the Hasmonean period. The author, a fervent admirer of the Hasmonean house, who lived in the Land, describes the history of the revolt and the establishment of the new state. The first sentence is enough to show that this is in no way a Hellenistic book, but a work—rising on occasions to poetic heights—designed to create a scriptural atmosphere in the style of the earlier Prophets. The deliberate adoption of the biblical style does not affect the vitality of the work in any way. On the contrary, it was more successful than any other work in recreating the atmosphere of the holy war conducted by Mattathias and Judas Maccabaeus. As a historical source, the book is of the greatest value: the objective narration, the frequent use of documents, the copious factual content, place it in the front rank of Jewish historical works.

The Hebrew Language

154

Josephus Flavius   The approach of the historian Joseph son of Mattathias (Josephus Flavius) was quite different; he was a Palestinian Jew of priestly family who went to Rome after the fall of Jerusalem in 70 C.E. to enter the service of the Caesars. It was there that he wrote his two great works, *The Jewish War* and *The Antiquities of the Jews*. The former, published between 75 and 79 C.E.—that is, a few years after the events described—was a work of contemporary history. It was a work that Josephus was well qualified to write, for he was not only an eye-witness of the events described, but had played an active part in them as a Jewish military leader. Thus he was well acquainted with both camps. But his objectivity and freedom of expression were undermined by the fact that he was writing under the direct auspices of the imperial house, and so his work assumed the character of a song of praise to the Flavian dynasty. His historical objectivity was subjected to its severest test when he had to describe the Jewish freedom fighters; generally he adopted an attitude of reserve toward them. It is worth noting, however, that the broad lines of the war were not distorted. The heroism of the fighters is conveyed completely by Josephus—particularly in his description of the deaths of Ele'azar Ben Ya'ir and his army at Massada.

The Jewish War is perhaps the most brilliant prose work of Hellenistic-Jewish literature, a great work even by the Greek and Roman standards of the time. Josephus' other major work, *The Antiquities*, which relates the history of the Jews up to the eve of the Great Revolt of 66 C.E., remains the main historical source for the period between the death of Simeon the Hasmonean (in 135 B.C.E.) and the outbreak of the revolt.

A contemporary, though an opponent of Josephus, was Justus of Tiberias, a historian who wrote in Greek and who was thought to have an even better knowledge of Greek than Josephus. Though almost none of his work has survived, he was well known for a considerable period among both Gentiles and Jews.

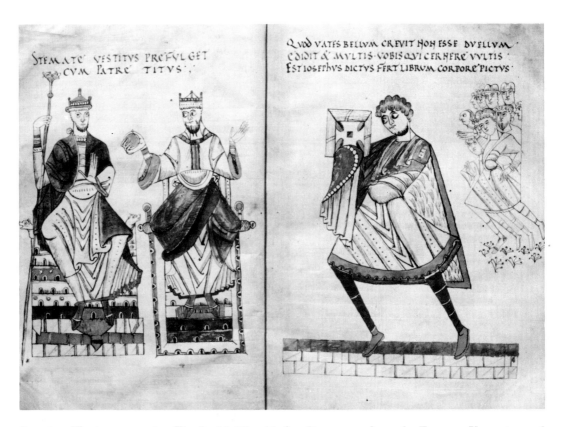

Josephus Flavius presenting *The Jewish War*, his first literary work, to the Emperor Vespasian and his son, Titus—from an 11th-century Latin version of the book. Josephus, a leader of the Jewish rebellion of 66-70 C.E., and later historian of the Jews, wrote this classic history of the Great Revolt under Vespasian's commission.

A frontispiece to the apocryphal book of *Judith*—from the 13th-century French Arsenal Bible (published in Acre). The pictures show Holofernes, the Assyrian commander, and his army; the Israelites in Bethulia; Judith rebuking the elders of Bethulia for wishing to surrender to Holofernes; Judith before Holofernes; Judith killing Holofernes; Judith showing Holofernes' head to the elders.

And Judith was left alone in the tent, and Holofernes lying along upon his bed: for he was filled with wine. . . . Then Judith, standing by his bed, said in her heart, O Lord God of all power, look at this present upon the works of mine hands for the exaltation of Jerusalem. For now is the time to help thine inheritance, and to execute mine enterprizes to the destruction of the enemies which are risen against us. Then she came to the pillar of the bed, which was at Holofernes' head, and took down his fauchion from thence, And approached to his bed, and took hold of the hair of his head, and said, Strengthen me, O Lord God of Israel, this day. And she smote twice upon his neck with all her might, and she took away his head from him, And tumbled his body down from the bed, and pulled down the canopy from the pillars; and anon after she went forth, and gave Holofernes his head to her maid; And she put it in her bag of meat: so they twain went together according to their custom unto prayer: and when they passed the camp, they compassed the valley, and went up the mountain of Bethulia, and came to the gates thereof—JUDITH XIII: 2-10.

Two post-biblical narrative works that have survived, *Judith* and *Tobit*, were probably written before the beginning of the Hellenistic period. *Judith* is widely regarded as a work of great literary merit. It tells, dramatically, how a Jewish woman saved her city by an act of great heroism, and in doing so reflects the atmosphere then prevalent in the Jewish towns of the Land. *Tobit*, which describes the everyday life of decent, ordinary people, and contains elements of folklore, expresses a common belief in the direct intervention of angels and demons in the life of man. Outstanding among the poetic works of the period are the Psalms of Solomon, written in Palestine (in Hebrew) soon after Pompey's occupation of Jerusalem (63 B.C.E.) but preserved in Greek and Syriac only: the book contains 18 poems, attributed to King Solomon. In them the author describes and laments the desecration of the Lord's sanctuary, condemns immorality and sin, and expresses his longing for Messianic redemption. Another important poetic work of the time is the *Scroll of Thanksgiving*, discovered among the Dead Sea writings. This work is a collection of psalms expressing gratitude for the constant mercies of God.

One of the finest examples of the apocalyptic literature of the period is the *Book of Enoch*, a collection of apocalyptic visions, Messianic yearnings, and moral discourses. The work had a considerable influence on world literature. But apart from its literary merits, it is invaluable as a social document, for it contains vivid passages describing the social conflicts in Judaea and denouncing the rich for obtaining their wealth by unjust means, for oppressing the poor, and for persecuting the righteous. In *The Ascension of Moses*, written some time after the death of Herod in 4 B.C.E., Moses is shown at the end of his life, foretelling the future to Joshua and describing events up to Herod's death. After Herod's death (according to the author) time would cease and the kingdom of God would appear. The natural order would be transformed: the sun would not give light, the moon's beams would be transformed into darkness. The Lord of the universe would come to wreak vengeance on Israel's enemies and to destroy their angels. Israel would be happy and exalted by God. One of the most famous and profound of the apocalyptic works is the *Fourth Book of Esdras*, a book of visions and reflections—on the problems of the generations that saw the destruction of the Temple, on the faith of Israel, on the longed-for destruction of Rome, on the redemption of the Jews. This work was probably written in the period of despair after the destruction of the Second Temple.

A work of a different type is the *Book of Jubilees*, a homiletical commentary on the stories of the Bible from the Creation to the Exodus. Noteworthy also is the apocryphal *Genesis Scroll*, discovered among the writings of the Qumran community.

The Great Revolt

THE GREAT CLASH between the Yishuv and the Roman Empire that came at the end of the Second Temple period was the outcome of a number of pressures and differences. In the ideological sphere, there was the painful contrast between the Jewish belief in Israel as a chosen people, and the reality of an empire in which Judaea was only one of many provinces under Rome's heel. The Messianic ideology and the faith in Israel as a chosen people had stimulated certain circles to action even in the early days of Roman rule: once again they called for revolt and an effort to cast off the yoke of Rome, which they regarded as an offense to the Jewish religion. The profound faith of the Jews imbued their fighters with confidence and led them, until the Temple was destroyed, to expect Divine intervention that would save the sanctuary and rout the enemy. It was a belief that even infected some Gentiles. The tyranny of Imperial rule and the idolatry that was involved in even its political aspects—the cult of the emperor, for example—sharpened the conflict between the Yishuv and Rome. Caligula's attempt to impose Caesar-worship on Judaea had revived the emotional atmosphere prevalent in the days of Antiochus, and convinced the people of the grave danger involved in the continuation of foreign rule in Judaea. Many features of Roman rule were an affront to Jewish feelings. The presence of a foreign army on Judaean soil and the harsh taxation system were degrading enough. But what aroused the fury of the Jews more than anything else was the support given by the Roman administration to the Greek and Syrian population of the province. These communities, whose status had declined during the great period of the Hasmonean dynasty, were now increasing in power at the expense of the Yishuv. Furthermore, they were becoming a privileged class, for the occupation forces were recruited mainly from the Hellenistic cities—especially Sebaste and Caesarea. Relations between the foreign elements and the Yishuv became dangerously strained. Gentiles in Yavneh and Ashkelon were among those who took the lead in instigating Caligula's affronts to the Jewish faith, and even after his death the people of Dor continued to molest the Jewish inhabitants of the town. The conflict between the Jews and Gentiles of Caesarea was particularly violent. This tension acquired increased significance during the decades immediately preceding the revolt, when more and more members of the Greek elements rose to ever higher positions in the Roman administrative hierarchy. (Even the procurator of Judaea was a Hellenist.) Once appointed, these officials naturally tended to support the citizens of the Greek towns, and it was no coincidence that Florus, the worst of the procurators, was a Greek from Asia Minor.

The revolt against Rome was also a social revolution in many ways. The debt-ridden and landless lower classes together with refugees from the border areas provided the backbone of the rebel forces. There were also some extremist groups, ardent revolutionaries whose leaders (posing as kings or Messiahs) regarded the revolt as a war not only against the Romans but also against those members of the upper classes who had collaborated with the authorities. The extremists pursued these definite ends from the beginning of the revolt, setting fire to the archives of Jerusalem in order to destroy loan contracts, and using terrorist tactics against the leading representatives of the upper classes.

Jews from every part of the Land took part in the rebellion. The leaders came from various places: Menahem, leader of the extremists at the beginning of the revolt, Ele'azar Ben Ya'ir, the hero of Massada, and Yohanan of Gush Halav (Gischala) came from Galilee, while others came from Jerusalem and Transjordan. It is difficult to estimate the part played by Diaspora Jews, some of whom helped in the defense of Jerusalem, but it seems that (except at Alexandria) they did not start disorders serious enough to divert the Roman military commanders. If the rebels counted on outside military support from one or other of Rome's enemies, they must have been bitterly disappointed: the Parthians, Rome's principal rivals, continued to maintain good relations with the empire throughout the revolt. For a while, the rebels were helped by the bitter civil war that raged within the Roman Empire (between the summer of 68 and the end of 69 C.E.), but by the spring of 70 C.E. a powerful Roman army was able to lay siege to Jerusalem.

Unlike the Hasmonean rebellion and the rebellion of Bar Kochba, the Great Revolt did not produce a central personality who could command the confidence of all. And absence of a united leadership was a major obstacle to the effective deployment of Jewish forces at various stages of the revolt. Nevertheless, Judaea was the only eastern province to rebel on a large scale against the Roman Empire in that epoch.

The immediate causes of the revolt were the anti-Jewish policies of the Hellenistic authorities in Caesarea and the decrees of Florus, the procurator. Jews left Caesarea *en masse* as a result of clashes in the city, and the news roused the population of Jerusalem to arms: then Florus confiscated a large sum of money from the Temple treasury, and the Yishuv's fury exploded. The revolt had started. When it became clear that the auxiliary forces in the country were quite unable to suppress the Jewish forces, the governor of Syria was forced to intervene personally at the head of his legions. His forces were routed in the hills of Judaea near Beit-Horon. **Clashes in Caesarea**

The victory had striking political consequences. A provisional Jewish leadership was set up in Jerusalem, and almost the entire Yishuv was united against the Roman forces. The leaders in Jerusalem sent commanders to all districts: Galilee was placed under the command of Joseph son of Mattathias (Josephus, who, as we saw, became famous as the historian of the war). In addition to the official commanders, other leaders who had proved themselves in guerilla warfare against the Romans continued to organize their forces, notably Shim'on Bar Giora, and Yohanan of Gush Halav.

The Emperor Nero could not ignore the Jewish revolt. For in addition to imperiling the province of Judaea—the heart of an area vitally important to the empire—the rebels had disrupted Nero's military plans for further conquests in the east. The governor of Syria's defeat compelled him to send additional legions to the Judaean front. The command of these legions was entrusted to Vespasian, one of the empire's most experienced generals.

In 67 C.E. Vespasian entered Galilee, his first objective, at the head of a tremendous army. The most sturdy resistance was put up by the fortress of Jotapata, where the best fighters of Galilee, under the command of Josephus, managed to hold off the major part of Vespasian's forces for 47 days. But, despite the heroism of the defenders, the fortress was taken, and in a comparatively short time the whole of western Galilee was in Roman hands.

The imperial army was now free to march against the other Jewish centers. Jaffa, in particular, was important to them since the Jewish fighters there were endangering

Roman maritime transport along the coast and interfering with communications with Egypt. The city was taken by a Roman column, the Jewish ships were destroyed in a naval battle, and an occupation force was left in the city to control the neighboring towns and villages, which had large Jewish populations. Tiberias did not put up any serious resistance, and—though the defenders of Gamala, in the Golan, showed great courage—the liquidation of Jewish resistance at Mount Tabor and Gush Halav virtually set the seal on the Roman re-conquest of the north. The only Galileans to continue fighting were the refugees who somehow escaped to Jerusalem. (Among these were the daring forces of Yohanan of Gush Halav.)

These early defeats dealt a heavy blow to the official leadership, and the zealots of Jerusalem tried to take command. Civil war developed, and almost the whole country, including Transjordan, was occupied by the Romans. Vespasian himself, at the head of the main force, conquered northern Judaea, and in 68 C.E. joined up with the column that had subdued Transjordan. Civil war in Rome held up further operations against Jerusalem, but at the beginning of July 69 C.E. Vespasian was crowned emperor by the legions in the east, and in the spring of the following year his eldest son Titus was able to lead the Roman forces against the capital.

The rebels had failed to exploit this golden opportunity to set up a united leadership and strengthen their military position. There had been constant disagreement between the three leaders, Yohanan of Gush Halav, Ele'azar Ben Shim'on (a priest), and Shim'on Bar Giora (the zealot leader who controlled the upper city), and no joint defense plan had been worked out before the siege began.

The Siege of Jerusalem

Titus' siege operations started in the early spring of the year 70 C.E. and were completed only five months later, in the late summer. During this period he deployed all the force at his disposal to break the Jewish resistance. The attack began (as was usual in a siege of Jerusalem) from the north. After the « third wall » and then the « second wall » were taken, the Romans were able to start operations against the citadel of Antonia (which was defended by Yohanan) and the Upper City where Bar Giora was in command.

The fall of Antonia opened the way for a direct assault against the Temple Mount, and during the first half of the Hebrew month of Av (July-August) the Romans succeeded in overcoming its defenders. Titus ordered his troops to burn the Temple to the ground, intending by this action to destroy the main root of Jewish strength and inspiration. With the burning of the Temple, the Jews' last hope of victory vanished. The stragglers fled to the Upper City, but that too fell to the Romans.

Caesar shouted and waved to the combatants to put out the fire; but his shouts were unheard as their ears were deafened with a greater din, and his hand-signals went unheeded amidst the distractions of battle and bloodshed. As the legions charged in, neither persuasion nor threat could check their impetuosity: passion alone was in command. . . . Most of the victims were peaceful citizens, weak, and unarmed, butchered wherever they were caught. Around the Altar the heap of corpses grew higher and higher, while down the Sanctuary steps poured a river of blood and the bodies of those killed at the top slithered to the bottom. The soldiers were like men possessed and there was no holding them, nor was there any arguing with the fire. Caesar therefore led his staff inside the building and viewed the Holy Place of the Sanctuary with its furnishings, which went far beyond the accounts circulating in foreign countries, and fully justified their splendid reputation in our own—Josephus Flavius, The Jewish War.

Two Roman legionaries, from a first-century relief in Turkey: Roman domination of the Middle East lasted until the Arab conquest in the seventh century.

159

In the end not a man failed to carry out his terrible resolve, but one and all disposed of their entire families, victims of cruel necessity who with their own hands murdered their wives and children and felt it to be the lightest of evils! . . . they quickly made one heap of all they possessed and set it on fire; and when ten of them had been chosen by lot to be the executioners of the rest, every man lay down beside his wife and children where they lay, flung his arms round them, and exposed his throat to those who must perform the painful office. These unflinchingly slaughtered them all, then agreed on the same rule for each other, so that the one who drew the lot should kill the nine and last of all himself. . . . So finally the nine presented their throats, and the one man left till last first surveyed the serried ranks of the dead, in case amidst all the slaughter someone was still left in need of his hand; then finding that all had been dispatched set the palace blazing fiercely, and summoning all his strength drove his sword right through his body and fell dead by the side of his family—Josephus Flavius, The Jewish War.

Massada, where the last Jewish rebels took their own lives to evade capture by the Romans (as related above): recent excavations show Herod's fortress, and (bottom right) the Roman camps.

Once Jerusalem had fallen, the war was really over. Only a few isolated centers continued to hold out. The last of these was Massada, which was defended by the remnants of the rebels, under the command of Ele'azar Ben Ya'ir, until the year 73 C.E. The heroic death of Massada's defenders, who remained faithful to the principles of liberty and preferred to die by their own hands rather than fall into Roman captivity, provides a sublime and tragic epilogue to the Great Revolt.

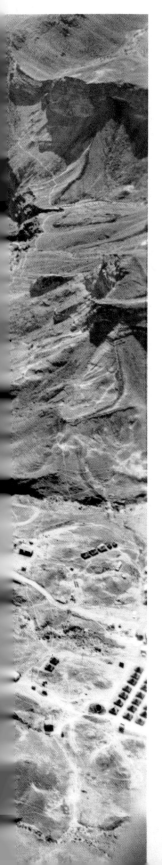

Repressive Measures

The revolt forced Rome to recognize that a considerable military effort was required to preserve order in Judaea, and that a new policy had to be formulated. As a result Judaea was made an ordinary imperial province, to be governed by a member of the senatorial order. Under his command was a force of regular soldiers, the Tenth Legion *(Legio X Fretensis)*, established in the ruins of Jerusalem. The regiments of auxiliary troops (composed of men from Sebaste and Caesarea), whose conduct had been largely responsible for the unrest, were removed. The main center of Roman military strength was transferred to the Jerusalem area so that more effective control over the Jewish population could be imposed. Veterans of the Roman forces that had participated in the war settled in various parts of the country. One such Roman settlement (known as *Colonia)* was established at Motza, just outside Jerusalem. Some of the provincial cities of the Land were even raised in status, and Caesarea and Jaffa were recognized as Roman colonies. A new city was established in Samaria (near ancient Shechem), named Flavia Neapolis.

The destruction of Jerusalem brought bitter suffering to the Jews. Tens of thousands had been killed in battle, tens of thousands had been taken captive; large areas of land had been confiscated. Some of the Jewish land was taken over by the Roman state, which either leased it out or used it to settle newcomers. Many of the Jews remained as tenants on land that had previously belonged to them. Taxation was heavy—particularly the tax for Capitoline Jupiter, principal god of the empire.

Considerable changes were made in the distribution of the Jewish population. Jerusalem, the largest Jewish center in the country for generations, was depopulated. Many of the Jewish villages had been destroyed during the fighting, and most of the Greek cities had been cleared of Jews early in the war. But some settlements had suffered less, and these were re-settled soon after their occupation. There were also places that had surrendered to the Romans immediately, or put up only brief resistance—Sepphoris and Tiberias, for example, the urban centers of Galilee.

An important role was now played by the Jewish centers in western Judaea, especially in the Shefela: apparently these were even more prominent in the life of the community than the Galilean cities. Yavneh, which had a predominantly Jewish population even before the revolt, now became the spiritual and social center of the entire Yishuv and the seat of Jewry's new leaders, Rabban Yohanan Ben Zakkai and Rabban Gamliel the Second. Lod (Lydda), the center of a thickly populated area, also became outstanding as the home of such famous sages as Rabbi Eliezer Ben Hyrcanus and Rabbi Tarfon. There were also important Jewish settlements at Emmaus, Gamzu, Gophna, and Jericho—in fact, in all the remaining towns and villages of what was formerly Judaea. During the 60 years that followed the destruction of the Temple, Judaea was repopulated, and the areas near Jerusalem became the focal points of Bar Kochba's revolt. One sign of the resilience of the Jewish population was the fact that Jews settled again in Caesarea and Acre, and in other non-Jewish coastal cities.

As grievous as the material disaster that followed the Temple's destruction was the spiritual vacuum that had been created. For generations the Temple had been the religious and social center of the entire nation. It was directly associated with many religious customs and had become, also, the focal point of the nation's supreme institutions. Now the nation was left leaderless and without a spiritual center.

The task of regenerating Jewish society was undertaken mainly by the great Pharisee sages, and in the first and most difficult stage by Rabban Yohanan Ben Zakkai, already a notable figure before the destruction. He succeeded in transferring the religious center to Yavneh, and in establishing there a court and an academy. Later, Rabban Gamliel the Second made this court the supreme national authority. The 60 years following the destruction were tranquil ones. Even when—toward the end of Trajan's reign—the Jews of Egypt, Cyrenaica, Cyprus, and Mesopotamia fought a desperate war against Roman rule, the Yishuv did not participate actively. (Though there was some unrest in the Land, the Roman authorities apparently took quick and effective steps to prevent the outbreak of actual revolt.) The struggle created havoc in parts of Rome's Eastern Empire, but weakened Diaspora Jewry.

The Bar Kochba Revolt

THE YISHUV'S second great revolt against Rome broke out between 132 and 135 C.E., during the Emperor Hadrian's rule: this was to be the last great military clash between the Roman Empire and the Jewish nation. The revolt arose out of the Jews' determination to preserve the Jewish character of the Land (and the Jewish religion) at any price: they could not stand by silently and watch its transformation into an ordinary Hellenistic-Oriental imperial province.

Hadrian had decided to rebuild Jerusalem and to establish—in place of the ruined Jewish city—a new heathen city containing a temple in honor of Jupiter: the city was to be called Aelia Capitolina. Furthermore, the emperor followed up previous laws against mutilation with an edict forbidding circumcision—and though this was not directed expressly against the Jews, it did strike a direct blow at the Jewish religion. These measures made the Jews desperate; they could see no alternative to armed revolt.

Rome, at that time, was at the zenith of its power, with nothing to fear from any foreign foe. Thus Hadrian was able to send his finest legions into action against the rebels. But this time the revolt was carefully planned, and the rebels had a single, determined leadership.

According to the Roman historian Dio Cassius, the Jews bided their time. While Hadrian and his legions were in Egypt and Syria they did not make a move—except to damage the weapons they were forced to make for the Roman soldiers. But once Hadrian had left the region, they launched their revolt. From all accounts it seems to have covered most of the Jewish areas of the Land, and to have had Samaritan support as well. There was also unrest among the Jews abroad, but the main rebel force was concentrated in Judaea—and it was only there that the rebels put up stiff and prolonged resistance.

Right, arrows found in the Bar Kochba caves, in the eastern Judaean desert. Far right, a view from inside one of the caves. The Bar Kochba caves, west of the Dead Sea, were used as rebel hideouts in the last stages of the revolt against the Romans in 135 c.e. These almost inaccessible caves are set in steep gorge walls, often hundreds of feet from the ground. When they were explored in 1960-61 a good deal of invaluable material and evidence was discovered: fragments of the Bible and Hebrew prayers on parchment or papyrus; letters (one from Bar Kochba himself) and various documents in Greek, Aramaic, Hebrew, and Nabatean; coins, vessels, weapons, and even fabrics and articles of clothing.

The leader of the rebellion was Shim'on Bar Kosiba—known as Bar Kochba—who acted as nassi or prince of Israel. (Although many considered him to be a Messiah, Bar Kochba did not assume the royal title.) Bar Kochba was supported by Ele'azar the priest—whom he intended to make high priest of liberated Judaea—as well as by the greatest sages of the generation, led by Rabbi Akiva Ben Yosef, who exercised a tremendous influence over the people.

Jerusalem was captured by the rebels and held for a while, despite the resistance of the Tenth Legion. Attempts by the governor of Syria to suppress the revolt failed, and an entire Roman legion was destroyed. Hadrian was forced to resort to extraordinary measures: legions were despatched from various parts of the empire and placed under the command of Julius Severus, who was recalled from Britain. Uncertain of the size of the rebel army, but knowing its courage, Severus refrained from open combat, hoping to crush the rebels—as he did—by degrees.

In the last stages of the revolt, the center of Jewish resistance was Beitar, south-west of Jerusalem, and it was there that Bar Kochba fell. Jewish losses were tremendous: Dio Cassius wrote of the destruction of 50 fortresses and 985 villages, and the killing of 580,000 men. The Romans themselves suffered heavy casualties—so heavy, in fact, that in his report to the Senate, Hadrian omitted the customary formula: ‹ I and my army are well. ›

But, for the Jews, the defeat was disastrous. Rigorous anti-religious measures were taken in Judaea. And although these were withdrawn by Hadrian's successor, Judaea ceased to be the center of the country's Jewish population.

And God roused the spirit of the king of the Ishmaelites in the four thousand nine hundred and fiftieth year of the creation, and a spirit of wisdom and courage descended upon the king. And he and all his army came up from Egypt, and laid seige to Jerusalem. And God delivered the city into his hands. And he commanded a proclamation be sounded throughout the city, to old and young, to speak his words to the people of Jerusalem: That any who desired could return to the city of the sons of Ephraim, of the survivors of the Assyrian exile and those scattered to the ends of the earth.

SALADIN AND THE JEWS   A CITIZEN OF JERUSALEM TO YEHUDA ALHARIZI

Part Four

Professor Benzion Dinur

From Bar Kochba's Revolt
to the Turkish Conquest

135 C.E. -1517

Rome's long-drawn-out campaign against the Jews in Palestine during the Bar Kochba revolt was marked by singular brutality, and it brought about grave changes in the position of the Jews in their Land—some resulting directly from the savage battles, some from the repression of the revolt and from the new policy adopted by Rome after she had gained complete domination over ‹ rebellious Judaea, the vanquished. ›

The broad effects were threefold: devastation of the country; decimation of the community; laws to uproot the Jewish religion and force conversion.

In practice this meant a policy of scorched earth—fields bared, trees uprooted, towns sacked, and houses destroyed—to starve into submission the rebels and their sympathizers who were isolated and encircled by the Roman legions. The Roman historian Dio Cassius tells of a land turned into a bleak wilderness, of jackals and wolves howling in the city streets. A Jew writing as long afterward as the third century C.E. summed up Hadrian's ravages in a single phrase: ‹ only now are olives again to be found in Palestine. ›

The awful decimation of the Jews is fully documented. Dio Cassius' figures—50 fortified towns and 985 villages razed to the ground, 580,000 Jews killed in battle—were probably not greatly exaggerated. His estimate of the number of Jews who perished of hunger or disease and of those who were burned to death appears to have been taken from contemporary accounts, from eyewitnesses of an extermination so thorough that only a fragment of the people survived. Some Jews escaped to near or distant shelter, some were taken prisoner and sold into slavery; but the great majority were killed. The scale of the slaughter that followed the collapse of Bar Kochba's revolt is revealed by contemporary and later allusions to a devastated land, to uncountable deaths, and to ‹ rivers of blood › flowing into the Mediterranean. However, the gravest threat of all was the new policy ceremoniously proclaimed with the fall of Beitar, or even possibly before. This policy found expression in three ruthless and symbolic acts. On the Temple mount (Moriah) in Jerusalem, the Roman commander, Postumus Faustinus Julius Severus, burned a scroll of the Law and set up a graven image in the sanctuary; all Jewish buildings were demolished and the entire area plowed up. The very name « Judaea » was abolished and « Syria Palaestina » replaced it as the Roman name for the country.

These acts were followed by a series of anti-Jewish laws and persecutions. The scroll of the Law, containing the rejected statutes of an extinct city, had been burned:

Left, a relief from the triumphal arch of Titus, erected in Rome (in either the late first or early second century C.E.) to commemorate the conquest of Palestine by Titus in 70 C.E. and the destruction of Jerusalem's Temple: the relief shows Romans carrying sacred and precious objects from the Temple. Right, a coin of Vespasian (69-79 C.E.) bearing the inscription *Iudaea Capta*; it depicts a weeping Jewess (symbolizing the Jewish people) and the victorious emperor.

any person who disavowed their annulment was in open rebellion to Caesar. If a Jew assembled congregations and taught the *Torah* (the Mosaic law), or gave judgment according to its ordinances, or appointed judges to deliver such judgment; if he observed the Torah's precepts or showed himself to be loyal to its customs— then he was guilty of defying Caesar's authority, and would be punished as a rebel.

Jerusalem's Fate

Jerusalem had been obliterated, name and remembrance had to be blotted out once and for all. To ensure this, a new Roman city, Colonia Aelia Capitolina, was built on Jerusalem's ruins. A statue of the Roman god Jupiter was placed in the sanctuary, and beside it a statue of the Emperor Hadrian, the god's partner in rule upon earth. The new city was proclaimed a colony, and colonists were introduced from among the Gentiles of Palestine and elsewhere. A large part of what was formerly Judaea was assigned as the urban enclave. The city was redivided into suburbs and quarters and its own government set up, complete with constitution and senate, a people's assembly, and a staff of officials. All Jews were expelled, forbidden to reside in the city on pain of death.

The renaming of country and capital spoke plainly. What Rome had done in Jerusalem, it was prepared to do throughout Palestine. The object was clear: to stifle the political breath of the *Yishuv* (the Jewish population of the Land) and to make Palestine an entirely Roman country. It was not enough to forbid the conduct of Jewish courts of law or proceedings based on the canons of Israel, or to liquidate any institution whose existence reflected even the slightest shadow of Jewish autonomy. Every tie between the Jews and their Land had to be cut; Judaea had to be struck off the map, all remembrance of the Jews wiped out. And the fact that « the Land of the Jews » did not belong to them but to their neighbors and oppressors had to be proclaimed publicly.

These laws applied to Palestinian Jewry alone. Elsewhere in the Roman Empire, Jews were treated more leniently. It is true that they were denied the rite of circumcision—but so was every sect: it was a total embargo, and published as such. The anti-Jewish decrees in Palestine were decided upon by the Senate at Rome, following the political inferences it drew from the Jewish revolt and its repression. But the method of application was undoubtedly determined by Hadrian himself, and seems very much an attempt to revive the decree of Antiochus Epiphanes in Roman dress. It bears all the marks of a Hellenistic Caesar.

167

How the new laws were translated into judicial, administrative, and military measures is recounted by tradition and folklore. The first among « 10 martyrs of monarchy » were the high priest and the president of the *Sanhedrin* (the assembly of 71 ordained rabbis that functioned as a supreme court); the remainder were great rabbis, who ‹ assembled congregations in multitude, › taught the Torah, and ordained disciples as ministrants and *dayanim* (judges). « Interpreters » who explained the Torah to the people, scribes who wrote the scrolls of the law so that they could be read widely, and Jews who ventured publicly to affirm the existence of a Jewish community and the Jew's duty to die for the sanctification of the Holy Name, were executed. Tradition ascribes a most important place to the Roman procurator Tyrrhenius Rufus and his legions for carrying out these measures.

The changes in the situation of the Jews in their homeland brought about a sharp turn in the Yishuv's history. In the days of the Bar Kochba revolt the nation had fought—for the last time—a national war, with its own forces on its own soil. It had fought a courageous war, standing alone against a mighty enemy, conqueror of dominions, ruler of the world. The Yishuv had to battle hard and strive for its very existence, for the lives of every one of its sons, for the soil they tilled and dwelt on; for the organic unity of a self-created, self-ruling community that Rome—however reluctantly—had recognized; for its religion and its culture. Unswerving in faith, it was the selfless guardian of a spiritual testament and of a people's living continuity, of the links between Israel in its Land and its brethren in the Diaspora. In later periods, there was Jewish insurrection in Palestine, Messianic agitation, and mutiny against alien overlords: in every generation, Jews were politically conscious and active. But from then on, even though risings were an integral part of a long-continuing struggle by the nation for its existence and unity, they were touched off by the existing political, communal, and social circumstances.

The Yishuv's Resistance

168

Left, a map showing the first appearance of Jews in countries outside Palestine: the defeat of Bar Kochba at Beitar, and Rome's cruel policy of oppression in Palestine, forced many thousands to flee to the Diaspora. Above, an edict of Constantine the Great (dated 321) ending the exemption from public office previously granted (on religious grounds) to the Jews of Cologne: since only landowners were eligible for public office, it would seem that Cologne already had a substantial Jewish community by this time. Right, two Chinese figures of Jews (from the 7th-10th century); both are traders, both wear Persian costume.

The Jews of the Land were never a passive minority. For almost 18 centuries a struggle was fought by many anonymous individuals—as well as by organized congregations—to defend life, home, and identity against innumerable obstructions and reprisals. The strength of resistance, and its success, naturally varied with the community's size and authority, with differing forms of government and administration. Yet the mainspring of this dogged self-preservation—the character of the Yishuv itself and the links with the Diaspora—remained constant. Even in exile, the Jews were united by their ancient bond. There were always « Exiles of Zion, » « Mourners of Zion, » « Awaiters of Redemption, » and « Hasteners of the End, » rabbis and Karaites, extremists and schismatics, sharing a determination to maintain, augment, and glorify Jewish existence in the Land.

Somehow, the Yishuv survived. Even the Crusaders, guilty as they were of destroying communities, of slaying and burning captives, of expelling survivors, could not break the chain of history: once the tempest had calmed and some kind of stability returned, the Yishuv always came back to life.

But the Yishuv perpetuated more than the urge to return to the Land: its achievements were cultural and social as well. It ensured the continued use of Hebrew as the medium of private and public speech, a high level of Bible knowledge, the ordering of worship and prayer, the retention of the traditional domestic habits and family manners, the preservation of communal institutions and organizations. The source of the Yishuv's religious authority over Diaspora Jewry was its Judaic wholeness. The Yishuv was composed of Jews faithful both to the Land and to the complete Jewish cultural tradition. At all times, in all parts of the Diaspora, these elements formed the main driving force of *aliya* (immigration to the Land).

The Yishuv's indestructibility made it a magnet for all Jewish spiritual movements. The pious ferments, the Messianic urges, the various tides of aliya, were all responses to that unique magnetism: they were an indivisible part of the Yishuv's history.

Our Rabbis have taught: once the wicked government [Rome] decreed that Israel should no longer occupy themselves with Torah. There came Pappos Ben Yehuda and found Rabbi Akiva attracting great assemblies and studying Torah. He said to him, 'Akiva, art thou not afraid of the wicked government?' He replied, 'I will tell thee a parable: to what is the matter like? To a fox who was walking along the bank of the stream and saw some fishes gathering together from one place to another. He said to them, "From what are you fleeing?" They answered, "From nets which men are bringing against us." He said to them, "Let it be your pleasure to come up on the dry land, and let us, me and you, dwell together ever as my fathers dwelt with your fathers." They replied, "Art thou he of whom they tell that thou art the shrewdest of animals? Thou art not clever but a fool! For if we are afraid in the place which is our life-element, how much more so in a place which is our death-element!" So alas is it with us: now while we sit and study Torah, in which it is written, "For that is thy life, and the length of thy days," we are in such plight, how much more so if we go and neglect it!'— from the Talmud.

The bust of a first-century Roman senator, found at Caesarea. After 135 C.E., governors of Palestine were of senatorial rank.

The Rule of Pagan Rome

FOR 190 years after Bar Kochba's revolt, the Land was ruled by pagan Rome. The political framework remained unchanged throughout these years, but the shocks and setbacks suffered by the empire affected and conditioned events in Palestine. The empire's headquarters moved from West to East, and as it weakened, centralized control became slacker and eventually, in the third century C.E., disintegrated completely. The climax of Roman rule was reached with the reforms of the emperors Diocletian (284–305) and Constantine (306–337), designed to bring all classes under the imperial heel and to merge all peoples and territories into one Christian union. The first generations of this period of Roman rule (138–235) saw, eventually, the cancellation of the anti-Jewish decrees. The Yishuv was rehabilitated, scholarly activity enhanced and enlarged, Jewish autonomy with all its offices restored, communal bye-laws issued, and a number of important rabbinical works, such as the *Mishna*, were completed. But the next century (235–330) saw tyrannous impositions, the swift decline of the Yishuv, sharper social differences, less autonomy, the impoverishment of the countryside, and an increasing number of Jews leaving the Land for the Diaspora.

The fighting quality, courage, military organization, and persistence displayed by the Jews in the Bar Kochba revolt forced Rome to take special measures to deal with insurrectionary outbursts that might, at any moment, replace passive resistance.

170

Two full legions (out of the 30 that Rome could muster) as well as auxiliary troops were permanently maintained in the Land, even though no external enemy threatened it. The tiny province of Syria Palaestina was raised to consular dignity; its governors were all of senatorial rank, all former consuls, all experienced administrators. And since Jews were no longer permitted to appear before their own judges or to be tried by Mosaic law, still more highly-trained public officials had to be brought into the country.

Naturally, the intrusion of Roman elements into the innermost life of the Yishuv was strongly resented. Contemporary rabbinical writings and commentaries are bitterly censorious and hostile, mingling dislike with contempt, anger with derision. After the defeat at Beitar, when dread of the victors was widespread, the critics were more circumspect; they cloaked their gibes in allegory, writing of a ‹ Sodom › where the judges were ‹ prevaricators and liars, men of meanness, of corrupt judgment, robbers of souls › who gave a semblance of justice to oppression and confiscation, and whose ordinances tricked the simple mind. The implication was that the procedures described in this ‹ Sodom › matched those prevailing under the Roman occupation. Other circumspect writers referred to Rome as ‹ Edom › or ‹ Esau, › the kingdom of evil-doing, whose symbol was the swine: ‹ Just as the wallowing pig stretches out its cloven hooves as if to say « see how pure I am, » so Edom robs and ruins, and yet claims to be just. ›

Some rabbis disdained the cover of allegory and preached openly against the so-called justice of the procurator, declaring: ‹ This place [the courts] where there are attorneys is a place where there is bribery, where agreement deceives, where sophistry cheats, and where prejudice is rampant. › Rome's power was said to rest on the threats and exactions of tyrants, ‹ crookedness of ways, decrees innumerable wrought against us. › The petty despots that Rome inflicted on conquered territories were judged to be only ‹ great or little beasts. ›

But there were sages who counselled the people to keep the peace and to pray for the welfare of the empire, who reminded them that God had bound Israel by oath not to rebel against kingship but to be seized with fear of it. To justify their pacifism they would declare that Israel had been crowned in heaven and that peace would come only when the nation was redeemed by the Messiah, not by flesh and blood.

Antoninus Pius

Under Antoninus Pius (138–161) life became easier for the Yishuv. The Romans preserved a record of Antoninus' ordinance permitting Jews to circumcise their sons. Jewish tradition remembers Yehuda Ben Sh'moa and his comrades, who assembled at night before the mansions of Rome's leaders and called out: ‹ In the name of Heaven, are we not your brethren? Are we not the sons of one father? Are we not the sons of one mother? Are we different from every other nation that you make harsh laws against us? › And (so the story goes) the appellants ‹ did not move from there until three commandments were vouchsafed to Israel: to circumcise their sons, to keep the Sabbath day, to worship their own God. ›

Reading between the lines, it would seem that the provincial governors brought back an earlier edict protecting the Sabbath and were willing to respect the original ban on imperial statuary in synagogues of Palestine and the Diaspora. Rescindment of the anti-Jewish decrees under Antoninus restored prerogatives Jews had not enjoyed for many generations—including exemption from general edicts likely to affront their religious susceptibilities. (Circumcision, it should be noted, was permitted to Jews alone). The new policy brought with it a relaxation of the severe administrative methods that had made the oppressive measures even more onerous than was originally intended.

But life was difficult for the Jews, and the intervals of peace were brief. The chronicles of the Antonines tell of Jewish rioting and uprisings, and even though

PALESTINE AFTER
THE FALL OF JERUSALEM

171

the references are not always detailed and generalization is frequent, they may be taken as reflecting the true picture. There are hints in the *Talmud* of notables helping the Romans to outwit the Jewish guerrillas, those ‹ thorns in the vineyard. › And there is the popular tale of a scholarly disputation on the merits of Roman culture: Rabbi Shim'on Ben Yohai decried it, arguing that ‹ whatever Rome instituted, it instituted for its own purposes—markets to instal whores, bathhouses to sweeten proconsular torsos, bridges to collect tolls. › According to legend, the outspoken rabbi was forced to hide in a cave for the next 13 years.

Though the stories may well be folklore, they stem, nevertheless, from fact. Together, they suggest that while Palestine may have remained peaceful on the surface, the people were never at ease and hated their Roman overlords. Jewish writings of the time on the wars between Rome and Persia confirm this opinion. Shim'on Ben Yohai's comments are typical: ‹ If you see a Persian horse tethered to a grave in Palestine, there is prospect of the Messiah. › Another scholar wrote: ‹ If you see benches full of men in rags, there is prospect of the Messiah the King. › And another: ‹ the destroyers of the Second Temple are like to fall at the hands of Persia. ›

While the harsh anti-Jewish decrees were in force, it was impossible for the Yishuv's members to perform orderly communal work. As soon as that terror was lifted, systematic efforts were made to repair the wreckage. But first it was essential to rid the people of a sense of emergency and to guide them back to normality, to accustom them to the new conditions after the long years of war and pillage, of life under the lash of the Roman taskmasters and the foreigners they imported to help them.

The first decisive step toward normality was the convening of sages at Usha in Galilee by disciples of Rabbi Akiva, Galileans who had survived the period of persecutions—Rabbi Yehuda Bar Ilai of Usha, Rabbi Yosi Bar Helpta of Sepphoris, Rabbi Meir of Tiberias, and Rabbi Shim'on Ben Yohai of Tekoa in Upper Galilee. The watchword was: ‹ Everyone that has learned, let him come and teach, and he that has not learned, let him come and learn. ›

At the convention, the sages resolved that no man might escape the duty of supporting his children by shifting the burden to the community. A father had to supervise his children's education, and to bring them up until the age of 12. A man who made over his property to his children in his lifetime as a fiscal relief was entitled to be kept by them (together with his wife) until death. It was agreed, too, that no man should give more than a fifth of his possessions to charity—an attempt to prevent people who expected the coming of the Messiah from giving away everything in the hope of bringing redemption nearer.

The convention and the rules it made were widely publicized and accepted, and long after the delegates were honorably styled « the men of Usha. » Possibly at a later meeting a Sanhedrin was re-established in Usha under the presidency of Shim'on, son of the great patriarch, Gamliel of Yavneh; other members were Rabbi Nathan (of the family of the Babylonian exilarch) who became head of the judicature, and Rabbi Meir, a distinguished pupil of Rabbi Akiva, as *Hacham*. For a while, friction between the three embroiled the court in controversy, but the patriarch emerged triumphant. Thus a national leadership, exercising popular authority, came into existence again—though the Sanhedrin's status as such was not officially recognized until the patriarchate of Yehuda, Shim'on's son. Shim'on's rule was characterized by modesty and pacifism. His skill in winning the allegiance of the rabbis of Galilee confirmed and enlarged the power of the Sanhedrin and encouraged his colleagues to turn their attention to the local seminaries, to attract the people to them, and to teach the Torah openly. In this way the towns and villages of Galilee—which had no scholastic tradition—became centers of biblical study, and gradually their opinions, practices, and interpretations became generally respected.

Rabbi Akiva (right) instructing his pupils—from a 13th-century Spanish *Haggada*. Rabbi Akiva was the greatest scholar of his age, and his support won Bar Kochba wide following. When (in 135 C.E.) the Roman authorities prohibited the study of the Torah, Akiva ignored the decree and continued to preach publicly; he was arrested as a rebel, imprisoned, and executed at Caesarea.

Rabbi Akiva said: 'Jesting and ribaldry lead a man to lewdness. Tradition protects the Torah, tithes protect wealth, vows protect virtue, silence protects wisdom—the Mishna.

Sequestration and Poverty

Even after the worst of the Roman repression was over, everyday life in Palestine continued to show signs of bitterness and unrest. There was still personal suffering. But far more important, the Yishuv's very existence was threatened by its poverty, especially in the countryside, and by the wide-spread sequestration of Jewish estates. Foreign elements swarmed into the towns, restricting all Jewish activity; the rate of emigration, draining the Yishuv's lifeblood, rose alarmingly. The farmers were in particular difficulty because so much land had been devastated by the Roman legions during the fighting and because so much had been confiscated.

Confiscation of the lands of vanquished nations and their transfer to imperial ownership was always the common practice of Rome. The Emperor Vespasian, too, had ordered that ‹ the whole land of the Jews › be transferred to the treasury as the property of Caesar. But in those days the « transfer » had only a legal-fiscal meaning: the former owners of confiscated land remained on their land as tenants and paid a special tax to the treasury. After Beitar the system changed. Owners were evicted wherever possible; lands not reserved for foreign colonists were sold or leased to friends and servitors of the administration. Rabbis and laymen, led by the Jewish courts, refused to acknowledge the new system of ownership or the legality of any « sale » to a third party. The Palestinian Talmud has a vivid passage: ‹ The sons of Esau [the Romans] or their wicked agents would go and take our fields and sell them to others, and then the new landlord would come, bringing havoc with him. ›

It became very clear that if land were not repurchased from the dispossessors it would be alienated for all time, and that continued denial of the rights of third-party ownership would lead to the total landlessness of the Yishuv. So a rule was made recognizing third-party ownership—but only in Judaea: elsewhere the rabbis, accepting the risk, still recognized only the original owners. It was an ambivalent state of affairs—*de facto* ownership and *de jure* ownership, one recognized by Rome, and the other by Jewish law—and it was only resolved in the days of Yehuda Hanassi, when a special tribunal decided that after the sale of a plot of land had been held up for a year because it was owned by a « knifer » (one of the many Jewish epithets for land-grabbers), it could be bought by anybody—provided that the purchaser paid a quarter of the land's value as indemnity to the « legal » owner. The Jewish legislators had one purpose constantly in mind—to sustain the Yishuv. They accepted the new reality clear-sightedly, with the intention of safeguarding what counted most: keeping Jewish soil in Jewish hands.

Jewish farming was intensive. It supported a large and compact population, and though it was wedded to traditional techniques it possessed the characteristic inventiveness of a people that drew its sustenance from the soil. Clearing rocks and undergrowth, improving the soil, manuring, irrigating the land, making and perfecting tools, introducing foreign fruits and vegetables from lands to which they exported other agricultural products—these were the principle features of their economy. Such intensive cultivation demanded the farmer's constant attention: dedication and vigilance were the prerequisite for success.

During the war years, farms had been abandoned and become derelict. The loss was inestimable. When life returned to normal, the ruined holdings could scarcely yield a pittance. Incomes slumped, and in a widespread depression that sometimes forced two or three rabbis to share one cloak, the farmers themselves often starved. The situation was aggravated by the concentration of large estates in the hands of the people to whom the Land had been given over: for not all the sequestrated acres were offered for sale to third parties. A good deal of land was retained. This vast landlordship, condoned by imperial authority, was fatal. The land deteriorated, trees were felled, sheep and goats bred at the expense of farmland.

For three generations, the Yishuv made a concerted effort to overcome the crisis. Rabbis issued rules and gave decisions, preachers encouraged and heartened, the simple peasants sweated and struggled in sacrificial attachment to the soil they loved. It was forbidden, except in Syria and the Palestinian deserts, to breed sheep and goats, although they might occasionally—especially on the eve of festivals—be imported and stall-fed. For the fallow *(shmita)* years, directives were issued to protect fields, vineyards, and orchards. Everyone was urged to fertilize and hoe his own plot, and to live by its yield: ‹ If a man make himself a very serf to the soil, he shall have bread in plenty. If you have worked the soil [so went the sermon praising husbandry] you have truly worked; if you have not worked the soil, you have not worked at all. › Numerous rabbinical pronouncements in Jewish writings like the Mishna and the Talmud, and in sermon after sermon give detailed instruction on the farmer's tasks—plowing and manuring, laying out beds and rows, propagating new varieties of plants, irrigating the trees and fields.

About Jerusalem which is situated among mountains: These mountains have such an abundance of every kind of tree and sweet scented wild grasses and herbs that they can be compared to Mount Ida in Crete, as can their climate and other peculiarities. The earth which is cultivated above the rocks, is cut in steps, which shows the diligence of the Jews of the past in husbanding the earth. . . . The Jews, having such infertile earth, not fit to bear vines and fruits, rendered these hills fertile with great labor, the masonry of which has lasted from the time when the Jews were the absolute rulers of Jerusalem, which shows their great diligence and application and keeps something of its past greatness. . . . The side of the aforesaid mountains which faces East is thick with vines, fruit trees, olive trees, figs and pomegranates—P. Belon, Observees (1553).

A second-century Palestinian glass vessel, in the shape of a bunch of grapes—then one of the country's main agricultural products. Palestine's glass industry was famous throughout the Roman Empire.

Foreign Elements

In the end these measures were successful, and their success undid Rome's plan to erase the name of Israel and turn over the Land to strangers. Jewish land still gave its harvests to its faithful sons. (From these days comes the saying that Israel's enemies derive no benefit from their farming in Palestine.) However, the rising population of foreigners remained a serious concern. Agriculture could be restored by hard work, but this alien intrusion could not be openly resisted or fought, since Rome was behind it. It could be resisted only by constant, cautious, and wise application. It was a long and arduous business, with two salient characteristics: regulations and constraints that made it difficult for strangers to enter the Land, and for those already there, to settle down; and directives and counsel toward amity and understanding between Jews and Gentiles. A Jew, for example, would not let a house or a field to a Gentile, but if he bought a house from a Gentile he could get his written deed of sale even on the Sabbath. Yet there was also a genuine attempt to maintain peaceful relations with the Gentile element. In towns of mixed population, the *parnassim* (the presidents of the Jewish congregations) were directed to collect dues from Jew and Gentile alike, and to give alms to both the Jewish and Gentile poor. The Gentile dead were eulogized and buried and Gentile mourners comforted. Gentile poor were also allowed to gather gleanings from the cornfields.

Many Jews protested that this policy weakened the Yishuv and strengthened the foreigners, who profited both from the power of Rome and from Israel's benefactions. They argued that the more Jewish charity the Gentiles received, the more they multiplied, while Jewry diminished and enjoyed no comfort; that families who taught the Gentiles their crafts were supplanted by their pupils; and that only Jews who did not pass on their skills made a living. These criticisms had little effect, and the sages' policy continued to influence and shape the Yishuv's character.

Stemming Emigration

Yerida—emigration from the Land—was another serious obstacle to recovery, for many Jews were driven from Palestine by the hard conditions that continued to prevail there: the Roman administration was still far from mild; the scholars lived like paupers and the farmers and householders were impoverished too; and, to make matters worse, there was the growing influence of Gentile culture in the Land. Again attempts were made to cure the ill by injunction, preaching, and moralizing: ‹ There is no departing from the Land unless two measures of grain cost a sela ›—that is, unless the price rose astronomically. Rabbi Shim'on Ben Yohai went further: ‹ As long as grain is obtainable, then even if one measure cost a sela, ye shall not depart. › Also: ‹ If a woman intends to go abroad and the husband says « No, » she must stay, and if she insists then she goes without her *ketuba* [marriage contract]; if the husband intends to go and the wife says « No, » he must stay, and if he still insists, he must give her her ketuba. ›

The rabbis taught that the Land is inherited by living in it, and that only therein lay Jewish security: ‹ In your Land ye dwell securely, outside it ye do not dwell securely › . . . ‹ property outside the Land brings no blessings › . . . ‹ Ye shall always dwell in the Land of Israel even though it be in a city where most are Gentiles; ye shall not dwell outside the Land though it be in a city where most are Israelites. › Injunction followed injunction: to abide in Israel was ‹ worth all the other commandments › . . . ‹ all that dwell in Israel are without sin › . . . ‹ all that dwell in Israel and recite the *Shma* [Judaism's confession of faith] at dawn and dusk and speak in the holy tongue are certain of the world to come › . . . ‹ the Land of Israel is holiest of all lands . . . and who dies therein shall be the first to live again in the days of the Messiah. › Some rabbis went so far as to say: ‹ Jews that die abroad have no life hereafter. ›

These exhortations were not without effect. The existence and locality of hundreds of Jewish villages during this period of rehabilitation are recorded in Talmudic literature, in inscriptions on the ruins of ancient synagogues, and in the writings of contemporary Gentiles. Most of the names have been preserved haphazardly, and thus cannot represent the whole of the Yishuv. But they are enough to reveal some main features.

First, the Yishuv dwelt in every zone and area of Palestine: in all the coastal towns—Gaza, Ashkelon, Ashdod, Jaffa, Apollonia, Caesarea, Dor, Haifa, Acre, Achziv, Tyre, and Sidon; in the south and the Negev, in Hebron and its environs, from Beersheba to Etzion Geber and the islet of Yotvata in the Gulf of Eilat; along the shores of the Dead Sea from Jericho to Zoar; in Upper and Lower Galilee, in the Valleys of Jezreel and Beit She'an; even, when the anti-Jewish decrees were revoked and Roman authority slackened, in Judaea and the outskirts of Jerusalem. The only region without any Jewish inhabitants for generations was the ‹ royal mountain, › the western Hills of Judaea, where Gentiles would murder Jews who returned.

Second, the greatest concentration of Jews was in Galilee, including the Valley of Jezreel, the eastern shores of Lake Kinneret (the Sea of Galilee)—the region of Susita—and the Jordan Valley from Tiberias to Beit She'an. Northern Galilee was a solid mass of Jewish settlement, and thousands of Jews from Jerusalem and Judaea fled there after the revolt. The hamlets and towns, particularly Sepphoris and Tiberias, were bustling centers of Jewish life.

Third, not all refugees went north. Many went south, to the settlements in the Negev and Transjordan. True, the Romans saw the advantages of keeping Jewish villages alive on the southwestern shore of the Dead Sea from Ein-Gedi to Ramata, where persimmons grew, just as they valued the Jewish settlers on the Mediterranean coast north of Acre as collectors of murex for dye-stuffs and as artists in glass. But the increased Jewish population in these areas was the result of migration and the help given to newcomers by Jews already settled there.

Where the citizenry was mixed and mostly Gentile (as it was along the coast) the Jews were usually found in tight suburban blocs of habitation. There were such blocs, for example, at Haifa and Acre—where they were economically dependent upon the large Jewish population of Galilee and the Valley of Jezreel—and also at Gaza, Ashkelon, and Caesarea. Each of these Jewish « suburbs » formed a Jewish enclave under the foreign rule of the « sea-cities. » Even in Judaea, where Jewish resettlement was slow and difficult, there was a belt of Jewish localities, the most important of which were Ono, Bnei Brak, Lydda (Lod), and Yavneh.

Fourth, it seems that the Jews were a majority in Galilee and a minority in Judaea and in the self-governing coastal towns (which tried to exclude them). It is not clear whether they formed a majority of the whole population. But it is certain that their numbers were very great and that most of the land was farmed by them. At the end of the third century, rabbis were arguing whether Jews owned the bulk of the land; at any rate the evidence shows that in addition to their own land, the Jews also farmed a good part of the state-owned land and Gentile property.

The Yishuv, now large, concentrated, settled, well-organized, and living on (and off) its own land, exercised an important political influence during the reign of the house of Severus. Its importance was particularly marked when Pescennius Niger and Septimius Severus were rivals for succession in Rome at the end of the second century. Their vital battles were fought in Syria and Palestine. Niger, Proconsul in Syria, had been proclaimed emperor in a temple built by the Syrian king, Antiochus Epiphanes, in Antioch—which perhaps explains why the Palestinian Jews preferred Septimius. Most of them supported him, even fought for him, in what was the Yishuv's first bid to earn Roman goodwill since the Bar Kochba revolt, 60 years earlier. Even when Persian Jewry fiercely held off the legions of Septimius in the Parthian War—a victorious campaign that the Senate proclaimed a triumph—their action did not lessen the standing of the Yishuv.

176

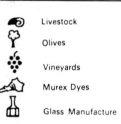

Livestock

Olives

Vineyards

Murex Dyes

Glass Manufacture

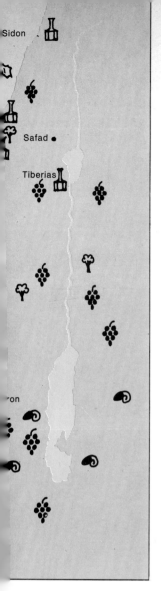

Above, the tombs of famous rabbis in the Galilean town of Safad. In the Roman period, Galilee had the largest Jewish population in Palestine, and its numbers were constantly swollen by devout Jews who came to die in the Holy Land. Left, *Murex brandaris*, the shell-fish gathered by inhabitants of northern Palestine for the extraction of precious Tyrian purple dye.

Once in power, the Severi followed a new policy toward the Jews. No doubt this was partly in return for Jewish support (under the patriarchs of the house of Hillel) in their long struggle for power; but whatever the reason, the Severi's general policy tended to strengthen the eastern provinces and to honor their ancient civilizations. Contemporary statutes provide evidence of Rome's new, more liberal outlook. A law made by Septimius Severus and his son Antoninus (Caracalla) typifies the change. It permitted Jews to hold high office and to undertake the obligations of office: this meant that local government was reestablished, and that Jews could be town mayors, tax collectors, and judges of civil cases. (All this had been denied to them since the anti-Jewish decrees, and even when these were anulled, Jewish courts of law were in fact illegal, though the government took no steps against them.) It is true that an ordinance of Septimius condemns « judaizing, » and fixes a heavy penalty for proselytes and proselytizers, but it must not be inferred from this that his reign was hostile to the Jews as such. The ordinance was drawn up in 202 C.E., during the emperor's second visit to the Middle East: it signifies only that he had observed the extent of conversionist activity, and decided to proceed against it and its agents.

177

There were probably other statutes of the house of Severus in favor of the Jews. A biographer records that Alexander Severus (222–235 C.E.) safeguarded the privileges of the Jews. The elevation in status of the patriarch was apparently the direct act of the Caesar. At this time the patriarch was officially recognized as the head and spokesman of the Yishuv, and his family given the leasehold of spacious estates in Judaea and northern Transjordan. In a letter of Origen, a Father of the Church, patriarchal authority is defined in terms that indicate how strongly national leadership had become inherent in it. The patriarch is ‹ empowered as by consent of Caesar, › so much so that ‹ there is hardly any difference from him who used to reign over the people ›; and there is mention of judgment according to the Torah—even the death sentence—being passed by the patriarch, ‹ not without the emperor's knowledge. › This situation is also reflected in Jewish writings, which offer a good deal of evidence to show that Jewish courts enjoyed official recognition and that their verdicts were, in fact, carried out by the government authorities. These writings also point to a rise in the status of the patriarchate in the days of Rabbi Yehuda. Jewish preachers saw him as the Yishuv's appointed savior in Roman times, ‹ as were Shim'on the Righteous and Mattathias, son of Yohanan, in Greek times. ›

As head of the people and supreme judge, the patriarch possessed certain powers in matters of local taxation, and local administrative procedures apparently extended those powers. Under Yehuda, the patriarchy developed into an all-powerful institution. The patriarch and his court ordained rabbis, enacted legislation, and laid down regulations. There was a council chamber, where dayanim debated *halacha* (the legal part of talmudic literature), arguing and proving, clarifying and correcting; the *yeshiva* (theological seminary), where scholars and students discussed and interpreted the law, analyzed every suit, took part in public debates, and passed on ‹ the words of the scribes ›; and there was the college, where the people gathered to hear the rabbis lecture, interpret the Torah, and comment on everyday affairs. All three institutions were ancient, but now, under the patriarchate of Rabbi Yehuda, in Beit She'arim and Sepphoris and later in Tiberias they formed the central Jewish self-governing authority.

The oral law—the part of Jewish lore that explains and supplements the written law of the Torah—was codified and collected into one work, the *Mishna*, in about 200 C.E. (as explained on page 179). The Mishna itself became subject to interpretations and discussions, and these additions were collected together to form the *Talmud*. There are two compilations: the Jerusalem Talmud (written in Palestine in c. 400 C.E.) and the Babylonian Talmud (written in Mesopotamia in c. 500 C.E.). The latter is now the sole authoritative work, and it is to it that the term Talmud strictly applies. A page of the Talmud is shown, left: in the central column is a section of the Mishna (shaded) and the discussion and elucidation of that section the *Gmara;* around this column are commentaries and notes on the Gmara that were written in later periods.

The patriarch presided over the Sanhedrin, which was made up of his fellow judges, the « elders » nominated by him and his advisors from members of the council-chamber, the rabbis, and the college. As president he determined the times of feasts and festivals, acted as link between Palestine and the Diaspora, appointed town scribes and teachers, and commissioned inspectors of general education and Bible study. The patriarchate and its offices—which were extended and consolidated by Yehuda Hanassi, and further embellished and developed by his grandson, Yehuda II—endured for 250 years, until 425 C.E.; they formed the Yishuv into an independent national-religious entity, unique in the Roman Empire.

Yehuda Hanassi was the only patriarch to have unchallenged authority over all the self-governing organs of the Yishuv: he was patriarch and head of the courts, chairman of the council, principal of the yeshiva, chancellor of the college. The numerous legends about his noble character and vast scholarship, about his mastery of the Torah and majestic personality, testify to the great authority he wielded in his own time and the continuing influence of that authority in later generations. It was this authority that enabled him to carry out the historical cultural project that was to have such a tremendous impact: the compilation of the Mishna.

The Mishna

Within the scope of a single work Yehuda Hanassi reassembled all the varied traditions of halacha—as taught orally in the colleges and theological seminaries and as written down in « secret » manuscripts. The Mishna is divided into six orders, or *sedarim: Zeraim* (seeds) is concerned mainly with the religious laws pertaining to farming; *Mo'ed* (seasons) deals with laws for the Sabbath, festivals, and fasts; *Nashim* (women) with laws of the family; *Nezikin* (damages) with civil and criminal legislation; *Kodashim* (holy things) with the laws regulating ritual slaughter, sacrifices, and consecrated objects; *Tohorot* with the laws of ceremonial purity. Each of these orders is broken down into tractates, of which there are 63 in all; each tractate is divided into chapters (523 in all), each chapter into passages, or *Mishnayot*.

It is impossible to overrate the historical significance of this authoritative codification of the oral law, written in the precise Hebrew style of « the Language of the Sages, »

EXCERPTS FROM THE MISHNA

Rabbi Hanina Ben Dosa used to say: 'When one's deeds are even greater than one's knowledge, the knowledge is effective; but when one's knowledge is greater than one's deeds, the knowledge is futile.'

Ben Zoma said: 'Who is wise? He who can learn from every man. Who is strong? He who can control his passions. Who is rich? He who can feel satisfied with his lot. Who is honored? He who honors mankind.'

Rabbi [Yehuda Hanassi] said: 'Don't look at the pitcher but at what it contains. Sometimes a new pitcher is full of old wine, and an old pitcher is empty even of new wine.'

EXCERPTS FROM THE TALMUD

Why was man created on the sixth day? To teach that if he is ever swollen with pride, it can be said to him: a flea came ahead of thee in creation.

Rabbi Hanina Ben Hama said: 'Everything is in the power of Heaven except the fear of Heaven. God in His providence determines beforehand what a man shall be and what shall befall him, but not whether he shall be righteous or wicked.'

The story is told that a heathen came to Shammai with the request to be accepted as a convert on condition that he was taught the whole of the Torah while he stood on one foot. The Rabbi drove him away with the yardstick which he was holding. He then went to Hillel with the same request; and he said to him: 'What is hateful to yourself, do not to your fellow man. That is the whole of the Torah and the remainder is but commentary. Go, learn it.'

as it had been handed down over the centuries. It became the basis of all Jewish religious and civil law, and its meanings and applications were discussed endlessly in seminaries throughout Palestine and the Diaspora. It shaped every aspect of Jewish life and became the all-embracing textbook, though teachers added explanations and comparisons and there were many disputes over its interpretation: for different circumstances of time and locality demanded different interpretations.

The Mishna was more than a compendium of ancient scholarly testaments; it was a signpost to juridical and civic unity, to a uniformity in manners and faith for Jews throughout the world. And from it there evolved another important Jewish work, the Talmud—in essence an interpretation and amplification of the Mishna. Yehuda's personal authority and that of his many students from the Diaspora—particularly from Mesopotamia—who came to study at his yeshiva, gave the Mishna an unshakable religious authority. Furthermore it did a great deal to strengthen the bonds between the Diaspora and Palestine. Because of it, the Diaspora came more and more to accept the teachings and rulings of the Yishuv.

Between the death of Alexander Severus (235), and the establishment of Christian Byzantium (330), the Yishuv, together with all other imperial provinces, declined rapidly—a direct consequence of a crisis within the Roman Empire. The crisis had really resulted from the shifting of all responsibility for sustaining the empire, with its administrative complexity and growing social unrest, from Rome to the provinces. Rome recruited troops from each province for its defense and the defense of its neighbors, and the local inhabitants had to lodge and feed them and to underwrite the often extravagant budgets of local Roman officials by raising additional taxes. Previously the emperors had maintained good relations with the cities, which were the mainstay of provincial authority and communally responsible for collecting taxes. But the citizens could no longer shoulder the heavy liabilities that were being foisted on them. And as they fell ever deeper into debt, more and more municipal control was taken over by Roman officials. Many of the landowners (newcomers and natives) who really belonged to a privileged class, managed to avoid being « affiliated » to the debtor cities: they paid their taxes directly to the authorities, which meant that they escaped liability for any but their own assessments. At the same time many villagers, exhausted by the burdens of mobilization and its dues (exemption from the army had to be bought), began to leave their lands.

Sometimes Rome did try to give the provinces a larger share of political responsibility; an edict of Caracalla (212), for example, granted Roman citizenship to every freeman in the empire. Attempts were made to build up a provincial army but this only encouraged nationalist desires to establish independent principalities. And to make matters worse, the legions and their commanders—the real rulers of the provinces—usurped the right to appoint and dismiss Caesars: in one province after another, they would proclaim this or that general emperor; in one after another, they would discard him.

The decline was swift. Security deteriorated, desolation and neglect were widespread; there was constant insurrection, open or underground. Though the Yishuv was not singled out for exceptional treatment, it still suffered more than other colonies since—in the bitter war that raged between Sassanid Persia and Rome—Palestine became a Roman military base. Disciplinary squads pursued tax defaulters and deserters throughout the country, and the leaders of the Jewish congregations were constantly forced to buy them off. There was, it seemed, ‹ neither judge nor justice › in the Land.

True, during the Severan era new towns were built in Palestine, the Jewish element in these mixed towns became larger, and Jews began to take part in municipal

A fourth-century sardonyx cameo commemorating the capture of the Roman Emperor Valerian by Shapur I of Sassanid Persia in 260 C.E.: Valerian spent the remainder of his life as Shapur's prisoner. The war that raged between Persia and the Roman Empire in the third century, and the instability of the Roman regime, impoverished Palestine and brought misery to its inhabitants.

management. True, relations between Jew and Gentile improved, and there was even some adoption of the Greek language. But the paralyzing indebtedness of the towns and their councils to the imperial exchequer together with the arbitrariness of local overlords (who changed continually as governors were made or unmade and consequently sought to grasp ever larger revenues in ever briefer spells of authority) eventually broke even the affluent, who had to pledge their assets for the whole body of taxpayers and to clear municipal debts as well. Naturally, these affluent few tried—sometimes successfully—to evade the burdens of municipal leadership and (in a contemporary phrase) ‹ would smuggle themselves out of imperial control, › either by leaving or by disassociating themselves from the town and its commitments. As a result the villages, already in desperate straits, were placed more and more at the mercy of a capricious and exacting soldiery that did not even respect the patriarch: he could not journey to the proconsul—which he did with a military escort—and be certain, under its « protection, » of returning whole in purse or limb. So, throughout the empire, populations shrank and settlements disintegrated. In Palestine, there was a special historical significance to the process of decline. It was on the edge of the desert, and for centuries nomadic desert tribes had been striving to gain a foothold on its farmlands; already in this period they had managed to penetrate the south and east—to such an extent that Jews referred ironically to the desert as ‹ the insolent land that gave us of its fruits in plenty. › This nomadic infiltration was encouraged by the nationalist tendencies of some of the legions to proclaim as emperor the natives of provinces whose immigrants already lived in and around Palestine: thus the legions proclaimed Philippus (Philip the Arab), a native of Bostra, in southeast Syria, and also Septimius Odainath (Odaenathus) of Tadmor (Palmyra).

The necropolis of Beit She'arim: left, the entrance to one of the inner burial chambers, flanked by a carving of a *menora*; right, a burial chamber, showing the niches where bodies were interred. Beit She'arim, on the Haifa-Nazareth road overlooking the Jezreel Valley, was made the seat of the *Sanhedrin* at the end of the second century C.E. by Yehuda Hanassi. When this celebrated patriarch died and was buried there, it became the principal burial place for leading rabbis and Jewish notables from both Palestine and the Diaspora. The town of Beit She'arim was destroyed by the Romans in the middle of the fourth century, and the cemetery abandoned. Excavations since 1936 have revealed, in addition to the ruins of a prosperous town, an extensive necropolis; and so far 26 catacombs have been unearthed there. Each catacomb is approached by a courtyard cut out of the side of the hill and entered through openings covered by carved stone doors (many of which still turn easily on finely cut stone hinges). The doors lead to long halls, and it is from these that the burial chambers proper open out. The catacombs are profusely decorated with reliefs, engravings, and paintings, showing not only traditional Jewish motifs—like the menora, the Ark, the ram's horn, and so on—but also Roman subjects. There are ornamental carvings of garlands, eagles, and bulls' heads; and, surprisingly, portrayals of human figures and even subjects taken from Greek mythology. These decorations, and the many inscriptions—mostly in Greek, but also in Hebrew and Aramaic—are important sources on the social history of the period.

The rabbis regarded immigration to Palestine and settlement there as being of the highest religious value. But while it is true that many scholars did come to settle there and that their teachings were respected and their influence on the Diaspora was great, many others emigrated to Mesopotamia and elsewhere. Nevertheless, belief in Palestine's sanctity grew, and the remains of many Jews who had died abroad were reinterred there. Beit-She'arim, burial place of the Patriarchs, became a central cemetery for the rich and great of the Diaspora, and many epitaphs there and in other places show how widespread the practice of re-interrment was. After watching a caravan of coffins from overseas, one rabbi was moved to quote the phrase, ‹ And ye shall come and pollute my land ›—a typical attack on Jews who lived abroad throughout their lives and returned only in their shrouds.

Diocletian's Reforms

The reforms of Diocletian, who became emperor in 284, greatly reduced the rivalry between contending commanders and the arbitrary treatment of the subjected peoples by the soldiery. Diocletian strengthened the authority of the central government and improved administration in the provinces—but even so he could not halt the process of decline. The new emperor respected the Jewish faith, and his personal attitude toward the Yishuv was apparently fair. Under his new territorial organization the Sinai peninsula and the Negev, each with a sizeable Jewish community, were annexed to Palestine. A tiny Jewish congregation, the « holy congregation, » was

allowed to worship in Jerusalem, and the belief grew that the divine presence had not departed from the Western (or «Wailing») Wall—thought to be the original western wall of Herod's temple. Once again pilgrims were drawn to the city. But these concessions did little to ease the social conditions of the Jews or make the structure of servitude less rigid: the official was still the slave of his position, the artisan of his craft, the farmer of his soil, the citizen of his class and duty. Caste and class were still sharply emphasized, and the growing social divisions were a feature of this period of decline. ‹ Whoever visits your house, › ran the adage, ‹ comes to steal your field. › Jews pitied and comforted themselves: ‹The almighty will restore the dwellings of the righteous ›—an optimistic reaction to the existing situation of houses destroyed or fallen to ruin. And who were the ‹ righteous ›? Simply, men who did not steal—for under the pressure of anarchy and want many did. In plays and mimes, neighboring peoples mocked the Yishuv's poverty.

Commandments and precepts of good farming were neglected, and the once strictly enforced fallow year was disregarded. The rich were loath to pay tithes and contributions to the synagogues, despite threats and appeals by the rabbis, who preached in vain the virtues of charity. The rabbis condemned theft and extortion of the poor, and argued that charity matched all commandments and surpassed all sacrifices, entitling even the wicked to greet the divine presence. But their exhortations were of little avail. The gap between a hungry proletariat and the wealthy few who

183

The stone "Cathedra [chair] of Moses" from the third-century synagogue at Korazim, in Galilee. Chairs of this kind were installed in ancient synagogues for the principal teacher of the law, or for a person the community wished to honor.

somehow managed to cling to their wealth and status, sharpened and deepened class distinctions. Among both rabbis and laymen the patriarchate lost much of its prestige. It was called a « pinchbeck government, » accused of favoring only the « aristocrats » and of appointing them, and their kinsfolk, as judges and parnassim—to such an extent that the households of the judges were labeled a « dynasty of governors. » Since parnassim handed their office on from father to son, a hereditary aristocracy came into existence: ‹ A family of scribes puts forth scribes, a family of scholars puts forth scholars, and the rich put forth the rich. ›

Growing opposition to the patriarch came from the rabbis (increasing in number and reputation as students passed out of the great seminaries of Sepphoris, Tiberias, Lydda, and Caesarea), the erudite members of the Sanhedrin, the principals of colleges, and the leaders of the council chambers and academies—all people of considerable standing, who demanded recognition of their rights, their status as scholars, and the importance of their place in the community. Tiberias was a conspicuous example: since the time of Rabbi Yohanan Bar-Nafha, a great scholar and the town's chief spokesman, the Tiberias yeshiva had molded the spiritual shape of the Yishuv. Yohanan never tired of praising scholars. ‹ They are builders, › he would say, ‹ because all their lives they are busy building the world, › and he held that only they should be parnassim. If scholars are preoccupied with ‹ heavenly things, › he argued, ‹ surely the townsfolk are bidden to do their work for them. › In general, it was accepted that scholars were excused impressment—the practice of exempting them from taxation was introduced in the days of Yehuda Hanassi and had continued ever since. Nevertheless, the rabbis were discontented with the way the patriarch appointed ignorant judges and then forced the real scholars to teach them law. They also complained that he did not give enough assistance to those scholars who studied for the sake of scholarship rather than to gain a living. The general state of decline and impoverishment forced the patriarchs to resort more and more to bribing the ever-changing administration, and to ally themselves with the moneyed class. They resisted attempts of the rabbis to set up an independent judiciary—independent, that is, of the patriarch and his well-to-do friends. When news of the clash reached Diocletian, he immediately disavowed the separatist courts, and reaffirmed the rights of the patriarch.

The double conflict—between the patriarch's aristocratic and wealthy urban party and the rabbis, and between these two privileged parties and the oppressed populace made for turbulence and ferment in the Yishuv throughout the reigns of Diocletian and Constantine. Then came the rule of Christian Byzantium.

Opposition to the Patriarchate

184

The Rule of Christian Byzantium

CONSTANTINE (a convert to Christianity) was the first Christian emperor to rule the Holy Land. His reign was marked by anti-Jewish decrees, by an intensive program of church-building, by assiduous protection of Christian holy places and the enforcement of the « colonate »—that made tenants slaves to the soil they tilled. The new elements in the decrees were the religious overtones and the spirit of hatred of both Jews and Judaism. They made it clear that from then on religious and church considerations would guide the imperial attitude to the Jews even more than political considerations. This meant that the Yishuv would fall victim to the Church's doctrine on Judaism and its policy of mass proselytization.

And, indeed, in the first 20 years of Byzantine rule, the decrees of the Christian emperors and the conduct of the administration showed clearly the influence of Church doctrine. The Jews were not a nation but only a sect, ‹ an unclean and pernicious sect ›; their members were ‹ impure beings, › ‹ creatures without law, › ‹ vile men of abomination ›; and their religious assemblies were gatherings of the sacrilegious. If a Jew married or converted a Christian woman, if he converted a slave or maltreated Jewish apostates, he was put to death: if he circumcised a slave, the slave was given his freedom. And eventually, Jews were forbidden to keep slaves altogether. The ban on Jews dwelling in Jerusalem was reimposed, and its small congregation dispelled. To emphasise the expulsion, Jews were allowed to visit Jerusalem on the ninth of the Hebrew month of Av (the anniversary of the Temple's destruction) to weep in its ruins.

The "Wailing Wall," the supposed western wall of Herod's Temple in Jerusalem—a picture painted in Jerusalem (in 1922) by the British artist Isaac Snowman. Except while the Old City was in Jordanian hands (1948-67) the wall has been the principal place of Jewish pilgrimage.

The emperor, his family, and his courtiers competed in their zeal to multiply Christian edifices, showing that their aim was not simply to convert the Jews, but to remove all vestiges of Judaism and make Palestine an entirely Christian country. To the Christian administration, Palestine was not merely a small province, differing from the others only in its bitter hatred of Rome and its refusal to submit to foreign authority: it was a Holy Land, and its rocks and stones, its air and waters, its heaven and earth were charged with the Redeemer's presence. The Church's failure to convert the Yishuv *en masse* made it all the more determined to Christianize the Land: to the Church Fathers, a Palestine where Jews dwelt and kept the Holy Scriptures, where Jews frequently taught Christian pilgrims, monks, and scholars from these writings and even served as their guides to the Holy Land, was a denial of Christian victory. The Jews had their synagogues, colleges, and sages not only in Sepphoris and Tiberias but also in Nazareth and Capernaum, Migdal and Kfar Kana, and in all the Holy places; they continued to live there and to deny the holiness of Christian shrines, even when pointing out to pilgrims the precise place in the synagogue where the young Jesus had sat and studied. The administration, therefore, built churches throughout Galilee (even in places where the population was entirely Jewish) subsidized the construction of monasteries, reinforced Christian settlements, and strove to limit the number of Jewish settlements by all possible means.

The colonate law, which forebade tenants to leave their land, was imposed in Palestine in 388. (This law had been enacted in the empire in 332, but Palestine was one of the countries where its enforcement had been delayed). The law, designed to protect state revenues, meant the enslavement of the greater part of the Jewish rural population, which was mostly a population of tenants. But neither this, nor any other of the empire's strictures could force the Yishuv to submit to the new faith. The numerous and persistent efforts of the Church to win over the Jews in their masses failed, despite the active help of the emperors and the local administrations. The Church leaders were sadly disillusioned. They had thought their task of conversion would be easy. Now they realized they could not overcome the stubborn refusal of the Jews to become apostates. For the Jews, the edicts of Christian Byzantium were only a passing evil. A blasphemous government could not confound them. After all, the sages of a former generation had foreseen that: ‹ The son of David shall not come until all the kingdom has become blasphemous . . . when the days of the Messiah are nigh, the whole kingdom shall pass into blasphemy. ›
For this reason, the Jews believed that redemption was near, and they continued to preach their religion. God had warned Israel: ‹ If ye shall not tell of my divinity to the people of the world, then I shall deal harshly with you; › and ‹ the Almighty gave the Torah to Israel so that all the nations might enjoy it. › The Jews believed that they had suffered in the past because of their own sins and blasphemies, and thay they could now atone for these by dying for their faith, and by defying their tyrannical overlords. The Jews would not be aroused by the Christian world that called to Israel: ‹ How long will ye die for your God? Come to us and we shall make you dukes, premiers, and generals. › They remained faithful to their God. The failure of Christian proselytism among the Jews was certain; it was even predictable, considering the age-long Jewish ostracism of « blasphemers, » and the degeneration of the original groups of Christianized Jews in Palestine. Nevertheless, both government and Church were amazed at their failure to Christianize the land. Despite all their efforts there were comparatively few Christians in Palestine, according to Christian sources at the beginning of the fifth century: the Jews and Samaritans were in the majority, and in fact made life difficult for the Christian converts. Admittedly, it is known that in the fourth century there were 25 Christian congregations, but they were small and almost all in the coastal towns, or in Judaean towns

THE BYZANTINE EMPIRE 450 C.E

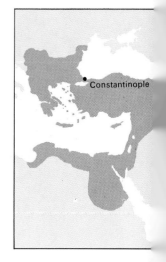
Constantinople

that already had sizeable non-Jewish populations. There was not a single congregation in any region of close Jewish settlement—not even in places associated with Christian tradition, such as Lower Galilee and Nazareth.

The central government had to accept the fact of its failure, for it was unwilling to embark on a tough campaign against the stubborn and unyielding Jews at a time when war with the new Persian Empire was a constant feature. Already, in the reign of Constantine, the Jews had risen up against mass conversion, and a report by one of the Church fathers speaks of the harsh punishment inflicted upon them. But it seems to have had little effect, for there was a similar rising—about which we have more details—under his son Constantius in 351, when Roman forces were assembling in Syria to attack Persia, and relations between the Yishuv and the government and also with the soldiery were very strained.

Jewish Rising

The rising itself was sparked by a specific incident. A converted Jew, once a member of the patriarch's entourage, had been given a charter by the emperor to ‹ construct churches in Jewish towns and villages, › in places where ‹ none had hitherto been built because neither pagan nor Samaritan nor Christian lived there. › The proselyte was given high rank and a special appointment, and the local councils were ordered to finance his building projects out of imperial funds. He was instructed to begin erecting churches in Tiberias, Sepphoris, Nazareth, and Capernaum. This so enraged the Jews that they fell upon the builders, most of them converts, and stoned them as idolaters. The emperor immediately sent in more legions and ordered that rioters be burned to death.

A deputation of rabbis approached the regional military commander, who is said to have received them sympathetically, but fragmentary accounts of military demands in Sepphoris show that the situation had worsened. The army insisted, for example, that bread be baked on the Passover, and work be done on Sabbath and festivals, even on the Day of Atonement. Since acquiescence meant betrayal of the Torah and the fundamental tenets of Judaism, most Jews felt compelled to disobey these demands. The results were inevitable. Resentment soon exploded into open rebellion, the Jews hoping they could count on Persia as an ally, and encouraged by their faith in the imminence of Messianic redemption.

According to Roman historians, the Jews of Sepphoris launched a surprise attack on the legionaries by night, routed them, and then chose themselves one Patricus as king. The rising soon spread to Tiberias and Lydda (Lod), which both had large Jewish populations, and many Romans, Greeks, and Samaritans were killed. Eventually, Gallus, eastern commander of the Roman army, sent in reinforcements from Antioch and after bitter fighting the legions regained command. Sepphoris was burned down, and all its inhabitants condemned to death. (Those who escaped were forced to live in nearby caves for many years). Lydda and several other Jewish towns were also burned down.

After 354, when Gallus was executed by imperial command, the situation improved somewhat: Sepphoris, Tiberias, and Lydda were rebuilt, and the other Jewish towns of Palestine—which had taken no part in the uprising and been spared Roman reprisal—could breathe more freely.

Julian the Apostate

In 361, Julian the Apostate (Flavius Claudius Julianus), nephew of Constantine, became emperor. He made no secret of his contempt for the alliance his two predecessors had made with the Church. He was an intellectual: learned, perceptive, and wise—and a violent critic of Christianity. Loathing the organized Church, he set his heart on reviving paganism in the empire, but also resolved to allow every nation and country to live by its ancestral laws and to worship according to its own rites and rituals.

Above, Julian the Apostate, emperor of Rome from 361-363 C.E.—a contemporary gold coin. Left, a woodcut from a book of *minhagim* or customs (Amsterdam, 1823) depicts the blowing of the *shofar*, the ram's horn that was blown in synagogues all over the world in celebration of Julian's reforms: normally the shofar is blown only during the month of *Elul*, on the New Year, and at the close of the Day of Atonement.

Restoration of Jerusalem

Julian reigned for only 20 months. In that time he proved himself to be a wise, energetic, and humane ruler, flexible in his planning and execution. His aim was to atone for the errors of the past imperial policy and to restore the glory of Rome. And an organic part of this general policy was his desire to right the wrongs that Rome, pagan and Christian, had done Jewry. After lengthy discussions with leaders of the Jewish community, Julian decided to restore Jerusalem to its owners and reestablish it as a Jewish city, to expel the usurping Christians (who had not only taken the place of the Jews, but had denied them the right to return), to rebuild the Temple, and to give fresh sanction to traditional Jewish law.

In one imperial decree, Julian called on the Jews to return to their homeland and govern it again in the manner of their forefathers. In a second, he announced the abolition of a long list of taxes that had been prepared for imposition on the Jews, declaring that he would end their oppression at the hands of ‹ the barbaric of spirit and presumptuous of heart, › the favorites of Constantius. Furthermore, he advised the brethren of the noble patriarch to abolish the communal envoy tax, and to refrain from oppressing the people with taxes. He added that after victory in the Persian War, he would rebuild the Holy City of Jerusalem, which ‹ you have been yearning so long to see rebuilt, and I will come with you to do homage to the Omnipotent One. › Julian's decrees were phrased (no doubt deliberately) in the biblical style of Cyrus' historic proclamation (see page 111). Both these and his discussions with prominent Jews impressed the Yishuv profoundly, and rabbis began to believe that—if not full redemption—at least days of peace and salvation had come at last. Contemporary Christian writers record the tremendous excitement that stirred the Jewish communities in Palestine and the Diaspora; the wild enthusiasm, the blowing of the *shofar* (the ram's horn, normally blown in synagogues only on the New Year and the Day of Atonement), the collection of great sums of money for aliya and reconstruction, the wide-spread belief that the age of prophecy had returned, that Israel had been reborn.

Julian's Death

In some circles there was hesitation, as fragments of rabbinical disputations reveal: ‹ just as Israel was banished by the utter despot, so it will be saved only by the perfect Redeemer. › But Julian was seen as ‹ defender of Israel, › and because of this ‹ he is elevated by the Lord. › Some rabbis argued that redemption would come by degrees: that Israel was greatly troubled, and that if redemption came at once, the relief would be beyond human bearing. Others argued that the Temple would not be rebuilt after Israel's rebirth, but before it: ‹ until the Temple has risen again, the royal house of David cannot be re-enthroned. › This general mood of optimism was felt and shared by all the Jews of the Diaspora, notably those nearest to Palestine—in Syria and Asia Minor, for example.

The emperor, faithful to his design, appointed a close friend (a former proconsul in Britain) to supervise the rebuilding of Jewish Jerusalem; and he ordered the authorities in Palestine to help him. Jews entered Jerusalem once again, and opened a synagogue near the Temple mount. But progress was not as swift as the emperor anticipated, and some historians claim that Julian's advisors were less enthusiastic about the project than he. Christian writings tell of columns of fire rising from the foundations, scorching the laborers and hindering work. Apparently cooperation between the emperor's agents and the Jews was not close; and there is evidence in later Christian writings that the delays were due to Christian influence.

The rebuilding of the Temple was halted by the death of Julian in 363. His death struck a grievous blow to the Jewish community, but seemed to justify the skepticism of the many rabbis who, as we saw, had always doubted that Roman hands would usher in redemption.

Renewed Oppression

After Julian's death, Rome's policy toward the Yishuv changed radically. The most significant event was the reintroduction, toward the end of the fourth century C.E., of the colonate law. Throughout the empire, it was Roman practice to concentrate large estates in the hands of single owners, and local circumstances in Palestine—particularly the recurrent insurrection that led to the confiscation of large areas of Jewish land—prompted and even hastened the process. Ever since the second century C.E. (when Antoninus Pius ruled) and especially in Severan times, Rome had shown itself anxious to reduce the area of friction between its administration and Palestine's rebellious Jewish population, and had initiated a system of long-term tenancy: this was also designed to ensure regular tax payment, since taxes were collected from the landowners. Many farmers welcomed the system, preferring the sure relationship of tenant and landlord to the status of « independent citizen, » which placed them at the mercy of officials and tax collectors. As a result it became quite common for landlords to sell their fields to become tenants.

The mechanics of the system were quite simple. The proprietors, Jews and Gentiles, would hand over their land to lessees, against payment of an annual sum (pre-determined according to area and soil and irrespective of yield) and to tenants, who would pay the landlord, or in most cases the landlord's head lessee, part of the annual yield, usually a third. The landlord, or the head lessee, was liable for his tenants' taxes, and the authorities would deduct this from the crop paid to him by his tenants. As a rule, tenancy lasted for two or three years, though it could last for a lifetime; in some cases the tenancy could even be inherited. Many of the tenants were poor, and on occasions had to join the beggars who went from field to field searching for ungleaned wheat. However, the landlord had no personal rights over the tenant. The tenant was a free man and could leave his land whenever he liked—and could even, occasionally, claim compensation for any improvements he had personally made to the land.

So the Jewish farmers had held grimly to the soil and to their freedom. Indeed, their system of tenantry suited the imperial tax collectors, and must have made the

Roman authorities hesitate to impose the colonate law upon Palestine. But it was the very freedom of this tenant status among Jewish farmers in Palestine that now led to its enforcement. The new law altered the status of the tenant fundamentally: there was to be no distinction of tenancy, all tenants were to become servitors with no personal freedom, all were to be placed in perpetual bondage to the tenanted land and to its owner. (Owners might even employ tenants as personal servants.) There was little difference between this tenancy and serfdom: tenants could be transferred to a different owner together with the land they farmed. Many Jewish tenants came to serve Gentile masters, and there is evidence of their interminable conflict.

As a result of the colonate law more and more Jews gave up farming. Though this process of a declining agriculture was common throughout the empire, it had particular affect in Palestine, weakening, as it did, the Jews' footing in their own country. The Romans argued that the law did no more than bring Palestine into line with the rest of the empire. It is true that at the time there were rebellions and uprisings throughout the empire of serfs and slaves who flocked to join subversive sects, advocating—directly or indirectly—emancipation and equality; and the government felt it absolutely necessary to block every breach in the structure of serfdom. But there was a second, hidden motive: the Jewish tenants could not be allowed to enjoy a status superior to that of Christian tenants elsewhere in the empire. The Church fathers had done everything in their power to introduce anti-Jewish discrimination into imperial legislation; yet here were Jewish tenants enjoying discrimination in their favor: for most of the tenant farmers in Palestine were both Jewish and freemen. This situation would not be tolerated. They had to be made equal with the others. And such « equality » would bring about « degradation. »

The militant anti-Jewish policy crystallized and became fully articulate during the first half of the fifth century. It comprised many different elements: literary polemics by the scholars and sages of the Church, unceasing political pressure by the Church's leaders, unrestrained incitement by its preachers and monks, assaults and riots by inflamed mobs. Synagogues were burned and looted, Jewish houses were destroyed and Jewish property plundered. There was extensive and detailed legislation, designed to serve three purposes: to maintain law and order; to give form to the passions of the populace; to render political assistance to the Church leaders. Though this policy was common throughout the empire, its enforcement in Palestine—the home of thousands of Jews and the center of Judaism—created a battlefront in the cruel war declared on the Jewish faith by the Church when it won control of the empire. The Church sent its greatest scholars, writers, and monks to Palestine, many of whom had studied Hebrew and biblical interpretation with Jewish sages. There were also many intensely fanatical monks, some gathered in monasteries—built at holy places associated with the history of Christianity—others living as hermits in remote and isolated huts in the deserts of Palestine and its neighboring countries. And there were numerous pilgrims, who came from all the Christian countries to search for holy relics or other vestiges of ancient holiness.

The Christian scholars produced argument after argument to prove the manifold errors of the Jews, whom they termed heretics. They declared that the Jews' plight after the destruction of the Temple was absolute proof of this heresy—their freedom lost, their sanctuary in ruins, their revolts crushed. And they pointed to the widespread religious persecution that the Jews had suffered at the hands of the Christians whose influence and power grew from day to day. The Christian scholars held that refusal to acknowledge the truth of Christianity after its great triumph was sheer obstinacy, while their leaders felt duty-bound to demonstrate the truth of their declarations by increasing attacks on ‹ these wretched Jews that deserve no mercy. ›

A sixth-century silver plaque shows St. Simeon Stylites, the first Christian "pillar saint." St. Simeon (who lived in the third century) spent most of his life on a 60 ft. pillar in the Syrian desert so as to withdraw from the sinful life of the world. Here, he resists the temptations of the snake, the symbol of evil.

Looting of Synagogues The principal agents of the Church's attack were the monks: they were its army, men for whom war upon the enemies of the Christian creed was a sacrament, a holy life's work. But there was also the rabble, who ransacked synagogues, had them consecrated, and then handed them over to the Church. Such rioters were said to be doing good deeds and promise of the hereafter (as well as the promise of material gains in this world) made Palestine all the more attractive for a certain type of pilgrim. From time to time, the emperors did issue decrees against attacks on synagogues: ‹ The Jewish religion, › they stated, ‹ is not forbidden in the empire; › they declared that the noble patriarch's dignity was to be protected, and one order exempted ‹ the patriarchs, the heads of the Jewish Assembly and the elders › from paying certain taxes that the Church's clergy and servants had already been excused. But these were only brief lapses in the storm. For the most part the emperors accepted the doctrine that if hooligans pledged a looted synagogue to the Church, then it remained ecclesiastical property for ever. And to rub salt in the wound, they banned the building of new synagogues. (Synagogues verging on collapse could be repaired, though—and the restriction was rigidly enforced—there was to be no improvement or re-decoration.) Jews were excluded from imperial service and from most honorary municipal appointments—except the ones carrying obligations, which most citizens sought to avoid.

This process, which continued for several generations, inevitably reduced the Yishuv's size and led to more and more synagogues being burned down or destroyed: but it did not succeed in driving the Jewish community from its Land. Direct and detailed accounts of its activity in the last decades of Byzantine rule are lacking, but from the Talmudic literature and contemporary stories on the extent of the Jewish revolt in the final years of that rule, it is evident that the densely populated settlements of Galilee survived and figured prominently in the last rising: most places seem to have had Christian inhabitants, but all had some kind of Jewish

191

community, often large. The Jews detested their overlords, accused them of having
‹ meddlesome and crooked ways, › of oppressing the poor and robbing the weak,
of being riddled with ‹ every sin the Almighty detests. › The Jewish people's spirit
was not broken. This fact was acknowledged even by the Romans, who called them
‹ a fierce people thirsty for battle, courageous and warlike. › The Jews retained their
trust that ‹ in the end the Kingdom of Edom will fall into the hands of Israel. ›
They were still confident that ‹ the legions of Rome and Byzantium will be conquered
by the Messiah-King, who stands behind our Wall . . . and peers between its cre-
vices. › In the campaign of Church and government against the Jews and Judaism,
one of their most important battles was that waged fiercely and systematically against
Jewish local government in general and against its principal institution—the patriarchate—in particular. The internal organization of the Yishuv was an intricate complex
of organizations and institutions covering all phases of living, with its committees,
leaders, treasurers, and trustees. There were tribunals of civil magistrates or arbi-
rators, the provincial courts, and the great Sanhedrin; there were the yeshivot
and colleges with their sages and students and the synagogues with their presidents
and cantors.

The patriarch had supreme control; he nominated or appointed communal leaders **The**
and judges, scribes, teachers, and even minor officiants in the synagogue. He sent **Patriarchate**
his agents at fixed intervals to inspect communal affairs. All officers in every Jewish
town or settlement were appointed in his name after local opinion had been taken
into consideration. Generally his choice fell on the men of whom it could be said:
‹ the people delight to talk of him and say he is good and pious and fit for authority. ›
Everyone who accepted office had to make a solemn pledge: ‹ to be ready to give
his life for Israel. › And it was customary to appoint not one, but at least two persons
to an office of high responsibility. Every community, however tiny, had its judge,
‹ even if there was but a single family in the town. ›
The government recognized all appointments made or vouched for by the patriarch,
who had rabbinical advisers and his own *Beth-Din* (court of law). It would seem
that the patriarch was partly responsible for taxes due from the Yishuv, or at any
rate assisted the government, as « head of the Jews, » in their collection. The patriarch
was not only the head of the Yishuv but of all Jews in the empire. He could levy
special taxes on them—such as luxury or envoy taxes—and conduct fund-raising
campaigns for the upkeep of colleges and the administration. He had his own
militia—to enforce the judgments of Jewish Courts, and generally to keep law
and order in Jewish centers.

The patriarch's authority was very real, and a pillar of protection. The rabbis **Patriarchal**
held that only a man who swore to ‹ bring the nation back to life, replant it on its **Authority**
own soil and defend it, › was fit to be a judge in Israel, and these were the essential
aims of the patriarchate. Though the rabbis might question the patriarch's religious and judicial authority, or complain among themselves about the taxes, they
did so quietly: for there was quite enough outside criticism from senior imperial
officials and from churchmen who were always scheming to undermine the patriarch's
political status and influence. Yet the continuity of his office, which had safeguarded
the organizational forms of Jewry ever since the days of the Second Temple, its
organic connection with the development of the oral law from the days of the
Patriarch Hillel to these of the Patriarch Yehuda and his successors, and the way
it determined religious life for both the individual and the community, assured the
patriarchate the nation's unswerving allegiance.
On the whole the patriarchs adopted a wise attitude to Roman power, avoiding
involvement with Messianists, rebels, and fanatics. They accepted the existing

BYZANTINE EMPERORS

Constantine the Great
                        306-337
Constantine II ⎫
Constantius II ⎬   337-350
Constans   ⎭
Constantius II,
  sole emperor   350-361
Julian   361-363
Jovian   363-364
Valens   364-379
Theodosius I   379-392
Theodosius I   392-395
Arcadius   395-408
Theodosius II   408-450
Marcian   450-457
Leo I   457-474
Leo II   474
Zeno   474-491
Anastasius I   491-518
Justinus I   518-527

Justinian   527-565
Justin II   565-578
Tiberius   578-582
Maurice   582-602
Phocas   602-610

Heraclius I   610-641

situation themselves, and they taught the people to do so. There is no doubt that the tradition of patriarchic learning, wisdom, and majesty had originally influenced imperial attitudes considerably. For, after all, the patriarch was the acknowledged leader of Jewry, his revenues were great, and he was a lavish benefactor of the government and its officials. Indeed, the patriarch ranked officially among the highest imperial grades of office and honor. (Theodosius I is said to have put a senior official to death for affronting Gamliel V and intriguing against him.) Thus it was natural that the patriarch should become the central target for the Church's virulent anti-Semitism, and that his power should be gradually undermined.

The division of Palestine, in 399, into three provinces worsened relations between the imperial authorities and the patriarchate. The centers of Jewish population—the Valley of Jezreel, Galilee, part of the Decapolis, and northern Transjordan—constituted Palaestina Secunda, and Beit She'an was made the capital. There were also Jewish settlements in Palaestina Prima, which took in Judaea, the Negev, the Shefela, the Sharon, and part of Transjordan. But the patriarchate had direct authority only in Palaestina Secunda. The administration now had an ideal opportunity to extend its control and inspection over the patriarch's actions. Collisions were sharp and frequent, and eventually the situation exploded when the Patriarch Gamliel VI was officially charged with infringing the new anti-Jewish laws.

Gamliel built new synagogues, his courts assumed jurisdiction in suits between Jews and Christians; furthermore, it was said that he had dared to convert slaves. He was the last patriarch—Honorius II, emperor of the west, and Theodosius II, emperor of the east, decreed that the patriarch be stripped of his titles and removed from office. Gamliel died in 429, and with his death the patriarchate was abolished. Its treasury was sequestered by the government, the envoy tax was continued to enrich the imperial exchequer, and power to appoint parnassim and congregational officers was vested in the « little Sanhedrins » of the two Palestines. A central administration of a kind did persist, though it was spiritual rather than political, and internal; its main authority was the Tiberias yeshiva, its rabbis, and their writings.

The statute book of Theodosius II (dated 438) is mainly a compendium of legislation by the Christian emperors after Constantine; and in it most of the « Jewish » laws are set out. For two generations after Theodosius—until the reign of Justinian (527–565)—we hear of no anti-Jewish laws, either general or aimed specifically at the Yishuv. The period was one of prolonged religious schism and bitter, uncompromising polemics, that taxed the energy of Church and empire: neither had the time or the physical resources to deliver fresh onslaughts on the Yishuv or on Judaism, or to enforce anti-Jewish ordinances. During the respite a number of new synagogues were built, as extant ruins and inscriptions (at Beit Alfa for instance) show, and there was a restoration of the congregation in Jerusalem. But Palestine itself remained a center of sectarianism and religious controversy, and many different proponents came to live there, adding to the Christian population.

The anti-Jewish campaign broke out again under Justinian. To begin with, Justinian slightly amended an anti-Jewish law of Theodosius II, which had required all Jews in the empire to turn to the common courts and to be judged by Roman justice, as Roman citizens. Previously, however, the law had excepted proceedings related to Jewish religious law, in which Jewish courts still had authority. By striking out one word, Justinian empowered Christian courts to adjudicate in such proceedings as well. Justinian played havoc with Jewish domestic affairs. Synagogues using Greek translations of the Bible were compelled to employ the Septuagint

Left, three Byzantine emperors: Constantine the Great (top); Justinian (center); and Heraclius.

193

version exclusively; no discourse on the oral law was allowed in synagogues; Jews were not allowed to observe the Passover festival if it fell on a date preceding Easter. Since Justinian considered Judaism to be one of many heresies, he resolved to treat the Jews as heretics. A series of laws and decrees deprived the Jews of general rights, and civic status: they were dismissed from municipal posts and city councils; concessions that had been granted to holders of communal and ecclesiastical offices were withdrawn; the admissibility of Jewish testimony in court was limited; and the conversion of Jewish children was officially encouraged.

By his new legislation, Justinian aimed to root out the Jewish religion and force Jews to convert. To show how serious this intention was, he put the enforcement of his decrees in the hands of local church leaders. Nor did he rely on indirect measures alone. He forbade the building of synagogues, turned existing synagogues into churches, and commanded Jews to accept Christianity. But the Samaritans, who at this time were still very much involved in the theological differences of the Church, were his particular victims. (The Samaritans had already revolted in 485 under Zenon, an emperor notorious for his Jew-baiting, whose reaction to pogroms in Antioch had been: ‹ a pity they burned dead Jews, not live ones. › The rising— which began at Shechem and enveloped the Valley of Jezreel, the Shefela and the coast as far as Caesarea, capital of Palaestina Prima—had been crushed ruthlessly, and a church built on Mount Gerizim, site of the Samaritan synagogue. This act of provocation led to a second revolt, which broke out at the beginning of Justinian's reign, in 529. The Samaritans reached Beit She'an, which they took, wrecking churches, burning down monasteries, and killing bishops and monks. For a while they managed to hold the captured area, but eventually they were crushed again—even more barbarously: thousands of men and women were massacred or sold into slavery, and the few who survived were forbidden to hold religious services.) This was only part of the story. Apart from the legislation and the repressive measures taken against all Jews, there was the physical damage done to the Yishuv. Churches were built on sacred Christian sites where Jews were dwelling, and since Jews were not permitted to own land where a church stood they were driven out unceremoniously. Jewish autonomy in the islet of Yotvata (in the Gulf of Eilat), which previous emperors had left in peace, was abolished: Procopius, a contemporary historian, records that the islanders were ‹ Hebrews who, from time immemorial, had lived by their own laws and customs. › But under Justinian, they were forced to submit to the rule of Rome.
Justinian's policy of annihilation was continued by his successors—often harshly, sometimes less so—right through to the reign of Heraclius (610–641), the last emperor of Byzantium to govern Palestine.

The Samaritans

Throughout the three centuries of Christian Byzantine rule, Israel's struggle for independence and survival, for its religion, and for its soil never let up: it was a struggle that united the Yishuv socially and spiritually, yet in the end exhausted and weakened it politically. As a result of the Yishuv's stubbornness, Christian opposition became ever more aggressive. Just how staunchly the Yishuv clung to its faith is shown in Jewish writings of the time—in the Jerusalem Talmud in Aramaic versions of the Bible, in *aggadic midrashim* (interpretive homilies or sermons) and in later anthologies of discourses and legends.
The prayers and beautiful liturgical poetry of the time reflect the spirit of the Jewish people in those dark days of oppression. A most important development was the revival of Hebrew as the language of the Land. Greek and Aramaic began to be used less and less, children were given Hebrew names, inscriptions in synagogues were written in Aramaic and Hebrew-Aramaic, legends that had been written down

Poetry and Prayer

A sixth-century bowl inscribed with an Aramaic incantation against harmful devils (found in Nippur, Iraq); bowls of this kind were used by Jews to protect women in childbirth and sick people. The superstitious belief contrasts with the oath administered by Jewish physicians to their pupils in sixth-century Palestine—part of which is quoted below.

Take heed that ye kill not any man with the sap of a root; and ye shall not dispense a potion to a woman with child by adultery to cause her to miscarry; and ye shall not lust after beautiful women to commit adultery with them; and ye shall not disclose secrets confided unto you; and ye shall take no bribes to cause injury and to kill; and ye shall not harden your hearts against the poor and the needy, but heal them; and ye shall not call good evil or evil good; and ye shall not walk in the way of sorcerers to cast spells, to enchant and to bewitch with intent to separate a man from the wife of his bosom or a woman from the husband of her youth. And ye shall not covet wealth or bribes to abet depraved sexual commerce. And ye shall not make use of any manner of idol-worship to heal thereby, nor trust in the healing powers of any form of their worship—from The Book of Medicine, by Asaf Harofeh (sixth century).

in Aramaic, or that were usually recited in Aramaic, were translated into Hebrew. Almost all halacha was written in Hebrew, and liturgical verse was composed in an everyday Hebrew that was considered a holy tongue, fit to be used in prayer to God. Hebrew became the medium for a number of midrashim on redemption— many of which described ways of salvation, and comforted the Yishuv in its hours of distress with simple but vivid tales drawn from biblical commentary and ancient legends. These legends, describing the various steps that had to be taken in the long ascent to liberation from slavery and exile, were gathered together by the rabbis of Palestine's yeshivot: by those at Tiberias, Sepphoris, Lydda, and Caesarea in particular. (The Tiberias yeshiva remained preeminent. The extinction of the patriarchate had done nothing to destroy its authority, and a century after that event, in 520, it could boast of having—in Mar Zutra—a descendant of the house of David in its rank, now returned from Mesopotamia.)

The Jerusalem Talmud

The countless and detailed compilations of the oral law produced by the yeshivot confounded the Christian claim that the Jews had invented the law, and that it had no religious validity. The Bible translations had obvious social implications: they were not literal, but sprinkled with legend, with consolation and encouragement for the persecuted, with explanatory passages linking written and oral law.

The Jerusalem Talmud, which followed the exact order of the tractates of the Mishna (see page 179), incorporated the halachic disputations and arguments of the rabbis of the yeshivot. Written in a mixture of Palestinian Aramaic and Hebrew, it was mainly intended to minimize abstract theological argument and to turn thought toward practical discipline. For the most part it followed the tradition evolved by three distinguished Tiberias jurists, Rabbi Yohanan, Rabbi Ami, and Rabbi Assi, and by another of the yeshiva's leading sages, Rabbi Ze'ira.

The colleges also compiled works on general sciences, particularly on medicine. The *Book of Medicine*, for example, written in beautiful Hebrew and in the polished style of the sages at the very end of the Byzantine period, was a compendium of medical doctrines and usages as taught in the medical schools of Palestine. And we also know of discourses on medical matters from much earlier writings.

195

Above, the central panel from the mosaic floor of the sixth-century C.E. synagogue at Beit Alfa, in the Jezreel Valley; it depicts the signs of the Zodiac and the symbols of the seasons. Right, a sketch of the floor's layout: the upper panel shows ritual objects, the lower one the sacrifice of Isaac.

As we saw earlier, the development of *aggada* and religious poetry in this period was exceptional. One contemporary wrote: ‹ Since we are sick of slavery, all a man asks for are words of benediction and comfort. › The sages of Palestine produced a great many aggadic works, and the people would flock to hear them read aloud. The maxims and adages of these sages, their anecdotes and parables, their veiled allusions to current affairs, their polemics (overt or hidden) against Gentile incitement, their strictures on the exactions and hypocrisy of wicked « Edom, » and their certainty of its impending doom kept the people firm in faith and calmed their rebellious spirits. Probably the greatest of the aggadists (writing in the second half of the third century and at the beginning of the fourth) was Rabbi Abahu, a pupil of Rabbi Yohanan: his discourses, his disputes with Christian leaders, his fearless and fiery defense of the Yishuv, did much to boost the community's morale.

Liturgical poetry began to develop at quite an early stage. Prior to Bar Kochba's revolt, an officiant, rising in the synagogue to pray according to the rites and forms determined in Yavneh (then the seat of the Sanhedrin), would often add prayers and verses of his own to make his rendering more personal and also more relevant to the times. When Justinian came to power, this custom became a regular and organic part of prayer. And when the emperor forbade the rabbis to deliver interpretive sermons (or midrashim), the poets inserted the midrashim into the liturgical verses normally read in the synagogues.

The most famous of the Hebrew poets were Yosi Ben Yosi, Yanai, and Eliezer Hakalir from Kiryat Sefer, south of Hebron. They drew on the nation's spiritual heritage, and gave it expression in prayers for the renewal of man's faith in God. But above all, these poets expressed the people's longing for redemption and freedom—as does Yosi Ben Yosi in the following lines:

> *Remember the bird within your house,*
> *Seek out the silent dove.*
> *Summon it with the ram's horn's blast,*
> *Call it with ringing voice.*

Yanai's words could be more somber:
‹ Our land is not ours, what is ours is not ours, strangers possess our strength, and aliens take the fruit of our labors. › But his writing was charged with faith:
‹ As in the days of the going forth from Egypt, when the enemy pursued and swept and drove, the desert raged, the sea barred the way, in our straits we called you, from the depths wast thou called, from afar wast thou beheld, and from nigh wast thou found . . . [thus, even in our days, in the days of enslavement to Edom]. And if it be said: this is a time of hurt, thou shalt answer: it is a time of God's will. › At times, Yanai could even be profoundly optimistic:‹ Set watchmen to guard Thy city, day and night, and darkness shall be bright as day. ›

Jerusalem, as depicted on a mosaic map of the Holy Land (on the floor of a sixth-century church at Madaba, Transjordan): the city is shown from above, with its main streets and buildings detailed.

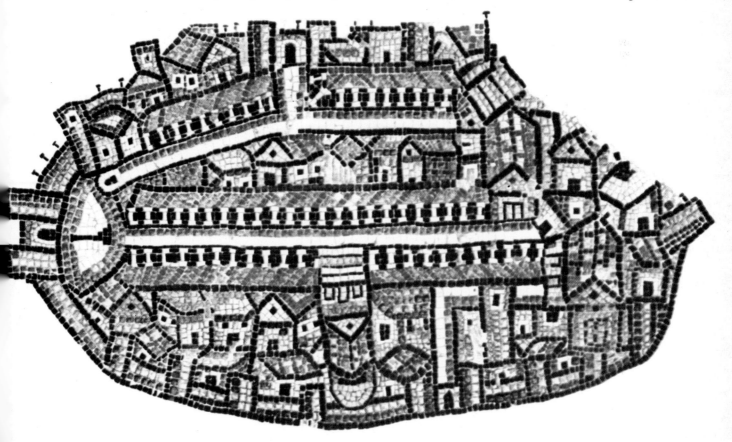

Yanai's optimism was premature. As we saw, the emperors who followed Justinian upheld his Jewish policy, and the anti-Jewish decrees—disguised as law and justice—continued. The Jews were not murdered or exiled, but they were subjected to all the administrative orders and pressures aimed at crushing their religion and forcing them to convert. The Jews' reply to this relentless religious persecution and degradation was to side with the Persians when they invaded Palestine in 614. It appears that they greatly assisted the conquest (the only conquest of Palestine during the long period of Roman rule), fighting in the Persian ranks and by their thousands and ten of thousands in special battalions. In return for this support, the Persians promised the Jews self-government in Palestine within the framework of the Persian Empire, the rebuilding of Jerusalem as a Jewish city, and the restoration of its Temple.

There is evidence to show that the alliance between Persia and the Yishuv was planned ahead by the Persian king, Khosrau II. At any event, when the war broke out, he revised the official attitude to the exilarchy in the Persian Empire. (Eighteen years earlier, the exilarchy had been suspended, and the king had tried to destroy the house of David. Now Khosrau appointed the last survivor of that family head of the Babylonian Exile.)

The new Persian policy encouraged Jews from Mesopotamia, Syria, and from other countries to follow the Persian banner; and when the Persian army marched on Jerusalem in 614, it was joined by battalions of Palestinian Jews. These Jewish battalions took part in the storming of Jerusalem; they participated in the battles for the coastal towns in the north, and they made an abortive attempt of their own to seize Tyre with a force of 20,000 men. For three years the Jews were apparently in full control of Jerusalem: recalcitrant Christians were held firmly in check, many apostates were sentenced to death as idolaters, and materials were gathered for the rebuilding of the new Temple.

The mass participation of Jews in the war indicates that the Yishuv was large at the time, though it is impossible to gauge what percentage of the overall population was Jewish. But we do know that most of the Palestinian Jews in the Persian army came from the Galilean hills—from the neighborhood of Nazareth and Tiberias in particular—and that there were substantial congregations in the coastal towns, in the Negev, and in Transjordan. (It seems unlikely, therefore, that the bulk of Palestine was already Christian in the fourth century as some scholars claim: the gradual diminution of the Yishuv occurred mainly in the fifth century—and in the second half of it at that; and even then, a Jewish majority persisted in Galilee.)

Persia's pact with the Yishuv was short-lived. The conquerors came to terms with the local Christians, a bishop was appointed to govern Jerusalem, and the Jews were expelled once again. Though there is no detailed historical record of events and their causes during the 14 years of Persian rule, it would seem that the Persians' shameless betrayal of the Yishuv impelled the Jews, especially the wealthy ones, to side with Heraclius, the Roman emperor. We have record of the emperor's promises to Jewish deputations from Tiberias, Nazareth, and the many small villages of Galilee that ‹ offered him gifts and blessed him and entreated him to grant them security. › The emperor was staying at the time in Tiberias, at the home of a wealthy Jew, Benjamin, the former leader of the pro-Persian forces who now supported the Roman leader and his attendants.

The emperor gave his word that the Jews would not suffer with the reinstatement of Roman authority. He signed a solemn contract, a written guarantee of Jewish safety—and almost immediately dishonored it when the Christians of Jerusalem demanded the slaughter of every Jew in Jerusalem and Galilee, arguing that the very existence of the Jews there placed them in grave danger, and that the Jews would certainly side with any enemy that attacked the Christians, as they had with Persia. The Christians promised that a fast would be observed to atone for the imperial breach of faith. Heraclius gave way, and we are told that he killed every Jew he could find in the vicinity of Jerusalem and Galilee; many hid, or fled to the desert and the hills, or across the frontiers.

So began the worst and last of the anti-Jewish campaigns. Many Jews—Benjamin of Tiberias among them—accepted Christianity, either because their faith had been broken by the bitter succession of disappointments, or simply to save their lives. But those who had escaped to the wilderness and those who waited as refugees in neighboring countries were among the first to join the invading Arab armies when they came, and—as we shall see—did a great deal to help them conquer and then rule the land.

Arab Rule

ARAB rule in Palestine lasted for 460 years—from the capture of Jerusalem in 638, to its overthrow by the Crusaders in 1099. The period falls naturally into four parts: the conquest, and the first occupation up to 660; the Mu'awiyyad dynasty, 660-750; the Abbasid dynasty, 750-969; and the Fatimid dynasty, from 969. Throughout these periods there were certain common features that shaped the historical, social, and political character of Palestine, and also its religious and demographic characteristics.

There was, first of all, the constant penetration of nomads into Palestine, which was then, as always, a corridor from desert to cultivated lands. This recurring influx made it impossible for the Arabs there to become an ethnic or cultural unity, and no distinct Arab national or territorial formation could emerge. For the same reason, large-scale social or political integration was out of the question, and the division of the Arab population into tribes and clans remained.

These conditions were bound to produce unrest, and the spells of peace and order during this period were few. It was said that ‹ for him that goes forth as for him that enters there is no peace. › Social and organizational forms were unstable. Aspiring religious and political rivals contrived to introduce more and more partisan sects and tribes into the Land. As a result, Palestine was swept by unending waves of Arab immigrants, adherents of this or that religious or political group.

The Caliphate

During this period, Palestine was always part of what may be called a large Arab state (greater under the caliphate, smaller under the Fatimids), and its regime was part of the overall Arab regime. (The caliph was Mohammed's representative and master of all the faithful; the caliphate was hereditary, though each caliph had, in theory, to be the unanimous choice of his people.) State revenue came mainly from taxes imposed on « unbelievers »; later, it was derived from newly settled Arab townsfolk and farmers.

At first the administration depended on an army conscripted from the desert tribes, whose only concern was to loot. But the caliphs eventually disbanded the desert army and relied on Seljuk and Turkish mercenaries. In all these shifts and turns, only one thing remained constant: a government that was thoroughly lawless, corrupt, and wide-open to bribery.

The assimilation of Palestine into the Arab world was vital to the general development of the Islamic Empire, which covered a great land mass from Spain and the Atlantic Ocean to Lake Aral and Khorasan (in northeast Iran), from southern France and Sicily to the borders of India and the Sunda Isles. Arabic became the common language of all these countries, the language of commerce, science, and culture. They were all connected by a special network of highways, and shipping and trade caravans linked them more closely still. Economic progress was swift and vigorous, and provided the social basis for Arab cultural ascendancy: every country within

A map made in 1154 (according to the Arab conception of the world) by Al-Idrisi, the Moroccan cartographer to the court of King Roger of Sicily. Arab maps of this period were drawn with the south at the top, and for this reason the Indian Ocean appears *above* the Mediterranean. Al-Idrisi believed the world to be 22,900 miles in circumference, and 'stable in space like the yolk of an egg.' *Bodleian Library, Oxford (MS. Pococke 375, f.3ᵛ-4ʳ).*

the Arab Empire, Palestine included, became part of the Arab cultural complex. The Arabs discouraged the forcible conversion of Jews to the Arab religion, and regarded Jewish Scriptures as divinely revealed and authoritative. Those faithful to Islam were bidden to respect the variant creeds, to make pacts with the « unbelievers, » and to protect them. The political and juridical status of the Jews was largely decided on the same principle: their community lived under the aegis of the state, its laws safeguarded them. The state was thus answerable for their lives and their possessions.

The Islamic regime was theocratic. It had a socio-religious form; its law was religious law, state and religion were synonymous. Any religious community living under its aegis would obviously have to be organized in a similar fashion, its laws and customs extending beyond the limits of creed into the realm of politics and sociology: thus Islam encouraged communal autonomy. In Christian lands, the Jews were the only separate religious community. But in Arab Palestine there were other— notably Christian—groupings, and with them the Yishuv constituted (in the first phase at any rate) a substantial part of the population. The state could hardly fail to recognize it, or exclude it from its own body politic.

The Islamic Regime

If the Arabs were not anxious, initially, to convert Jews or Christians to Islam, it was partly because the faithful were exempt from taxation—and the conversion (and consequent exemption) of so many people would have imperiled the solvency of the state. So it was their policy to minimize apostasy, and grant all « Peoples of the Book » adequate freedom to observe their familiar practices and precepts, while ensuring that they still paid their government dues.

It must be remembered that the Arabs were desert dwellers who had suddenly become lords of populated, well-developed territories. They lacked experience in the intricacies of administration and the management of state revenues, and at times could not even grasp the arithmetical problems involved. Consequently they were forced to seek Jewish help and guidance in the ways of political and fiscal administration, and trusted the political loyalty of the Jews implicitly. Christians and Jews played an important part in the administration, and so earned the authorities' tolerance and goodwill.

Since authority in the caliphates was not centralized, provincial governors also found themselves in need of Jewish expertise in administration and economics, and this fact enhanced the status and situation of the Jews throughout the empire.

Renewed Immigration

The Yishuv served the Arabs conscientiously, and naturally pinned great hopes on their victory. This made for a special relationship—particularly under the Omayyads, and in times of war. Influential Jews in the Diaspora would intervene at the caliph's court to defend the Yishuv against local iniquity, and many Jews immigrated to the Land. Jewish pilgrimage brought the local administration and its officials a considerable income, and they were not slow to exploit it or (through it) the Yishuv. Furthermore, the visits of devout Jews and Christians emphasized and drew attention to Palestine's sanctity. Jerusalem was holy to Muslims, and later, as the Muslim religion became more powerful and extreme, they sought to extend the sanctity of Jerusalem to the whole country. Many Jewish shrines, which lacked the powerful guardians that protected Christian shrines, were taken over by the Muslims.

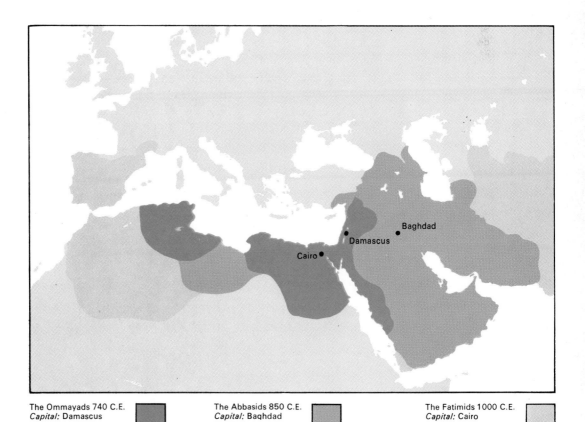

The Ommayads 740 C.E.
Capital: Damascus

The Abbasids 850 C.E.
Capital: Baghdad

The Fatimids 1000 C.E.
Capital: Cairo

The Arabs were quite aware of the Yishuv's rebellious attitude to Byzantium, even before they conquered Palestine: reports of Jews fighting against Rome in the Persian ranks had reached Mohammed himself. There is also evidence of Jews fleeing from Palestine to Arabia, and later of the refugees returning.

When Mohammed planned his Palestinian campaign he made treaties with the Jews of Eilat and Makna (the small harbor in the south of the Gulf) and those of Badruh and Jerba in southern Transjordan. And so, when the Arabs opened their offensive, there were many Jews among them—not only members of the Yishuv, but also Jews who had escaped to Arabia during the persecutions of Heraclius. A contemporary Armenian historian claimed that ‹ all the remnant of the Children of Israel joined the Arabs, and with them made a great host. › According to the same historian, the leaders of this combined army wrote to the emperor in Byzantium, asking him to relinquish Palestine, ‹ the inheritance of the sons of Abraham, › and to return to the Jews ‹ the Land of their Fathers. › In return they promised that they would not do battle on ‹ territory that was not theirs. ›

Arab records acknowledge the value of Jewish and Samaritan support, though they tend, on occasions, to play down its value. One speaks of a Jew proposing a way to capture Jerusalem, another of a Jew prophesying its overthrow, a third of a Jew witnessing the city's formal surrender. The Arab historian Ya'quibi, writing in the second half of the ninth century, tells of a treaty made by the Caliph Omar with the Jews, concerning Jerusalem, whereby they could dwell there once again. (Christian historians of a subsequent era have suggested that the Christians induced Omar to forbid Jewish residence: this, as Ya'quibi shows, is untrue—though it may be that Jews were not allowed to dwell within the Christian quarter.)

At the outset, only 70 Jewish families were reinstalled in Jerusalem. They showed the conquerors where the Temple had stood and helped in beautifying the Temple mount (where churches had been built during the Byzantine period). Jews were allowed to pray on the mount and to build a synagogue there, apparently next to the Wailing Wall. In the country at large the Jews returned to their former settlements, and re-established synagogues and colleges. Immigration to Palestine was resumed, and Jews took back their lands that had been seized after the abortive rising against Heraclius.

Allowing the Jews to take back their land was in keeping with the general policy followed by the Muslims throughout the empire, which was never to dispossess the previous landowners—for they had to pay a poll tax and a land tax, as well as part of the budget of the local garrison, and this solved the regime's fiscal problems. The owner could sell his land to a coreligionist but not to a Muslim. The early caliphs were careful to preserve this system and to prevent Muslims from becoming landowners. They were to be kept instead as a large army group, fed and supported by the conquered territory, and would thus be enabled to continue their wars of conquest. The lands of cities or countries that failed to negotiate a treaty beforehand, and were taken by force, were deemed the property of all Muslims in common, or rather of the state; but, again, the first caliphs would return them to their original owners. The victors, at that stage, never cultivated them.

As allies, the Jews had little difficulty in repossessing their estates. The Christian tenants had long since abandoned them, and the Arabs were anxious to find working owners who would take over their civic duties. The Jews, for their part, were only too ready to accept the responsibilities. Immigrants could be absorbed on the regained acres, and Jewish farming could start again. In these circumstances, it is hardly surprising that many Jews saw in the Arab conquest and its after-effects the usual encouraging signs of approaching redemption—a mood reflected in the poetry of Eliezer Hakalir and the mystic literature of the time.

Hopes of Redemption

Arab Repression In the end these high hopes proved false. There was nothing in the Arab method of government to raise hopes of redemption, even though so much had changed for the better and the anti-Jewish laws had been annulled. Jews began to understand the nature of the «Ishmaelite conquest,» Arab aims in Palestine, and their real attitude toward an organized Yishuv. The capital of the caliphate was moved from Medina, in the Arabian Peninsula, to Damascus in Syria, which meant that Palestine was now in the very heart of the empire.

The Arabs tightened their methods of administration and security, and they soon made clear their intention to make the Land of the Jews a land of permanent Arab settlement. More and more Arabs began to come into Palestine, and it was apparent that they intended to take over the sanctity of Jerusalem and the rest of Palestine. At first Jews and Arabs had equal rights to all Jewish Holy Places (notably Jerusalem and Hebron). But after a while, the Jews were edged out altogether. Jewish privileges on the Temple mount, for example, were gradually curtailed. At first Jews were permitted to make pilgrimages there and to hold regular services; and on the Feast of Tabernacles they were even allowed to erect booths there. But in the end they were denied these rights, and barred from the site. Since they could no longer pray on Mount Moriah, the Jews turned to the Mount of Olives, for ‹ the Divine Presence had rested upon it. › They would assemble there on festive days to bless the House of Israel, country by country, its elders, and its benefactors.

This series of expulsions and deprivations may at first have been linked with the Omayyads' desire to accentuate the holiness of Jerusalem (for they were battling for power with rivals in the « Holy Cities » of Mecca and Medina). But as time went on, the whole Muslim world followed their example, and Jews were forced out of all their ancient shrines.

The new phase of Arab rule was marked by the process of Arab settlement in Palestine and the sequestration of Jewish lands. Even though the political and military system of the first caliphs had opposed the settlement of Arabs on conquered territory, to all intents and purposes there were already in that period the beginnings of an Arab peasantry in Palestine, for the Arab soldiers were followed by their wives and children who settled near the military camps. In Tiberias we hear of the citizens being ordered to share all houses equally with the troops; and in a second town, we are told, soldiers were given abandoned homes and fields. Near every army camp villages sprang up, and these were soon full of Arab settlers.

From Caliph Mu'awiya onward (660 C.E.), settlement was specifically encouraged and facilitated, and state lands that had originally been leased to private occupants were even reclaimed for the purpose. Mu'awiya was the first caliph to own land personally: in all the territories he ruled, he took over former royal estates (whether those of Persian kings or Byzantine emperors) and settled former soldiers, Arab or non-Arab, on them. In theory all Jewish holdings in Palestine belonged to the state, and, as we saw, the Jews were either tenants or sub-tenants. The caliphs could thus claim that they were simply evicting random settlers—whereas in actual fact they were stealing, and divorcing a nation from its soil. The Jewish farmers, faced with servitude to the military colonists, preferred to leave their villages.

By the beginning of the eighth century the burden of taxation and Muslim fanaticism had become very heavy indeed. Jews were prompted to cry out that: ‹ The Almighty will hear the people's lamentation over the deeds of the sons of Ishmael in the Land at the End of Days. › In the second half of the ninth century we find a *Gaon* (the intellectual leader of a community) referring to earlier Gentile theft of Jewish property and proclaiming the principle that land stolen from Jews in this way was still legally theirs: the sages, he declared, made it quite clear that the territory of Palestine belonged to the Jews, that there was ‹ no son of Israel but has four square ells of his own in the Land of Israel. ›

Jews (wearing their traditional colored costumes) consult a 120-year-old elder in Damascus, who tells them that Mohammed was a Messiah and the last prophet to come into the world—a 16th-century Turkish miniature based on an original 10th-century Arab text, *Siyer-i Nebi* ("The life of the prophet"). In this period there was constant theological discussion about the respective roles of the three great monotheistic religions—Judaism, Christianity, and Mohammedanism.

The Abbasids

As we saw, Arab intolerance toward other religious groups first showed itself under the Omayyads, at the beginning of the eighth century; under the Abbasids it became even more marked. Although the extent of the change was influenced by factors of time and place, it was common to all the Islamic countries. With the development of the caliphate and the growing needs of the empire, the Muslims' exemption from paying taxes ended: there was thus no longer any financial or political reason to stop dissemination of the new faith among the « Peoples of the Book. » The expansion of Islam resulted, after several generations, in a Muslim majority and a corresponding reduction in the economic importance of the rest of the population. Moreover, as Arab cultural enlightenment grew, the state's dependence on Jewish help lessened: indeed Arab envy of competitors and their hostility to the rule of unbelievers was aggravated.

In this period many new tribes and peoples—Berbers, Turks, and Seljuks—penetrated the caliphate realms as mercenaries in the caliph's service, and their military powers helped to fan Muslim intolerance—for the Arabs had to compete with the new champions for the top military and administrative appointments. Naturally, the new-comers tended to put their trust in the loyalty of Jews and Christians rather than in the Arabs whose places they had taken. To counteract this, the Arabs emphasized their common religion and encouraged fanaticism. The fanatics' aim was not to convert Christians and Jews, but to demean them, for forcible conversion could only weaken the position of the Arab intelligentsia by presenting it with many new and privileged competitors. Thus, even at the end of this period, forced conversion was unknown to Islam.

Muslim fanaticism expressed itself exclusively in humiliation, abuse, extortion, violence, and pillage of the non-believers; but there was no attempt to win them over to the « true faith. »

204

In Palestine, the policy resulted in the persecution of the Christian and Jewish communities, and aimed to drive them out of the Land and to impose Islamic customs on the country. Early in the Abbasid period, this persecution was linked automatically with military action against rebellious partisans of the Omayyads. Many Christians were forced to flee to Byzantium, while the Jews of Jerusalem were subjected to the kind of harassment that could mean only one thing: a systematic attempt to drive them from the city. Nevertheless, they held on. Incidentally, the Christians joined with the Arabs in harassing the Jews, and Christian attacks on their Jewish neighbors in Jerusalem were a common feature of the 10th century. In that century, the Muslims followed the same policy toward the Samaritans, forcing them to evacuate their central towns and live in scattered villages. Most of their land was taken, and many Samaritans emigrated to Egypt.

A significant factor in this new anti-Jewish policy was the appropriation of Jerusalem and of all Palestine as an area holy to Islam. Among other things, land adjacent to the Temple mount (and part of the mount itself) was turned into burial ground for distinguished Muslims. The Jews regarded this transformation of ‹ the courtyards of the House of God › into ‹ courtyards of the dead › as an outrageous profanation. They considered that the sanctity of the mount had been ‹ brutally trampled on by the spiters of the Lord › when ‹ Ammonites, Moabites, Ishmaelites, Edomites, and Hagarites came bringing coffins and all kinds of unclean things to it. › Ironically, it was the Jews who had told the Muslims of the Temple mount, who had advised them on the preservation of its sanctity, and served as caretakers of its holy places. (Before long these officers were dismissed and forced to work as refuse collectors on the mount: eventually even this degrading job was taken from them.)

Arab Dominance

All these processes changed the face of Palestine and the Yishuv: Arab culture had ascended rapidly, and Judaism was being repressed. On top of this, the Arab population was growing steadily. Even the insecurity of the Arab regime contributed to the process, for the active participation of local Arabs in the controversies and conflicts of the Muslim world not only brought more Muslims to Palestine, but also strengthened their ties with their brethren in other countries. Arab domination in Palestine was furthered by the country's involvement in the struggles of rival Arab states and dynasties, tribes and clans, factions and forces. This strengthening of ties between the Palestinian Arabs and the rest of the Arab world was paralleled by the gradual worsening of their relations with the Jews.

The Arabs in Palestine were not at all perturbed by their instability. To these former desert nomads, insecurity was normal and expected—no more than a continuation of their previous existence: it was unlikely to affect their settlement in Palestine. Nevertheless, the formation of an integrated Arab majority in the Land was a slow process. Arab historians writing at the end of the ninth and at the beginning of the 10th century (such as Ya'quibi and Ibn-Hawqual) indicate that the Arabs did not constitute a majority even in this period, and that the population was still divided into separate ethnic groups. The Jews, on the other hand, were always conscious that theirs was a history of unbroken settlement in the Land, and since they had managed to remain there through the 1000 or so years after the destruction of the Second Temple, they felt sure that they would ‹ no longer know exile. ›

Information on the Yishuv's size and make-up during the period of Arab rule is available only from the 10th and 11th centuries—mainly periods of deterioration for the community. Most of the extant records were found in the Cairo *Geniza* (the depositary for ancient sacred books) and consist mainly of legal documents and correspondence between Jewish communities in Egypt and their brethren in Palestine. These sources mention some 50 communities from different parts of the Land, including all the coastal towns—from Tyre to El-Arish—most of the important inland towns, and small villages. Though this information can only supply a partial record of the composition and size of the Jewish population in Palestine, it does give an impression of the Yishuv's nature.

Apparently, Jews lived not only in the towns specifically mentioned, but also in the areas surrounding them. There is reference to Jews living in ‹ Tyre and all Galilee, › in ‹ Ramleh and its environs, › and to ‹ the numerous inhabitants of the Shefela and the Sharon Valley ›; apparently Jews dwelt in ‹ the vicinity of Hebron, › and in ‹ Gaza and neighboring communities. › There were also different forms of Jewish settlement, with congregations living in ‹ the fortresses, the towns, and the villages. › From what we know of Jewish agriculture under Arab rule, it would seem that these references to the environs of towns indicated small villages and farming settlements near the urban center.

The Jewish population of Palestine formed a religious and political entity, under the general administration of the Muslim Empire: but it was autonomous in religious matters. The Jews preserved all their old forms and institutions of self-rule, and these were accorded official recognition. At first the center of Jewish autonomy was at Tiberias, then at Jerusalem: in later periods it moved to Ramleh and to Haifa, and eventually to the Diaspora.

The Sanhedrin

The organizational structure of the Palestine Sanhedrin preserved the unbroken historic tradition. At its head was the *gaon-nassi* (patriarch), who presided together with the chief justice, another deputy, and five other judges. Then there were the sages, who taught and interpreted the Torah, and other learned rabbis. These dignitaries commanded great respect and enjoyed rights inherited from earlier times: they were exempted from taxation, and had full religious authority. The historical continuity apparent in the Jewish forms of governmental organization was closely linked to the hereditary nature of authority. During the first period of Arab rule, the office of gaon was apparently held by members of the family of Mar Zutra III, who had immigrated to Palestine from Mesopotamia (where his father had been exilarch) and become head of the Sanhedrin 120 years before the Arab conquest: a list of eight of his descendants who filled this post exists. After them the office returned to the family of Rabbi Yehuda Hanassi (members of the house of Hillel), and we know of eight presidents from this family too, heads of the yeshiva of «Geon Ya'akov» in Jerusalem. We also know of 10 geonim—descended from two families of priests *(cohanim)*—who presided over the Sanhedrin from the end of the 10th to the beginning of the 12th century. There are records of rivalry between these families, and of attempts by the exilarch in Mesopotamia to take advantage of the rift and become president of the Jews in Palestine.

The yeshivot were organized on the same lines as the Sanhedrin. The presidium appointed rabbis and members of distinguished families as heads of communities and judges: also included among the leaders of the community were the *hazanim* (cantors)—who were also poets and interpreters—the scribes, and the teachers. The Palestinian yeshivot were centers of learning, and their religious authority was recognized even by distant Jewish communities abroad. The rabbis were jealous of their authority, and in the 10th century the head of the Jerusalem yeshiva, Aharon Ben Meir, even tried—unsuccessfully—to make the Palestinian scholars sole arbiters of festival times, as they had been in earlier generations. But over a period of some 250 years (from the first half of the eighth century to the second half of the 10th) the authority of the yeshivot over the Diaspora declined: Diaspora Jewry was caught up in violent religious controversies in which Palestinian Jewry became involved—and this involvement weakened the Yishuv's religious authority abroad. The fact that the Yishuv was able to maintain the stability of its internal organization during its continual struggle for existence, and, indeed, the fact that the Yishuv itself survived, was due in the main to the deep consciousness of its historic continuity in the Land, a consciousness heightened in time of crisis and prompting greater unity. On the religious side, the awareness of an unbroken spiritual continuity was perpetuated by the orthodox scholastic and religious traditions upheld by the Sanhedrin, the yeshivot, and the rabbis of Palestine, and by the esoteric traditions of various ancient sects dedicated to the study of schismatic « hidden doctrines. » The religious heads of Palestinian Jewry insisted on the supreme authority of the Land's religious tradition. For generations they denied the validity of any rulings made by the rabbis of Mesopotamian Jewry—even when the latter tried to unify Jewish religious practice and to make the Babylonian Talmud and its teachings the sole *halachic* (or legal) source binding all Jewry, annulling all local practices and traditions, Palestine refused to comply. It still remained the center of Jewish zealots, Messianic visionaries, and « Mourners of Zion, » who refused to resign themselves to exile and submission and continued to wait for redemption and the coming of the Messiah. The « hidden doctrines » of the various Palestinian sects varied considerably: some advocated militant opposition to their oppressors, seeing active rebellion as a prerequisite to redemption; others taught that the only way to attain salvation was to lament the fall of Zion. (The followers of this second philosophy, the Mourners of Zion, wore mourning, lived in hovels, and would not eat meat or drink wine.)

These traditional elements, the essence of Judaism's historic, spiritual continuity, became active forces in Jewish life. They were, on the one hand, part of the political, religious, and social conflict of the times; on the other hand, they were precursors of the powerful Messianic and religious movements—and particularly of Karaism, which was most widespread. Although Palestine was not necessarily the only source of these forces and movements, it was their pivot and source of inspiration.

"The Mourners of Zion" Recurrent crisis in the caliphate forms the general historical background to the great Jewish Messianic resurgence—the proliferation of contentious Muslim sects, religious upheavals, class conflict, clashes between various factions, and civil war during the struggle between the Omayyads and the Abbasids. To the Jews, it seemed as if the Arab Empire was about to disintegrate completely. At the beginning, the Yishuv had helped the Arab conquerors, hoping—as we saw—that the new rulers would be the « saviors of Israel. » Now hope of Islam's fall and of imminent redemption led the Jews (especially the Mourners of Zion) to agitate and participate, wherever possible, in the Muslims' wars. It was hopes of this kind that prompted Abu Issi, the first « herald of Redemption » and a member of the tribe of the « Sons of Moses » (an Arabian-Jewish tribe), to visit the eastern Jewish communities. Abu Issi, who was killed in battle against the army of Al-Mansur, the second Abbasid Caliph, was closely connected with the Mourners of Zion. He tried to come to terms with both Islam and Christianity by preaching that Mohammed was a prophet sent to the world, and Jesus a prophet sent to the Jews. He seems to have been a man of daring and revolutionary Messianic vision who exemplified the spiritual originality and visionary force of the Mourners of Zion.

There was also a social background to the messianic zealotry of the Mourners of Zion. The style, tone, and social content of their teaching reflected the widespread resentment felt against those dignitaries of the Jewish communities who had become wealthy and powerful by exploiting the vicissitudes of the times. Palestine had become a refuge, however insecure, for aggrieved and destitute Jews, and consequently a hot bed of resistance to the central, internal Jewish leadership that had been established in Mesopotamia, and which was composed of aristocrats, rabbis, and friends of the authorities. The prosperity and status of these Jewish leaders enabled them to form close ties with Muslim intellectuals and live at a high standard.

207

A 10th-century Karaite manuscript: though it is in the Hebrew language and has the vowel points of Hebrew, the characters are Arabic. Arab and Jewish cultures were closely linked in this period.

As a result they were seduced into easing the « burdens » of religion—and they became adroit at supplying halachic justifications for their laxity. This stiffened the Yishuv's determination to preserve the strict religious tradition, and to ignore attempts to annul all local practices and traditions. Its hatred of the Mesopotamian leadership was reinforced by social and cultural opposition to assimilation and love of luxury.

With the spread of Karaism and the religious polemics it engendered, Palestine became the movement's center. Karaite colleges were built in Jerusalem, and the activities of Daniel Ben Moshe Al-Kumisi strengthened Karaism enormously. Al-Kumisi tried to bring the movement back into harmony with its original Messianic and social aims. He was one of the original Mourners of Zion, and had immigrated to Jerusalem from Persia. He believed in asceticism, and delivered angry and abusive sermons against the people's leaders and their behavior. Again and again he called on the Jews to steep themselves in mourning for Zion, and preached that salvation and atonement could only be won by immigration to Jerusalem: he also founded Jerusalem's Karaite community.

The propagation of Karaite doctrines was planned and organized by colleges and schools, headed by the « Great Teachers, » who were the sect's leaders. The teachings of these colleges were based on the concept of the individual as prime bearer of religious responsibility. The Karaites believed that the individual's first duty was to study, and to become capable of deciding his own course of action on every occasion. Karaite scholars were taught to develop their powers of judgment and criticism, and to reach their own conclusions on even the most crucial religious and moral matters. The colleges were the centers of Karaite literary and polemical

The Karaites

activity, and produced the most exceptional preachers of Karaism in that period. Most of the Karaite colleges were situated in Jerusalem, which became the center of militant Karaism. Immigrants from all over the Diaspora came to Jerusalem, and as a result the city's influence spread among Jews everywhere—for any ideas originating in the Holy City had an intrinsic authority. Ultimately, however, Karaism weakened the Yishuv's religious authority over Diaspora Jewry; for the more serious circles regarded Karaism as blasphemy, and its concentration in Palestine tainted the religious authority of that country. Many rabbis were prompted to immigrate to Palestine to suppress the blasphemy and preserve religious purity there, and their literary outpourings against Karaism were formidable.

The Fatimid Dynasty	THE YISHUV'S position changed dramatically with the establishment of the Fatimid dynasty in 969. Jews had played an important part in the Fatimid conquest and in helping to consolidate their power, and during the first years of Fatimid rule in Palestine Jews held important posts in both the civil and military administration. Most of the Muslims in Palestine were Sunnites, and regarded the Fatimids as blasphemers and usurpers who had no right to the caliphate. They opposed the new regime fiercely, obeying the authorities only under duress, rebelling frequently, and helping nomadic tribes to invade from the north and east. Even in later periods, when the Fatimids were securely established, the authorites could not trust the local Muslim inhabitants.

The Fatimids built fortresses in the coastal towns and on the borders, which served as the main pillars of their authority, and it is no accident that many of these fortresses were manned by Jews—particularly those at southern Hazor (Rafiah), at Haifa, and at Dan, in the north. The special political status enjoyed by the Jews under the Fatimids is reflected in a contemporary poem, dedicated to an important Jewish official, Adia Ben Menasheh Ben Avraham Ben Al-Kazaz, in which the poet calls Adia's father Menasheh ‹ as great a commander as Joab son of Zeruiah, › and says: ‹ He struck fear in the hearts of the people of Damascus, Zoba, Tyre, Sidon, and Ramleh. He... subdued the nomads and cast them into wretchedness. ›

The Yishuv's Status	The fortress at Haifa was given to the Jews with the caliph's consent. At the time Haifa was an important Jewish town and seat of the Sanhedrin, and the fact that Jews were allowed to man the fortress there and hold administrative positions confirms that the Yishuv was held in high esteem. Furthermore, it seems that the administration was interested in strengthening the Yishuv and its leadership, and it supported and upheld the authority of the yeshivot and the gaon. The power of the Jewish leaders in this period and their influence on the authorities is emphasized by the fact that local Arab officials and dignitaries repeatedly asked Jews to recommend them to the central administration.

But though its leaders were honored, on the whole the period was one of decline for the Yishuv. As usual the rural population had suffered most from the general insecurity, and we find that Jewish farming deteriorated greatly toward the end of the 10th century and at the beginning of the 11th. The country was swarming with troops, who could not be trusted, even when expressly sent by the caliph.

Military commanders held the rank of governors, often behaving as independent rulers: even the towns were unsafe, and their garrisons could not always be relied upon. More and more Jews felt compelled to leave Palestine and to emigrate to the neighboring countries, particularly to Egypt. (There is extensive information from the 11th century on communities of Palestinian expatriates in Egypt, grouped according to the towns they came from. Many of the families were even named after their towns of origin.)

The decrees of Caliph Al-Hakim (996-1021) precipitated the emigration. At the time, Palestine was overrun by troops sent in to fight the Bedouin; these troops had conquered a considerable part of the country and even tried to appoint a caliph of their own in Ramleh. In 1012, Al-Hakim ordered the forcible conversion of Christians and Jews to Islam, and the resulting persecution in Palestine was fiercer than is generally supposed. The Cordoban scholar and poet Rabbi Yosef Ben Avitur, who was in the country at the time, wrote a dirge on the events that took place. The troops played a major part in the pogroms, and the poet tells of ‹ pregnant women disembowelled and the blood of old men and babies freely spilt, synagogues destroyed by ravening beasts, victims of the sword in Zion left without burial; › he speaks of rape and ruthless mutilation, of Jews being forced to convert and to ‹ forget their covenant with their Lord, and their cherished Land. ›

Even though Al-Hakim's decrees were eventually revoked, and the policy of religious toleration restored, the Yishuv was badly hit by the persecution. This was a decisive point in its decline; from then on the dominant trend was increased emigration from the Land. And since there was also less aliya (immigration to Palestine had become too hazardous) the Yishuv was depleted in size and political importance. But despite the fact that the Yishuv's very existence was in jeopardy, internal conflicts continued. The more recent immigrants to the Land grouped themselves in separate communities according to their countries of origin. Thus in addition to religious schism (between rabbis and Karaites) and social conflict, there was inter-communal rivalry. And since the veteran population had been weakened by emigration abroad, the immigrants and their controversies attracted most attention. Some help came to the Yishuv from Jews in the Diaspora, who were shocked by the Fatimids' persecution of their brethren. Palestinian expatriates, especially in Egypt, were very active in organizing aid. But according to the information we have, the assistance given by the Jewish communities of Egypt, Italy, and Spain went mainly to where it was most needed: to Jerusalem, to its many poor (mainly destitute immigrants), to its yeshiva and its rabbis, and to synagogues in small depleted communities. Elsewhere in the country, despite the hardship, the Yishuv remained self-supporting.

Jewish literary works written in Palestine during Muslim rule were mostly in Hebrew. For a considerable period Arabic even failed to replace Aramaic as the language used by Jews for everyday speech. One source (from the end of the ninth century) informs us that the Jews of Palestine spoke Aramaic, and that Hebrew was only spoken in a few small circles. But another (from the first half of the 10th century) states that even women and children spoken Hebrew—and they were so meticulous in preserving the correct pronunciation, punctuation, and vowelling, that their usage served as an authoritative linguistic basis for halachic rulings. The language of the literature of that period was mainly the « Language of the Sages »—classical Hebrew. College classes were held in this language, and the rabbis used it in their discussions. But spoken Hebrew continued to infiltrate the literary language—especially the religious poetry.

There is no doubt that the Palestinian Hebrew literature of this period was a product of the Yishuv's struggle to preserve its cultural and spiritual heritage, and its continuity. Its greatest achievement was the codification of the traditions of pronunciation, vowelization, and stress, to which generations of scholars and teachers dedicated their lives. The codification meant determining the precise spelling, whether full or shortened, of each word in the Bible (in full accordance with tradition); it meant finding a system of symbols to represent and convey the exact pronunciation of the original Hebrew; it meant preserving the technique of reading scripture aloud before the congregation and of correctly accenting the text.

The codification helped to revitalize Hebrew and to make it popular again. Most historians (even from early periods) regard this as the beginning of systematic research into the Hebrew language. Indeed, the first work on Hebrew grammar was a book on the vowels, written by Rabbi Moshe Ben Asher of Tiberias at the end of the ninth century.

The creative Jewish literature of this period had some distinct aspects—indicative of its close connections with contemporary events: it was didactic, it had the appeal of folklore, it was rousing and original in its presentation. These qualities were especially apparent in the aggadic literature, which developed in Palestine at this time, and survived for centuries. The aggada was created for the people and was intended to teach them. It is full of allusions to contemporary problems, full of criticism and polemics—whether castigating the Muslims by comparing them to Ishmael (‹ whose hand is against every man, and every man's hand is against him ›), or whether mocking and condemning the Karaites and other opponents of the rabbis. Most of the aggadic literature of this period is pseudepigraphous—that is to say, the authorship of contemporary or near contemporary works was ascribed to ancient historical personages. (The *Essays of Rabbi Eliezer*, for example, written in the eighth century C.E., were ascribed to Rabbi Eliezer Hyrcanus, who died in the second century C.E.) There were books of aggada on special subjects, such as the festivals; or books devoted to specific literary forms—proverbs, parables, tales, and anecdotes. The authors were teachers (that is, heads of yeshivot, tutors, and preachers) cantors, translators, and grammarians. They wrote for the man in the street as well as for scholars, students, and pious Jews. Their writing was direct, simple, and conversational in style—intended always to be read aloud. This is what gives it its folkloristic nature. Even halachic writings displayed some of these qualities—as when ‹ the differences of custom between the people of the Land of Israel and the people of the East [Mesopotamia] › were described.

Literary Innovation

Originality of form was a common feature of all the different categories of literary creation. We find many and varied combinations of halacha and aggada; insertions of biblical interpretation and exegesis into aggada; the mingling of aggada with excerpts from polemical writings and from stories; letters composed of polemics, descriptions, and reminiscences. But the greatest innovations seem to have been in the field of religious poetry. Apart from the magnificent verses of Rabbi Eliezer Ben Ya'akov Hakalir (of Kiryat Sefer) only a fragment of the poetry from the Arab period has survived. And yet we know the names, and a few of the poems of some 20 Palestinian poets, among them Rabbi Pinhas Hacohen of Cafra (near Tiberias), Rabbi Yosef Beirabbi Nissan of Shveh Kiryatayim (in Transjordan), Rabbi Shmuel III (a member of the Jerusalem Sanhedrin at the end of the 10th century) and Aharon Hacohen Ben Merion of Acre, who was apparently writing at the time of the Crusader conquest.

Each poet enlarged the existing poetic form—either by including allusions, by linking each stanza with a biblical text, or by technical innovation. But the poets shared their themes. They were concerned with the Sabbath and the festivals and their customs and prayers, with the nation's glorious past and its hopes for the future, with the confrontation of man in all his misery and sin with his omnipotent and omniscient God. One theme stands out in all the poetry of this period: the recurring complaint that the Jewish people had been left (in the words of Aharon Hacohen) ‹ As a cedar in the wilderness, a child in an alien bosom, / As an old man among deriders, a sage amidst fools, / As a poor man clamoring at the gates, / a bird's soul trapped in a boy's hand. › And always there is the appeal to God—here expressed by Moshe B'rabbi Yitzhak of Tyre: ‹ Raise from the depths a people wandering among the Gentiles, / Erect my plundered tent. ›

Mounted Crusaders leave their castle to pursue a group of Saracen soldiers—a miniature from a 14th-century Venetian "handbook for Crusaders". *Bodleian Library, Oxford.*

THROUGHOUT the period of 192 years that elapsed between the Crusader conquest of Jerusalem (in 1099) and the fall of Acre to the Mamelukes (in 1291), the Crusaders were forced to fight for their domination of Palestine. All this time battles, raids, and invasions were unceasing, even when the Crusaders actually ruled the whole Land: Palestine was swept from end to end by war, murder, and plunder. This war took place in a country that had been decimated by the ravages of mercenaries and their commanders and by the arrogant rule of distant overlords; its villages and farms were already decimated and its inhabitants in misery.

Yet in this small impoverished land, the armies of many nations fought what was, in fact, a kind of world war lasting almost two centuries. On the one side were Frenchmen, Germans, Italians, Normans, Englishmen, Scots, Spaniards, Danes, Greeks, and Armenians; on the other were Arabs, Seljuks, Turkomen, Mongols, Turks, and Tartars. They invaded the Land, destroyed its cities, desolated its fields; they settled in it and founded principalities, built fortresses, and erected monasteries. The Crusader wars were not confined to Palestine; they reached from the Bosporus to the Nile, from Asia Minor to the fringes of the Arabian desert. But their supreme objective was always Jerusalem and the Holy Land, and these had no respite from the fighting. As wars of conquest against the Arabs, the campaigns had both a religious and a colonizing purpose. The Crusades were organized by the Church but their declared aim was not only the defense of the Christians in the East against a ‹ cursed people, › whose ‹ heart had not turned to God, › who had attacked the Christian countries, destroyed churches, and massacred their worshipers; not only the salvation of the Christian holy places from the rule of heretics and blasphemers. The Church spoke also of the conquest of ‹ a land more fruitful than any other land, like Paradise in its beauties, › by the people of an over-populated Europe. Thus the wars were a counter-attack on Islam by Christianity, by the West on the East.

Not surprisingly, the Crusades attracted ambitious churchmen, preachers, rabble-rousers, and frenetic monks, who gave the Crusades their quality of uncompromising religious fanaticism. Not surprisingly either, the wars, which started as a campaign to free the holy places and rescue persecuted Christians, expanded into a general offensive against all the enemies of Christianity and the Church: against the Islamic Empire, against Byzantium and the schismatic Orthodox Church, against heretics in southern France.

Unending war, deepening hatreds, and a general state of insecurity—these were the features of life in Palestine even after its conquest. The Land was covered by a network of fortresses and castles, but it was dangerous to venture outside their bounds. One of the religious attractions of the Crusades was the promise to the Crusaders of complete absolution from their sins, and so the country was overrun with rapacious hordes, who had received religious sanction to murder and rob. The Crusaders' attitude to conquered heretics was presaged by their massacre of Jews in Europe, and their looting of Jewish property, at the start of the Crusades.

212

In Palestine, the colonizing aspect of the Crusades—to conquer the Land and to rule over it as a lawful heritage—determined the composition and character of the population under Crusader rule. What the Crusaders really wanted was to appropriate the Land, to settle in it as overlords, and to profit from its produce and riches. And many ordinary farmers who came to fight in these wars wanted simply to escape from their restrictions of class, to raise their status, to enrich themselves, to become masters in a new land and to enslave its inhabitants.

And, indeed, the rural population of Palestine became a class of serfs, bound to the land taken over by the Crusaders. They were naturally hostile to their new rulers and a continual source of insecurity and insurrection: one of their most effective and subtle methods of resistance was to ensure that the land did not yield sufficient food for the urban population, which was mainly composed of alien invaders. (The Crusaders' fierce battle for naval domination was aimed not only at fighting off invasion by the strong Egyptian fleet, but also at ensuring a regular supply of provisions for the conquerors, whom the country could not support.)

The Conquest of Jerusalem

The Crusader conquest of Palestine was, as we know, ruthless and bitter. In a letter sent by Godfrey of Bouillon (leader of the first Crusade) to the pope on behalf of ‹ all the army of God that is in Palestine, › the French Crusader tells of his men riding ‹ in the corridors and in the temple of Solomon . . . the blood of Saracens as high as the fetlocks of their coursers. › Contemporary records indicate that the carnage was not limited to the actual wars of conquest, or to the battlefield: ‹ On the third day after the victory, at their commanders' orders, the Crusaders carried out a dreadful massacre of all the people who still survived in the city. The Christians

The Crusader assault on Jerusalem (1099)—a miniature from *The Story of Godofroy de Buillon and Salehadin*, a history of the French Crusaders up to St. Louis, written (in France) in 1337.

gave themselves wholly to their murderous urges, and not a suckling babe, not an infant, escaped the sword; the streets of Jerusalem were strewn with the corpses of men and women, and the shattered limbs of children. ›

According to the few refugees who managed to escape from the city, ‹ the Franks killed all the Ishmaelites and Israelites in it, › and only a few were taken prisoner. The Jews were given special treatment: ‹ They were assembled inside their synagogue, which was then put to the fire. › Of the prisoners, ‹ there were many Jews captured alive in the vicinity of the Temple. › Evidently these Jews were collecting corpses for burial, but ‹ when they were recognized [as Jews], they were all sold into slavery. At Tancred's order, 30 men were sold for one piece of gold; many were taken overseas, to Apulia and other places, and some were drowned or beheaded on the way. › The bishop who recorded this last description concludes: ‹ And thus they purified the whole city [Jerusalem] of its contamination. ›

The Jewish communities in Judaea and those in the towns and villages near Jerusalem suffered the same fate. Fragments of a dirge written in this period (incidentally mentioning Haifa as the city of the Sanhedrin) tell of the destruction of the communities of Jaffa, Ono, Lydda, Hebron, Usafiya on Mount Carmel, and Haifa. The last few lines of the manuscript are missing, but presumably they continued the references to other communities that came to the same end.

Apparently, however, the situation in Samaria and in Galilee was slightly better. In a description of the conquest of Shechem, we are told that ‹ an arrogant nation › from the West ‹ killed many people in the city of Shechem, and took many Samaritan prisoners, men, women, and boys. › But there is no mention of a general massacre: this may well have been because the inhabitants opened the city's gates to the Crusaders. Caesarea, too, surrendered to the invaders and the Jewish community was spared. That many of the Galilean towns also capitulated can be inferred from the fact that most of the Jewish communities that survived were in Galilee.

Although the dirge on the destruction of Jewish communities describes the ‹ murderers › as falling upon the Jews ‹ suddenly, › the Yishuv must surely have heard about the Crusades' beginnings three years earlier, and of the persecution of the Jews in Europe and those encountered *en route*. From contemporary letters it would seem that while the Jews had heard of disturbances in Europe, their information was vague and misleading and had led them to see those events as a great movement of peoples heralding the coming of the Messiah. There were widespread rumors that ‹ the Germans in their thousands, with their wives and children and all their possessions › had been ordered to go forth by the Ten Tribes, who had emerged from the ‹ Hills of Darkness, › from the cloud that had hitherto enveloped them. Many believed that this was actually a prelude to the war of Gog and Magog, in which God would assemble the wicked peoples of the earth for battle in the Valley of Jehoshaphat near Jerusalem, and command the people of Israel: ‹ Arise and thresh, O daughter of Zion! ›

But meanwhile the Crusaders advanced, and the Jews began to have premonitions of the approaching disaster: ‹ The Germans conspire to descend upon us, and evil reports of them confound us, and we know not what to do. › Most resorted to their ancient remedy: prayer for themselves and their brethren. Yet when the Crusaders laid siege to the towns of Judaea, the Jews were among the foremost defenders and fighters. A contemporary Crusader account of the conquest of Jerusalem acknowledges the valor of the Jewish fighters: ‹ And here, in front of us, were the foreigners, Jew, Turk, and Arab, fighting for their lives with slingstones, with catapults, with fire and venom . . . and when the end came upon the foreigners, they withdrew from one battlefront, only to find a second battlefront facing them. And though there was terror on all sides, none put down his sword; the Turk, the Arab, and the Jew were among the fallen. The Jew is the last to fall. ›

214

CRUSADER KINGS OF THE KINGDOM OF JERUSALEM

Godfrey of Bouillon	1099-1100
Baldwin I	1100-1118
Baldwin II	1118-1131
Fulk of Anjou	1131-1143
Baldwin III	1143-1162
Amalric I	1162-1174
Baldwin IV	1174-1183
Baldwin V	1183-1186
Guy de Lusignan	1186-1192
Conrad de Montferrat	1192
Henry of Champagne	1192-1197
Amalric II	1197-1205
Mary, under a regency	1205-1210
John of Brienne	1210-1225
Frederick II	1225-1250
Conrad IV	1250-1255
Conradin	1255-1268
Hugh I	1269-1284
Henry II	1285-1291

CRUSADER PALESTINE

The Defense of Haifa	There is more detailed information on the defense of Haifa. As we saw earlier, Haifa was an important Palestinian city. In the previous generation it had been the seat of the Sanhedrin, and most—if not all—of its inhabitants were Jews: it was fortified, it had its own shipyard, and (by special agreement with the Egyptian caliph) its garrison was manned by Jews. The Crusaders felt that ‹ this city hindered the way of God more than any other city, for its fortifications were mighty and its townspeople of consuming pride. › Consequently, in 1001, they decided to attack Haifa before the other coastal towns, and laid siege to it by sea and by land, encircling it with engines. Crusader accounts of the conquest describe the brave stand made by ‹ the enemies of the Lord in the city of the Devil, › and how the occupants cursed Christendom and glorified in the fact that the city had never been Christian. When the city fell, all its defenders and ‹ all who were in the city › were put to death. Apart from a few places in the south, we have no information about Jewish participation in the defense of other Palestinian towns; but there is no reason to suppose that Jerusalem and Haifa were exceptional cases. Most of the Jews in the cities taken by the Crusaders were killed, or captured and sold as slaves; the rest fled with the Muslim inhabitants to neighboring countries or to the uncaptured cities and were helped by the local Jewish communities. From letters written by refugees and their helpers—those who concerned themselves with rescuing survivors and redeeming prisoners—it would seem that after the foundation of Crusader rule the survivors began to return to their villages and to rehabilitate themselves. (The Crusaders did not actually prohibit Jewish settlement anywhere except in Jerusalem, where Jews were not even allowed to set foot, though one witness reported that Jews and Saracens were also driven from Hebron.) In the towns of Judaea, apparently, there were very few Jews left. Binyamin Metudela (Benjamin of Tudela), who visited Palestine in the 1170s, wrote that he found only one Jew in Lydda, one in Jaffa, two in Bethlehem, two in Beit-Nevo, and three in Beit-Govrin. In Jerusalem—despite the ban—he found four Jews working a dyeworks they had leased from the Crusader king, with a country-wide monopoly. The few other Jews in Judaea were also dyers.
Galilean Settlements	As against this, we know of 10 Jewish settlements in Galilee (some are also mentioned by Benjamin of Tudela), and of Jewish communities in Tiberias and Safad. The largest communities were in the coastal cities of Tyre, Acre, and Caesarea; it seems they were engaged in naval commerce. Benjamin of Tudela mentions Jewish shipowners living in Tyre. And a 14th-century document, written in a fine and meticulous Hebrew, contains the charter agreement of a ship from Tyre, giving details of its equipment, its sailing arrangements, its operation, the insurance of its cargo, and so on. All this points to a tradition of shipping among Palestine Jewry. As we saw, the Crusaders were dependent upon imports because of the food shortage, and it can be supposed that those Jews in the coastal towns with Western connections participated in overseas trade. Indeed, we have details of commercial transactions with the East among the Jews of Spain and other European countries. We also have evidence of Jewish doctors, money-lenders, and glassblowers, and of peddlers wandering from village to village. There were also Jewish guides, since the Christian pilgrims regarded the Jews as experts and authorities on the holy places of Palestine, on its geography, and on its history.
Messianic Hopes	The Messianic fervor aroused during the first Crusade continued throughout the 12th century. From its stirrings among the Jewish communities of Byzantium, where it first emerged, the fervor passed on to the communities of Palestine, Syria, Mesopotamia, Persia, the Yemen, Morocco, Spain, and France. Hardly a single Jew doubted that the persecutions and massacres were a prelude to the days of the

215

Messiah, and none could conceive that those who had started the campaign against Palestine would remain as its occupiers and rulers: all were certain that the Crusaders would not become Palestine's rulers. Jewish thought was preoccupied with the problems of redemption, and the reasons for the Messiah's delay. The prevailing mood was expressed in the following poem of the time:

‹ My spirit is impatient and my soul faileth from the rigors of strangers and servitude to tyrants. Is my strength as the strength of rocks, my flesh as bronze to endure and to suffer these tribulations? How long wilt Thou be silent and dumb, and when wilt Thou lift us up from the depths and gather us in? See how the defilers of purity dwell in Zion!›

Out of the anguish and the yearnings for redemption came the call for Jews to return to the Land of Israel as a preparation for redemption: the most powerful and eloquent expression of the new spirit can be found in the poetry of the Spanish poet, Rabbi Yehuda Halevi:

Yehuda Halevi

> *Doves who flock in distant lands—*
> *Whose wings droop—rise up!*
> *Yours is not a place of rest.*
> *Your home is troubled.*

The poet was convinced that the only way his people could obtain redemption was by returning to Palestine. He believed that this return would bring about the reinstatement of prophecy in the Land, and that this was a necessary precondition to the Messiah's coming. (These ideas were developed and substantiated in his philosophical essay *The Book of the Kuzar*). The poet calls to the dispersed people of Israel (the ‹ distant dove ›):

> *Turn to thy cote, come to thy tent, Zion.*
> *Rise, return to the Land of thy glory!*

Halevi resolved to put his ideas into practice, and together with a number of like-minded friends set off from Spain for Palestine. But he never reached the Land—though he got as far as Egypt: travel from Egypt to Palestine was then extremely difficult (it was the time of the second Crusade), and apparently ill health and his friends' entreaties persuaded him to stay in Egypt, where he died. But his example and his work (even though unfulfilled) made a deep and lasting impression.

The conquest of Acre—a miniature from a 14th-century French history of the Crusaders by William of Tyre: Acre was taken by the Crusaders in 1187 and remained their capital until 1291.

Saladin's Victory

The defeat of the united Christian army and the conquest of Jerusalem by the Egyptian sultan, Saladin, in 1187, strengthened the appeal of Halevi's poetry—for immigration to the Land became much easier. According to the poet Rabbi Yehuda Alharizi, who visited Palestine in 1216, Saladin issued a proclamation urging all Jews, young and old—and especially refugees from Crusader rule—to return to Jerusalem. Within just a few years Jerusalem's Jewish community was reestablished: Jews ‹ gathered from every corner, and dwelt within its bounds, › and ‹ from the day the Ishmaelites [the Arabs] took Jerusalem, the Israelites inhabited it. › As was customary in Jerusalem, the immigrants were organized according to their countries of origin and Alharizi in fact refers to the ‹ congregation of Westerners › and to the ‹ congregation of North Africans › there.

The revival of the Jerusalem community encouraged other Jews to immigrate to the Land. The distinctive feature of the new immigrant groups was the fact that they were headed by the greatest scholars and religious authorities of the time. Among the most distinguished of these immigrants were a group of 300 rabbis from France and England, a group of Spanish Jews and—later in the 13th century—a large group of German Jews.

A Hebrew chronicle (apparently from the first half of the 14th century) relates how, in 1211, ‹ The Lord aroused the rabbis of France and England to go to Jerusalem. › They numbered over 300; the king (apparently Saladin's brother) received them with great honor, and they were allowed to build synagogues and colleges. At the head of this group stood two famous French rabbis: Rabbi Shimshon Ben Avraham of Schanz, and Rabbi Yonatan of Lunel. Rabbi Shimshon was a leading critic and opponent of Maimonides—the most important philosopher, halachist, and medical writer of the times, who died in 1204. (Rabbi Shimshon was especially critical of Maimonides' method of codifying halacha and compiling it without mentioning the names of the sages and rabbis who had originated it, and of his religious philosophy.) Rabbi Yonatan, on the other hand, was a champion of Maimonides and was instrumental in arranging for a Hebrew translation of *The Guide to the Perplexed*—Maimonides' great work explaining the fundamentals of Judaism and its laws in simple terms for the layman. And so the new wave of immigration embraced the different extremes of Jewish religious thought. It exemplified the widespread influence of Rabbi Yehuda Halevi's conception of aliya as a means to redemption—as though the intensified persecution of the Jews had come to warn them to return to their land while there was still time.

The Bodleian Bowl, most probably used to collect funds for the many scholars who immigrated to Palestine in the early 13th century. This finely cast bronze bowl was made in France, but found in East Anglia in 1696.

Immigration of scholars and their pupils from France continued during the next generation. The new immigrants included another great French scholar, Rabbi Yehiel of Paris, who came to Acre in 1259 together with his yeshiva (comprising 300 students). There was also immigration from Spain—apparently on a large scale, to judge from the Spanish royal prohibition of the ‹ transportation of Jews to the East, › and from the numerous obstacles the Spanish port authorities placed in the way of Jews attempting to embark on ships bound for the East. Despite these restrictions, one of the foremost Spanish-Jewish scholars immigrated to Jerusalem in the 1260s—Rabbi Moshe Ben Nahman (Nahmanides), Talmudic authority, philosopher, biblical interpreter, and doctor. Nahmanides had defended Judaism with great skill in a religious disputation held before the king of Spain, and published an account of the proceedings—which infuriated church leaders.

When he came to Jerusalem, Nahmanides found the city in ruins (the Tartars had destroyed it in 1260) and only two Jewish inhabitants—both dyers. His first act was to found a synagogue, and little by little he reestablished a Jewish community in the city. Nahmanides also founded a yeshiva, attracting many people from the neighboring countries. But eventually he transferred it to Acre, which had the principal Palestinian Jewish community of that period.

Immigration to Palestine from Spain continued after the death of Nahmanides, who had gone so far as to rule that settlement in the Land was a religious duty, binding every Jew. Among the newcomers was the cabbalist Rabbi Yitzhak Ben Latif, both an admirer and a critic of Maimonides. One of Rabbi Yitzhak's pupils, who accompanied him to the Land, described the aliya: ‹ And now many rouse themselves and offer to go to the Land of Israel; and many think we are nigh unto the coming of the Redeemer, for they behold how the nations of the world oppress Jewry almost everywhere, and they discern other signs that the humble recognize. › German Jews, too, began to immigrate. Their greatest religious scholar, Rabbi Meir of Rutenberg, left Germany with a large group of followers for Palestine. However, he never reached his destination; a converted Jew informed the authorities of his plans, and at the emperor's command the rabbi was arrested in Lombardy (in 1286). He remained a prisoner until his death.

This settlement of a large number of important scholars in Palestine over a comparatively short period raised the spiritual standard of the Yishuv and enhanced its religious influence over the Diaspora. Palestine became a center of the controversy then raging over the works of Maimonides. The community of Acre, which contained most of the leading immigrant rabbis, was foremost in these polemics, and a center of opposition to Maimonides' teachings. Its scholars conducted a lively correspondence with their colleagues in the Diaspora. Acre was also a center of Jewish mysticism, or Cabbala (see page 241). One of its most important rabbis, Rabbi Yitzhak Ben Shmuel, a native of Palestine, continued to teach cabbalistic lore in Italy and Spain after the destruction of the Acre community in 1291.

Among the signs of « imminent redemption » that served as an important stimulus to immigration were some that were clear to all in Israel—and not only to the humble and the mystics. The most obvious was the Crusaders' failure to dominate Palestine. This failure became obvious in the 13th century and served as a source of hope and encouragement to the Jews. A scholar from the south of France, Rabbi Meir B'rabbi Shim'on of Narbonne, declared openly that the fate of peoples ‹ not of our faith that dwell in the Land of our glorious inheritance › was a judgment of God. ‹ Day by day, › he went on, ‹ we see the Land bleak and barren and all in it are wasted, the sons of Ishmael and then the sons of Esau. Wherein is the fulfillment of the promise: « And I made waste the Land and your enemies that dwelt therein were wasted upon it. »

A page from a 13th-century illuminated German manuscript of the *Mishneh Torah* of Moses Ben Maimon (Maimonides), the great philosopher and halachist (1135-1204); the miniature at the bottom of the page illustrates the Talmudic tale of how, when the Israelites came to Mount Sinai, God engulfed them in the mountain, saying: 'If you accept the Torah, it is well; otherwise this mountain will be your grave.' The Mishneh Torah is a full and systematic compendium of the *halacha*, and covers the entire field of Jewish law. The work was completed in 1180 and became the subject of strong rabbinical criticism—since Maimonides did not name the Talmudic sources he had used and gave his own opinions as law on matters about which the Talmud expressed only divided views and gave no final ruling. Below, Maimonides' vision of the Messianic age—as expressed in his Mishneh Torah.

Let it not enter the mind that anything in the world's system will cease to exist when the Messiah comes, or that any novelty will be introduced into the scheme of the Universe. The world will go on as usual. The statement of Isaiah, 'The wolf also shall dwell with the lamb, and the leopard shall lie down with the kid' (XI: 6), is a metaphorical expression signifying that Israel will dwell in safety among the wicked of the heathens. . . . In that era there will be neither famine nor war, neither jealousy nor strife. Prosperity will be widespread, all comforts found in abundance. The sole occupation throughout the world will be to know the Lord. And men will then be very wise, learned in things that are now hidden; they will attain all the knowledge of the Creator that is within the capacity of mortals—Moses Maimonides, from the Mishneh Torah.

Nahmanides was equally outspoken. When he arrived in Palestine he saw ‹ much desolation in this wide and once fruitful land, › and observed that when the Gentiles enter the Land they ‹ boast of the Holy City and say: it is given to us for an inheritance . . . Yet though they find all things to delight the eye, they flee as if from the sword, even though there are none to pursue them. › Nahmanides explained that this happened ‹ because they are not fitting for you [for the Land], and because you do not deserve them. ›

If the failure of the Crusades and the desolation they brought to Palestine showed the Jews that the Land was intended for the House of Israel alone, the Crusades also taught them the importance of aliya and of political negotiation to secure their return to the Land. A cabbalist of the early 13th century wrote: ‹ For, by permission of the kings of the nations, and with their help, shall Israel go back to its land. › The alternation of different rulers in Palestine made this all the more possible: a Muslim sultan, Tartar monarch, or even a Christian king might ‹ proclaim throughout his kingdom that we should return to our Land. ›

Maimonides also spoke of the process of redemption: ‹ If there shall be a king of the house of David, a scholar of the Torah performing the Lord's commandments

219

according to the written and the oral law, and if he shall constrain all Israel to walk in their light, to establish them and to defend them—he shall do all these things by virtue of his being the potential Messiah. If he succeeds and conquers all the peoples about him, and builds the Temple in its place, and gathers in all the remnants of Israel, then will he indeed be the Messiah. But if he fails to do these things, or is killed, then he is not the Messiah promised in the Torah, but as any of the ordinary— albeit perfect and righteous—kings of the house of David who have died. ›

Here Maimonides offers not only a rationalistic interpretation of the Talmud's rulings on redemption, but also a realistic glimpse into Crusader patterns and an attempt to delineate a realistic policy of redemption. This is inferred from the preparatory steps to redemption that he outlines: education of the people, emphasis on the importance of learning the art of war, the need to unify the Jewish people under a supreme leadership (the Sanhedrin).

Nevertheless, the new « Messianic realism » and all the speculations about the possibility of redemption under the existing political conditions did nothing to change the actual situation in Palestine. Rabbi Yitzhak of Acre was not the only Palestinian scholar to leave the country in this period. One of the Land's foremost sages, Rabbi Tanhum B'rabbi Yosef of Jerusalem, a biblical scholar, an exceptionally learned grammarian and philosopher, and a great admirer of Maimonides, was forced to leave and go to Egypt: there he composed a commentary on the Bible (in Arabic) that earned him the name of « Ibn Ezra of the East, » and a Hebrew-Arabic dictionary *(Sefer Hamaspik)*, intended to elucidate the linguistic style of Maimonides' *Mishneh Torah.* (Ibn Ezra was a 12th-century Spanish poet, scholar, and biblical commentator: he wrote only in Hebrew and became the leading authority on Hebrew grammar.)

But emigrants from the Land were sons of the very scholars who had immigrated at the beginning of the 13th century: the latter had, indeed, succeeded in changing the character of the Yishuv, but not in consolidating its foundations. Persecution, murder, and enslavement had weakened its structure, decimated its population, and shaken its agricultural basis. The Land was so desolate that the scholars' sons could not make a living: it was said that ‹ even their fathers, out of the fear that men might sin for a slice of bread, › advised them to leave Palestine and to find work in the Diaspora.

THE MAMELUKES were originally mercenaries and slaves in the service of the caliphs of the Egyptian Ayyubid dynasty. In the middle of the 13th century they overran Egypt and consolidated their rule by defeating the Mongols at Ein Galud (now Ein Harod) in 1263, and by conducting a successful campaign against the remnants of the Crusader armies in Palestine. The campaign ended with Acre's fall in 1291. For 225 years—from the fall of Acre to the Ottoman conquest in 1516—the Mamelukes ruled Palestine, unhampered by outside attacks or by any major internal insurrections. After centuries of unrest, security and order were brought to the Land, though the price was a stern and cruel martial rule, and widespread serfdom.

The Mamelukes' army of mercenaries, made up of slaves from many countries (especially Turks and Circassians), established a unique and enduring regime that gripped the country for generations. The regime was strictly military, and its first concern was the interests of the army; but to give itself an aura of legitimacy it enthroned true or supposed descendants of the Abbasid dynasty as its puppet caliphs. It also gave itself a semblance of religious authority by assembling Muslim religious judges from every college in Islam: this religious sanction strengthened the Mamelukes and inspired them to increase their persecution of infidels and to follow a policy of religious fanaticism (which appealed to their Muslim subjects).

**Mameluke
Rule**

220

Mameluke archers manning a warship (a 16th-century Egyptian shadow theatre cutout): the maintenance of an efficient navy was essential to the all-military Mameluke regime.

Cairo •

The country was totally subjected to this regime: state revenues financed the army and the central government, and filled the royal treasury; estates were given to the governors and their officials, as well as to the sultan and his court; senior appointments were filled by army officers (Emirs), who administered the country in the army's interest. But each privileged position was of limited duration. Governors, officials, or military commanders were not allowed to become too attached to their lands or offices, or to form too close connections with influential citizens. Nor were merchants allowed to earn too much.

The state had many needs, and simple ways of extracting funds to satisfy those needs: fines, confiscations, currency devaluation, purchase of agricultural produce at low prices fixed by the authorities—and even extortion and robbery, direct and indirect. Private enterprise was discouraged, businesses were prevented from expanding. People set aside charitable endowments to ensure themselves a life in the next world, and to provide a modest living for their heirs in this one.

Policy and Administration

Though the Mamelukes' policy decimated Egypt and impoverished Palestine (their links were close), rule in the Land was secure. Any rebellions or conflicts that did break out were usually internal struggles between rival lords, and the subjects had no part in them. Palestine—like all countries within the Mameluke Empire—was divided into district kingdoms, but parts of it (Jerusalem and Gaza, for example) belonged to the « kingdom of Damascus » for a considerable time. Safad rose to importance in the Mameluke period as the center of a principality that comprised Upper Galilee, Tiberias, and the coastal towns from Atlit to Tyre.

Although economic decline was general under Mameluke rule, Palestine suffered even more than her neighbors since—to lessen the chances of Christian invasion—the Mamelukes destroyed almost all the country's harbors. By doing this they cut

221

off Palestine from world trade, and its position as link between the merchants of Europe and the East was promptly seized, with the assistance of the Mameluke authorities, by the port of Alexandria, in Egypt.

During the Mameluke period, Palestine's sanctity as a Muslim holy place was increasingly emphasized, and Muslim fanaticism mounted. Since the days of Saladin, the rulers had continued to found many theological colleges where Muslim teachers preached and indoctrinated large classes of eager pupils. Endowments were made to provide for these scholars and their students, who indulged in continual religious incitement against « infidels »—Christians or Jews.

What little information we have on the Jews of Palestine during this period comes mainly from contemporary letters and travelogues. According to these sources, only 15 Jewish communities existed: in Jerusalem, Mitzpeh, Lydda, Ramleh, Hebron, Gaza, Safad, Beit She'an, and Gush Halav; and in a few places in Transjordan (among them Badhruh, Ajlun, and Malka). Jewish population of these places was not always stable, since it was influenced by local conditions and the extent of immigration to the Land. The largest communities were those of Safad (300 families) and Jerusalem (250 families).

Most of the inhabitants were peddlers and artisans—many goldsmiths or weavers of silk. All members of the family did some kind of work, the women often producing the goods and the men selling them. Peddlers went from village to village during the week, returning home on Fridays for the Sabbath. From contemporary accounts it would seem that while profits were low, expenses were too: ‹ The necessities of life are cheap. ›

Contemporary sources indicate that the Jews were generally on good terms with their neighbors: ‹ The Arabs are friendly to us, they never strike us and do not usually rob . . . the Jews ply their trades among the Ishmaelites, who neither envy nor provoke them. › In Jerusalem there were many Jewish shops ‹ in the best [part] of the city ›; there were ‹ many Ishmaelites around, yet none part their lips to speak evil ›; we read also that the highways were ‹ very, very safe. ›

The Jewish Communities

Spiritually the Yishuv was in a very low state. True, newcomers to the country related how the Jews of Palestine still respected ‹ scholars of the Torah › in all the villages of Galilee; we hear of how, in Jerusalem, ‹ a poor and wretched remnant takes comfort in the Lord's name, ever in prayer, morning and evening, and among them is no sinful laughter or levity or whoring. › But the scholars' level of learning and the study of the Torah was very modest. Throughout this period there were no outstanding Palestinian-born scholars and no original works by Palestinian Jews. Circumstances were by no means conducive to aliya, despite the comparative security; nevertheless, immigration to the Land continued throughout the Mameluke period. Sometimes there were many newcomers, sometimes few. But the flow—or trickle—was constant. (The main spur to immigration was the persecution of Jews in the Diaspora.) For the most part, immigrants were absorbed into the existing communities—though some did settle in places that had had no previous Jewish population, or in places with only a few Jewish inhabitants, and laid foundations for new communities. In 1306, for example, a group of exiled French Jews, led by Rabbi Ishtori Hafarhi, settled in Beit She'an and reestablished its Jewish community. Documents show that there were many immigrants from Germany in the second half of the 14th century, and that they formed the majority of the Jerusalem community. In the 15th century there was considerable immigration from Italy.

The increased immigration caused an intensification of anti-Jewish feeling among Muslim fanatics, but at the same time encouraged the authorities to exploit the influx as a source of income. Muslim fanatics destroyed the Jerusalem synagogue,

Spiritual Revival

222

and the administration extorted large sums from the Jews as payment for the permission to rebuild it. This was in 1473, and was apparently associated with an increased wave of immigration at the time. The Turks had occupied the Balkan peninsula shortly before and taken Constantinople, thus opening a new outlet for Jewish immigration from Europe. Until then it had been obstructed by papal decree. (In 1428, the pope had commanded the cities of Italy, which controlled all sea traffic with Palestine, to stop the transportation of Jews to the Holy Land: as an excuse the Church claimed that Jews had been responsible for the erection of a mosque on Mount Zion, the traditional site of David's tomb, arguing that the Jews wished to acquire it for themselves and first sought to shake Christian rights to the site. The pope's edict had been a serious blow to Jewish immigration to Palestine in the decades before the Turkish conquest of Constantinople.)

Hafarhi and Ovadia

Although aliya was not extensive, it greatly strengthened the Yishuv and raised the spiritual standard among the Jews of Palestine. Among the immigrants who had great influence in this period were two of considerable historic importance; Rabbi Ishtori Hafarhi, the founder of scientific research on Palestine, who (as we saw) came to the land in 1306; and Rabbi Ovadia of Bartenura, interpreter of the Mishna, who came to Palestine from Italy in 1485, and settled in Jerusalem. Rabbi Ovadia was appointed head of the community, and devoted himself to improving its social customs and to raising its moral standards. He founded a yeshiva, and managed to reestablish Jerusalem as a spiritual center. Rabbi Ovadia, famous for the sermons he gave in Hebrew, was admired and respected by the entire Jewish population of the Land.

It was in Jerusalem that Rabbi Ovadia completed his great commentary on the Mishna, and, as we shall see, his letters from Jerusalem are an important documentary source on the history of the Yishuv: on the eve of the expulsion of Spanish Jewry, the creative activities of this distinguished scholar did much to enhance the importance of Palestine and to prepare the way for the new—and massive—wave of immigration to come.

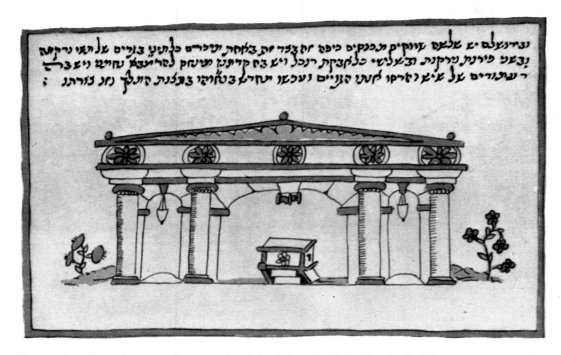

The ancient Jerusalem synagogue depicted (and described) in *The Casale Pilgrim*, an anonymous 16th-century illustrated guide to the Holy Places of Palestine. The Hebrew inscription concludes: 'There is an ancient synagogue attributed to Rabbi Moses, son of Nahman [Nahmanides]. In it are four pillars of marble. The Gentiles destroyed it, but recently it was rebuilt by order of the King.'

223

Israelites, unique nation, whom, in thousands of years, lust of conquest and tyranny have been able to deprive only of their ancestral lands, but not of name and national existence.

Arise! Show that the former overwhelming might of your oppressors has but repressed the courage of the descendants of those heroes whose alliance of brothers would have done honor even to Sparta and Rome, but all the two thousand years of treatment as slaves have not succeeded in stifling it.

APPEAL BY NAPOLEON BONAPARTE TO THE JEWISH NATION

Part Five

Dr. Izhak Ben-Zvi

Under Ottoman Rule
1517-1917

Before the conquest of Palestine by the Ottoman Turks in 1517, the Jewish community there was small, unstable, and economically poor, and its spiritual state was hardly better. At that time Jews were constantly migrating to the eastern Mediterranean countries, for the Catholic Inquisition's barbarous decrees against the Jews of Spain and Portugal had forced hundreds of thousands to quit their homes and flee the Iberian Peninsula. Many of these refugees reached the Islamic countries of North Africa, but were not made welcome, and for the most part wandered on—some to Italy, others to Turkey. There they were warmly received by the Sultan Bayazid, who allowed them to live where they pleased and to practice their own rites and customs. Although most of these Jews settled in the Balkans and Asia Minor, a minority moved on to Egypt and Palestine, which were still under Mameluke rule.

A clear picture of life in Jerusalem in the late 15th century emerges from the letters of contemporary Jewish travelers, such as Meshullam of Volterra or Ovadia of Bartenura. Taxes—including an extortionate poll tax—were intolerable, and the impositions of arbitrary and high-handed governors made life precarious. All responsibility for collecting the poll tax was forced on the leaders of the community. For this purpose the governor appointed a deputy, who in turn appointed five Jewish elders to collect the tax and to impose heavy penalties for failure to pay. The overall assessment was fixed rigidly, and although the number of Jews constantly declined, the remaining members of the community were made to pay the sum in full. This hit the affluent in particular and many began to leave the city.

In 1481 Meshullam could find only 250 Jewish householders in Jerusalem. Seven years later, Ovadia wrote: ‹ Jerusalem for the most part is ruined and derelict, and needless to say there is no wall around it. The population within might, from what I was told, number 4000 householders, but of Jews there survive today only 70, all extremely poor, without any form of livelihood; hardly a man among them but lacks for bread. Here, if he can find sustenance for a year, he is called rich. And in a time like this there are many widows, old and lonely, Ashkenazi and Sephardi, and of the other tongues; far too many women in the city, seven to every man. ›

But Ovadia also saw a pleasanter side: ‹ Jerusalem, for all its desolation and havoc, has four long streets of bazaars, very pleasant indeed. I have not seen the like of them elsewhere. They are at the end of Mount Zion, all arcaded over with domes, offering every manner of wares, and divided each according to its kind: a bazaar for merchandise, a bazaar for spices, another for vegetables, a fourth for all sorts of cooked foods and loaves. ›

About this time the arbitrary poll tax was abolished. But conditions were slow to improve: a ban on building new synagogues remained in force, and no Jew could erect or repair a house without obtaining a special permit—that is to say, without bribery. Time and time again Jews were charged with offences against the Muslim faith and had to buy their way out of trouble. Consequently they were always deep in debt; and if anyone fell behind in his payments his belongings were often auctioned off—even sacred articles and ancient scrolls of the Law. These were usually bought by Christian dealers who sold them in Europe.

Eventually, life for Jerusalem's Jews became somewhat easier—partly because of the efforts of Ovadia, who had come as a scholar from Italy but who remained to become Chief Rabbi of Palestinian Jewry and to labor to improve conditions in Jerusalem. Spanish and Portuguese refugees arrived, and one source claims there were 1600 Jews in the city by 1455. Jerusalem's intellectual life revived. To attract scholars, the community made special rules and provisions for their welfare. One stipulated that full-time scholars (even if wealthy) were exempt from all taxes except the poll tax; and that in the event of dispute their cases should not be judged by

Messianism, a major force in Jewish life throughout the 16th, 17th, and 18th centuries, was partly a product of continual persecution. Above, the prophet Elijah leads the Messiah to the gates of Jerusalem (from a German Passover Haggada, dated 1753): Jewish legend held that the Messiah's coming would be heralded by Elijah blowing 'the trumpet of redemption.'

the congregation, as was usual, but be brought before the *Nagid* (the titular leader of all regional Jews) in Cairo.

Galilean Communities

Conditions in Galilee were better. Joseph di Montagna of Italy, visiting the ancient city of Safad in 1481, wrote: ‹ It is a pleasant community of 300 householders, including the villages round about which are within the city bounds. › In Kfar Kana, near Nazareth, there were then ‹ about 70 respectable householders, with Isaac, a scholar, prominent among them. › In 1495 an anonymous traveler (a pupil of Ovadia) wrote of ‹ the good and healthy land, its waters exceptionally salubrious. And it is solemn truth that there I saw men a great deal older than 60 and 70 years, and one actually 130, yet still robust, virile, and healthy. ›

Most of the Galilean Jews were vendors of spices, cheese, oil, pulses (edible seeds), and fruit; their lives were peaceful but not always prosperous. As Ovadia wrote: ‹ The Jews in Safad and Kfar Kana and everywhere in Galilee are safe and tranquil, and no ill befalls them from the Ishmaelites [Arabs]; but the majority are poor, lodging in the villages, peddling their wares in houses, courtyards, and countryside. › Many of the fugitives from Spain were beginning to reach Safad and other towns in the north of Palestine; some of these were professing Jews, others Marranos. («Marrano» is a general term applied to Jews who were compelled by Spanish and Portuguese authorities to renounce their religion—for themselves and for their descendants—but who, in many cases, had secretly practiced the rites of Judaism for centuries. Ovadia observed that half of Hebron's Jewry was of Marrano origin; and he discovered other Marranos in Jerusalem.) The official lists of Safad's taxpayers for the year 1525-26 name four Jewish quarters. The Musta'arabim quarter (that of the old inhabitants, descendants of Jews who had never left the Land) had 130 householders, the Frank had 46, the Portuguese 21, and the North African 33. If bachelors (who were not included in the tax register) are added to these figures, the total matches the estimates given by Joseph di Montagna and others.

Throughout the Crusades and the Mameluke period small Jewish communities had managed to hold together in the coastal towns of Gaza, Ashkelon, and Rafa; but by the time of the Turkish invasion only the Gaza community, which had lingered since the era of the Talmud, remained. In 1481 Rabbi Meshullam of Volterra visited

227

the town and, in his book of travels, praised its natural beauty and harvests, noting that only the Jews engaged in wine making. Meshullam found some 60 Jewish families, as well as four Samaritan families: among the Jews were planters and farmers. The assessment given in contemporary Turkish documents was rather different—95 Jewish families, 25 Samaritan families.

During the Mameluke period there were Samaritans in Jaffa, but no record exists of Jews dwelling there at the time. Caesarea had a few Jewish families that lived by trading with the adjacent villages and the mountain dwellers. In Hebron, Ovadia counted some 20 families, and an ancient synagogue suggests the permanency of this settlement. Shechem (Nablus) had a dozen Jewish families—all that remained from a considerable community that existed before the Arab conquest. And in Sidon (near Beirut, in the Lebanon) there were 20 Jewish families.

IN 1517 Palestine was conquered by the Ottoman Turks under Sultan Selim I, and for the next 400 years the Land formed part of the vast Ottoman Empire, which stretched from Persia to Budapest. The Jews of Palestine were at first enthusiastic over the advent of the Turks. The kindly attitude of the Sultans toward the fugitives from Spain and the Turks' general behavior toward their Jewish subjects inspired the hope that they would behave equally well in Palestine. At first harmony seemed within reach: for instance, many Jews aided the Turkish army, and some (such as the physician Moses Hamon) reached high positions. **The Ottomans**

This friendliness between Turks and Jews did not escape the notice of the Mamelukes and their Arab servitors: as a result anti-Jewish demonstrations broke out in both Palestine and Egypt. Safad's Jews especially suffered. The vanquished Mameluke soldiers fell upon them, and the neighboring Arabs seized the chance to loot Jewish goods and property. Fortunately, these destitute Jews were saved by their coreligionists in Egypt, who collected clothing and money to help in their rehabilitation. In Cairo a mob was incited to attack the Jewish quarter, but the Jews fought back bravely and after several desperate days drove the rioters off. This could, perhaps, be called the first modern case of Jewish self-defense in the Middle East.

The Jews of Jerusalem only occasionally experienced outbreaks of this kind—in fact, conditions in Jerusalem began to improve. The Street of Spices was now in the Jewish quarter and there were four congregations: Sephardi, Ashkenazi, Moroccan (North African), and Musta'arabim. The largest was the Sephardi, with its exiles from Spain and Portugal. Next came the Ashkenazi, comprised of 15 very old families (descendants of Jews who had come in the days of Maimonides) as well as more recent arrivals from Europe, including immigrants from Italy. The Musta'arabim, as mentioned earlier, were descendants of the Land's early inhabitants. With the Turkish victory, *aliya* (immigration to Israel) began from Turkey and North Africa. Most of the people who now began to settle in the Land were Spanish refugees and Marranos, but immigrants from Italy and Ashkenazi Europe also began to arrive—merchants, artisans, scholars, even dreamers of Messianic dreams. Workshops and factories appeared; some fishing was revived on Lake Kinneret (the Sea of Galilee); orchards were planted and field crops sown in Galilee. And once again Palestine became a spiritual center: Talmudic seminaries and colleges of the mystic *Cabbala* were opened; in the larger towns, the congregations revised their constitutions along democratic lines. Rabbinical courts came into existence, and new educational and charitable institutions were founded. And included among these new developments was the construction of a fortified court in Safad, to protect the Jewish inhabitants against marauders.

The Turks never actually encouraged immigration, nor did they hinder it. Indeed, three successive Sultans—Selim I (1512-1520), Suleiman the Magnificent (1520-1566),

I am David, the son of King Solomon (may the memory of the righteous be blessed), and my brother is King Joseph, who is older than I, and who sits on the throne of his kingdom in the wilderness of Habor [Chaibar], and rules over thirty myriads of the tribe of Gad and of the tribe of Reuben and of the half-tribe of Manasseh. I have journeyed from before the king, my brother and his counsellors, the seventy Elders. They charged me to go first to Rome to the presence of the Pope, may his glory be exalted—David Reubeni (c.1522).

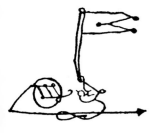

Two false Messiahs who fired the imagination of Jews everywhere in the early 16th century with their plans for conquering Palestine at the head of a Jewish army were David Reubeni and Solomon Molcho. The opening passage of Reubeni's travel diary (*Bodleian Library, Oxford,* shown right and translated above) and Molcho's pretentious signature with its incorporated pennant (left), reveal the arrogance and artifice of these two men—who even succeeded in winning the temporary support of the pope and the king of Portugal.

and Selim II (1566-1574)—refrained completely from meddling in the lives of their Jews and discriminating against them. (Several Jews even held high government positions.) Jewish newcomers to Palestine were concentrated largely in Safad and Jerusalem, but Safad had the stronger pull: for half a century it was the magnet and metropolis for Jewish immigrants.

Messianic Stirrings

The fall of Constantinople in 1453, the triumphs of Islam on the eastern margin of the Mediterranean, the rising tide of Christian fanaticism in the west that culminated in the Inquisition's rule over the Iberian kingdoms and the expulsion of the Jews from Spain and Portugal—such major upheavals had shocked all Jewry, and conditioned it emotionally to Messianic visions and expectancy. In Jerusalem, students at the *yeshiva* (theological seminary) prepared themselves for redemption by keeping long penitential vigils and by intensive study of the Cabbala. Rumors circulated of miraculous happenings—of pillars tumbling in the Dome of the Rock (a Muslim mosque, in the Temple area), of the twisting of the crescent on the Dome's roof.

These rumors spread to the neighboring countries and encouraged Jews to visit Palestine to witness the «Ingathering of the Exiles» and the approaching redemption. In 1523, David Reubeni, a self-styled emissary of the tribe of Reuben, came to Palestine from Chaibar in Saudi Arabia and told of the existence of the « Lost Ten Tribes of Israel» beyond the hills of Ethiopia. (The Ten Tribes that formed the kingdom of Israel had dispersed with the destruction of the kingdom by Shalmaneser in 722 B.C.E.—see page 63.) Reubeni expounded his plan to free Palestine through an alliance between the Palestinian Jews and the monarchs of Europe. Two years later his disciple Solomon Molcho, a Portuguese government official who had been forced to adopt Christianity but later returned openly to Judaism, passed through Damascus, Safad, and Jerusalem, declaring that the redemption would come in 1540. Eventually both Reubeni and Molcho were executed by the Inquisition—Molcho in Italy and Reubeni in Spain.

IN THE EARLY years of the Ottoman occupation, the Jews of Jerusalem endured a great deal of slander and official troublemaking from the Arabs of the city and had constantly to pay heavy bribes to obtain even a modicum of security and ease. It was an impoverished community, obliged to borrow (usually from rich Arabs) at exorbitant rates of interest. And because of this its existence was often in jeopardy. Without the generosity of fellow-Jews in Cairo and Damascus, the Jewish congregation of Jerusalem would never have been able to survive. A contemporary letter gives a detailed picture of the situation: ‹ Our neighbors have charged us this past year with all manner of wrongdoing. We thought that if merciful Heaven did not intercede for us, we should be expelled from the Land. Anyhow, this holy congregation contrived to pay 3000 florins in three days to mollify our masters . . . . Poverty is dire, but all have taken loans from wealthy Muslims at a rate of interest that devoured their means each day, until our brethren in Egypt succored us with 600 florins. Even in Damascus, where the cup of misery is brimming over too, they volunteered to help a little in this payment and presented the suzerain with 8000 florins, and Egypt then provided 3000 more. All in a single year! ›

Further evidence of the prevailing poverty comes from the *Booklet of Ordination* by Rabbi Levi Ben Habib: ‹ Whoever is lucky enough to buy a sheep's head or a goat's guts for the Sabbath or festivals regards himself as one veritably freed from serfdom. › Women who worked at sewing or weaving were given a « bit » (a minute silver coin) for a week's work, which was hardly enough to buy a barley

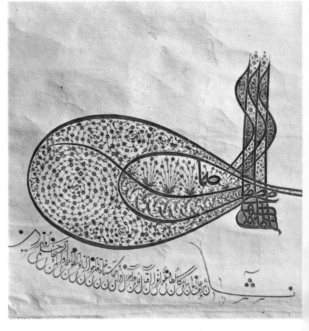

Left, the Sultan Suleiman the Magnificent and, above, his signature. Suleiman did much to improve the living conditions in Jerusalem and protect the city against marauders. The wall he built—shown right in an etching by the 16th-century Flemish artist Frans von Hoghenberg—still surrounds Jerusalem's Old City.

loaf. There were a few prosperous merchants who dealt in clothes and condiments. The rest were shopkeepers or peddlers who moved from bazaar to bazaar and from village to village. Their living was made even more precarious by the fact that Jews were forbidden to trade in the public square, or to sell wine to Muslims —though many did, and risked severe punishment. These limitations and the general insecurity caused many Jews to leave Jerusalem for Safad.

The situation improved under Suleiman who (between 1536 and 1542) built the great wall that still encircles the Old City today, constructed a reservoir (the Pools of Solomon), and repaired Jerusalem's sewers and cisterns. With the water supply guaranteed, life became easier for Jerusalem's inhabitants, and Jews were attracted to return. An official census for 1526 put the number of Jewish householders at 200. By 1539, according to one source, there were 224 householders and 19 bachelors. And by 1555 there were as many as 324 householders and 13 bachelors.

But toward the end of the century the tyrant Abu Sufain (Master of the Two Swords) became governor of Jerusalem, and the situation worsened. In 1586 the Nahmanides synagogue, which had been the Jewish place of worship for 320 years, was taken from the Jews and turned into a warehouse by the Arabs. Yet in spite of such tribulations, groups of pilgrims still came to pray at Jerusalem's holy places or to settle in the city as so many had in the past. Perhaps the most unique of these groups was the Karaite community, which had come to Jerusalem from Hebron. This sect rejected Talmudic authority, basing itself on individual interpretation of the Bible.

Its members were concentrated in the city around an ancient cave, near what is now called the Courtyard of the Karaites. The cave was believed to be the Cave of Anan, founder of the sect, and remained their place of worship for centuries. The Karaites in Jerusalem were supported by contributions from the Karaite communities of Damascus, Egypt, Istanbul, the Crimea, and Persia.

Jewish communities had continued to exist at Hebron, Gaza, and Shechem. The small Hebron community had survived since Mameluke days; and in fact the Jewish quarter, a courtyard surrounded by stone houses, was not abandoned until the massacres of 1929. In the 16th century, Hebron was an important place of pilgrimage and, small though its Jewish community was, it included a number of renowned rabbis and biblical scholars who had come from Safad and Jerusalem to be near the tombs of the Patriarchs. Among them was Eliahu di Vidas, author of the ascetic moralist work *Reishit Hochma* (The Principles of Wisdom), whose own tomb became a shrine after his death in 1578. And among the next generation of scholars to come from Safad was the German-born Rabbi Adani, who wrote his commentary on the *Mishna* (the oral law) at Hebron.

The community of Gaza was strengthened by the arrival of refugees from Spain. The registers for the years 1533-39 give the number of Jewish householders as 98; by 1549 the number had risen to 116 and five bachelors. The Jews of Gaza were mostly merchants who flourished at this crossroads of the great caravan route to Egypt. Others cultivated vineyards and manufactured wine.

Unlike Gaza, the ancient town of Shechem was impoverished. Much of the town's importance derived from the fact that convoys of pilgrims passed through annually on their way from Jerusalem to Galilee and the holy places of the area—the tombs of Joseph the Righteous; of Ele'azar son of Aaron, in Avarta; of Joshua son of Nun, in Kfar Heres. Six years after the Turkish conquest, there were only 12 Jewish householders (all Moriscos) and a small synagogue in Shechem. The census for 1533-39 gave the total as 71, which by 1549 was reduced to 40. Shechem had also a substantial Samaritan community.

Safad's Golden Age

Safad, always more prosperous than Jerusalem, had quickly developed into both a great spiritual center and an economically prosperous city. Set in fertile country, it was surrounded by a number of Jewish agricultural villages. By 1549 there were at least a dozen Jewish settlements in Galilee, three urban, the rest rural. All were in close contact with Jewish settlements in Syria and the Lebanon. The Jewish farmers of Galilee exported fruit (especially grapes), wheat, sheep, wool, and honey to Damascus and to the European provinces of Turkey. And Safad merchants imported goods from Syria, Constantinople, and other maritime centers to be sold to their neighbors and to the Turkish garrisons.

Among the Jewish newcomers to Safad were experienced merchants who quickly adapted themselves to local conditions. Many engaged in wholesale and retail trade; others became money brokers, dealing in gold and silver. Workshops were opened by goldsmiths and silversmiths who employed skilled craftsmen. Other Jews exchanged currency or ran booths in the produce bazaars. Clothiers had a bazaar to themselves, and several of them were owners of spacious stores. Weavers, knitters, and dyers flourished, and the uniforms made by the tailors of Safad for soldiers of the Turkish sultan were popular all over the empire, as far away as the Peloponnese, and were marketed from Venice to Alexandria—even rabbis and scholars worked at weaving cloth and making up garments. The town also boasted a few coffeehouses, and at night watchmen patrolled the narrow streets to keep thieves away from the shops and stores.

Safad was the best protected of Palestine s towns. In 1549, Sultan Suleiman built a wall around the city (as he had in Jerusalem) and a Turkish garrison was posted

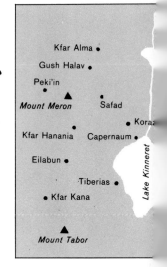

there as protection against marauders from the neighboring villages. Later in the century the Jews built themselves a huge *khan*, or fortified compound, containing houses, shops, and warehouses. For nearly 100 years this remained their place of refuge in times of violence. A hundred families could live within the khan, and once its gates were barred at dusk and the special guards had come on duty they could feel relatively safe from intruders.

The Renewal of Ordination

Safad's spiritual prominence in this period attracted Bible students by the hundreds from all over the Diaspora. In 1577 a Jewish printing press was established there—the first in Palestine. The most outstanding of Safad's scholars was Rabbi Jacob Birav, who arrived in 1524, became chief rabbi, and founded an important yeshiva. To attract scholars from other countries, he personally undertook responsibility for their upkeep and freed them from the burden of taxation.

Birav's main ambition was to restore the Jewish court of law (the *beth-din*) with powers to inflict fines and bodily punishment. In this he followed Maimonides, who, in the 12th century, had sanctioned the renewal of rabbinical ordination in Palestine, provided all the rabbis then in the country, or at least a majority of them, agreed. Ordination, which bestowed on the recipient the considerable authority of a judge, had been officially abolished by Roman decree early in the Byzantine era, but there is reason to believe that it was restored at various times up to the end of the 11th century—for instance, in the period of the *Geonim* (the heads of the yeshivot in Tiberias and Jerusalem from the sixth to the 11th century).

Jacob Birav strove to prepare the nation for redemption, and saw ordination as an initial phase, aware of Isaiah's words: ‹ And I will restore thy judges as at the first, and thy counsellors as at the beginning.... Zion shall be redeemed with judgment. › After arguing the question for two years with the scholars of Safad and gaining their consent, Birav called an assembly of Safad's 25 leading rabbis (in 1538). The assembly formally approved the renewal of ordination, ordained Birav, and empowered him to ordain others.

But the rabbis of Jerusalem, led by their most distinguished scholar and chief rabbi, Levi Ben Habib, vigorously opposed the resolution, insisting that the renewal of ordination required the unanimous approval of all the scholars in Palestine, and that the Safad ordination was thus not valid. In the end the opposition from Jerusalem proved too strong. Some of Safad's rabbis withdrew their support of Birav, quarrels broke out, and finally the disagreements undermined the whole endeavor—even though the organizational and political instrument that Birav envisaged might easily have developed into a unifying political force in Jewish Palestine and created an important spiritual center for all Jewry.

The uproar that followed forced Birav to flee to Damascus, but before he left he ordained four of his pupils—among them Joseph Karo, author of the *Shulhan Aruch* (a compilation of the laws applying to daily Jewish life) and the great jurist Moses Mitrani. They in their turn ordained pupils of their own, including Moses Alsheikh, Moses Galanti, and the cabbalist Haim Vital; in this way the right of ordination lasted for three generations.

A few years later, Jacob Birav returned to Safad, but he died shortly after (in 1545). He was succeeded by Rabbi Karo, who reigned unchallenged for 30 years. Karo came from a Spanish family that had fled to Turkey, and before coming to Palestine had been principal of a yeshiva in Adrianople. It was there that he began to write his great commentary *Beit Yosef* (House of Joseph) on the code of Jewish law of the 14th-century Talmudic scholar Jacob Ben Asher. But it was the *Shulhan Aruch* that made him famous; this compendium of Jewish oral law was acclaimed and accepted as binding throughout the Diaspora. Karo died in 1575, and Rabbi Mitrani (1505-1580) succeeded him.

Among the other famous Jews living in 16th-century Safad were the cabbalist poet Solomon Halevi Alkabetz, composer of the hymn *Lecha Dodi* (Come My Beloved); his pupil, friend, and brother-in-law, the great cabbalist Rabbi Moses Cordovero, author of *Pardess Rimonim* (A Grove of Pomegranates); Rabbi David Ben Zimra, a famous rabbinical authority; the preacher Moses Alsheikh; and the cabbalist and moralist, Rabbi Eliezer Azikri, author of *Sefer Haredim* (The Book of the Pious). Their writings and legal rulings are considered authoritative to this day.

Safad was particularly famous as a center for study of the Cabbala, partly because the city was close to Meron, burial place of Rabbi Shim'on Ben Yohai. (Tradition ascribed to Yohai the authorship of the *Zohar*—Brightness—the greatest cabbalistic text, which first appeared in the late 13th century.) Another exceptional mystic who lived and worked in Safad in the 16th century was Rabbi Isaac Luria Ashkenazi —whose initials, in Hebrew, formed the word « Ari, » meaning « a lion, » and who was therefore called « the Ari. »

The Ari revealed his doctrines directly only to Rabbi Haim Vital, his veteran disciple, allowing him to transmit them to a few other chosen disciples. This small band of disciples, nicknamed « the lion's whelps, » also put the stamp of mysticism on much of the *halacha* (the traditional oral law derived initially from the Torah). The fame of the Ari and his doctrines spread throughout the Diaspora. On the basis of the phrase in Genesis (XLIX: 10) ‹ until Shiloh come › (*shiloh* being another word for lion) many believed the Ari to be the herald of redemption— and that the final redemption would come in 5335 (1575). But his death in 1573 ended their hopes.

Poets as well as cabbalists made their homes in Safad—poets like Alkabetz, whose moving *Lecha Dodi* (expressing longing for redemption and for Israel's exaltation) was recited enthusiastically wherever Jews gathered, and still forms part of the Jewish Sabbath Eve Service. But the greatest poet of the period was Israel Najara (1555-1625), who wrote both religious and secular poetry. Many of his religious hymns and songs, originally published in an anthology entitled *Songs of Israel*, have since been incorporated into the prayer book and are still sung today—in synagogues and at private gatherings. The Ari, too, wrote poems in Aramaic, the language of the *Zohar*, and even today there are congregations that still recite and sing them over their Sabbath meals.

Tradition has it that 290 rabbis were teaching in Safad under Karo, to whose final verdicts all would consent. Zachariah Alzahari, a traveler from Yemen, described one yeshiva where ‹ approximately 200 worthy and talented students sit on benches as the master sits in the chair and expounds on the subjects. › And throughout this remarkable period of spiritual development in cabbalism, Hebrew poetry, and Bible instruction the expectation of imminent redemption remained strong. Only when Safad's Jews despaired of a redemption achieved naturally by settlement in town and village, by ordination, by a supreme beth-din, and by a centralized administration, did Messianic beliefs overcome the tenacious community. This cabbalistic Messianism reached its climax in the latter half of the 17th century (as we shall see shortly) with the appearance of Shabbetai Zvi.

Outside Safad, the Jews of Upper Galilee lived among villages, which they visited occasionally to buy milk, cheese, wool, and wheat, and in which they sometimes settled as shopkeepers, peddlers, smiths, tailors, or physicians. Some hawked their wares around the villages, returning home for the Sabbath. Others rented shops in the villages or among the Bedouin, returning home only for the festivals.

When Safad was hit by plague or famine (as it very often was), its Jewish inhabitants would flee to villages where they could stay for a while among their coreligionists. Their stay sometimes became protracted and the villagers were

Left, the walled town of Tiberias—a 17th-century woodcut. Tiberias was reestablished as a Jewish center in the mid 16th century by Donna Grazia Mendez and Don Joseph Nasi, who built the city's walls in 1564 and restored many of its houses. Right, a contemporary medallion (made by Pastorino de Pastorini) shows Donna Grazia at the age of 18.

obliged to support the transient townspeople. Of special interest to these refugees from Safad were the many tombs scattered across Galilee, said to contain the remains of prophets. Jews would visit the shrines to pour out their hearts in prayer—a custom that was particularly widespread in the heyday of cabbalism.

The literature of this period often alludes to rural communities of Jews. The village of Peki'in was first mentioned in 1522 in the travel memoirs of Rabbi Moses Bassola, but it was well established before the Ottoman conquest. Turkish registers for 1555-56 and 1572-73 listed 45 Jewish householders there—simple peasants, grain farmers, and fruit growers. Peki'in is the only one of these ancient Jewish settlements where Jewish families have continued to live up to our own time. Kfar Yassif, a settlement near Acre, had 29 Jewish householders in the mid 16th century—traders, artisans, and farmers. By 1573 the number had dwindled to 18.

Rabbi Bassola found 15 Jewish families farming in Kfar Alma, a settlement north of Safad: some of these moved to Peki'in, where they were called Almanis. The Jewish population of Kfar Hanania (also known as Kfar Anan), a settlement situated between Upper and Lower Galilee, consisted of 30 householders—mostly Moriscos—and possessed a synagogue that survived throughout the 16th century. In the Druse village of Julas, in Galilee, there was a Jewish community that is first mentioned in the Mameluke period. In Kfar Kabul, five miles northeast of Shfar'am, the Turkish census of 1555-56 noted 15 Jewish householders out of a total of 26 families. In Kfar Kana (situated between the towns of Nazareth and Tiberias), we are told that there were no less than 77 Jewish householders at the end of the 16th century. In Ein Zeitim, near Safad, Bassola found 40 Jewish householders (mostly Moriscos) and even a yeshiva. There were 19 Jewish families in the ancient settlement of Biria, where Rabbi Karo lived for a time and concluded his *Orach-Haim* (The Way of Life). Jews also lived at Kfar Hakok (Yakok), Banias, and Eglon (Ajlun).

Jewish agriculture in Galilee took on new life as Safad flourished. The rabbis turned their attention to the agricultural laws, and proclaimed a fallow year in 5264 (1503-4) according to the reckoning of Maimonides, the reckoning still followed today.

Donna Grazia Mendez

Not all the refugees from Spain and Portugal went straight to the cities and settled areas of Palestine. Many of these brave and energetic people wanted to colonize the waste areas. Some Portuguese refugees appear to have settled at Zeida and Korazim, on the shores of Lake Kinneret, where they lived as fishermen. Others settled among the ruins of Tiberias.

235

Murad III, sultan of Turkey (1575-95). Murad was generally sympathetic to the plight of Palestine's Jewish population and to its appeals against the extortions and oppression of corrupt local governors. Below, an order (dated 1576) for the deportation of 1000 Jewish families from Safad to Famagusta in Cyprus—it was later rescinded by Murad.

Order to the Sanjaq Bay of Safad and to the Qadi of Safad: At present I have ordered that a thousand Jews be registered from the town of Safad and its districts and sent to the city of Famagusta in Cyprus; I command that as soon as [this order] arrives, without delay and in accordance with my noble forman, you register one thousand rich and prosperous Jews, and send them, with their property and effects and with their families, under an appropriate escort, to the said city. Once Jews have been inscribed in the register, do not afterwards, by practising extortion, remove them [from it]—part of an order from the Sultan.

236

In 1549, a Christian tourist found a tiny and impoverished Jewish community in Tiberias. But there were soon to be great changes there, thanks to Donna Grazia Mendez and her son-in-law Don Joseph Nasi, members of a wealthy Marrano family that had escaped the Inquisition and settled in Turkey. Don Joseph had distinguished himself at the sultan's court and been made duke of Naxos (an island off Greece). Now, together with Donna Grazia, he worked on the idea of restoring Tiberias as a Jewish center. In 1561, Sultan Suleiman consented to the plan, and in 1563 Don Joseph's envoy, Ibn Ardit, arrived in Tiberias.

His first task was to build a wall for the town's defense. But he came up against a number of difficulties. First the pope, encouraged by the Christians of Palestine, conspired with the grand vizier to thwart the restoration. Then a local sheik frightened the Arab workers and made them desert by declaring that the completion of the wall would mean the end of Islam. But with the intervention and help of the pasha of Damascus, work was eventually resumed, and by the end of 1564 the wall (almost a mile long) was complete.

The next step was to rebuild the town itself. The settlers repaired the ruined old houses as best they could, and built new ones. A palace was built for Donna Grazia near the hot springs (though it is doubtful whether she ever reached Palestine); and soon Tiberias had blossomed into a prosperous Jewish town and an important center of learning. Jews from Safad and the neighboring towns moved there, and eminent Jewish scholars came to open a seminary.

This gratifying development was halted after the death in 1574 of Sultan Selim, Don Joseph's close friend and patron. Five years later Don Joseph himself died. But not long afterward another savior appeared in the person of Don Solomon Ben Ya'ish, a Marrano. He reached Turkey in 1585 and soon became Grand Commissioner of the Ottoman Empire. For 15 years, until his death in 1603, he directed Turkey's foreign policy, and Sultan Murad gave him the dukedom of Mytilene. As soon as Don Solomon reached Constantinople he became interested in the resettlement of Palestine. But his particular enthusiasm was for Tiberias. He was given the concession of the town by the sultan, and sent his son Jacob there as his agent. Jacob Ben Ya'ish built many houses in Tiberias and a fine castle; but (on his father's own admission) he was a poor administrator, and spent most of his time studying the Bible and the Cabbala. Still the Arabs liked him immensely, and the Jewish community of Tiberias was temporarily saved.

The Decline of Safad

BY THE second half of the 16th century, Turkish authority was on the wane and security in Palestine was badly shaken—especially in Galilee. Bedouin and Druse tribes cast greedy glances toward Safad and its rich warehouses, and in 1567 burst into the town and ransacked it. Many Jews fled to the hills or nearby villages. In 1576 the Safad community complained to Constantinople, accusing the governor and several of his officials (one of whom was a Jew) of extortion and cruelty, of torturing affluent Jews, and of bringing fictitious indictments as a means of blackmail. The Sublime Porte instructed the pasha of Damascus to hold an inquiry, but the defiant local governors continued to do as they pleased.

Things went from bad to worse. In 1587 Safad was plundered again and its printing press destroyed. Recurring disorder led to calamities that resulted in further flight and dispersal. Some of the refugees went as far afield as Sidon, Beirut, Damascus, and even Egypt; others went south to Jerusalem. But that was not all. In 1599 Safad was hit by drought, plague, and famine, and most of the Jews who had remained in the town were compelled to seek help and asylum wherever they could. Committees of distinguished Palestinian scholars went to the Diaspora for help. In 1600 a relief center was set up in Venice. In 1601 the heads of Venetian Jewry decided to help Safad by levying a tax of a quarter ducat on every taxpayer in the community. Messages were sent to the Jewish communities in Germany, Poland, and Russia, asking them to share in this charity. A rabbi in Istanbul, Elijah Ben Haim, wrote: ‹ We are again this year concerning ourselves with the plight of the people of Safad, and are collecting money to send them wheat. ›

But despite all this, Safad remained in a desperate state. Its commerce had dried up, its workshops for weaving and tailoring had either closed down or were struggling to keep open. Seminaries were empty. Teachers and students left, one after the other, and were not replaced. Then in 1602 plague came again. Safad never really recovered from this plague and in 1604 fell easy victim to Druse onslaught.

It was a desperate fight for survival. In 1621 a Prague cabbalist, rabbi, and author, Isaiah Halevi Horowitz, declined an invitation from the Jews of Safad to dwell among them and went on to Jerusalem, remarking: ‹ The Ashkenazi congregation in Jerusalem is double that of Safad and grows every day.... They dwell behind walls, unlike Safad ... where they are exposed to tremendous thievery, for they live in an area that is open on all sides. ›

This appears to have been an accurate picture of life in Safad. Yet its dwindling community hung on doggedly. In 1628 the Druse seized the town again, and dominated it for several years, oppressing and despoiling the small Jewish population. In 1633 the Druse chieftain Fahr-al-Din was routed by the pasha of Damascus; but the victors were as bad as the vanquished had been. In 1636 the Druse took and devastated the town once more. In the fighting that followed between the heirs of Fahr-al-Din, both factions plundered the Jews of Safad. Most were forced to flee the city.

Tiberias was just as badly off. By the beginning of the 17th century it had only a tiny, impoverished congregation. Haim Vital mentions the synagogue in which Rabbi Luria, the Ari, used to pray. There, too, Rabbi Horowitz, who fled from Jerusalem to Tiberias in 1624 to escape persecution, prayed until his death in 1628. In 1660, the town was destroyed completely and for the next 80 years Jewish Tiberias lay in ruins.

Gradually hunger, disease, and pillage exhausted Galilee and almost erased the 16th-century Jewish villages. Only faint traces of Peki'in and Kfar Yassif were left. The Jewish farmers of Kfar Alma, Kfar Hanania, Kfar Kana, Kfar Kabul, and Julas (Julis) were gone. Historians of the time mentioned Jewish merchants and peddlers still living in the countryside of Upper Galilee, but their allusions were generally to the fate of some unhappy traveler, murdered by *fellahin* or Bedouin.

AS SAFAD sank, Jerusalem rose—both materially and intellectually. In 1587 Rabbi Bezalel Ashkenazi gave a letter to Rabbi Isaac Shechmi, an emissary from Jerusalem to Italy, in which he wrote: ‹ The Land is steeped in learning as it never was in ancient days. There is a religious school [*Talmud Torah*] with more than a 100 youngsters ... also a college where the pupils study day and night ... and the great synagogue [the reference is to the synagogue named after Nahmanides] will speedily be reconsecrated ... for already the great [Muslim] Judge of the Holy City and all his colleagues have petitioned the Palace concerning it ... we know that His Majesty's word will come forth saying that Jerusalem be rebuilt ... and all this will cost much money. ›

Rabbi Ashkenazi's optimism was premature, for the synagogue was never restored. But he did achieve his ambition to preside over a yeshiva in Jerusalem (among his pupils was Rabbi Solomon Adani, author of *Mlechet Shlomo*, a commentary on the Mishna). Ashkenazi instituted several reforms, including one whereby one sixth of all overseas collections by Ashkenazi emissaries was allocated to the Sephardi *kolel*

The Seventeenth Century

(communal body); but when he died (sometime between 1591 and 1594) the Ashkenazi community revoked the law.

At that time there were a number of distinguished Ashkenazi scholars in Jerusalem, headed by Rabbi Ephraim Fisch, son-in-law of the Ari. There was Rabbi Simon Annesburg (who came from Frankfurt-on-Main in 1589), Rabbi Simon Bak, Rabbi Uri Feibish, and Rabbi Tevlin, all of whom went to Germany to raise money for their congregations and for immigrants. (Most of the immigrants of that period from Turkey, North Africa, Italy, and Germany made for Jerusalem rather than Galilee, particularly the North African and Italian newcomers, who favored it as the place to found their congregations.)

<table>
<tr><td>Jerusalem's revival</td><td>

The anonymous author of the famous letter *Hurvot Yerushalayim* (The Ruins of Jerusalem) refers interestingly to contemporary progress: ‹ More of our people now inhabit the city of our Lord than have done so since Israel was exiled from its Land. Daily many Jews come to settle there, in addition to the pilgrims who come to pray to Him who stands beyond our Wall, to behold the countenance of God . . . and they give generously, each according to his means, to sustain the community. And the news is abroad that we dwell in peace and security, and the streets are filled with children, and from there springs forth knowledge and wisdom . . . to all the world. There are many colleges open to all . . . ›

On his arrival in 1621, Rabbi Horowitz had found twice as many Ashkenazim in Jerusalem as in Safad—that is, an Ashkenazi community of 500 as well as the 500-strong Sephardi community. All occupied a single courtyard fortified for defense against marauders and bandits. ‹ The Jews of Jerusalem, › Horowitz wrote, ‹ are increasing by the hundreds and erecting huge structures. We regard all this as a sign of redemption. › In a letter from Jerusalem to his son he wrote: ‹ In a brief space, if God wills, you will learn that the Ashkenazi congregation is to be extremely numerous and powerful for I know many will yet come to join with me. ›

One result of this wave of immigration was the revival of an ancient prescript that ‹ there shall be no division in this holy congregation, be it for the sake of Bible scholars or for the good of the treasury, except the Ashkenazi community; and none shall spread disparaging words concerning our holy communities. › It was natural that the Ashkenazim (whose number and resources were larger than those of any of the Oriental Jews) should want to keep control of their treasury and to look after Ashkenazi immigrants themselves: however, their attitude caused the other congregations to form a united front.

Two years later, disaster struck Jewish Jerusalem. In 1625 Mohammed Ibn Farouk, a wealthy Nablus tyrant, bought himself the office of pasha. His reign was one of the blackest in the city's history. He imprisoned the Jewish leaders and notables, took their property, and imposed heavy taxes that eventually forced the Jews to borrow 50,000 *grush* (about 12,500 gold florins) at an annual interest of 10,000 grush.

The situation is described in a letter from an Italian Jew then living in Jerusalem: ‹ The Jews are made to dress like Turks, and failure to do so means punishment by death . . . they are as full of debt as a pomegranate is of seeds, and are greatly to be pitied. › There were two synagogues in Jerusalem ‹ which from morning to evening and from midnight to morning are never silent. › The congregations ‹ sit on the ground and, in dirge and lamentation, mourn the destruction of Jerusalem. › The writer mentioned a small Karaite community numbering about 20, who dressed like Jews ‹ but did not mix with them. › He gave details of the Ashkenazi congregation, which, he said, was smaller than the Sephardi, and was headed by two Sephardim According to him the community numbered about 2000, and it was agreed that the Ashkenazim should cover a fourth of the communal budget, and the Sephardim the rest.
</td></tr>
</table>

An aerial photograph shows Safad's position in the hills overlooking the Sea of Galilee.

The Jews were even held responsible for acts of nature. In 1637, for example, there was drought. In the words of an English priest: ‹ The Turks [meaning the Muslims] prayed abundantly, and when their prayers remained unanswered, they threatened to put the Jews of Jerusalem to the sword unless rain fell within three days. The Jews fasted and cried out to Heaven. On the third day they assembled at the tomb of the prophet Zechariah, and prayed till noon, whereafter dark clouds gathered; a great downpour came and all the reservoirs overflowed with water. ›

Succeeding governors were no better than Ibn Farouk. They, too, brought false charges against the Jews, robbed and plundered them, threw them into jail and then demanded ransom. If the unfortunate hostages could not buy their way out, the entire community would be blackmailed. And if the community could not meet the price and outside help was not forthcoming, they were persecuted. There was a typical incident in 1643: the governor inflicted a burdensome tax on the community, and since the community was quite incapable of paying it, he jailed all its notables. As a result emissaries had to be sent to the Diaspora for help—to Turkey, Italy, Morocco, Holland, Germany, Persia, and India. This happened again and again during the period, forcing the Jews to leave the city. By 1663 most of them had gone to Ramleh, abandoning their property in Jerusalem.

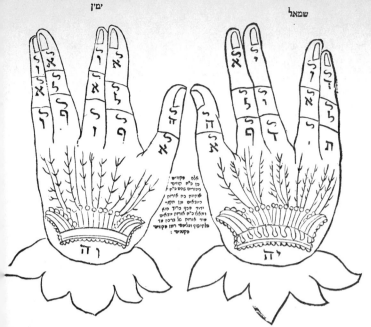

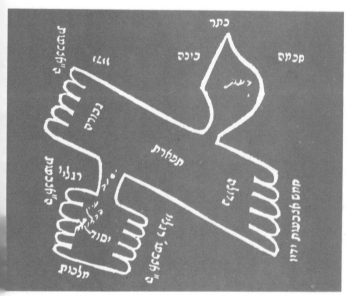

A vital influence on Jewish life in the 16th and 17th centuries was the large body of mystical thought known as the Cabbala. To the cabbalists speech was the medium of God's revelation and his means of creating the world. Thus, they held language to be sacred, something that contained immense depths of mystical meaning in itself. Abraham Abulafia (1240-1300) took this conception of language to its extreme: he regarded the letters of the Hebrew alphabet and their combinations (whether they formed words or not) as objects of mystical contemplation—and held that through contemplation of these combinations the devout might ascend through ever more abstract levels of experience and thereby achieve ecstatic knowledge of God and prophetic vision. (Abulafia's own explanation is quoted below.) A later example of the mystical use of the alphabet is shown above left (in a figure from *Shefa Tal*, by the 17th-century German cabbalist Shabbetai Horowitz): it depicts the channels of divine emanation in the form of hands. Lines of emanation issue from the wrists—each wrist bearing two letters of the Hebrew name of God—and from these, in turn, issue 28 sources of emanation (in the fingers) in the form of 28 combinations of letters.

An example (from *Pardess Rimonim*) of the common use of the first letter of the alphabet, *Aleph* (which denotes "One," and thus symbolizes the unity of God) is shown, left: the letter represents the "body" of God—the diagonal section symbolizing his "hands," the lower projection his "feet."

Know that the method of Tseruf [combination of letters] can be compared to music; for the ear hears sounds from various combinations. . . . And from the ear the sensation travels to the heart, and from the heart to the spleen (the center of emotion), and enjoyment of the different melodies produces ever new delight. It is impossible to produce it except through the combination of sounds, and the same is true of the combination of letters. It touches the first string, which is comparable to the first letter, and proceeds to the second, third, fourth and fifth, and the various sounds combine. And the secrets, which express themselves in these combinations, delight the heart which acknowledges its God and is filled with ever fresh joy—Abraham Abulafia, Gan Na'ul.

The Spread of Cabbala

After the death of Rabbi Luria (the Ari), his mystical doctrines spread rapidly among all classes of Jewry. The Ari had ordered that his teaching be kept secret; and indeed, his principal disciple, Rabbi Vital, attempted to restrict it to a small circle. Nevertheless, this form of cabbalism spread throughout Palestine and on to Italy, North Africa, Poland, and other countries of the Diaspora.

The Ari's disciples and their students were zealous in propagating his cabbalistic system—notably Rabbi Joseph Ben Tabul, a rival of Vital, and an Italian rabbi, Israel Sarok. Particularly active was Jacob Semach, a Portuguese Marrano who had openly returned to Judaism in Salonika at the age of 35. Semach studied the Cabbala, first in Safad and then in Damascus, with Rabbi Samuel Vital, Haim Vital's son. When he came to Jerusalem, Semach discovered a manuscript of Rabbi Haim Vital's last and final exposition of the Ari's doctrine (kept secret until then) and was inspired to open a college for the study of the Cabbala.

Jewry, and particularly Diaspora Jewry, became steeped in expectations of a miraculous, supernatural redemption that was to be brought about by cabbalistic means. With the beginning of Safad's decline at the end of the 16th century, the centers of Cabbala shifted to Hebron and Jerusalem. And so, in Jerusalem too, a climate was created for the expectation of supernatural redemption.

In 1662 Shabbetai Zvi came to Jerusalem from Smyrna. Safad and Tiberias had just been devastated by the Druse; Tiberias lay in ruins, and only a sprinkling of Safad's former inhabitants returned after its destruction. Almost the whole of Palestine Jewry was concentrated in Jerusalem, Hebron, and Gaza—though, as related earlier, most Jews were forced to flee to Ramleh.

Shabbetai Zvi behaved as an ascetic, and his mortifications and fervent prayers at the tombs of holy men attracted both scholars and unlearned people. His standing was such that the heads of the community felt confident in sending him on an errand of mercy to Egypt. At Gaza, he met Nathan Ben Elisha Ashkenazi (1644–80), who later became his chief disciple. Nathan of Gaza's talks with Shabbetai Zvi strengthened his conviction that here indeed was the long-awaited Messiah. In Egypt Shabbetai Zvi was welcomed with great honor as the emissary of Jerusalem by Joseph Raphael Jilibi, a wealthy and influential scholar (and a close friend of the viceroy of Egypt) whom he had met years earlier on his way from Smyrna to Jerusalem. Shabbetai Zvi « revealed » himself as the Messiah, and Jilibi gave him 4000 grush (an enormous sum, worth about 1000 florins) for the needy of Jerusalem. But instead of delivering the money to the community Shabbetai Zvi spent it on his own activities. As a result, the heads of the community excommunicated him. When he refused to give way, a complaint was lodged with the governor, and Shabbetai Zvi was forced to flee, first to Gaza and then to Smyrna—a flight that led Nathan to proclaim that holiness had removed itself from Jerusalem to Gaza.

Meanwhile, belief in Shabbetai Zvi spread like wildfire through the Diaspora, and he gained considerable support in Palestine as well, despite the opposition of Jerusalem's scholars. Early in 1666 Shabbetai Zvi set out with a great retinue for

No Invitation was now made in Smyrna by the Jews, nor Marriage, or Circumcision solemnized, where Sabatai was not present, accompanied with a multitude of his followers, and the Street cover'd with Carpets, or fine Cloth for him to tread on.... And having thus fixed himself in the Opinion and Admiration of the People, he began to take on himself the Title of Messiah, and the Son of God, and to make this following Declaration to all the Nation of the Jews, which being writ Originally in Hebrew is thus translated into English:

'The only, and first-born Son of God, Sabatai Sevi, the Messiah and Saviour of Israel, to all the Sons of Israel, peace. Since that you are made worthy to see that great Day of Deliverance, and Salvation unto Israel, and Accomplishment of the word of God, Promised by his Prophets, and our Forefathers, and by his beloved Son of Israel: let your bitter sorrows be turned into Joy, and your Fasts into Festivals, for you shall weep no more, O my Sons of Israel, for God having given you this unspeakable comfort, rejoyce with Drums, Organs, and Musick, giving thanks to him for performing his Promises from all Ages, doing that every day, which is usual for you to do upon the New Moons; and, that Day Dedicated to affliction and sorrow convert you into a Day of Mirth for my appearance: and fear you nothing, for you shall have Dominion over the Nations and not only over these who are on Earth but over those Creatures also which are in the depth of the Sea: all which is for your Consolation . . . .'—The Counterfeit Messiah (1666).

The wave of Messianic expectation that swept Palestine and the Diaspora in the mid 17th century reached its climax when the "Prophet" Nathan (Levi) of Gaza acclaimed Shabbetai Zvi in 1665. Left, the title page of *The Counterfeit Messiah, or False Christ of the Jews*, by 'an English Person of Quality,' show Shabbetai Zvi blessing the Jewish congregation of Smyrna

Constantinople, but he was arrested on landing and taken in chains to the capital. There his courage failed him and he denied his divinity. Given the choice of conversion to Islam or death, he chose the former.

When news of Shabbetai Zvi's conversion reached Palestine, his followers renounced him and his movement in an uncompromising change of face. But he had played havoc with the moral, social, and economic life of Jewish Jerusalem. The community had been split, and its economy neglected. Even the emissaries dispatched to raise money in the Diaspora had sadly neglected their duties.

Hebron's Communities

The Jews of Jerusalem often took refuge in Hebron from pestilence or persecution—such as that instigated by Ibn Farouk. But Hebron's sources of livelihood were meager; its Jewish community was virtually dependent on foreign charity. Nevertheless, a number of the Ari's most outstanding disciples settled there during the 17th century: Rabbi Eliahu di Vidas, Rabbi Adani (the author of *Mlechet Shlomo*), Rabbi Abraham Azulai (author of *Hessed Le'Avraham*—Compassion for Abraham), Rabbi Isaac Ben Arha and his son Eliezer, and, much later, Rabbi Haim Abulafia, a descendant of Rabbi Birav. Abulafia, a contemporary and fierce opponent of Shabbetai Zvi, was forced to leave Hebron when the Shabbetaists brought some false charges against him.

There were also Ashkenazim among the Jews who settled in Hebron in the 17th century. The small Karaite community established there in the previous century had ceased to exist, and the new settlers bought and took over its synagogue and property. Samuel Ben-David and Moses Yerushalmi, two Karaite travelers who visited Hebron in the mid 17th century, confirmed that no Karaite Jews remained there.

The fervor and fanaticism of Shabbetai Zvi and Nathan of Gaza captured the imagination of Jews and non-Jews alike. Above, an engraving from a popular German broadsheet (dated 1666) envisages Nathan leading the Jewish people from exile.

Even though the Hebron community was small, it was not spared the plagues and oppressions suffered by Jerusalem and Safad. In 1619 a great plague ravaged the town, and other communities—principally the Jews of Italy—came to its aid. Committees were set up in Verona and in Venice to raise money. Rabbi Meir Rofeh, a native of Safad, conducted a major fund-raising campaign in Italy, Holland, and France. The money he raised was dispatched to Samuel Abuhav in Venice, who belonged to a family well known for its support of Hebron; and Abuhav, in turn, sent the money through Italian merchants to Jerusalem and finally to Hebron. In 1652 Abuhav wrote to Hebron about Rofeh and praised him highly: ‹ Thanks to his untiring efforts in these parts, despite the constant danger, the amount of money collected comes to much more than expected. ›

Rabbi Rofeh founded two Hebron yeshivot: one, *Hessed Le' Avraham*, endured for several generations as the center of Jewish intellectual life in Hebron. Most of Hebron's scholars supported Shabbetai Zvi, and when Messianic enthusiasm was at a climax, the staff of the yeshiva wrote to Abraham Pereira (the head of the Jewish community in Amsterdam) saying that from then on they did not want his contributions, but wished him instead to come and join them in beholding the ‹ sweetness of the Lord. ›

A certain Hiya Dayan left Hebron shortly afterward on a mission to North Africa. In their letter of recommendation (it was in 1661) the Hebron leaders bemoaned the town's plight, their subjection to the neighboring sheiks, and the constant feuding among the local Arab tribes. They recalled the plague that had struck them in 1660 and the consequent attack on the Jewish quarter and synagogue.

Gaza— Center of Shabbetaism

Throughout these years Gaza had more tolerant and enlightened governors, and its Jewish community continued to flourish. At times it was swollen by refugees from Jerusalem and Hebron, many of whom became permanent residents—as scholars pursuing intellectual interests, or as merchants and businessmen profiting from Gaza's position on the caravan routes between Syria, Palestine, and Egypt. In this way the Jews of Gaza made contact with the desert tribes and established trade connections, just as the Jews of Safad had once done in Galilee and Transjordan.

The head of Gaza's rabbinical court at the close of the 16th century was Rabbi Isaac Ben Arha, a pupil of the Ari, who had come with his family from Safad to escape the plague. He died in about 1600. His son Eliezer succeeded him, but in 1619 moved to Hebron, handing over authority in Gaza to Israel Najara, the famous poet. Najara was succeeded by his son Moses, who in turn was succeeded by his son Jacob, a fervent Shabbetaist.

At this point, Gaza—that small town of orchards on the Mediterranean coast— became famous throughout the Diaspora. Shabbetai Zvi arrived to dream his dreams, to be proclaimed by Nathan of Gaza, who saw visions of Israel redeemed by this new Messiah and who wrote to the Diaspora proclaiming the Messiah's coming. In Gaza Shabbetai Zvi received the recognition from scholars that he had failed to get in Jerusalem. A contemporary wrote: ‹ And it came to pass when he entered Gaza, that the prophet Nathan proclaimed aloud: « This is the saviour of Israel, the anointed One of the God of Jacob. Israel has no other redeemer, and it is of this one that all the other prophets prophesied. » ›

Thus Gaza became the fountainhead of Shabbetaist propaganda. From Gaza, appeals went out to all the exiles of Israel to fast, repent, and come to Palestine to see with their own eyes the countenance of the Messianic king. In a letter describing the birth pangs of the Messianic age, Nathan proclaimed: ‹ And none shall be saved from suffering save those that dwell in this place [Gaza] where the ruler of the kingdom [Shabbetai Zvi] lives, for the name of the city signifies « the might of God. » › (The Hebrew name for Gaza is *Aza*, which Nathan broke into two

An illuminated marriage contract (*ketuba*) from Padua, dated 1670. Nostalgic landscapes of Jerusalem were a common feature of the many highly decorative illuminated *ketubot* produced in various parts of the Diaspora throughout the 17th century.

parts that could be interpreted as meaning « the Lord is mighty. ») But as with Jerusalem, so with Gaza. The community was shattered by Shabbetai Zvi's collapse, and by the end of the 17th century its fame and prosperity had dwindled away. Meanwhile the tiny Jewish congregation of Shechem (Nablus) had been struggling on. The Karaite traveler Samuel Ben-David found in 1640 a synagogue and 12 Jewish householders there, as well as a community of Samaritans. And Moses Yerushalmi wrote in 1656 of a Jew he called ‹ Rabani › who took him to pray at the tombs of Joseph in Nablus, of Joshua and Caleb at Kfar Heres, of Ele'azar, son of Aaron, on the hill of Phineas (his son) at Avarta. When Abraham Yerek, rabbi of Casale, wanted to emigrate to Palestine in 1660, he asked Samuel Abuhav to suggest a good place to settle. Abuhav mentioned the better-known towns, but added some newly settled areas, such as Shechem and Lydda, and their environs. In the poll-tax register of 1690-91 there is record of 34 Jewish taxpayers in Shechem.

In the second half of the 17th century, despite grasping and oppressive governors, Jerusalem regained its feet, largely due to the efforts of Jacob Hagiz, who came to Jerusalem from Fez in Morocco, in 1658. With the backing of the wealthy Viga family in Italy, Hagiz established a yeshiva in Jerusalem called *Beit Ya'akov* (House of Jacob). The yeshiva attracted eminent teachers and scholars, and before long its graduates were serving as rabbis and communal leaders throughout Palestine and the Diaspora.

Some Egyptian rabbis visiting Jerusalem at the time wrote of Rabbi Hagiz: ‹ With his faithful waters he assuages the thirst of all human creatures; from him goes forth a light to the world. His is a sanctuary and a hall of holiness. ›

At the end of the 17th century Jerusalem contained some 300 Jewish householders. This was more than the quota previously established by the Ottomans, and the community had to bribe the authorities to keep their eyes closed to the excess. Some Jews were apprehensive, and protested that newcomers should ‹ not be able to dwell in Jerusalem, apart from a quorum of householders, and those who come after them must go to other places. › But Rabbi Moses Hagiz (a great-grandson of Jacob Hagiz) fought fiercely to safeguard the rights of newcomers to the city: ‹ I cannot deny that this gathering of exiles into Jerusalem has caused some congestion and distress to the established residents . . . and the nations of the world have an excuse for criticizing. What is there for us to do? All Israel are companions, not omitting those who dwell in this Land, and since all children of Israel are equal [in the Land], who is there, and what is he, that can hinder their path. . . ? ›

Most of the Jews in the capital were poor, and lived off communal funds and the city's yeshivot. But there were some wealthier Jews with businesses and investments outside Palestine. These well-to-do men paid taxes to the community and a special levy to the sultan's exchequer as well, each according to his means. The community had annually to raise between 5000 and 6000 *lions* (then a common currency in western Europe). Yet its income came to only about 850 (400 from householders, 300 from bachelors, 150 from the meat tax). The rest had to be found abroad. The income from the Diaspora was not always sufficient, and the community sometimes had to borrow money from the Arabs at high rates of interest, which strained their resources even more. According to Rabbi Mordecai Malki, the community of Hebron needed only 1000 lions annually and the community of Safad slightly more than 2000—which shows that the Jerusalem community was, in fact, the largest in Palestine at the time.

Right, a chart showing the comparative value of currencies used in Palestine under Ottoman rule.

SILVER COINS:

1 Lion	1 Grush
1 Peso	1 Grush
1 Piaster	1 Grush
1 Zolota	¾ Grush
1 Grush	1 Taler
1 Taler	25gr. Silver

GOLD COINS:

1 Douro	¾ Florin
1 Florin	1 Ducat
1 Ducat	1½ Talers
1 Ducat	3.5gr. Gold

FOLLOWING the Ottoman defeats in Europe at the end of the 17th century, Turkey's grip on Syria and Palestine loosened. Local sheiks and feudal lords were quick to exploit every opportunity to shake themselves free from the yoke of Constantinople. Some rebelled openly, and at the beginning of the 18th century led revolts in Jerusalem and, later, in the north and other parts of Palestine.

The great revolt in Jerusalem broke out in 1703, when the sultan's agents came to collect the money due to the royal treasury. The government usually appointed local officials to collect the *haraj*, or land tax, and they always sought to collect more than the proper sum, using every delay in payment as a pretext for further extortion. Each spring the money had to be handed over to a pasha who came from Constantinople, but the local officials would often refuse to admit him or his escort to the city. Thus there were occasions when the pasha had to go back empty-handed—either because he had come with only a small force, or because he did not dare to violate the sanctity of Jerusalem. When the sultan's envoy came in 1703 to collect the haraj, a full-scale revolt broke out that was not quelled until 1706 when a second pasha came with a large army and overran the city.

It is hardly surprising that in this atmosphere of greed and cruelty the Jews were often victimized by the Arabs. Often they feared to walk in the streets. Defaulting debtors were punished by torture on the rack. Soon the community was forced to consider whether the *parnassim* (the presidents of the congregation, who were held responsible by the tax collector) should go into hiding; and it was agreed that whenever a parnass was arrested his ransom should be paid from communal funds. The ransom of one parnass, Rabbi Meyuhas Ben Samuel, is known to have cost 146 Turkish gold coins.

The communal debt continued to grow. Arab moneylenders charged up to 40 per cent interest and the interest was added to the principal, which thus increased geometrically. The Jews were not allowed to engage in any form of manual work and since there was no commerce in Palestine, the economic situation of Jewish Jerusalem became hopeless. In the end the parnassim, the scholars, and the affluent few left the city. The poor could not. Immigration stopped and help from the Diaspora was reduced. Within a space of three or four years, the Jewish congregation in Jerusalem, bereft of leadership, disintegrated.

Help came just in time. A group of influential and single-minded Jews in Constantinople, following an appeal for help from Jerusalem, formed a permanent seven-man committee that was supplemented by a committee made up of Constantinople's most outstanding rabbis. Their first task was to ascertain how much was owing to the Arab creditors—who immediately advanced impossible claims. Eventually the sultan interceded, and a sum was fixed. The Jews of Constantinople undertook to pay this, and also sent a representative to administer communal affairs in Jerusalem and to see that further debts were not incurred. The Constantinople committee imposed special taxes on the wealthier Jews in Jerusalem: Jewish creditors were not permitted to collect their debts from the community council until all debts to the Arabs had been paid in full. No gift could be made or will drawn up without permission and the private selling of gravestones was forbidden. (This was to enable the community to realize the full income from this source.) The committee also assumed control of all fund raisers sent to the Diaspora. Emissaries were sent to Yemen, Egypt, Syria, Persia, and all the cities of Turkey to establish special funds and organize collections.

Thanks to the Constantinople committee a new era dawned for Jewish Jerusalem. Once again scholars began settling in the city. Rabbi Haim Ben Attar came from Sali in Morocco in 1742 with 30 disciples and founded a yeshiva called *Midrash Knesset Yisrael* (The College of the Assembly of Israel). At about the same time

The typical blue and purple costumes worn by middle-class Jews of the Ottoman Empire—two 18th-century Turkish paintings.

Gedalia Hayun, a wealthy cabbalist from Constantinople, founded the yeshiva *Beth-El*. This yeshiva was a center of cabbalistic study and prayer based on the teachings of the Ari. Among its students were Rabbi Shalom Shar'abi, a noted Yemenite cabbalist; Rabbi Abraham Gershon of Kitov; Rabbi Yomtov Algazi, later chief rabbi of Jerusalem; and Rabbi Haim Joseph David Azulai.

By the middle of the 18th century, even the depleted Ashkenazi congregation, which had suffered most from the exorbitant demands of Arab creditors, began to show signs of revival and expansion. Their leader, Rabbi Moses Hacohen, had traveled tirelessly throughout the Diaspora between 1688 and 1692, raising money to pay their debts. As a result the Ashkenazim had managed to pay the first installment of 80,000 lions before 1707. But when they were unable to pay the next, the Arab moneylenders set fire to the synagogue, which was destroyed with all its contents.

Rabbi Gershon was probably most responsible for the Ashkenazi revival. He came to Palestine with his family in about 1746, settling in Hebron before moving to Jerusalem in 1752. At first he appeared as an Ashkenazi, although dressed as a Sephardi *hacham* (rabbi). But the next year he wrote to his brother-in-law, the Baal Shem Tov (founder of *Hassidism*, a pietist movement), that the Ashkenazi scholars, with the assent of the Sephardim, had asked him to become their head.

248

It became the custom for the wealthy Jews of Turkey to visit the Holy Land on pilgrimage. They came frequently and in large groups, the favorite time being before the festival of *Shavuot* (Pentecost), when a number of ships carrying Jews from the Diaspora would dock at Jaffa. Moses Yerushalmi, who lived in Jerusalem in 1768 (and often served as a guide to the pilgrims), has described the visits of these Turkish and Italian Jews in detail: some came grandly, bringing several attendants— a butcher, a man to prepare the coffee, another to keep the tobacco dry, another to prepare the hookah, a scribe to record descriptions of the shrines, and so on. Yerushalmi served them variously as guide, secretary, and coffee-maker. He reported that the pilgrims would often donate large sums of money for the repair and adornment of holy places.

As well as organized visits and immigration from Turkey, there was immigration from North Africa and other parts of the Muslim world, though it was more gradual—for, unlike the Turkish immigrants who were able to support themselves or rely on regular assistance, these Jews were poor and unsupported. Many of the new arrivals feared the hardships that Jews were experiencing in Jerusalem, and settled in Safad and Tiberias. Nevertheless, the Jewish population of Jerusalem grew steadily. In a letter to the Diaspora written in 1741, the scholars of Jerusalem claimed that there were 10,000 Jews in the city.

This expansion resulted in further repressive legislation. In 1782, for instance, Jerusalem's Jews were forbidden to bury their dead on the Mount of Olives. A contemporary document records: ‹ Many years ago we purchased a plot as a burial place on the Mount of Olives, and there we have buried hundreds and thousands of rabbis and great ones of the world, peace be upon their souls . . . and it was for these that our eyes darkened when the wicked men [meaning their Muslim oppressors] rose up against us . . . they began to dig up every grave and disturbed the last rest of the dead of Israel, and mourning was loud and bitter in all the House of Israel . . . . We were forced to annul the decree by paying a huge sum to all the lords of the Land. ›

As if official persecution was not enough, disease and natural disasters added to Jerusalem's troubles. In 1757 smallpox killed ‹ more than 150 infants ›; in 1760 there was an earthquake; in 1772, during a revolt led by the rebel Ali Bey against the rulers of Egypt (he was attempting to establish an independent Mameluke Empire), there was a drought, and though a truce was declared to allow provisions to be brought to Jerusalem, prices were inflated and there was famine. In 1787 another drought was again followed by famine; then snow fell for five successive days, and the synagogue of the Constantinople Jews collapsed. People were unable to leave their homes—even to bury those who had perished in the storm.

These, then, were the tribulations faced by the Jews in Jerusalem during the 18th century. Throughout it there was a unique endeavor to reorganize communal life, to improve the economy, and to strengthen the spiritual life of the Holy City. Throughout, on the other hand, there was Arab enmity, official tyranny, public disorder, plague, and drought. Both the Constantinople committee and the Jews of Jerusalem fought to counteract these evils, but external events threatened to defeat them, and on more than one occasion Jerusalem seemed about to collapse again. Though the city remained a religious and scholastic center, economic and security factors halted its advance. And by the end of the 18th century Galilee had become once more the center of immigration.

The Jewish community in Hebron remained static throughout the 18th century. According to Rabbi Gedalia of Semiatitz, who arrived in 1700 with Rabbi Judah Hassid, there were some 40 householders in Hebron, all living in a single compound. The community had been split on the issue of Shabbetaism, and was deeply in debt to the Arabs. The administration was never stable, and there are records of constant fighting between the governors and the sheiks, of power passing from hand to hand, and of the governors' victimization of the Jews by means of exorbitant taxes and threats to destroy the synagogue or the cemetery.

Internal disorders among the local Bedouin tribes also affected the Jewish community. In 1724 war broke out between the local Arabs within the town itself and continued for three years. In 1727 the heads of the Hebron community wrote abroad: ‹ Because of the wars that have afflicted the city these three years, the place is divided into two opposing factions. We, situated in the center, are liable to violent death at all times, for the lead bullets fly back and forth and most fall within our compound, taking life after life out of Israel. Moreover, the two contestants now threaten to plunder our compound, burn our sacred scrolls, and hand our dwellings over to soldiers, so that we have had to pay a bribe to the commanders of 3000 pesos—a sum that we raised by borrowing at an interest of 30 per cent. ›

True to its splendid tradition, Constantinople was the savior once more. In 1729 the Constantinople Jews sent 2000 *zolotas* to Hebron in part payment of their debt of 46,000. But the amount was soon spent on current needs and the peril from the creditors remained. In Constantinople the Jews were dismayed: ‹ These Gentiles menace exceedingly: their voice, like a serpent, spits poison on the egg of Israel. The stillborn and the dead are dragged out from their graves and their bones are strewn all about. ›

More drastic measures were necessary. In 1733 the Jerusalem cabbalist Rabbi Gedalia Hayun went to Constantinople on behalf of Hebron and prompted the establishment there of a « Committee of Servants of Hebron. » The new committee undertook to pay off the community's debt, and sent a representative to Hebron for the purpose. But conditions continued to be difficult. Two outstanding emissaries were sent abroad on a fund-raising mission—Rabbi Haim David Azulai and Rabbi Haim Isaac Karigal. Rabbi Azulai, one of the greatest scholars and most powerful personalities of his time, visited western Europe twice—in 1753 and 1773. Rabbi Karigal also traveled extensively: in 1754 he visited Egypt, Syria, Iraq, and Turkey; in 1757 and again in 1768 he went to Europe and then on by sea to Jamaica; and in 1772 to Philadelphia, New York, and Newport, Rhode Island. In 1773 he went first to Surinam and then finally to Barbados, where he served as rabbi of the *Nidhei Yisrael* (the Exiled of Israel) congregation until his death in 1777.

Despite all the efforts on their behalf the Jews of Hebron still owed 25,000 pesos in 1765 and were under threat of expulsion. During the revolt of Ali Bey and the Russo-Turkish war of 1773, the Hebron community suffered dreadfully. Communications were severed, prices soared, money from abroad came irregularly. The Hebron committee in Constantinople again interceded on its behalf and persuaded Sultan Abdul-Hamid I to issue an order directing Arab creditors to reach agreement with the Jews as to the amount of the debt and the terms of payment.

Nevertheless, the Jews were sometimes unable to find the necessary money, and their failure led to renewed violence. In 1775 the Arabs accused the Jews of murdering the son of the ‹ Great Sheik, the king of the land, › and of throwing his corpse into a cesspit. The Arabs confined all the Jews, ‹ men, women, and children, › into one place to ‹ wreak vengeance. › They escaped only by paying a huge bribe to the local sheik.

But the community continued to grow slowly. In 1780 there were 300 Jews in the town—despite the continuing torment and extortion. In 1782 the heads of the community were thrown into jail when a debt installment was not paid (the interest alone was 40,000 florins). In 1798 the debt had risen to 120,000 grush—80,000 owed to the Arabs of Hebron and 40,000 to the neighboring villages. Once more the

Above left, the great Hebron scholar Rabbi Haim Isaac Karigal (1733-77). Karigal traveled throughout eastern Europe and America on behalf of the Hebron community before settling in Barbados, as rabbi, in 1763: the title-page of the famous sermon he delivered at Newport, Rhode Island, in May 1763, is shown on the left. Above right, the cabbalist and bibliographer Rabbi Haim David Azulai (1724-1806): he went to Western Europe to raise money for Hebron's impoverished community.

The Marquis de Thomé, a Christian savant, came to see me with great demonstrations of respect as well as another Christian of mark and an 'Italian abbé.' They stayed nearly two hours and I answered their questions. At the end the Marquis asked me to bless him: I blessed him, as well as the other Christians, it is strange—from the Travel Diary of Haim David Azulai (1755).

committee in Constantinople prevailed upon the sultan to cancel all interest on the debt on the understanding that the Jews would pay 10,000 grush annually. (The committee undertook to pay 8000 of this.) This temporarily alleviated the situation though it did not cure it.

Gaza and Shechem Little is known about the Jewish community in Gaza during the 18th century. The first information that a community still existed there during that period is contained in some notes on a manuscript of the Jerusalem physician and warden Raphael Mordecai Malki (apparently written by his son Ezra). The notes say that the manuscript was written in Gaza in 1711, and it may well be that Malki was rabbi there. Another reference to Gaza appears in the travel journal of Rabbi Azulai. In January 1754 (while on a fund-raising mission to Egypt from Hebron) he stopped over in Gaza and had to wait more than 50 days for a caravan to Egypt. But when Napoleon's army reached Gaza in 1799, any community that existed there was smashed completely; by 1811, not a single Jew remained.

Of Shechem's Jewish community, too, there is only slight and fragmentary information. The Shabbetaist Nehemiah Hayun lived in Shechem between 1698 and

251

1702, and we may assume that a small Jewish community existed there. But apparently there was no rabbi or rabbinical court and prior to 1749 all marriages and divorce cases had to come before the court in Jerusalem: it is recorded that the rabbis of Jerusalem sent ‹ to learn the facts about the people of Shechem. › Rabbi Joseph Sofer mentioned the Jewish community of Shechem in 1760, and subsequently a rabbinical ordinance was issued in Jerusalem to the effect that every man or woman coming to pray at the holy places in Shechem had to give four lions as a donation to the local community. The Christian minister Ezra Steel, later president of America's Yale University, recorded in his diary that when he discussed the synagogues of Palestine with Rabbi Karigal at Newport in 1773, Karigal mentioned that there was a small synagogue in Shechem as well. But it seems that efforts to expand the community in Shechem failed, and only a few Jews remained.

The reason for Safad's poverty and decline have already been detailed. In 1722-23 the Jews there fell victim to further famine, and five years later the town was swept by virulent plague: in 1728 the governor forbad the Jews to bury their dead in their old cemetery, claiming that they had acquired the property unlawfully. He also threatened to destroy existing graves, and again it was a question of paying heavy bribes to have the decree rescinded.

The Reemergence of Safad and Galilee

After the decline of the Ashkenazi congregation in Jerusalem, Safad was the only remaining place in Palestine where Ashkenazim could live in safety. As a minority group there they began to speak, dress, and behave like the Sephardim—preserving only their own form of prayer. However, Safad's Ashkenazi community grew as immigrants from Europe, unable to settle in Jerusalem, came to live there. According to a document of 1727, ‹ the city was resettled and its ruins rebuilt. › But, ironically, the improvement merely increased the community council's burden, for many of the immigrants had no means of livelihood: ‹ Expenditures for charity and for the scholars increased tenfold. › As the population grew, the local governors made greater demands upon the Jews. In a letter of 1736 the heads of the community voiced their indignation: ‹ Our heartbreak is as deep and wide as the ocean because of the hatred of the oppressor. His oppression has silenced us. › To make matters worse, plague struck again in 1743 ‹ and many of Israel perished. › Then, in 1760, houses and synagogues were destroyed by two severe earthquakes.

But nothing could stop the flow of immigrants from eastern Europe—many of them disciples of the Baal Shem Tov, and of the Gaon of Vilna (a celebrated Lithuanian Talmudist). In the second half of the century, there was a mass influx of hassidim—from Lithuania, Volhynia, Wallachia, and the Ukraine—under the leadership of Rabbi Menahem Mendel of Vitebsk.

Rabbi Mendel brought more than 300 men, women, and children to Safad, but though their enthusiasm was great, they were not wage earners, and had to subsist on charity from Russia. At the same time Rabbi Mendel continued to lead his followers in the Diaspora and appointed an assistant—Rabbi Shneur Zalman—to represent him there. Among the others who helped to keep the Diaspora hassidim together and materially assisted those in Palestine were Rabbi Levi Isaac of Berdichev, and the rabbis of Shpitovka and Sanovitz: these rabbis established special funds for the resettlement of Palestine that were invaluable to the new immigrants.

But, despite help from the Diaspora, Safad's economic condition worsened. In 1793 plague and famine came again and the community was forced to borrow 50,000 grush. In 1799 the rabbis of Safad wrote: ‹ The cruel adversary [meaning the sultan] has inflicted an enormous levy upon us, far and away beyond 23,000 douros . . . and the communal organizations are forced to obtain the cash immediately from barbarous overlords, at savage rates of interest. › In the same year Napoleon retreated from Galilee and the Jewish population became the traditional scapegoat

Tiberias in the early 19th century—a lithograph made by the French traveler Léon, Comte de Laborde, after his visit there in 1828.

for local anger. The Swiss traveler J. L. Burckhardt wrote of Jewish quarters in Safad being pillaged by ‹ the Turks, › apparently meaning the Muslim Arabs.

But in this same period Tiberias was revived—after 80 years of desolation. The main architect of the renaissance was the rabbi of Smyrna, Haim Abulafia, who was born in Hebron, had lived in Jerusalem, and was at one time rabbi of Safad. Abulafia had been approached by the enlightened Bedouin sheik Daher-al-Omar, ruler of Galilee, who was anxious to develop the area and prized the energy and capacity of its Jewish inhabitants. (He had similarly encouraged settlement of Cypriot Greeks in and around Acre.) Daher wrote to Abulafia: ‹ Arise, come up and inherit the land of Tiberias which your forefathers possessed. ›

Abulafia reached Tiberias in 1740. The sheik received him royally, dressed him in fine robes, and granted everything he requested. In two years Abulafia had built houses and courtyards for the Jews, and a synagogue more beautiful than any in the Land. He also built a fine bathhouse, shops for market day, and a press for sesame oil; and he rebuilt the wall around the Jewish quarter and began to construct roads. He ordered the Jews to plant fields and orchards, and consequently his popularity with the local rulers increased each day. ‹ The people of Tiberias are all healthy and happy, for the Land is free from all evil and fear. ›

It is clear that Abulafia viewed the rebuilding of Tiberias as the beginning of an ‹ Ingathering of the Exiles › as well as an immediate necessity. But he remained faithful to Sheik Daher throughout—even when a violent dispute broke out between the sheik and the Turkish authorities in Damascus. Involvement exposed Abulafia and the Jewish community to great danger, but Abulafia respected Daher's ability and believed that he would continue to support Jewish immigration. The opportune death of the pasha of Damascus closed the incident.

Abulafia's primary concern was to create prosperity in the community by developing trade and crafts, in addition to farming. As a result of his far-sighted policy the economy continued to expand even after Sheik Daher had fallen and had been replaced by a violent and intolerant Turkish governor. In 1798 (50 years after Abulafia's death) the heads of Tiberias' Jewish community wrote complaining of their vexations and debts. But in the same letter they spoke of urban construction: ‹ We have kept well to the dimensions of the building, which will be used as a college. Indeed, we are at work on a number of buildings in the town, and a new synagogue. ›

Another example of Daher's enlightened attitude to Jewish settlement was the restoration of the Jewish agricultural settlement at Kfar Yassif, near Acre. Here

The great mosque erected in Acre in 1781 by the tyrannical al-Jazzar Pasha, governor of the city from 1775 until his death in 1804.

Rabbi Solomon Abbadi, author of *Sha'arei Rahamim* (Gates of Mercy), played an important role. Kfar Yassif had existed for many generations. In 1741 Rabbi Abraham Hai Ishmael Sanguinetti and his associates, who had reached Palestine with Rabbi Haim Ben Attar, visited the place, and found that it had been ruined by siege and invading armies. Rabbi Abbadi restored it as an agricultural settlement, which survived until the mid 19th century.

There was a similar revival at Shfar'am, credit for which is traditionally given to Abulafia. A missionary named Schultz recorded that, when he came to Kfar Yassif in 1754, he was told that its rabbi had gone to Shfar'am. Evidently the Shfar'am community grew after Daher's son Ottman built a fortress in the village. It is also known that a rabbi from the west settled in Shfar'am and completed a book on rabbinics there in 1773. The British traveler J. S. Buckingham (in 1816) also spoke of the presence of Jews in Shfar'am. David Hillel, visiting the village in 1825, found some 20 families (all farmers), a tiny synagogue, and a large cemetery. And Sir Moses Montefiore's wife Judith referred to Shfar'am as a Jewish agricultural settlement in her memoirs: the settlement existed until the outbreak of World War I.

During Sheik Daher's reign, Jewish settlement was also strengthened at Peki'in. A number of settlers came to live there, and links with the other Jewish settlements in the area were tightened. In 1760 Rabbi Joseph Sofer came to live in Peki'in, and five years later Rabbi Simha of Zalazitz visited the settlement. He estimated that there were 50 Jewish families living there.

Sheik Daher also infused new life into the ancient city of Acre, which soon became an important administrative and commercial center. He repaired the fortress and port, and developed a prosperous foreign trade; and he also encouraged Jews, Cypriots, and Greeks to settle in the city. In 1746 Rabbi Moses Haim Luzzatto, a poet and cabbalist of Italian origin, arrived in Acre, but he died soon after in an epidemic, and was buried at Kfar Yassif.

Al-Jazzar Pasha and Farhi

With the fall of Sheik Daher and his sons, Acre came again under the jurisdiction of the Wali of Damascus, and a freed Bosnian slave, Ahmad al-Jazzar, was appointed governor. Jewish merchants began to come from Damascus to the port of Acre to do business. One of them—Haim Farhi—was invited by Jazzar to serve as his financial adviser. Farhi used his great influence with the government to get anti-Jewish decrees revoked and to check the extortions of local rulers. These kindnesses often infuriated the ruthless and cruel Jazzar. In one outburst he ordered that one of Farhi's eyes be gouged out and the tip of his nose cut off. But the two men were reconciled and Farhi returned to Jazzar's service.

(When Jazzar died in 1804, Farhi went into the service of Suleiman Pasha—formerly Jazzar's deputy—and helped him to become governor of Acre. Suleiman died young—in 1818—and Farhi acquired the governorship for his pupil Abdullah, Suleiman's son. But after two years in office, the corrupt Abdullah ordered the death of his benefactor. On August 24, 1820, Farhi's body was thrown into the sea.)

This drawing [below] exhibits the Pacha [al-Jazzar] in the act of counting his beads, at the time when he is condemning a man to lose his eyes. On the left appears his secretary [Farhi], a robust well-looking man. Some years ago, Jazzar sent this person to purchase some merchandise for him; when, on his return, thinking he had defrauded him, he put out his right eye, and cut off his nose; to make him, as he said, 'look like a lion.' Afterwards, however, finding that he [Farhi] had been just, he heaped innumerable presents on him, and has, ever since, remained firmly his friend—F. B. Spilsbury, Picturesque Scenery of the Holy Land and Syria (1803).

In 1799, Napoleon's armies entered Palestine. Napoleon planned to pass through Palestine into Syria and Asia Minor, seize Constantinople, gain control of the whole Ottoman Empire, and incidentally smash British trade in the Mediterranean. At first Napoleon hoped that Ahmad Jazzar (being of Bosnian origin) would join him against the sultan; but Jazzar, who ruled absolutely over the greater part of Palestine, was not tempted. Napoleon then resolved to conquer Palestine, to consolidate his conquest of Egypt, and thus assure provisions for his troops. His objective was not Jerusalem but the strategic points on the route to Constantinople. Napoleon took Jaffa on March 6, and there are records to show that after his army entered the town a delegation of Jews came and told him of the Messianic hopes they had pinned on his victory. Stiff resistance from the Turks hampered his advance toward Acre, and his army came to a standstill for several weeks before mounting an attack on the town.

Napoleon's army storming the walls of Acre. Napoleon abandoned the siege (and his plans to conquer Palestine) on May 26, 1799, and withdrew his army to Egypt: three months later he set sail secretly for France.

The Jews of Acre, led by Haim Farhi, sided with the Turks. Napoleon, thinking that if he could befriend Farhi he would be able to take the fortified port and proceed with his plans, sent emissaries to win Farhi over. But Farhi remained faithful to Jazzar, who obtained supplies and arms from a British fleet under the command of Sir Sydney Smith and succeeded in holding Napoleon off.

Meanwhile a French force led by Kléber had won a decisive victory near Mount Tabor (April 14, 1799). Napoleon then hoped that the Jews would join him, and on April 20 issued a proclamation calling on the Jews of Asia and Africa to rally to his flag for ‹ the restoration of ancient Jerusalem. › Many Jews did in fact enlist in Napoleon's army, and it has been suggested that he formed a Jewish brigade for the capture of Jerusalem. But the Jews of Acre remained unmoved, and in May 1799 Napoleon finally abandoned his attempts to take the town and withdrew his army to Egypt.

Napoleon's Appeal to the Jews of Asia and Africa

General Headquarters, Jerusalem, 1st Floreal, April 20, 1799, in the year 7 of the French Republic.

Israelites, unique nation, whom, in thousands of years, lust of conquest and tyranny have been able to deprive only of their ancestral lands, but not of name and national existence!

Attentive and impartial observers of the destinies of nations, even though not endowed with the gifts of seers like Isaiah and Joel, have long since also felt what these, with beautiful and uplifting faith, have foretold when they saw the approaching destruction of their kingdom and fatherland: And the ransomed of the Lord shall return, and come to Zion with songs and everlasting joy upon their heads: they shall obtain joy and gladness, and sorrow and sighing shall flee away (ISAIAH XXXV: 10).

Arise, then, with gladness, ye exiled! A war unexampled in the annals of history, waged in self-defence by a nation whose hereditary lands were regarded by its enemies as plunder to be divided, arbitrarily and at their convenience, by a stroke of the pen of Cabinets, avenges its own shame and the shame of the remotest nations, long forgotten under the yoke of slavery and, also, the almost two-thousand-year-old ignominy put upon you; and, while time and circumstances would seem to be least favourable to a restatement of your claims or even to their expression, and indeed to be compelling their complete abandonment, it offers to you at this very time, and contrary to all expectations, Israel's patrimony!

Bonaparte, Commander in Chief of the French Republic in Africa and Asia, to the rightful Heirs of Palestine.

Jerusalem, in the month of Nissan, of the year 5559.

Although there is no need to add anything to the letter which the man after God's heart, Bonaparte, that great and highly enlightened Commander in Chief of the French Armies in Africa and Asia, has directed to you, I, Aaron son of Levi, of the tribe of Levi, by the mercy of our God, Jehova Zebaoth, after the passing of numberless generations again first Rabbi and Priest in this Holy City, have, for the sake of the weak, thought fit to remind them of the words of Joel, son of Pethuel, Chapter IV, and of Zephaniah, son of Ehudi, Chapter II, and Malachi, Chapter II, 3.

Brethren, the so glorious prophecies contained therein have been, as to their larger part, already fulfilled by the victorious army of the great nation, and it now depends only on us to be not as the children of harlots and adulteresses, but true descendants of Israel, and to desire the inheritance of the people of the Lord, to behold the beauty of the Lord, and to inquire in his temple (PSALM OF DAVID XXVII: 4).

Take, then, unto yourselves the wings of the eagle and the strength of the lioness, like unto our fathers in the days of Nehemiah, son of Hachaliah, and Ezra, son of Seraiah, to rebuild the walls of the orphaned city and a temple to the Lord in which His glory shall live from now and for evermore.

Proclaim this to all nations among whom Jacob's seed is scattered, sanctify a combat, arouse the stronger, let all men of Israel capable of bearing arms gather and come up to us, let even the weak also declare I am strong! (JOEL III).

May the God of Abraham, of Isaac and of Jacob bless the work of our hands! May He do and accomplish this, as He hath sworn to our fathers! May He remember for good all that the great nation has done unto us (EZRA VII), and let the whole people speak as of Gideon, son of Joash (JUDGES VII).

Hear the word of the Lord and Bonaparte!

Aaron, Son of Levi, Rabbi of Jerusalem, to the Children of Captivity in the Lands of Sunrise and of Sunset, of Noon and of Midnight.

Napoleon's appeal (above) is thought to have been made at the gates of Jerusalem in 1799: its authenticity is confirmed by a report in the official French news sheet *Moniteur*, and by a transcript found in the papers of Wolf Fleckeles, head of the Prague community in the early 19th century.

BY THE END of the 18th century the decline of the Ottoman Empire's power was quite apparent; the weakness of its domestic civil administration, the enfeebled condition of its army, and its generally inept conduct of international affairs had taken their toll. This weakness, rooted in developments that began in the 17th century, did not become obvious until the end of the 18th century, when Selim III (1789-1808) failed in his attempts to modernize his army and administration and was assassinated by his opponents. The clouds over the sultan's court darkened. The rulers of Europe began to intervene in the internal affairs of the Ottoman Empire, referring to the empire as ‹ the sick man of the Bosporus. › Austria had already grown belligerent in the 18th century, and her attitude was shared early in the 19th century by both Russia and France.

Strategic, political, and religious factors raised Palestine (and all Syria) to international importance during this period. After the Crusades—and especially after their annexation to the Ottoman Empire—Palestine and Syria became outlying provinces of little importance to the masters of Constantinople. The revolts of Fahr-al-Din (a Druse), Daher-al-Omar (a Bedouin), and Ahmad Jazzar—all of whom dreamed of widening their spheres of influence and enriching themselves by imposing high taxes in those lands—were not important enough to disturb Constantinople, which continued to regard them as merely minor annoyances.

Then in October 1831 the Egyptian Ibrahim Pasha (son of Mohammed Ali, ruler of Egypt) invaded by land and sea. His forces took Jaffa without a fight, and generally met little resistance until they reached Acre. There, Abdullah Pasha and his garrison held the Egyptian army at bay for a while. Again the rulers in Constantinople miscalculated: thinking to weaken two dangerous leaders at once, they delayed sending help to Abdullah. In May 1832 Acre fell to the invaders and Abdullah was captured. The Egyptian's advance could not now be halted and he swept into Syria. Only the threats of Russia and Great Britain prevented Ibrahim Pasha from marching on Constantinople itself.

Ibrahim Pasha was a brilliant general and statesman, and a wise administrator. At first he retained the Muslim officials of Jaffa and Jerusalem who had been appointed by Abdullah, and only later began to replace them with members of families newly risen to power—such as the Abd-el-Hadi family of Shechem and the Kassim family of Jerusalem. Apart from regional civil governors, a number of military governors were appointed. Ibrahim was not satisfied with making only administrative changes, but tried to revolutionize the society itself. He abolished the administrative taxes and the collection of tolls from the devout and pilgrims—and, for the old system whereby the officials lived on whatever money they could extract from the people, he tried to substitute a system of regular government wages. The reforms infuriated the local potentates, and conscription for military service (applicable to all Muslims) hardly endeared Ibrahim to the fellahin.

As part of his campaign to enforce law and order, Ibrahim saw that the rights of Christian and Jew were safeguarded. He permitted the Jewish community to repair four synagogues in Jerusalem, and in another allowed them to replace a roof of cane and mud with a dome built of stone. (Technically synagogues could only be restored to their former state.) According to a Christian writer, the restorations cost 1,000,000 piasters. But despite these reforms—intended to raise the economic, social, and cultural level of the Land—and the vigorous and sincere efforts to maintain public order, most of the populace was hostile to the Egyptian regime. In the spring of 1834 the Arab peasants in Palestine revolted: they took Jerusalem, Tiberias, and Safad, and besieged Jaffa and Acre. The direct cause of the uprising was the military conscription of Muslims. But it was the sheiks and the other feudal lords—unwilling to surrender their prerogatives or accept Ibrahim Pasha's administration—who incited the Muslim populace, calling Ibrahim an « infidel. »

258

Above, the court of Selim III: Selim's far-sighted attempts to revitalize the Turkish army and administration were nullified by the incompetence of his ministers and the pomp of his court. His assassination in 1808 accelerated the disintegration of the Turkish Empire. Below, the Empire as it was at the close of the 18th century.

HE OTTOMAN EMPIRE 1800 C.E.

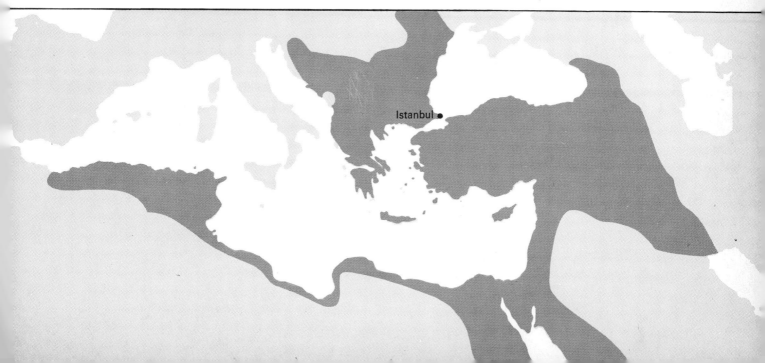

Istanbul

Ibrahim was forced to send to Egypt for help. When it came he crushed the revolt ruthlessly, giving the troops free license to kill, without discriminating between Jew and non-Jew, innocent and guilty. Many of the Jews in Safad were slaughtered. In Hebron, too, the soldiers indulged in a wholesale pogrom—and again the Jews were the principal victims. The Jews of Jerusalem were luckier, and their casualties were few. In Tiberias, the Jewish congregation averted disaster only by handing over all their possessions to the rioters.

In 1840, the intervention of the European powers forced the Egyptians to withdraw. In October Acre fell after a joint offensive by British and Turkish naval forces. (After this, Acre declined rapidly and Haifa and Jaffa became the main ports of Palestine.) One by one the Arab tribes surrendered to Turkey. By the end of December the shattered Egyptian army had been beaten back across the border, and Turkish forces reoccupied the whole of Palestine.

Although Napoleon had abandoned his plan to conquer Palestine, the Turks continued to suspect the Jews of conspiring with him. The early years of the 19th century were hard ones for the Jews of Jerusalem, and this Turkish suspicion brought fresh oppression. Not only the governor but his assistants and military commanders used every opportunity to exploit the Jews. Apart from the regular poll and land taxes they were compelled to pay a « government aid tax, » festival taxes, and a monthly tax. Nevertheless, the community grew. The arrival of Rabbi Menahem Mendel of Sheklov (a disciple of the Gaon of Vilna) in 1816 heralded the expansion of Jerusalem's Ashkenazi community. And the Ashkenazim lost no time in making themselves a force to be reckoned with.

In 1820 Rabbi Shlomo Pah was sent to Constantinople in an endeavor to get the time-honored debts of the Ashkenazim written off. Pah succeeded—and from then on Ashkenazim could dwell unchallenged in Jerusalem again. But their main synagogue was not restored immediately and the congregation had to await the governor's edict, releasing them from outstanding obligations, before they could go ahead with its repair. The edict came in 1824. In 1825 an uprising of fellahin prevented all thought of repair. The governor of Acre, Abdullah Pasha, was charged with putting down the revolt. His artillery shelled the city into early surrender. Then Mustapha, pasha of Damascus (who was still tax-master for Jerusalem), suddenly demanded an indemnity of 100,000 lions from the Jews alone—more than half their annual income—though they had taken no part in the rising.

Although many emissaries went to the Diaspora, the funds that reached Jerusalem did not cover the community's debts and ordinary needs. Not all Diaspora communities responded generously to the fund appeals; some complained that the expenses of the emissaries were excessive, being enough to ‹ build castles of gold and silver. › But details of the community's needs, income, and expenditure exist in *Tov Yerushalayim* (The Goods of Jerusalem) by Isaac Farhi, then communal treasurer. Four funds were established in Jerusalem to aid the needy: the Scholars' Fund, the Poor Fund, the Sick Fund, and the Orphan Girls' Fund. The Scholars' Fund (which had an average yearly income of 12,000 grush) was designed to help theological students: all but one tenth of this income came from local offerings in memory of the dead. The Poor Fund provided Jerusalem's numerous poor and helpless inhabitants with food every Sabbath, fuel in winter, and special food for Passover: the fund was replenished by a regular tax paid by all receiving money from abroad. And every Friday the wardens of the community went from door to door collecting loaves of bread for the poor. The Sick Fund paid for medical treatment and helped with funeral expenses. It was supported by the relatives of the deceased who paid either 40 or 25 grush, depending on whether they were wealthy or middle class. The Orphans' Fund saw to the upkeep, schooling, and marriage of

260

The synagogue of Rabbi Yohanan Ben Zakkai in Jerusalem: it was built on the spot where the sage is said to have prayed after the city's destruction in 70 C.E. by the Romans.

orphan girls: it was replenished by the sale of clothing bequeathed by deceased members of the community.

Part of the money collected abroad naturally went to meet the expenses of travel. Other portions had to be given to harsh governors as a means of dispelling slander or annulling some unpleasant decree. And some of the money was needed to pay interest on usurious borrowings. Consequently very little of the money collected actually reached the destitute in Jerusalem. Isaac Farhi spoke of the many widows and orphans in the city, and every new immigrant ship increased the burden. Despite the many hardships, the Sephardi community decided to restore its old synagogues, which were badly in need of repair. At first the Jews were denied the special permit without which, as members of a non-Muslim religion, they could not undertake the work. But when the Egyptians conquered Palestine the heads of the community renewed their request, which was granted in 1835. The community then found it could not afford to undertake the necessary repairs, but decided that it must begin, for fear that the permission would be revoked and that great expenses would then be required to secure it again. Fund-raising emissaries were sent to the Diaspora and in August 1835 the work began.

Above, Jerusalem—as depicted on the wall of a 19th-century German *succa* (tabernacle). Right, the seal of the Austro-Hungarian Jewish community of Jerusalem.

The Ashkenazim had earlier received permission to restore the ruins of their old synagogue, named after Rabbi Judah Hassid. But just when the Ashkenazim had cleared away the ruins the Egyptians conquered Palestine and negotiations had to be started anew. In 1836 Rabbi Abraham Solomon Zalman Zoref went to Egypt for the purpose. With the help of the European powers (who saw the Jews as a means of expanding European influence), Rabbi Zoref succeeded in obtaining a decree ordering the creditors to reach a compromise with their Ashkenazi debtors.

Fresh impetus to the rebuilding of Jerusalem was given by the visits to Palestine of the British philanthropist Sir Moses Montefiore. His love of the Land and of Judaism brought him to Palestine seven times to examine conditions and to seek ways of bettering them. He sent regular contributions to the towns of the Holy Land, both from his own pocket and from funds he raised. He planned and established public institutions and economic projects in Palestine and was particularly interested in the advancement of agriculture.

Sir Moses Montefiore

Sir Moses first visited Palestine with his wife Judith in 1827. While his purpose was to become acquainted with the Holy Land, he lavished money on educational and charitable institutions. He began to launch projects during their second visit, in 1840. He instructed his secretary, Eliezer Halevy, to compile a detailed census of the Jews in Palestine. Ostensibly this was to serve as a basis for carrying out various projects to improve the condition of Palestine Jewry; actually, it merely served for the distribution of alms.

From the census it is clear that Jerusalem had become the pivot of Jewish life in Palestine—with a population of 2943, about 46 per cent of the total Jewish population of Palestine. Of these, 2450 were Sephardim and Orientals, and 493 Ashkenazim.

I shall apply to Mohammed Ali for a grant of land for fifty years. . . . This grant obtained, I shall, please Heaven, on my return to England, form a company for the cultivation of the land and the encouragement of our Brethren in Europe to return to Palestine. Many Jews now emigrate to New South Wales, Canada, etc.; but in the Holy Land they would find a greater certainty of success; here they will find wells already dug, olives and vines already planted, and a land so rich as to require little manure. By degrees I hope to induce the return of thousands of our brethren to the land of Israel. I am sure they would be happy in the enjoyment of the observance of our holy religion, in a manner which is impossible in Europe—from the Diaries of Sir Moses Montefiore (1839).

Right, the British philanthropist Sir Moses Montefiore, who encouraged many of the early Jewish settlements in Palestine.

The Ashkenazim were divided into three groups—34 were of Dutch and Hungarian origin, 41 hassidim, and 418 of miscellaneous European origin. The Sephardim and Orientals were united in one organization. The ratio of Jews in Jerusalem to those in the rest of Palestine remained fairly constant until after World War I. Thus in 1914 Jerusalem's 45,000 Jews comprised 45 per cent of the country's Jewish population. But after the Balfour Declaration (in 1917) when Palestine came under the British Mandate and the third wave of immigration began, the overall Jewish population increased tenfold while that of Jerusalem only doubled (to 100,000).

According to Montefiore's census, 80 of Jerusalem's Sephardim and seven Ashkenazim were brokers, peddlers, money changers, or dealers in livestock, cheese, wine, and books. Other professions included weavers, tailors, porters, bakers, butchers, barbers, millers, cobblers, carpenters, metalworkers, smiths, bookbinders, household workers, hatters, a watchmaker, and several physicians—in all 229 Sephardim and Orientals, and 29 Ashkenazim. There were also 407 students and scholars—289 Sephardim and Orientals, and 118 Ashkenazim.

Montefiore's visit in 1840 coincided with the notorious blood libel in Damascus (accusing the Jews of ritual murder), which eventually led to the Jerusalem blood libel of 1847. In letters to Montefiore, the leaders of Palestine's Jewish community spoke of the need to develop new sources of livelihood by providing technical and agricultural training. Emphasis was laid on the question of education for children and the need to train them in profitable trades. The first people to concern themselves with this problem were the Christian missionaries, who also provided medical services and aid to the poor. But the Jews were reluctant to trust them.

In 1855 the Eliza von Lemel School was founded in Jerusalem and in 1864 the Evelina de Rothschild School. Montefiore founded a number of charitable institutions and aid funds to help the poor of Jerusalem, though owing to bad management many of these never bore direct fruit. He also financed the building of houses outside the city walls, a radical innovation. Up to this time most Jewish dwellings (and a number of synagogues) were rented from Arab neighbors: it required great

263

courage to move outside the city walls into an area open to bandits and robbers. One after another the new quarters went up. Yemin Moshe (built by Montefiore in 1856) was the first; Nahlat Shiv'a was built in 1869; Me'a She'arim (today the ultra-religious quarter) and Even Yisrael in 1873; Beit Ya'akov and Mishkenot Yisrael in 1875; and many more followed. By the end of the century, more than half the Jewish community was living outside the city's walls. Many Jews became expert masons, stonecutters, and bricklayers—all trades entirely new to the Jews. Homes were built for orphans and the aged, as well as dispensaries, clinics, and hospitals. In 1870, the Alliance Israélite Universelle (an international organization founded by French Jews in 1860) started the first agricultural school at Mikveh Yisrael, and in 1882 a trade school in Jerusalem where teaching was in French.

The city's intellectual life continued to develop. Jerusalem's first printing press was founded in 1842 by Israel Bak (with Montefiore's help); Bak's press at Safad had been wrecked by fellahin in 1834 and by earthquake in 1837. Soon both Jews and European Christians brought more printing presses to Jerusalem, and newspapers began to appear (papers like *Halbanon* and *Yehuda Veyerushalayim*), as well as a great many books, pamphlets, and maps.

Jerusalem was the exception; elsewhere the story was much less happy. Hebron was in a precarious state and quite unable to keep up with the development and expansion of other towns. Immigrants were slow to come to Hebron, though occasional new settlers moved in. In 1819, for instance, a rift between rival rabbinic schools caused 15 hassidic families to move to Hebron from Tiberias. The hassidim established themselves as a separate community, sending their own emissaries to the Diaspora. During the campaign of Ibrahim Pasha (when the local Arabs rose against the Egyptians) the Jews of Hebron suffered more than any Jewish community in the Land—for the Egyptian troops stormed the town and ruthlessly slaughtered the rebels without pausing to differentiate between Jew and Arab. After this disaster, the new hassidim united themselves with Hebron's Sephardi community; and in 1834 they jointly sent an emissary to Europe to seek aid.

But Hebron started to recover when Rabbi Elijah Mani, a distinguished scholar from Baghdad, came to settle there. He devoted himself immediately to the betterment of Hebron's Jewish communal life. He founded the Beit Ya'akov yeshiva and a synagogue, and turned Hebron into a center of scholarship for young people. When their rabbi, Moses Pereira, died in 1865, the Jews of Hebron asked Mani to become their leader. At the time he was busy helping the victims of a plague that had recently struck the town; but once the plague had subsided, he accepted the office—on condition that he received no salary.

Communal life was reorganized and Jews from Oriental countries began to immigrate to Hebron in large numbers. During a drought in 1872, Rabbi Mani went abroad and succeeded in obtaining substantial help for his community. Later he went again to raise money to redeem the Cave of Machpelah from the Arabs. (According to the Bible, this was the cave bought by Abraham as a burial place for his family.) He also actively encouraged agriculture, and wrote to Sir Moses Montefiore that plots of land around Hebron should be purchased from the Arabs for settlement and cultivation by Jews.

Another champion of Hebron's community (as well as of the other Jewish communities in Palestine) was Rabbi Haim Hezkiyahu Medini, author of the 18-volume *halachic* encyclopedia, *Sdei Hemed*. A native of Jerusalem, Medini had served for 33 years as the rabbi of Karassobazar in the Crimea, where he revolutionized and revitalized Jewish life. In 1899 he returned to Palestine and in 1901 settled in Hebron. Gaza had suffered heavily from Napoleon's occupation in 1799. The Jewish community grew smaller and poorer and in 1811 the few remaining Jews left the town

Hebron's Revival

264

Above, the town of Hebron—a photograph taken in the second half of the 19th century. Left, the seal of Hebron's Ashkenazi community: it depicts the Cave of Machpelah, tomb of the Patriarchs.

for Hebron and Jerusalem. (Contemporaries related how the Jews from Gaza brought with them the doors of Gaza's old synagogue and fixed them to the ancient synagogue in Hebron. The doors, which existed until the destruction of Jewish Hebron by the Arabs in 1929, were decorated with the Star of David and other carvings.) It was half a century before Jews returned to Gaza, though major Jewish settlement took place further north at Gedera and Birtuvia. Gradually these two settlements brought new life to Gaza, and by the 1890s there were about 75 Jews living there, many reasonably well off. Gaza was famous for its barley, and ships called regularly at its port to load grain for brewers abroad. Later, when World War I broke out in 1914, Jews of British and French nationality were banished from Gaza. And when the fighting approached the town, the remaining Jews were expelled.

The End of Shechem's Community

The Shechem community was extremely small in the 19th century. Rabbi David Hillel visited Shechem in 1832, and found about 10 native Jewish families and a tiny synagogue. The following year, Rabbi Mendel of Kamenitz noted that there were two Sephardi *minyans* and one Ashkenazi. (A *minyan*, consisting of 10 males above the age of 13, is required for formal worship.)

In 1837 Shechem was hit by an earthquake and Rabbi Israel of Sheklov wrote that ‹ houses and all the shops collapsed and about 60 lives were lost. › The Montefiore census of 1839 records that there were 25 families—approximately 75 people. But only two families were natives of Shechem; the majority came from Syria, Persia, Yemen, Jerusalem, Rhodes, Constantinople, Sarajevo, North Africa, and the West. Some were merchants, but most were artisans, plumbers, smiths, woodcutters, cobblers; one was a tailor. According to Montefiore's second census of 1866, there were only 12 Jewish families in Shechem: four merchants, eight cobblers, smiths, a silk worker, and a watchmaker—all extremely poor. Seven children studied at the school, which was a room in the synagogue.

No new Jewish settlements were established around Shechem, and gradually its Jewish occupants departed. A publication of 1896 gives the number of Jews there as 50. Three or four years later, as the scholar and geographer Abraham Moses recorded in his *Almanac*, the total was 31. After that the exodus quickened, and when the present author visited the city in 1908 he was unable to find one Jew

265

Above, Polish Jews wait to embark at Jaffa after a pilgrimage to Jerusalem (*c.* 1850). Right, the seal of Jaffa's community (1892), bearing the biblical phrase: 'Unto the great sea . . . shall be your coast.'

there: except for a few tombstones that had escaped the vandalism of the local Arabs, there was absolutely no trace of the 700-year-old Jewish community.

Until the 19th century, Ramleh had no permanent Jewish community. But as the nearby port of Jaffa developed, Ramleh became a convenient overnight stopping place for people traveling from Jaffa to Jerusalem; and in 1896 David Yudelowitz wrote that a number of Jews had gone to settle there. The new settlers included carpenters and metalworkers who had come with the help of Nissim Behar, at whose school in Jerusalem they had learned their trades. Ramleh remained static after World War I—principally because the introduction of the automobile robbed the town of its « stop-over » advantages. According to the British Mandate census of 1922, there were still 35 Jews. By 1931 (after the anti-Jewish outbreaks of 1929) there were no Jewish inhabitants left in Ramleh.

Napoleon had sacked Jaffa in 1799 on his march north from Gaza, but Mohammed Abu Nabut (a vassal of Jazzar) rebuilt the city early in the 19th century. He created the harbor and the market place, and soon vineyards and orchards were flourishing again. The fact that Jaffa served as a transit station for immigrants and pilgrims to Palestine aroused the special interest of Turkish Jewry. In 1820 Isaiah Ajiman, treasurer to the commander of the Janissary Guard in Constantinople, visited Jerusalem. When he saw how the Jews had to be put up in Christian houses on arrival in Palestine, he bought a compound in Jaffa and built there a lodging place for Jewish pilgrims and travelers.

A group of Moroccan Jews came to live in Jaffa in 1838 and they were said to be the first to resettle there. But Montefiore's census of 1839 shows that Jews from

Resettlement of Jaffa

Turkey, Egypt, Smyrna, Bulgaria, and Yemen were already living there. When the Crimean War ended in 1856, Jewish Jaffa began to flourish again. Christian pilgrims came much more frequently, and passed through the town on their way to holy places. At this time, too, Jerusalem's commerce was expanding and merchants from Jerusalem began to settle in Jaffa. Among them was Haim Amzalek, formerly of Gibraltar, who opened a commercial establishment in Jaffa with several partners. (Eventually he was appointed British vice-consul there.) A few years later a group of Jerusalem Ashkenazim founded Jaffa's first Ashkenazi community.

Upper Galilee

The series of disasters that struck the towns of Galilee in the preceding century had prevented the strengthening and expansion of their Jewish communities. But after the earthquake of 1754 and the revolts and pillaging that followed it, the communities of Safad and Tiberias began to increase; and the arrival in 1808 of disciples of the Gaon of Vilna (led by Rabbi Menahem Mendel of Sheklov) breathed new life into them. Other immigrants followed, and in 1810 Burckhardt reported that there were 150 Jewish houses in Safad.

Rabbi Mendel moved from Safad to Jerusalem with several families in 1816, and was succeeded by Rabbi Israel of Sheklov, leader of Galilee's *Mitnagdim* (disciples of the Gaon of Vilna). Israel was a brilliant scholar and communal leader, who worked tirelessly for the welfare of the community. But he had much to contend with. When the 19th century opened, the Jews of Safad still had the help of Haim Farhi, Jazzar's adviser in Acre. Farhi protected Safad's community from persecution and helped it financially. But after Farhi's assassination his murderer, Abdullah, began to persecute Safad's Jews. In 1826 some scholars wrote from Safad: ‹ Since the day on which the proud Father of Israel [Haim Farhi] was torn down, the entire being of the community has been upset. › Then locusts and drought returned, and the communal debt had soon reached 300,000 piasters.

An earthquake struck in 1822. In 1825 and 1833 there was torrential rain; houses collapsed and were washed away. Another earthquake in 1834 was followed by a fellahin uprising. For 33 days the Arabs plundered and wrecked the Jewish quarters. In 1837 still another earthquake shook Safad, Shechem (Nablus), Tiberias, and some 30 villages in Upper Galilee. Two thousand people were killed in Safad alone, many Jews among them. There was to be no respite. In the summer of 1838 the Druse revolted against Ibrahim Pasha, and the Jews were the scapegoats once again.

After Ibrahim's withdrawal to Egypt and the restoration of Turkish authority in Palestine, the fighting in Galilee ceased; but terrorism of Jews by the Arabs and officials continued. Documents show that the Jews of Safad protested to the authorities in Beirut, Sidon, Tripoli, and Acre. The response was often sympathetic; but the authorities' directives, when given, were disobeyed, or obeyed for only a short period, and persecution continued.

Tiberias shared Safad's fate. In 1802 Rabbi Joseph Ben Samon, an emissary from Tiberias to India, gave a depressing description of the town's condition. During the peasant uprising against Ibrahim Pasha the Jews there had to pay heavy bribes to avoid destruction. And their losses in the earthquake of 1837 were considerable: it is estimated that 700 Jews were killed. But the community held on. The tomb of Rabbi Meir, « the Miracle Worker, » was a source of both comfort and revenue. Jews in the Diaspora sent regular contributions in memory of Rabbi Meir, and the Jews of Tiberias supported themselves with these.

As the 19th century progressed, Tiberias began to expand again. In 1843, there were 50 Ashkenazi and 80 Sephardi families (about 650 souls). In 1848 the Jewish population numbered 1514; 881 were Ashkenazim. In 1887 Schumacher counted 2035 Jews. Luncz, in 1895, counted 3200. And the Turkish census of 1911 recorded 3389 Jews of Ottoman nationality.

Throughout this whole period, the Jews of the Diaspora never forgot their homeland, never relinquished the desire to plow their own soil again. At first newcomers were forced to live the lives of a persecuted minority in the cities. But as immigration increased and the great powers became more tolerant, the new immigrants turned to the fields and began to establish Jewish villages and settlements where they could live in peace. The Jews of Palestine were tired of living on charity from abroad, and hastened to make themselves independent.

A significant start was made by Israel Bak between 1837 and 1839. A practical man with a deep faith in the Jews' ability to rebuild the Land, he began working as a pioneer in agriculture and industry—with his own hands and his own money. On arriving in Safad in 1832 he tried to establish a printing press, but failed because of the disasters already described. Then he approached Ibrahim Pasha and asked for a plot of land to cultivate: he was granted the abandoned Druse village of Jermak on Mount Meron. Bak moved there after the earthquake of 1837, built houses, planted gardens, and sowed fields. According to one source, five Ashkenazi families followed him there, and engaged in vine culture.

The visits of Sir Moses Montefiore and his wife greatly stimulated this agricultural trend. Montefiore wrote in his diary that at Safad he had become convinced that the Jews there wished to free themselves of their economic plight and turn to agriculture. He also wrote of several Jews who had leased land near Safad that they cultivated in partnership with the Muslims.

In 1839, Mordecai Zoref of Jerusalem proposed to Montefiore the establishment of a Jewish agricultural colony, near Gaza; and the heads of the Safad and Jerusalem communities submitted a series of memoranda containing proposals for the establishment of Jewish farm settlements. The heads of the Sephardi and Ashkenazi communities of Safad affirmed that ‹ the Jews are joyfully prepared to work the earth and thus earn their bread, or be herdsmen of sheep and cattle, although they have no previous experience of this. › They implored Montefiore to ‹ buy or rent for them a plot of sown land, there to plant vines or olives, there to do work of herdsmen, to breed oxen and sheep, or any allied occupation, so that they might hope to eat the bread of their own toil. ›

Montefiore took their appeal to heart. When he returned to England he developed a plan for the renting of 200 villages in Galilee to be settled by Jews—and he submitted his plan to Mohammed Ali, then governor of Egypt and Palestine. To finance his plan Montefiore undertook to establish a bank with a capital of £1,000,000 (then about $435,000). His letter expressed a wish ‹ to meet the pasha at Alexandria to ask him to protect the Jews of the Holy Land, especially the inhabitants of Safad and Tiberias who are always liable to pillage and slaughter . . . to repair the ruins of Tiberias . . . to permit the Jews to rent areas of field and vineyards for a period of 50 years on condition that lessees be exempt from all taxes and levies except the rent. ›

The outcome of the meeting was not very encouraging. Mohammed Ali said that he viewed the plan with favor and promised to give Montefiore his reply and approval in writing. Montefiore's secretary Eliezer Halevy, who was present at the interview, recorded: ‹ I gathered from his [Ali's] words that the proposal to found Jewish settlements in the Holy Land and Syria had caused him to fear that the Jews intended to set up a new state in their ancestral homeland. › Meanwhile the Egyptians were forced to quit Palestine and further negotiations with the governor of Egypt were pointless. Montefiore was persistent, and sought discussion with the authorities in Turkey—but to no avail.

Sir Moses Montefiore's noble plan did not then materialize. Apart from adverse political factors, the Jews of Palestine were not psychologically or technically ready for the inevitable struggle. Consequently, Montefiore's efforts had no immediate

Some of the first students at Mikveh Yisrael, the pioneer agricultural school founded by Karl Netter on behalf of the Alliance Israélite Universelle in 1870.

effect. But they did plant the seed for the future. The concept of a Return to Zion appealed strongly to thinkers, statesmen, and writers the world over. The British especially displayed a remarkable interest in returning the Jews to their ancient Land, and began to consider practical steps to help them.

The great re-awakening of interest in Palestine also affected other Christian centers. Two Scottish missionaries who were sent to Palestine, Turkey, and the Balkans in 1839 told in their journals of conversations with Wallachian Jews from whom they heard about Rabbi Yehuda Bibas of Corfu. Rabbi Bibas was visiting Jewish communities, preaching self-help and encouraging the Jews to study science and worldly subjects, ‹ to learn the military arts and wrest Palestine from the Turks under the leadership of the Messiah, just as the Greeks had rescued their fatherland. › Later the missionaries met Bibas: ‹ Immediately he began to speak of the Promised Land. He thought that collections for the Holy Land ought to be abolished, and that the Jews there ought to be forced to work, even at bayonet point. . . . He thought Sir Moses Montefiore's plans to buy lands in Palestine would prove useless so long as there was no security for property there. ›

Bibas made a great impression wherever he spoke, and his ideas created a favorable climate of opinion for the great « revivalists » who followed him—men like his pupil Rabbi Alcalai (formerly rabbi of Zemlin on the Danube) who traveled extensively, rousing Jews to action and winning support for his ideas in Vienna, Berlin, London, and Paris. Alcalai's oratory and his writings attracted scholars, intellectuals, and businessmen: and to implement his ideas he founded the *Hevrat Yishuv Eretz Yisrael*— « the Palestine Settlement Society. »

As a result of Alcalai's work (and of such leaders as Sir Moses Montefiore and Rabbi Bibas before him) the way was paved for the pioneers who were to rebuild the Land of Israel in the next three generations.

It is the natural right of the Jewish people, like any other people, to control their own destiny in their sovereign state.

Accordingly we, the members of the National Council, representing the Jewish people in the Land of Israel and the Zionist Movement, have assembled on the day of the termination of the British Mandate for Palestine, and, by virtue of our natural and historic right and of the resolution of the General Assembly of the United Nations, do hereby proclaim the establishment of a Jewish State in the Land of Israel - The State of Israel.

FROM THE DECLARATION OF INDEPENDENCE   MAY 1948

Part Six

David Ben-Gurion

From the Founding of Petah Tikva
to the Present Day
1878-

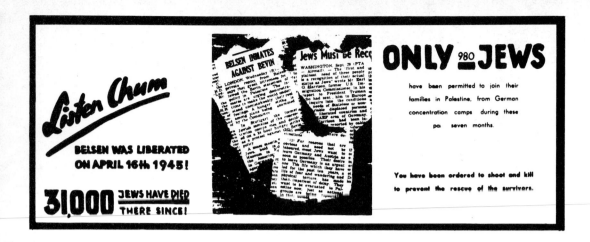
The longing to return to Zion and in Zion to renew the independence of Israel was ever in the hearts of the Jewish people. But in the last quarter of the 19th century there was a fundamental change in the nature of this aspiration. Till then, the focus of the longing had been a mystic faith in the coming of the Messiah. Till then, Jewish farmsteads had continued to exist in the Land, especially in Galilee, but they had attracted no newcomers. Jews driven from Spain and Portugal, and later Jews from Russia, gravitated to the four holy cities of Jerusalem, Hebron, Safad, and Tiberias. Now Jews began to settle and cultivate the land itself.

The great historic turning point was the independent effort of Jews themselves to become workers on the land, to found villages in which they themselves would settle, and later to develop industry and shipping as well. It is to them and the heirs of their tradition in the following 70 years that credit must be given for the resurgence of the State of Israel.

The first protagonists in this historic drama were a small group of veteran Jerusalemites, led by Joel Moses Salomon. Born in the walled Old City in 1838, Salomon preached his plan in *Halbanon* (the Lebanon), the first Hebrew newspaper to appear in Jerusalem in 1863. His was a plan of down-to-earth farming by Jews. With the help of two energetic Hungarian Jews, David Guttman and Yehoshua Shtampfer, Salomon's dream was realized. Together the three bought 844 acres of land in Arab Muleibis, not far from the Yarkon River, and established a Jewish village there which they called Petah Tikva (Gateway of Hope). That was in 1878. Two years later, together with 60 others, they purchased 2725 additional acres. But the place was infested with malaria, which wreaked havoc among the settlers in 1880 and 1881, killing many and compelling the survivors to leave.

A second village, Gei-Oni, in Upper Galilee, was settled at the same time by Jews from Safad. Its first inhabitants, indigent folk, endured great hardships, and soon practically all of them left. But, in 1882, Jews from Romania came and resettled the spot, giving it its present name, Rosh Pina.

At the time these two settlements were founded, the Jewish population of Palestine was estimated at about 24,000. More than half of these Jews lived in Jerusalem, and nearly all the rest in Hebron, Safad, Tiberias, Jaffa, and Acre. In the 16th century, at the beginning of the period of Ottoman rule in Palestine (see page 232), Safad had been the spiritual center of the Land and of Judaism. In the 19th century Jerusalem gradually assumed this position. In 1841 Israel Bak, who had founded a printing plant in Safad, moved it to Jerusalem, where it became the first in that city. In 1854 James Rothschild of Paris established the first Jewish hospital in Jerusalem. At the same time the first secular Jewish school—named after a German-Jewish merchant, Simon von Lemel—was founded in Jerusalem. And in 1864 the Evelina de Rothschild School for Jewish Girls was founded.

Above, Eliezer Ben-Yehuda, architect of the modern Hebrew language. Ben-Yehuda fought fiercely to revive Hebrew as the living language of a pioneering Yishuv—despite the fact that he was ostracized by the leaders of orthodox Jewry, who accused him of profaning a holy language. Today, Hebrew is an organic part of everyday life in Israel. Far left, one of the many Hagana "protest" leaflets distributed clandestinely to British soldiers sent to police Palestine in 1945.

The Revival of Hebrew

Until the 1890s, the majority of Jews in Jerusalem were *Sephardim* of two types: descendants of Jews expelled from Spain, who spoke a dialect of Spanish (with an admixture of Hebrew words) called Ladino; and descendants of North African Jews from the Maghreb, who spoke Arabic. Immigrants from the Caucasus spoke Georgian. The *Ashkenazim* (mainly German Jews) spoke Yiddish. When the leaders of the different Jewish communities came together, however, they spoke Hebrew. The first person to introduce Hebrew into his home was Eliezer Ben-Yehuda, a Lithuanian Jew (born January 7, 1858), who studied medicine in Paris and came to the Land in 1881. With everyone he spoke only Hebrew. He devoted his entire life to a study of Hebrew, enriching it, reviving it as a spoken language, and composing a Hebrew dictionary of 17 volumes, the last 12 volumes of which appeared after his death (in 1922) in Jerusalem.

A friend and collaborator of Ben-Yehuda was Yehiel Michal Pines, who was born in the Grodno district of Russia in 1843, came to the Land in 1878, and settled in Jerusalem. When Ben-Yehuda came to Jerusalem the two men, together with a number of enlightened teachers—such as David Yellin, Yosef Meyuhas, and a few others—established a society called *Tehiat Yisrael* (Revival of Israel) with the aim of making Hebrew the spoken language of the Jewish people, settling the land with Jewish farmers, and developing trade and industry.

The center of the Jewish world then was Europe. In 1880 there were 7,750,000 Jews in the world, almost nine tenths of them Europeans—the majority in tsarist Russia, which at that time included part of Poland, Lithuania, Latvia, Estonia, and Finland. Emancipation, after the French Revolution, gave birth to two contrary tendencies: assimilation, which tugged at the Jews of Western Europe, and national rejuvenation, a powerful force in Eastern and Southern Europe. The ancient ardor for national revival now cast off its mysticism, its faith in miracles, and donned a *halutzic* (pioneering) garb. A belief spread that it was possible for a Jew to win control over his destiny, as well as the destiny of his people. This faith was nourished by the renewed influence of the Bible, illuminated by the Enlightenment Movement and 19th-century Hebrew literature (including Mapu's *Love of Zion* and the verses of Chaim Nachman Bialik, greatest Jewish poet of these times) and also by the national and social revolutions that were beginning to convulse Europe. Jewish youth learned to appreciate the dignity of man, and to respect people who fought for freedom. They came to perceive the strength and significance of workers and peasants. Thus they were inspired to carve out a new road to the longed-for redemption: *aliya*, the traditional "going up" to the Land of Israel, but now with the aim of working the soil.

In Kharkov and other Russian cities, Jewish students formed an organization called *Bilu*, the initials of the Hebrew words for 'O House of Jacob, come, let us go!' The first group of Bilu members reached the Land in the summer of 1882 and went to work as day laborers at Mikveh Yisrael. Although pogroms and anti-Semitism in the early 1880s precipitated a mass exodus of European Jewry, especially from the East, they did not determine the goal and direction of the emigration; least of all did they direct the exiles toward aliya and settlement in the Land of Israel. The Jewish immigrants who began to pour into the Land at the start of the 1880s were drawn, magnetically, by the vision of Jewish redemption. The immigrants included not only young people but older men and women who gave up the security of their existence in Europe to make a new life on the land in Israel. These were the founders of the first settlements after Petah Tikva—Rishon Le-Zion, established by Russian Jews on the dunes south of Jaffa; Zichron Ya'akov in Samaria on the hills overlooking the Mediterranean, and Rosh Pina—both founded by Jews from Romania. The establishment of these three settlements in the same year, 1882, aroused great excitement among the Jews left behind in Russia and Romania. Now many of the founders of Petah Tikva came back to Palestine and with a group of Jews from Russia (especially from Bialystok) resettled some distance from the Yarkon River, source of their previous trouble.

In the same decade five more colonies were founded: Yesud Hama'ala, Ekron (later renamed Mazkeret Batya), Nes Ziona, Mishmar Hayarden, and Gedera. Few of the settlers had previously lived on the land or had any notion of farming. Most came from generations of city-dwellers: clerks, shopkeepers, students of theology. Besides the lack of agricultural experience, they were plagued by many other problems. The majority were poor, lacking the capital to build houses or buy tools and livestock. They were oppressed by corrupt Ottoman officials, and often attacked by their Arab neighbors.

The Biluim

Immediately after the establishment of Rishon Le-Zion, Joseph Fineberg, an energetic, intelligent man, well versed in European languages, was sent abroad to seek assistance. After visiting Austria and Germany without success he reached Paris, where Chief Rabbi Zadok obtained an interview for him with Baron Edmond de Rothschild, a man destined to play such a decisive role in Jewish settlement in Israel that he came to be styled Father of the *Yishuv* and the Great Benefactor— although he stipulated, when he gave Fineberg the aid he sought, that his identity should not be divulged. In the years that followed, the Baron lavished a greater bounty on the Yishuv than any other Jew—perhaps more than all the rest of the Jewry of the Diaspora combined, until the actual rebirth of the state.

But Rothschild was not merely a philanthropist. To assist in resettling the Land was not for him a charitable hobby. It was a vision of redemption for the Jewish people. He began modestly, but went on to great accomplishments. From the support of a few infant settlements he proceeded to the creation of new villages and the purchase of land throughout the country—both east and west of the Jordan—

The Rothschild Settlements

Petah Tikva, the first *moshava*, in its early days: the moshava was finally founded in 1883, after an earlier attempt at settlement (in 1878) had failed.

On November 3, 1878, the first settlers arrived in Petah Tikva, equipped with twelve span of oxen, five horses, and some donkeys. Their first task was to dig a well, and soon water was found, at a depth of 21 metres. The settlers rejoiced. This was the first Jewish well. They constructed a pulley over it, like the ones the Arabs used. That winter the rains were plentiful, and they bought European plows and big Syrian oxen, and went out to plow and sow their land. The neighboring Arab villagers were greatly impressed by this, as they were used to their own primitive plows and to the small local oxen. The Jewish settlers also began to build their houses, without waiting for licenses—Moshe Smilansky, Episodes in the History of the Yishuv.

fired by a far-sighted, politico-strategic purpose, recoiling from no obstacles, no difficulties. During his first visit to Palestine, in the spring of 1887, he expressed his faith that 'we shall yet be privileged to see the in-gathering of the exiles, and Israel dwelling securely in its land.' He understood, also, what many of the first colonists themselves did not: the crucial importance of self-labor, of Jewish sweat in working the land. He urged the settlers to speak Hebrew and to teach the language to their children. He opposed those who cherished and spoke French, even though it was his own language. His days were deservedly many and he lived to see pioneering settlements, from 1907 onward, coming into existence without his aid. In 1957 Rothschild's heirs, headed by his son James in London, gave all his property in Israel to the state.

In 1890 two villages were established by immigrants from Russia who were unwilling to be subsidized by the baron: Rehovot in Judaea and Hadera in Samaria. Rehovot became noted for its love of Hebrew speech and culture, Hadera for its boundless and selfless patriotism. Hadera was surrounded by swamps, and malaria decimated the villagers. There were many fatal cases, often three or four deaths in a single household. Yet not a man left, and in the end the pestilence was stamped out completely by draining the swamps. (As a result Hadera became one of the most flourishing places in the country.)

By 1897—date of the First Zionist Congress—there were 19 settlements in the Land, covering 45,000 acres and having a total population of 4350 souls. In addition there were unsettled Jewish lands of some 10,000 acres west of the Jordan and almost 20,000 acres in what was then Transjordan. Forty-five thousand Jews lived in nine cities or towns, 28,254 in Jerusalem alone. So the entire Jewish population of Palestine at the close of the 19th century was about 50,000.

The First Zionist Congress was convened in Basel by Dr. Theodor Herzl, a Budapest-born Viennese journalist who in 1896 had written an 86-page brochure entitled *The Jewish State,* advocating that immediate plans be made for an orderly exodus of Europe's Jews to a land of their own. Before the Congress adjourned, a World Zionist Organization had been formed. This body, offspring of the *Hovevei Zion* (Lovers of Zion) movement that had spread over Europe some 20 years before, did a great deal to foster self-respect and national pride among the ghetto Jews in Eastern Europe and brought many in Western Europe back from the embrace of assimilation to the bosom of nationalist Judaism. Herzl opposed what he called infiltration—that is, any form of Jewish settlement in Palestine that was not licensed by the Ottoman government. And at the time most Zionists agreed with him. Herzl made several attempts to obtain a charter from the sultan in return for an undertaking to pay off Turkish debts to the governments of Europe, and for a while he believed he would succeed in the end. However, after a series of fruitless meetings with the sultan he abandoned this hope and turned to the British government. Here he met with sympathetic attention. At first he was offered the lands of El-Arish (an oasis on the northern fringes of the Sinai Desert) for Jewish settlement, but Lord Cromer, British high commissioner in Egypt, disliked the plan. Next, Joseph Chamberlain offered him Uganda, an idea the Russian Zionists vigorously opposed.

Herzl's life was tragically brief. In 1904, at the age of 44, his heart gave out and he died. At the next Congress a majority rejected the Uganda plan. The Zionist Organization split. The minority, calling themselves Territorialists, looked for a land outside Palestine for a Jewish state, while the majority, the Zionists of Zion, remained faithful to the land of their ancestors. Herzl's death was a crushing blow to the Zionist movement. In all Jewry there was no one as magnetic and inspiring. Almost all the strength and influence of the Zionist Organization in its early years stemmed from this great, prophetic personality, product though he was of an assimilated Jewry.

If I were to sum up the Congress in a word—which I shall take care not to publish—it would be this: At Basel I founded the Jewish State.
If I said this out loud today I would be greeted by universal laughter. In five years, perhaps, and certainly in fifty years, everyone will perceive it—from Theodor Herzl's Diary (September 3, 1897).

Right, Dr. Theodor Herzl, founder of political Zionism. Herzl was driven to action by the rabid anti-semitism he encountered while covering the Dreyfus case as foreign correspondent for the Viennese *Neue Freie Presse* in 1895. The prophetic entry in his diary (shown and translated above) was made at Basel, in 1897, during the first Zionist Congress.

David Ben-Gurion (center) with his fellow-workers at the wine cellars of Rishon Le-Zion in 1907.

The Second Aliya

The death of Herzl and the split in the Zionist Organization might have undermined the entire Zionist movement had not a new development taken place, nourished both by the aspiration for national revival that had given birth to *Hibbat Zion* (Love of Zion) and to the Zionist movement, and by the revolutionary trends then developing in Russia. This was pioneering immigration by Jewish youth, who regarded labor as the principal agent in the rebuilding of the homeland, and who threw themselves, heart and soul, into working in the Land itself. Their aim was to create a new life in Israel for the Jewish people: a free workers' society, with everyone equal in rights; a nation with neither exploiters nor exploited.

This wave of immigration was known as the Second Aliya. Its chief guides and mentors were A. D. Gordon and Berl Katznelson. Gordon, who came from a quite wealthy Russian family, settled in the Land in 1904, when he was already 48 years old, to live by the labor of his hands, working on the land in Sejera, Kinneret, and Degania, where he died in 1922. Through his articles and essays he became the philosopher of "the sanctity of labor". Katznelson arrived in the Land in 1909 from Russia, where he had been an active socialist. He worked first as an agricultural laborer in Hadera, Sejera, Kinneret, and Ben Shemen, and was active in the young labor movement. He founded and edited the labor daily *Davar,* and had a great influence in the Zionist pioneering movement throughout the world, being its brain, conscience, and spokesman. He combined a shrewd personality with creative initiative and revolutionary energy.

277

It was the Second Aliya that forged the patterns of a Jewish labor movement befitting a nation and a land awakening to a new life. The first settlers in the 1880s had carved out, under conditions of unparalleled difficulty, a new road for Jewish agriculture. As the great thinker of the Hovevei Zion movement Asher Ginsburg (known by his pseudonym Ahad Ha'am) wrote: 'They came to the Land of Israel in the flower of their youth, for the sake of a sublime ideal, and dreamed of a happy future; liberty and honor; honest, holy work; national resurgence.' But their idealism did not last long, as he wrote in 1912: 'For 20 years a never-ending flood of gold has descended from above and washed everything away: love of labor and the ability to work, national idealism and a sense of human self-respect—leaving nothing behind but bitter hearts and dejected spirits.'

In 1904, the year the Second Aliya began, most of the workers in the Jewish settlements were not Jews. In 1900 a census of Jewish workers in the villages registered 312 in 12 settlements; 161 others worked in the wine cellars of Rishon Le-Zion and Zichron Ya'akov, which were required to employ Jewish workers for religious reasons. In the same settlements there were 3000 Arab workers.

The men of the Second Aliya knew that the fate of Jewish resurgence depended on Jewish labor, and that without it nothing would be built in the land of their fathers but one more wretched ghetto. And in the end it was their pioneering vision that triumphed. A working class was created in all branches of the economy, especially in agriculture. Israel was to be transformed, by the will of history, into a working nation. In the process, the pioneers of the Second Aliya laid the foundation for labor settlements, creating the *kibbutz* (communal or collective cooperative settlement), and the *moshav* (smallholder's settlement), with all their economic, social, and moral values. They organized credit and consumers' and producers' cooperatives. They established trade unions in the cities and in the country. They founded a labor press that played an important role in the development of a new Hebrew literature in the Land. They worked wonders in helping to revive Hebrew as a spoken language. Eventually they founded the *Histadrut,* the federation of Jewish labor, with its complex of cooperative and cultural institutions that have few counterparts in other labor movements. And within the fabric of the Histadrut, they incorporated vocational and cultural education, the absorption of immigrants and the building of settlements, all in one framework, resting on a membership consisting of workers, wage earners, and the self-employed. They fought for the right of Jews to guard their own homes and defend themselves. *Hashomer* (the Watchman), the first Jewish armed force in modern Israel, was their creation.

Under Ottoman rule the Land was given over to anarchy. Bedouin from time to time raided Arab villages. And in the Arab villages unending internecine war went on between two Muslim sects, the Qaiyasin and the Yamanin. The isolated Jewish settlements were attractive and easy targets for brigands and robbers, whether from neighboring villages or from roving nomad caravans. It was in Sejera, with the formation there of Hashomer, that modern Jewish defense was born. Ostensibly, Sejera was an agricultural school for farm hands. But after a year or two a student would be given a plot of land in the settlement and would become an independent tenant farmer. In Sejera, too, a first attempt was made in communal settlement. It was virtually the only settlement in which all work was done by Jews—though guard duty was entrusted to a Circassian from Kfar Kama. The farm manager feared that any change might provoke Arab reprisals. But one night in 1908, after the Circassian was found to be sleeping every night at home when he should have been on guard duty, he was replaced by a Jew. For several weeks there were, as predicted, shooting attacks on Sejera by Circassians. But when it became clear that the Jewish settlers

One of the first groups of Jewish watchmen, at Mes'ha in Galilee (1904): Israel Shohat, Hashomer's first commander, is in the center.

were not to be terrorized, the Circassians desisted. Thus the first Jewish armed force in the modern history of the Land came into existence. Its founder and first commander was Israel Shohat, a young Russian Jew who had been one of the founders of Jewish self-defense in Grodno.

Little by little the idea of Jews performing guard duty spread to other settlements—though not without clash and conflict, in which some of the first watchmen fell at their posts. But, undeterred, Hashomer stood by its policy: to resist by force the attacks of Arab marauders, while at the same time attempting to develop friendly relations with Arab neighbors. The policy was also to found settlements in which members could farm, for Hashomer did not wish to turn its members into professional guards.

Collective Settlement In 1908 the *Keren Kayemet Leyisrael* (the Jewish National Fund), which had been founded by the Zionist Organization in 1901 to acquire land as the property of the Jewish nation, founded a farm on the southern shore of Lake Kinneret (Sea of Galilee) on both sides of the Jordan. Hired Jewish laborers were employed, as usual; but when a dispute broke out between them and the manager because of a deficit at the end of the year, the organization of workers known as *Hahoresh* (the Plowman) demanded that the workers be permitted to manage the farm themselves. Under the agreement that was worked out, seven of the best farmhands in Galilee were permitted to cultivate the Um Juni lands, to the east of the Jordan—75 acres in all. They were given a monthly wage of 45 francs and half the annual profit. The year ended with a profit of 4000 francs. The group left, however, for they had undertaken the project only to establish the right to work. They were replaced by another small group whose monthly pay was raised to 50 francs. This group, led by Yosef Bussel, named the place Degania (God's corn).

We arrived [at Um Juni] in summer. It was very hot down there, two hundred metres below sea level. The air buzzed with mosquitoes and it lay heavy and close between the hills. The flat valley was like a hot plate. . . . Everything was burnt brown. The river was a trickle. But when the rains came, it flooded the land and when the waters withdrew they left swamps and mud. For months on end we were cut off by mud—Joseph Baratz, A Village by the Jordan.

The guiding principle was cooperative labor, but little by little the farmers arrived at a communal form of life—in work, in property, in bringing up their children. At first they lived in Arab hovels, but during the summer of 1911 their numbers rose to 15, and they built themselves permanent housing. And so a new chapter was opened in the annals of settlement of the Land. Degania, the first *kvutza,* became mother of the communal settlements.

Degania's founders believed that only a limited and compact membership could establish a kvutza and keep it alive. But in 1921 Shlomo Lavi, a member of Hashomer and of the kvutza at Kinneret, proposed the establishment of a large kibbutz, with hundreds of members, open to anyone willing to work on it. The members debated loud and long whether this was feasible. In the autumn, the council of the recently founded Histadrut decided to try out Lavi's idea at Ein Harod, with 150 families. Agricultural experts, wedded to the idea of the small, intimate kvutza, predicted disaster. But today there are flourishing kibbutzim with upward of 1000 members. The social basis of the kibbutz is the complete partnership of all workers, without distinction between experts and ordinary laborers, between bachelors and fathers of large families, according to the principle: from each according to his ability, to each according to his needs. There are neither wages nor private wealth, the farm being the common property of the whole settlement. Each member, whether he has been in the kibbutz for decades or has just been accepted that day, has equal rights.

The first Zionist Congress had supported Dr. Herzl in his objection to 'infiltration'; but in 1908 the Palestine Office was organized under the direction of Dr. Arthur Ruppin, a German Jew with experience in commerce, who came to the Land to manage the practical work of the Zionist Movement and cooperate with the men of the Second Aliya. He was given a yearly budget of 30,000 francs to foster farming and manufacturing. The Jewish National Fund purchased land at Hulda and Ben Shemen in the Judaean foothills, and at the spot where the Jordan flows out of Lake Kinneret. At first it founded settlements that employed labor, but Degania's success encouraged it to dispense with paid supervisors and hired farmhands.

Two men were mainly responsible for persuading the Zionist Organization to take up settlement work. Dr. Chaim Weizmann, born near Pinsk, in Russia, had been a Zionist since boyhood, had studied chemistry in Switzerland, and was already

The Jewish National Fund

Left, Arab mud huts at Um Juni—which later became Degania, the first *kvutza*. Degania's founders made these their homes when they arrived in 1910. Above, a members' meeting in progress at Ein Gedi, a *kibbutz* founded in 1953 on the western shore of the Dead Sea. By the 1960's, most of the settlers in Ein Gedi were young pioneers (born and educated in Israel) who came to live in this isolated desert spot after completing their army service.

establishing an international reputation for himself as a scientist. Menahem Ussishkin, a spokesman for Russian Jewry, had been a leader of Hovevei Zion even before the Zionist movement was established. Eventually he was to settle in the Land of Israel (in 1920) and become head of the Jewish National Fund.

When Ruppin arrived in 1907, 10 years after the First Zionist Congress, some 80,000 Jews lived in Palestine: 45,000 in Jerusalem; 8000 in Jaffa; 8000 in Safad; 4000 equally divided between Haifa and Tiberias; and 1000 in Hebron. There were also 30 Jewish villages with a total population of some 6000, as well as 8000 or so Jews on undeveloped land. The only Zionist institution in the country before Ruppin's arrival was the Anglo-Palestine Bank, founded in 1903.

For a while the successful experiment in communal settlement made in Degania was not made known to the public at large, and the opinions of the German-Jewish sociologist, Dr. Franz Oppenheimer, continued to carry great weight. In 1896, Dr. Oppenheimer had published a fundamental treatise on producers' cooperatives in town and country. When Dr. Herzl, who was interested in such ideas from the beginning, became acquainted with Oppenheimer and his plans, he invited him to address the Sixth Congress in 1903 on the problem of settlement in the Land.

At the Ninth Congress, which met at the end of 1909 in Hamburg, Dr. Oppenheimer succeeded in convincing the delegates of the importance of cooperative settlement and a resolution was unanimously adopted that 'the system of cooperative settlement should be adopted within the framework of the Zionist Organization's activities.' To implement this resolution, the Jewish National Fund was requested to lease the land necessary for the establishment of a cooperative settlement.

The 2500 acres in the Valley of Jezreel, bought in the following year, were at first placed under the control of a farm manager, but within two or three years the all-Jewish workers had gained collective control and ran it successfully as a kibbutz.

Organizing Labor

Jewish labor began to organize itself, politically and professionally. In 1906 two parties had been formed: *Hapoel Hatza'ir* (the Young Worker), which inscribed on its banner 'The Conquest of the Right to Work'; and *Poalei Zion* (Workers of Zion), the Zionist Socialist party. Within a year Hapoel Hatza'ir began to put out a weekly, and in 1910 Poalei Zion also started a paper, called *Ha'ahdut* (Unity). The greatest writer of the period, Yosef Haim Brenner (who was killed by Arabs

The editorial board of the *Poalei Zion* journal *Ha'ahdut* (The Unity), founded in 1910. From left to right: Izhak Ben-Zvi, Ya'akov Zerubavel, David Ben-Gurion, and Rachel Yana'it.

in 1921), contributed to both. Hapoel Hatza'ir also published a series of popular books under the imprint *La'am* (For the People). It was supported by most of the Yishuv's intelligentsia, while Poalei Zion had a greater influence among the workers, counting among its members almost all the men of Hashomer, which played such an important role before World War I. There was also a substantial group of independents who were active mainly in the Agricultural Workers' Union, which was organized in 1911 in Judaea and Galilee, and afterward extended to Samaria. In 1912 a Workers' Sick Fund (*Kupat Holim*) was created and eventually became the largest health-insurance scheme in the country: today it has a membership of over two million.

A unique feature of Palestine's labor movement was the fact that the agricultural workers took the lead in organizational matters and influenced the town workers. It was the laborers on the land who became the most progressive pioneering force, creating new social patterns and remaining to this day the spiritual guides of the entire movement. The first urban workers to organize themselves into a union were the printers of Jerusalem, supported by Poalei Zion, and printers' unions were later established in Jaffa and Haifa as well.

In the summer of 1908, some Jews from Jaffa—members of a society called *Ahuzat Bayit*—purchased a stretch of sand dunes northeast of the town and decided to build a Jewish suburb. They called the first street in this new place Herzl Street, and at the end of it they allotted land for the *gymnasia* or high school that had been founded by Dr. Matmon-Cohen in Jaffa in 1905, and which they now called Gymnasia Herzliya. The original intention was to build houses for just 60 families, but the new quarter steadily expanded and in time became Tel-Aviv, the largest city in Israel, and the first all Jewish city in the Land. The high school, with an original enrollment of 14 pupils, became the major high school in the country. Many of its graduates are today high in the economic, political, and intellectual life of Israel. A few years

Founding of Tel-Aviv

later a second high school was established in Jerusalem, where Izhak Ben-Zvi—a future president of the State of Israel—became a teacher.

The Haifa Technion

A landmark in the history of higher education in the Land was the establishment of the Institute of Technology in Haifa. In 1907 Paul Nathan, leader of a German-Jewish philanthropic (but anti-Zionist) organization called *Deutsche Hilfsverein,* visited Palestine and decided to establish a technical college (or *Technicum,* as it was known in Germany) to spur on the development of the country. He later met a Russian tea merchant, K. Z. Wissotzky, who had inherited a considerable fortune from his father, one of the leaders of the Hovevei Zion. Under the terms of the will, the heirs had to contribute 100,000 rubles (the equivalent of almost $50,000) from the estate every five years to some public institution, and the son agreed that the first contribution should go toward the establishment of a Jewish technical college in the Land.

Nathan chose to build the institution in Haifa, though at the time Haifa was a small town of 20,000 people and only a few thousand Jews. With great difficulty a small plot of 12 acres was acquired on the southern slope of Mt. Carmel. In 1911 the necessary permit was received from the Turkish authorities, and the main building was completed in the spring of 1913. A *Realschule,* or technical secondary school, was established in affiliation with the Technicum.

One of the first matters to be settled was the language of instruction, which Nathan and his associates wanted to be mainly German. There was a storm of protest—which some Zionist leaders abroad regarded as a sign of chauvinism, but for the workers and the intelligentsia in the Land it was a matter of primary importance, for they were aware that the language would be instrumental in determining the cultural character of Israel.

When the board of governors met in October 1913, Nathan insisted that Hebrew was not advanced enough for instruction in technical subjects. The majority accepted his views, and the Zionist members resigned. The protests in Palestine gathered strength, and as a result the opening of the college was postponed. Finally, the American governors, under the influence of Dr. J. L. Magnes (who was later to settle in the Land and become the first president of the Hebrew University in Jerusalem), decided that 'the use of the Hebrew language must be instituted immediately, as far as possible, and extended after seven years to all subjects except where adequate staff and textbooks are not available.' Nathan still objected, but in the meantime World War I broke out and the Hilfsverein took over complete charge of the Technicum.

Tel-Aviv's founders meet (in 1908) to draw lots for land on the sand dunes outside Jaffa—site of the proposed Jewish suburb.

Above, Turkish prisoners of war, captured by the British at Megiddo in September 1918: the British victory ended Ottoman rule in Palestine. As in the past, Megiddo's position at the center of the Jezreel Valley—where the main overland routes crossed—made it the site of a decisive battle.

As a result of the German defeat in World War I, the Hilfsverein lost control of the Technicum, and an agreement was signed in Berlin in February 1920 transferring the college to the sole jurisdiction of the Zionist Organization; the Hilfsverein received over half a million marks as compensation. The Realschule (in Hebrew *Beit Hasefer Hare'ali*) opened immediately with Dr. Arthur Biram as headmaster, the teaching being conducted in Hebrew. The Histadrut pressed for the immediate opening of the technical college, for which the poet Chaim Nachman Bialik coined a Hebrew name: *Technion*. After exhaustive discussions, it was decided that the highest possible scientific standards should be maintained. On January 7, 1925, the first course—on building and roadmaking—was opened, in Hebrew. New departments were gradually added and today the Technion, the Israel Institute of Technology, Haifa, is one of the world's foremost institutions of its kind.

In 1914 there were 85,000 Jews in the Land (12 per cent of the population), of whom 73,000 lived in the towns, many on *haluka*, charitable aid received from Jews in the Diaspora. But in two towns—Haifa and Jaffa—self-supporting communities had developed, men and women of the new Yishuv, who were sturdily independent. Once Turkey joined the war on Germany's side, the majority of Palestinian Jews, being of Russian origin, were regarded as enemy aliens and many were compelled to leave the country. Among them was Yosef Trumpeldor, a former student at the University of St. Petersburg, who had been cited in the Russo-Japanese War for heroism at Port Arthur, where he lost an arm. He was the only Jew in the tsar's army with an officer's rank. After arriving in Alexandria, where most of the Jews from Palestine had gathered, he organized a Jewish unit in the British Army—the Zion Mule Corps—which fought at Gallipoli.

Two students from Palestine who were studying law at the Turkish university in Constantinople—Izhak Ben-Zvi and David Ben-Gurion—returned home at the outbreak of the war and, together with a group of prominent Jews who possessed Ottoman citizenship, began a propaganda campaign to persuade their fellow Jews to acquire Turkish citizenship so that they could remain in the Land. They also applied to the Turkish commander in Jerusalem, Zaki Bey, for permission to organize a Jewish military unit for local defense on the understanding that it would not be sent to any other front. The authorities agreed and scores of young Jews, including the writer Yosef Haim Brenner, volunteered and began training. But when Jamal Pasha, one of the ruling triumvirate of Turkey, was assigned to the Egyptian front, he gave orders for the disbanding of the unit. He also took repressive measures against Arab nationalists in Syria and Palestinian Jews. A number of Arab leaders were hanged in Beirut; and although Henry Morgenthau Sr., the American ambassador in Constantinople, took the Palestinian Jews under his protection so that none was hanged, many leaders were expelled to Constantinople. Ben-Zvi and

World War I

Ben-Gurion were condemned to 'perpetual exile from the Ottoman Empire,' and went to America. Israel Shohat, the head of Hashomer, and other Jewish leaders were exiled to Turkey.

An espionage group called Nili was organized by Aaron Aaronson, a renowned Jewish botanist. Its work for the British provoked the Turks to take more severe measures against the Yishuv. Some Jews were arrested, some were even sent to prison in Damascus, and some were executed. The Jews of Tel-Aviv were expelled. The condition of the Yishuv became desperate. By the end of the war the Jewish population of the Land numbered only 56,000.

The Balfour Declaration

On November 2, 1917, after the British army had begun its Palestine campaign, the British government addressed the following declaration to Lord Rothschild:

> Dear Lord Rothschild,
>
> I have much pleasure in conveying to you, on behalf of His Majesty's Government, the following declaration of sympathy with Jewish Zionist aspirations, which has been submitted to and approved by the Cabinet.
>
> His Majesty's Government view with favour the establishment in Palestine of a national home for the Jewish people, and will use their best endeavours to facilitate the achievement of this object, it being clearly understood that nothing shall be done which may prejudice the civil and religious rights of existing non-Jewish communities in Palestine, or the rights and political status enjoyed by Jews in any other country.
>
> I should be grateful if you would bring this declaration to the knowledge of the Zionist Federation.
>
> Yours sincerely,
> Arthur James Balfour.

This, the famous Balfour Declaration, was obtained mainly through the efforts of three illustrious Jews: Herbert Samuel, a member of Asquith's Liberal government; Nahum Sokolow, eminent Hebrew writer and journalist; and above all, Dr. Chaim Weizmann, who was then a lecturer in chemistry at Manchester University and already a close friend of Balfour, the British Foreign Secretary.

The jubilation of Jewry throughout the Diaspora and in the Land was tremendous. There was, however, a certain mild self-delusion in it. It had to be pointed out that, although the British occupied the whole land, from Dan to Beersheba, it would not become Jewish once again merely because Britain had so agreed.

The Jewish Legion

The immediate practical result of the declaration was the raising of Jewish battalions in the British Army—in Palestine mainly through the Labor movement, in America through the activity of Poalei Zion, and in Britain mainly through the activity of Ze'ev Jabotinsky. Jabotinsky who was born in Odessa on October 5, 1880, studied in Berne and Rome, and soon became known as a brilliant orator and journalist. In the Zionist movement he belonged to the extreme right wing, and all his life fought the Jewish labor movement, which was mainly socialist. In 1925 he founded his own party, the Revisionists. He opposed the moderation of Weizmann and in 1935 —after the Zionist Congress of 1931 had rejected his proposal to proclaim the Jewish state as the final aim of Zionism, and the labor group had become the largest at the 1933 Congress, its representatives assuming leadership of the Zionist Organization—Jabotinsky established the New Zionist Organization as a rival of what he called the "old" one. In the name of the new organization he organized a popular petition to the British king and to the secretariat of the League of Nations demanding a Jewish state on both sides of the Jordan. He died in New York on

With the establishment of a Jewish Legion in the British army (early in 1918), extensive recruitment began. Above left, a Hebrew poster calling for Palestinian volunteers—it begins with *Shma Yisrael* (the opening words of the Shma, the prayer stating the basic creed of Judaism), which it repeats as a motif: 'Hear, O Israel! Hear the voice of your heart: do we not need to repossess our Land and to affirm our right to it? Hear the voice of your reason: can we watch the British fight, and remain idle until they give us a country which they alone have won with their blood? Hear the voice of your honor: can we accept such an offering, such a gift from our redeemers, if we do not give our lives for it with them....' Above right, in an American Yiddish journal the allegorical "Daughter of Zion" declares: 'I want your Old New Land! Join the Jewish Regiment.'

August 3, 1940. After his death the New Zionist Organization was disbanded and some of its members rejoined the old organization.

With the aid of Dr. Weizmann, Jabotinsky persuaded the British government to let Jewish residents of Russian nationality be conscripted into all-Jewish battalions. In America Justice Louis P. Brandeis (who had recently been appointed to the Supreme Court by President Wilson) supported an effort by Pinhas Rutenberg and the two exiles, Ben-Gurion and Ben-Zvi, to form a Jewish battalion in the American army to fight on the Palestine front. Wilson was sympathetic but pointed out that America had declared war only on Germany, not on Turkey. He therefore advised them to put the proposal to the British War Office, which they did, but for a long time the British refused to accept the two stipulations made: a strictly Jewish unit, and service only on the Palestine front. But after six months of negotiation the terms were wholly agreed to, and an appeal was issued for young American Jews to volunteer for service in a Jewish battalion of the British army. Thousands responded, although only young men exempted for various reasons from American conscription could be accepted.

In the Land itself the task of enrolling volunteers was undertaken by Eliahu Golomb, Dov Hos, and Rachel Yana'it, the future wife of Ben-Zvi. Most of the Palestinian volunteers were workers. Among them were Golomb, Hos, and Ya'akov Dori, the future builders of the *Hagana* (defense force).

286

| Union of Workers | When the American battalion (also, to a large extent, made up of workers) met the Palestinian battalion, the idea was conceived of a union of all the Jewish workers of Palestine within a single professional, political, and cultural framework. Six men—two of Poalei Zion, just back from America (Ben-Zvi and Ben-Gurion), two non-party men who had joined up in Palestine (Katznelson and Yavne'eli), and two civilians (David Remez and Yitzhak Tabenkin)—issued a proclamation for the establishment of a union of labor. |

There was an enthusiastic response and when the battalions came home after the armistice in November 1918, fervor mounted even more. In February 1919, a meeting was called of agricultural workers' delegates, representing the largest and most important trade union then in existence. By a vote of 48 against 12 they decided on unification, and immediately, at a general conference of urban and rural workers, the delegates established *Ahdut Ha'avoda,* the Zionist Socialist Union of Workers in the Land of Israel. It was the first Zionist party to proclaim the need to establish in the Land a free Jewish state that would be, until the creation of a Jewish majority, under the protection of the League of Nations. The conference also decided to establish a Palestine Workers' Bank, which was set up a short time later and was to become one of the principal banks of the country.

Only a minority of Hapoel Hatza'ir joined the new union, the majority remaining a separate party. But the ferment for unity did not cease and in December 1920, only 18 months after the establishment of Ahdut Ha'avoda, a general conference was held in Haifa at which 87 delegates representing all the workers in towns and settlements decided to establish a General Federation of Labor (the *Histadrut*) to unite hired and independent workers who lived entirely by their own labor. The purpose of the federation was to represent all the economic and cultural interests of the working class and to help build a Jewish labor society in the Land of Israel. The Histadrut gradually became the main factor in building up the State. Starting with a membership of 4433 in 1920, it had by the beginning of 1970 a membership of over a million, including about 50,000 Arabs and Druse.

| The Zionist Commission | At the end of the war, with the Land occupied by the British and still under military control, an official Zionist Commission (in Hebrew *Va'ad Hatzirim*) came to Palestine, with the agreement of the British government, to examine the country's needs and plan for the future. The Chairman was Dr. Weizmann. He arranged a meeting with Emir Feisal, son of Sherif Hussein of Mecca to whom the British had addressed the MacMahon Declaration in 1916, pledging liberation of the Arab countries from Turkish rule and support of Sherif Hussein as king. Palestine had been excluded from the area of this newly liberated Arab kingdom, but Dr. Weizmann felt it proper to establish friendly relations between the Jewish National Home and the prospective Arab kingdom. He met Feisal at Aqaba in June 1918, and on January 3, 1919, signed an agreement with him in Paris providing for cordial relations between the two states. |

| The Defense of Tel Hai | Feisal's goodwill was not shared by the Military Administration in Palestine. On the excuse that it was only an occupational authority, it would not permit any transfer of lands; and the only immigration it permitted was of prewar residents. It completely ignored the Balfour Declaration and displayed an attitude of hostility to the Jewish community, an attitude that quickly infected the Arab leaders. |

Trouble began in the north. For a long time Upper Galilee had been disputed territory between Britain and France. On September 15, 1919, the two countries agreed on a provisional demarcation line, and in November British forces withdrew from the north of Upper Galilee. French troops were unable, however, to occupy the evacuated area immediately, and the Arab villagers began to arm and rebel.

There were four Jewish settlements in the area: Metula—by now 23 years old and accustomed to heroic resistance to Druse attacks—and three workers' villages founded during the war, Kfar Gil'adi, Tel Hai, and Hamara. The disturbances began with disputes between Muslims and Christians, and for some time did not touch the Jewish villages. But at the end of December 1919, Tel Hai was attacked. The settlers defended themselves and the attackers fled. But the attack was repeated, the Arabs demanding that all four settlements join them in their fight against the French. The Jews declared that they were remaining neutral. At first the Arabs accepted this decision, but not for long. Soon all the villages were under frequent fire, surrounded by tens of thousands of attackers. Help came from Jews in the south, led by Trumpeldor, who discovered on his arrival that the food supply at Tel Hai and Kfar Gil'adi was running out and that the situation was desperate.

On March 1, 1920, Tel Hai was attacked by large numbers of armed Arabs, on foot and on horseback. They said they had come only to see if any Frenchmen were hiding there and meant no harm to the Jews. Trumpeldor permitted a few officers to enter. When the Arabs saw an armed Jewish girl and tried to seize her weapon, Trumpeldor shot at them. Thereupon the Arabs began a mass attack. Trumpeldor was mortally wounded and handed over command to Pinhas Shneourson, a member of Hashomer. As dusk fell, reinforcements arrived from Kfar Gil'adi and took away the wounded. Trumpeldor died on the way. With his last breath he whispered: 'No matter, it is good to die for our country.'

On March 3 a formidable Arab force, with field pieces, approached Kfar Gil'adi and Metula. The defenders of Kfar Gil'adi were compelled to evacuate the village and take refuge in the hills to the west with their friends the Mutawallas. The sheik, Kamil al As'ad, gave them supplies that enabled them to continue on southward; their hosts could not believe that this handful of 80 or 90 men had held their ground so long against an enemy 40 times as numerous. That same night the defenders of Kfar Gil'adi reached Ayelet Hashahar, bringing all their arms with them.

At the end of July the French finally took over the area and two months later the members of Kfar Gil'adi and Tel Hai returned to their villages. Late in December a treaty was signed in San Remo under which the entire area—including Metula, Kfar Gil'adi and Tel Hai—was placed under British administration, thus becoming

Below, the *kvutza* of Tel Hai: it was temporarily abandoned after a desperate stand against strong insurgent Arab forces in March 1920. Yosef Trumpeldor, the heroic commander of the Jewish defenders, was killed in the fighting. Right, a map showing the borders of Palestine after the San Remo agreement of 1920.

part of the Jewish National Home. The defense of Tel Hai had ended with a temporary retreat, but it became an example and a symbol for the new generation in the Land. Because of it, the entire northeastern area was included in the territory of the British Mandate—and in the State of Israel when it was established.

The Passover Riots

In 1920, shortly before Passover, the Arabs celebrated the Nebi Mussa festival. (Nebi Mussa is a spot east of Jerusalem not far from the Dead Sea where, according to Arab belief, Moses is buried—*Mussa* being Arabic for Moses. Palestinian Arabs traditionally made a pilgrimage there each spring.)

Hundreds of Arabs poured into Jerusalem from Shechem. On the first day of Passover—April 3, 1920—with the arrival of more celebrants from Hebron, known for their fanaticism and cruelty, the pogrom broke out. The sheik who led the Hebron delegation finished a harangue to the crowd by shouting: '*Itbahu el-Yahud!*' (Slaughter the Jews!) Immediately the attacks began.

The mob broke into Jewish shops and stoned passers-by. They rushed through the narrow lanes of the Old City leading to the Jewish quarter and attacked the Jews there. Arab shops were marked with distinguishing signs and Christian shops with a cross. They remained untouched. But Jewish shops were looted and wrecked. Arab constables and police officers joined the rioters in their murderous deeds. Cries were heard: '*T'hafush, e-dawla ma'ana!*' (Don't be afraid, the government is on our side!). In the New City, the authorities were busy rounding up and arresting the Jewish defenders.

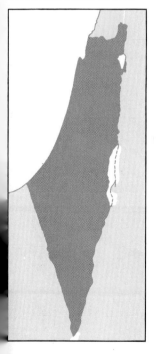

THE BRITISH MANDATE 1920

The pogrom in the Old City lasted three days. Six Jews were killed, more than 200 were wounded. Jewish women were raped, Jewish property was stolen or destroyed, synagogues were burned. However, there were some cases of Arabs sheltering their Jewish neighbors. The Military Administration held up the news of what had happened—and it was nine days before the first report was published in a London newspaper.

On the last day of the fighting Jabotinsky and 19 other members of the defense organization were jailed. They were accused of being in possession of arms and conspiring in a devilish plot to incite looting and murder. Jabotinsky admitted responsibility for all the weapons seized and for the establishment of a defense organization. He was condemned to 15 years' hard labor, which was to be followed by expulsion from the country. The others were sentenced to three years' hard labor. Within three months all were pardoned by Herbert Samuel, who had recently taken up his post as Britain's first high commissioner to Palestine.

Samuel had been elected to Parliament in 1902 as a member of the Liberal party and eight years later had entered the cabinet as postmaster-general—the first Jew in Britain ever to occupy that post. In 1916, as home secretary, he had helped to obtain the Balfour Declaration. Now, at the age of 50, he had the task of administering Britain's Mandate over Palestine.

The National Council

After the Balfour Declaration and the occupation of Judaea by the British, Bezalel Yaffe and several other leaders of the Yishuv summoned a conference at Petah Tikva; there it was decided to convene a constituent assembly to establish a representative body on the basis of democratic elections throughout the Yishuv. An attempt in this direction had been made in 1903 (in Zichron Ya'akov) by Ussishkin, who tried to establish an Association of the Jews in the Land of Israel; but the attempt failed because of the split over the Uganda question. This time representatives of all the Jewish organizations met (at the beginning of 1918) in the hall of the Girls' School in Jaffa, and a Provisional Committee of the Jews in the Land of Israel was elected. That summer a second constituent assembly was called, with delegates from Jerusalem

289

also taking part. There was heavy participation in the balloting for members of the Elected Assembly (*Asefat Hanivharim*) that took place on April 19, 1920—partly a reaction to the Passover riots, which had shocked the Yishuv. At first the British Military Administration would not permit the Assembly to meet, but when it did— in Jerusalem, on October 7—a National Council (*Va'ad Leumi*) of 38 members was elected, with a presidium of three: Izhak Ben-Zvi, Ya'akov Thon, and David Yellin. Within a fortnight the elected institutions had been officially approved.

Occupation of the Land by the British had led many to think that Jewish self-defense had become superfluous, for was not the country under the rule of a progressive European power known for its fairness and liberality to everyone? The riots of Jerusalem opened their eyes. There were still those (led by Jabotinsky) who wanted to rely only on the Jewish battalions, under British command. But the men of Hashomer and Ahdut Ha'avoda agreed that it was impossible to rely on any force, even a Jewish one, that was entirely dependent on a foreign administration. What they now demanded was a completely independent Jewish defense force.

The Hagana

The first Histadrut conference at Haifa in December 1920 decided that the organization of defense was within its scope. Hashomer, after much heart-searching, had agreed to dissolve, and Ahdut Ha'avoda (at its Kinneret conference in June, 1920) resolved to undertake the responsibility of organizing the defense force and of assuring its national and social character. Command over the *Hagana* (defense force) was later transferred to the Histadrut. Later still—when the private farming element agreed to join—the Hagana was placed under the control of the Yishuv's executive body, the Va'ad Leumi.

Pioneering immigration started after the war, stimulated by the Balfour Declaration and the Russian Revolution. At first it was a tiny trickle, for up to 1920 the country was under an unfriendly military administration. After 1920, with the appointment of a civil administration, headed by Sir Herbert Samuel, immigration increased. During the first six years—from 1919 to 1924—close on 50,000 immigrants arrived, most of them young pioneers. Their first tasks were making roads (under the self-management of the workers as contractors), draining the swamps, and preparing the land for settlement.

The Third Aliya

The men of the Third Aliya, as it was called, built the road from Tzemah to Tiberias along the shores of Lake Kinneret and the Haifa-Jedda and Afula-Nazareth roads. The great majority would have preferred to engage in cooperative agriculture, but at that time the Zionist movement had no funds to devote to the purpose. At the end of the summer of 1920, the new immigrants, together with some veterans, founded *Gedud Ha'avoda al shem Yosef Trumpeldor* (the Yosef Trumpeldor Legion of Labor) as a countrywide commune, with the aim of setting up a comprehensive commune of all the workers in the Land. A second body established by some members of the Third Aliya was *Hashomer Hatza'ir,* which sprang from a youth movement created in the Eastern European countries. At first it was purely a national movement, opposed to any form of class consciousness, zealous in promoting the speaking of Hebrew, and determined to settle on the land in communal groups. In a few years, however, it absorbed the doctrine of communism, and became the extreme left wing of the labor movement.

In the summer of 1920 a Zionist Conference met in London, the first since the outbreak of World War I, and established the *Keren Hayesod* (the Palestine Foundation Fund) in addition to the *Keren Kayemet,* which had been founded at the Fifth Zionist Congress in 1901. While the latter was dedicated to the redemption of the soil, the new fund was to be used for agricultural settlement, education, and the absorption of immigrants. The new immigrants had a strong desire for agricultural settlement

290

Winston Churchill, then Britain's colonial secretary, during his visit to Jerusalem in 1921. On his right is Sir Herbert Samuel, the British high commissioner to Palestine at the time. Churchill expressed great sympathy with the Zionist cause, and in his White Paper of 1922 reaffirmed the Balfour Declaration of 1917.

and when 17,500 acres of land in the Valley of Jezreel—known as the *Emek* (Valley)—were acquired in 1921, hundreds settled on the soil. The first large kibbutz, Ein Harod, was established, and the first workers' moshavim were set up. These differed from the kibbutzim in that every settler was solely responsible for the area allotted him. The moshav was based on the following principles: national land, allocated on hereditary leasehold; personal labor (called self-labor) by the settler, and mutual assistance by all members; cooperative purchasing and marketing; and assistance to sick members in working the farm.

Settlement and Industry

Only two settlements had been set up in the Emek before World War I—Tel Adashim, by a Hashomer group, and the cooperative farm of Merhavia. Between 1911 and the end of 1924, 27 kvutzot and kibbutzim were established, with 1340 working members and 189 children, farming an area of more than 2000 acres.

Immigration reached a peak in 1925, the last year of Sir Herbert Samuel's term, when 34,386 immigrants came in. Most of the newcomers streamed to the towns, especially Tel-Aviv, Haifa, and Jerusalem. Many newcomers found work in large-scale building operations, and the Histadrut's public works office was reorganized in 1924 as a workers' contracting company called *Solel Boneh* under the direction of David Remez, later Israel's minister of communications and minister of education. Solel Boneh eventually became the largest single building and road-making contractor in the country.

Tel-Aviv absorbed almost two thirds of the immigration and by the end of 1925 had a population of 40,000. Jerusalem had 42,000 Jewish inhabitants, Haifa 14,000. Industry, too, began to grow. An important role was played by Pinhas Rutenberg,

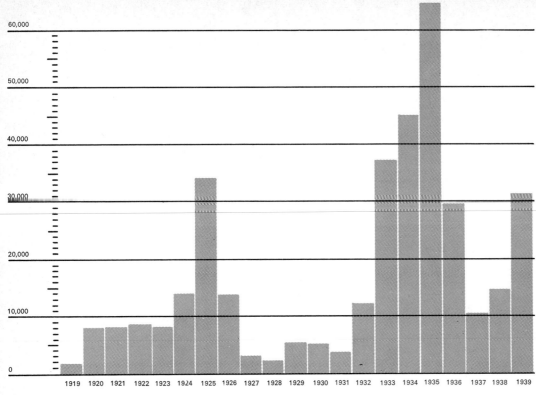

60,000

50,000

40,000

30,000

20,000

10,000

0

1919 1920 1921 1922 1923 1924 1925 1926 1927 1928 1929 1930 1931 1932 1933 1934 1935 1936 1937 1938 1939

IMMIGRATION 1919-1939

a Russian Jew whom Ben-Zvi and Ben-Gurion had met in the United States in 1917 when they were all working for the creation of Jewish battalions. There Rutenberg began to devise a plan for the electrification of Palestine with water power from the Jordan and Yarmuk rivers. After the war he settled in the Land and devoted all his energies to this plan. In 1921 he received a concession from the Mandatory Power to generate electricity everywhere except in Jerusalem, where a British company operated. He built his first power station in Tel-Aviv in 1923 and two years later stations were operating in Haifa and Tiberias; this made it possible to set up larger industrial undertakings.

In March 1925, the foundation stone of the Hebrew University was laid on Mount Scopus, Jerusalem, in the presence of Lord Balfour and Dr. Weizmann. On June 1 *Davar,* the labor movement daily, started to appear, with Berl Katznelson as editor. In the same month Sir Herbert Samuel completed his term of office as the first high commissioner. His appointment in 1920 had aroused great joy and much hope in the Yishuv: the British prime minister, David Lloyd George, had undoubtedly appointed Samuel because he knew him to be a Jew who believed in the creation of a Jewish . State. But Samuel not only disappointed the hopes of the Jewish people, which were perhaps exaggerated at the time; he also failed to carry out obligations that Britain had incurred in accepting the Mandate—to place the country 'under such political, administrative and economic conditions as will secure the establishment of the Jewish national home' (Article 2); to 'facilitate Jewish immigration under suitable conditions' (Article 6); and 'to encourage close settlement on the land by Jews, including state lands and waste lands not required for public purposes' (Article 6). In his report to the colonial office, Samuel admitted that the administration had found few opportunities of supplying land for Jewish settlement, that all the burden of educating Jewish children had been placed on the shoulders of the Jews themselves —and that state funds, which came mainly from the Jews, had been used exclusively to maintain Arab schools.

When Samuel addressed the Mandate Commission in 1924, he said that the basic principle of the administration's policy had been to deal with the Arabs as if there had been no Balfour Declaration. He might have added that for the most part he

292

Workers at Nahalal, in the Jezreel Valley (in 1922), beside the swamps they were fighting to drain. Nahalal was the first fully-planned landscaped settlement.

had also behaved toward the Jews as if there had been no Balfour Declaration, or any obligation to facilitate immigration and encourage close settlement by Jews on the land. Samuel temporarily suspended Jewish immigration after the riots of May 1921. State lands were distributed to Bedouin—who already had a surplus they could not cultivate—and the Jews were deprived of their right to land. Jewish workers were not given a fair share of employment in public works. The first White Paper, which was ostensibly drawn up by Winston Churchill (then secretary of state for the colonies), in fact came from Jerusalem and was drafted by Samuel: this document excluded Transjordan (the greater part of Palestine) from the scope of the promised National Home, and subjected immigration to the fetters of economic absorptive capacity, which was artificially determined by the Mandatory government.

Samuel was succeeded by Field Marshal Lord Plumer, who behaved amiably and justly to both Jew and Arab and observed the provisions of the Mandate. For some reason Plumer was removed from his post after two years; he was replaced by Sir John Chancellor, previously a senior official in Rhodesia who was accustomed to looking on the natives with the contemptuous attitude of a colonial governor.

Problems of Immigration

The large-scale immigration of 1924 and 1925 led to an expansion of building work, which absorbed most of the workers among the new immigrants. But building does not provide a permanent source of livelihood, and there was considerable unemployment from the second half of 1926. In 1927, there were 13,440 unemployed, and immigration fell off. In 1926, 13,855 immigrants had arrived—the great majority in the first half of the year; in 1927 the figure dropped to 3034; in 1928, it dropped as low as 2178, and there were as many emigrants leaving the Land as there were immigrants coming in. It was only in 1929 that the flow of departures was stemmed and immigration gathered strength, rising to 5249.

In that year, however, there was a new wave of Arab attacks on Jewish settlements, provoked by the Mufti of Jerusalem—who had been appointed head of the Supreme Muslim Council by Sir Herbert Samuel against the wishes of the majority of its members. Attacks started on isolated Jewish quarters in Jerusalem on August 23, 1929. The next day there was a barbarous slaughter of Jews in Hebron: 59 men, women, and children were butchered—and it was only after the attack was well and truly over that British troops arrived from Jerusalem. The disturbances spread throughout the country. Many of the inhabitants of Motza (a small village near Jerusalem) were murdered, and their homes were demolished. Other small villages were destroyed—among them Ein Zeitim, in Upper Galilee; Hartuv, Kfar Uria, and Hulda on the Judaean foothills between Jaffa and Jerusalem; and, after a particularly heroic defense, Be'er Tuvia in Southern Judaea. At Mishmar Ha'emek, the police ordered the settlers to leave, and then watched while the Arabs looted the place. The attack on the Jews of Safad was particularly brutal. In one week 105 Jews were murdered and 187 wounded throughout the country; property worth hundreds of thousands of dollars was destroyed and plundered. Isolated quarters and small settlements suffered, though they were defended heroically; in the large villages and towns the Arabs did not dare to attack. The Jews who survived in Hebron abandoned the town but most of the destroyed villages were soon rebuilt.

Lord Passfield (Sidney Webb), secretary for the colonies in the British Labor government, appointed a commission to enquire into 'the immediate cause' of the outbreak and to make recommendations as to the steps that should be taken to avoid a recurrence. The report was published at the end of March 1930, and its conclusions challenged the basis of the Mandate. The Commission found that the outbreak was 'an attack by Arabs on Jews', but it ascribed the responsibility to Jewish immigration and the Jewish Agency's land policy, not to the Mufti's incitement. Only one of the Commission's members, Mr. Harry Snell (a Labor member of parliament), dissented from its conclusions. As a result, Prime Minister Ramsay MacDonald asked Sir John Hope-Simpson, who had previously taken part in the resettlement of Greek and Turkish refugees, to report on immigration, settlement, and development in Palestine. Even before his arrival, the Palestine Administration—on instructions from London—suspended 3300 immigration certificates that had been delivered to the Jewish Agency three days earlier. The Hope-Simpson report justified the suspension of immigration and severely criticized the colonization policy of the Keren Kayemet, which was based on self-labor.

The report was published in October 1930, together with a White Paper signed by Lord Passfield, which placed new and grave limitations on Jewish immigration and settlement. In protest, Dr. Weizmann resigned from the presidency of the Zionist Organization. Under the influence of the Palestine workers' representative in London (Dov Hos) Ernest Bevin, leader of Britain's largest trade union with 15 members in Parliament, informed the prime minister that these members would vote against the government unless the injustice of the White Paper was rectified.

In the face of this dual pressure a cabinet committee, headed by foreign secretary Arthur Henderson, was appointed to "interpret" the White Paper, and finally a letter, drafted by Henderson but signed by MacDonald, was published. This letter in fact annulled the limitations imposed by the White Paper. A new high commissioner, General Sir Arthur Wauchope, was appointed. He made a sincere effort to carry out the obligations of the Mandate.

The
Hope-Simpson
Report

294

By the 1960's Nahalal (above), a large cooperative small-holder's village (or *moshav ovdim*), had private farms encircling its communally-owned buildings and facilities.

Political Unity

At this point an event took place inside the labor movement that was to have far-reaching results in determining both the character of the Yishuv and the influence of the homeland on the Jewish people in the Diaspora. At the unity conference held in Petah Tikva in 1919, Hapoel Hatza'ir had lost only a few members to Ahdut Ha'avoda, and it was reinforced by new immigrants—so that at the foundation conference of the Histadrut it had only 11 delegates fewer than the larger party. But the demands for political unity did not die down, even after the establishment of the labor federation. At the second Histadrut conference, held in 1923, Ahdut Ha'avoda had an absolute majority, and its majority increased at the third conference in 1927. But the party's leaders persevered in the demand for unity. When the Hapoel Hatza'ir Council met in 1929, voices were raised in favor of unity and negotiations began between the two parties. The question was submitted to the members of the two parties, in the atmosphere of tension that preceded the riots of August 1929. Unity was carried by a large majority in both bodies.

The unification conference met in Tel-Aviv on January 6, 1930, with 134 delegates from Ahdut Ha'avoda and Hapoel Hatza'ir and 28 non-party men. The new party was called *Mifleget Poalei Eretz Yisrael* (the Party of the Workers of the Land of Israel), known from its initials as Mapai—or in English, the Palestine (later Israel) Labor party. (Only Hashomer Hatza'ir did not join the new party though it did not yet proclaim itself an independent party.) At the 1931 Zionist Congress a Mapai representative was elected to the Zionist Executive—Haim Arlozoroff, then just 32, who had been one of the founders of Hapoel Hatza'ir in Germany in his university days. (Arlozoroff was murdered in the summer of 1933 while strolling along the Tel-Aviv seashore with his wife; his murderer was never found.)

The establishment of Mapai revolutionized the status of the Jewish worker. The organized Yishuv was now headed by a labor representative, Ben-Zvi. The 1933 Zionist Congress saw leadership in the Zionist Organization pass from representatives of Diaspora Jewry to leaders of the labor movement in the Land. At the 1931 Congress the labor group had received only 75,810 votes out of the 233,730 cast—32.4 per cent. At the 1933 Congress labor received 226,058 votes out of 535,113—42.2 per cent— and became the largest party. Three of its representatives, David Ben-Gurion, Moshe Shertok (later Sharett), and Eliezer Kaplan, were elected to the Executive in Jerusalem, together with Yitzhak Gruenbaum (of the radical group), who was close to the labor movement, and Arthur Ruppin, an old friend of the workers.

At the end of 1933, following Hitler's rise to power in Germany, David Ben-Gurion addressed the Fourth Conference of the Histadrut (of which he had been secretary-general) on the policy of the new Executive. He said:

'The disaster that has befallen German Jewry is not limited to the territory of Germany alone. Hitler's regime cannot last long without war—war against France, Poland, Czechoslovakia, and the neighboring countries, or against Soviet Russia with its vast expanses . . . The world is in danger of war during the next five years. For us here, this danger is of sevenfold gravity, and so that we shall be able to stand firm when the catastrophe comes, we must double our numbers in this period and consolidate our internal position to the utmost. This must be our five-year plan.'

The plan was fully realized. Immigration, which was only 9553 in 1932, rose to 31,327 in 1933, to 42,539 in 1934, and to 61,854 in 1935. During this time, too, one of the largest land purchases was carried out—the Hula area of 10,500 acres, the most fertile land in the country. The Jews of Germany played an important role in the growth of immigration, bringing with them knowledge and skill, initiative and capital. Some settled on the land and established moshavim. Those with capital invested in citrus, and 5000 acres of new plantations were added in the years 1932-34. Sixteen agricultural settlements were founded in 1932, 28 in 1933, 12 in 1934, and 15 in 1935. In 1935, too, the Palestine Land Development Company purchased the concession for drainage of Lake Hula.

Two political complications arose during this period of prosperity—the Ethiopian war in 1935, and the Arab riots that followed in 1936, fomented and financed by agents of Mussolini and Hitler in collusion with the Mufti in Jerusalem.

On Monday, April 19, 1936, 16 Jews were killed by a savage mob in Jaffa. Three days later the Arab Higher Committee declared a general strike and closed the port of Jaffa, then the country's principal port. Almost all foreign trade and passenger traffic through the port was Jewish, but not a single Jewish worker was allowed to work there. By closing the port, the Arab leaders thought they would stifle the Yishuv. They proclaimed three slogans: stoppage of Jewish immigration, prohibition of the sale of land to Jews, and the establishment of a government responsible to a local parliament elected by the people.

The Zionist Executive demanded that the high commissioner either operate the port of Jaffa or permit loading and unloading at Tel-Aviv. On May 15, 1936, the high commissioner informed the Jewish Agency that he had no desire to use force to open the port, and had therefore decided to approve the building of a jetty at Tel-Aviv. This was followed by the spread of the disturbance throughout the country. The terror affected the Arabs as well. Some of the Mufti's Arab opponents were murdered and resentment against their leaders grew among the Arabs. The strike had ruined Arab merchants, shopkeepers, and artisans. The orange harvest was approaching, and members of the Arab Higher Committee, which had proclaimed the strike, included many large orange-grove owners. They cared little about the injury to the masses, but were very worried about the loss of their own incomes. On October 11, 1936, the Arab Higher Committee announced the stoppage of the strike and the disturbances—ostensibly at the request of the Arab kings of Iraq and of Saudi Arabia. During the strike the number of Jewish workers in the villages increased

Above, *moshav* Beit Yosef, in the Jordan valley—one of many isolated "stockade and tower" settlements established during the Arab disturbances of 1936-1939. These prefabricated settlements would be erected with lightning speed—always in less than 24 hours—to forestall the attacks of Arab gangs. They comprised huts, dining hall, showers, a stockade of wooden frames filled with gravel, a surrounding barbed-wire fence, and a water-tower equipped with a searchlight, which served as lookout post. The cost of erecting these settlements, and of defense generally, was met by *Kofer Hayishuv*—a tax imposed by the National Council on various commodities, and which included the sale of a special stamp (shown left).

dramatically, and the economic independence of the Yishuv was consolidated. Despite violent provocation, the Jews never overstepped the bounds of defense or stooped to vengeance. Their brave and constructive behavior made a good impression in Britain, but the disturbances once again confronted British public opinion (and not only the government) with the entire complexity of the Palestine problem.

The Royal Commission

In 1936, a Royal Commission, headed by Lord Peel, was appointed to examine the situation. Formally it was not authorized to change the Mandate, only to examine whether it was being correctly interpreted. But it was not the formal terms of reference that decided the issue.

Dr. Weizmann was the principal Jewish spokesman to appear before the Commission when it reached Palestine. His picture of the 6,000,000 Jews of Europe, whose aspirations and hopes—indeed, whose very lives—depended on settlement in Palestine and the establishment of the Jewish state, made a tremendous impression.

The Commission's report was published on July 7, 1937. The first part contained a review, written with great skill and remarkable impartiality, of the history of the country and the Jewish people; the unbreakable historic bond between Israel and its Land; the distress of the Jewish people in the Diaspora; the constructive achievements of the Yishuv; the eternal values that the Jewish people had created in their homeland; the great heritage they had bequeathed to humanity. The report told of the tenacity with which the Jews had clung to the Land even after it had been devastated, of the determination that Jews had cherished in their hearts throughout the Exile to rebuild the Land one day; and it spoke also of their modern-day achievements in town and village, in industry and agriculture, education, and culture. All these historical facts were faithfully described. The Commission also pointed out the benefits that Jewish work had bestowed on the entire country.

The Commission stated that in general the Arabs had received their fair share of the material benefits that Jewish immigration had brought to the country; that the obligations of the Mandate in this respect had been fulfilled; that the Arab economy, in general, had not been injured by the National Home. It also revealed for the first time the original intentions of the Balfour Declaration. 'We were permitted to examine the documents', the report states, '. . . and it is clear to us that by the words "establishment of a national home in Palestine" His Majesty's Government recognized that in the course of time a Jewish state was likely to be established, but it was not in their power to say when it would happen.' President Wilson was quoted as saying on March 3, 1919: 'It is clear to me that the Allied Powers, in complete accord with our government and our people, agreed to foundations of a Jewish Commonwealth being laid in Palestine.'

The Commission pointed out that the Emir Feisal, who represented the Arabs at the Peace Conference, had consented to the Balfour Declaration, and in an agreement with Dr. Weizmann had promised cooperation 'between the Arab state and Palestine and encouragement for the immigration of Jews into Palestine on a large scale and their settlement on the land as quickly as possible.'

Nevertheless, the Commission concluded that the Mandate was unworkable and that Palestine west of the Jordan must be partitioned into two unequal parts, with a view to establishing a Jewish state in the smaller part (in the north and west) and—combined with Transjordan—an Arab state in both the south and the east. Immediately after publication of the report, an article by Lloyd George, entitled "The Scandalous Report," was published in a London weekly. The former prime minister, who had been in office when the Balfour Declaration was issued, bitterly denounced the partition plan as a violation of the undertakings to the Jewish people. But Lloyd George's was a solitary voice. The entire British press, from right to left, daily, weekly, and monthly, almost without exception, praised the report and supported its conclusions. The government announced, in a White Paper published simultaneously with the report, that the British government had examined the report, and that it was in general agreement with the arguments and conclusions of the Commission.

On July 19 a two-day debate took place in the House of Lords, followed by an all-day debate in the House of Commons. In both houses vigorous criticism was leveled at the proposals on three issues: the smallness of the area suggested for the Jewish state, the exclusion of New Jerusalem from its territory, and inclusion of the Negev in the Arab state. As a result of this devastating parliamentary criticism, the British government was compelled to retreat from its earlier position—or perhaps the criticism served as a good excuse to abandon the idea of a Jewish state—and a non-committal resolution was adopted: to submit the matter to the League of Nations and to allow the British government, after adequate inquiry, to submit to parliament specific proposals, taking into full account the recommendations of the report.

At the 20th Zionist Congress, which met in Zurich in August 1937, the American delegates and some of those from Palestine vigorously opposed the partition plan, and a resolution was passed by a large majority in which the Congress declared that the scheme of partition put forward by the Royal Commission was unacceptable. Meanwhile, dark clouds lowered over Europe. Britain and France abandoned Austria and Czechoslovakia to Hitler's Germany, and the rumblings of a new world war drew closer and closer.

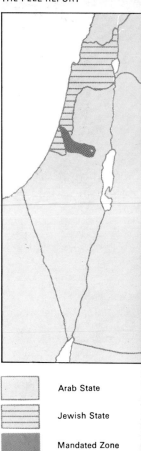

Arab State

Jewish State

Mandated Zone

Illegal Immigration

During the four years preceding World War II, 86,094 people reached the Land of Israel, many of them illegally. The first attempts to bring in immigrants without the permission of the British authorities were made in 1927, when, as a result of growing unemployment, the government cut down the immigration certificates to vanishing point. With the aid of the French government, a training farm was established in Syria, which was under French mandatory rule at the time; this farm served as a

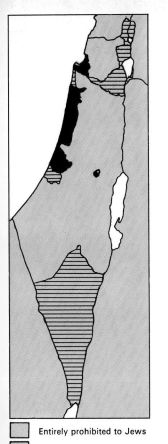

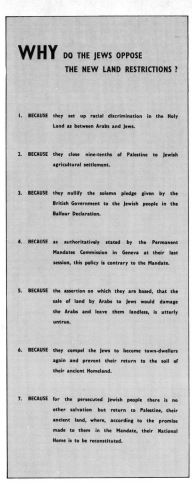

Far left, the Peel Report's recommendations for the partition of Palestine. Above left, in February 1940 the British government followed up its White Paper by imposing restrictions on the transfer of land in Palestine to Jews, as shown in this map. The official Jewish reaction to the new land regulations is expressed (above center) in a leaflet issued by the Jewish Agency at the time. Above right, a poster in Jerusalem calling for a general strike in protest against the British government's Palestinian policy as laid down in the White Paper.

transit point for immigrants who came in across the Syria-Palestine frontier. Others arrived with tourist visas and remained in the Land. At the end of 1933 the first ship carrying immigrants without certificates—a small Greek vessel called the *Velos*—arrived. It had a capacity of 150, but was packed with 350 pioneers from Poland, who had reached Athens by rail from Warsaw.

Organized illegal or unpermitted immigration was renewed in 1938, when the government imposed political restrictions on immigration. In 1939 ships started arriving with 300, 800, and even 1400 passengers. The governments in the countries of departure were of great assistance, and altogether 115,000 illegal immigrants were brought in: 105,000 by the *Mossad La'aliya Bet*, the Institute for Immigration (under the auspices of the Histadrut and in the charge of Shaul Avigur, a veteran of the Hagana), and the rest by private agents and the Revisionist organization.

The London Conference

At the beginning of 1939 the British government invited Iraq, Jordan, and Egypt, the Palestinian Arabs, the Jewish Agency, and Jews in Britain and America to send representatives to London to discuss the political future of Palestine. The Arabs refused to meet with the Jews, and two separate sets of meetings were held: there were even two separate Palestinian Arab delegations, which would not sit together. The meetings took place at St. James's Palace under the chairmanship of Neville Chamberlain, the British prime minister, who was accompanied by Lord Halifax,

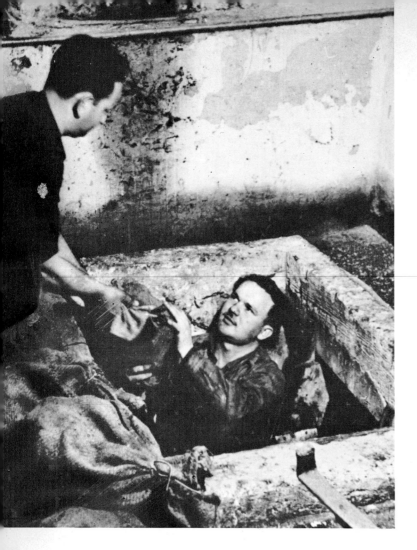

שמור
בלבך
כל הידוע לך
לרגל תפקידך

Above, a Hagana appeal to the Yishuv: 'Keep in your heart all you know as a result of your mission.' Left, illegal arms are stored in a secret cache at a leather factory in Tel-Aviv—the entrance to the cache was concealed beneath a machine.

the foreign secretary, Malcolm MacDonald, the colonial secretary, and their aides. Before the conference Dr. Weizmann, president of the Zionist Organization, and David Ben-Gurion, chairman of the Executive, had a personal meeting with Malcolm MacDonald, who in previous years had shown great sympathy for Zionism and for Jewish work in Palestine. Dr. Weizmann asked him if the British government really intended to condemn the Jews to remain a permanent minority in the country, for if so there was no point in the conference. MacDonald assured the two Zionist representatives that the government had no such intention, and that there was no basis for this suspicion.

At the sixth meeting between the Jewish and British government delegations, MacDonald proposed that for a period of years a certain maximum quota should be imposed on Jewish immigration, and that afterward it should be permitted only if the Arabs agreed. After an unstated number of years Palestine would become an independent state.

Ben-Gurion replied that he had arrived in Palestine under the Turks 33 years before as an illegal immigrant, because the Turks had forbidden Jewish immigration and allowed visitors to enter for three months only. He and many others had violated this law because they had obeyed a supreme law that had existed long before the British and the Turks came to the Land—a law that had been recognized even by the British Mandate: the unbreakable bond between the people of Israel and the Land of Israel. The Jews would not agree that their return should depend on anyone's consent. Immigration could not be stopped without resort to British bayonets, nor could Palestine be transformed into an Arab state without the constant aid of British bayonets—and even then the Jews would not be frightened. The right of the Jews to the Land of Israel was historic, and no power in the world would rob them of it.

300

The White Paper

On May 17, 1939, the Chamberlain government issued a new White Paper on Palestine. It stated that no further Jewish immigration would be allowed after another 75,000 Jews had come in; in 10 years' time a Palestine (i.e. an Arab) state would then be established and the Jews would be allowed to acquire land in only five per cent of the country's area. This document was a complete and utter disavowal of the Balfour Declaration and of Great Britain's international obligations under the Mandate.

On May 18, Dr. Weizmann sent a cable to the British prime minister in which he made the following declaration:

'The proposal to abolish the Mandate, freeze the Yishuv at a third of the population, and contract the area of Jewish settlement to a tiny sector, is in our eyes a shattering of Jewish hopes and the handing over of the Yishuv to a regime of the Arab gangsters who are responsible for all the terror. The Jews will make the ultimate sacrifice but will never capitulate to such hegemony.'

On May 23, 1939, the House of Commons approved the White Paper policy by a moderate Conservative majority, despite strong opposition from the Labor party, the Liberals, and several Conservative leaders, among them Churchill and Amery. At the 21st Congress, which met in Geneva in August 1939, Dr. Weizmann declared that during the three years of the Arab terror, which began on April 16, 1936, the Yishuv had carried out great achievements: 50 new settlements had been established; a Jewish port had been built almost overnight; a powerful defense organization had been founded; and economic independence had grown. The Jews would stand united in defense of their rights in Palestine, which had international validity, and the eternal chain that bound the Jewish people to their land would not be broken.

World War II: The Jewish Brigade

A short time after the Congress, World War II broke out. Ben-Gurion declared: 'We shall fight side by side with Britain in our war against Hitler as if there were no White Paper, and we shall fight the White Paper as if there were no war.'

On September 3, 1939, the Zionist Executive in Jerusalem published a call to all young people to enroll in Jewish units to fight Hitler. In a few weeks 130,000 men and women had registered. The British government at first refused to accept Jewish volunteers, unless an equal number of Arabs came forward. However, few Arabs volunteered; most of their leaders in Palestine and the neighboring countries supported Hitler and prayed for his victory. Finally, Jewish volunteers were accepted, and after training were sent to the North African front; but it was not until September 1944, as a result of Churchill's personal intervention, that a Jewish Brigade was formed, which fought in Italy and took part in the decisive battles. Moshe Shertok (Sharett), head of the Political Department of the Zionist Executive in Jerusalem, and Dr. Weizmann played important roles in this achievement.

America's entry into the war made it clear that the decisive force when peace came would be not Britain but the United States, and so Ben-Gurion went there to mobilize American Jewry for the struggle to defeat the White Paper policy and establish a Jewish state after the war. In May 1942 representatives of all Zionist parties in America met, for the first time, at the Biltmore Hotel in New York. The following resolution was adopted:

'The new world order that will follow victory cannot be established on foundations of peace, justice, and equality unless the problem of Jewish homelessness is finally solved. The Conference urges:

1.   that the gates of Palestine be opened to Jewish immigration;
2.   that the Jewish Agency be vested with control of immigration into Palestine and with the necessary authority for up-building the country, including the development of its unoccupied and uncultivated lands;

3. that Palestine be established as a Jewish Commonwealth integrated in the structure of the new democratic world.'

This resolution, which became known as the Biltmore Program, was submitted by the chairman of the Executive to the Zionist General Council in Jerusalem on October 15, 1942, and approved. It was later adopted by all the Zionist organizations in the world, and became the official program of the movement.

On May 7, 1945, after Germany's surrender, Ben-Gurion had a frank and friendly talk with the colonial secretary, Colonel Oliver Stanley. He conveyed the impression that Britain was unable to give the Jews of Palestine what they wanted, or to give the Arabs what they were asking for, and was not ready to fight either Arabs or Jews. Ben-Gurion became convinced that before long the Mandatory Power would have to leave Palestine entirely. In that case the Yishuv would soon be faced not only with Palestinian Arabs but with the armies of all the neighboring Arab states, and that would mean a real war, for which preparations had to be made.

The youth of the Yishuv could be relied upon, but arms were needed. Ben-Gurion went to New York, where (on June 23, 1945) Dr. Stephen Wise told him that he had been assured by President Roosevelt, upon his return from the Yalta Conference, that Stalin was not against the Zionist program, in fact that he was in favor of it, and that Churchill could be counted on. Even this news did not change Ben-Gurion's mind, and he asked Henry Montor, then head of the United Jewish Appeal, to give him a list of 20 or 30 reliable friends.

Montor asked no questions. The next day he appeared with a list of 17 men—in New York, Toronto, Los Angeles, Pittsburgh, Philadelphia, Miami, Minneapolis, Houston, Cleveland, Columbus, Baltimore, Atlanta, Newark, St. Louis, and New Haven. Telegrams were sent inviting all 17 to a meeting at 45 East 57th Street, New York City, at 9 A.M. on July 1. All the men appeared at the appointed place on time. Also present were Eliezer Kaplan (later minister of finance in the first Israel government), Meyer Weisgal, the late Reuven Shiloah, and Henry Montor.

Ben-Gurion told the meeting that in the near future Britain would give up the Mandate and that the Jews of Palestine would have to face the armies of all the neighboring Arab states; that these armies could be defeated if the young people of the Yishuv were equipped with the necessary arms—tanks, heavy artillery, heavy machine guns, fighter planes, and warships; that because it might be difficult to acquire such weapons illegally, it was necessary to build up a military industry in the Yishuv. He pointed out that in Europe the war had ended and that soon Japan would be defeated and forced to surrender. America would then undoubtedly dismantle a great part of her military industry, and the necessary machinery might be acquired cheaply. Ben-Gurion concluded his talk by asking if those in the room were ready to help.

The meeting started at 9 A.M. and did not end until 5 P.M. Many questions were asked and answered. Before the end of the afternoon those present agreed to provide the necessary funds. Engineer Haim Slavin, manager of the Hagana's underground defense industry, was asked to come immediately to New York and—together with Ya'akov Dori, head of the Hagana, who happened to be in America—he was charged with buying the necessary machinery. During the next two years Slavin and Dori acquired a considerable quantity of machinery, which was immediately transported to Palestine; and although the Administration was then searching for arms in all the Jewish settlements, the machinery came in undetected by the British.

The British Labor party obtained a majority in the postwar elections, and there were growing hopes in the Zionist movement that the end of the Chamberlain-MacDonald White Paper policy had come. Labor had opposed the White Paper in 1939, and had proposed a vote of censure on the government over the 1940 land law, which limited Jewish rights to buy land in 95 per cent of the country In 1944 the Labor party conference had passed a resolution demanding the establishment of a Jewish state, and added a proposal which the Zionist movement had never advocated: the transfer of the Palestine Arabs to the Arab countries.

In August 1945, a World Zionist Conference was held in London. Hopes were high as a result of the change in the composition of the British government, but Ben-Gurion warned the delegates not to rely too much on the Labor party: 'What a party says in opposition is no indication of what it will do when in power,' he said. Within a few weeks it became clear that the Attlee-Bevin government had no intention of annulling the White Paper, and a bitter struggle began· in Palestine.

The Struggle for Independence

On November 13, 1945, Ben-Gurion and Shertok (Sharett) were summoned to the colonial office, where the colonial secretary, George Hall, gave them the text of a statement that the foreign secretary, Ernest Bevin, was making in Parliament that day. He said that in a few days' time he would invite them to meet Bevin and himself so that they could submit their observations personally, but for some reason the meeting was never arranged. In Bevin's statement there was no mention or hint of the Labor party's declared attitude on Palestine, although as recently as April 25, 1945, its National Executive had unanimously adopted a resolution that stated: 'The Committee reaffirms the policy accepted by the annual Conference in December 1944 on Palestine. It therefore calls upon the British government to remove the present unjustifiable barriers on immigration and to announce without delay proposals for the future of Palestine in which it has the full sympathy and support of the American and Russian governments.'

Bevin's statement declared that there were irreconcilable antagonisms between Jews and Arabs, and that Palestine would therefore have to be placed under 'international trusteeship.' In other words, the British occupation would continue without the Mandate and its obligations.

Underground Resistance

An Anglo-American Committee reached Palestine in March 1946. It recommended the immediate admission of 100,000 Jews, but Attlee announced that he would not accept the report. So the struggle went on. Illegal immigration was stepped up; the Yishuv organized itself for resistance; bridges were blown up and telephone lines destroyed. In defiance of the organized Yishuv and the Hagana, two underground break-away movements—*Irgun Zva'i Leumi* (National Military Organization, called *Etzel*) and *Lohamei Herut Yisrael* (Fighters for the Freedom of Israel)—engaged in acts of terrorism. On July 22, Etzel blew up a wing of the King David Hotel in Jerusalem, which housed the government administration, and about 100 Jews, Britons, and Arabs were killed. The Va'ad Leumi and the Jewish Agency Executive immediately published the following statement:

'The Executive of the Jewish Agency and the Executive of the Va'ad Leumi express their horror at the unparalleled atrocity committed today by a band of criminals who attacked the government offices in Jerusalem and shed the innocent blood of scores of civil servants and other civilians, Britons, Jews, and Arabs. The Jewish community in the Land of Israel is called upon to rise up against these loathsome crimes.'

The army authorities issued an order of the day laying responsibility for the deed on the entire Yishuv, and threatened punitive action. On Saturday June 29, 1946 (on the Jewish Sabbath), all the members of the Zionist Executive and hundreds of other leaders of the Yishuv were arrested and detained at Latrun. The chairman of the Executive, Ben-Gurion, happened to be in Paris at the time, so the British were unable to arrest him.

At the 22nd Zionist Congress, which met in Basel in December 1946, both the

*They are coming. Driven by suffering they have taken the one way of light for Jews in this world—the road to Israel. The world and the nations' hearts are closed to them. Only one hope exists—homeland. Only one heart is open—that of the Yishuv, the heart of brothers. Cruel laws will not stop them, barbed wire will not frighten nor bayonets deter them; if denied, their spirits will not break. They come and will continue to come to their homeland, the Land of Israel—*from a Hagana poster.

president of the Zionist Organization, Dr. Weizmann, and Ben-Gurion demanded a Jewish state as the only solution to the problem. But differences arose over the attitude to Britain, and Dr. Weizmann was not reelected. The Congress undertook 'to give the Yishuv all possible aid in its determined struggle for the defense of the Jewish people's vital interests and irrevocable rights, including the right to immigration, settlement and defense.' At the same time it condemned 'acts of murder and the spilling of innocent blood as a means of political warfare,' and called upon the separatist groups to 'refrain from bloodshed and accept the national authority of the organized Yishuv and the Zionist movement.' At the Congress, the chairman of the Executive, Ben-Gurion, was appointed to serve also as head of the Defense Department. Ehud Avriel and Yehuda Arazi were sent to Czechoslovakia and other countries to purchase arms, some of which were delivered to the Hagana just a few weeks before Israel's declaration of independence. But the bulk of heavy weapons could not be imported until after the state was established.

The opposition to the continuation of the British Mandate was not confined to the Yishuv and the World Zionist Organization, but extended to the Arab population as well. Bevin tried again to convene representatives of Jews and Arabs in London, but could not reach an understanding with either group. He offered the Jews the admission of 96,000 further immigrants in two years, a new trusteeship under the United Nations, and the summoning of a constituent assembly in four years to prepare a constitution for an independent Palestine, which would come into force only with the consent of the majority of the Jewish (and also of the Arab) representatives. Both Jews and Arabs rejected these proposals and demanded the departure of the British from Palestine. The British government was therefore compelled to submit the Palestine problem to the United Nations General Assembly. The foreign secretary did not say whether his government would regard itself bound by the

Far left, illegal immigrants bound for Palestine. Fifty-eight of the 63 immigrant ships that sailed clandestinely for Palestine between April 1945 and January 1948 were intercepted by the British. Left, a Hagana poster affirming the immigrants' determination to reach Palestine (a translation is given on the opposite page). Above, an illegal immigrant—whose ship has been intercepted by Mandatory forces—is interrogated by British soldiers.

conclusions of the UN; and as subsequent developments showed, it did in fact refuse to carry out its decisions.

In the middle of May 1947, Ben-Gurion was summoned to appear before the General Assembly, where he met, among others, Mr. Andrei Gromyko, delegate of the Soviet Union, who expressed sympathy with the demand for a Jewish state and publicly supported it in the Assembly:

'It will be unjust,' he said, 'if we do not take account of this aspiration of the Jews to a state of their own, and if we deny to the Jews the right to realize this aspiration. The denial of this right to the Jewish people cannot be justified, especially if we take into account everything that the Jewish people underwent during the Second World War.'

The UN Committee The Assembly decided to establish a committee—the United Nations Special Committee on Palestine (UNSCOP)—representing the five political and geographical blocs, excluding Britain and the Arab states. Mr. Gromyko urged that the Jewish people's right to a state of their own should be taken into account, and that the preparation of suitable proposals should be an important function of the committee.

At the end of June 1947, the committee arrived in Jerusalem and visited various parts of the country before hearing evidence. At first the Arabs refused to appear. Ben-Gurion, testifying before the committee, explained the possibilities of the country which could, according to expert opinion, absorb millions of Jews without displacing a single Arab; he pointed to the way the Arabs had flourished in Western Palestine, where hundreds of thousands of Jews had settled, in contrast to the stagnation in Transjordan, where Jewish immigration had not been allowed. He concluded by expressing the hope that the establishment of the Jewish state would in course of time lead to an Arab-Jewish alliance in the Middle East.

305

At the end of August the Zionist General Council met in Zurich, and on September 1, while it was still in session, the conclusions of the UN Special Committee were published. Certain recommendations were agreed to by all the members, including:
1. the termination of the British Mandate at the earliest possible date;
2. independence for Palestine as soon as possible;
3. the shortest possible transition period;
4. the United Nations should be responsible for the administration during the transition period.

The committee was divided on the nature of the regime to be set up after the transition period. A minority proposed a federal state, with a small Jewish region and a large Arab region. The majority proposed the partition of the country into two states, Arab and Jewish, bound by an economic union, with Jerusalem as a separate body under international administration.

The Zionist General Council noted with satisfaction that a sizable majority of the committee had recommended the speedy establishment of a sovereign Jewish state. The final attitude of the Jewish people would be determined after the Assembly had adopted a decision on the Palestine question.

This majority resolution was opposed by three parties: by Ahdut Ha'avoda, Hashomer Hatza'ir, and the Revisionists. The first two demanded 'a regime founded on reciprocal non-domination and equality between the Jewish people returning to its land and the Arab people dwelling in it; in the transition stage the British Mandate should be replaced by an international civil and military administration, with an Arab-Jewish council on a parity basis, until the United Nations decided at the end of a transition period on the final form of the regime in an independent Palestine.' The Revisionists proposed the continuation of efforts for the immediate establishment of a Jewish state in the historic boundaries of the undivided Land of Israel, but they did not explain how a Jewish state could be set up immediately in an area containing 1,200,000 Arabs and only slightly more than 600,000 Jews.

On October 10, 1947, the Zionist Executive adopted three proposals submitted by Ben-Gurion:
1. to mobilize and train a Jewish armed force with the utmost urgency;
2. to prepare an administration for state service;
3. to prepare stocks of food and supplies to meet the vital needs of the economy.

A committee of five—consisting of Ben-Gurion, Peretz Bernstein, Golda Myerson (later Meir), Eliezer Kaplan, and Moshe Shapiro—was appointed to prepare all the military and economic measures.

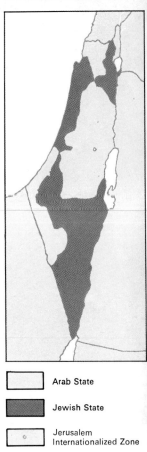

Arab State

Jewish State

Jerusalem
Internationalized Zone

The discussion in the United Nations Assembly lasted over two months; but finally, on November 29, 1947, the Assembly agreed by a majority of over two-thirds to accept the majority report. Thirty-three countries (including the United States and the Soviet Union) voted in favor, and 13 voted against: six Arab states—Egypt, Syria, Lebanon, Iraq, Saudi Arabia, and Yemen; four non-Arab Muslim states—Afghanistan, Pakistan, Persia, and Turkey; and three others—India, Greece, and Cuba. There were 10 abstentions, including Britain.

**The
UN Decision**

The Assembly decision aroused universal enthusiasm and joy among the Jews in the Land and the Diaspora. Even the Communists, who had obstinately fought the idea of a Jewish state, became devotees of the idea after Gromyko's speech.

The Arab rulers had publicly declared that they would frustrate the Assembly's decision by force of arms. Britain had abstained, but had announced that she would not implement the decision against the wishes of the Arabs. Britain still controlled the country, with an army of 75,000-100,000 men. The best Arab force at the time was the Arab Legion, which was under British command and stationed in Western Palestine. The Egyptian and the Iraqi armies had also been trained by British officers.

A Jewish volunteer posts up a Hagana appeal to the Arabs of Palestine (December 1947): part of the appeal is translated below.

The Jewish Hagana organization exhorts you to peace and calm and at the same time presents you with a firm ultimatum. For the past two days the peace of this country has been disturbed by a group of incited Arabs who have engaged in shooting, arson, and murder. We have stressed that our aims are peace and good relations with our neighbors. . . . Now we offer you peace, but we also extend a grave warning. If the bloodshed continues we shall be forced to resort to extreme measures. . . . We call on you to take our appeal for peace to heart. Heed our warning—from a Hagana poster.

The Zionist Executive and the Va'ad Leumi had begun to mobilize the youth into the ranks of the Hagana; but the British navy and air force kept a meticulous watch to prevent any arms reaching the Jews (who could receive supplies only by sea or air, while the Arabs obtained their weapons overland from neighboring countries).

On November 30, the day after the adoption of the UN resolution, the Arabs launched their assault. An Arab band ambushed and killed seven Jews traveling to Jerusalem. The Arab Higher Committee proclaimed a three-day strike in protest against the Assembly decision, and on December 2 an Arab mob set fire to the Jewish commercial center in Jerusalem; the British police stood by and only obstructed the efforts of the Hagana to come to the assistance of the victims.

The Arabs Flee

At the beginning of December the Arabs began to flee from the area allotted to the Jewish state. On page 23 of the Arab Higher Committee's report of 1951 the following statement appears:

'It was natural that those inhabitants of Palestine who found it necessary to flee took refuge in the neighboring Arab countries, and preferred to remain there and be in contact with their country so that it would be easy to return when the opportunity arose, as had been promised in the declarations of the Arab leaders. These

307

leaders exaggerated greatly, so that many believed that this opportunity would come in a very short time. These declarations were a factor that encouraged the emigration of many residents, especially those with large families, who preferred to leave with their families, believing that the stabilization of the position in Palestine in accordance with Arab interests would take only a very short time. Most of the inhabitants in the northern area of Palestine emigrated to Syria and Lebanon; those in the southern part turned to Egypt and the Gaza Strip, while the majority of the inhabitants in the center migrated to other parts of Palestine and Transjordan.'

The Arab flight continued until the establishment of the state. Many Arab villages were completely evacuated. Habib Issa, editor of the Arab newspaper *Al Huda*, published the results of his inquiries into the Arab flight in June 1951. He concluded: 'The Secretary-General of the Arab League, Abdel Rahman Azzam Pasha, published numerous declarations assuring the Arab peoples that the occupation of Palestine and of Tel-Aviv would be as simple as a military parade for the Arab armies. He pointed out that the armies were already on the frontiers, and that all the millions the Jews had spent on land and economic development would be easy booty, for it would be a simple matter to throw the Jews into the Mediterranean. . . . Brotherly advice was given to the Arabs of Palestine to leave their land, homes, and property and to stay temporarily in the neighboring states, lest the guns of the invading Arab armies mow them down. The Palestine Arabs had no choice but to obey the League's advice and believed what they were told by Azzam Pasha and the other responsible League leaders: that departure from their lands and their country would be only temporary, and would come to an end in a few days, when the Arab punitive operation against Israel was completed.'

Two weeks after the Assembly resolution, the Arab League met in Cairo and decided to send troops from the neighboring countries into Palestine under the guise of volunteers. This invasion by foreign forces met with no obstruction from the British authorities, who refused to cooperate with a UN committee appointed to facilitate the transition from Mandate to independence.

In the meantime the Mufti had managed to organize bands in all parts of the country, and recruiting centers had been set up in the neighboring countries. For a while the attacks were concentrated on Jaffa, Jerusalem, and Haifa. Most of the Palestine *fellahin* (Arab peasants) at first shied away from involvement but it was obvious that this was only a beginning; and, indeed, Arab lawlessness did soon begin to spread. There were over 300 Jewish points of settlement scattered around the country, many isolated from the rest of the Yishuv. Each point had to be defended, and the settlements could not be maintained without lines of communication between the villages and towns—and since there was hardly a single continuous area of Jewish settlement, almost all the roads were in Arab hands.

It was only in Haifa that the Jews had the upper hand, because the town was surrounded by Jewish settlements. The Arab merchants urged the Arab Higher Committee to keep the peace in Haifa, since all the wealthy Arabs had fled to Lebanon. By the end of January, over 20,000 had left the city. A delegation of three Arabs, led by Archbishop Hakim, went to Egypt to try to persuade the Mufti to withdraw his bands from Haifa, otherwise all the Arabs would have to leave; but the Mufti would not agree.

In Jerusalem the position of the Jews was more difficult. Jerusalem had no direct link with any Jewish settlement, and in the city itself the Jewish quarters were scattered and intermingled with Arab districts. The Arabs had four roads open to Jerusalem: north (from Nablus and Ramallah), south (from Hebron and Bethlehem), east (from Jericho), and west (from Jaffa through Ramleh). The Jews had only one road—from Tel-Aviv—and day by day it became increasingly difficult and dangerous for traffic to move along it. The authorities undertook to preserve freedom of movement on the road, but this promise—like most others—was broken. Since Jerusalem would be faced with famine and drought if the road were cut, it became essential to go from defense to attack.

As the member of the Executive responsible for defense, Ben-Gurion (at the end of March 1948) ordered the Hagana command to muster a large force to break open the way to Jerusalem. The command estimated that 400 men were needed, but Ben-Gurion thought that this was not enough. The Arabs also understood the importance of the city, and they rightly believed that the sack of Jewish Jerusalem would be a deathblow to the Yishuv as a whole. Against 400 Hagana fighters they would mobilize at least 4000, and Ben-Gurion therefore demanded at least 1500 men for the operation. Ascertaining the number of men on each front, he ordered half the fighters and arms to be taken from each, with the exception of Galilee, where the position was particularly grave. All the commanders received the order with understanding and complied speedily.

Operation Nahshon

The first Jewish offensive was organized in a few hours. It was named Operation Nahshon, after the prince of the tribe of Judah who, according to tradition, was the first to jump into the Red Sea after the Exodus. The Jerusalem road was breached and the Castel, the high hill overlooking the road, was taken. The Arab commander Abdel Kader el-Husseini fell in the battle. Both British and Arabs were taken aback by the Jews' courage and power of attack.

On April 6, 1948, a few days after Operation Nahshon, the Zionist General Council met in Tel-Aviv, and Ben-Gurion surveyed the situation. During the four months since the beginning of the Arab attacks in November, 900 Jews had been killed.

THE CASTEL AREA

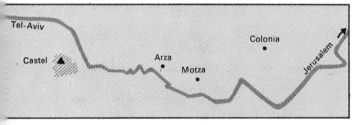

Below, the Castel, the hill five miles west of Jerusalem where the Arab outpost harassed Jewish convoys to Jerusalem. Scene of some of the most bitter fighting of the war (it was one of the principal objectives of Operation Nahshon), the Castel was eventually taken by Israeli forces on April 9, 1948. Left, a map of the Castel area, showing the road dominated by the hill.

All the roads were in danger and Jews could travel only at peril of their lives. Many Jewish villages had been attacked, in Galilee, Samaria, the Jordan Valley, Judaea, and the Negev. In the three cities—Jerusalem, Jaffa, and Haifa—not a night passed without skirmishes. Thousands of Arab soldiers had invaded the country from the neighboring states, and their number was growing. They were coming mainly from Syria, Iraq, and Transjordan, but also from Egypt. The government was doing nothing to prevent them entering. Worse still, the Arab Legion was actually stationed in Palestine itself.

The administration was disintegrating, but it was doing all in its power to hamper and obstruct the Yishuv's self-defense. In violation of UN decisions, it had refused to free Tel-Aviv port by February 1. British warships cruising along the coasts maintained an effective blockade of the Jewish population, while the land frontiers—north, east, and south—were open to the Arab invaders. The Jews in Palestine were outnumbered fortyfold by the local Arabs and those from the neighboring countries. Six Arab states were represented in the United Nations, and the seventh—Transjordan—was Britain's official ally.

Nevertheless, not a single Jewish settlement, village or town, had been taken or evacuated. Although Jerusalem had been cut off at times from the rest of Jewish Palestine, the position inside the city had improved, for the Arab quarters were being abandoned and their residents were in flight. The most serious trial, however, was to come on May 15, after the departure of the Mandatory Administration. There was no doubt that the country would then be invaded by all the Arab armies.

In Palestine (including Transjordan) there were only 650,000 Jews and almost 1,200,000 Arabs; in the neighboring countries there were another 30,000,000 Arabs, and their armies were equipped with artillery, airplanes, tanks, and ships of war—weapons that the Jewish defense forces did not as yet possess, for they could not be obtained secretly.

The Jews could never equal the Arabs in numbers, Ben-Gurion pointed out. Their main strength lay in their qualitative superiority and they would win only if they mobilized that advantage to the utmost. For this purpose, five things were essential:

1. to mobilize all manpower for fighting and production on rational lines, subject to one overriding consideration—defense needs;
2. to manufacture and acquire the necessary equipment that had never been in the Hagana's possession—including vehicles for land, sea, and air—in line with the preparations that had been made over the past three years;
3. to organize all branches of the economy and the distribution of food and raw materials in accordance with the requirements of the emergency;
4. to establish in the Yishuv a single, central, supreme authority, which would be in control of all manpower, the army, the economy, industry and agriculture, finance and public services;
5. when the Mandate terminated, to discard defensive tactics, and attack all along the front—not only in the area of the Jewish state, and not only on the territory of Palestine, but at every point where it was necessary to undermine and crush the power of the enemy.

In theory, the Hagana was subordinate to the Va'ad Leumi, the Zionist Executive, and the local authorities; but in practice it was self-governing. Outside the Hagana there were the two separatist organizations—Etzel (also called *Irgun*) and Lehi (Lohamei Herut Yisrael), also known as the Stern gang. There was also a Defense Committee of the Yishuv. But discipline in the Hagana was not complete, and, obviously, war could not be waged against regular armies under such a regime. There was one independent unit in the Hagana: the Palmah (*Plugot Mahatz*— "Assault Companies"), then numbering some 2500.

The Hagana contained the finest of the country's Jewish youth. It was built entirely on a voluntary basis, and its strength lay in its free initiative. But in view of the war with the Arab armies that was to be expected after May 15, all the young men would have to be drafted, whether they were ready to volunteer or not. They would face regular armies, and without strict military discipline and subordination to a single supreme authority they would be unable to fight. Now that the State of Israel has been in existence 26 years, this is obvious to everyone, but in those days—even after months of Arab attack—it was not easy to bring the idea home to the members of the Hagana. It was even more difficult to convince the separatist organizations, who would not accept the authority of either the Yishuv or the Zionist Movement.

The Provisional Government

The Executive Committee of the Zionist Organization, overriding *Mapam* and Revisionist opposition, decided to establish a Jewish state and government once the Mandate ended; and, as a preliminary measure, to set up a Provisional Council of State, with 37 members and a Provisional government of 13. Until the Mandate expired, the larger body was to be known as the Thirty-Seven, and the smaller as the People's Administration, which would be responsible to the Thirty-Seven.

In the unofficial war that began immediately after the UN Assembly's resolution of November 29, 1947, the Yishuv had to face local bands, as well as Syrian, Iraqi, and Jordanian soldiers who had entered the country unofficially as individuals, and also the so-called Liberation Army of Arab irregulars from Syria under the unofficial leadership of Fawzi Kaukji.

In most of these battles the Hagana had the upper hand. The Arab bands were routed in Tiberias, Haifa, and Safad in the second half of April 1948, and finally in Jaffa as well, a few days before the departure of the British. The Arabs of Tiberias and Safad fled, on the orders of the Arab Higher Committee, immediately after the Hagana victory. It was only in Haifa and Jaffa that a few thousand remained. The fugitives obeyed the instructions of the Arab command, relying on its promise that they would soon return together with the conquering Arab forces from the neighboring countries. In the New City of Jerusalem, too, all the Arab quarters were abandoned, while the Jewish minority in the Old City held its ground until after the invasion of the Arab armies.

On the day before the Declaration of Independence the Etzion bloc—a group of four Jewish villages not far from Hebron—fell after a desperate assault by the Arab Legion. The men were taken as captives to Transjordan, while the women and children were brought to Jerusalem. Two other Jewish villages north of Jerusalem, Atarot and Neveh-Ya'akov, had to be evacuated and abandoned.

In the battle that raged around Mishmar Ha'emek at the beginning of April, Kaukji used artillery and powerful fighting forces many times larger than those of the Jewish defenders. But, like his previous assault on Tirat-Zvi in the Beit She'an (Beisan) area, his attack ended in failure. The attack on Ramat Yohanan by a Druse battalion, which had been brought across the Jordan, was held off; after this battle the Druses took no further part in the fighting against Israel.

Among the victories, there was one that did not redound to the honor of the Jewish population. On April 9, 1948, the two separatist underground forces, Etzel and Lehi, which did not accept the Hagana's authority, attacked the village of Deir Yassin near Jerusalem. More than 200 villagers, including women and children, were killed. On April 13, 1948, a group of 94 members of the staff of Hadassah Hospital and the medical faculty of the Hebrew University—which were both located on Mount Scopus—were returning there from Jerusalem when they were ambushed by a large Arab gang near Shiekh Jarrah, and murdered. Many were so badly burned when their cars were set on fire that their remains were beyond recognition.

In the weeks immediately preceding the declaration of the state, the People's

Administration had many critical decisions to make. For example, what should the reborn state be called? There were many suggestions, among them Zion, Judaea, and The Land of Israel (Eretz Yisrael), but a majority finally voted for Israel. There was also disagreement over whether the Declaration of Independence should specifically mention the borders of the state. Ben-Gurion's arguments against being specific were that the Declaration of Independence of the United States made no mention of borders, and that, during the inevitable war that would soon occur, the frontiers might be changed and improved. The vote against naming boundaries was five to four.

While such questions were being decided, attempts were made in the UN General Assembly by the British government and by the state department of the United States to annul the resolution of November 29. Some of Israel's friends were frightened by experts who predicted that the Jewish state would be unable to stand up to the Arab armies and that the Yishuv would be doomed to annihilation. There were also a few in the Land who had similar apprehensions. However, the People's Administration did not waver in its decision to bring the state into existence. On the morning of Friday, May 14, 1948, Ben-Gurion, on behalf of a committee of five which had been appointed to draft Israel's Declaration of Independence, presented to a meeting of the People's Administration a proposed text of 14 short paragraphs. There was only one amendment and then the approved text was given to a Tel-Aviv artist to copy onto a piece of embellished parchment.

On the afternoon of Friday May 14, 1948, shortly before 4 P.M., the leaders of Jewry in the Land assembled for the official declaration of the state in the Tel-Aviv Museum, since Jerusalem was under siege and there was no possibility of getting there that day. The fact that the state was to be declared at this time was not publicized, for fear that the heads of the British Administration (scheduled to leave the country at midnight that night) would make some last-minute trouble.

The members of the National Council and other leaders who were cut off in Jerusalem could not come. Only Rabbi Maimon succeeded in getting to Tel-Aviv by Piper Cub airplane. Present in the hall were those members of the National Council who could get there, representatives of the World Zionist Organization and the Va'ad Leumi, literary and artistic figures, journalists, party leaders, the chief rabbis, the Hagana chief of staff and his associates, and representatives of the community's economic bodies.

News of the event spread among the public despite the attempt at secrecy, and thousands poured into the streets, especially near the museum, carrying flags of blue and white, which had been chosen as the colors of the state about to be born.

Inside the auditorium, behind the dais, hung a photograph of Theodor Herzl. The Tel-Aviv Philharmonic Orchestra played "Hatikva", which had been made the new state's national anthem. On this solemn occasion the words had more meaning than ever before in history. Ben-Gurion read the Declaration and then Rabbi Maimon pronounced the traditional *shehehiyanu* benediction, giving thanks to the Almighty, 'who has kept us in life, and preserved us, and enabled us to reach this day.' Ben-Gurion was the first to sign the Declaration, then his colleagues signed in alphabetical order. Spaces in the same order were reserved for those in Jerusalem. One thousand eight hundred and thirteen years after the defeat of Bar Kochba, a sovereign Israel had arisen once again. In the streets the throngs sang and danced.

That night the young state received its first official recognition when the president of the United States, Harry S. Truman, announced *de facto* recognition—for which Dr. Weizmann, who was then in the United States, was largely responsible.

On May 17 *de jure* recognition came from the Soviet Union. More countries followed suit, one after the other: Poland, Czechoslovakia, Romania, Hungary, Yugoslavia,

312

Ben-Gurion signs the Declaration of Independence (shown on the left). Seated beside him is his foreign minister, Moshe Sharett, who had led the Palestinian delegation at the U.N. and was later to become prime minister.

Finland, Uruguay, Paraguay, Venezuela, Guatemala, Costa Rica, Panama, and South Africa. Great Britain recognized Israel only after the end of the fighting, on January 30, 1949. Australia did likewise on the same day, and was followed by Holland, Belgium, Luxembourg, and Switzerland. Two days later, on February 1, 1949, came *de jure* recognition from the United States Government. On May 11, 1949, before the completion of its first year, the State of Israel was accepted as a member of the United Nations Organization, but only after it had faced the momentous test of an attack by the neighboring Arab states, which did not end until January 7, 1949.

The last British high commissioner, General Cunningham, left Palestine at midnight on May 14, and at the very same moment the armies of Egypt, Lebanon, Syria, Iraq, and Transjordan invaded Israel.

The Eve of Invasion

Seldom, if ever, in the annals of mankind has there been any parallel to the birth of Israel. A new state had been established with the blessing of world public opinion, on the basis of a resolution by the United Nations, and supported by the two greatest world powers, the United States and the Soviet Union; and yet it was attacked by all its neighbors, 44 times as numerous, the moment it emerged into the light of day. The young state had not even time to establish a regular army for its own defense. Those fighters who emerged from the underground had only light weapons—no artillery, no tanks, no fighting planes, no ships of war; for although heavy armaments had been acquired during Mandatory days in Czechoslovakia and France, it was difficult to bring them in under British rule. The first consignment of Czechoslovak arms arrived by air at a secret airfield at the end of March 1948. It consisted of rifles and machine guns, which were sent immediately to the fighters in the campaign for the liberation of Jerusalem. But heavy machine guns, artillery, tanks, and fighter planes

313

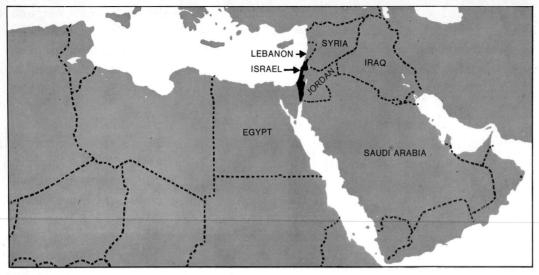

ISRAEL AND THE ARAB STATES 1948

could not be brought in until the British had left. During the first month, therefore, a small number of Hagana volunteers, almost unarmed, faced five well-established and well-equipped armies.

The first campaign against the invaders lasted four weeks. On May 17, Acre, the city that Napoleon had been unable to conquer, surrendered to the Hagana. Almost all its Arab residents stayed where they were. On June 11, a four-week truce was instituted, at the Security Council's demand. In the early days of July, a United Nations emissary requested Jews and Arabs to renew the truce. Israel agreed, but the Arabs refused, and the fighting recommenced on July 9, continuing until July 18. Again a truce was declared at the UN's demand, this time of unlimited duration. Both in the north, in the face of the Syrian assault, and in the south, due to the Egyptian advance, a few settlements had to be evacuated; but otherwise the defenders held their ground on all fronts. Supreme heroism was displayed by Jewish Jerusalem. **The First Campaign**

After the invasion, it was completely cut off from the rest of the Jewish population, and all the power of the Arab Legion was directed against the beleaguered city. Bombardment by the Legion's artillery and bombing by the Egyptian air force did not cease for a single day. Food had almost run out. On May 28 the small Jewish community in the Old City surrendered to the Legion. All the young people fit to bear arms were sent as prisoners of war to Transjordan, while the women, old people, and children were transferred to the New City. There were only 40 fighters among the prisoners. This was the most serious defeat in the entire War of Independence. The resistance of the New City under a hail of shells and bombs is faithfully described by Dr. Dov Joseph, governor of Jerusalem during the war, in *The Faithful City*.

At the fourth session of the Provisional State Council, on June 17, 1948, the prime minister reviewed the events that had taken place during the first four weeks of the state's existence, dwelling particularly on the battle of Jerusalem: **The First Truce**
'For centuries the entire Christian and Muslim worlds have claimed that this city, which was sanctified in history by the prophets of Israel, had also become a Holy City to them, and by virtue of the claim that Jerusalem is sacred to the three great world religions it was decided that it should be placed under international rule. And now the Holy City has been bombarded for four weeks by Muslim forces from the desert, with the aid of British artillery and officers—an unbridled, cynical, barbaric and brutal bombardment, battering down all that is sacred in the city, destroying synagogues—and all the Christian world looked on in silence. . . . Forgotten was the sanctity of

Jerusalem, forgotten were the memories binding this city with all the great religions. There was only one people, one small, isolated people, who—though left defenseless by the Mandatory government that held sway here—stood alone, bearing untold suffering, in supreme heroism, against the unremitting bombardment. Thus it was clearly shown to whom this city is truly precious and holy, and to whom the sanctity of Jerusalem is no more than empty and lying verbiage.'

The Altalena

It was in the days of the first truce that the incident of the Irgun Zva'i Leumi ship *Altalena* took place. After the Zionist General Council meeting of April 1948, the Irgun undertook to disband of its own free will after the state had been established, but it did not keep its word. On June 1, after negotiations that followed the establishment of the state, the Irgun leader signed a number of general undertakings providing for the disbandment of the Irgun as a military formation, and committing its members to hand over their arms and contacts and to enlist in the Israel Defense Forces.

These undertakings were only partially fulfilled. On June 18, 1948, during the first truce, it became known that the Irgun had brought into Israeli waters a ship containing arms and had refused to hand it over to the government. The ship made its way to Kfar Vitkin, and the government decided to prevent by force the unloading of the ship by the Irgun. Many Irgun men serving in the forces left their units and came to Kfar Vitkin. But the revolt failed. The Irgun men surrendered to the Defense Forces, and signed an undertaking that all the arms, ammunition, and military equipment in Irgun hands in the Kfar Vitkin area would be handed over intact to the local Defense Forces commander. During the night, however, the *Altalena* slipped away, reaching Tel-Aviv in the morning.

The government met and decided to order the Irgun to hand over the ship to the government of Israel; otherwise, it warned, force would be used. The ship, which was under orders of the Irgun commander, refused to comply and the army did its duty by firing on it. When the ship caught fire, the men of the Forces helped the passengers and crew to reach land safely. The State Council approved the government's decision. This was the gravest internal test the young state had yet been forced to face.

The second underground organization, Lohamei Herut Yisrael (Lehi), disbanded unconditionally immediately after the establishment of the state, but some of its members continued to operate. On September 17 an underground group murdered Count Bernadotte (The United Nations emissary) and his adjutant, the French Colonel Saraut, in Jerusalem. This was the young state's second grave trial.

The government decided to liquidate this remnant of separatism and revolt. On September 20, 1948, the Army issued an ultimatum to the Irgun: within 24 hours it must undertake to obey all the laws of the state, and all Irgun members liable for enlistment must serve in the Israel Defense Forces, not in separate units. If this order was not complied with in the course of one day, the army would deploy all its forces against the dissidents. The Irgun surrendered and handed over its arms to the army and its members reported to the Forces as individuals, with the same status as other soldiers.

The Battle for the South

During the 10 days that followed the Arab refusal to renew the first truce, Israeli forces occupied Nazareth and the villages around it (on July 16, 1948), and the village of Lubia fell into their hands without a shot being fired, thus opening the way to Tiberias. The road between Haifa and Tel-Aviv was cleared. Lydda and Ramleh were taken, and most of their inhabitants fled. The Lydda airfield was also occupied. Only the attempt to take Latrun, in order to clear the Tel-Aviv-Jerusalem highway, failed. But the capture of numerous villages in the Shefela (see page 14) allowed an alternative road to be laid to Jerusalem.

Part of a convoy carrying supplies and reinforcements to the besieged city of Jerusalem in May 1948. Jerusalem remained cut off from the rest of the country until the middle of June.

Kaukji, who still did not consider himself bound by the UN decision and the cease-fire, continued to attack settlements in Galilee, but he was repulsed in every clash with Israeli forces. The Egyptian army was spread out across the length and breadth of the Negev. Under the terms of the truce it was obliged to allow the Israel Defense Forces to supply the Israeli settlements and troops in the south with all necessities. The Egyptians violated the condition and would not permit the Israeli forces to cross the Mejdal-Beit Govrin line, which was in their hands. The local UN representative did not have the power—or perhaps the will—to assure Israel free passage from north to south to bring in supplies. At first the army sent in supplies by air, for after the first truce Israel had gained control of its skies with fighter planes acquired abroad before the establishment of the state. But after the impotence of the UN representatives had been revealed, and after the Egyptians on October 15 had attacked a food convoy to the Negev, the army was ordered to break through by force. It bombed the Egyptian airfields and cut the Egyptian line between Iraq Manshiyeh and Beit Govrin, but an assault on Iraq Manshiyeh itself failed.

On October 21 the army entered Beersheba, and the whole of the northern Negev was in its hands. The young navy sank two Egyptian warships off Gaza. (The Egyptians made a valiant stand at Faluja, where they were commanded by Sudanese officers. Although completely surrounded and facing starvation, they refused to surrender.) Kaukji continued to attack in the north until, at the end of October, a combined Israeli force, which included a Druse company, was sent into the attack and defeated the enemy in two days. Kaukji fled, his liberation army disintegrated, and the whole of Galilee was purged of the invaders—except for the veteran village of Mishmar Hayarden, east of the border, which remained in Syrian hands even after the second truce. This was the only point in the territory designated for the Jewish state to remain in enemy hands until the armistice agreement was signed.

The Egyptian army, which had been routed in the northern Negev, concentrated in the Gaza Strip and began to attack nearby Israeli posts, with the aim of recapturing Beersheba. The attacks were repulsed and Israeli forces took the Iraq-Suweidan police fortress, opened the road to Sdom, and dug in at Kurnub and Ein Hussub in the Arava, south of the Dead Sea.

On November 16, 1948, the Security Council decided that Israel and Egypt must open peace negotiations. Israel welcomed the decision and complied; the Egyptians evaded it on various pretexts. Israel informed the United Nations that, as Egypt refused to comply with the Security Council's decision, it must reserve freedom of action so as to hasten the coming of peace and defend its Negev territories.

The operations to liberate the Negev started on December 23. The road from Beersheba to the Sinai border was entirely held by the Egyptian army. To expel the invaders the Israeli forces were compelled to lay a new road across the sands in record time. The operation was a success, ending with the road in Israeli hands.

Supplies presented tremendous difficulties, for Israeli forces in the Negev were hundreds of kilometres from their bases in the north. All three arms of the Israel Defense Force took part in the Negev operations. The attack began by sea and air, the navy bombarding the Egyptian coast and the air force harassing Egyptian air power. The

Below, a Jewish settlement in the Negev. The full-scale Israeli offensive to break the strong Egyptian cordon and relieve the 27 Negev settlements began on October 15, 1948—after the Egyptians had violated the truce by attacking an Israeli food convoy.

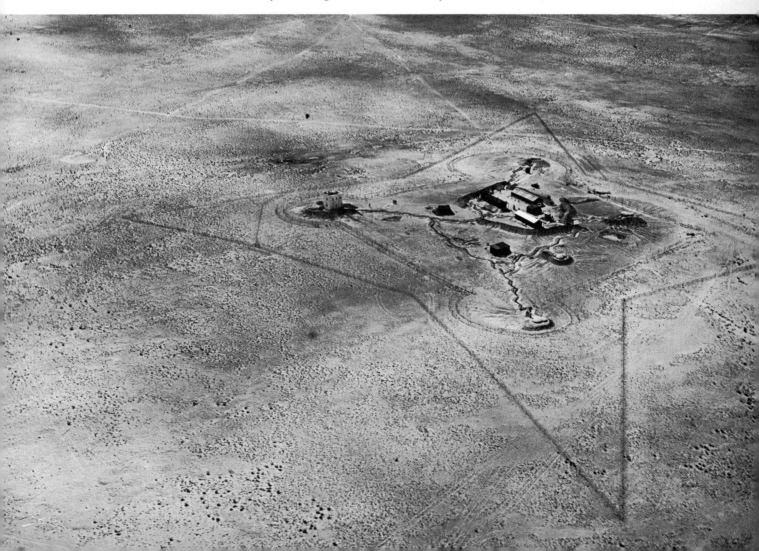

Egyptians, on the other hand, operated in strength on land only. Israel mounted a diversionary attack on Gaza that lasted four days, but the true objective was El-Auja on the border, which was taken. Next came Bir Asluj and the road was cleared of Egyptians. A large part of the Egyptian army in the Negev was captured; the rest fled.

On the entreaty of the Security Council, the fighting was brought to an end at 2 P.M., January 7, 1949. The Egyptians remained only in the Gaza Strip, and stated that they were prepared to conduct negotiations with Israel in accordance with the Security Council's decisions of November 4 and 16, 1948. The negotiations began in Rhodes with a representative of the Egyptians and the Assistant UN Secretary-General, Dr. Ralph Bunche. On February 24, 1949, the first Armistice Agreement was signed. Article 1 stated:

Armistice

'The establishment of an armistice between the armed forces of the two parties is accepted as an indispensable step toward the liquidation of armed conflict and *the restoration of peace in Palestine.*' (Author's italics.)

Israeli forces were then ordered to advance toward Eilat on the Gulf of Aqaba, which is in the territory of the State of Israel. The Arab Legion, seeing the forces advancing, retreated to Transjordan, and the flag of Israel was hoisted at Eilat on March 10, 1949. The problem of Jerusalem was again placed on the agenda of the UN Assembly in the autumn of 1949. An extraordinary coalition, consisting of three blocs—the Catholic states, the Communist group, and the Arab countries—was established in the Assembly, and obtained a decision by a two-thirds majority on December 10 for the complete internationalization of Jerusalem, instructing the Trusteeship Council to draft a constitution for an international city. The United States and Britain voted against the resolution.

The prime minister told the *Knesset* on December 13, 1949:

'This resolution cannot be implemented on any account, if only because of the categorical and determined opposition of the people of Jerusalem. In the tempest of war,' he continued, 'when Jerusalem was beleaguered, we were compelled to establish the seat of government for the time being in the official quarter near Tel-Aviv. But the State of Israel has had, and will have, one capital alone: Jerusalem the Eternal . . . . Immediately after the end of the fighting we began the transfer of government offices to Jerusalem and the creation of the conditions required for a capital city. The necessary arrangements are approaching completion, and there is no longer any obstacle to the return of the Knesset to Jerusalem.'

The Knesset and the government offices—except for the ministry of defense—moved to Jerusalem, which thus became, in practice as well as in principle, Israel's capital.

But the State of Israel was not established for the purpose of battle and military victory, or even to ensure the peace and welfare of its citizens alone. It was charged with a unique mission: the ingathering of Israel's exiles and the developing and populating of the country's waste areas. And although war was forced upon it on the day of its birth, it has never diverted its attention from these two historic goals. On the day the state was proclaimed, the Provisional Council announced that the White Paper and all the immigration and settlement laws based upon it were null and void, and that the gates were open to unlimited immigration.

During the first seven and a half months of the state, 101,819 immigrants arrived; in 1949, 239,076 followed. First came the internees from Cyprus—illegal immigrants expelled from Palestine by the Mandatory government and housed on the island; then came refugees from the concentration camps in Germany. In the following two years, 343,306 more immigrants came in, and the Jewish population also rose by 88,338 as a result of natural increase during these four years. These were the

The Gates Open

318

A group of Kurdistani Jews in transit to Israel. "Operation Ali Baba", the massive airlift to bring in 120,000 Jews from Iraq, began in 1951.

years of flood tide in immigration, in which the number of Jews in the country (650,000 at the founding of the state) was doubled.

During the first year there was no difficulty in housing the immigrants. Most of them settled in abandoned towns and villages, and found work in the existing economy. In the second year, however, these resources came to an end. Thousands of soldiers were demobilized and had to be given employment, and the newcomers found it difficult to get work. The housing problem also became serious. Difficulties arose in educating the children of the newcomers. There was a shortage of teachers and schools. The problem of educating the adults was also critical. They, too, had—and wanted—to learn Hebrew. Special adult schools called *ulpanim* were set up to teach the language to adults, especially professional men: doctors, engineers, book-keepers, and the like. Vocational training courses were organized in building, carpentry, hairdressing, sewing, and many other trades.

In those years, complete communities were brought over from exile: almost the whole of Yemenite Jewry, a majority of the Jews of Iraq, and nearly all the remnants of Polish Jewry. During the first four years, the number of agricultural settlements was doubled. During the half-century before the state, fewer than 300 villages had been established, cultivating some 125,000 acres. By the end of 1951, Jews were cultivating 850,000 acres. A major building operation was also set in motion—in 1949 buildings containing 33,556 rooms were built, and by 1951 the number had almost trebled. The massive immigration also led to rapid industrial development.

The organization of the Israel Defense Forces (*Zahal*), which were set up in haste during the War of Independence, began only after the adoption of the Defense Services Law by the Knesset in September 1949. This was designed to endow the army with two basic qualities, military skill and pioneering capacity. A special corps was established in 1950, called *Nahal* (initials of *No'ar Halutzi Lohem*—Fighting Pioneer Youth), which was given agricultural as well as military training. In the first two years it set up 15 agricultural settlements, most of them on the borders with Egypt, Syria, and Jordan.

319

On November 4, 1948, at the 21st sitting of Israel's Provisional Government, it was decided to hold general, direct, equal, secret, and proportional elections to the Constituent Assembly (which later became the Knesset). The number of seats in the legislature was fixed at 120. Every man and woman aged 18 or over had the franchise, while men and women over 21 were entitled to stand for election. On November 8, 1948, a census was held which showed a population of 782,000 (713,000 Jews and 69,000 non-Jews); 506,667 of these had the right to vote. The elections themselves took place on January 25, 1949, nearly three weeks after the end of the fighting. Twenty-one lists of candidates were submitted, but only 12 parties won one or more seats. Mapai, the Israel Labor party, came out on top with 155,274 votes and 46 seats; Mapam, the United Workers' party, was runner-up with 66,018 votes and 19 seats.

General Elections

The Constituent Assembly was ceremonially opened on February 14, 1949, at the headquarters of the Jewish Agency by Dr. Chaim Weizmann, president of the Provisional Council. A Transition Law was passed, establishing that the legislature in Israel would be called the Knesset and the Constituent Assembly would be the first Knesset. The official gazette was named *Reshumot*. On February 16 the Knesset elected Dr. Weizmann as president of the state. On February 24 the president entrusted David Ben-Gurion, the prime minister designate, with the task of forming the first elected government.

Ben-Gurion wanted to include all the parties that had taken part in the provisional government, according to the new relative strengths established by the elections, which had improved the position of Mapai. He proposed a cabinet of 12, with five members from Mapai, two each from Mapam and the Religious Front, and one each from General Zionists, Progressives and Sephardim. But the General Zionists refused to join, arguing that they should be represented according to their weight and not their numbers. Mapam refused unless it received the portfolio of defense. As a result, a cabinet of four parties was formed: Mapai had seven members; Religious Front three; Progressives one; Sephardim one.

The First Knesset

Party posters on display in Tel-Aviv during January 1949, just prior to Israel's first general election.

The main laws passed by the First Knesset were: the Defense Services Law, under which Zahal was established; the Free Compulsory Education Law; the Law of the Return, giving every Jew (except those working against the Jewish people, or those endangering the security of the state or public health) the right to settle in Israel, and making him a citizen the moment he announced his intention of settling in the country.

In September 1950, the government assembled a widely representative gathering of American Jewry at the King David Hotel in Jerusalem. The prime minister reviewed the changes that had taken place in Israel and the tremendous tasks it still faced. The government, he said, had decided it was necessary to organize among the Jews of America and other prosperous countries a long-term (12-15 years) low-interest development loan. By the end of 1963 it had brought in $651,325,000.

A crisis arose in 1951 over the right of parents to decide whether they wanted their children to attend religious or non-religious schools. When the Religious Front voted against the government's policy of free choice, the government resigned—on February 14. An alternative government could not be formed and new elections were held on July 30, 1951. Again Mapai had a majority—with 45 seats—and the president again called upon David Ben-Gurion to form a government. Another attempt to expand the coalition did not succeed, and on October 7, 1951, a government of 13 members was presented; it incorporated eight Mapai members, two Hapoel Hamizrahi, one Mizrahi, one Agudat Yisrael, and one Sephardi.

Reparations from Germany

At the beginning of January 1952, an extremely vehement debate was opened in the Knesset. It was concerned with the demand for reparations from Germany, which followed on a note sent by the government of Israel in March 1951 to the four occupying powers (United States, United Kingdom, Soviet Union, and France), presenting Israel's claim for reparations totaling $1,500,000,000 from the two parts of Germany (East and West).

Referring to the annihilation of one third of the Jewish people by the Nazis, the note said:

'A crime of such vast and fearful dimensions cannot be expiated by any measures of material reparation. All that can be done is to secure the indemnification of the heirs of the victims and the rehabilitation of the survivors. The Jews have been killed, but the German people continue to enjoy the fruits of the carnage and plunder perpetrated by their erstwhile leaders. In the biblical phrase, they have "killed and also taken possession".'

On September 27, 1951, Dr. Adenauer, chancellor of West Germany, stated in the Bundestag at Bonn that his government was prepared 'to reach a solution of the problem of material reparations through negotiations with representatives of the government of Israel, which has absorbed a large number of homeless Jewish refugees,' and with the representatives of the Jewish people.

A conference of Jewish organizations met in New York on October 26, 1951, and in the name of the Jewish people approved Israel's demand for reparations. But in Israel itself opinions were divided. Mapai (the Israel Labor party), Hapoel Hamizrahi, and the Progressives, who had a majority in the Knesset, were in favor of reparations; the General Zionists and Mapam were against. But the most vehement opposition came from Herut, the party of the extreme right.

A few hours before the debate in the Knesset, the Herut leader, Menahem Beigin, addressed a street meeting in Jerusalem and (as his party's newspaper reported next day) told his hearers, among other things: 'When they fired at us with cannons [referring to the *Altalena* episode], then I gave the order: No! Today I will give the order: Yes! This will be a fight for life and death.' And indeed the incited and uncontrolled mob attacked the Knesset during the debate, threw stones into the

David Ben-Gurion at *kibbutz* Sde Boker (in the Negev). After his resignation from the government in 1953, he went to live in this outlying settlement.

House, and assaulted with sticks and stones the police who had come to protect it. More than 100 policemen were injured and the inflamed mob trampled them underfoot. Eventually troops were summoned to restore order.

During the stone-throwing, Beigin was on his feet addressing the Knesset, arguing that reparations were 'the abomination of abominations in Israel; there has been nothing like it since we became a nation.' He said he had told the mob assembled in the street: 'Go, arise, surround the Knesset, as in the days of Rome when a Roman Procurator wanted to place an idol in the sanctuary. If necessary, we shall be killed together with you, and there shall be no reparation from Germany!'

The members of the Knesset, of course, were not terrified by the stone throwers, or by Beigin's threats, and decided in favor of reparations. The sum agreed with the West German government was DM3,450,000,000. (Beigin was suspended from the Knesset for three months for his lawless behavior.)

On November 9, 1952, the president of the state, Dr. Chaim Weizmann, died. More than any other man in his generation, he had prepared the way—by his political work, by his scientific greatness, and by his initiative in land settlement—for the establishment of the state. For over a year, with all his tremendous vitality, he had wrestled with the angel of death until he succumbed. In all of Jewish history in the Diaspora, few Jews had earned such international standing as Dr. Weizmann—in Britain, in America, and in many other countries—even before he became president. On December 8, 1952, the Knesset elected as president Izhak Ben-Zvi, one of the pioneers of the second Aliya and a founder of Hashomer in the Ottoman days. He had been expelled from the Land of Israel in spring 1915 by Jamal Pasha, and helped to found the Jewish Legion in the United States during World War I. Through his researches into the history of Israel's "tribes" in the Diaspora he gained the affection of all communities and sections.

The Death of Weizmann

Break With Russia

The prime minister's efforts to expand the coalition were partially successful, in December 1952, when the cabinet was joined by four representatives of the General Zionists, who had received 20 seats in the elections to the second Knesset.

On February 9, 1953, a band of hooligans committed a serious political crime by throwing a bomb in the yard of the Soviet embassy. Three people were injured. The government immediately issued a statement expressing its 'horror and detestation' of the 'dastardly outrage', its 'deep regret and apologies', and its readiness to pay compensation for the injuries and material damages sustained. Nevertheless, three days later the Soviet foreign minister handed the Israel embassy in Moscow a note stating that it had been decided to recall the Soviet mission from Israel, and demanding the recall of the Israeli mission from Moscow. Diplomatic relations between the Soviet Union and Israel were not resumed until July 20, 1953, shortly after the death of Stalin.

At the end of 1953, the prime minister informed the president of the state that he felt compelled to resign from the government for a year or two because of the great tension and tremendous emotional strain under which he had lived since his meeting with the Peel Commission in 1936, as chairman of the Zionist Executive. He first received two months' leave from the government and spent the time on a thorough review of the security position and the army's needs. On October 10, 1953, he submitted to the government a three-year plan for the strengthening of security, which the government approved. On December 7 he officially submitted his resignation to the government and went to work as a member of kibbutz Sde Boker, in the southern Negev.

A New Prime Minister

Mapai chose Moshe Sharett, the foreign minister, to take Ben-Gurion's place, and on January 25, 1954, Mr. Sharett presented his government to the Knesset. There was no change in its composition except for the appointment of Pinhas Lavon as minister of defense. In presenting the new government, Mr. Sharett stated that it 'regards itself as a direct continuation of the previous government and remains faithful to the basic principles presented by the previous prime minister.'

The new minister of defense apparently thought otherwise and strained relations developed between him and the prime minister. Mr. Lavon also had strained relations with the director-general of his ministry and with the chief of staff. On the other hand, there were close ties between the minister and one of his senior officers, though in the end relations with this officer deteriorated as well. In February 1953, the minister of defense demanded that the prime minister dismiss the director-general of the ministry and this officer—otherwise he would resign. The prime minister refused and the minister submitted his resignation, which was unanimously approved by the government on February 20. Members of the cabinet complained that during Mr. Lavon's term of office they had known nothing of what was going on in the ministry of defense.

The prime minister approached Ben-Gurion in Sde Boker and asked him to return to the ministry of defense. The latter proposed one of his colleagues, a veteran of the Hagana, for the post, since he felt it necessary to continue his work in Sde Boker for another year. The person proposed refused to accept the nomination, and Ben-Gurion, aware of the confusion and lack of confidence that had reigned in the army during the past year, felt it his duty to return. On February 21, 1953, the Knesset confirmed his appointment as defense minister.

The 1955 Elections

On May 29, 1955, the prime minister of Burma, U Nu, accompanied by his wife, arrived in Israel, the first prime minister to pay an official visit since the establishment of the state. On June 4 of the same year an agreement was signed in Washington for cooperation between the United States and Israel in atomic research for peaceful purposes, and the United States undertook to erect an experimental atomic pile in Israel.

At the end of June the term of the second Knesset came to an end. In the elections, which took place on July 26, 876,085 ballots were cast—Mapai again receiving the largest number of votes and seats. On October 18 the president again entrusted Ben-Gurion, who had headed the Mapai list, with the task of forming a government on as broad a basis as possible, and on November 2 the new government was presented to the Knesset. In his Knesset speech, the prime minister stated that with the worsening of the border situation during the past few years, defense occupied a central place in Israel's preoccupations. 'With us, it is not merely a problem of independence, territory, borders and regime,' he said, 'it is a question of security for our actual physical existence. Our enemies are preparing, as many of them openly proclaim, to throw us all into the sea . . . . Let us not forget that during World War II most of the Arab rulers were devotees of Hitler and looked forward to his victory.' The prime minister paid particular attention to the recent "commercial transaction" between the Czechoslovak government and Egypt, and the fact that ships carrying heavy armaments were on their way to Egypt, loaded with tanks, artillery, jet planes, and submarines. Cairo radio had declared: 'The day of Israel's destruction approaches.'

Renewed Hostility

Two months later, on January 2, 1956, the prime minister in the Knesset again surveyed the security situation, which had continued to deteriorate. He declared: 'Our neighbors, not content with violating the UN Charter and defying the provisions of the armistice agreements, have also organized a guerrilla war against the citizens of Israel. Here the Kingdom of the Jordan was in the van. Bands of saboteurs and murderers would cross Israel's border and ambush any Israelis they came across.

'These incidents . . . increased in number, particularly from 1951 onward. In 1951, 137 Israeli citizens were wounded or killed by these bands of murderers . . . . In 1952, the number of casualties rose to 147, including 114 victims of gangs from Jordan. In 1953 the number rose to 162, gangs from Jordan being responsible for 124. In 1954, Egypt began to compete with Jordan in this sphere, and the casualties rose to 180, Jordanians responsible for 117 and Egyptians for 50. In 1955 the Egyptians gained the lead. Out of 258 casualties inflicted on Israel by gangs of murderers from across the border, only 37 were due to attacks from Jordan; 192 were the work of the *fedayun,* especially organized Egyptian gangs whose function at first had been to fight against the British during the Suez Canal dispute, but who had been transferred to the Gaza Strip when the dispute ended . . . . These fedayun gangs were also sent by the Egyptian military junta to Jordan and Lebanon, to attack Israelis from there, although the authorities in those countries did not always regard these operations with favor.

'The Egyptians also became expert in minelaying on Israel's roads, and in 1955 alone, 49 of their mines took toll of life and limb in Israel.

'During the past five years we have suffered 884 casualties from the operations of regular and irregular military bands, including 258 last year alone. . . .

'Egypt's representative in the United Nations Assembly and the Security Council [Mahmud Fawzi on June 16, 1951, Abdal Hamid Galib on February 16, 1954, and Azmi Bey on March 13, 1954] expressly declared (in flagrant contradiction of the armistice agreement) that Egypt continued to regard a state of war as existing between herself and Israel, and for this reason would not comply with the Security Council's decisions or the findings of the UN observers in regard to freedom of navigation in the Suez Canal.

'Nor did Syria remain inactive. In May, 1951, a Syrian military unit crossed the

324

border north of Lake Kinneret [Sea of Galilee] and attempted to occupy Israel territory at Tel-Muteila. In the battle that ensued with the Israel Defense Forces 40 Israeli soldiers fell, while the Syrian unit suffered heavier casualties—more than double ours—and was compelled to retreat to its own territory.'

Clashes in the North

In the middle of November 1954, at a four-power conference (the Soviet Union, the United States, Britain, and France), the West tried to dissuade the Soviet Union from encouraging the arms race in the Middle East further, but without success. And once again the trouble started in the north. On December 10, Syrians opened fire on an Israeli patrol boat on Lake Kinneret. That night an Israeli force answered by blowing up the Syrian post from which the shots had come, and then immediately evacuated Syrian territory. Fishing on the lake was renewed without interference. But the attacks from the Gaza Strip and Sinai multiplied.

Speaking in the Knesset on April 22, 1956, the prime minister warned the House that during the last few months the war against Israel had grown to an intensity unparalleled since the War of Independence. On January 24, he recalled, the United Nations Secretary-General, Dag Hammarskjöld, had come to Israel, after visiting Egypt and talking to Nasser about compliance with the armistice agreements and the cease-fire. Although Nasser had told Hammarskjöld that he was interested in both these matters, he had refrained from giving any undertaking to comply with them. Firing from the Gaza Strip had continued as before, day by day. In February and March there had been 38 Israeli casualties (31 wounded and seven killed). In April the position had become still more acute. Between the 1st and the 19th of the month, there had been 82 military and civilian casualties—18 killed, 64 wounded—including the victims of the loathsome murder of children in the Shafrir village synagogue.

Sharett Resigns

On June 18, 1956, foreign minister Moshe Sharett resigned because of differences of opinion between himself and the prime minister regarding foreign policy, and in his place the Knesset approved the transfer of Mrs. Golda Meir from her post as minister of labor to the foreign ministry. In that same month, a chain of new settlements was set up along the Gaza Strip and the Egyptian border of the Negev. In July two new destroyers of the Israeli navy, *Jaffa* and *Eilat,* which had been acquired in Britain, reached Haifa.

On September 23 the people of Israel were aroused by a murderous Jordanian attack on the members of an archaeological convention who were inspecting the excavations at Ramat Rahel in Jerusalem. A burst of machine-gun fire came suddenly from an Arab Legion post, killing three people and wounding 18. The Jordanians stated that the attack had been carried out by 'a Legion soldier suffering from an attack of madness,' but on the same day Jordanians killed two other Israelis—a plowman in Maoz Haim, and a woman from Aminadav, near Jerusalem.

Tension also grew on the Egyptian border when, in October, five Jewish travelers were murdered on the road from Sdom to Beersheba. The foreign ministry announced that 'if the UN authorities are not capable of forcing the Arabs to honor agreements and observe the cease-fire, Israel herself will see to it that the lives of her citizens are not taken with impunity.'

Despite this warning a Jordanian band perpetrated another murder in the heart of the country. Infiltrators broke into an orange grove near Even Yehuda (not far from the road between Petah Tikva and Beit Lid), killed two laborers working in the grove, and cut off the ears of the victims to show their masters that they had faithfully carried out their mission. In reply, the next morning the Israel Defense Forces destroyed the Jordanian police post of Kalkilya, opposite the spot.

During the second half of October the Egyptians renewed their aggression in the south. Fedayun units laid mines on Israel territory and three Israeli soldiers were killed when their vehicle touched one off.

The threat to Israel's security reached its peak on October 25. After the victory of pro-Nasserist elements in the Jordan elections, a tripartite military alliance was concluded between Egypt, Jordan, and Syria; the armies of the three countries were placed under the command of the Egyptian chief of staff, Abdel Hakim Amer. In view of this, Israel was compelled to mobilize its reserves and station the maximum number of troops on the borders. On Sunday morning, October 28, the prime minister and the minister of defense submitted to the cabinet a proposal for an all-out offensive against Sinai and the Gaza Strip.

In the evening of October 29, Israel Defense Force units entered Sinai to liquidate the nests of murderers and to extirpate the forces from which they came. The Israel army was faced by about three Egyptian divisions: one in the Gaza Strip; a second in the expanses of the Sinai peninsula, mainly in the El-Arish and Abu-Ageila area; and a number of units scattered over the peninsula—at Ras el-Nakb, Thamad, Kusseima, Jebel Libna, Nakhl, a-Tur, Ras Nasrani and Sharm el-Sheikh. These three divisions numbered over 30,000 men, and reinforcements of more than two brigades arrived during the fighting. The Egyptian air force and navy also went into action, and an Egyptian destroyer reached Haifa, where it was captured by the Israel navy.

On the first night of the operation, Kunteila, Ras el-Nakb, and Kusseima were taken; the next day Thamad, El-Basis and El-Ofra in the heart of Sinai. On October 31, Bir Hasana was occupied without resistance, as well as Nakhl; Abu-Ageila was

An Israeli commander briefs his officers for battle during the Sinai Campaign of 1956.

taken after a fierce engagement. On November 1, all the fortified approaches to Rafa were taken, as well as El-Gafgafa (on the Nitzana-Ismailiya road) and the first outpost of El-Arish. Toward morning of November 2, El-Arish was captured after stiff resistance, and Gaza surrendered three hours later without offering any serious opposition. On November 3 two important points were taken on the western shore of the Gulf of Aqaba, Dahab and Ras Nasrani. By this time practically the whole of the Sinai peninsula was in Israeli hands, except a small bay, Sharm el-Sheikh, on the Red Sea coast opposite the island of Yotvat (Tiran); the bay was fortified with long-range artillery and equipped with an airfield. This last Egyptian post fell to Israeli forces on the morning of November 5.

On the second day of the fighting an ultimatum from the British and French governments was received by both Egypt and Israel, demanding the withdrawal of their forces to a distance of 10 miles from the Suez Canal. Israel complied, since from the beginning she had had no intention of invading the soil of Egypt proper.

The Cease-Fire

France and Britain, whose ultimatum was rejected by Egypt, launched attacks on Port Said and tried to seize the Suez Canal. After the Security Council had failed to reach a decision because of the Anglo-French veto, the United Nations Assembly was immediately summoned to an emergency session; it decided to demand that all parties institute a cease-fire. On November 3, Israel informed the UN Secretary-General that her forces had complied. The Assembly was not content with the cease-fire, and (on an American proposal) demanded that Britain and France immediately evacuate all their forces from Egyptian territory, and that Israel withdraw her troops behind the lines established in the armistice agreement of February 24, 1949.

The Assembly also adopted a Canadian proposal to set up a UN Emergency Force. On November 7, the Israeli prime minister received a note from Marshal Bulganin, prime minister of the U.S.S.R., and next day a letter from President Eisenhower of the United States. Bulganin's note was redolent with hostility and full of threats. President Eisenhower's letter was couched in friendly tones. He stated:

'There is being dispatched to Egypt a United Nations force in accordance with pertinent resolutions of the General Assembly. That body has urged that all other foreign forces be withdrawn from Egyptian territory, and especially that Israeli forces be withdrawn to the General Armistice line. . . .

'I need not assure you of the deep interest which the United States has in your country. . . . It would be a matter of the greatest regret to all my countrymen if Israeli policy on a matter of such grave concern to the world should in any way impair the friendly cooperation between our two countries.'

In reply, the prime minister assured the president that 'we will, upon the conclusion of satisfactory arrangements with the United Nations in connection with the international force entering the Suez Canal area, willingly withdraw our forces.'

The political struggle continued for four months, from the beginning of November 1956 until the beginning of March 1957. There were three stages. During the first, which continued until February 11, Israel was opposed, with hardly any change in the situation, by almost the entire world.

On that date, Mr. John Foster Dulles, the American secretary of state, issued a memorandum to Israel's ambassador in Washington, with the approval of President Eisenhower, noting that Israel still held the Gaza Strip and Sharm el-Sheikh, in contravention of the Assembly's decision. On the Gaza Strip he wrote:

'We recognize that the area has been a source of armed infiltration and reprisal back and forth contrary to the Armistice Agreement. . . . Accordingly, we believe that the United Nations General Assembly and the Secretary-General should seek that the United Nations Emergency Force, in the exercise of its mission, move into this area and be on the boundary between Israel and the Gaza Strip. . . .

327

A "Tournalayer"—the giant mobile steel mold used in the crash building program begun in 1948. Concrete would be poured into the mold to form the outer wall for one story of a house.

'With respect to the Gulf of Aqaba and access thereto—the United States believes that the gulf constitutes international waters and that no nation has the right to prevent free and innocent passage in the gulf and through the strait giving access thereto. . . . It is of course clear that the enjoyment of the right of free and innocent passage by Israel would depend on its prior withdrawal in accordance with the United Nations resolutions.'

Toward the end of February 1957, France and Canada took a hand, concluding the second stage and beginning the third and final stage of the struggle. These two countries had supported Israel throughout, but they knew that a two-thirds majority could not be obtained in the Assembly in support of Israel's conditions for evacuating Sharm el-Sheikh and the Gaza Strip. They therefore proposed that a number of important countries, especially maritime states, should announce in the Assembly that they supported:

1. freedom of navigation in the strait;
2. Israel's right to self-defense (under Article 51 of the UN Charter) if anyone interfered by force with Israeli shipping in the strait.

A similar declaration would be made about the Gaza Strip: that the United Nations Emergency Force should remain there until peace was assured.

The Israeli foreign minister announced in the Assembly that Israel would evacuate the Gaza Strip and Sharm el-Sheikh on the understanding that freedom of navigation in the strait was assured, that the UN force would remain in both places, and that Israel reserved the right to defend freedom of navigation in the strait in case of any interference by force. As agreed in advance, similar statements were made by the delegates of the United States, France, Argentina, Costa Rica, Panama, Holland, Norway, Belgium, Australia, New Zealand, Sweden, Britain, Canada, Portugal, Italy, Denmark, and others.

On March 3, President Eisenhower wrote to the prime minister:

'I believe . . . that Israel will have no cause to regret having thus conformed to the strong sentiment of the world community . . . .'

The government then decided to withdraw from Sharm el-Sheikh and the Gaza Strip. The Danish ship *Birgitte Toft* was the first to reach Eilat after the withdrawal of the Israel Defense Forces from Sharm el-Sheikh on March 10. On April 7 an American tanker reached Eilat with a cargo of 15,600 tons of crude oil. Freedom of navigation in the Red Sea Strait had become a fact.

Oil Projects

In the meantime, the laying of an oil pipeline from Eilat to Beersheba, which had been started on December 15, 1956, was completed. On the eve of Passover, April 14, 1957, the oil began flowing from the tanks in Eilat through the pipeline to Beersheba; from there it was taken by rail to the refineries in Haifa. The oil flowed at a rate of 70 tons per hour, covering one and a quarter miles in that time. It was decided to build a pipeline of larger diameter, which would continue north to Haifa, and during a visit to France the minister of finance succeeded in obtaining $20,000,000 for that purpose. The larger pipeline was completed on July 10, 1958.

The evacuation of the Gaza Strip was a bitter disappointment to the settlements on the border. After five months of complete security all along the Strip, mine-laying and infiltration started up again. Generally, however, there was relative quiet along the border with Egypt, and the center of attack shifted northward, to the Syrian border. Despite constant interference and attack by the Syrians, the drainage of Lake Hula, over an area of 15,000 acres, was completed by November, 1957. Another great settlement enterprise—the Lachish area—was started in the south, opposite the Hebron Hills, in an area of 125,000 acres. Forty-five agricultural settlements were established—32 moshavim, eight kibbutzim, three *moshavim shitufi'im*, and two agricultural schools. Three thousand families settled on land that had been desolate for many years; most of them had come from Asian and African countries, though the kibbutzim were manned mainly by natives of Israel.

New Towns

In 1955 a new town in the Negev, between Beersheba and the Dead Sea, was founded by immigrants from Morocco; it was given the biblical name of Dimona (JOSHUA xv: 22). In a few years it became the textile center of the Negev, and now has a population of over 22,000. In 1962, a second new town, called Arad (NUMBERS xxi: 1), was established in the Negev, and in October 1964 a third, called Carmiel, in Galilee. On September 23, 1955, Israel's first petroleum deposits were discovered at Heletz, in the northern Negev, at a depth of 4,905 feet.

The rapid growth of the population under the state called for the expansion of agriculture as well as for vigorous development of industry and handicrafts.

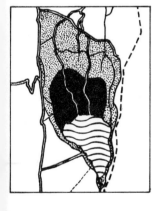

Below, a section of soil in the Hula Valley—after drainage. The Hula Lake area (in northeast Galilee) was acquired by the Jewish National Fund in 1934, but the massive task of draining the lake and its surrounding marshes—the largest swamp area in Israel—could only be begun in 1948: the work was carried out by the J.N.F. A map of the drainage scheme is shown on the left. When it was completed (in 1957), swamp and lake had disappeared, leaving 15,000 acres of highly fertile soil.

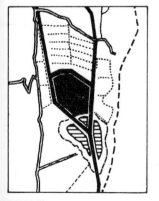

 Swamp Area

Peat Area

Lake Hula

Fishponds

During the state's first 25 years, many new industries have been started: metals, chemicals, petrochemicals, electronics, automobiles, arms, and planes. Before 1948 industry was mainly concerned with finishing and assembly; since independence it has gone into basic production, and its output has quintupled, growing by over 10 per cent a year. Diamonds are now Israel's most important industrial export, and the country's largest single enterprise is its aircraft industry, which employs more than 14,000 people.

There have also been great changes in handicrafts, and a signal improvement in the position of the Arab artisans, for whom special funds have been set up. The landscape of Israel has also been transformed. Bare hills and sand dunes have been covered with green woodland, and by 1970 the cultivated area of the country was 1,028,000 acres. The change in the human landscape has been even greater, with the total Jewish population of the Land rising from 758,702 in 1948 to 2,561,400 in 1970. (The total population of Israel in 1970 was 3,001,400.)

No less great has been the cultural transformation. At the first census, in 1949, Jews listed more than 20 different European and Asiatic languages as their media of speech. Almost a half (337,276), however, already spoke Hebrew alone; in addition, 139,293 noted Hebrew as their main language, and 33,434 as a supplementary tongue. Only 128,483 were limited to various foreign languages. At a later census, in May 1961, when 1,932,536 Jews were registered, 1,391,403 spoke Hebrew.

Immediately after the reestablishment of the State of Israel, free, universal, and compulsory education was instituted for all boys and girls between the ages of 5 and 14. It was in the field of education that the difference was most clearly marked between the immigrants who arrived before the destruction of European Jewry and those who came after—especially those from the Muslim countries. The latter (except those from Iraq) were poor and uneducated. Home conditions naturally tended to discriminate against the children of the poor—and during the years of mass immigration it was impossible, for lack of teachers and schools, to find means to put this right. From 1955 onward, however, steps were taken to rectify the position. Backward pupils spent more hours at school; youth clubs were established where children from poor families could prepare their lessons with the aid of instructors; graded (in some cases nominal) fees for poor children were instituted in secondary schools; scholarships were given to talented students (especially from the oriental communities) for post-primary and higher education. During this period, too, standards of education and scientific research rose rapidly, especially in the Weizmann Institute of Science in Rehovot, founded in 1949. Today just under a million pupils attend educational institutions (as compared with 140,000 in 1948), and education is the third largest item on the state budget.

IMMIGRATION	1948-1961
1948 (May-)	101,828
1949	239,576
1950	170,249
1951	175,095
1952	24,369
1953	11,326
1954	18,370
1955	37,478
1956	56,234
1957	71,224
1958	27,082
1959	23,895
1960	24,510
1961	47,638

A signal event, of no little educative impact on the youth of Israel and on public opinion universally, was the trial of Adolf Eichmann, chief nazi instrument in the murder of 6,000,000 Jews during World War II. A group of nameless Jewish volunteers allowed themselves no rest until they had ferreted out his place of concealment in Argentina, brought him to Israel, and handed him over to the Israel police. A year was spent in collecting material on Eichmann's crimes from all over Europe, and on April 11, 1961, he stood in the dock of the District Court of Jewish Jerusalem. The German lawyer Servatius, whose expenses and fees were paid by the government of Israel, defended him; Israel's Attorney General Gideon Hausner, prosecuted.

Some foreign jurists and journalists entertained misgivings at the outset as to the likelihood of a fair trial in Israel, where so many of the victims of nazism and their kin had found asylum. But as the hearings went on, the doubters recanted. This

Expansion and Transformation

Assimilating the Newcomers

The Eichmann Trial

Sections of the giant pipes (shown ready for installation) used in the large-scale scheme to divert the waters of the north down to the parched Negev desert.

The trial of Adolf Eichmann in 1961 served to remind the world—and the youth of Israel in particular —of the calculated inhumanity that caused the extermination of 6,000,000 Jews. Here, young Israelis stand before a life-size concentration-camp photograph at an exhibition in Jerusalem, one of many such exhibitions to have been mounted in various parts of the world.

was the first time that the monstrous chapter of genocide, without parallel in the history of mankind, was unfolded in all its stark horror. At Nuremberg, the Jewish holocaust had, somehow, been drowned and smothered in presenting the evidence of all Hitler's countless atrocities. Israeli youth, born and brought up after the end of the war, now heard of the dreadful doings for the first time; hundreds of thousands of citizens sat at their radios day after day, listening and seldom speaking. Eichmann was found guilty and on December 15 was sentenced to death. On May 29, 1962, the Supreme Court set aside his appeal, and two days afterward he was hanged. His body was cremated and his ashes were scattered in the sea.

On April 23, 1963, President Ben-Zvi died after a severe illness. His passing was observed with national mourning in Israel, and throughout the world. There was no man in the Land before him so beloved by so many sections of the population. He was buried in Jerusalem near the grave of his father, in accordance with his will. Zalman Shazar was elected Israel's third president on May 21, 1963. (He held office until May, 1973, when he was succeeded by Professor Ephraim Katzir.)

The following month Ben-Gurion announced that for personal reasons he was giving up the premiership. He recommended Levi Eshkol—then minister of finance —as his successor, and after consulting the various parliamentary groups President Shazar invited Eshkol to form a government. On June 24, 1963, the new prime minister introduced his cabinet to the Knesset. He declared: 'The new government is a continuation of the preceding one: its working programme will be guided by the same principles'.

The assassination of President Kennedy, on November 22, 1963, came as a great personal shock to the Israeli people, and the Knesset assembled in a state of mourning to pay tribute to the dead president. Early the next year Mr. Eshkol visited America, where his discussions with President Johnson included problems of defense and the setting up of a joint desalination programme.

On November 9, 1964, the prime minister announced the resignation of General Moshe Dayan from the government. General Dayan stated that he was resigning because of 'differences between himself and the prime minister'. Chaim Gvati succeeded him as minister of agriculture.

On March 16, 1965, Mr. Eshkol told the Knesset that the Federal Republic of Germany wished to establish diplomatic relations with Israel, and that his government was in favor. There was fierce opposition from the right-wing Herut party, as well as from two left-wing parties, but the government's decision was approved by 66 votes to 29, with 10 abstentions.

Elections to the Sixth Knesset took place at the end of that year, and on January 12, 1966, Prime Minister Eshkol introduced his cabinet, expressing deep regret that Mrs. Golda Meir, the foreign minister, had decided to leave the government after nine years of intense activity, adding that the prestige Israel enjoyed throughout the world was to a large extent the fruit of her labor. Abba Eban was named as Mrs. Meir's successor.

During the first years of the State, the Knesset possessed only temporary headquarters. In 1957 James de Rothschild (son of Baron Edmond de Rothschild, who did so much to encourage Jewish settlements in Palestine) wrote to Ben-Gurion saying that he wished to donate six million Israeli pounds towards a new Knesset in Jerusalem. James de Rothschild died shortly after, but his widow, Dorothy, wrote to Ben-Gurion: 'Needless to say the six million pounds will be forthcoming.' In fact, Baroness de Rothschild increased the sum to ten million and the building was completed in 1966.

Intentions to Annihilate Israel   Ever since the Sinai Campaign of 1956, and the steps taken by the United Nations and the Maritime Powers to ensure free navigation through the Straits of Tiran, the Israel-Egypt frontier had remained relatively quiet. Even though President Nasser made no secret of his intentions to annihilate Israel, he at first remained apart from the guerrilla war that Syria was attempting to wage in the north. But on May 14, 1967, he sent his chief of staff to Syria to co-ordinate operations against Israel. The next day he submitted a military and political plan in five stages, alleging—

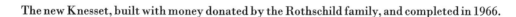

The new Knesset, built with money donated by the Rothschild family, and completed in 1966.

Above, a Lebanese newspaper cartoon of May 31, 1967 shows the cannon muzzles of eight Arab states pointed at a quivering Israel. Above right, another cartoon of the time symbolizes the effect on Israel of the closing of the Tiran Straits.

falsely—that Israel was concentrating troops on the Syrian border. When this mythical troop concentration was denounced by the Soviet Union, Eshkol wrote to Kosygin: 'When the organs of Arab propaganda claimed that Israel was massing troops for an attack on Syria, I invited your ambassador to visit the frontier to see for himself that there was no truth in the allegation. To my regret, the ambassador did not respond to my invitation.'

On May 16 Nasser demanded the withdrawal of the United Nations Emergency Force. Two days later U Thant, the UN Secretary-General, acquiesced, ordering the force (which numbered 3400 men) to withdraw from the Egypt-Israel border, from the Gaza Strip, and from Sharm el-Sheikh, which commanded the Tiran Straits. On May 19, the Egyptian Commander of the 'Israeli Front' announced that the UN troops had handed over their positions, and the following day Egyptian troops moved into Sharm el-Sheikh. Two days later, during a visit to his troops in Sinai (which by now numbered 80,000 men), Nasser announced that the Tiran Straits were closed to Israeli shipping. Thus, when the UN Secretary-General arrived in Cairo on May 23 to discuss the situation, he was faced with a *fait accompli*: Egyptian guns on the borders of Sinai, an Egyptian naval force in the Straits of Tiran. At a Cairo press conference Nasser declared: 'Sharm el-Sheikh means in fact confrontation with Israel. The step we have taken means we must be ready for total war with Israel. This is not an isolated act. . . . The battle will be total and our basic aim will be the destruction of Israel.'

All these threats forced Israel to mobilize a large part of her reserves, and General Moshe Dayan was called back to the government as minister of defense: more than any man he commanded the complete confidence of the Israeli people. Meanwhile Foreign Minister Eban flew from capital to capital in a vain attempt to gain support from the Maritime Powers and find a diplomatic solution to a situation that was worsening daily.

334

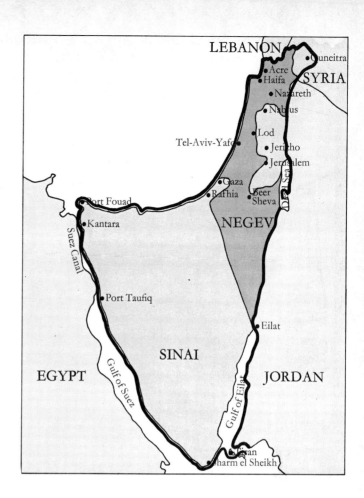

Israel

Territory occupied by Israel during the Six-Day War

Neighboring countries

The Order to Attack

Time was not working in Israel's favor. On May 30, King Hussein of Jordan flew to Cairo to sign a military pact with Egypt, placing the Jordanian army under the Egyptian command. On June 2, troops from Algeria and Kuwait entered Egypt, and troops from Iraq and Saudi Arabia joined forces with Jordan's Arab Legion. Then, at dawn on June 5, an Egyptian armored unit was seen moving towards Eilat. Israel was now left with no choice, and the order to attack was given. From Israel's point of view the military situation was grim: there were seven to eight Egyptian divisions, two of them armored, deployed in Sinai, and 900 tanks lined up along the border—200 of them opposite Eilat, poised to cut off the southern Negev. Along Israel's eastern border there were 60,000 Jordanian soldiers and 300 tanks, with the Jordanian army under Egyptian control and Iraqi forces ready to fight beside them. On Israel's northern border, 50,000 Syrian soldiers were dug in on the heights overlooking Israel's villages and kibbutzim, their positions fortified and protected by concrete and steel.

At 10.40 on June 5 General Dayan broadcast the following message: 'As yet we do not have precise reports on the fighting. Our planes are engaging enemy planes, our land forces have moved forward to silence Egyptian artillery which has been shelling our units near the Gaza Strip. We have also moved to check Egyptian tanks advancing towards Eilat. The Egyptian General Mourthagi, commander in Sinai, has just broadcast the following message to his troops: "The eyes of the whole world are turned towards you in this, your Holy War. You must, by force of arms and by your brotherly union, occupy the land of Palestine." Soldiers of Israel: our aim is not to occupy, but to prevent the Arab armies from occupying our country and to break the vice that is closing on us. The Egyptians have mobilized and taken under their command Syrian, Jordanian, and Iraqi forces. They may outnumber us, but we shall win.'

Meanwhile Israel's air force launched a brilliantly coordinated attack against

335

Egyptian airfields and defenses. Ten major bases were destroyed simultaneously, and then a further nine—in Sinai, in the Suez Canal region, in the heart of Egypt itself, and in the south. In less than three hours, Israel's pilots had destroyed the greater part of Egypt's air defense. Then they turned their attention to Jordan, Syria and Iraq.

At 1.00 on the night of June 5-6, General Yitzhak Rabin, Israel's Chief of Staff, announced: 'In the northern region of Sinai our forces have occupied Rafa, and El-Arish; other units have occupied Kham Yunis and Deir El-Balah, and are now at the outskirts of Gaza. In the central zone the outpost of Auja El-Masri and Tarat Um Basis have been taken; and in the south, bases in the Kunteila region have been occupied. During the day Israeli planes delivered a mortal blow to the air force of Egypt, Jordan and Syria, giving us complete supremacy in the air. The commander of the air force will give you details.' General Mordechai Hod then reported: 'We have destroyed 288 Egyptian planes, including 30 Tupolev-16's, 27 Ilyushin 28's, 12 Sukhoi-7's, 99 Mig-21's, 75 Mig-15's and 17's, 32 transport planes and helicopters. We have lost 19 of our own pilots, 8 killed and 11 so far unaccounted for.'

Fighting continued during the night, and on June 6 Gaza was occupied and the Israelis continued their advance along the west coast. There was bitter fighting on the El-Arish-Jebel Libna axis, while to the south Israeli forces occupied Um-Katif, Abu-Ageila, and continued toward Kusseima and Bir Hasana. By the following midday the Israelis were west of Rumani, had penetrated the Bir Gafgafa region, occupied Bir Hasana and their advance troops had reached the Mitla Pass. The entire Kunteila region was in their hands, and Sharm el-Sheikh fell after a combined air and sea operation.

That same night General Yitzhak Rabin announced: 'Today, the greater part of the Egyptian army in Sinai was crushed. All that prolongs the battle is the enemy's attempt to reach the Suez Canal.' During the night of June 6-7, and all the following day, a violent tank battle raged west of Bir-Gafgafa and in the Mitla Pass, as the Egyptians tried to battle their way to safety. The remains of their air force came into action, but to no avail. Finally, on June 8, Nasser announced his willingness to accept a cease-fire. Almost the entire Sinai Peninsula, as well as the Gaza Strip and Sharm el-Sheikh, had been taken by Israel in just under four days.

On June 5 Jordanian artillery had begun to shell Mount Scopus, north of Jerusalem, and Ramat Rahel to the south. Jordanian positions opened fire along the entire length of the Armistice line and Jordanian planes began to strafe Israeli troop emplacements. Prime Minister Eshkol responded by sending an urgent message to King Hussein through General Odd Bull, head of the UN Truce Supervision Organization. It read: 'We shall not initiate any action against Jordan. However, should Jordan open hostilities, we shall react with all our might and he [Hussein] will have to bear the full responsibility for all the consequences.'

The Jordanian Front

Hussein chose to ignore Israel's overtures, and at 13.00 launched an attack on Government House, the UN headquarters. Israeli forces counter-attacked and drove the Jordanians back. Israel then brought her planes into action, attacking the Amman and Mafraq airfields and destroying all of Jordan's Hunter interceptors. Meanwhile, Israeli infantry and armored units encircled Jenin and occupied other areas on the West Bank of the Jordan. On June 6, in the face of continued shelling, Israeli forces occupied Nebi Samuel, north-west of Jerusalem, the Jordanian Police School, and reached the walls of the Old City itself. The Latrun area was cleared, and Israeli forces moving south took Ramallah and Kalkillah. On June 7, Sebastia and Nablus fell, and in the Jerusalem sector Israeli troops battled their way through the narrow streets of the Old City. At 10.00, after bitter fighting, they reached the Temple Mount and the Western (Wailing) Wall. To the south of Jerusalem, Jericho was

General Moshe Dayan (center), Israeli Minister of Defence, enters the Old City of Jerusalem shortly after its capture. He is accompanied by General Yitzhak Rabin, the Chief of Staff, and Brigadier-General Uzi Narkiss, G.O.C. Central Command.

taken, as well as Bethlehem, Gush-Etzion, and Hebron. The following night, King Hussein announced his acceptance of a cease-fire on all the Jordanian fronts. The entire West Bank of the Jordan, which since the 1948 War of Independence had been part of the Hashemite Kingdom, was now in Israel's hands.

The Syrian Front

A few hours after the fighting between Eygpt and Israel began, the Syrians opened their attack. Syrian Migs strafed a number of villages in the Haifa region, and the Israeli air force hit back—destroying 52 Syrian planes: 30 Mig 21's, 20 Mig 17's, and 2 Ilyushin 28's. On June 6, attacks by three Syrian armored columns were beaten back, but most of the settlements and built-up areas near the frontier found themselves under continual fire from Syrian positions in the commanding Golan Heights: and the Syrian attack continued even after Egypt and Jordan had accepted the cease-fire.

At first Israel's attention was focused on the Egyptian and Jordanian fronts, but on June 9, at about midday, Israeli infantry and armored vehicles reached the Syrian frontier. In the face of murderous fire, they fought their way up the steep slopes of the Syrian Heights—where five infantry and four armored brigades were concentrated. Fighting continued throughout the night as Israeli forces inched their way forward, struggling to break through the massively fortified enemy lines. The battle flared until the evening of June 10, when Israeli troops finally overran the Syrian positions and pressed on to Kuneitra, 20 kilometres east of the Israeli border. At 18.30 both parties accepted the cease-fire.

The Khartoum Conference

For the third time in the first twenty years of her existence, war had been forced on Israel; but it did not bring the peace she desired. The Arab reply to the Israeli demand for direct peace talks and a negotiated settlement was given by Nasser at the Arab Summit Conference, held at Khartoum in August 1967: 'No peace with Israel, no recognition of Israel, no negotiations with Israel.' Nevertheless, Israel's official policy remained unchanged, as Foreign Minister Abba Eban reiterated in an address to the UN Security Council on November 22, 1967: 'We shall respect and fully maintain the situation embodied in the cease-fire agreements until it is succeeded by peace treaties between Israel and the Arab States ending the state of war, establishing agreed, recognized and secure territorial boundaries, guaranteeing free navigation for all shipping, including that of Israel, in all waterways leading to and from the Red Sea, committing all signatories to the permanent and mutual recognition and respect of the sovereignty, security, and national identity of all Middle Eastern States.'

Such peace treaties were not to be. In September 1968 Egypt began a series of large-scale artillery barrages across the Suez Canal, and these were stepped up the following spring as President Nasser began his 'war of attrition' against Israel. Israel used her air force to blunt the Egyptian attack, but the situation worsened as the Soviet Union's involvement increased, and the Russians began to assemble (and man) a growing number of ground-to-air missile sites. In an effort to defuse the situation and reopen talks via Gunnar Jarring, the UN envoy, the American government proposed a cease-fire and military standstill on both sides of the Canal. Egypt and Israel agreed, and the cease-fire came into effect on August 6, 1970. **War of Attrition**

Meanwhile, terrorist incursions persisted along Israel's other borders. Israel retaliated by striking hard at terrorist bases and by maintaining vigilant patrols in the border areas. As a result, King Hussein was finally forced to clamp down on terrorist operations from his territory: this led to a bloody civil war in Jordan in the summer of 1971, during which an estimated 700 guerrillas were killed by the king's troops. Many others fled to Syria, and also to Lebanon, where over 3000 were gathered in bases at the beginning of 1972, compelling Israel to mount a series of reprisal raids into both Lebanese and Syrian territory. Since then, El Fatah, Black September, and the various other guerrilla groups, frustrated in their attempts to penetrate Israel or to stimulate any real resistance in the administered territories, have sought out civilian targets in Western Europe: hijacking attempts, the massacre of Israel's athletes at the 1972 Munich Olympics, the sending of letter bombs, have been the outcome. Israel has had to take its own measures to curb terrorism and hijacking; but the problem is an international one—as Golda Meir, who succeeded Eshkol as prime minister after his death in 1969, has emphasized repeatedly: 'If the states of the world do not curb terrorism, then terrorism will destroy civil aviation.' **War with the Guerrillas**

The challenge facing Israel today is as great as at any time in its history. In the past two years or so, in the face of international pressure, some 50,000 Jews have managed to leave the Soviet Union and make their way to Israel—many of them old, and almost all of them destitute. Whatever the pressures on her economy and social services, it is Israel's duty and privilege to ensure that they are made welcome, assisted, and given every opportunity in their new homeland. Formidable too are the problems presented by the areas administered by Israel since the Six Day War. Israel's policy toward the million Arabs under her control in these areas is an enlightened one. Although she has provided substantial aid in the fields of education, social welfare, health and agriculture, Israel does not interfere in any way in their day-to-day life, other than to control law and order. The inhabitants may travel overseas through Israel's airports and harbors, while "open" bridges over the Jordan permit regular trade with the Arab States and free movement of person either way for family reunions, work, or study. **The Challenge**

Israel realizes that her fate is integrated with the fate of all humanity, that her peace depends on peace among the nations. The heritage of her prophets and the vision of the latter days—as expressed by MICAH (IV: 15) and ISAIAH (XI)—guide her steps **A New Order** on the international scene. At home, she strives for the ingathering of the exiles, the fructification of the wastelands, economic independence, the advancement of the individual, progress in education and science, and the creation of a society founded on liberty, equality, tolerance, mutual aid, and the love of one's fellow man. In her foreign policy she aspires to friendly relations with all peoples, irrespective of their internal regimes, and for permanent peace and cooperation with the neighboring countries, so that the Middle East may be tranquil and prosperous.

Israel is well aware that only by the closing of the material and spiritual gap between the wealthy, highly developed nations and the poorer, still developing ones, and by the establishment of a true partnership between all states, will world peace be ensured. With all her heart, Israel is ready to make her modest contribution to this universal partnership.

Age and youth planting trees together typify Israel's pride in the past, faith in the future.

Glossary

Abaya (Arabic): The long cloak worn by Arabs.

Aggada (pl. *aggadot*): Literally « a tale. » That part of rabbinical literature illustrating, exemplifying, and augmenting *Halacha*—generally by means of tales, legends, anecdotes, parables, and fables.

Aggadic Midrash (pl. *a. midrashim*): A form of commentary and interpretation of the Scriptures, based primarily on legends, tales, and parables.

Agal (Arabic): The headband worn by Arabs to hold their headdress in place.

Agudat Yisrael (« Society of Israel »): The world organization of orthodox Jews, founded at Kattowitz in 1912. Formerly opposed to Zionism, A.Y. is now represented, as a party, in Israel's parliament. It advocates strict religious observance and rabbinical jurisdiction in the administration of the state.

Ahdut Ha'avoda (« Labor Unity »): (1) The Zionist-Socialist Workers' Party in the Land, inspired by Marxism and founded in 1919. A.H. joined with *Hapoel Hatza'ir* in 1930 to form *Mapai*. (2) A leftist group that broke away from *Mapai* in 1944, and—with *Hashomer Hatza'ir* and the left wing of *Poalei Zion*—formed *Mapam* in 1946, and in 1954 broke away from Mapam to form the present-day Ahdut Ha'avoda-Poalei Zion party.

Aliya (pl. *aliyot*): Literally « going up. » Immigration of Jews to the Land.

Aliya Hadasha: An organization of German and Central European Jews formed in the late 1930s to represent their special interests. It later became a political body that put forward lists of candidates for election to various Jewish representative bodies in the last years of the British Mandate.

Alliance Israélite Universelle: A Jewish international organization founded in 1860 by a group of French Jews—to defend Jewish civil and religious liberties the world over and to provide education and material aid for backward Jewish communities. The A.I.U. still maintains a network of schools—mainly devoted to French studies and systems—in a number of eastern countries.

Arava: The southernmost part of the rift valley in the Land extending from the southern shores of the Dead Sea to the Gulf of Aqaba.

Ark of the Covenant: The shrine in which the two Tablets of the Law were kept. It was transported from place to place during the Israelites' wanderings in the desert—and later in the Land—until installed permanently in the inner sanctum of the First Temple. (See EXODUS XXV: 10-22.)

Asefat Hanivharim (« Elected Assembly »): The elected assembly of representatives of Palestinian Jewry that functioned during the British Mandate. It first met in October 1920.

Ashkenazim (sing. *Ashkenazi*): The biblical name of a people descended from Ashkenaz (GEN. X : 3; JER. LI : 27). In post medieval times the term was extended to refer to all Central and East European Jews and later to Jews of Central and East Europe (except the Balkans) who settled in other countries. The A. possess their own ritual and Hebrew pronunciation (as distinct from the *Sephardim*): they comprise over 80 per cent of all Jews.

Av: A lunar month of the Jewish calendar. The fifth month in biblical times, the 11th month in post biblical times.

B.C.E.: Abbreviation of « before the Christian (or common) era. » It equates exactly with « B.C. »

Bedouin: A nomadic Arab.

Beitar: A fort southwest of Jerusalem, which was the last stronghold of the Jews (under Bar Kochba) against the Romans. Now the name of the rightist Zionist youth movement *(Brit Yosef Trumpeldor—* « Yosef Trumpeldor League ») founded by the *Revisionists* in 1923; it now forms part of the *Herut* party.

Ben: Literally, « son » or « son of. » Frequently used in personal names (in the same way as the Arabic *Ibn*). Also *Bar, Bei,* or *B'.*

Beth-Din (« court »): The rabbinical court of law that—in the Second Temple period—had jurisdiction in civil, criminal, and religious cases. In Israel today, it is authorized to deal with such personal questions as marriage, divorce, and—if all concerned agree—inheritance.

Bilu *(Beit Ya'akov Lechu Venelcha*—« O house of Jacob, come ye, and let us go »): One of the first modern Zionist pioneering groups, founded in 1882 at Kharkov in Russia by Jewish students reacting against the Russian pogroms. Its members established some of the earliest Zionist agricultural settlements in Palestine.

Cabbala (« Receipt »; i.e. something received down the centuries.): A system of Jewish mystical philosophy. See page 241.

C.E.: Abbreviation of « Christian (or common) era. » It equates exactly with « A.D. »

Cohen (« Priest »): A descendant of Aaron (elder brother of Moses). Aaron and his descendants were designated by the Lord to form the clan of priests of the Israelites. Also, a common Jewish family name.

The Covenant of Confession: The solemn and public contract—initiated by Ezra and Nehemiah and signed by the *Yishuv's* leaders (*c.* 433-432 B.C.E.)—in which the people confessed to its past sins (particularly to the widespread intermarriage), repented, and renounced all heathen practices. (See NEHEMIAH, VIII-IX.)

Davar: An Israeli daily newspaper, founded in 1925. It is the official organ of the Jewish Trade Union organization *(Histadrut)* in Israel.

Dayan: The judge of a rabbinical court.

Deutsche Hilfsverein: A German-Jewish charitable and educational organization founded in 1901 to aid Jews in Eastern and East European countries. It was dissolved in 1941.

The Diaspora: The collective term used to denote all Jewish communities outside the Land. (Also called: *Gola, Galut* or *Exile.*)

Druse: Members of a religious sect dwelling chiefly in Syria, Lebanon, and Israel. Their religion—an offshoot of Mohammedanism—was founded in the 11th century C.E. by the Fatimid Caliph of Egypt. The D. are represented in Israel's parliament and serve in the Israel Defense Forces.

Etzel *(Irgun Zva'i Leumi*—« National Military Organization »): A Jewish terrorist organization active in Palestine during the British Mandate. It was founded in 1937 and disbanded in September 1948.

Exilarch: The title given to the head of Babylonian Jewry.

Fedayun (Arabic): The Egyptian terrorist gangs that raided Israeli territory during the 1950s.

Fellahin (Arabic): The Arab peasantry.

Gadna: *(Gedudei No'ar*—« Youth Regiments »): The Israeli para-military youth organization.

Gaon (« genius »): The title given to an outstanding spiritual leader. From early medieval times to the 11th century, the title of the leading rabbinical authority in Mesopotamia.

Gedud Ha'avoda al shem Yosef Trumpeldor (« Yosef Trumpeldor Legion of Labor »): The country-wide organization of workers established in Palestine in 1920 to train workers for various fields of labor and for defense.

Gerusia: The council of 71 elders that assisted the High Priest in administering the Land. The G., which originated during the Ptolemaic period, became the *Sanhedrin* during the period of Roman rule.

Great Assembly: See *The Great Convocation.*

The Great Convocation (or Great Assembly—*Knesset Gedola*): The institution embodying the traditional spiritual leadership that constituted the supreme religious and legal authority of the Jewish people at the beginning of the Second Temple period, forming a link between the last of the prophets and the first of the rabbis. It is identified by some scholars with the people's assembly—presided over by Ezra in the Temple court—that accepted the Covenant of Confession. (See NEHEMIAH VIII-IX.)

Ha'ahdut (« The Unity »): The newspaper published in 1910-1915 by *Poalei Zion.*

Hacham (sage): The title given to the head of a *yeshiva* during the days of the *Sanhedrin;* also the title applied today to the rabbi of a *Sephardi* congregation.

Hadassah: The Women's Zionist Organization of America, founded in 1912 by Henrietta Szold: it runs an extensive health organization in Israel as well as social welfare, vocational training, *youth aliya* and land redemption projects. The new Hadassah hospital and medical school at Ein Kerem, near Jerusalem, is the largest and most modern in Israel.

Hagana (« Defense »): The clandestine self-defense organization founded by the *Yishuv* in 1920. With the establishment of Israel in 1948 it became *Zahal*—the Israel Defense Forces.

Haggada: The book containing the text of the ritual service recited during the Passover *Seder.*

Hahoresh (« The Plowman »): The organization of Jewish farmers established in Palestine in 1907 to encourage Jewish farming.

Halacha (pl. *halachot):* The traditional oral law constituting legal precepts that were initially derived from the written law (the *Torah*). Also, a precept of the oral law.

Halbanon: (« The Lebanon ») The Hebrew periodical founded in 1863 (in Jerusalem) by Yehiel Brill.

Haluka (« Distribution »): Charitable funds raised by Diaspora Jewry to support the scholars and poor of the Land. (The system shrank considerably after World War I and has almost disappeared.)

Halutz (pl. *halutzim)* : An agricultural pioneer.

Hapoel Hamizrahi (« The Mizrahi Worker »): An Israeli political party established in 1921 as part of the Zionist Organization; it advocated the rebuilding of Palestine and the rehabilitation of Jewish labor on religious principles. Since 1956 it has formed part of the *National Religious Party, Mizrahi-Hapoel-Hamizrahi.* It also represents the special requirements of religious people in the various trade unions within the framework of the *Histadrut.*

Hapoel Hatza'ir (« The Young Worker »): (1) The Zionist labor party founded in Palestine in 1906. Its principal aim was the establishment of a Jewish labor movement and the protection of labor rights. In 1930 H.H. amalgamated with *Ahdut Ha'avoda* to form *Mapai.* (2) The name of a weekly newspaper published by H.H. (since 1907), and now by *Mapai.*

Haraj: The land-tax imposed on the Jews by the Ottoman rulers of Palestine.

Hashomer (« The Watchman »): The organization of Palestinian-Jewish workers founded in 1909 to defend Jewish settlements and to establish the rights of Jewish workers to employment.

Hashomer Hatza'ir (« The Young Watchman »): The Zionist youth movement, founded in 1913, with a strongly Marxist pioneering ideology. It formally became a Palestinian political party in 1946, and part of *Mapam* in 1948.

Hassid (« a pious or righteous man »; pl. *hassidim):* A follower of *hassidism.*

Hassidism: A popular religious movement founded by Israel Ben Eliezer of Medzibozh *(Ba'al Shem Tov*—« Master of the Good Name ») in the first half of the 18th century: it attracted the great majority of East European Jewry. H. called for the worship of God through simple prayer (as opposed to study), through joy and mystic ecstasy, and through sincerity of emotion. It was a reaction against the formalistic aridity of the traditional Jewish religion and the dominance of a learned elite. H. was strongly influenced by the mystical ideas of the *Cabbala.*

Hatikva (« The Hope »): The national anthem of the State of Israel—previously the Zionist anthem.

Hehalutz (« The Pioneer »): A pioneering youth movement concerned with the agricultural and pioneer training of Jewish youth, and their immigration to Israel. It was formed in the U.S.A. (in 1915) and was later active in Russia and other European countries.

Herut (« Liberty »): (1) An Israeli political party, founded in 1948 by members of the *Revisionist* party, the *Beitar* movement, and by former members of *Etzel*. It advocates territorial integrity within the historical boundaries of the Land of Israel—on both sides of the Jordan—private enterprise, and social reform. (2) The daily newspaper published by the Herut party.

Hevrat Yishuv Eretz Yisrael (« Palestine Settlement Society »): The society—advocating the colonization of Palestine—founded by Rabbi Yehuda Alcalai in the middle of the 19th century.

Hibbat Zion (« Love of Zion »): The Zionist movement that arose in Russia in 1882—largely as a result of the pogroms of 1881.

The Histadrut (*Hahistadrut Haklalit shel Ha'ovdim Ha'ivriyim Be'eretz Yisrael*—« The General Federation of Hebrew Workers in the Land of Israel »): The Israel trade union federation, founded in 1920.

Hovevei Zion (« Lovers of Zion »): The Zionist movement established in Russia in 1887 after the federation of the various societies included previously in the *Hibbat Zion* movement.

ICA (Jewish Colonization Association): A Jewish philanthropic organization founded by Baron Maurice de Hirsch in 1891 to resettle European and Eastern Jewish emigrants (mainly in agricultural settlements in the Argentine, but also in Palestine).

Ihud (« Unity »): A society of Jews in the Land—founded in 1942—advocating closer cooperation with the Arabs of Palestine and the foundation of a bi-national state.

Iyar: A lunar month of the Jewish calendar; the second month of the Jewish year in biblical times, the eighth month of the calendar in post biblical times.

Jewish Agency: Originally, a public body recognized during the British Mandate. Since the establishment of Israel, an international non-governmental organization concerned mainly with the promotion of immigration, the absorbtion of immigrants, and education.

Karaites: A Jewish sect (originating in the eighth century C.E.) that denied the authority of the oral law, accepting only the written law and its almost literal interpretation.

Kefiya (Arabic): The long head-scarf worn by Arabs—and held in place by the *agal*.

Kehilla (pl. *kehillot*): A Jewish community or organized congregation.

Keren Kayemet Leyisrael (Jewish National Fund—J.N.F.): Literally, « The Perpetual Fund for Israel. » A foundation set up in 1901 by the World Zionist Organization to buy, develop, and afforest land in Palestine as national property.

Ketuba (pl. *Ketubot*): The marriage contract containing the obligations of a bridegroom toward his bride; the K. must be signed by the bridegroom and two witnesses.

Kibbutz (pl. *kibbutzim*): The form of large cooperative settlement that evolved in Palestine from the *Kvutza*. In the K., all work, property, amenities, etc., are shared equally, and all profits plowed back into the community. Administration is by an elected secretariat, though matters of principle or important practical matters are decided by the corporate body of members. The economy is based primarily on agriculture, but industry and other occupations may form an important source of income. Children are cared for and educated on a strictly communal basis.

Knesset: The parliament of the State of Israel, situated in Jerusalem.

Kolel: The term applied (mainly in the 19th century) to a community of Palestinian Jews from a specific country of origin living on *haluka* from that country.

Kupat Holim (« Sick Fund »): The health service of the *Histadrut*. It provides medical care, free of charge, to members of the Histadrut and their dependents under a form of health insurance. It also cares for the medical needs of new immigrants to Israel, and for members of various affiliated organizations.

Kvutza (pl. *kvutzot*): The system of cooperative settlement from which the larger *kibbutz* evolved. The communal principle was essentially the same; but the K. generally had only 15-25 members, was administered by the full body of members, and concentrated on only a few branches of agriculture.

Lehi (*Lohamei Herut Yisrael*—« Fighters for Israel's Freedom »): A Jewish terrorist organization (also known as the « Stern gang ») active in Palestine in the 1940s. It was founded as a breakaway group from *Etzel* (in 1940) and disbanded with the establishment of the state in 1948.

Ma'bara (pl. *ma'barot*): one of the temporary transit camps erected in Israel (between 1948-50) to house the many thousands of new immigrants.

Malben: A foundation for the care of handicapped immigrants to Israel; it was established by the American Joint Distribution Committee in 1950.

Mapai (*Mifleget Poalei Eretz Yisrael*—« The Party of the Workers of the Land of Israel »): The Israel Labor party, founded in 1930 through the merger of *Hapoel Hatza'ir* and *Ahdut Ha'avoda*. M. has remained the largest single party throughout the entire period of statehood and the dominant power in successive government coalitions.

Mapam (*Mifleget Poalim Me'uhedet*—« United Workers' Party »): An Israeli socialist party (standing left of *Mapai*) founded in 1948 through the merger of *Hashomer Hatza'ir* and *Ahdut Ha'avoda*. M's philosophy is based on socialist, Marxist, and Zionist principles.

Mekorot: An Israeli public (non profit-making) corporation engaged in tapping Israel's water resources and supplying water to the population.

Midrash (pl. *midrashim*): The interpretation and amplification of the scriptures. An exegetic exposition appended to biblical verses, often in the form of a homiletical sermon. In some cases the M. established the law; in others, it found scriptural support for laws already accepted.

Minyan: The quorum of 10 male adult Jews (i.e. above the age of 13) required for communal prayer.

Mishna: The codification of the oral (rabbinical) law, compiled *c.* 200 C.E.

Mitnagdim (« Opponents »): The name given to the opponents of *Hassidism*—i.e., adherents of traditional authoritarian Judaism (mainly in the 18th century).

Mizrahi: A movement founded in 1901 as part of the Religious Zionist organization. With the foundation of the state, its members formed a political party which amalgamated with *Hapoel Hamizrahi* in 1955, and—in 1956—became the *National Religious Party, Mizrahi-Hapoel-Hamizrahi*. The general concern of the movement has been with religious education and the establishment of religious settlements and of various religious institutions.

Moshav (pl. *moshavim*): An agricultural cooperative smallholders' village. All land on a M. is privately owned and cultivated, but some central organization does exist—there is a village secretariat, common marketing of produce, cooperative supply of household goods, common ownership of machinery, and so on.

Moshav Shitufi (pl. *moshavim shitufi'im*): A semi-cooperative settlement based on a combination of the principles governing the *moshav* and the *kibbutz*. Each family forms an integral unit with a home of its own. Administration is by an elected secretariat. The principle of communal responsibility governs land and machinery, cultivation, marketing, etc. All profits are plowed back into the community.

Moshava (pl. *moshavot*): An agricultural village in which land is owned and cultivated entirely on a private and individual basis.

Musta'arabim (pl.; also *Moriscos*): The term applied during the Ottoman period to the descendants of Jewish families that had remained in the Land from ancient times and never been exiled.

Mutawilla (Arabic): The name of a Muslim sect belonging to the Shia creed. The sect's adherents live mainly in Lebanon and Galilee.

The National Religious Party, Mizrahi-Hapoel-Hamizrahi: An Israeli religious party founded in 1956. It stands for the administration of the State on a religious basis.

Oral Law: The traditions of interpretation, amplification and practical application of the written law (i.e. the *Torah)* preserved orally by the generations of scholars until they were codified in the *Mishna* and *Talmud*.

Palmah *(Plugot Mahatz*—« Assault Companies »): The underground striking force of the *Hagana*. The P. was founded in 1941; it disbanded in 1948 when its members were incorporated into the Israel Defense Forces.

Parnass (pl. *parnassim*): The lay head of a Jewish congregation. Originally the P. had a religious function, but today his responsibilities in the community are mainly administrative.

Passover (Heb. *Pesah*): The Jewish festival (lasting eight days in the Diaspora, seven in Israel) that commemorates the Exodus from Egypt.

Patriarch (Heb. *Nassi*): The official title given by the Roman authorities to the heads of the Yishuv (from the second century C.E.).

Pentateuch: The Five Books of Moses.

Pentecost: See *Shavuot*.

PICA (« Palestine Jewish Colonization Association »): The organization founded by *ICA* in 1923 to administer the settlements that were being financed in Palestine by Baron Edmond de Rothschild.

Poalei Agudat Yisrael («Workers of Agudat Yisrael»): An Israeli religious pioneer workers' movement (founded in 1924); originally the labor movement of the extremely orthodox *Agudat Yisrael*. It became an independent party after the establishment of Israel.

Poalei Zion (« Workers of Zion »): An international Socialist Zionist party, founded in 1907. Its principles are derived from a socialist interpretation of Zionism. Three Israeli political parties have evolved from P.Z.—*Mapai*, *Mapam*, and *Ahdut Ha'avoda*.

Reshumot: The official Gazette of Israel's parliament.

Revisionists: The right-wing Zionist party founded in 1925; it advocated a more aggressive Zionist policy and the achievement of the biblical boundaries of Palestine (on both sides of the Jordan). The party, led by Ze'ev (Vladimir) Jabotinsky, seceded from the World Zionist Organization in 1935 to form the New Zionist Organization, which remained in existence until 1946. The R's followers founded *Etzel* and *Lehi*, and later the *Herut* party.

Sabra (Arabic): Literally « prickly pear. » The modern term for a person born in Israel.

Sanhedrin (Originally the *Gerusia*): The assembly of 71 ordained scholars that constituted the Supreme Court, the legislature, and the chief religious authority in Palestine from the first to the fourth century C.E. The S. was presided over by the patriarch *(Nassi)* and the Chief Judge.

Seder (pl. *sedarim*): Literally « order. » (1) One of the six sections of the *Mishna* or the *Talmud*. (2) The service conducted in Jewish homes on the first two nights (in Israel on only the first night) of Passover.

Sephardim (sing. *sephardi*): Originally the name given to the Jews of Spain, before their expulsion in 1492; now a term loosely applied to Jews from various oriental countries. The S. have their own ritual and Hebrew pronunciation as distinct from the *Ashkenazim*.

Sephardi Union: The political organization of *sephardim*, formed to fight the elections to Israel's first parliament (January 1949).

Shavuot (« weeks »): The Jewish festival of first fruits that falls at the time of the wheat harvest. S. traditionally commemorates the giving of the law on Mt. Sinai. (The festival is sometimes called by the Greek name of *Pentecost*.)

Shefela: The lowland region of southwestern Israel between the Judean Highlands and the Mediterranean.

Shehehiyanu (« Who has kept us alive »): The blessing recited by Jews after they have undergone a joyous event, and on festivals; the reciter thanks God for preserving him and for granting him the new (or renewed) experience.

Shma *(Shma Yisrael*—« Hear O Israel »): The basic affirmation of the creed of Judaism, attesting to the oneness of God. The S. is recited three times daily—at morning and evening prayers, and before retiring to bed at night.

Shnat Shmita (« Fallow year »): A sabbatical year, occurring once every seven years, during which—according to biblical law—all land must be allowed to « rest. » S.S. is still observed by ultra-orthodox Jewish farmers in Israel.

Shulhan Aruch (« Set Table »): The standard authoritative and concise code of Jewish religious law and practice. It was compiled by Rabbi Joseph Karo in 1565, and later revised by Rabbi Moses Isserles.

Solel Boneh: An Israeli building and industrial concern, established by the *Histadrut* in 1924 as a worker's contracting company. It has three semi-autonomous units: a building contracting company, an industrial holding company, and a section that deals with harbor services and overseas contracts.

Talmud (« Teaching »): The definitive and final codification of the oral law—amplifying, interpreting, and supplementing the *Mishna*. See page 178.

Talmud Torah: The general term for Jewish religious study. It is specifically applied to a type of religious school, more elementary than the *yeshiva*.

Technion: The Israeli Institute of Technology. Originally called the « Technicum. » The T. was founded by the *Deutsche Hilfsverein* in 1912.

Tell: A mound formed by successive layers of ancient settlement.

Torah: The *Pentateuch* (which includes the written law of Judaism) or, in a more general sense, the whole body of Jewish religious precepts.

Tosefta (pl. *toseftot):* A supplement to the *Mishna.*

Ulpan (pl. *ulpanim*): A special school where new (adult) immigrants to Israel are given an intensive course in the Hebrew language.

Va'ad Leumi (« National Council »): The representative body of Palestinian Jewry under the British Mandate. Its members were first elected (from the *Asefat Hanivharim)* in October 1920. The V. L. was dissolved on May 14, 1948.

Wadi (Arabic): The channel or bed of a watercourse, dry except in the rainy season. Also, ravine or gully.

Yerida (pl. *yeridot*): Literally, « going down. » Emigration from the Land.

Yeshiva (pl. *yeshivot):* A religious seminary, devoted mainly to the study of the Talmud and rabbinical literature.

The Yishuv: The collective term for the Jewish population of the Land.

Youth Aliya: An organization founded in 1934 to bring children and young people to Israel and to rehabilitate and educate them there—mainly in agricultural settlements and institutions.

Zahal (Zva Hagana Leyisrael): The Israel Defense Forces, founded in 1948.

Zionism: The movement for the return of the Jewish people to the Land. Political Zionism—which aimed at founding a Jewish State—was conceived and defined by Theodor Herzl.

Zionist Congress: The regular congress of representatives of the Zionist movement, instituted by Theodor Herzl (at Basel) in 1897.

Torah, 106, 114, 115, 117, 118, 120, 121, 122, 123, 125, 127, 128, 129, 130, 132, 133, 143, *151*, 152, 167, 168, *170*, 172, *173*, 178, *178*, *179*, 186, 187, 206, 220, 222, 234, 343; egalitarianism, 129; ethical sections, 125; forbidden by Rome, 167-8; *Mishneh Torah*, *219*; and patriarchs, 178; and Pharisees, 143; sovereignty of, 132, 152; *Talmud Torah*, 238; *see also* Law, *Mishna*, Talmud
Transjordan, 14, 15, 28, 31, 34, 50, 51, 56, 59, 60, 75, 87, 89, *137*, 138, 139, 158, 178, 211, 222, 244, 293; Assyria and, 63; and David, 52; early Israelite settlement, 42, 43, 45; Greek cities, 137, 140; Hasmoneans, 141; invasion from, 310; Jews in, 120, 124, 134, 140, 147, 151, 176, 193, 198, 202, 222, 275; Roman, 147, 148, 158; Tobiads, 126-7; and White Paper, 298
Tribes, 27, 29, 31, 73, 87, 214; alliances, 44-6, 49; Covenant of, 12, 89; democracy among, 74; early movements, 31, *35*, 44; inter-tribal disputes, 89; "Lost Ten," 229; names of, 38, 43, 44; origins, 30; unification of, 34, 76, 86, 89; *see also* individual names, and Israel, Israelites, Judah
Truman, Harry S., 312
Trumpeldor, Yosef, 284, 288, *288*
Turkey, 10, 199, 204, 212, 214, 220, 223, 226, 227, 232, 240, 250, 260, 268; Jews from, 228, 239, 249, 267; Jews in, 226, 228, 248, 249, 267; Russo-Turkish war, 250; Sultan Abdul-Hamid I, 250; Sultan Bayazid, 226; in World War I, *284*; *see also* Ottoman Empire
Tyre, 14, 58, 59, 108, 112, 120, 121, 122, 130, 137, 176, 197, 205, 206, 209, 211, 215, 221; Ladder of, 14; power in Middle East, 52, 55; William of, *216*; *see also* Jezebel
Tzemah, 290

Uganda, 276, 289
Um Juni, 279, *280*, *281*
United Jewish Appeal, 302
United Nations: Arabs in, 305, 306, 310, 318; Committee of, to facilitate transition from Mandate to independence, 308; discussion and resolution on Israel, 306, 312: Emergency Force of, 327, 328, 334; Israel becomes member of, 313; resolution to international-

ize Jerusalem, 318; and Suez, 327; and War of Independence, 314, 316, 317
U.S.A., 250, *251*, 252, 323-4; aid to Israel, 321; recognition of Israel, 312; in World War I, 286; in World War II, 301
Ussishkin, Menahem, 281, 289
USSR, *see* Russia

Va'ad Leumi, 290, 307, 310, 312, 343
Velos, 299
Via maris, 10, *11*, 14, 15, 32, 57
Vital, Haim, 233, 234, 238, 241; Rabbi Samuel, 241

Wailing (Western) Wall, 183, *185*, 202
Wauchope, Sir Arthur, 299
Webb, Sidney (Lord Passfield), 294
Weisgal, Meyer, 302
Weizmann, Dr. Chaim, 280-1, 285, 286, 287, 294, 297, 300, 301, 304; death, 322; president of Israel, 320
Wilson, Woodrow, 286, 298
Wise, Stephen, 302
Wissotzky, K. Z., 283
Workers' Sick Fund, 282
World War I, 263, 265, 266, 284
World War II, 301

Yaffe, Bezalel, 289
Yahweh, 47, 54, 61, 65, 74; covenant with, 34, 76; *see also* God, religion
Yana'it, Rachel, *282*, 286
Yarkon, river, 12, 14, 47, 48, 272, 276
Yavne'ehi, Shmuel, 287
Yavneh (Jamnia), 64, 65, 141, 149, 157, 196; center of Yishuv, 161
Yehuda, Rabbi, 178; Yehuda II, 179
Yellin, David, 273, 290
Yemen, 215, 234, 247, 324; Jews from, 265, 266, 319
Yemin, Moshe, 264
Yerek, Rabbi Abraham, 246
yerida, 173, 175, 181, 209-10, 220, 343
Yerushalmi, Moses, 243, 246, 249
yeshiva (-*ot*), 178, 180, 184, 192, 193, 195, 206, 209, 210, 211, 218, 223, 229, 343; *geonim*, 233; in Hebron, 244, 264; in Jerusalem, 233, 246, 247, 248; in Safad, 233; in Tiberias, 233

Yesud Hama'ala, 274
Yishuv, 108, 109, 114, 117, 120, 129, 130, 136, 176, *277*, 303, 304, 343; arms for, 303; character of, 295; extent, 107, 108-9, 175-6, 205-6, 210, 222; "Father of," 274; help from Diaspora, 152, 210, 230, 237, 240, 244, 247, 248, 249, 260, 267; indestructibility, 169; influence over Diaspora, 142, 218; the new, 284; poverty, 127, 173, 183, 222; resistance to Christianity, 186ff; revolts of, 147, 149, 155, *155*, 157-61, *160*, 162-3; wholeness, 169, 207
Yitzhak, Moshe B'rabbi, 211
Yosef, Rabbi Tanhum Berabbi, 220

Zadok, 114; the Pharisee 150
Zadok, Chief Rabbi, 274
Zahal, 319, 343; *see also* Hagana
Zaki Bey, 284
Zalman, Rabbi Shneur, 252
zealots, 150, 157, 159, 169, 207
Zebulun, 30, 40, 42, 45, tribe; 89
Zechariah, book of Bible, 70, *72*, 101, 102; king of Israel, 61; prophet, *72*, 102, 109, 113, 240
Zedekiah, king of Judah, 66, 80, 82, *98*, 99, 107, *108*
Ze'ira, Rabbi, 195
Zephaniah, 73; book of Bible, 21
Zerubavel, Ya'akov, *282*
Zichron Ya'akov, 274, 278, 289
Ziklag, 51, *51*
Zion, 52, 95, 100, 102, 233; "Exiles of," 169; "Mourners of," 169, 207, 208; return to (from Babylon), *107*, 109, 110, 122
Zion Mule Corps, 284
Zionism, 343; *Hibbat Zion*, 277; *Hovevei Zion*, 276, 278, 281, 283; New Zionist Organization, 285, 286; World Zionist Organization, 276, 279, 284, 312
Zionist Commission, 287
Zionist Congresses: (1897), 275-6, 280; (1903), 281; (1909), 281; (1920), 290; (1931), 295; (1937), 298; (1939), 301; (1946), 303-4
Zionist Executive, 301, 306, 307, 310, 311
Zionist General Council, 302, 306
Zoref, Mordecai, 268
Zoref, Rabbi Abraham Solomon Zalman, 262
Zoroastrianism, 101, 111, *112*

Acknowledgments

The Editors would like to thank the following for their valuable advice and assistance:
Text: *Donald Berwick, Dr. Moshe Brawer, Douglas Hill, Moshe Pearlman, Robert St. John.*
Art: *Dr. Meir Benayahu, Joe Davies, Dr. Michael Heymann, Dr. Jacob Kaplan, Arie Kindler, Michael Kitson, Edna Kram, Dr. Lothar Rothschild, Miriam Talisman, Mme. E. Sed.*

Editorial Team:

Editor: *Jeremy Robson*   Art Editor: *Felix Gluck*
Editorial Assistants: *Jonathan Lamede* (Text), *Anthony van Kampen, Sheila Muir* (Art), *Desmond Green, Jennifer Mulherrin, Patricia Quick* (Research).

Illustration Credits

Key: (B) bottom; (C) center; (L) left; (M) middle; (R) right; (T) top; and combinations, e.g. (BR) (TL).

Photo John Allegro, p. 143; Alliance Israélite Universelle, p.241 (B); Archaeological Museum of Istanbul (photo Hirmer), p.18, 159 (B); Ashmolean Museum, p.217; Associated Press, p.313 (R); Ben-Zvi Institute, Jerusalem, p.229 (L), 235 (R); Bezalel National Museum, Jerusalem (photo A. Bernheim), p.119, 223, (photo Maitek), p.262; Bibliothèque Municipale, Dijon, p.123; Bibliothèque Nationale, Paris, p.72, 79, 83, 133, 155, 156, 181, 213, 214 (T), 216, 230 (L), 241 (T); Bollingen Foundation, New York (photo Fred Anderegg), p.49, 80-81, 85, 127; British Museum, London, p.59, 60, 64, 91, 108, 110, 111, 112, 120, 128, 129 (L), 193 (B) (T), 195, 231, 235 (L), (photos Freeman), p.28, 208, 225, 227, 253, 255; from J. Carne: *Syria the Holy Land and Asia-Minor*, London, 1845, p.261; , Artist Kevin Carver, © Aldus Books, p.335; Cecil Roth Collection, Jerusalem, p.223; Central Zionist Archives, Jerusalem, p.272, 273, 275, 276 (L), 280, 288, 297 (T), 299 (R), 300 (R), (photo Z. Oron), p. 282, 291, (photo Dr. N. Gidal) p.305 (R); Chester Beatty Library, Dublin (photo, Rex Roberts), p.94, 236; from Cornfeld (Ed.): *Adam to Daniel*, Hamikra Baolam Ltd., Tel-Aviv, 1961, p.26; photo Yvan Dalain, p.281; Everadan Materaradan (photo courtesy Editions Cercle d'Art, Paris), p.103; French Government Tourist Office, p.71; from T. Fuller: *A Pisgah Sight of the Holy Land*, 1650, p.44; Geographical Projects Ltd., London, p.13, 37, 115, end papers; from E. R. Goodenough: *Jewish Symbols in the Greco-Roman Period*, Bollingen Foundation, New York, 1964, p.196 (R); photo Ara Guler, p.204, 230 (R); Haaretz Museum, Tel-Aviv, p.174; Hagana Archives, Tel-Aviv, p.279, 286, 297 (B), 300 (L); from T. Herzl: *Old-New Land*, Haifa Publishing Company Ltd., 1960, p.276 (R); Imperial War Museum, London, p.284; Embassy of Israel, London, p.277, 334, (photo Soskin) p.283; Israel Government Department for Landscaping and Preservation of Historic Sites, p.139, 182, 183, (photo Arie Volk); Israel Government Press Office, Tel-Aviv, p.16-17 (TC), 177 (T), 184, 295, 319, 320, 322, 326, 328, 339, 349, (photos Fritz Cohn © Aldus Books) 25, 126, 131 (L), 153; Israel Labour Archives, Tel-Aviv, p.269, 293; Istanbul University Library (photo Ara Guler), p.248; Italian Synagogue, Jerusalem (photo A. Bernheim), p.251 (R); photo Izis, p.90, 332 © G. A. The Jerusalem Publishing House Ltd., p.333, 337; Jewish Museum, London (photo Behram Kapadia), p.135; Jewish National Fund, p.329 (R); Jews' College (photo Freeman), p.178; after Julius Jotham Rothschild, p.55 (B); Kadman Numismatic Museum, Tel-Aviv (photo Arie Kindler), p.122, 137, 167, 188 (R), 214 (C); Kunsthistorisches Museum, Vienna, p.62; Kunstsammlungen der Veste, Coburg, p.243; Hungarian Academy of Sciences, Kaufmann Collection, Budapest (photo Behram Kapadia), p.219; Lehnart & Landrock, Luxor, p.22 (T); photo Meyer Levin, p.304 (L); Louvre, Paris, p.56, 58, 66, 67, 191, (photo Studio Josse-Lalance), p.58, 66; MAGNUM, photo Robert Capa, p.316; MAGNUM, photo Jerry Cooke, p.317; Mansell Collection (photo Alinari), p.87, 145 (B), 166; Maritime Museum, Haifa (photo Sadeh), p.142, 146 (BR), 148 (T), 177 (B), 256; Metropolitan Museum, New York, p.19 (R); Museum of Ancient Art, Haifa, p.21 (R), 170; Museum of Turkish-Islamic Art, Istanbul (photo Ara Guler), p.107; National Library, Hebrew University, Jerusalem, p.242, 245; courtesy Oriental Institute, University of Chicago, p.22 (B), 24, 48, 116; photo Palphot, p.196 (L); from E. Pierotti: *Jerusalem Explored*, 1864, p.149; photo Hans H. Pinn, p.307; from J. B. Pritchard: *Ancient Near East in Pictures*, Princeton University Press, New Jersey, 1954, p.23; Rijksmuseum van Oudheven, Leiden, p.30; from David Roberts: *The Holy Land*, London, 1855, p.266 (T); Rubens Collection, London (photo Behram Kapadia), p.169 (R), 188 (L), 263 (R); Sammlung für Völkerkunde der Universität, Zurich, p.53; Samuel Snowman (photo Freeman), p.185; Sassoon Library, Letchworth (photo David Swann), p.36, 173; Scala, Florence, p.193 (C); Ben Shahn, p.54; Staatliche Museen zu Berlin, p.39,221 (T); Staats und Universitätsbibliothek, Hamburg (photo Kleinhempel), p. 33(T). photo Shabtai Tal © Aldus Books, p.16 (TL), (BL), 17 (TR), 20, 35 (R), 41 (T), 160, 240, 309 (B); Topkapi Palace, Istanbul (photo Ara Guler), p.259 (T); Vatican Library Rome, p.125, 169 (L), (photo courtesy International Publishing Co. Ltd., Jerusalem-Ramat Gan), p.131 (R); from Zev Vilnay; *The Holy Land in Old Prints and Maps*, Rubin Mass, Jerusalem, 1963, p.263 (L), 265 (B), 266 (B); photo Arie Volk, p.183; photo Michael Wolgensinger, p.11, 21 (L); courtesy Yale University, New Haven, p.251 (TL) (CL); Zemaljski Museum, Sarajevo (photo Behram Kapadia), p.88, 151; photo Zur and Avnon, p.139.

Acknowledgment is made for permission to reprint excerpts from the following works:

Jewish Travellers edited by E. N. Adler, published by Routledge & Kegan Paul, 1930; *A Village by the Jordan* by Joseph Baratz, published by the Press Department of Ichud Habonim, 1956; *Wisdom of Israel* by Lewis Browne, published by Michael Joseph Ltd., 1949, reprinted by permission of Random House Inc.; *Selections from the Teachings of Maimonides* by the Rev. A. Cohen, published by Shapiro, Valentine & Co.; *Thespis* by Theodore H. Gaster, copyright © 1950, 1961 by Theodore H. Gaster, reprinted by permission of Doubleday & Company Inc.; *A Source Book of Jewish History and Literature* edited by Julius Hoexter and Moses Jung, published by Shapiro & Valentine & Co., 1938; *The Jewish War* by Josephus, translated by G. A. Williamson, published by Penguin Books Ltd., 1959; *Notes and Documents from Turkish Archives* by Professor Bernard Lewis, published by the Israel Oriental Society, 1952; *Oath of Asaf Harofeh* Oxford Hebrew MS. 2138, translated by Dr. Süssmann Muntner, copyright © Dr. Süssmann Muntner, 1952; *Ancient Near-East Texts Relating to the Bible* by James B. Pritchard, copyright © 1950, 1955 by Princeton University Press; *Major Trends in Jewish Mysticism* by Gershom G. Scholem, copyright © 1941 by Schocken Publishing House, Jerusalem, copyright © 1946, 1954, by Schocken Books Inc., Thames & Hudson, 1955; *The Letter of Aristeas* edited by H. St. J. Thackeray, published by the Society for the Promotion of Christian Knowledge, 1917; *The Dead Sea Scrolls in English* by G. Vermes, published by Penguin Books, 1962; *Trial and Error* by Chaim Weizmann, published by Hamish Hamilton and Harper & Row, 1949; *Illustrations from Biblical Archaeology* by D. J. Wiseman, published by the Tyndale Press, 1958; *The Goodly Heritage* by Avraham Yaari, published by the Zionist Organization, 1958.

Extracts herein taken from the Authorized Version of the Bible, which is Crown Copyright, are included with permission.

If the publishers have unwittingly infringed copyright in any illustration or quotation reproduced they will gladly pay an appropriate fee on being satisfied as to the owner's title.